From Now On

New and Selected Poems, 1970–2015

Clarence Major

The University of Georgia Press
Athens and London

Published by the University of Georgia Press
Athens, Georgia 30602
www.ugapress.org
Designed by Melissa Bugbee Buchanan
Set in Mendoza ITC and ScalaSans
Printed and bound by Sheridan Books
The paper in this book meets the guidelines for
permanence and durability of the Committee on
Production Guidelines for Book Longevity of the
Council on Library Resources.

Most University of Georgia Press titles are
available from popular e-book vendors.

Printed in the United States of America
19 18 17 16 15 P 5 4 3 2 1

Library of Congress Cataloging-in-Publication Data

Major, Clarence.
 [Poems. Selections]
 From now on : new and selected poems, 1970–2015 / Clarence Major.
    pages ; cm
 ISBN 978-0-8203-4796-7 (pbk. : alk. paper) —
 ISBN 978-0-8203-4830-8 (e-book)
 I. Title.
 PS3563.A39A6 2015
 811'.54—dc23

                        2014043940

British Library Cataloging-in-Publication Data available

CONTENTS

FOREWORD

Clarence Major's Cosmopolitan Vision

No other voice in American poetry sings quite like Clarence Major's, and his new collection, *From Now On: New and Selected Poems, 1970–2015,* elucidates ample proof. Of course, some poets and critics have attempted to trace the lineage of Major's voice and vision to the objectivists (because of his unembellished language), especially to Louis Zukofsky and George Oppen, and even to Denise Levertov; others associate him with the jazz-influenced poets aligned with the Black Arts aesthetic, and still other critics and poets have intoned Ezra Pound as a primary influence. However, anyone who knows contemporary American poetry, especially African American poetry, knows that Clarence Major, an iconic wordsmith, is also a gifted painter, novelist, essayist, and anthologist; but more than anything, he's always himself. And this new collection speaks for itself.

Major has artfully resisted being pigeonholed. In fact, here's a poet we can call a school of one; he fits that bill but not because he's trying to be different. I believe his work is naturally different. Highly personal, yet universal, Major's poetry is usually serious but playful, through technique and tone. His work achieves a middle register—not high or low—the same way some of our great jazz stylists search for the grace note, always dependable but edgy and democratic; like those musicians, Major is someone who adapts a phrase or melody and then bends it until it is completely his, through feeling. Major knows how to make profundity seem accidental; his almost casual phrasing makes this possible. His poems are not consciously trying to be poems in an imagistic or rhetorical sense. And of course, this concept of easeful engagement is an aspect of the poet's genius.

Major's practice as a painter at the Art Institute of Chicago informs his craft as a poet, his method of weaving and dovetailing elements of sound into his unique way of seeing the world. At first, reading a poem by Major, one may think he or she knows the narrative, but then one realizes this poet is no tool or fool for the expected. His work embodies echoes—language as feeling. An example of this is the last poem of the book's first section; the title, "Something Is Eating Me Up Inside," makes one think he or she already has a clue to the poem's meaning. But let's see if that's truly the case; the poem opens this way:

> I go in and out a thousand times a day
> and the fat women with black velvet skin
> sit out on the front steps watching.
> "Where does he go so much?"
> I think often, not "much."
> I look like a hood from the 1920s
> in my Ivy League black shirt with button-down collar.

We may not know where we've traveled, but we know we have been on a voyage pushed and guided by feeling by the time we get to the phrase "There is a tapeworm inside philosophy." And moreover, we may be that "tapeworm" because of our bloated assumptions about each other. But also, for me, the "tapeworm in philosophy" could be about Major's poetry, the mechanics of the speaker's psyche, or perhaps the line is about the artist compelled by language as a system of thinking. Major's poems articulate the quotidian, but they are also naturally philosophical, and each defies any narrow-minded trajectory; all the senses are employed—mind and feeling as organism. "Something Is Eating Me Up Inside" ends with the following lines:

> The sun is blood in my guts
> as I move from gin to sin to lakesides to sit down
> beside reasons for being in the first place.
> In the second place?
> in the second place looking outward
> for a definition to a formal ending—.

And yes, that dash is so instructive. Major's poetry relies on what is said and remains unsaid, and one enters his vision at the risk or the obligation of becoming a participant, an interloper within spaces of casual preciseness. The playfully simplistic is always more; in fact, it is a dynamo when queried by a feeling, thinking reader. And that is how Clarence Major seems always to be having fun in each poem, but the poem is never simply funny, slapstick, or bravura. Edgy and Socratic, his poems often pose questions through short declarative phrases amassed—syncopation.

Major has a way of making a poem accrue. "Beast: A New Song" seems like a template for reading many of his poems composed of longer phrases. Here's the poem in its entirety:

> The cage. Tiger. Stripes. From sun up to midnight the
>   pacing tiger steps
> softly. Caged. Soft traction. Across. Turns. Back. Up.
>   Down. Turns.
> Back across. Eyes? Headlights. Dark clues. Turns. The way
>   things go
> on. Pacing. Trapped. Absolute. Absolute cage. Absolute
>   song.

Here, we see the underbelly of process and meaning converge. Pace and rhythm—words—almost work like colors laid down on a canvas in brushstrokes. Much of the music in *From Now On* whispers to us; it beckons, seduces, and then holds us accountable for what we are thinking. We chide ourselves and might even find ourselves mouthing that almost edible conjunction: "But . . ." This poet teaches us there are few *buts* and *ands* when reading or hearing his poetry. One enters an emotional-psychological contract with a voice that can be defined as Clarence Major. His language is himself. We are challenged to grasp his style. This voice is bold and straightforward, as in "Conflict," wherein the astute reader is with the speaker when he proclaims:

> I claim that knowledge—
>
> outside and beyond Verlaine, Baudelaire and Rimbaud.
>
> That conflicting disorder
> was not disorder—it was order.

In many ways, like the jazz musician, or any other artisan or craftsman who has earned the salt in his or her daily bread, Major has honed a cosmopolitan style that belongs to him, though in fact it may have been shaped out of the earthy stuff of southern blues. Always measured, paced, and syncopated, each poem in *From Now On* makes us feel and know language is music, and of course, style is shaped through practice until it is earned. Insinuation and humor are always at the center of Major's poetry, and it seems appropriate that the final poem, "The Things You Hear," in this fine collection ends on this trope:

> It doesn't come in a bottle
> but it's also an effective medicine to drink.
> Drink it slowly.

Yusef Komunyakaa

A NOTE ON THE EARLY POEMS

Poems from *Swallow the Lake* were written between 1955 and 1965; poems from *Private Line* were written in 1968; poems from *Symptoms and Madness* were written between 1965 and 1969; poems from *The Cotton Club* were written in 1970. The poems from *The Syncopated Cakewalk* were written between 1969 and 1972. Poems from *Inside Diameter: The France Poems* were written while living in France between 1981 and 1983. The poems from *Surfaces and Masks* were written between 1984 and 1985 while living in Italy.

ACKNOWLEDGMENTS

The selections from *Swallow the Lake*, published by Wesleyan University Press, Middletown Connecticut, in 1970, are reprinted by permission of Clarence Major. Copyright © 1970 by Clarence Major.

Selections from *Private Line*, published by Paul Breman as volume 15 in the Heritage series, London, England, in 1971, are reprinted by permission of Clarence Major. Copyright © 1971 by Clarence Major.

Selections from *Symptoms and Madness*, published by Corinth Press, New York, New York, in 1971, are reprinted by permission of Clarence Major. Copyright © 1971 by Clarence Major.

Selections from *The Cotton Club*, published by Broadside Press, Detroit, Michigan, in 1972, are reprinted by permission of Clarence Major. Copyright 1972 © by Clarence Major.

Selections from *The Syncopated Cakewalk*, published by Barlenmir House, New York, New York, in 1974, are reprinted by permission of Clarence Major. Copyright © 1974 by Clarence Major.

Selections from *Inside Diameter: The France Poems*, published by Permanent Press, London and New York, in 1985, are reprinted by permission of Clarence Major. Copyright © 1985 by Clarence Major.

Selections lll, Vl, XI, XV, XX, XXVI, XXIX, XXXll, XXXlV, XXXVlll, XXXIX, XL, XLI, XLll, and XLlV are reprinted by permission from *Surfaces and Masks* (Coffee House Press, 1988). Copyright © 1988 by Clarence Major.

From Now On

From *Swallow the Lake*
(1970)

Abbreviation of the Blues

Modest, he comes out of a cloister.
What, twenty-two? Just out of college and in limbo,
irregular from the wretched asylum of a ghetto.

Young Mississippi, they called him. His voice so soft
you could break it with your efficiency anytime.
He's like slate and noiseless.

Not even San Francisco put the city in him.
His was a repressed encampment of anger.
Yet he was dignified and beautiful.

He was shameless in stand-up moments.
We found him coming out of clairvoyance.
Now we see him

pumping in street demonstrations,
asserting his pride
in an ancient African egoism.

Air

The breathing the air the clearance the air the breathing of air

the math of air the figures of breathing the mind the men

the life the ring repeat in out repeat in out breathing

the life the women the men give to air to the breath

to the clearance a clear convincing math of things

out in the country the trees some irregular plants

not here now in this city of destruction to breathing

to hands even to eyelids to the sounds to the lips

that pave the pavement of flesh to the air to the way we walk

out in the country to get air to use our hands

that touch and break the soft mud out there under eyelids

Blind Old Woman

Spots on black skin.
       She is dry.
How time, how she waits here
in her dingy wool, shabby,
       the fingers on her cup.
So frail, a woven face, so oval,
such empty charity. How she remains
so quiet, quiet please.
             How the cup shakes. And
it is not straight. Nothing
is.
She does not sell candy or rubber-
bands. Like the blind man
at the other end. Of the silence. The sounds
       of one or two pennies
in the bent-up tin. Up her canvas stool
at the end of the shadows.
       How they return before her,
through these 1960 Indiana streets.
As she shuffles into street sounds.

Longlegs

Her cool was a northern thing brought from the South.
She really stretched out in New York City.
Longlegs now steps silently in narrow streets in the Village;
sleeps on easy floors.
In the dark she travels on high-tongue eye-trips
or on her indispensable devotion to music.
She works for her cool.
She really stretches out like a reel.
In protective winter nights: her yoga.
Her diluted footfalls through parks of drums: a challenge.
Night challenges her tender pot reek, her LSD.
Beyond the challenge of night her unknown codes linger.
Yet she handles the pressure
of rigid situations—Europe, Mexico, West Coast,
and again New York City.
Cities show her, define her—but not necessarily.
She is just a rapid position girl.
Change! Movement! Change of self!
Movement of self!
She is a self-sufficient girl,
a girl of efficient calmness.
She is in her private rites.

Segregated Self

He never knew she hurt
so way down at the mother level

of self, herself throbbing and breaking
between her and her man who broke.

She had this memory of her happy self,
a child, despite the gigantic holes

her mother kicked in her delicate flesh
in her instinct.

But she held to her man now.
She held her man together now—

what little there was left for the children.
She stopped idealism,

said fuck the hurt
down at the mother level, the pain.

He never knew so much broke inside her,
so much ran deep inside her,

as she tried to make ends meet
to end the failure of self:

herself on the floor clutching stink,
herself in the mirror unknown.

Flies in the baby's mouth,
flies on the bottle.

No, he was so washed up
he left that kind of life.

Grimness
was what she was left with.

Something Is Eating Me Up Inside

I go in and out a thousand times a day
and the fat women with black velvet skin
sit out on the front steps watching.
"Where does he go so much?"
I think often, not "much."
I look like a hood from the 1920s
in my Ivy League black shirt with button-down collar.
I go in and out to break the boredom,
the agony in the pit of my stomach.
I go out for a cigarette, for a drink, bumming it.
The floor is too depressing.
I turn around inside the closet
to search the floor for a dime, a nickel.
I turn my pants pockets inside out.
But seriously something is eating me up inside.
I don't believe in anything anymore—science, magic,
you name it. There is a tapeworm inside philosophy.
I go inside, maybe inside you—
certainly not anybody else.
In the middle of going—the inscrutable!
That something is getting itself deeper into me.
In time, I mean, it is pushing in against my eardrums,
against my time. This is what I move full of—slow,
young, strong and sure of nothing.
Myself a gangster of the sunshine!
The sun is blood in my guts
as I move from gin to sin to lakesides to sit down
beside reasons for being in the first place.
In the second place?
In the second place looking outward
for a definition to a formal ending—.

From *Private Line*
(1971)

A Mother's Pride

I played it, forgot it

I spoke it and

played it against the sophistication of the self—

its disappearance into print.

I played reel upon reel

after the cruel turn.

Turning, we built its center.

Playing, we destroyed its appearance.

Yet, it never turned back on us.

Being in the presence of my mother was key.

And she forgave herself in me.

Private Line

Direct, without the priest, you tried to transfer your sins to me.
You led me along a street
to the backside of a high school gym

and in the dark you used me
in the wet grass and I fell for it
while somebody's TV screen threw a light on us:

a large hull, your gray triangle—
obscured by my own ego.
You divided me, the hero of those weeks,

into whipped lubber. I look back now
with anticipation, a fitted, adjustable spirit.
You've turned me into broken parts

with your motherliness, your constant questions.
You now worry about and dream me so often
your husband is ready to leave you.

Rock Music USA

See the seventy-two-thousand-ton

butterfly floating over New York City

song sounds of the Beatles

emerging from its metal night

time flight—an electrical moth

the helpless star of its own light

show blinking in Times Square

to music from its own exterior.

From *Symptoms and Madness*
(1971)

Picnic

Historical episode, 1955

Sunday morning outside the arm of the city:
friends among friends

in the city's elbow under trees dusty green.
On the wooden table

beer cans and paper plates galore.
In summer dresses and T-shirts

they eat fried chicken
and plums and beets and baked apples.

Their smiles are carbohydrate
soda-pop glucose clean.

Their faces are buttered—one girl's especially.
Alma is her name—my first puppy love.

Her figure is an S. This is Baptist faith,
like crystals in that commercial.

Dream

Then I woke and discovered myself sackcloth naked.

It was like cinema.

An outcast from my own tribe,

for I was running but unable to get back to the temple.

A scribe, still naked.

Tears of shame running down my cheeks.

I stopped and smoked a cigarette.

I was broke.

I couldn't find the place or the moving door

but I had something anyway—

whatever it was,

somehow it was heavy by volume.

The Backyard Smelled of Deodorant

Summer outdoor beer party

of smiles and popped cans

brewed with Milwaukee sky blue eyes.

We dream of how and when to feel rich.

We are summer life

unable to kill what we eat.

Conflict

Smell. What smells? Is it the air of stale milk?
I was under the influence of Rimbaud, Baudelaire, and Verlaine,

the French decadents. Who do you contrast them with?
What did they smell? Ah, the fishy odor of a boat

where something happened.
I was a boy in a small boat swaying on the water

at Fox Lake, Indiana, 1953. See two girls and another boy
on the grass at water's edge?

On the Chicago trolley sweaty men
coming from the stockyards in their dirty overalls.

So much depends on what hits the nostrils.
Or consider the deep decline of Fullerton Hall

at the Art Institute, 1954,
with its impersonal odor of walls and floor.

Shadows circled heads.
Quick red splashes clash with earthquake force

into the gentleness of vestal green.
I claim that knowledge—

outside and beyond Verlaine, Baudelaire, and Rimbaud.

That conflicting disorder
was not disorder—it was order.

Not This—This Here!

My horoscope said
I am the kind of person

who would like living
spring and summer

in New England.
Maple sugar. Shoe shops.

Waterfront lobstermen.
Rich children.

Electronics workers.
Nantucket. Ah! Nantucket!

Is there in Nantucket a sign
that shows how far Nantucket is

from Rome and Moscow
and Calcutta and Bombay?

My horoscope is ink on paper.
I am not my horoscope.

This Temple

A flight of pigeons scattering peanuts
on Drexel in front of the Park Theatre.

My arms at my side.
I will never be that old man feeding birds.

The pigeons scatter trash;
they scatter sound;

they scatter the colors sound creates
in the exact time it takes to tag or

to frighten them away.
They always catch my eye.

But I wrote of doves for Ron's mag.
I even said the dove is a symbol

comparable to the arms of a crucifixion:
nails driven into the temple

to hold the warm blood in,
to destroy the paradox of life.

But it was all about love—
the pigeons or the doves.

Holy Ghost Woman

Sister Patty Johnson. Ex-slave to nothing but motion.

Midday silver leaves. The moment of the front porch.

Everything they gave she ate.

Off this Georgia highway she catches the sun.

Sister Patty Johnson. Near a shack she meets voices

soft honey sweet, trusting voices. She ate hard.

Pretending to be not even flesh. Wind talking through her.

Coming on with a flat devotion. Sister Patty Johnson.

Everything they gave she ate.

Theater

1. The bone. Stand still flesh: weeping or speaking. O mother wife sister, I trust. I trust everything that is. I trust your lies. I trust the child in me. I trust the children we are. O mother wife sister. I came from somewhere. I trust I came from somewhere. You are warm, my beginning. Is it a pose? What lurks in the pose? Am I in it too? He walks tall and beautifully on the stage. I am he for an hour projected somewhere. *Thank you, ladies and gentlemen, thank you!*

2. Above footlights: the Venus Theatre Troupe on stage. Venus and her girls: they are girls exercising the night's delight, girls against a bamboo backdrop. Photogenic. Lovely: Venus goddess on a small budget. Red lips, long legs in black stockings, rubber rears studded with beads.

3. In gin-mill stage lights, Venus has her hair piled on her head, a vast crown curled in a thousand dark loops. Her voice is naked as she sings to guitar music. *She is beautiful!*

4. Just two years ago—seems so many years ago: a young actor I used to know did not feel beautiful unless he had an audience. He jumped through his rooms practicing for parts. He stood on the kitchen table and read his lines. Last time I saw him I saw in his eyes whisky bottles and soggy cabbage.

The Distance between Tomorrow and Me

There is motion in my stomach. I cannot find enough space in the crevice of time. I am not moved until you move me. My mind had no business thinking back in time. Like some Roy Rogers returning from tomorrow, roughing it, engineering it, I ride the ghost of Halley's Comet. Venus is no longer riffing on the promise of love but instead she sings a song of natural resources. Researchers are assigning a new birth date to the image of Neptune. No matter what, I shall require a new spirit as I pass my point of no return to emerge luminous like nothing you can now imagine.

Float Up

Like a child with wrist against wall, I float up without anchor. Seeing

me float up there is fun in my mother's eyes. My sister has gone

away in shame. I remember her round face pressing against the train

window. The steps at the station were like those in a mystery movie.

I see the steps on a winter morning. I float up as my mother takes

my hand for the first time. We enter a bakery shop. She buys a large

sponge cake—her favorite, not mine. With memory of my sister in the

train window as the train starts moving slowly out of the station, from

the bakery mother and I go away into my first happiness. In it, I float

up!

My People Are in Centers

Cab drivers, heavy with sweaty asses on leather, move the future.

Italians make sausage. My house, it looks out of its own red windows

toward the nervous conspiracy outside on trial in all people. Who

drives us, cheekbone to cheekbone, through institutions? Some build

their houses of nightmares, not straw or mud. My people are far from

the dump yards. Bubblegum characters: they scream with joy. Ours is a

generation of astonished love.

The Rose and Satisfaction

What of wine and the wonders of smartly dressed ladies? What of

the mildness of the ladies? Take one lady! When she comes to her

mother's house, she takes a deep breath of fear. When will she be free

of her guilt? She takes her car at the curb. Smartly dressed she wants

me to notice, but only women come—and envy her. What of those

first days of drunken sweetness? And the night she came late with two

college boys to my door and knocked, showing me her pouting lips.

All I remembered was her voice a long way off over a phone saying

nothing new.

From *The Cotton Club*
(1972)

1915 Interior

Sister,

you open like a beautiful fan.

You must be the opening

to the greatest secret,

the truth: the ancient riddle.

Sister,

you spread, and

your center is never revealed.

You grow wider and smoother,

and your depth is unending—

opening without pressure, lightly;

giving me light, giving me myself.

1919

My mother was one year old that year.

Boys were just back from the war.

At the parade of soldiers

this lady stepped into the street

to embrace a black boy with one leg,

hopping on crutches. She was so proud

that year, proud of the boys.

She took him by the shoulders and

she held him back to get a good look.

"I'm so proud of you!

I'm so, so very proud of you!"

In the Interest of Personal Appearance

I wait for you to cut my hair.
I wait on your stool while you cut hair
so close to the bone the skull shines.
With your clean, dainty hands, you clip close.
You use a razor on the neck,
leaving circles around the ears.

Last night I couldn't speak to you
at that crazy party—
too many people around you.
Anyway, I don't go often
to these dizzy parties
where they wear masks
and ceremonial objects,
parties under indirect light.

I burn the invitations
and stay in touch with myself
in my din.
I'm working on our history,
on our folklore—its emotional side.
I sit straight at my desk.
But I keep coming to you because
although your mouth might lie,
your fingers don't.

Ladies Day 1902

Women in long dresses and bright hats,

men in summer suits and straw hats:

Sunday, on the Harlem River,

in long narrow boats,

people are dressed up in their Sunday best.

They sit stiffly and grimly

as the boats move slowly downriver.

It's true, people have simple habits,

and going out on the Harlem River

is one of them, but where is the fun?

No one is having any fun.

The Bust

You call me from a dream and I remember your soft voice, your

beautiful face, the skin of your arms. And I am not sure where it

happens or if it really happens in a dream. I wake up laughing,

remembering you laughing at the boys telling corn-planting jokes.

Busting up, actually. Busting up over the hog-head and peas bit. And I

remember your whole family thing—your mother, your wife working.

She hated her father, an accountant. Did I get that right? She grew up

on the Nicodemus from Detroit thing, the ghosts and snakes jokes.

She knows her father tricked her. He hated all women like he hated

account figures.

Like Family

You were booked into court as an offender of the law for making gin in a bathtub. You didn't rob anybody. You didn't sell it. You just made it and drank it. Your brother comes to bail you out. He's not your real brother, but he's like family. He knows the law. He says he knows the old men on the bench. Still, they might cook your goose till your skin is loose. Although there has been talk of changing the law, don't hold your breath.

Quick History of an Untarnished Sad Moment in Time

The painter and I met through a wasted man,
a poet, fumbling blindly
in his Lower East Side walk-up of sandy walls.

When I began thinking
that metallic things and art
were not so different from agriculture,
leaves, and trees,
he took down his watercolors of farmlands,
oceans, and lakes,
took down his big oils,
even took down the things he didn't do.

His wife, a lovely goddess,
turned from him about that time.
She started worshipping the deity
growing inside her own body,
growing from a tiny spirit
to a larger spirit—she called it Elquis.
She and her spirit moved away.

The painter was a genius, I thought,
and he should never have stopped painting
his trees and seas. But I have no idea
what the argument was about,
yet we stopped speaking.
Last I heard he'd gotten a nine-to-five
in New Jersey
as a principal in a high school.

Rig

Artie took us out on our first sail.
He made the boat move
smoothly
across every wave it took.

Rich guys were looking,
but we knew
they were not so polite
and modest as Artie, yet

when we were out
a ways, we waved
to those back on shore—
those rich guys.

When we were out a long way
on a calm sea,
Artie turned off the motor
and we drifted peacefully

while the three of us
went down below
and ate cheese and drank tea.
Remember, not feeling fit,

in the back toilet you threw up?
Artie was sympathetic.
Here was a man who could share
himself without thought of profit.

From *The Syncopated Cakewalk*
(1974)

Bruce and Nina

Nina got out of herself

while Bruce unsnapped the things holding her.

And himself. But nothing really helps for long.

You have to keep making the world new

and interesting. Some go crazy over large things.

Others simply wait a minute and do it again.

Bruce now stands waiting for Nina to change his life,

where there is nothing to work with but ideas.

Outpost

It must be fifty below.

The hungry dogs out back eat their own mess.

I cut enough wood two days ago to last a week.

A week ago, Blacky brought soup

from Ma's place, but it's all gone.

The Craw Stage Coach from Dead Point

won't get here before tomorrow noon.

I can't leave anyway. This is my job.

My horse got the fever,

had to shoot her three weeks ago.

A bunch of Negro cowpunchers

rode through late yesterday,

probably headed down to Boxhorn.

Yeah, it must be fifty below—or worse.

And though snow stopped this morning,

everything is covered with ice.

H

A tribal woman speaks

I am happy that you are the man
who brought the night storm into my belly
and did not lie to me.
I am happy that you are the man
who did not talk to me about silly love
or worthless romance.

I want you to help me plant the forest
and direct the winds
that drive the snow south
and help me carry the sunlight
into the North
across its plains and bluffs and valleys.

Can you become the flame
eating the stripped earth?
This will renew my people and me;
this will open the way
into another brighter place
where we can survive,
where we can touch
and still remain separate.

The Ground

The ground is still damp from the hard rains.

I keep dreaming of that pretty lady

in a long yellow dress in Baxter.

I had a lamp, but it burned out.

Thank God, I'm still sane, but I have no scheme.

Mr. Tough, my dog, died yesterday.

Since then, I have no one with me. No friends.

I am not free and I travel by night on back roads.

Sometimes I go through the woods. It's safer.

Tonight, the sky is clear.

The moon is yellow. At least there is no sleet.

I wonder what Jenny will do, seeing me tomorrow,

after fifteen years? My feet are swollen.

I have no teeth left.

Except for the ride with the medicine man,

I have walked for a month.

I Depart Some Months for Whole Areas

I've just come back from spearfishing.

Now, I will mend tissue to make new nets.

I check the long stretch of my skin

my heart my brain my eyes my teeth my feet

my back my bones my joints my muscles

my hands and my arms.

Okay. So much for a success story.

Everything seems to respond promptly.

It all leads to this thoughtless comfort

with fish on the grill as I relax,

finding it all fascinating—

these campaigns through here—

this spearfishing

to mend tissue to make new nets.

Law Magic

The three figures are irrigated and irrational;
they are duplications of each other.
They're yeasty but never seem to rise;

they seem to sink, black robes and all,
with their law books and appointment books,
with all of their stuff. They sink deeply;
they sink under the wide sink
of prohibited briefs and ceremonies.

You know, you've seen them: their eyes—
disembodied eyes—peep up
over the ceremonial rim
at us like human fragments.

And they remain speechless
for lack of character.
I see them as large houseplants
that should be watered
every morning.
And out of kindness, I would
keep their dead leaves clipped.
Even give them lots of sunlight.

The High Purpose

In the blue cash register of soft shades,
money casts a purple shadow
as its ringing spreads.
Its tones
from night till morning signal a lust
for things and the power of things.
It's a kind of bank. Willie Sutton said,
"That's where the money is."
Stop telling it. It opens wide
across white space. *Show it.*
Show how it opens.
It has a title, a trademark, a history.

The blue cash register
is as delightful as a living creature.
But don't tell us! Make us feel it.
I might decide to keep it for a pet.
Play with it. Rub its belly.
Stroke its ears. Certainly,
when it speaks,
I will listen to its high purpose.

Doodle

We are in the classroom.
He giggles and falls on his face.
I say stand up
and read the Papaya poem!
He goes into the poem from its rear,
struggling through its warm blood,
clawing his way. A Charlie Chaplin wobbler,
this boy is a doodle-squat.
He walks to the wall
and with it holds a conversation.
Look, kid, I say,
if you want to make it
through Word Diving 101,
you must stop
bringing me rotten onions.
How about a few Idaho potatoes?
The idea cracks him up.
He leaps on the table
and makes like a frustrated monkey,
jumping up and down, waving his arms.
The girls and boys laugh.
Listen: is this any way for a poem to act?
His pink-tinted sunglasses
are frosty from his own breathing.
The girls scream
when he suddenly takes out
his tiny notebook. He reads:
"I am a frog with bat wings.
I want to eat cars on the freeway.
I want to stroke my mother's butter."
Look, I say, go stand in the corner
and write a hundred times:
I will understand
what it means to be a poem.

Gothic Westchester

Dracula sleeps in the basement,

inhaling black smoke.

On the dark stairway

the bulldog is barking in his sleep.

In the living room the guests have no eyes.

Out back the lady of the house

floats over the empty pool.

Dracula lives in the basement.

His egg-yoke eyes

are stretching wider and wider.

In his black suit, he sits upright.

Spooky doors open.

Fog, the most obvious clue, drifts in.

Her Emotional Nature

In Philadelphia she was unhappy.
He'd changed—he'd reached his peak.
The New Year was an emotional trap.
Should she take a lover?
She slapped him
and fled to Boston—snow and sleet.
A week in Boston she
reached for happiness,
hanging out with a jazz group,
enjoying their company—they, hers,
but she felt like a toy.
Then, back together again.
Back in Philadelphia, on pills,
mattress on the floor,
she was a cocktail waitress,
an expert at drinks; still,
she felt untipped, incomplete.
After making him search through her,
she could not find cover.
Her profile was not her own.
Seriously, should she take a lover?
And her ability to sleep went out
somewhere on its own.
While he went on knowing
the pounding surf of her blood,
she grew to fear silence and men.
Her bones wiggled at their joints.
Some force was growing in her.
She reached into him for stars
but pulled out only stardust.
It was the color of his stupid cufflinks.
So she moved to Boston for good.

Zigzag Patterns

Rome, August 14, 1971

It's late.
Bats wing low over the pine garden.
They fly crazily.
We're riding a double bicycle.
The bats continue to shoot over us.
Now you understand us

here among trimmed pine trees,
dodging bats
and wheeling
between and around
people with bulldogs
in dog jackets.

It's very late—
dark in Rome.
This, after Florence
and Michelangelo. Back in the hotel
I dream—no, I have a nightmare.
I fall
locked in an antique elevator—
squeaky! SJS is at the mirror
talking to herself of Garda.
The downward motion goes on
plunging down center,

smashing panels
till it slams to the bottom,
killing thousands of bats.

Mountain Man

Imported from over the hill is this lively
fandango music on Friday market day.
To the music, I help Mary sell red peppers.
When I ask her to dance she blushes a lot.

We listen to what the people say.
Red peppers: some she crushes.
We exchange some for mango and sugar.

Nearby, in French, our grandbaby says goo-goo and bye-bye.

I am too old now to go down to Port-au-Prince
to find tourists and their big money.

This is my favorite seat outside our place in the sun.
Our bamboo hut needs repair but it is heavy work.

Anyway, I can still slit the throat of a pig.
But it's been a long time since we've had meat.

Mary's hoe broke a month ago
so she can't work the doctor's land.
He used to give us salted pork—but no more.
Each time I promise myself I will not beg,
the pain in my gut breaks that promise.

Old Car

I had two hundred bucks.
Paid, let' see, forty,
for the greasy bastard,
not pretending to know cars.

She ran all right for one day,
then forgot how.
Got sick.

Miscellaneous mechanics
fingered her undersides
till she coughed.
They screwed her screws
and stuck their fingers
deep into her curves.

To let them do this
cost me sixty bucks.

She was really worn out—
not worth my crazy eagles
with feet full
of the possibility of stars;
and to prove it,
I had to *pay*
to have her taken away.

Queen Pamunkey

The Quenn of Pamunkey . . . entred the chamber with a comportment gracefull to admiration. . . . [She] was cloathed in a mantle of dress't deer skins with the hair outwards and the edge cut round 6 inches deep which made strings resembling twisted frenge from the shoulders to the feet.

Thomas Jefferson

In drag, but hard as British morality
in the New World,
they, with honor,
delivered it themselves,
this twenty-year-late crown,

to a dead woman. Called her Queen Anne,
but her name was Chief Pamunkey.

Grief.

She lost Totopotomoi
and the warriors and never forgot
nor forgave. English ends

turned up in the Society
for the Preservation of Virginia.

The Powhatan at the James River, 1706–15

The Jefferson Company

I did not spy on your place.
It showed in your face.
Your two hands.

Brentwood and Oakville.
Black section,
where your best friend

from high school
turned into a beer belly
and a TV set.

The Jefferson Company?
One walked Cass Avenue
as it turned to the Mississippi.

Remember he beat you across
the MacArthur Bridge?
Remember Highway 70?

Remember the lady
with the shopping bag
dripping hog guts?

I smell them now
and ragweed now.
Near the railroad tracks

you felt each other's muscles.
His were bigger. There was no need
to spy on Hillside or Pine Lawn.

I saw the names
in your eyes,
touched them on your lips.

The Other End of the Land

I didn't mean to come back to this place—not just yet.

Mildew fungus here.

Everything from the loudspeakers to the keeper,

dressed in emerald green, turns me off.

Yet, here I am—but not for long.

I plan to finish up here

and go down through the mosquitoes

and dragonflies and fight my way

across the river to the lilac foliage

and by the time I arrive,

the autumn night will surround me.

Once I reach the cottage at the other end of the land

I will sleep, wake in the morning,

and clean away the cobwebs and water the dahlias

and the chrysanthemums and the larkspur.

Then I will write this poem on green paper.

American Setup

The scene opens as in a movie:
Cops and robbers straight out of cartoons.

A smile a day on the corner keeps the doctor away.
It's a great life. It's groovy!

Everybody says it!
A lady with diamonds and lace.

Over and over the scene expands.
"It's a great life if

you don't weaken."
A cop with a bulldog face.

He hustles a drunk cowboy
off the street.

"I'm an American citizen
just like you!"

We are all burning our bridges
behind us. This is nothing new!

Homeless man in a tattered coat.
Homeless man on crutches.

You would think the war had just ended.
Run of the mill. So what? Take a pill!

And out of the clear blue
the drunk breaks his wine bottle

on the sidewalk
in honor of the church.

Behind the man at the throttle
on the el train

a black girl
in a pretty dress, speaking,

"I'm sick of working
at the hospital,

cleaning up the mess
on people."

A man in the subway
relieving himself

in a corner:
"These people crazy as bedbugs!"

Stripper on a stripper pole:
"All I see is horny old men!

I'm sick of it all!"
A baby-faced bank president:

"An apple a day
keeps the doctor away."

"Did you see Jack Benny last night?
So funny!"

"Did you see Ben Casey on TV?"
We have our heroes.

See Lincoln! See Washington!
See Jefferson! See Kennedy!

See Martin Luther King!
See Malcolm X! It's late!

Everybody's got a hero!
Who's yours? It's 1968!

See those buildings in flames!
See the riots! These are not games!

See the assassinations!
What a nation!

In her seat, Grandma Moses
selling her paintings

along with canned jars of fruit!
What a treat!

The washing machine
breaks down!

Call the repairman!
The furnace stops working!

Call the repairman!
Bubble Gum Kid Clown

blows his bubble gum.
And somebody

closes the refrigerator door
on puppy's nose.

Boy flying his kite
above a high-rise.

Exhausted men
in coveralls

stumble out from factories,
stumble up

from coal mines,
out into daylight.

Charlie Chan catches his man.
Jesse James shoots up the place

and rides off on Roy's Trigger.
Spinning Top Johnny

drives his leaky jalopy
into the Smithsonian.

"Here," he says,
"this is where this thing belongs!"

Mother Hubbard
dances a war dance

at Broken Bow.
Billy the Kid on horseback

blocks traffic on the Brooklyn Bridge.
A man on vacation

falls into the Grand Canyon!
Pan American jets

fill the skies, purple as wine,
with futuristic sounds.

Odgen Nash writes the words.
John Williams composes the music.

People up on Sugar Hill
all dressed up and fine.

People in the countryside
cooking barbequed ribs.

The whole neighborhood
will have a good time.

The Gold Coast smells of chitterlings.
Phew!

Everybody's eyes are burning
from too much television.

Hot-dog dinner!
Popcorn lunch!

Mack the Knife is back in town!
Eat and Sleep

declares he's turning a new leaf.
The city expands its reach.

Cadillac
  (a ballad)

When he is five years old,
Cadillac Johnny thinks

he will be five forever.
He dreams of driving a Cadillac—

with a body by Fisher.
He and his grandmother live

at the end of her lost dreams.
He loves his grandmother.

She raises him.
But he's growing up too soon.

His father drives him
from one promise to another.

Cadillac Johnny grows up
near windows day dreaming.

This is his way of scheming!
He looks out at the moon.

He will soon be grown,
out on his own and smart.

With nothing to do
Cadillac Johnny collects junk

from the rubble
of a burned-down factory,

stores the stuff in a trunk.
Not a treat!

He is ten years old.
At twenty-five

he knows he will not live forever.
So he buys a Cadillac!

At the zoo
he talks to a shark that talks back.

Cadillac Johnny is handsome;
he's sharp. He wears a suit.

Women think he's cute.
He can love and talk well.

He keeps track of his thoughts.
He respects the church bell.

He participates
in his own quietness.

He likes to walk in the park.
He listens to his own heart.

His dreams are many.
He uses his mother wit.

He puts rude people on
a crosstown bus.

Cadillac Johnny takes chances.
He's a badass in his wet beanie.

He learns to race and to dance.
He falls in love at his own pace.

Her name is Minnie.
He learns to ski

and to ride a horse.
He sees everything

he can see.
When in a trance

he shakes himself free.
He's pushing thirty

He falls
from a runaway horse.

With a broken leg,
he keeps trying

to explain to the nurse
how hard

the hospital light is
on his eyes.

How hard it is to see!
She understands.

She dims the lights.
But he can't sleep nights

with all the noise
in the hallway.

The nurse touches his hand.
At forty

Cadillac Johnny sips tea.
He falls out of love.

He divorces.
Pass the sugar please!

He is lonely.

He can't keep track
of anything.

Pass the cream please.
At fifty

a fifty-year-old woman
loves him.

He loves her back.
Yet angels beat at his window.

He takes it as a sign,
so he moves to the apartment above.

From *Inside Diameter: The France Poems*
(1985)

Beaulieu

Red mullet: rosy in its sleepy profile.
Red mullet: subject on a white plate.
Blue tablecloth—as frame.

Mullus smiles up from its dead eye.
Olive oil glows on its scales.
Red mullet, red mullet, smiling in its bed of herbs.

Before you eat the red mullet, embrace at the table—
especially if you are not a mullidae expert.
The goatfish will kick.

Pray to the Red Sea and the Suez Canal.
Become skilled at fishing and fishing around the bones.
Do not tickle its erectile barbels.

It will not laugh at itself.
Tickle your own whiskers.
Scrape the slime from your body.

If your hair is matted, clip it.
And don't forget to clean your fingernails.
Don't come to the table unhappy.
Come with joy!

Bouquet for Lovers

I am tired of lovers.
They droop too much.

They smell like goats and remote plants.
They tend to stoop a lot.

They rant till they're yellow in the face.
They depend on appearance to get them in the loop.

In Nice or North Africa, it's the same.
I am fed up with lovers—*and* their toys.

They refuse to ride the circus horse around in a circle.
What could be easier?

What better way to express the absence of duress?
I meant to say what better way to display joy.

Lovers blush a lot.
Lovers have problems with their spines.

They cling to cigarettes.
Lovers light up after lovemaking.

So, I am quite finished with lovers—
finished with their inability to make love in the farmyard,

in the picture window where Monique sat
hoping to sell to lady passersby
her handmade hats.

Inside Diameter

Consider the straight-line segment
leaping through the center of the circle—
it starts from one position and ends at another.
Tension and conflict are involved and unresolved.
Consider the end points.

Gladiators lose their thrust.
Battles are lost. People praise the wrong works:
those early things, inspired dullness—no tension.
Putting it in a silk screen doesn't get attention either;
putting it under acetate overlay doesn't create conflict.

Jokes about Noah's Art—pardon me:
Noah's Ark—with a panoply of animals!
Watch the horse's eye flutter
just above the buckle on the strap:
it is an attempt to resolve conflict.

Machinery rusts by contact with stagnant water.
You want the intensity of warm-flowing liquids.
From across the room the guests look futuristic,
as if held down by a printer's correction color,
which when applied and stroked on, creates energy.
The working instrument resembles a phallus.

Once things are going,
you can stick a well-known face in a battle scene,
place a sword in her hand,
and let her gallop forward toward the surface.

But it's difficult to make any scene glow—
no matter how intense.
Unlike in art, holy wars cannot escape.

In nightclubs women in black stockings
shake themselves intensely at warriors
with hatchets in their belts.
Tension is sometimes hard to locate
in the cathedral of the imagination—which,
itself, is a cracked surface of conflict
shaped like Barcelona.

You can see variations in the imagination.
Mediterranean masqueraders
down on their luck surprise us all
with their creative powers
as they go about their business
under wriggling skies.

Yet, something, like broken mirrors,
is plowed under with inexhaustible anger.
Battles are won or lost to no avail.
Crutches are propped under the performers
after war to keep them from falling
out of their own bodies.

When it happens, prophets have their say.
A nun jumping rope in a room
with three inches of water.
Here, where they speak a language
I cannot speak well;
life for me is far from spontaneous.
Again, watch the horse's eye:
there is a message in the fluttering.

Losing Control at Nice

Get up carefully from the stool and go barefoot.

You are lucky the musicians are playing your song.

It's so easy to fall, except when you want to.

One might want to fall into a pool of circus light.

One might want to fall into a bed of sleepers.

One might want to fall from a helicopter.

Are the musicians still there? Listen to the music.

They are teachers. Try not to sneeze.

Lift yourself from bruised hands and knees.

Go carefully and firmly on both feet.

Over Drinks at Café au Charbonnage

They know us here now.
We don't have to ask—they know.

You come here to sketch;
I come to drink to your sketching,

say, of an old man with bent head,
gripped by trembling hands.

The waiters like us.
You are sketching the garden

of the parsonage across the way.
In it, an old woman in black shawl

walks among the flowers.
As you sketch,

it's important that I hold my glass
with as much skill

as you hold your pencil.
Look! There! In the distance:

those workers are going home
silhouetted black

against the silver sky.
Sketch quickly! Capture the motion.

In the City of Motorbikes

Give 'em the walled city,

poverty of the pushcart fisherman

on his knees before the manger

with the three wise men

bearing gifts

    ("Surprised," a friend said,

    "revisionist historians

    haven't chosen to alter

    the presence of a black man

    as wise")

and the wealth of Lascaris—the family

with its private chapel upstairs!

Give *me* the walled city.

I know what to do with it!

Last Days in France

My days were falling stars—each with a number.
On the promenade, I smelled the beach at Nice;

in the yard,
I smelled freshly slaughtered rabbits

suspended upside down
from hooks.

The smell got my goat.
I was up to my old detection.

Old Town bins of spongy tripe: larva—
or Crispus Attucks's brains.

My lungs filled with the fullness of the moon.
My days were carefully counted.

We drove a mile in no particular direction.
Flower vendors beckoned.

My wife smiled no thanks;
then we bought anyway—

as if we were planning to stay.
Coffee in sunlight

on Cours Saleya.
A sadness clouded my coronas.

Selected Moments in France

I ate a Gervais from a stick.
University students lined up in front of La Sorbonne.

A wino sleeping in Place Wilson
opened one eye and smiled at me.

The slime of moules was deep in my diet:
curse of living by the sea.

Winter now vanishing.
Postcard sellers still in the park.

I bought one showing a beach
with bathers in suits

circa 1923, Place des Ponchettes.
Philippe Brejean: "C'est beau, c'est bon, c'est chaud."

I ate the news from Monaco.
Grace was no longer in Monte Carlo.

I listened to Puccini and Powell.
I moved silently through May.

My Simca pissed me off.
In the English bookshop I was told,

"Picasso is expecting you in Antibes."
But isn't he, uh, dead? I said. "Are you?"

Picasso and I talked only once,
while listening to a guitar player

play and sing, "I feel like, I feel like
I'm on my journey home."

And: "Sometimes
I feel like a motherless child."

In the British bookshop
I was a sight to behold.

Radiguet was my double—my defense!
On my way home

I threw ten francs in the basket
of a beggar pretending to be 1923.

Years have it hard.
People have it harder.

From *Surfaces and Masks*
(1988)

She takes him into *The Rape of Europa*.
He takes her by surprise
    by playing the Avocadore di Comun.
She delights him as Puttana, then again as Odalisca.
He scares her as Nobilgiovine Veneziano
    and again as Cuoco of the Hotel Saturnia.
He scares her nearly out of her senses
    when he does his Compagno della Buona Morte act.
He is her cavalier-servant.
    He helps her lace her underclothes,
to take off her tight corset.
The music they live by is made for chambers.
He takes her duck hunting
    at the mouth of Tagliamento in the winter.
He puts her up in the best room at the Palazzo Gritti.
    They got no interest in Harry's
nor Martini Montgomery.
    In the summer they fight off zanzare
and spend much time on the islands.
    They go onto the mainland Sundays or Saturdays
and drive along Monfalcone and through Latisana.
    Once with Bill and Franca
they ate the best spaghetti in butter
    in Casale sul Sile.
They toasted Carlo Goldoni's humor
    and saw in his home
the only play Picasso ever wrote.

VI

Nothing in me goes out
    to the stuffy one
who comes over from the Lido
    because he has to,
to buy some cheap thing or other,
    and resents having to bump shoulders with the people,
nothing, absolutely nothing,
    whether we're talking about 1921 or 1985:
nothing, nothing, nothing!
    Everywhere you step you step gingerly
to avoid dog shit. She was smoking a cigar.
    He was causing a ruckus.
The tourists were beginning
    to come in greater numbers.
You could easily keep count
    of the big ships coming in
this time of year. Flooding didn't matter.
Unlike John Evelyn, I was not constantly surprised.
    I was at home,
as I imagined myself among the best of them!
    Them?—Again. Poor Dickens, poor Disraeli!
Goosebump weather!
    "—Oh , / How beautiful is sunset
when the glow / of Heaven descends
    upon a land like thee, Thou Paradise of exiles . . ."
I won't say "Italy!"
    Damned fool!—Did he never know?
I tried to be patient.
    I was not Lord Chesterfield's son
waiting for a letter from dad.
    Tightly woven missiles
of moral purity were never aimed at me.

Peggy G's home, with its Enchanted Forest,
      is open,
hard gray and iron black
      against the soft pinks across the Grand Canal . . .
Empire of light.
      Angel of the Citadel.
The place itself is Alchemy.
      You can go out in the stone yard and sit
and see the boats go by.
      The Zoomorphic couple will not come out and join you.
They are hopelessly entangled in their own tentacles.

      Also—go, then, to "feast the eyes" on the gold and silver,
the reds and blues, of Salome dancing
      with Herod's head held above her own.
Shapely, shark quick,
      and not a drop of blood spilled on her mink
(and see Herod before he's beheaded
      interrogating the Three Magi
as they plead and dance on their toes
      without upsetting their crowns).
And touch the brilliant rough surface of yellow gold
      behind Madonna Nicopeia's black-covered head.
She holds the Christ child against her stomach.
      He's a piece of wood held like a wooden block,
a little man whose red lips know no smile,
      whose eyes are more untrusting than his mother's.
Follow him, grown, as he rides a jackass,
      with the face of an upstate farmer, into the City.
Outside—a boat on spaghetti waves bringing back the Body—
      stiff and in skullcap,
very holy looking, this body.
      Patron, patron!
Sailors lower the white sails
      as the vessel nears the lagoon.

You may then want to go back inside.
    They go. We go. She goes back inside.
I go back inside, and there is Noah, poor Noah,
    sending out the raven and the dove
from both hands held together.
    You will like his sturdy face.
You can tell he trusts the birds.
    You may notice his hands:
small, with fingers
    you expect of a twelve-year-old girl.
And since you're there,
    touch the surface of La Pala d'Ora in the Basilica—
    rubies
    emeralds
    sapphires
    pearls
laid in a network of gold.

Then go across the city
    by way of the small calli
to look up at the Assumption
    (retouched, I think)
with a Venetian sky
    just behind the earthbound worshippers reaching up;
all except the messenger man.
    He's looking up at the cherub-packed heavens.
It's enough for one day.

XV

PG? The sister, the nose, the money.
  But then—hey!—most people have silly lives,
as silly as hers.
  The long early stretch without work—
then art collecting.
  It's the only thing you can do most of the time, (Faulkner).
We went (what a way to begin!) to see Eleonora,
  dramatic Eleonora, sitting forward on the edge of her chair
there in the dark room,
  fully dressed, bejeweled but sad, sad in Asolo.
With Bill and Franka again!
  Early spring.
You know those sudden thunderstorms in Venice.
  And sun again, so we escaped Venice,
and the tourists coming in,
  in the manner of real Venetians.
(They were, anyway—*she* certainly, from the beginning).
  Went to visit the great poet!
First, in the yard, I lost myself climbing
  into the hedges hanging from the wall
of his grand villa.
  Bees nearly stung me to death.
Colder, later, inside than out in the sun
  with the mountains behind.
("Did you say pasta or basta?")
  The great poet wasn't home,
but the caretaker let us in,
  and we studied the furniture,
the stone floor,
  the scenes of his life
left in the things possessing him,
  his rare books, his rarer manuscripts,
his priceless great chair.
  Leaving, in the yard we were caught in thunder
of an approaching storm.

Rain came like bullets.
To escape, we hid under hanging vines.

In the car going back Franka sang the poet's songs
remembered from liceo

when she was made by the maestro di scuola
to sing them.

XX

Beckett didn't come here, at least
    not on the same day Christopher Marlow
chose a darkness in the tower—no, campo;
    the music by S. (He's over there on the island now.)
But it's more *b* than *c* I'm talking about.
    Not Burgess though!
Venice has nothing to offer that is not already in the spirit.
    Already a lot was done with doubt.
Byzantines doubted not.
    The dama Veneziana came grandly into the campo.
No doubt.
    Those who raped Europe had no doubt in their thrust.
People in Harry's Bar seem to doubt nothing on earth;
    they lift their glasses to their lips
with dead certainty.

XXVI

Badly sick in bed but only for a quick week,
I drew a picture of my own stomach
      to show the doctor next time.
In this, our bedroom,
      with no Turner view
of the Grand Canal!
      It was not a tomb,
floating all the way out to the sea.
      Commander of profound stillness,
the bed became my workshop.
I became familiar with the ceiling also:
      gaudy decorations in gold and white,
pale green, sick yellow, feverish pink.
      Hangover silver.
I could go on, like Rilke, about blue.
      My illness was no romantic comedy,
though it was crowded with opera figures
      pretending to take real life very seriously.
All there on my bed, spread out before me,
      pretending to be print
on the pages of books, in magazines.
      And Pamela had to do all the shopping alone,
and bring up the water,
      and talk Italian
with anybody who rang the doorbell.
      But like I said,
the week went swiftly,
like a bleeding sunset
      at that time of year.

XXIX

Shy. She keeps a stiff upper lip,
  dresses like a twelve-year-old boy
forced to be clean—with tie and polished shoes—
  in some sedate military academy.
Proud. She works hard
  at hiding her total self-interest.
She pants like a drill sergeant,
  folds her hands across her stomach,
speaks out the side of her mouth like a guy
  (to the one behind him) in an Attica line
on the way to license-plate making.
  Her eyes! Her eyes are sharp and clear.
She is in control. Her brushes are clean.
  Her canvases are stretched
with the unmistakable tightness of a firm wind
  against a sail in sun
on distant Mare Adriatico.
  She is ready. Exhibition gallery.
Her show opens.
  She stands at the entrance greeting the guests.
They come from the expected philosophical positions,
  but the unexpected drifters please her most—
even if they are stupid,
  they mean her no harm.
The others she knows too well.

XXXII

I was back in Longmont, Colorado,
      one night,
yet my body stayed in bed in Venice.
      As I drove down the main street,
I saw gray, fashionable hotels
      right alongside feed stores
and hardware stores.
      The sun was almost completely down,
and the sky straight ahead
      was full of blue cavalry riders
in lemon-colored uniforms.
      Their horses galloped
across a beach stretch of banana fish.
      I smelled the lagoon.
No question about those odors.

      I stopped at the light.
The Venetian Lagoon Company boat,
      on a trailer, stopped by my Ford.
I looked at the driver.
      He had some good advice
on where I could buy tourist junk.
      No thanks.
It took them ten minutes at the Danieli Royale
      to find my reservation.
While waiting I scrutinized the people in the lobby:
      mostly Italian cowboys, farmers with red necks,
guys sure they made the right decision
      when they quit high school to become men.

Twenty minutes later,
    on the fondamenta and walking
toward a sky now onyx,
    filled with jujitsu arm-swings
my sails furled, my mainstay flew to pieces.
    Some kind of helmsman,
I ran along an embankment,
    walked two blocks down Riva degli Schiavoni,
past the elegant ones out for a stroll,
    mingling with the cowpokes
and innocent people on cheap tours,
    trying their best to remain unchanged
in the face of this, the oldest republic.
    Gondoliers steered their gondolas
along the asphalt, hawking, barking, singing sweetly,
    waving to the girls of Longmont.

XXXIV

Spring truly is here.
    The upward swing of feeling
matches the day.
    You place offerings
on the graves of pirates at San Michele.
    In the silence you hear political whisperings
from across the lagoon from the sea,
    which is still,
like a killer crouched behind your front door,
    but only half the time.
Maybe, just maybe,
    from as far away as Leningrad or Washington,
spring is whispering political thoughts.
    Meanwhile you try to hold the future
to maintain a balance
    of your own strength and pulse together
while listening to the voices.
    You know they touch you
but exactly how leaves you with dumb questions:
    "Can you tell who's coming by the sound of the walking?"
You seek distraction
    by exploring Como Bergamo Cortina d'Ampezzo,
by seeking out Adriana Ivancich,
    and by getting friends to write to the officials,
urging them to decorate you with an honor,
    perhaps the Cavaliere di Gran Croce al Merito,
so that you can strut through the city,
    cross every bridge at least once,
and proclaim the city
    your own personal playground.
This distraction, you realize,
    from the beginning,

may be your own way
     of sandpapering the rough surface
of your own political consciousness.
     And once it is smooth, then what?

XXXVIII

We drove over to Padova.

    The students built a platform
for G. to lecture from
      so they could hear him better.
I stood on it
      but couldn't get anybody's attention.

I am in charge of the trapdoor.
      The grave robbers know me.
The hunters bring the gaunt boar
      and the wild dogs,
and the farmers the sheep.
      Horses are too large.
At all times
      I keep a carcass available . . .
on the floor
      in case the officials
should come
      into the room
of our anatomy lessons
      (we can easily drop the corpse—
to switch—
      down the trap to conceal it).

So far no student
　　has leaked our secret.
It is for the good of humanity.
　　It is amazing how well
they all realize it
　　and even give presents,
on holy days,
　　to the families
of the grave robbers.
　　They are good boys, all two hundred,
and at least eight
　　will become great doctors,
I bet you . . .

XXXIX

The storm had no evil intentions.
    We knew that
and that
    it denied its own name.
Pure wind came
    from over San Giorgio,
once a place of skulls,
    and we crawled into the traghetto,
hovering like starving dogs
    across the Ice Age.
We could not locate the exact place
    of frostbite,
out of season
    because the message from our brains
no longer connected
    to the tips of our fingers.
The storm
    renamed the calli and canals.
The mind froze
    to the degree it could not
recollect the names
    each of us had before,
leaving us as stems without buds.
    The storm was not here to stay.
You have transgressed;
    Venice must sink;
pay for ill intentions.
    No, it spoke another language:
that of warm glacial sheets
    far out of rhythm
with any frigid texture of meaning.
    It made only gestures,
lashing out at San Giorgio
    with as much force

as it whipped against La Giudecca
    in its loneliness, width, and repose.
Then it pointed to its mouth
    (like some horrible god-devil,
demanding to be fed)
    where there was no tongue.

XL

Sitting here at our table
    in front of the coffee shop
in Chioverate de Simon
    with the closed hotel
adjacent the casa
    at the end
(the one I drew)
    where the shadows seem tangible
as hieroglyphic tablets,
    I feel the utter quarry-like surface
of this spring (or is it already summer?)
    as hidden relief
from the cruel theater
    that passed itself off as winter.
Even the strike today,
    with shops closed
and having to resort to canned goods
    for lunch and possibly dinner,
is no greater bother
    than the Jacobin winds
rushing between these buildings,
    or the sirocco from the desert
of North Africa.
    This day, blue and free of paranoia,
makes up for the malicious chill
    that hung over us so long,
wrenching us apart from ourselves,
    or the best of ourselves.
I know the Adriatic is still out there,
    and so be it.
Marinetti was so, so wrong:
    Venice should not be destroyed,
not on purpose (it will go down soon enough).
    And at worst

we will remember only the nosy thieves
        and witty pirates,
as we gaze at the lagoon
        from the factory town, Mestre.
And will the Socialist
        and the Christian Democrat
finally shake hands
        as she sinks?

XLI

They had just arrived.
    He was going to write
a long poem on Venice.
    She was going to paint up a storm.
They came like a couple
    dragging a dead horse.
We took them to the terrace
    of the Palazzo Gritti
for drinks and pointed
    to the windows
of Hemingway's suite
    just above us.
They were impressed,
    being literary snobs.
Then looking at the gondoliers
    standing, rowing their gondolas
as though they were participants
    in the Regata Storica,
as if everything depended on winning,
    she said, "My, my how romantic!"
And I thought of Mario
    the gondolier, our friend,
who worked nights mostly
    and whose smile
was like a swinging door
    held opened with a lot of light
coming from inside,
    and I thought of Mario
when he was angry,
    his flailing, his grunts,
his tipsiness
    (for he was never drunk!),
and I remembered the trip to Chioggia
    on the big ship, the crowds,

the sun, the children screaming,
    and there was Mario with his family,
going to visit relatives,
    out of his zanzara darkness,
        no longer in need of night vision,
insisting that we join him.

XLII

Any excuse for a celebration?
    Excitement cannot be manufactured
and held up to the light like plastic flowers.
    Yet the invention of Vogalonga
was not unlike that of fine columns,
    signed and dated. May 8.
We got a good spot
    on the Lido near the middle.
Going by were more boats
    than I could count.
They'd started at that place
    where the Grand Canal touches
Riva degli Schiavoni
    and moved toward San Giorgio.
There, you can hear the cannon go off,
    but we chose not to deal with the crowd.
Boom! Boom!
    There, that's loud enough for me.
I felt a rush.
    They were moving with a grace
as tangible as the lines
    on that triumphal dome
of San Giovanni at Macerata,
    toward Malamocco,
that "charming village,"
    as they say,
where the oarsmen will be fed
    and celebrated.
Some, of course, will cheat—have, already!—
    by taking a short cut
to the finish, but the main fun is not spoiled,
    as the balmy winds of the sirocco
push the vessels along.
    I know, everybody said

it was best to see it from its beginning.
    Prince Charles and Princess Diana
were there. All the more reason
    to seek another spot.
And once the boats passed
    we took the vaporetto back to Venice
and had coffee at the Canale di Cannaregio,
    where the oarsmen would pass again,
on their way back to the Grand Canal.

XLIV
(Envoi)

. . . and when we saw the slides,
    the perspective! Wow!
In the little red Fiat Junior, we drove
    from the Veneto down to Casino.
Nine hours.
    In the morning
climbed to the rebuilt monastery—

    up here no Monte Sant'Angelo,
the basilica to Michael.
    A procession of cure seekers
carrying olive branches
    coming toward the church
from a big blue bus
    with silver fenders and Goodyear tires.

A red donkey cart, a red car,
      a woman in red.
      But those bread eaters, peasants
with bent backs
      hobbling up the narrow sidewalk
and coming up on the big glossy blue buses,
      all mournful, worshipful, intent on prayer,
seeking cures—stumbling down
      the dungeon steps
with them deep into Saint Michael's sanctuary
      gave me both a sense of shame and awe.
I clung to the wall,
      so overpowering and sincere
was their faith and its expression.
      They made offerings.
They came with sores.
      They were the aged, close to death.
They came with incurable diseases.
      (Perhaps first time off the farm.)
They came. (And years—centuries!—ago a group
      of sheep keepers took refuge here
and were protected by the saint from the enemy.)
      So they still come.

In Rialto at Vietri you see the sea all the way.
      First the sea. Then more of the sea!
Salerno with her history
      is now also one dirty street after another,
one smelly alley after another,
      but San Benedetto
has not forsaken the dirtiest ditch.
      You can drive the narrow winding roads
from Vietri and see Ravello.

It was raining, and the road was narrow.
And the drivers drive like madmen.
I come around the curve
like a man who simply wants to stay alive.

At Paestrum
birds nest high in the basilica beams
where moss and buffalo grass grow
from cracks in Hera's honor.
Here at the base of Neptune's Temple
I see a large black tree in foreground.
Very Japanese! I love it! Gymnasium.
A Chinese artist sketching it.
Amphitheater Square. Italian kids yucking it up.
Sunday before noon.
Lunch, the reward for enduring boredom.
At Paestrum a priest and two nuns
herd the children toward the Roman building
north of the Athenaion. Politeia! Echo of Aristotle!
We squat in the shade
till the legs are ready to move again.
Again we move.
Not a picnic ground,
yet they bring sandwiches and corked wine.
The guards will not notice.
Greasy paper in the Italic Temple!
We walk along the wall of the town.
Sky? Hot metal. No hat.
Shadows are directly under things.
Back to the red Fiat.

"Whatta ya say when ya're in Pompeii?"
You say, Which way!
    Drove first nearly to the top
of the volcano,
    but the red dragon got stuck
in the ash and started sliding down,
    so we shot the excavations
and watched the birds bathe
    in the bird bath. Parrots, really.
Then the positions English gents laugh at,
    making mental notes to copy.
Why are the men all dark
    and the buxom women all so pink?
What's the correct word
    when one thinks of hot lava
pouring down? Encasing everything.
    And a dumb guidebook says, "The good fortune was."
In Julia Felix's Hotel!
    There, we stayed and dined in grand fashion.
My wife pressed a flower between the pages of a map.
    Deep purple.
Julia's garden, too, was grand.
    We walked about in it.

Once I stayed at Sittius's Inn.
    Didn't get first-class treatment.
No Albergo di Sittius for me—ever again!
    The "for rent" sign there was always up.
At Julia? Rarely!

In the House of the Bear
the mosaic in the entrance framed our pause;
   in the House of Cornelius Rufus
we got wet from the steam
   coming from across the street,
where bathers had no regard for anything
   but their pleasure and pain.

In the House of the Faun
   we heard the unexpected whisperings
of the goddess Fortuna Augusta.
   She really was arrogant
about her claim that only the "best people" came
   to her little village
("it's not the quantity that counts here;
   it's the quality").

Some Observations of a Stranger at Zuni
in the Latter Part of the Century
(1989)

Some Observations of a Stranger at Zuni in the Latter Part of the Century

I

A stranger to the desert,
I come here with my jaw jammed shut

so that speech does not spill out
like fish falling from a net.

Yet I speak. Having chosen Zuni
leaves a darkness roaring in my ears.

The decision is . . . a sharp fin:
We enter not by road alone.

If, during the trip inward—
in an unending switch-system

as on a train rail—
the upper body tumbles over

a top-heavy house,
do not be alarmed.

We are approaching
the end of the century,

yet Kothluellakwin
is where Salimopiya will continue

to carry his yucca switches
and whistle through his blue snout.

I will be his escort
between the parked Fords and pickups.

The dogs leap—leap fast at him.
Okay, we have entered.

Incest binds the people together
in the color of Corn Mountain.

Brother and sister,
trusting each other's heartbeat,

swim the Morningstar
as it rises from Spirit Lake.
They are surrounded
by powerful, powerful medicine.

Medicine men forgive them;
priests hypnotize them

as they watch themselves
reflected and lose focus in the lake.

Only where rules are unbreakable
will I break them.

With no reason to fear Unseen Hands
or the ancestors Cliff Bullneck,

Dirty Water, Warm Springs,
the others "even if you become a priest"

(they told her) you will never
make the prayersticks or enter the kiva.

You'd think she could have turned
to the antelope, to the great Star,

or to Forbidden One. I could not help.
I wrote only her name

with a stick in the land, in the sand.
The stick turned into a horned serpent.

One of her moccasins
was stolen from her foot.

The wolves did not take it.
Spider Woman had no interest

in a single moccasin. In the house
there was a cooking bowl, a stone knife.

In the house
there was a digging stick by the door.

On the porch there was a firestick
and a portable radio.

Those who came out of the suds—
Siiwhu, Siwa, Siiwilu, Siyeetsa—

being unfamiliar with hard surfaces,
watched the white line

in the middle of the highway
with special care.

Nobody called
either of the two girls a squaw.

Those times had passed.
If the head needs to be held up, use hands.

Ears will insist on a certain type of music.
Even our Lady of Guadalupe

cannot contain the body
once it starts shaking.

The Catholic Daughters of America
probably did not have an extra chair.

You peeped
through the parsley-colored maze

at her plumage, peeled back
from her shimmering body.

You wanted to seduce her for the seeds,
in search of calmness;

you had no idea
how framed and otherwise locked she was.

She remains.
Somewhere between Gallup

and the crow's secret
you were right to give up.

You had no claims on the pueblo.
Although your presence was tense,

your toes might well have exchanged
with your heart or nose.

I meant to say all of this earlier.
I hand her a scarlet flower.

The Bow Priest will not hang me
from the beam and beat me.

There are rules, laws within laws.
Yahaaaaheeeeyoohoho Yahaaaaheeeeyoohoho

Ask me no questions—tell you no lies:
Spanish word "Zuni"

is a questionable corruption
of the Zuni "Shiwi." Pueblo's Keresan.

It sounds like Chinese
and can't be linked comfortably with any others.

The Slavic shop-owners sell junk.
The tourists buy junk.

The paddy wagons
pick up drunk Indians in Gallup.

The customers of the Indian prostitutes
are rednecks and Mexicans.

She told me early
that sheepherding and silverwork

were in their blood. I said how long.
It didn't matter.

Her own jewelry
was hammered out of her ancestor's

flesh and bones. In his red pickup,
Ciwanakwa waited behind the big rock

at Yellow Rock.
He kept his bedding at Sack of Flower Place

because the lone girls came there
to fill the family jugs with clear spring water.

She grew up weary of errands.
She told me about being the Rat Girl

singing in the silence of her own mind,
in fear of the owl.

She said she was always among the Hawikn,
shaking the gourds, insisting on support.

They gave her oxfords—shoes—
when she graduated high school.

At Hawikuh she sang
and listened to the echo of her voice

bouncing back from the rocks. She said
the Crane Mother protected her there.

The Great Turtle who declared a truce
with Coyote also held her hand

in dusk light. Thin dust rose
in red sunlight as the sun sank

into sacred earth:
the belly of a starving child.

First Plaza was where kachinas danced
in darkness when they came back

to touch the people. She feared
her own footprints:

they might trace her steps.
She could hear their hearts beating

in her ears. The dwellers woke.
The warriors tipped out of shadows.

They ran—they ran they ran—
when they saw the Ghost Dancer

dancing; they came back
only when her brother took off

his Ghost Dancer mask.
They swore witchery was in the air.
Women locked windows.
Menfolk went to the kiva to pray.

Even if it was a joke, it was not funny.

    II

Goose-bump weather, this.
Blazing-Star Eater stands on the fence

keeping the motorcycle gang out
with her strong sense of The Center

of the World: Here. Anybody can drive
onto the reservation but—

and this is a big but—
people are expected to respect

the customs. You know? I count to four,
no, ten, not to get angry.

When we gather in the home
around the stove

and she says give me an "e,"
she is barely noticed

in her unlighted corner.
Only when the fire dies

does her singing reach them:
with its fire. The rhythm of bedsprings

in the night; snoring from another direction:
her bare feet on the stone floor . . .

at the window, the garden in moonlight.
Will the night-dwelling ancestors betray her?

At Halona, will they boo her?
At Wimia, can they send her back

to The Center? At Hampasawan,
will they drive her east?

At Hawikuh, could they join the farmer
and learn to be useful?

I stop at Heshokta
(available from the U. S. Government Printing Office

only upon demand), up on the mesa
five miles to the northwest,

and up there the ancient ones
question my interest,

say, "But you have lived among the anglos
and your ways are not so different from theirs,

how can—" etc. She tells me that
to respond betrays a Larger content,

that at Kwakinawan, in the south-southeast
the ancient questions are not scornful,

not so narrow, not so culturally bound;
there, she says, the river talks to you.

The people of Kechipauan
and Kiakime will greet you—

a stranger whose face is a mirror
of their own. You will not beat your fists

against your chest in agony.
In the months of her cradleboard

she scratched her way out—
could not stand confinement.

She gave her father a toothless grin.
Shalako eyes. First-born,

she was a Winter Dancer
from the beginning.

III

Not only did she always want her own way,
she had it. In Kothuluellakwin

the question of physical location
was resolved—in the novel. You read that?

Those words on the seal—Ulohnan,
Do: Shonan Udeman Dehya' A: Deyaye—not found

over the entrance to the underground city.
But never mind, the city went beyond the words.

I had to make my story thrilling or die.
You see, the Bow Priest had me hung upside down

from a beam in the roofless old church.
I had no choice but to give it to him

like he never had it before:
as beautiful as the Chicago shoreline at night

all lit up and pretty as snake colors.
They wouldn't let her watch.

Fear, you know, fear she might witch them,
break their spirits. You see, the priest

had councilmen, men with clubs waiting turns.
I was more beautiful

than the great birds dancing in the dusk.
They cut me down before morning.

The rabbit fur around Nawisho's neck scared her.
This Hehea face couldn't be taken in hand easily.

When they found out she feared it,
they sicked it on her. Sickum boy!

She stood slightly behind her mother.
Nadir in his darkness showed no darkness.

She refused to hide in her mother's dress.
This was before my time but related.

Below, in the last light, Hemishikwe danced
with Nawisho, calling rain down.

Not even feathers scared her as much.
Awesome Uwannami danced for thunder.

She got lost running in his zigzag.
His face: a mass of clouds, head covered with clouds.

The butt feathers? Plucked from a chicken.
Kwelele danced. His gray face, white lightning

shooting down, down, and the laughter he inspired
spilled over into that given to mudheads,

stumbling along the walls of Sacred Plaza.
Her father was a Pautiwa dancer that year.

She liked his big dog-ears and the long feathers
jutting from his head. If only—oh, never mind.

She knew who was inside. At Shalako—
she wasn't the only thrilled runner fascinated

and driven. They came out the dressing house.
Six. Sayatasha. Hutut—two Yamuhuktos,

Salimopiyas—two of these too. Made bird sounds.
The alternate dancers stored their energy

for the long night to come.
The beehive oven was a good thing

behind which to hide. Only thing:

as each bird was escorted, you couldn't go
in six directions at once to watch each

one stoop to be led
into the bright electric lighted house

of some newness. You followed the sound
of no more than one wooden beak, clacking.

It was no doubt cold, December cold.
You remember summer and hammering

done on the houses: shirtless young men
sweating over boards or electricity wires

dropping from roofs. Tar paper too.
Or new bricks, new plaster or window frames.

Perhaps from your father's shoulder
you see through the window

of the house chosen: Salimopiya with yucca switches
and fun in his movement . . .

You wanted to test the pipe nose.
The big lighted room (framed) by the window

glowed—full of dancing giant birds!
Salimopiya's yellow topknots and his blue snout

led the eye. Mudheads danced along the sides
inches from the feet of the seated spectators

with backs to walls. The drums went on and on.
This particular house was Sayatasha's—

Great Rainmaker in black and white gown.
He came to the window and spoke through glass,

wishing you good health.
Calculated movements of dignity and grace:

all week, each night all through each night,
each step was a spoken thing—something

perfectly designed to drum up something else.
This, by the way, ya know, was not the Yaaya.

At this time
there was only talk of reviving it.

IV

Look at your scuffed oxfords!
Mother's hands made the pretty Sayastasa

to pay for those shoes—promised for good grades.
"I'm learning. A girls' place is not just in the home!"

Yahaaaaaaaaaaaaaaaaaaaaaaaaaaheeeeeeeeeeeeeeeeyooooooohoho
Ya—

Self-disgust gave her a fantasy.
She put on a mask—comedian mask.

It was like entering . . . entering a different point of view,
not a Sioux winktas—one a little less complicated:

wearing a dress
for this one was culturally expected.

Gossip lasted and rested heavily in her;
men bled their lizards;

it was no fun knowing the difference
between an irrigation ditch,

a particular way of looking at something—
rear-tip feathers, for example.

Rage is a container: it is made. She feared
it would come to claim her, bitterly. "Oh, give me a home—"

V

She hears kachinas coming up the ladder.
The first is Pautiwa,

the chief kachina priest.
She screams in his blue face.

As he has his way with her,
one of his macaw tail-feathers falls out.

The other kachinas come up
from "where the deer and the antelope play"—

an area they crossed coming from the suds.
Pautiwa throws her to them,

and they huff and they puff
at her till there is little doubt she will give birth to a god.

One makes a cradleboard, places it in her lap,
before he hops away;

another takes foodstuff from his bag and feeds her.
Others begin dancing and shrieking,

making the oku call. Soon, they all are dancing.
This is when she makes her escape

to "where the buffalo roam"
and on beyond to Water's End.

Villagers intent on reviving the Yaaya Dance
interrupt her labor and take her back to the village
where the kachinas are still dancing, now in the Plaza—

around a little evergreen. Heshokta-folk pull her into the dance,
but she escapes again.

Leaving the village, she encounters three roads.
She takes the middle. It's a guess. It leads to Rat Place.

Dogs follow her. One snaps repeatedly at her bare feet.
Going across a yard she rouses roosting turkeys.

The he-turkey calls out to her. He wants her protection.
She has no time. And this is not the way back

to Water's End. Given another choice
she would go elsewhere. She calls out for help.

A blackbird comes and perches on her shoulder.
He directs her back to Water's End.

Just before they reach the place of shame,
the bird flies off and away.

VI

They told her to empty the chamber pot,
to fill the terra-cotta jug, to tend the hogs in the hog shed,

to roll up the reed mat, to rub the spindly legs of the old,
to tell the little children stories of Zuni glory,

of Ground Rat, Mouse, Owl, Horned Toad, Mole, Prairie Dog,
Porcupine, Skunk, Deer Youth, Bear Wife,

Mexican, Cloud Swallower, and War;
then, stories of house building and planting and weaving.

Later, she was made to tell Santu stories.
"O Lord Grant unto Them Eternal Rest." —Aashiwi.
Because it was habit, she fasted,

not fully believing in its power.
The old folks said she had to be careful:

there were only twenty-five thousand in the tribe.
Kyaklo's instructions . . .

VII

Right in church they deliver the Little Doll
from the Big Doll, but it doesn't matter

because in their terms (I speak as an outsider)
this ceremony is not sacred since it is partly Catholic

and the people left a long time ago. The Little Doll

says to the Big Doll: "I'm gonna go to Acoma," and she goes.
Wewha, the He-She, waves good-bye, an outsider himself—

they wisely put him in pants and buried him as the man he was.
That was in 1896. Half-breeds, too, waved good-bye.

An old Indian at Crownpoint saw Big Doll heading for Acoma.
When she squatted on the roadside

to relieve herself, all the tourists came out with cameras.
The Mormons over at Ramah sent their good wishes.

She was delighted to make new friends.
She wrote to the Little Doll,

telling her how concerned everybody had been.
Because everything was going so well,

they didn't expect any crooked horse-buyers
from California this year.

"One year we sold them one to eighteen dollars a head.
Everything happened in the history

and shadow of Vanderwagen. Sheep on credit."
Imagine an old man chanting to Uwanammi for rain.

He foams at the mouth. Imitate Shumeekuli.
Imitate the Horned One image Shumeekuli.

You are at the center of sixteen directions,
kneeling on your blanket on top of a mesa,

your jewels and other worldly possessions
on the ground by your knee

in a Maxwell House Coffee can. Down below,
in the valley, you hear, "Woopee ti yi yo ,woopee ti yi yoo,
get along little, little doggie." Sounds familiar,

like irregular breathing through scar tissue.
Since you have not declared a semkonikya

beginning to this prayer, there will not be a kenkia ending.
You will fast and plan to float in grace or disgrace

over the Sacred Lake like the spirit of the dead.
When you go down, you may speak to the family

that keeps the dolls, say, ". . . roadblocks between here and Acoma—
more than Carter has pills in his liver . . ."

leaving the understanding that the trip might require prayersticks.
Imagine her brother running from the men

who were supposed to whip him
at his initiation ceremony!

People on rooftops laughed bluntly.
Imagine her turning into the Little Doll! What a laugh!

VIII

She cried out at the first sight of Nawisho,
with its rounded head of buckskin

planted in a bed of turkey feathers,
the abstracted deer painted on his face

facing the eyes (such eyes!)
and the two vertical lines of thunder

standing for rain. He, like Hemishikwe,
was supposed to be pretty, a pretty god,

good gods both, gods of fruitfulness.
The old folks teased her about her crying

on sight of mudheads (dark with white markings,
zigzagging lines and eyeholes rimmed in white).

IX

This is a circle with a tiny central circle
sprouting eight stemmed flowers,
then the hard jagged lines of a cross with a square center:
it meanders inside stripes. Vertical swirls dance

through geometric triangles and frets
and expanding circles, larger than the first ones.

Look!—Hemishikwe's big square face
with its oblong slits for eyes

and the bush of feathers at the lower part . . .
Ah, what's the use? There's Nawisho—this is his circle too!

X

She sews me to her bosom.
She wears me sewn with the long thread of her thought.

She will wear me everywhere with pride.
She weaves the same kind of spell for the others.

Unseen Hands protect her, pour her coffee, and make her bed.
Winter flashlights are waved on the roads in the dark.

Her brown legs cast long shadows.
Unseen Hands hold the instruments.

I'm helping her smoothly, coming close:
she's wearing the Kokokci mask.

I place the Upikaiapona over it.
She reaches into my shadows.

My struggle is a dance.
I place the Tcakwena over the Upikaiapona.

What a heavy face! I go and get the Muluktaka
and place it over the Tcakwaina.

How many masks can a person's face hold?
I put the Pautiwa on her next.

Heavy, heavy face! I wear earmuffs and gloves;
I have trouble keeping my blanket around my shoulders.

She, on the other hand, is warm—at least in the face.
I hold onto the thread of her thought.
The Hopis stole Cholawitze, but he still brings us fire.
We are warm tonight because of it.

I never argue with drunk men:
they think they are warm when they are cold.

The jukebox was pretty loud—
but that's Gallup—yup!

XI

You watch the old man coming up the dirt road.
He's coughing a smoker's cough.

See the traditional headband around his head?
See the beads around his neck?

Although it's summer, baggy, dirty wool pants
hanging halfway off,

he carries a folded blanket balanced on his right shoulder.
When he reaches the point in the road

where you are standing, you see his profile for sure.
He turns and looks directly at you—
no, rather—*through* you:

tuna pikwayi!
Who is he—what does he—?

Yellow coyote eyes: they are flashlights.
You ask. He tells you he has come a long way to help you:

to prevent tununu—which is when the earth shakes
and splits open and birds fly backward

and horses break their legs running
and houses fall apart

and people by the thousands die in pueblo.
Koli, he says, is his name.

Somebody in the family was expected to die.
She told me to wear a velvet shirt

and a large western belt with a silver buckle,
jeans, and cowboy boots. She came in buckskin.

The earth was shaking,
but nobody thought it serious enough to panic.

Gravediggers had already dug the graves.
Church bells were ringing.

A burial blanket lay across the back of the couch.
Although it was summer, a fire roared in the stove.

In the yard, her brother was swallowing his first sword.
If he pulled it out without sign of blood,

they would let him into the Wood Fraternity.
Who was sick?

XII

She now had nightmares
about being dressed in white leather—
skirt in blue leather—armbands in blue leather—

helmet-mask and blue necklace and armbands again
and wrists and knee decorations: trappings!

133

She watched the older girls dance the Kiowa hoop dance
through butterfly eyeholes.

"Don't go to the rodeo! Don't go to the parade!"
She watched from the shade of her shawl,

the saffron one. She first wore it,
she told me, when she danced with the girls

in the dance for Achiyalatopa.
All of this was in the past—thank God or somebody!

She danced that winter in her black dress
and wore lots of strung coral,

silver beads, and turquoise around her neck
and on her ears and wrists and fingers

and felt fabulous!
It was the winter she began to feel like a woman.

XIII

This to string music!
Huh huh huh huh huhhuh!

I help her sing to Muluktaka and Nawisho
and a poor Cumte'Kaia and the sadness of Mokwanosana

and to snowflakes and Yamuhakto
with his armful of wood and to "The Old Dance Man,"

Koyyemshi, to the "Owner of the Springs," Tkianilona!
This—my chant! A ha a ha a ha!

But sadness is part of what I know.
Look, I can dance them all, all—the tricky friend said.

The silly suitor.
Sad, sad—the miracle in the cave, ice cave!

Taming of the mountain lion!
The three virgins! Horror of the wound puttees!

Land grabbers—!
Keep the music coming! The chanting and the singing

and the dancing, the sad music of joy!
Let the earth burn with the intelligence and brilliance of the sun.

We were no longer living in prehistoric times, I sadly said.
She had said as much many times.

Laselute
Laiiuaitsailu

Patrico Pino
Palowahtiwa

Yo—a! All good and well,
but—this was the twentieth century

(as if that meant something
profound!)

She said they had a story for every occasion:
the unappreciated wife,

the witch whose powers have been confused
with those of a priest,

how Navajos caused albinos among them.
And there was black Esteban—

making Zuni babies
to the sound of pizzicato notes

somebody from Spain remembered.
While all this went on, her telling,

I imagined glissando runs sweet enough to taste.
I help her hop the snowbird hop.

She wonders if I'm going to betray her,
trick her like all the rest.

I hope not.
I strut and wobble under my helmet-mask.

I blow my bubble gum for her.
I dog dance, deer dance, snake dance again, hop the snowbird.

She takes off her dark glasses to see me better.
I feel blessed by her Mother of Dawn.

She sings a cowboy song—Prince Albert Hunt
or the Herrington Sisters (I forget which group).

I feel protected—yet distressed Hoo-o! Ho-o-ota!
Lwolohkia-a-a! O-Ko-ko!

XIV

When you eat venison, save the fat
for Coyote, she said.

If he is not happy, drive him away with a stick.
Turn the logs in the winter stove.

One day Turtle says to Coyote,
"Would you go out on this limb—?"

You know the story:
(The Buzzard took the Monkey for a ride in the air . . .).

Coyote falls and breaks his canines.
Say! I remember another one—

How did Coyote get his yellow eyes?
Ahhhhhh! Ya know that one.

You used to listen to Annie Dodge Waineka on KGAK in Gallup?
The Navajos—they all said—were out front. I listened.

When you eat dog meat, don't tell anybody.
There are times when it is necessary.

When you feel safer, attend classes
at Navajo Community College.

Shiprock is not far. Take a flashlight with you
if you attend night classes. Yo-a!

XV

Frank Darden danced like a god,
and he drove his Thunderbird, with its blue eagle on the hood,

the same way. She thought she loved him,
this Window Rock boy,

thought he was a secret hospital
meant to cure her shivers.

He worked as a clerk at a trading post;
his father worked in the coal mines, mining silver.

Frank was tricky: a Navajo, he wore a T-shirt
with the Zuni sign of war.

He came barely able to hold the armful of gifts
he brought for her. He took her dancing at Window Rock.

He made her think she could win Miss Indian World.
Oiyosoa.

Coupling, said Frank Darden, is done
the way they bang trains together in Gallup.

If you are a woman and a Zuni,
there are questions to consider:

ways not to be.
One must not be an ill-mannered tomboy—

a tcakwaina mana, a shameless hussy,
with thoughts meant for Anglos . . . of genteel ways.

One must not wear nightmare leather
or give in to Pinawa wickedness.

No witching around!
No rock 'n' roll! No crazy medicine! No hanahha!

If you follow the Old Ways
and chew the tenatsali and wash with the yucca

and be a good ulani and keep a sacred toyallanne
and keep to one tilinne

and keep a sonahtehi life and pray—
"I sana nakwe . . ."

If you are a Zuni and a woman celebrate
("Ee——so!") the storytelling.

XVI

Kachinas dance around her,
menacing her with pelts and cedar-bark torches.

One beats at her bare legs with yucca switches.
She can't put her finger on exactly what she has done wrong.

Dressed in sagebrush
and decorated with see-through duck feathers,

I try to help to rescue her.
The kachinas accuse me of trying to imitate Salimopiya.

Sally Mop who? I turn
so they can see the hepakine design on the other side of my face.

I flap my parrot feathers in their faces.
I jut my snout at them. They are not impressed.

I go and sit in a pumpkin patch and sulk.
It's Sunday the fourteenth—if that means anything.

It's winter too if that has any meaning.
Back at the village I can hear them singing.

I hear the drums.
The folks are planting prayersticks in the Red Earth.

Pautiwa is expected? Those with masks wrapped in cloth
have gone to the field to dig little holes.

They will place the masks facing east in the holes.
The sun is resting on the top of the mountain.

XVII

You dress yourself in hawk feathers
and wear a halo of goat's hair around your head.

You decorate your ears with squash blossoms.
You cry raindrops. You have no idea who you are.

You paint your face yellow with clay from the lake.
They say it is Kokokci pink.

Your mirror is not good.
You wear your hair brazenly down your back.

They say you must submit to flagellations
to drive out the demons. You'll feel better.

XVIII

She let her mind wander like the line of a blue pencil
tracing a wavering direction on a map of the village,

moving along the streets
and through the yards and along the riverbank.

The smoky blue of sacred mountain
held its own power with stillness unrelated to its volcanic belly.

The fire god never slept.
He could come again and burn the villages

and roll the people in his ash.
She watched her thought follow the movements

made in the Lahewe dance;
it moved tracing the smell of the hot bread

in the beehive-shaped oven,
on, around and around, inside the rolled-up cedar bark.

Her line of thought followed the menfolk
out to sheep camp, smelled the bacon frying,

the spring earth. It cut like the metal of skates
into the ice on the frozen lake;

it splashed and rose
and fell like the arms of the children

swimming
in the government dam in August.

XIX

You bring in the firewood;
you go for the food stamps; you grind the corn,

store the cornmeal in jars and cook the lamb stew
for three days; then you bake the bread outside in the oven

and change the tires on the pickup;
you pick up the mail at the post office;

and you are careful not to fall asleep on some mesa
and get raped (it happens all the time)—

because you've seen how jannis are disgraced—whole clans!
You are careful to stay away from crevices in sandstone—

you know what can suddenly come out!
So you feed the hogs, feed the chickens,

empty the pee pot;
you know how to be a good girl.

No way will you give birth to an unwanted child,
falling out of the sky, miracle infant of some god-awful kachina

(who probably has a secret villa in Phoenix—no less).
This way you will not have to wear dark glasses

when you go to market or into Gallup even.

Don't let the boys shake their shuminnes at you.

Ignore their bravado. Don't buy their fetishes—
silly ears of corn with feathers attached!

They are ready to go all the way.
Dressed as Keyemsi

such a boy can clown his way into your heart.
Even the serious ones, like Kona—

with his big yellow head and leopard spots—
can throw you, misdirect you.

Don't get mixed up with the stuck-man
when you go to Punchkofmoktaga to fetch berries;

he's mystery itself, a thrower,
a striped dancer with green horns.

Stay away from Owl dancer, Mongwa; and Longbill—
he's just as bad,

wearing his white and red skins
and waving his green feathers.

Avoid at any cost Palakwai, the Hawk,
decked out in exotic feathers with headgear

of white and brown feathers,
waving his red tail at the flower dancers Tsitoto.
Cook beans for your family

but don't dance with the bean dancer,
Pachavuin mana, fully covered like a family secret

(but sacred, I'm told!), and it's probably just as well
that you stay clear of the corn dancers too.

Like the cow bride in black—
they carry the spirit of Angwushahaii.

XX

Not so absolute a stranger to the village
as to the desert in general,

I am able on occasion to surprise her
with my ability to call all the shots, plan the dances,

talk the talk. I told her things she never knew—
from being so close: Mastof, sober,

sober Mastof she never knew.
She laughed (properly, of course)

at blue-faced warrior Qaletaqa
but fell over the foot of the buffalo dancer,

Mosairu. Qoqlo?
Another laugh! But with good will.

XXI

These nonroad entranceways
and the things they lead (have led?) to—

Piptuka swinging his knotted stick
(though he swings it for the first time just now)

at the ogre, Toson, and at Kikwilyaqua
in his white man's clothes, shaking a gourd;

night rooms rimmed in blue smoke
and peppered with the slow bite of western voices,

of Zunis dressed as giant birds,
falling through the smoke that rises—

and the mudheads, on purpose, also falling
so we can hear ourselves cry out, *E-lu! He-lu! Hi-ta!*

The ways do not lead necessarily into the house
or souls or Spirit Lake.

They may make them expedient,
though to sleep off the bad dream

in a root seller
or in the granary will no longer work.

Glossary

Note: all words are Zuni except where indicated.

AASHIWI: Zuni; the people

ACHIYALATOPA: kachina of the Sword Swallowers ceremony which takes place every four years in winter

AH! AHI!: my poor old legs

AHAIYUTA AND MATSAILEMA: (also Ua nam atch Piahk'oa) sacred and terrible two or twin boys

AIYAYAODE: Hopi kachina

AKYU: he went

AKZEKI: boy (very small)

A'LEMO CA'LAKO: grandson!

ALIKSAI: (Hopi) once upon a time

ANELHAAWA: hawk

'A-SH'I-K'-YA: dead

ASH WAY: Milky Way

AT-E-YA-YE: here are some beautiful flowers

ATIIKYA: (interjection) dear me!

AWITHLUIANE: terrace or sacred terrace; the earth (symbol) as sacred altar for use by the gods

AWOKANA-WE: (male speaking) to all his sisters as group

AWONAWILONA: Zuni Supreme Being

A-YA-VWI: dangerously susceptible, tender, delicate

BELICIANA: Navajo word for Americans

CHALE: child, or the young of an animal

COMO LOS ZUNI: when in Zuni do as the Zuni

CORAL DIRECTION: old term for "south"

CUMTE' KAIA: father of legendary girl who is raped by kachinas

EE-E-E-E-SO: audience response to storytelling

ELE: girl

E'-LU: "how delightful"

E-LU-YA: beautiful ones

ESONOTEATU: surely or okay

ETAWA: turtle

HA HA WAHA!: laughter

HANAHHA: (interjection) Wow! God! Shit! Damn! etc.

HA-PA: ghost or corpse-demon

HAUKABEDE: Hopi kachina

HAWIKUH OR HAWIKU: Zuni or Cibola

HEHEA: wild men of sacred dance, runners to the priest clowns; type of
    face Nawisho has

HE'-LU: hurrah!

HEMISHIKWE: ceremony and kachina

HEPAKINE: Zuni design

HIM: a suppressed giggle

HI-TA!: Listen!

HOKUWAM: Hopi prayer

HONAYANE: ritual killing of an eagle

HO-O-O-AWIYEISHIKIA!: cry of victory

HOO-O! LWOLOHIKIA-A-A!: Murder! Murder!

HO-O-OTA! HO-O-OTA!: Come quick! Help!

HO-O-O-O THLAIA-A!: cry of distress

HUUTUTU: kachina; deputy of Long Horn

IKINA: youngest sister

'ISHANATAKYAPON: slick, slimy rocks

I-THLIM-NA: god or superior being

JANNI: younger siblings regardless of sex

KAKA: order of the Sacred Drama; a dance; mother's brother

KA'KAMO: (Host) Uncle!

KA'SEMO CA'LAKO: Nephew!

KAWA: oldest sister

KAZIKI: small girl

KECHU: (Hopi) animal figurine

KEKEI VIRKEN: (Hopi) Virgin Mary

KESSHE: hello or hi

146

KETCHIPAWE: calcareous sandstone

KEYEMSI: kachinakia-al-lan; water shield

KIAKIMA: extinct place at Zuni Pueblo

KIRTLE: (English) sash to cover genitals and buttocks

KOA: (Hopi, Pueblos generally) throwing stick

KOH-THLOU-WAH-AL-WAH: ceremony every four years to give thanks to the
kachinas for freedom from drought and infertility

KOKO: spirit

KOKOKCI: kachina of good or beauty

KOMNIN: (Hopi) notched-stick player

KOLI: kachina of earthquakes

KOTHLUELLAKWIN: City of the Kachinas (gods)

KOYYEMSHI: kachina

KUKU: father's sister

KURI: buttocks

KWARUPOR: (Hopi) movement of dancers toward the kiva after the
Uwepor dance

KYAKLO: kachina priest

LAHEWE: one-day corn dance

LE-PA-LO-K'IA: food—a red meat paste wrapped in corn husks

LII THLAIA-A!: Here!

LOLOMAI: (Hopi) "hello"

LONG HORN: kachina priest

MAKKI: woman, girl

MAPURIDE: (Hopi) women who sweep path for foot race

MAPURNIN: (Hopi) boy in a foot race

MASTOF: kachina

METATE: mealing stone for processing corn

MEWISHOKKWA: owl

MILI: "Breath of Life"

MI-LI-A-ME: corn baked and boiled on the cob; dumplings; griddle cakes

MITSIPOCA: a dwarf

MI-WE: corn on the cob

MOKWANOSANA: the twins who protect the Zuni; Great Lying Star—it rises
in summer and as early as midnight foretells of the coming of morning

MONGWA: winged, sacred kachina figure

MOSAKI: bald-headed man
MULUKTAKA: ceremonial mask, kachina
MUWAIYE: Sword Swallower's dance

NA'NAMO: (Host) Grandfather!
NA-TI TSA: meat of the deer
NATOAI: (Hopi) prayerstick
NATOYPOR: (Hopi) dancer's altar
NAWISHO: ceremony, a kachina
NCAI: National Congress of American Indians
NEWEEKWE: Clown Society
NICOTIANA ATTENUATA: wild tobacco

O AI o!: I knew it!
OEO (AT Zuni): Office of Equal Opportunity
OLLA: a type of milk
OLLA MAIDEN DANCE: civil dance open to public; done by the traditional
    Olla Maidens of Zuni
O'-LU-TSI-NA: very fine cornmeal
O'-WE: fine cornmeal

PALAKWAI: hawk kachina
PAPA: older brother
PA'PAMO: (Host) Elder brother!
PAUTIWA: chief kachina priest; has blue face, blue beak, furry ears
PEENY: penis
PI-A-LA-WE: cord or cotton shields
PIKI: (Hopi) type of bread
PINITU: (Hopi) spruce
POITAKA: (Hopi) eye man or tihikya (doctor)
POLLENWAY: life
PUNCHKOFMOKTAGA: extinct Zuni place

QALETAQA: warrior kachina

SA'-KO-WE: mish-yeast (leaven); coarse cornmeal
SALIMOPIYA: kachina
SAWANIKIA: to "see" an enemy is to take his life

SEMANAWA: to call

SEMKONIKYA: the end, thus ends my story, etc.

SHALAKO: famous Zuni winter ceremony

SHI-PO-LO-A: mist-enshrouded

SHI-U-NA: hazy, steam-growing

SHOHKOYA: playing a flute

SHOYAKOSHKWE: southeastern mesa at Zuni

SHUMMINE: (also tu'linne, tilinne, peeny) penis

SHU-TSINA: turkcy vulture

SIUIUKI: a demon (killed by Coyote)

SON'AHCHI: once upon a time, thus begins the story

SONAHTEHI: let us follow the ways of our ancestors

SONTIINOO: long ago

SOYAL (HOPI): house blessing ceremony

SUMKUP (HOPI): painted buckskin

SUWA: younger brother

SU'WEMO CA'LAKO: younger brother!

TA'-A OR A'-TA-A: corn (generic term)

TADA: (also tachchu) father or father's brother (uncle)

TALAAAAA: sound made climbing a ladder fast

TALAKI: males

TA'LEMO CA'LAKO: (Host) Son!

TA'TCUMO: (Host) Father!

TCAKWAINA MANA: ill-mannered girl. tomboy, shameless woman (a Hopi
   expression commonly used at Zuni)

TCAKWAINA: ceremonial mask

TCHU-KWE: silence

TECAMIKA: echo, echo man

TENATSALI FLOWERS: medicinal flowers (yellow and blue)

TENKIA: the end, it is all, etc.

TESESE: "sound of pottery drum, a large jar with skin stretched over its
   orifice" (Tedlock)

THLAWASHIE: (Hopi) prayer feathers

THLIM-NAH-NA: god or superior being

TISSHOMAHHA: (interjection) God! Wow! Hell! Shit!

TKIANILONA: kachina

TO'CLEMO: great-grandfather

149

TOSHIYA: so you've come
Towayalanne: Corn Mountain, Thunder Mountain
TOYALLANNE: vagina
TSILLU: mother's younger sister
TSITTA-LUCCI: old mother; sister older than mother
TSITTA-TS'ANNA: little mother; sister younger than mother
TUNA PIKWAYI: look through or look fast
TUNGWAYANE: (Hopi) ritual naming of the baby before the sun with
  prayer meal
TUSAYAN: Hopi language

ULANI: females
UPIKAIAPONA: ceremonial mask, kachina
U'WAKAMO CA'LAKO: great grandfather!

WAVY: crazy

YAAYA DANCE: partly a social dance done around evergreen tree at plaza
  center; revived in 1969 after twenty years absence
YAMUHAKTO: kachina
YEPNA: substance of flesh, such as dried meat
YO-A!: What a pity!
YUCCA SUDS: soap

ZAWAKI: boy (older)
ZITTA: mother

From *Parking Lots*
(1992)

Parking Lots

All across America I travel and I remember Heather saying, "All I need is a
    post office and a liquor store."

But *I* need parking lots to feel I'm really in America. Parking lot diners and
    even dives next to department stores and wholesale stores,

all across America under good skies with clear afternoon light.
Up here in Elkins Park, in the house, in our brightest room,

the light is bright but out across the land of parking lots it is raining
in places dotted with fast-food joints. Up here or over in Jenkintown

or out on the wondrous freeway nobody worries too much
about anything—just park and eat. When the gas goes, call the gas man.

When the lights go call the light man. Just like in that resort town
we remember so rightly.

In searching across America for the essence of parking lots
I drive into the parking lot of my choice

for another order of crusty onion rings, a cold Coke,
and a hot fried filet of fish.

This is the only way to hit the visible crux, the tackiness aside. Notice,
    there are no sidewalks.

People on foot not welcomed. Moving by means of motor
you may be worth robbing yet luckily you are hard to reach.

You are moving fast, a whole technology unto yourself.
Pickup-truck drivers dodging stickup artists,

finding parking lots of drop-offs, fast romance, and lots of glances.
Vacationers hanging out as an ever-present chorus.

Lots of ordinary emptiness, none of it meant to be bluntly shocking.
Even so, I am shockproof. I find it hard to recognize my own image

reflected in the plate glass alas; you bet your ass.
Nothing here left for the senses to respond to. No heartache.

No boredom. We respond to despair at the graveside
of something lost. I respond! Back, then back upstairs on the seventh
      floor

in the drafty apartment I meant to feel safe and at the window
I watch the rain in the parking lot. So as not to misplace money

we put it on the kitchen table; easier than putting it away
and taking it out, counting and recounting it every day.

Now I take the train into the city twice a week to teach,
going through parking lots, walking in lots of emptiness,

seeing lots of empty buildings, crumbling buildings,
lots of vacant lots. Philly rubble, double rubble, and more rubble!

All of it on the way back into the earth. But there are rules.
There is order even in rotting wood and dust,

even in decomposing stretches of concrete—order like in a palm tree
or a flag or a pickup truck out front of McDonald's.

It's not like in a restaurant seeing, say, a waitress
you've never really looked at now out of place—in, say, the Laundromat

or the pet shop. Stop! You know the face but you can't place it backwhere
      you think it belongs. I'm not waiting on my inner landscape

to sprout a road on which to remember and travel. I'm after precious
and proven stretches of space, space filled with splintering silence

or first-rate noise—like that blasting from the front end
of the new Chevy pickup parked in front of the house.

Unlike in the parking lot, in the workshop I feel needed.
I point out to students their mistakes.
I tell them how to improve their poems.
They say, "You gave me comfort big as elephants,"

and I come home energized. I've made a difference.
I'm ready to rake leaves. They've come down

in the deliberate wind. They've covered the yard
and walkway. Against the coming storm,

I pile them against the fence and pack the stack tightly.
The first disappointment is real

and filled with surprise—like a moving violation
that leaves the car permanently parked, smashed

bumper and fender, stashed between a junked trailer
as silver as sky through plate glass and a stripped SUV

upside down. Oil stains can be taken as symbols

of machine mystery just like that line of hamburger stands
over there. Monuments to hunger and routine—unable to transcend

the point they make. I touch blacktop stone benches
at the bus stop. More dumpsters, more trucks. I drive up

my steep driveway. Today I saw an orange car
crashing head-on into a wall of concrete. This was not a test.

The boy was supposed to be parking a man's car. I park my car in the
     driveway and shut off the motor. On the highway there

were motorcycle gangs probably looking for billboards
of super-suspended breasts jutting out over beer cans.

Parking-lot regulars gone to pot in their exposed everydayness,
passing everybody while looking sideways

into the shiny chrome of transfer trucks, pretending
to be cartoon characters, roaring into parking lots.
They lumber into burger joints where I am searching
for that perfectly impersonal surface of concrete.

Give me a true surface—something not exactly a remote source of
    impersonality. Here is another parking lot near the university.

Nature here has some presence. Ants. Yes, ants.
I'm careful, as I cross, not to step on them.

They have a point of view, you know. I go into the nearby diner.
Ants on the Formica. I inhale the plastic surface

and listen to the vents in the ceiling sucking up the oily smoke
from the grill: a whole solar system up there spinning that stuff

up and out—just the opposite of flushing the toilet.
Everybody here looks like faces on the Most Wanted.

When we lived in San Diego the mass murderer came in
the drive-in burger joint and lined up all the teenagers

and old folks and mowed them down
with his *To Have and To Have Not*-Thompson machine gun.

And it was a nice day too.
The stale quietness had a streak

of drunken insanity running through it.
Surely, if psychosis is there, so is innocence; so are good intentions.

All three can serve you your death without telling you why.
The mass murderer lived in a mobile home down near the border

where it was always too hot. I'm not saying heat made him do it.
But what still amazes me is how quickly the shock passes.

From *Configurations:*
New and Selected Poems 1958–1998
(1998)

Round Midnight

You know my story.
They want to make me liable
to punishment for this picture.

So my spirit is closed.
I'm a delicate engraving
outlined
with semitones, curled
at the edges,
nearly worthless,
in mysterious trouble.

I walk the beach
at Scheveningen.
Drink myself blind in The Hague.
Piss in the bushes at Etten.

I redate all my efforts.
Reconsider a cluster
of old houses nearby,
but not the church behind it.
You know why.

Midnight is round.
Asleep, we go around in it.
So what if I fail
at the total—the whole?

Judith Te Parari
couldn't care less.
She swings low
in her sweetness
around midnight
as the diggers dig
the fields stacking mud
against gold panels.

When I come to trial
you will hear
in my defense, weavers
and rug makers, potters,
old men leaning on sticks—
people I trust—tree cutters,
tree growers, folks born
in the month of March.

In Harlem or Stuttgart
you can make anything work—
jazz with hard light
against the Rhine;
even a tiny red boat
tossed this and that way
along the tired face
of night's season.

You know the story.

I am held captive by winter light
at Nuenen next to an ox,
hooked to a cart, hopeless
in its sincere effort
to go on and on.

Judith holds the end
of the winter thread,
pushes it through the needle,
then through my lip
and through midnight and
sews it and me together.

My spirit rises.
I drink nectar from her Nefertiti
moon. It's midnight, exactly
and I hear—what? Piano keys?
Not from Rick's. It's the sounds

of water at the Gennep
Mill, turning, and
I am a monk, waiting,
holding a gift—
a token of reprieve
placed in my hand
by my defenders
who also wait now on
benches harder than mine.

Love against Death

Night odors: wet grass, wet trees;
sharp smell of skunk and roses.
Night sounds: outside the window:
burp of frog, the shrill instruments
    of crickets. Death,
she said, is the double cross—
in wood. There it is: in the ring
and splash of sunlight.
I want to pour mud into the sun
and jump the Wall of China. But
the moon drives me
to self-reflection—especially as
it comes through the window now.

Life is possessed by garlic and
the madness of Estelle, crisscrossed.

You stand in the yard, yours,
feeling crisscrossed, possessed.
Touch the whitewashed wall.
The rooster starts crowing at three.
Walk on the damp grass. You see
shadows crawling in front of you.

While waiting for Father Divine
and a miracle, my past lives with us.
The magic in Mineola placed him in
the powerful silence of maids
and white women from Canada.

In memory of my past—and in self-
forgiveness—my wife reached out
and touched her own broken leg.
It was a clam with a Universal Mind.
The long years of my history
grunt in her and my ears.
My black spats turn silver,
my brown derbies blue.
Welfare-check windows
fill with green smoke.

Estelle. Estelle was mad.
She was the aunt who raised me.
Her Christ overtook her life.
Whatever self she danced before me
was a widow of Death.

My wife and I now walk
through fall leaves.
What we say is reflected
upside down in the pond.

In the night, between the odor
and the sound, we hear the train.
It passes beneath a flexible bridge
with walkways on either side.
Without being down there, I know
a girl in a long white dress
watches it from the rail.
Though it's midnight, the sky above
    her is green.

The skunk comes by the window
two or three nights a week.
The boys come in and roll
the bed out into the sea.
I usually don't wake till
the dream of infancy ends
and I'm falling out the cradle.
I want to pour mud
into the cradle
once and for all.
I float back.

Death, she said, is not all
she's cracked up to be.
She's a little muddy and flat
with bark for a bed.
A harlot, perhaps! Something
tangible to look at!

With our love, dear, we fight death,
and we fight unclear meanings.
They are like air released
in a broken scream—
at three in the morning
when your legs turn to wood.

Embrace night odors.
Embrace each other.
Rub your hands
against the roughness
of the whitewashed wall.
For now, you are alive.

Train Stop

The train stops.
I'm trying to remember the name
of a woman at a train stop
like this years ago
who said she was possessed by demons
she called Enslaved Selves.
Gave them names
like Toxic Tamalina, Malignant Majesta.
But wasn't her real name Karen
or was it Karla?
I gaze out the window
at the city's lunch-counter lights,
wondering why
it feels like I've been here
In some subzero past stuck in time—
nickname and all.
Through the window
I see a railroad-crossing bar,
Sam's Diner,
and beyond, a run-down town,
one with nothing coming—either way.
Two tow trucks
stuck in mud.
A green light stuck on green.
The stillness is unfriendly—
dangerous as an uninspected dam.
I see the shadow of a woman
coming across the tracks.
Her name might be Karen.
Remember myself saying,
"Nice meeting you.
Hope you dispossess your . . . yourself—"
and her correcting me,
saying, "Selves," and "Thanks."
Very rational.

On second thought
her name might have been Karla
and the city might have been
Santa Fe or Savannah.
Caught between foot trails and foothills,
it's hard to say.
I've lived a long time
and made about as much impression
as a poly-pod
on the rest of the hope-and-grope garden.
Karen? The train was coming.
Red light stuck on red.
What I have to say about Karen
can be said in my last days
in the rest home
half out of my mind
on the sun porch
at midday midafternoon or midway
of a game of pool in the rec room.
She was kind, civil and kind—
and very rational. As sane
as any of us. Saner, underlined.
But will I live that long?
Surrounded by sandy rock-walls,
spruce, and sweet sedge,
with a blue-eyed nurse
taking my pulse
between her quick cigarette trips
out by the whitewashed wall.
But most likely
that other Karen
will be somewhere too,
with her memories
of having slipped her enslaved selves
off to places like Saginaw and Sacramento,
releasing them,
like little birds tossed up set free to fly.

She will watch them huff and puff,
up over the yucca and the yew.
They will beat their motorcycle wings—
crotch-rockets hit by a windstorm.
But don't count on any of this
or the special symbols:
emotional ports of entry,
lonely airports
where she might be spotted,
telling her story
to stranger after stranger.
Don't count on seeing her
on a ferry crossing over
from the mainland to the island,
or next to you on the train.
As I say, the name might be the same
but the heartbeat is purely individual.

Un Poco Loco

For Bud

To start, I have to draw blood,
find the right weakness,
show my grief,

just to get things moving:
sweep a bit,
dust my broom,
and since what I'm after
is so abstract, I bump
hard into chrome,
into the cluttered tables.

This one nearly killed me:
a lover I never wanted
to see again, a half-empty
glass of wine, lipstick
stuck in its brass tube,
a Cupid nailed to a globe,
half of an apple.

To keep going, I think
disconnected thoughts:
Chatter. Chew-tobacco.
Phoenicians. Rednecks.

To keep going I watch
my grandmother hold
the chicken by its legs—
bauk bauk bauk!
Chuck this time.
Cluck-Cluck last Sunday.

Keep going—the work
is the person said Peter
and proving it standing
there like that, silent,
before two hundred people.
That's one answer, the work
itself. No time to stop.

There's no time to stop—
for sickness or Jim Dine
or clever lines or the upshot
or the right note.

No time to remember
precisely—two glasses
left on the floor by the two
of us, gone down to
the level of plant life,
where we look so mysterious
and lovely that nobody's
going to care whether we
sprout next spring
or not. This is the problem
with a complete thing!
You can't lead it away
from the water it wants to drink.
It will kick your brains out!

Nazis drew blood a certain way.
They started something
they couldn't finish—they nailed Cupids
to crosses and fed apples to snakes,
raped on the Riviera
and kicked holes through the dance
motion of abstract painting
I expected to see later in Budapest,
where leaves on trees, birds on skies,
played Bud and whispered
Monk intimacies.
Take three. The Nazis
would have been better off
up in trees by Blue Lake.

The Pawnee is not going
to get nailed into a frame
of the Great American West.
Custer points his six-shooter
at the Indians' back:
only white space, the page's
margin between them:
the gun goes off:
a fluke of Nature: I bleed.

Take four. To start again
the light has to be just right.
I'm going to shoot the scene
before me: here—
Phyllis with that calculating smile!
And perhaps your brother
at the piano with polished fingernails
making bobwhite sounds.
Start again.

Take one. There are no miracles.
Take two. Being a little crazy
isn't the result of a
volcanic eruption.
Being a little off
places you in touch with Jene Ballentine's
Born Free, 1968,
with Whistler's gray and pink,
with lava and its flow.

Let's do it again from the top.
It's not art deco,
not locomotives of
brilliant returns from sparkling cities,
the polished nipples perched
atop Byzantine temples;
no, no—it's the return
to the unanticipated start
that continues to count:
one two three—Go!

Sure, I'm eclectic and electric!
My colors remain pure.
My columns won't shift.
Variety keeps the boats adrift.
Blue Lake absorbs the blood
and flows on, still blue.

No Time for Self-Pity

Always
I'm the one slightly slighted, he said.
But there is no why.
Desire is one thing.
The fall of events, another!
Take migrating birds, black ink spots against sky.
You navigate while I snap pictures.
Wrens go south, flapping,
light as leaf tissue.
No self-pity, they just go,
giving up their nests,
with rose-pink bitterroot hanging down—
        go, go, go—
like the girl said that time in Italy,
        go, go, go—
and if you could eat, say,
cherries in midair or eat spiders,
dig up earthworms and shit
from a telephone pole,
you too would have no time
for self-pity, no time
to ask yourself why
you get the cold shoulder.
You'd just go
pecking at tree bark when you could,
eating a lot of stuff that looks back at you.
To avoid death, you'd go
in cold weather to stay warm,
stopping, say, in some ash tree
to catch your breath. Then go on,
doing what comes naturally
on a long-distance flight.

September Mendocino

What do you hear up here?
Same Shasta air, same Nevada air,
same Sierra Nevada air, same rainsong air
that lured Walt Whitman when he heard it.

But it is easier to find what is left of Walt Whitman
these days, not in the sand, but
in a musty bookshop
over in Fort Bragg, where you sit,
rather than seeing him
imagining himself walking a logging road,
beating the underbrush with his long stick.

Now the question is:
How good are the muffins in the morning fresh?
They taste crunchy, still warm from the oven.
Would Whitman eat one, you think?
He would, he would, but he'd smell it first.

Can you smell the misty lands of the western shore?
Yes, but not like a big net full of fresh fish.
Not like that. You smell fresh pine in the wind.
And back on the hidden road
you really smell pine and redwood
as if they were still split open like watermelons
in the grass. Which grass? And back there,
on the track of a winding logging road,
giant log-trucks shooting by the turnoff
where we bought the dulcimer
at Mick's from Deb,
these trees whisper all day and certainly all night.

Can you come here without going to Russian Gulch
or to Primitive Horse Camp, the Headlands?
Skipping these, would you go away
with less than a tourist should?

Do we any longer see what is befitting
in these mountains?
No bark a foot thick here.
No. This is 1993, tree for tree.
How many of the giant spirits
of 1874 still stand as I wash
my hands in the California coastal water?

So is it necessary to still sing a California song?
The song has nothing to do with whether or not
this year is like Walt's imaginary time. It has to do with air,
this air, this new air, fresh still in all essential ways,
and singing through the redwoods' cold nights.

What else, then, do you hear?
We hear dulcimer strings—
that out-of-this-world sound. Nothing like it.
And other things we heard?
We heard about Jim's freshly baked muffins.
Heard about the cottage out back,
heard about the tree view,
heard about water towers one and two.
We heard about the pine furniture.
And we heard about complete privacy.
And friendly strangers around a breakfast table.
A fire in the fireplace after dinner.
We heard people up late downstairs
talking with great excitement.
We heard old Walt's wood spirits
talking all through the night.

What do you see through the trees?
Same giant redwood stand, back farther
than we can beat our way to by land;
same cold night corner-of-Pacific
from our bed-and-breakfast window
in old Joshua Grindle's house on the hill.
Through the redwood branches
we saw Walt swimming
out in the Pacific with his boots on,
but still being clear
about "your average spiritual man,"
and clear about the "voice
of a mighty, dying tree
in the redwood forest dense."

But it's not the same there, anymore. Walt:
Not in Jackson State Forest,
not in Damme State Park,
not in Pigmy Forest.

What do you see when you stand
out on Little Lake Road
and gaze at Grindle's house?
You see the big white frame house
with wraparound ten-pillow porch;
you see your upstairs window.

What do you hear from here?
We hear other tourists at breakfast
talking about where they came from,
talking about how long it's been
since they were last here,
back when the place was owned
by somebody else, not by Jim
and his wife. But we do not hear
the *crack! crack!*
of the chopper's ax Walt imagined.
They're farther back.

How deep is the river—is it as deep as it was?
It's deeper than the gift shops are high.
That's for sure. Deeper than
Rainsong Shoes or Paper Pleasures,
deeper than Papa Bear's Chocolate Haus
or The Melting Pot and Papa Bird's put together.
But really, how far down is that river?

Is this small cluster of shacks the remains
of the big camp shanties of the 1870s?
Pretty to think them
the type Walt wrote about, crowded together
boastfully strung along the coast.
Do you smell them—do they stink?
Do they smell of fish?
Fishermen think fish smell pretty good.
What is their "unseen moral essence,"
compared to, say, the trendy gift shops
and their objectives?

So what is coming up the mountain road for?
For the romance of the wood spirits, still.
And for our own romance in our ocean-view room
with its tiny sailboat wallpaper,
ships table and framed pictures of paddleboats.

And when we go away from here,
what do we want to remember?
What will we necessarily remember?
What we heard in the air.
What we smelled on the air.
The smell of fresh corn muffins!
Just the things a tourist needs.

Brief Visit to Venice

From the train window
coming here, I saw the Autostrada
stretching alongside tracks,
cars racing us, saw the names,
hip to all the games on signs—
Montellago, Scorze, Piombino.
In the countryside cracked my side
at the sign on a farmhouse—
Spend Summer Here!—pale pink,
paler green. Lean and mean boys
hawking at the train speeding
toward Venice. In Venice
we push our way toward St. Mark's
caught up in the remarks
and shuffle of tourists,
hip to nothing
but the red scarf
leading them. Good
at crossing bridges,
skipping steps,
we were out of step.
Called for help and got none.
Nuns in rows in the square.
Are they square, anywhere?
We played each other nights
like stringed instruments,
through the narrow streets,
walking in front of our own
long shadows, bright even at dusk.

Drawing from Life

I wake to sounds
of garbage collectors
banging cans,
making their rounds,
wake to taxi horns.
I wake to a dragon slain by Cadmus.
Must I wake—?
Must I stand tall?
To be both real
and drawn—that is reason
to stay, to endure the noise.
The window of this small room.
Poised in the room, I look out.
I see the rows and rows of wheat,
I see the pale green death-figure
whacking wheat left and left.
I see the death's-head moth,
floating around the booming
birth of Bacchus. Noise!
Everything today is water-
marked on Ingres paper.
I leave my dungeon
shirtless, shoeless, and wander—
by accident—
into Geronimo's cage
at the first World's Fair,
sit down with Geronimo—
endure the giggles,
endure the spitballs,
endure the peanuts,
endure the pennies,
the rotten apples.
Standing behind us
a grand old gorilla
lifts his unruly eyebrows,

wondering
what in hell
is he talking about.
Am I talking?
He strokes my clean
high cheekbones,
kisses my jawline.

The Slave Trade: View from the Middle Passage

I am Mfu, not a bit romantic, a water spirit,
a voice from deep in the Atlantic:
Mfu jumped ship, made his escape, to find relief

from his grief on the way, long ago, to Brazil or Georgia or Carolina.
He doesn't know which; but this is real, not a sentimental landscape
where he sleeps free in the deep waves, free to speak his music:

Mfu looks generously in all directions for understanding
of the white men who came to the shores of his nation.
Mfu looks for a festive reason, something that might have slipped.

Mfu looks back at his Africa, and there at Europe,
and over there at the Americas, where many of his kin were shipped
and perished, though many survived. But how?

In a struggle of social muck! Escape? No such luck then or now.
And Mfu hears all around him a whirlwind of praise, explanation,
insinuation, doubt, expression of clout—

"It was a good time to be white, British, and Christian" (H. A. C. Cairns).
And remembering the greed of the greedy white men of Europe, greed
for ivory, gold, land, fur, skin, chocolate, cocoa, tobacco, palm oil,

coffee, coconuts, sugar, silk, mulatto women, "exotic" battles,
and "divinely ordained slavery." And it was, indeed, with reverie,
heaven on earth for white men. But Mfu is even more puzzled

by the action of his own village: Mfu, a strong young man,
sold in half-light, sold in the cover of night and muzzled
(not a mistake, not a blunder); sold without ceremony

or one tap of the drum, sold in the wake of plunder—for a brush,
not a sum of money but a mere shaving brush, sold without consent
of air fish water bird or antelope, sold and tied with a rope and chain

(linked to another young man from Mozambique's coast,
who'd run like a streak but ended up anyway in a slave boat without a
leak or life preservers); Mfu sold to that filthy Captain Snelgrave,

sold by his chief, Chief Aidoo. Sold for a damned shaving brush. (And
Chief Aidoo, who'd already lived sixty winters,
never had even one strand of facial hair.) Sold for a shaving brush.

Why not something useful? Even a kola nut? A dozen kola nuts?
Six dozen kola nuts? Sold for a stupid shaving brush.
And why didn't the villagers object?

(After all, he'd not been sold from jail, like Kofi and Ayi and Kojo
and Kwesi and that girl-man Efua.)
And now Mfu's messenger, Seabreeze, speaks: "Chief Aidoo

wanted your young wife but before he could get his hands on her,
she, in grief, took her own life—threw herself in the sea."
Here in Mfu's watery bed of seaweed

he still feels the dead weight of Livingstone's cargo
on his head, as he crosses—one in a long line of strong black porters—
the river into East Africa;

in his seafloor bed of ocean weeds he still hears white men
gathered in camp praising themselves in lamplight,
sure of their mission—*Go ye therefore, and teach all nations,*

baptizing them . . . (Matthew 28:19). Mfu, raised from seed
a good boy—to do all he could—never went raving mad at his father,
never shied from work, one to never mope:

therefore when chief said hold the shaving mirror for the white man,
he held the shaving mirror for the white man,
teaching himself to read the inscription: Kaloderma Shaving Soap.

But now Mfu, like a tree, is totally without judgment or ambition,
suspended between going and coming in no need of even nutrition—
gray, eternal—and therefore able to see, hear, and know

how to shape memory into a thing of wholeness
and to give this memory not "the Negro revenged" voice of abolitionist
Wm. Cowper—bless him—but to see, say, what went into the making

of what, in those days, they called Negrophobia.
To understand the contour, Mfu must tour deep into Europe first,
explore its sense of Mother Nature: Mother Nature in Europe

is a giant pig with a black baby at one tit (this is good Europe: charitable,
kind, compassionate Europe) and a white baby at the other. A sucking
sound, plenty to go around!

And in the background, without thought of remission,
a band of white African catchers force Africans into submission
(this is bad Europe: evil, mercenary Europe) in order to chain them,

hand to hand and leg to leg, and ship them into slavery in the new land.
Both Europes baffle Mfu. Could it be solely for free labor and profit? But
he must try to understand it, first, the good Europe.

He pictures this: In a longhouse somewhere on the coast of West Africa
about fifty Africans in simple white cotton robes are gathered in dim light,
each awaiting turn to be dunked head-down into a big wooden bucket

of water. Two rosy Christian men, in slightly more elaborate white
robes, in attendance—linked, surely, to heaven—do the dunking. These
are good white men who wear Josiah Wedgewood's

medallion of a pious African face with the inscription "Am I not a man
and a brother?" (1787) But what is *really* happening?
One culture is modifying another, and in the process

(perhaps unwittingly) modifying itself, in the name of its god,
as a Liverpool slaver, with its wretched cargo, slides easily by
heading for the West Indies or Carolina port,

with people packed in the pit. The good monk on his knees
in prayer is not interested in gold of *Afric* or Bugaboo
or who looks more like an orangutan: Europeans or Ethiopians.

(And besides, the orangutan is not an African animal!) So
don't tell him stories of this man-of-the-forest kidnapping black babies,
thinking they his kin. Don't waste his time. Don't tell him a good savage

is one who will climb happily up a tree for you and fetch you fruit
like a good monkey. Don't tell him your heathen jokes.
Don't laugh at Casper, at the birth of Christ. Don't make fun

of the Hottentots. Don't try to convince him of African souls.
Souls are not proven. Period. The white monk has a secret vision
of the Queen of Sheba as a healing spirit for downtrodden people,

and though this secular dream is out of rhyme with his devotion,
much of his time is spent on a vision of the Sable Venus,
herself a Creole Hottentot, surrounded by chubby cherubs.

He prays to black Saint Martin and to black Saint Maurice,
in armor, patron saint of the crusade against Slavic people
(origin the word *slave*). The monk prays to the black Madonna,

who certainly must know something he doesn't know, prays to all the
white saints too (and you can name them) and to Jesus, Mary, and
Joseph. The monk prays that these lean Children of Ham

A Jamaican Creole noble lady sits on a porch while a black slave
fans her, her white lover inside sleeping off liquor!
Because of one slip, a Sambo, white as his tormentors,

is strapped over a barrel, beaten with a bullwhip,
and his backside beet-red with blood.
A giant snake, sixty yards long, drops from a massive, ancient tree

onto the back of a black horseman
and wraps itself around both horse and man, squeezing
till horse and man, taking all they can take, stop moving.

Snake then swallows first man, then horse.
Mfu can also see farther north—Georgia and Carolina:
Black men women and children bent working cotton, corn, and cane

from can't-see to can't-see, from birth to death,
with no stake in their labor. *Never will forget the day, never will forget
the day Jesus washed my sins away.* Who is that general dying,

lying on the ground dying out there as the Battle of Bunker Hill
rages on? And another general, who will become president,
fights his way free of a cluster of redcoats, while on horseback;

in the background, his slaves watch him. *Pharoah's army sunk in the sea;
Pharoah's army sunk in the sea; sho am glad it ain't me.*
And a Negro soldier (strong as a Wagogo warrior and brave

as KaMpande, King of the Zulu) aims his rifle at a redcoat
while a major points the frailest pinkie ever in danger of being shot off
in a revolutionary war. *Two white horses side by side, two white horses*

side by side, them the horses I'm gonna ride.
A newspaper item: And good white men have come to believe
that perhaps the sin is not in keeping the "niggers" in chains

but in releasing them ("Catch a nigger by the toe . . . ?"
"Let my people go!") A cartoon (1789): A black man dressed
like an English gent bludgeoning a poor, suffering white man

over the head with an ignorant stick. And in the background:
Similar configurations dot the diminishing landscape.
Message: Let them go and they will enslave you.

Rationale: Abolition is folly. Here is the white woman, France
(this time without the fabled black eunuch), with her arms outstretched
to receive slaves on knees before her,

their arms lifted toward her thigh, while Frossard watches
with light of an approving smile in his eye.
Jefferson strokes his chin, thinking about freeing his slaves,

but on second thought maybe not.
Here they come round the bend.
Rise, Sally, rise. Wipe your weeping eyes.

Washington, on his deathbed, frees his slaves. Thanks a lot.
On my way to heaven, yes, Lord, on my way to heaven,
on my way to heaven, anyway.

Mfu remembers an Ashanti Juju girl. She said:
We must believe that the good in human beings will prevail.
And on front: Nemesis, antique goddess with raised left arm,

right hand holding an olive branch.
Obverse: face of a young African man, sensitive and intelligent.
And the inscription: *"Me miserum."*

A Danish traveler, the girl said, gave this relic to her
from the West Indies, where he'd seen, without reverie,
the abolition of slavery in 1792.

Sister Mary wore three links of chain; Sister Mary wore three links of chain;
glory, glory to His name. Mfu says this is to strain against the insanity
that welcomes us at the other end:

Where one does not believe there is hope
and one strains, too, to keep the gentle face
of, say, Carl Bernhard Wadstrom, white man,

bent over Peter Panah, black man, teaching him to read.
And wish the configuration said more than it does.
Mfu remembers Equiano. Equiano (1789) saying:

"We are almost a nation of dancers, musicians, and poets."
And although we're much more, let's have a revival!
Why not celebrate? If nothing else, celebrate survival.

Bernardston

Excuse the unromantic place—
a few miles north of Greenfield
where wind rips

yellow leaves from October.
First time here,
in an old hotel with closed bar

downstairs. Mythic figures
of literature are far away.
Cows, I see, grazing on hillside—

above them: open sky.
Epics have no place here.
Listen! It takes a hill dweller

two hours to drive down
to the post office for a stamp!
Ash trees as symbols

are things I taught.
Now these sharp cold days,
in the room, filled with steam,

are for reading
and making love with my wife.
You'll find us at the intersection

of Massachusetts Highway 5
and Highway 10—
fifteen minutes to Vermont.

From here to there,
they're closing roadside stands.
We bought the last good tomatoes.

The white Fittonia veins
in the green surface
seem even, but they are not.

A profusion of leaves
in shade, by the window,
seem still,

but steam is moving them.
Long shadows of fall—
in here and out there—

are cool and vacant,
yet I know them, as I know Cezanne,
to contain life!

The sun on the Fittonias—moving fast.
Their veins glow white!
A midget downstairs

uses the public toilet
on the second floor.
When he hears me coming up,

he peeks
through the door crack:
one big red eye glaring

with a retarded blankness.
We came here from a different life.
I do not understand the midget:

yesterday across the road
he sat on the back of a donkey
in the shadows of an oak

near the liquor store,
whip resting across his shoulder,
short legs

hardly allowing his feet
to reach the rings!
Posture and mood

the same as the donkey's.
The metallic red, yellow,
and green of the TV screen

glows before us with warmth:
back view of a woman in pantyhose;
men in armor;

seated figures on a front porch;
news of murder;
an election;

the best deal in town;
the dark areas around the eyes;
soft, wet, glowing sensation;

still life with flowers;
hard and clear fences;
everything you can imagine;

the bone beneath the cheek;
red lips light and wet;
pink body-color turned yellow

with chalked-in outline,
finished with a fine brush.
Edges carefully worked smooth.

We grow sleepy before the screen.
In the dream I am worried
about the furnace:

I had to keep the fire burning!
Nobody liked waking up
in the night,

trying to dress in the cold.
Most of the guys
in the barracks

were from cities,
never seen a furnace.
Yet their turn came,

they stoked it too.
After feeding it
I returned to my bunk

to sleep for an hour.
I slept at the edge of a cliff,
an arm dangling,

the flames still yellow
with red centers at six.
And my relief didn't show.

Anyway, today the coast!
It's not far!
After a few days

all the leaves are
blown from the trees.
Stairway remains dark.

We hear groaning of big trucks
at the intersection.
I go on gazing at the Fittonias,

glancing at the midget's
inscrutable eye,
watching TV's bigots,

watching hooded mystery.
Then we are seized
by a lust to drive.

To get anywhere
we must drive.
In the thick fog

we follow the white line.
At the coast the wind
tears at the sails,

overturning small craft,
rocking even the big boats.
Women in long dresses

walk with their heads lowered,
pushing against the thrust,
their capes flapping.

Hats fly out to sea.
Barefoot children run
in the current.

We hold each other,
trudging through wet sand.
Man trying to anchor boat—

rope breaks,
boat tossed out beyond recovery.
His little red coat beats furiously

against his back
as he watches.
Coastal dreamtime?

"Serious" winter holiday coming—
proof: a holy figure
scratched deeply into the surface

of a rock. Her lines are old.
On her knee, two infants embrace.
A tear rolls down her cheek.

My wife and I embrace.
"I think we should buy a beach ball."
My wife bends forward

against the wind,
her jacket flapping in the storm.
She sits in the tide

and watches the photographer
snap picture after picture
of the surf model.

I watch her watching them.
She is not Phyllis in search of Aristotle—
not a symbol.

The hotel in Bernardston
is not the castle.
Neither wind nor sea will take her.

She has no miracle to reveal.
I am not a figure in action.
She is not Venus.

Yet, back in Bernardston
I dressed in blue armor—
charged forth with my sword out

before me, ready to strike!
Symbols, epics, mythic figures!
Caught up?

Think not!
I stood halfway
between dream and the room.
Clear, here we were safe,
though still dislocated.
Sword? Unreal, unnecessary!

I came out of the "forest"
and stood at the intersection
of Five and Ten.

It's late.
We are two lovers
in a meadow up near the border.

The sky is yellow.
Blue potato cart near gray fence!
A ladder lying against a haystack!

Vermont is prettier than Massachusetts.
We kiss.
Two figures carrying death

on a stretcher looming
between rows of olive trees.
Moonlight shows them to be mournful.

In the yard of beautiful flowers
blooming they let death down
into a limestone tomb.

Frenzy

Here is the little earthworm-eater,
she-kiwi.

She's in her frenzy of lust.
There she goes in her flightless

night journey, in mating season,
warm in her fur-feathers

poking her long bill, beaker,
with nostrils at the tip

sniffing and drilling
scratching and uprooting

with her powerful feet
pausing, maybe, to let

herself be mounted
furiously and briefly

by a he-kiwi whose
odor is to her liking.

Then there she goes again—
through the underbrush

(followed by her
faithful seducer)

back to her *querencia*
to burrow down

and wait and sometime
later she stands up

suddenly, and hatches
a big egg

nearly half the size
of her little body.

Finished, she steps away
and the father-to-be

steps in and sits
on the egg

warming it,
sits and sits warmly,

for three months
while she-kiwi, lustful still,

goes out looking
to get laid again.

Bricks and Sleep

In late afternoon,
the first row finished,
lined up neatly end to end,
with mortar still soft
as tree sap between them,
you start the second row,
cutting no slack,
staggering them firmly.
Night, you barely sleep—
still busy stacking
things now you can't see.

And in the morning,
with coffee cup warm in hand,
your bricks are hard
and you're somehow rested,
despite the busy night that
hums like motors in tanks.
Skin fresh to cool breeze
from the south, you start
your sawing. You're cutting
all morning, cutting two-
by-fours, then cutting your beams,
then cutting your planks. Now
you dump a keg of nails
out on your tarp like stars
spilling in a pattern
across deep black space.

In the afternoon when
the sun is too hot you go
upstairs and lie down, reading
a novel about a man
with a rake farming his own
land and you spill into sleep,
transplanted to his land
where the soil is moist
and, like his, your hands are brown.
When your work is done,
you seem to enter a dark hut—
like a cove—and
you build a fire
and with care, warm
those same hands by
the potbelly iron stove
you find there.

The Apple-Maggot Fly

In a Hudson Valley
winter apple orchard,
beneath one apple tree
in a row of apple trees,
snug inside your egg,
inside a rotten apple
hidden beneath red leaves,
you lay abed breathing
your slow larval sleep,
dreaming red,
without reason,
dreaming delicious,
longing too for the lost *she*
of your own delirious body,
through the long cold season.

Then, as pretty or ugly
as you want to be,
you chew your way
out of your own lace skin,
beginning to dream *lover*,
mindless of your fall,
mindless
of your puparium
cover—doing your own
maggot dance.

Lava-headed, cocky
and relaxed, and clear-winged,
you tunnel now into
the living corpse of winter
earth. You proceed where winter
hits with the least amount
of breast-pounding snow,
under the tongue
of a good layer of earth.

And in spring,
(I'm informed)
you are transformed,
(if you survived the wasps) into
a proud pupa, fit to sit
up, heavy and big
as you're going to get.

All to this end:
to wait quietly
on perhaps the same apple
tree till *she* sees you waiting
and decides you are the one,
the only one she wants
to catch her *ovi*.
On the lookout for birds,
and to let other
females know you are spoken
for, she leaves a trail
of her droppings
all around you so they will
know to whom you belong.

From *Waiting for Sweet Betty*
(2002)

Waiting for Sweet Betty

The sweetest waiting is waiting for Sweet Betty.
Pretty but messy, they say. Bird's-eye view
sees a blanket of shimmering pink and white
with green pods in sharp brightness.

Down beneath in the flower's cool shade,
in scattered shadows so dark, I wait
in uneasy restfulness,
waiting through sun and snow.
There's much to wait for.
I wait for plum rock to turn a darker purple.
I wait for the unmistakable black in white people to show.
I wait for black people to catch windflowers.
The sweetest waiting, though, is waiting for Sweet Betty.

Waiting is what I do.
I waited nine months to be born.
I meant to say something else.
In sleep I wait to wake.
I wait for the right moment.
I wait for the birds to finish with their nest of fussing.
I wait for the right book with the right cover.
I wait for the grass to take deep root.
I wait to see the bushes reach their fullness.
I wait for the grocer to fill my sack.

I wait in the hallway against the wall.
I wait for my students to finish the exam.
I wait for my students to start talking.
I wait for payday and I wait for the lottery.
I wait at the lake for the boat.
I wait offstage to have my say.
I wait at the zoo for the ram to stand up.

I wait in the waiting rooms, rest homes, recovery rooms.
I wait patiently as a patient in ward after ward.
I wait for the witch doctor to tell me something—anything.
I wait like a mechanic watching oil drain into a pan.

I wait for the axis to shift and the system to set.
I wait for the matrix to absorb the math of itself.
I wait for the big crunch to meet the big bang.
I wait like an astronaut strapped in a plastic seat.
I wait a light-year for light to travel through chaos.

I wait in Georgia sad on a base and in Illinois with a dime.
I wait in New York with a subway token and a briefcase.
Now we're recounting personal history.
I wait in fatigues in line in Texas, waiting and waiting.
I wait in the airport in Ghana and Liberia.
I wait in France for my identity papers.

I wait in the train station in Germany and in Holland.
I wait in Italy hoping time will stop for a rest.
I wait in Colorado and California without skis.
I await a Nebraska driving test and I fail.
I wait in the air and on the high seas, waiting calmly.
Who can tell how long I wait?

I wait for Skunk Bush to stop smelling.
I wait for Wandering Jenny to stop climbing the house,
to stop flying around and around the clouds
trying to kiss the upside-down boy. I wait for her
to move in another direction, to rest on a rock.

I wait the sweetest waiting of all—
I wait for Sweet Betty and she's won't bloom till next year,
but she *will* bloom next year.

In My Own Language

We can't cut this timber.
The convicts, with dreams of freedom,
gave it all they had. They
couldn't cut it. Little corrals
run all along here, no longer
used, cove converted, and also gone
the river running through here,
fished by folk from Mono Lake,
and mining gone, too, but we can mine
meaning and that action stands
up pretty well, like black roots
around a tree planted incorrectly.
A posse fought hard here,
bullets flying everywhere,
even knocking down an occasional orange
from a tree in that long row of orange
trees in that iron Santa Cruz sunlight.
It's a tight situation.
I move things around to make rock and tree,
water and land, connect
in their own language, but
only as I learn to speak it.

Unknown Presence

How to name what is unnameable.
The long road of history right up till now.
Think about Robert Johnson's deal with the Devil.
Unnameable, I think of you.
I know my demise is coded in your name.

But what does Unnameable know that I don't know?
In retrospect, oh, so that's how it all adds up.
We're in a new car driving along but
if something goes wrong
out here in the middle of nowhere,
no mechanic to deal with the problem.

The deal is that moment when no one knows
who has the ball, not even he, scratched and bruised, carrying it.

So, we keep bumping into one another,
used, our keys rattling.

You leave stage and come back dancing.
And I have no choice.
Watching your high kicks with a longing
that matches your tease.

And Lil at the piano at Bob's
A big deal for me.
We stayed up all night
listening to her play and
doing so made all mystery leave
at least for those few hours.

But the reality is, I bear the weight.
I listen to your screams coming up.
I no longer deny that
your voice and heartbeat are my own.

People are happiest when they forget.
Everyone forgot you that time in Kansas City
when Half Pint pitched high
and sang way up in a voice not his own.

Not unhappy, now I am inside you
crossing an imaginary stretch
as if you were an unending coastline,
too lovely to look at with the naked eye.
I couldn't have been dealt a better hand.

Mendocino

I could lose myself
in great bursts of work here,
cutting wood, planting a garden,
painting what I see,
or I could get lazy on our marine terrace.
First and last. I want to last.

We stand on ground mapped since 1587,
a long time for this our country
and what did Lorenzo do here?
Or for that matter, Antonio?
Colony and cove comfort.

Fog every morning obscuring coastline.
You need a warm sweater
and you come out of it by noon.
Victorian rows along unpainted lanes,
we walk searching for everything
and nothing in particular.
Agate, Blair, Caspar, Lansing, etc.

Off One, with groceries in trunk,
enough to last till next trek
ten miles south to ex-fortress.
Put frozen stuff away first.
Sun only hallway down.
Still time to catch its effect
and handcraft it to something reuseable
like leftovers,
bouillabaisse perhaps.

Photograph of a Gathering of People Waving

Based on an old photograph bought in a shop at
Half Moon Bay, summer 1999

No sound, the whole thing.
Unknown folk.
People waving from a hillside
of rippling grass
to people below
in an ongoing meadow.

Side rows of trees waving
in a tide of wind,
and because what is moving is not moving,
you catch a state of stasis.

Opposite of this inactivity
you image distant music
and buzzing of crickets
and that special hot smell of summer.

To the garden past the Bay
to the meadow,
cliff sheltered with low clouds,
offset by nodding thistle.
Tatter-wort and Stinking Tommy
along footpath worn down by locals.
But who or why?

In the photograph itself
you're now looking this way
to unknown clusters of houses.
Where forces are balanced
to near perfection.

Who could live
in such a great swollen silence
and solitude?
You hear church bells
from Our Lady of Tears
breaking that silence nicely
and just in the right way
so silence continues
as though nothing else matters
day after day.

Any anyway, each face seems so familiar.

What do you do when you wave back?
You wave vigorously.
You remember your own meadow,
your cliffside and town,
photographs forgotten,
the halfhearted motion of your hand,
your grandmother's church folk
gathering on a Sunday afternoon in saintly quietness.

You name the people
whose names are not written on the back.
You forgive them for wrapping themselves in silence.

You enter house after house and open top-floor windows,
and you wave down to future generations like this.

From the Train Window Going and Coming

I ride backward
to see what I'm missing.

Big pines and big skies ride up and down
and around with us.

Up and down and around!
Then for a straight stretch!

A red pickup shooting east
along a white highway with us!

I'm trying to call home
but cannot.

Sky and brush and pine
and salt earth curving sharply

from us!
Then tilting away from us!

A large natural tallness!
In the great distance,

blue mountains of comfort.
In the middle distance of Winnemucca

a darkness coming!
We are stopping by a pasture.

One cow gazes at us.
About two hundred cows

remain interested only in grazing.
I look forward to going back, either way.

Gathering Mushrooms: Cambria

A valley and hillside full of helmet-flowers
with that curious upper-sepal shooting out.
Not truly colorless, the color of life itself,
drinking air and spitting acid,
surviving on death, eating its flesh—
mold, mildew, bacteria.

More like musk of animal
than smell of vegetable. Stinkhorn stinks yet
dry out a toadstool and the smell is sweet

The girl's Airedale digs in the hillside,
turning back earth, spreading yeastiness in the air.
Overhead in trees—*stweet! stweet!*—
a sound securing the day.

She gathers mushrooms on the cliff.
Folk around here say they're stems
of old wives' hoods, friars' caps blowing
in noon's wind, a whiff of death full of life.

The girl insists they're both life and disease,
fertility, too, two by two—too many to count.
At ease, she carries a fistful of shoots,
spindly fleshy things.

They're both life and disease,
two by two. Too many to count.

An Eighteenth-Century Moment

A young married couple.
A comfortable domestic setting.
Upper class with expensive china
and glass, gold and green silk, but
furnished in terms of taste poorly.
A waste of money and music.

She wears a secret smile of pleasure.
She's been out all night.
He's been out all night, too.
Their little dog sniffs at the lace panties
hanging from his pocket.

I mean only to take this
as a point of departure.
This is where I depart,
go my own way, leaving
their shabby elegance
to the rhythm of Haydn.

It's a season but that's not why.
Gaudy figures on the fake-gold mantel.
Piss-poor paintings
all the way down the hall.
Tall windows with the best light.
A broken sword
hanging on the wall
for no good reason.

An embroidered pattern
of Macedonian reds and greens
in long zigzag competing lines.
This isn't bad but its presence is an accident.
The light gambles with everything.

Carrying an orange fruit bowl full of apples,
the snobbish steward comes and goes
splashed with pink heat.

He will tell you about the smell
of the meat market,
how both can't stand fruit
or lute music for that matter,
Macedonia or Haydn quiet or loud.

Looking out the window into the piazza
through midafternoon stillness
caressed and cuddled
by the usual steaminess,

I see a midget with stumps
for arms and no thumbs
making his way across from shade
to light where the church entrance stands
like a square of blackness
in a dream full of whispers.
He thinks he's unseen.

Here is the altar.
Some are already kneeling.
He will enter the church
of spheres and cylinders
and go down on his knees
in the circular dark, unaware

of the girl three seats away,
with a weedy broken heart,
sitting in an unholy unladylike manner,
knees apart, tears zigzagging
down her cheeks.

But what was it I meant to say
about this pathetic couple
in their pathetic life,
and the midget,
the piazza light and shadow,
the cool interior of the church?

Ah! Anyway, apples in an orange bowl.
Apples in an orange bowl!
See the light coming from inside each apple
as though holiday candles were glowing
from inside a tiny house?
And on the path of candlelight
a band of noble white mares
galloping out through the red skin,
filling the world with their thunderous music.

From *Myself Painting*
(2008)

The Red Bench

Pier stretches out a quarter-mile into ocean.
At its end this red bench vigorously illuminated,
as if to speak of its purpose.
I sit down.

Big morning sky clear and I am small,
grateful and grounded. Yellow oil shimmers
on ocean's hypnotic surface.

Close-cropped morning: presenting itself
as expansive. A slithering profusion:
more than yellow, yellow-orange, yellow-blue.

Purple, too, below a gleaming calmness.
I invite it in where color is needed.
Tides pound shore, leaving spray
standing in midair, eye-level.
Something overturned,
I feel it, something finished,
something returning to where it started,
to start again.

Plein Air

Look at Powell Street
with the trolley tracks
and the traffic jams
and the teaming crowds of tourists
and little motorbikes scooting about.

Oh, I know what the French had in mind.
Pasture with cows.
Beach house by the sea.
Hush of underbrush
where ducks suddenly shoot up
from the ticket. Last day of fall.
Sky full of dramatic clouds.
Last of the snow.
Rain over wheatfield.
Late afternoon sun
already out of sight
behind trees in the distance
and sky blazing with indirect light.
A drawbridge, a canal.
And Arles—one must not forget Arles.
Winter hills yellow and black.
Twilight on tall crop purple-green
with a touch of white light.
Midday shower in the yellow countryside.
Golden wheat harvest, no crows.
At water's edge,
empty boat slapping mossy rocks.
Summer at the beach with bathers.
And more bathers,
bathers pretending they're near a stream.
Golden autumn.
Poppy field under blue sky.
Mountain stream
with snow-capped mountains in the distance.

But what about Powell Street,
with its griminess and noise
and trolleys and crowds of tourists
and pollution with diesel fumes
billowing out of buses?
Is this not also Nature?
Who will set up an easel here,
who will defend Powell Street?

Windows and Women

This is Rome
where women beat rugs out windows.

Women hanging sheets and shirts and shorts
and baby diapers

on clotheslines
stretched from window to window.

Women and children in daylight
in the cobbled allies

between buildings crammed together.
Old women everywhere milling about,

pushing things, lifting things,
carrying things,

going to the hog butcher,
coming back from the market,

scattering the pigeons,
women stopping to talk with the ragman,

women stopping to talk
with the basket maker,

women stopping to inspect the goods
of the vendors

at the end of the street.
And in Australia

the Cathedral termite, too, stays busy
erecting cathedrals of sand

taller than women, taller than men,
building as much as they destroy.

The Young Doctor (1916)

At noon he smiles and nods
as he drives by,
thinking perhaps soon
she will be pregnant
coming to me,
but he's wrong.
He sees a long line
of pregnant women
packed like fish
in a net bursting out
the seams of their dresses.

Ah! Give me a cup of tea
and a back rub.
Blood and slime,
cupids and cherubs, no thanks.
Give me trees losing their leaves.

I'm okay. I pay the iceman,
and he brings ice
into the dark house,
inserts the block of it
into the icebox,
while church bells
go *dang! dang! dang!*
scaring the mice.

"Then again,"
as the fish man's nag
comes towing an old wagon
of trout, I turn about
to see who's driving by,
and I'm beginning to think
he is coming out of his way
maybe at least a mile
just to smile at me.
But no, that's crazy.

Against distant thunder
I watch my trout of many blues
being wrapped
in trodden newspaper
and blundered by shaky hands.
And I understand.

East Lansing, Michigan

September 10

There was no warning.
Rising from his rest
the dog bit the man's leg,
did it quietly,
then returned to his spot
on the front lawn to rest.
A solitary taproot
grows into a green bush
on which years later
a naked girl one day hangs
a wet bra to dry.
But the next morning
the dog's owner
came into the man's room
carrying a tray
containing croissants
and a pot of coffee,
and said, *Quick! Turn on the TV!*
Airplanes are flying
into the World Trade Center,
and the man knew then
that as fast as he would recover
from one season or reason
there would be no warning
from where the dog
or the airplane would come.
As fast as one plant dies
another grows.
The man is now a seedling
just starting
from the roots of 9/11
to grow again—but into what?

Black Snake Blues

Huts and houses, left and right.
Growth and gravel.
I can hear out of sight
both the nearby lake
and the wind over the lake.

Your world is tilted, swaying.
These wilted flowers
here in your house
are no longer vulnerable.

A countrywoman with one sock on
and the other hanging in her hand.
My memory of you.
You sit on her bedside,
gazing out the sun-drenched window
at the early morning.

Like a blade of light,
a black snake with a thick head
comes up from his hole
and into your Garden,
and I hear someone singing
"Crawling Black Snake Blues."

You sit on the bench counting ants,
miles of them. You are naked.
Somebody is waiting in your house.
Outside, your red pony chews blue grass.
Yours, a gray stone house
stuck beneath a big gray roof.

Somebody is waiting in that house,
waiting for your arrival.
On the roof a giant black chimney.
It really defines the sky
against which it stands.

In that other distance,
a seaside and sailboats and sea,
tipping under force of constant wind
with everything flapping and flying.
Three tiny people on the bridge waving.
White boat in the inlet, sails waving.
Rolling yellow meadow.
Tossed clouds over that purple range.

I'm outside walking your yard.
Everything here deeply rooted.
Mid-afternoon, orange glows yellow.
Nothing stays the same.
A profusion. Rose bushes.
A strange girl walks by in tears.
The buckeye stands by itself
like nothing else.

Difficult Pose

For Euan

Her back is to me.
She's standing on one leg,
with the other raised
and stretched out
as straight as possible

and with her whole upper body
turned to look back
over her left shoulder
so that I see her face;

and both arms are held out
at right angles
like a bird about to take off.

Ah! The long Egyptian curve
of her spine, the prominence
of her shoulder blades,

the curve of her buttocks,
with the overhead light
creating just the right shadow;

but the poor girl is in pain.
She is suffering.

The stretched-out body is
bent, twisted, curved.

She'll refuse to come back,
but what beautiful static rhythm,
like that of tree limbs in winter
or the simple geometry of a single flower
in a whisky bottle

or a blue steel rod casting a shadow
on a highly sculpted pear
whose each square inch of surface
reflects a different color of pear color.

But the poor girl is in pain.
I know she won't come back,
and I'll have to finish this one from imagination.

When the Model Does Not Show

What do artists do
when the model does not show?
The artist in charge calls her.
She says, oh shit! I forgot
or I'm sorry I had a death in the family
or I'm not feeling well, this morning.
I woke with the whole left side
of my body completely paralyzed
or somebody stole my car
or somebody stole my bike
or somebody stole my shoes
or somebody robbed my apartment
and I'm waiting for the police right now
or my cat is sick
or my dog ran away and I'm worried
because he's missed two of his shots
or my monkey got out of the cage
and somebody just called from across town
saying they found him
with my phone number on his collar.

Then the artists say, oh well,
and stand around
talking with each other
about how some models are so dependable,
and others, well, you get the picture.
They also start looking around the studio
at paintings and drawings on the walls
as though they've never seen them before
and at those left drying on easels.
They make a few more
awkward stabs at conversation.
Then one by one
or in twos

they start packing up their supplies,
thinking about the rest of the day
and how it is going to be,
wondering if this is a bad sign,
that one thing after another
will be a disappointment,
and they start getting ready to leave
but somebody had already made coffee
so a few of them stay to finish their coffee
or to have a second cup
and ask each other
about mutual friends
they haven't seen in a long time.

Three

She opened the door
to see who'd knocked three times.
It was the maid with her three children.

She said something about the procession
at Three Points. This is the procession
of the three wise men,

and as usual Casper is in third place
because that's where the first three
artists placed him. Actually,

she used her third finger
and the car door was open.
Anybody passing by could see.

And through the window, I see
the front of my car on the other side
parked in the rain on a Paris street.

Well, it could be Paris. *Ménage a trois.*
You could tell when it's Paris
because the three—I *think* there were three!—

green angels stand
with outstretched arms
showing no sign of hunger

or anger or angst. And she pulled open
her third eye to fish out the hair irritating it;
while one cluster of my entourage

hovered above us
like heavenly guests
and the other gathered below

around us like calm cattle
at the end of any day.
I gave each of the kids three pieces of candy.

Good candy!
Anyway, it didn't matter
how she later climbed the long stairway

to our hotel room, but as she went up
her dress fell off. It's how they make the clothes
these days—so flimsy. And

St. Sebastian looks up,
as if at her nakedness,
looks with dreamy eyes,

one arrow planted in his neck,
one in his stomach,
and the third in his left thigh.

And in the room just as I take her shawl
from her shoulders,
with her enchanting smell under my nose,

three familiar men gaze in
from outside the window,
waving wrapped gifts

like salesmen in an info commercial.
The driver had parked the car
three cars down and gone into a *tabac*

to buy cigarettes and that is how it happened,
how we got stuck
and couldn't get across the street

in the rain,
but we were safe
now in the room,

at least till morning
though the riots were still going on
in three sections of the city.

In Search of a Motif for Expressive Female Figuration

She, the many, concentrates with her hand
held in midair, waiting for the seer

in herself. Blue and naked, love arrives
with a heart half broken, in a sling,

walking on a crutch.
Ponytail. Bare legs.

Summer skirt: young woman on a ladder
painting her ceiling pink.

I stay as if she were land, new growth
everywhere and a warm day

pressing her skirt against her thighs.
Everything cut to the bone,

with hands folded in front of her,
just below the belly

like an answer to an unasked question.
Nothing slows her

or speeds her tissue thin.
The abating comes.

Her station wagon stands
in my driveway,

shadow directly beneath,
and two dogs or call it America,

with a red kitchen table.
She bakes, suns, runs, and rests.

Women dancing on the beach.
The girl twins in a burlap sack

together hopping across sand.
She is always a different she.

She moves like she is at the end
of a piece of twine.

Spring heat, winter wheat.
Her father in a casket: a living memory.

She, this: mosquito tents,
net and a dent left in myself

where she once pressed against me.
And the copper kettle's tea

will not completely comfort,
but then I was always crossing

in her headlights,
knowing even then her thighs

belonged to her knees and legs
like a train belonged to its rails.

And she could not swim
across the lake of her life

to save her life. I swear.
As she fixed her hair

she crossed her legs
and raised her arms

so that her armpits showed hairless.
Beginning blackness.

That unbearably lovely arm
extended, color of Tibet sunset,

in a thoughtless Degas gesture.
She belongs to a quiet moment,

arabesque all of its seconds.
She stands at the crevice

of the house and the fence,
arms crossed as in self-defense,

like when she sits uneasily
in the armchair in north light

wearing a blue bonnet
and white stockings,

a gold necklace
with a diamond pendant

and lots of bracelets on both arms,
disarming me: my Helga—

my Dora, my Marthe. My Saskia.
No surprise, she comes from memory

of self, a sick girl on her back
in an attic room and her dog sleeping

on the floor beside her bed.
She: I was a gingerbread gypsy

far from reach but now
in your colors I learn to teach

myself my lines, its music—yours.
And through rubble of self

my middle distance is yours too.
Pose me, she says, your gypsy woman

with red shawl draped over one arm,
no promise broken in unchangeable light.

Silk. Swish. Lights overhead blink.
Minus manners on the mezzanine,

leaning over the railing looking down,
we didn't care what people thought

or who saw us use catsup in public
or at the dance school for her daughter

where stumbling girls
are amazed at how long it takes

to calculate correctly unmapped steps
or where knees or elbows go

or when to fold or unfold,
brush stroke after stroke. But

what will break the stalemate?
Or to put it another way:

perhaps two old women
coming out a narrow passageway,

carrying straw baskets of wet laundry
balanced on their heads

is the answer—
even to what the wasp, entering a hole

in the old wooden cross
high on the wall above all heads,

wants to know.
She defends me, indefensible as I am,

even as the line dances in my name
in celebration across the surface,

rough or smooth, it's a pagan dance
with villagers gathered round and round,

till I find my way.
So secretive! Secrets keep secrets.

This is the image: scarfed, she is old
leaning almost out of confinement

where she lives, bread basket on arm,
charwoman cut in wood meant to stay,

and I do what I can
to hold her at the table

the way I love her, elbows on table,
reading that same letter over and over

looking up unwittingly,
eyes wet, memory molded to an absence.

And this image: in the dark theater green,
she sings red songs,

whole sad notes meant to be flat-out joy
but are not yet picked up

by washwomen with shopping bags
waiting at bus stops.

And like a body
coming up out of Nature she wakes

at daylight, looking at the floor,
her face saying *why* and *what*.

Kitsch figuration?
Not this one, bright-eyed in night
with a flashlight suddenly

turned upon her innocence.
Full face, three-quarters?

Sitting or standing or in motion,
Turning this or that way?

Turned completely around slowly.
Each limb, line, slope, tested on its quest.

She is sitting in a yard chair,
calming down

from the spearing of the day.
She runs, jumps over the pole.

Her shabby genteel gesture
unsealed completely by seamy half-light

and chapel bells ringing a knell.
She strolls bayshore, collar closed

with sparrow clasp,
or she sits quietly sewing.

At sea level, she's up again,
scarf thrown over bare shoulders,

she finds her way out into night sand,
gazing at antlike stars

and she's left dazed
or she's dazzled by another light:

walking the garden, watering plants.
She turns and comes back this way,

sits for my purpose,
bottom of her left foot a face-up spoon.

Fiddle-threaded fingers
through her hair and her twin sister

comes out of my imagination,
toes politely together, two sisters

in white dresses,
ribbon-tied and see them smirking.

I can't stop this or them:
her blank mirror looks back at me,

at them, blankly:
the girls and I in a trick mirror.

She dances to the beat of a broken set
of dishes, perfect disharmony, then repose.

And the pose must change.
Soldiers stepped on her dance-floor feet—

no canteen wallflower
warming a bench-seat.

She walks away, turns and comes back.
Sits quietly,

shoulder and arm in a tide of light,
the rest pulled back

in shadows of Hopper's hotel room.
She lies and prides herself

on not being a regular bride.
Her den, a dark gold Rembrandt.

She spans the grandstand
as if my trusted brush stroke bedded us all,

knowing life is smarter than us.
From her point of view,

one in this crowd of lace
leaps to light no faster than the next,

trying her best
to get through a long sitting.

She takes a straw broom
and sweeps the studio floor.

She sits on a cushion
and her body's light fills the canvas,

lighting the room,
twin daughters at her side, holding hands,

skylight light drinking their skin.
Gloomy, with a large hat full of fruit

and Matisse flowers balanced on her head,
head gently rocking

like a tree in wind.
The twine of my life, she says,

winds around everything twice.
I say, but surely there must be something

we share besides silverware,
Venetian blinds, pastel highlight.

She says a woman's life
is paid in full at birth,

it opens out
and it keeps opening all her life.

Heavy-hipped,
she walks slowly up a plank

into the shed. A soundless grayness

surrounds her. A gray opening in me
watches her change,

and watches over her
till I finish this, as I finish now.

From *Down and Up*
(2013)

Down and Up

Once up, nude or not,
they tend to come down—
gravity not withstanding,
with or without understanding.
They come down.
The woman carrying a lantern
comes down slowly,
inspecting the dark.
A woman fresh from her bath
comes down, damp and refreshed.
Somebody's niece or wife, in a chemise,
stands up and walks down the steps,
each one squeaking under her weight.
Two guards bring down an old woman
seated in a chair. Two boys
carry a woman, asleep in her bed, down slowly.
For the sake of art,
another woman, nursing her baby, comes down.
A man descends while reading a book
about sin and redemption.
They all come down,
down,
down
where everybody else is waiting to ascend.

No one is going up—yet.
The Calvinist minister must first finish her sermon.
The old woman with one shoe must stand up.
The man refinishing antique furniture
will try his luck when he finishes.
The bejeweled wealthy woman
may be too heavy for the staircase.
She stands on the landing,
inspecting the first step for its sturdiness.
Here is a young woman,
a pimple on the tip of her nose,
skeptical eyes, tight lips,
dimples, and fat cheeks.
She's waiting for her intended.
They are intent on moving
one way or two ways.

Evening Newspaper

Going home on the subway,
when you open the newspaper
you'd just picked up
at the corner
before coming down the steps,
there is always the person
next to you slyly reading
over your shoulder
and getting visibly upset
when you turn the page
before they finish the story
about some woman in Mexico or Brazil
discovering the Virgin's face in a mango
or seeing it in a puddle of water
in the road to the junkyard
or the Granada dig uncovering the bones
of people fallen in their tracks
during attacks in a medieval street battle.
Keep turning.

Father

I was there looking for the house
where my father died.
An old neighborhood,
clean and orderly,
with flower gardens flanking each front door.
Windows covered with white lace,
behind which nobody seemed to live.
Thanks to a restless cloudy sky,
a gray light hung over it all.
Despite the road sweeper's efforts
to smooth it over,
the main road was unpaved
and bore carriage tracks and car tracks.
And when I found the house,
at the deep end of the street, I knocked.
A woman came to the door
and said, Yes, he lives here
like a character in a gothic novel.
You see, when the storm came
and broke the levee, flooding the city,
leaving hundreds dead,
thousands stranded,
beach chairs and canopies blown away,
your father was a hero.
He got everyone out.
I knew it was a lie, but it was what I needed to hear.

The Rope

Let's follow the rope to where it takes us.
Lifesaver or hanging noose.
Roped off or roped in.
We depend on it.
Don't get distracted.
When we get there, take one end,
and I'll take the other.
Ignore the children
in sacks jumping around on the beach.
Don't get distracted by the blue trees,
the floating gulls, the busy sky. Keep walking;
stay close. We'll pass through
a silent city under white moonlight.
Pick up the pace. Ignore the piles of snow,
the crowing rooster. Boot prints
leading to that barn. The farmer's wife
in there killing a goose for dinner.
We're almost there. Boy pulling off his shirt,
making a turban. Over that hill a village
snowed in for the winter. Red Cross workers
can't get back in there till spring.
No one here was ever found guilty.
No one was up to it.
Even when tanks rolled through the city.
Seagulls perched on the ledge of that house.
Everyone in the casino has a scheme.
We now cross a pattern of planks.
People in boats are remote,
but we can still see them—even from here.
Everyone will soon gather at the dinner table
under a glowing chandelier. Cows
up to the shelter. There they go.
People walking across a stone bridge.
Others forbidden to cross.
No records are kept. Whitewashed pier,

six in the morning.
This is the way it is.
That was the way it was.
The shops are closed. A man in a blue suit
crosses the street. Rarely seen,
and always in a flash, the black stallion.
He knows when the flood is coming,
takes to higher ground.
We must not lose confidence.
A storm may be coming in.
We've lived through storms before.
We can survive.
Even armless, unguarded, we'll get there.
The rope will lead us there.
What to do with the eggs in the basket?
Rembrandt down in the cellar
with the slaughtered ox. The musicians
on stage ready to perform. Waiters
tall in yellow and black. A girl walking calmly
with books firmly against her bosom.
Here is my end of the rope.
This is your end.
Now that we are here let us look
back at where we were.

At the Movies

No real person will die in the dark this afternoon.
Many will pretend to die, pretend to ascend.
But the tendency of the body is to fall.
It is only here that we leave our bodies,
levitate up to the big screen
for a temporary weightless life.
We can choose our scenes
and our degree of participation.
They've gathered in large groups
listening to men shouting through bullhorns.
Holy men lifting tiny adults to their bosoms.
We expect tears and swooning.
A dancing nurse
jumping across the clinic floor.
A violinist playing chamber music.
We get more than we expect.
Medics bringing the wounded soldiers
down from the hills on stretchers.
Far out in the ocean
a lone swimmer doing backstrokes.
People in high box seats
shouting insults down at the diva.
A stage full of dancing women
in red dresses doing high kicks.
A man on a train
watching the scenery shooting by
while planning his murder.
A procession of priests and altar boys
marching piously into the cathedral.
A mob dragging a man through a village.
A detective searching a landfill
for the clue, kicking aside a wet mattress,
a rusty car fender, a pile of rotting dresses,
a rusty stroller. Then there it is, *the* clue.
A car chase through bumper-to-bumper traffic.

And there is that moment
when, between crates of fruit
stacked shoulder high, the harlequins
meet unexpectedly,
like Bud and Lou,
startled by each other's presence.
A cloud hides the moon.
The castle in the distance
is almost certainly locked.
An agent chases a Corot thief
flat-footedly through the Louvre.
The Louvre is surrounded.
All the docked boats are off limits.
One streetlight in this darkness
is not enough to show the way.

New Poems
(2015)

Plein Air

Ah! The erotica of ambition!
I cross the bridge across the stream

where lilac is blooming alongside it
on the embankment. Not far from the sea,

a seagull overhead circling something,
eyeing something. Almost a dream!

I pass the laurel. I remember its struggle to survive.
My senses are alive, revived

with the promise of the meadow.
Light through fluffy lettuce clouds,

bold and crisp. Name this gleam of light
shining on my gladness. In the meadow

I sit down and take out my sketchbook,
soon defeated by the power of red

and yellow, my pencil
no match for such splendor.

Inside Outside (Again)

To us our outings were famous and infamous too.
The fancy lady with a cigarette holder blew smoke rings

above our heads. They lingered like low-hanging clouds.
The barefoot man in a tux, the helmet boy on a rented scooter,

the man in a top hat and bomber jacket and spats,
and the others, all came along, but hot afternoons were best inside

for the memory of who we were out in daylight
on such trips. Compassion Guy stayed on his corner

asking passersby to define compassion. Maria's memory
of the confessional booth kept her outside no matter what.

We always go past the campus girls practicing archery.
It's the shortcut to the countryside.

Once a girl with a suitcase at a bus stop, seeing us,
decided not to run away from home. She joined us.

Crows in flight cawing, looking down at us, turned and followed us
to the meadow. Passing the old farmhouse half fallen in

was my favorite moment. It broke the monotony of long stretches
of astonishing loveliness. Two women held straw baskets

of tomatoes. "Ripe and delicious!" they called. But
hot afternoons are best inside, in our cool rooms.

On the Beach

Something seems to be going on down there.

Girls stop playing volleyball.

Couples stop sunbathing.

A man stops trying to inflate a plastic elephant.

A motley gathering of us starts moving in that direction:

men with big beer bellies,

old women with flabby arms,

pregnant ladies,

teenage boys carrying surfboards.

And this is what we discover:

across the lake a cluster of folk

onshore looking this way at us.

Leisure Dilemma

Are you up to a stroll through the Louvre?

Yves or trees? Ingres? Manet?

Morisot's purple impasto?

Or we could stop at that little café

we were told is so *you*.

We can talk Carot over coffee,

then walk along the Seine.

Take the train out to Auvers.

Or, on a dare, stop in on Henri

to see what he's up to;

or just do what *you* want to do.

What *do* you want to do?

Chase butterflies?

Play hide-and-seek?

Okay, okay!

We'll spend a week in the South by the sea.

Alchemy

My senses on high alert: I see ripples in frozen water, shaded.
Evading my responsibility, I help the priest carry the cross.
I defy my boss. I see the spilling of ink and blood.
This is my untold story without glory, without the Flood.

My senses in high alert: I see veins of leaves without trees.
I hear the slapping of water as swimmers swim. Evaded,
I trim the trees. I hear the scream of a man on a flying trapeze.
I smell the splash of a cook making a washtub full of soup.

My senses in high alert: Birds and bees keep me in the loop.
I see stone blocks pitted with age and moss over rocks.
I am duped! This is my fire burning, my desire burning.
I smell cab horses, no longer restless, standing curbside,

hooked to their carriages. Without lust, I see a girl
at a window holding her cat to her bosom.
I hear the crack of rifles as men shoot ducks from the sky.
I see scraps of skin-thin paper pasted together to no good end.

No one will contact my next of kin. I am careful of what I buy.
I hear the shout of people on rooftops above shops
waving at a procession of returning soldiers.
I see in the sky a looming darkness as welded bronze.

My senses are highly alert: I hear red slabs of earth
grinding together. This is my pain, my joy on a long train ride,
my golden leaf, my relief. I am alert to all.
This is my place in the shade, my trust. My trust in all.

Holiday at the Beach

What could go wrong? This is a place of moral certitude.
A pelican on a post. Gulls circling and searching the bay.
In the distance, drifting sailboats. Children flying kites
all day across a perky sky. People in green and pink swimsuits

on yellow sand. Girl with an attitude perched on a sea rock.
She leaps for a dive but becomes airborne. The bearded lady
under her beach umbrella reading about black holes.
A Yorkie chasing a butterfly. Children filling buckets

with sandy seaweed. The mime hasn't moved for two hours.
People sipping beer at the beach bar. Listening to the radio band.
Squinting at the lone swimmer far out in the ocean
doing backstrokes. He is moving so far out that even if he turns back

he might not make it. A dressed-up couple appear
on the boardwalk, apparently from afar.
They seem to be waiting for a formal introduction.
Yet, way, way out, in the misty and majestic distance,

beyond the lone swimmer, the ocean is turning black and blacker
against a blue-*blue* strip of sky. Sound of water like an earthquake.

Waiting for the Storm

Our jalousies slamming on their hinges.
Lights at the bottom of the stairway blinking off and on.
Candles laid out on the counter. Brooklyn Lantern too.
The road here is still open, but the bridge is broken.

I look out the back window at scrub grass.
It's the only thing holding up. Through the bay window
I see a gaggle of geese scratching in the sideswiped countryside,
somehow still hanging on. Downhill, below the house, Hank's

haystacks wet from last night's rain. Through the back window
work goes on: the river with side-by-side mahogany barges
in gray light as cranes lift kegs from shore to barge bellies.
We stayed up late eating oysters, drinking wine, and listening to jazz

and splatter. This morning, sunlight spilling across the old cotton rug,
I go to the kitchen. A pitcher of cold milk on a newspaper
on the kitchen table. The simple comfort of a blue teapot,
a sugar jar, and a few scattered apples.

Smell of ham and potatoes, peas and garlic and onions
in a pot cooking. My wife leaning against the sideboard
eating a piece of chocolate. Pretending to be calm.
I'm pretending too.

Ancestor Land

DNA says this is the land of my ancestors.
People here go around and around.
Today a wild dog followed me to the museum.
People at the market push. Beyond the market: the river.

A dog-eat-dog boat race under a swirling sky.
Yesterday, Cleopatra. Cleopatra claims she is the real Cleopatra.
Slowly moving eyes. Unlinking and unwinking.
Cheeks, nose, and chin claim otherwise.

She sleeps in her wedding gown.
Two birds with heads turned sideways flank her.
Twins here have special powers, doppelgangers too.
Mummies don't stay put.

They took the man pretending to be dead off a ship,
powdered his top lip, placed beads around his neck
placed him in a tomb on a bed of grass seeds at noon
with his head resting on a pillow of wood.

Their funerary portraits are never good likenesses.
My visit to the museum today was puzzling.
They said just take what you want.
Things need us, they said.

I took my ancestors' faces and put them in my briefcase.
Faces of my ancestors on panels,
worn and cracked,
smiled at my pathetic effort to understand this country.

Shop or Store

Morning,
my uncle the butcher stands in the doorway of his shop,
waiting for customers,
his arms folded across the bloody art of his apron,
my aunt getting the crates out.

She places them around the doorway and on the sidewalk
around the storefront. She says store. He says shop.
My job is to sweep the floor,
to empty the buckets under the meat counter.

The slaughtered hog hanging upside down in the window
dances on a chain.
My aunt outside checks crates of tomatoes and cabbage,
apples and bananas, beets and squash, lettuce and potatoes.

Across the street men read day-labor postings
in front of that government building.
The sun is coming up down the hill in shantytown.
Wives hang out wash in fresh morning air.

When they finish, they will come up here.
My uncle will sharpen his knives and wait for their orders.

Summer Visit

The Garden, they say, is the original,

if you believe, if you believe the Tree, it's there too,

but the ants are bad, big, and red,

and there will be a girl embracing a dove;

there will be Greeks and Syrians and everybody else.

Plenty of goats and a flock of geese.

We will follow the poppies

packed tightly together along the path.

Before returning

we can safely circle the lake this time of year.

Morandi

London, morning: a dying rose in a dish. Camellia in a glass.
On the windowsill: chrysanthemums drooping.
Desire: an apple, red, turning yellow. Chalk Farm produce.
Wine bottle with lips like roses. Plant in a jam jar.

Last night we stayed up late eating oysters, drinking wine,
listening to the splatter on the roof. You and the scent of light. Aphrodite
at Turnchapel Mews. As if friends are soon to arrive.
Adjust the candles, the door handles. Think of trees; think of pears.

I think of when we met. You were sitting primly on the edge of a park
bench reading a novel. The sky behind you was a slab of slate.
How could I best start a conversation? I could say, Is that a good book?
No, I thought. And just as I was about to break the ice

I thought I might turn out to be the plot complication
you would come to hate. But, no, that's not how we met.
You were a girl squatting under the boardwalk, holding a parrot, the
parrot saying, *Teatime, teatime, mother in the greenhouse*

clipping leaves, teatime, teatime, mother in the greenhouse
clipping leaves. That's how we met. I heard the parrot.
Then I heard you say hello. Now we are here
where the road crosses the train tracks. Now is now.

This morning you have a headache. Around the round table of cherry pie
and tea, you stand by the stove in self-derision. You regret last night. But
last night was ours for hours. Happy then. Now empty jugs and mugs,
bottles and glasses. *Look at them!* Standing as if posing for Morandi.

Ava

The greenhouse is full of flowers in bloom.
And the doomed flower faces are loud, clamped in a scream,
while in the stable Ava and her lover in love
talk late into the night among the horses.
And the horses watch with understanding.

Lover gone, in the quiet, near dark interior,
Ava sleeps
with her head thrown back, mouth open
and belly rising, winking, and sinking.

After sleep, a cup of coffee, coffee cup left on a table by a window.

Through the window are a scorched yard
and the boardwalk.
The black ocean quietly shifts and turns,
like a restless sleeper
under a flat colorless sky.
While sitting on sand, Ava in reverie for life
out there and inside.

She opens a book, begins to read: *a cup of coffee*
left on the corner of a table by a window
where sunlight started left, then moved right.
Outside a great sea under a great sky.
And by the sea a long stretch of sand.
And on the sand a quiet woman Ava reading this book.

Picking up the pace. Saturday night salon. For love of chamber music.
In a diamond choker, Ava having her usual.
The great composer at the piano in candlelight tonight
and every Saturday twilight.
Ava and her lover in love and within love.
Hostess and guest and mistress all in one.

Ava exhausted, sweat drenched, but the baby is coming out,
apart, in the arms of her lover.
But who knows what will rhyme?
Slit-open flounder with human legs sprawling in slime,
breaking pink smoke.
Fury of royal goddesses perched against painted iron.
But she recovers from her nightmare.
Picking up the pace, stoking the fire, tending the baby.
Still, who knows what will rhyme?
Pushing the tables together.
Picking up the pace.
Making a bed for new life.

Facebook

When I was younger, I had a lover who lived in the countryside
of ancient lava, quiet except for trains moving on hillside.
She waved her woven hat. But when she was moody,
she walked out to the valley, sat on an embankment,

watching cows and horses grazing. Our relationship was intense,
at times painful as birth. Unlike our lovemaking,
watching cows and horses in their slowness made her peaceful.
I had no good defense. Walking the dense forest

behind her house I had to cross a fence to reach a clearing.
She tallied her gains and her losses. She played her flute—
or was it a lute?—her music like lava spreading the earth.
She was short. I was tall. After gains and losses

she came back in to face the pull of bills and pills
and health issues and tissues for tears,
but that was not all. Best times we sat together in her swing
on the porch. From the porch we watched the sky eating earth,

earth in defeat under storm, storms rolling in over lava land.
Both in pain and in love we watched in heated horror
heavy black clouds hugging cliffs of ancient native art,
landing in blades of quivering wheat,

causing the roof to leak, the house to shake, trees to fall.
But that was all a long time ago. I was now in my den.
I hadn't thought of her in years. Then came a Facebook message.
She wants to be my friend. And I thought: again?

Mirror, Mirror

Ask about your puppet show.
The mirror didn't help the blind,
legless sitting on the sidewalk selling matches.
You say, But that was different.
Children yesterday lost interest,
uncapping fire hydrants, dancing in the blast,
infants in arms turned away.
The organ grinder packed away his organ.
Dear Mirror, what to do?
Your problems are nothing.
What of the homeless?
Days go by.
They die frozen in cardboard boxes in doorways.
Already the villagers are leaving,
starting the long trek up the dirt road out of town into the hills.
Puppets no longer speak the truth—truth about war,
about hunger. One war is over and another one begins.
Old women in black
make their way across the plaza to the chapel.
They pray for everybody.
They ask about their dead husbands.

Domestic Agenda

From outside, through the window,
you are watching the woman inside. You love her.

You left to walk the dog.
She was at the sink washing her hair.

You love her best when she is like this—washing her hair,
applying makeup, pulling on stockings.

Unconscious moments. Degas moments.
I watch you watching her.

The ocean a stretch of green,
seagulls overhead as you walk Smitty along the beach.

You pass people patiently enduring unhappiness.
You pass a pied piper, power walking,

a pack of happy kids trailing.
But who's in the houseboat making it rock?

Coming back to the smell of something baking,
cookies maybe, a warm house. She leans over the teapot,

testing it. You take a peach from the fruit bowl
on the table. You bite into its sweetness.

Today's War

A coast of embedded spring.
Today, in what is left of a barn, John tied a prisoner to a rack,
lay the woman on a stack of hay, went out,

pulled the boat back into the water.
Out there, standing in the open, one eye plucked out long ago,
the reaper sharpens his machete with a whetstone,

the screech cutting across the morning.
John piled the rifles in. I am in the main house.
The basement smells of dead bodies.

The dead organ grinder out there in the front yard.
Three girls coming up the road,
clawing their way out from under a frozen sky,

held up day and night by nearly naked trees,
trees not yet aware of spring.
Maybe every hope follows these girls
coming up from down in landlocked lives,

groping for a new trope of light.
John comes back in. Let's go.
An old horse standing in the yard

with his slow eyes slowly follows us to the boat.
And the ocean is a woman sleeping
with one arm flung out across her pillow. We push off.

War and Its Effects

This is what we see; this is what we know; this is what we feel:
Blood, gray blood. No one in sight in the town square.
East light on the columns,. on the pillars, on the rows,
on the government windows. Light on stone.

And light on the general on horseback,
his horse parade-stepping. And below the horse's lifted hoof,
a wounded warrior on one knee, crying out
as he pulls an arrow from his foot. Blood is everywhere.

This is what we see: Up from his seat the priest
giving the last sacrament over the deathbed.
One naked with a grenade in hand.
One in a shift, gazing into a handheld mirror,

seeing a face she's trying to forget.
Only the boy is worried. His eyes say so.
The rich man walks by.
Beggars camped on cathedral steps

scamper to their feet. This is what we feel:
They surround him with outstretched hands.
The old woman looks at the wall of black clouds
surrounding and closing in. She takes a deep breath.

She's not going to let it go. No one sleeping.
The family in grief slowly pacing the floor.
No place to go. Two maids outside by the door, weeping.
This is what we know: Secret lovers upstairs, above death.

If the kiss lasts long enough, the body begins to glow,
promising life forever. And if the kiss continues
longer than long enough, the body glows red.
A man in a stovepipe hat and cloak sits on a stool by the creek,

crows flying overhead.
Because of him something is lost in the rhythm of the kicker.
The ball will not meet the foot.
It should go sailing as a ship on a sea of air.

It should land somewhere intended,
in waiting hands. When we are coughing smoke
from improvised explosives, coughing smoke
as if from the eruption of Vesuvius, mesmerized by the flames,

too overcome to watch the game, still, we help the wounded,
lift them up. But a short distance south of here there is a hillside, golden
trees in autumn glory, reflecting long shadows
across the stream below, pink sandy shores, pebbles to pocket.

Water and Sand

Today. A scattering of fishing boats. A lost kite.
A scattering of geese and ducks.
Fishermen working ropes along a ropewalk.

Last night. In the night sky a falling comet,
like a stroke flashing down through the brain. No sound.
If sound, it would be that of a newborn screaming.

I need a nap. Out here on the beach a line of girls, knee to knee,
knitting a blanket spread from lap to lap. The pope resigned.
Last summer in Morocco young men gathered,

horseback riders of hope, competing in gunpowder games.
In a swelling blanket of dust they galloped across and back.
But today on this beach the comfort of the familiar.

The sky is a line of cancan girls in perfect harmony.
The ocean is clapping like a grateful audience,
regular as a train on its track.

Noon

Nice, Saturday afternoon.
Elderly men and women sitting on public benches,
along Avenue of the English, noses pointed to the sea.
Memories of war and trenches.

Sunlight striking uppermost edges of majestic hotels lining the avenue.
Noon shadows vanishing beneath.
I'm at Café Luc enjoying a coffee with my friend Darcy.
He's tapping his spoon.

Those old folks over there, many moons ago, he says,
on a day like this, would be working in the fields.
My grandfather, the pig farmer, he says, on Saturday afternoons,
sold pigs at Le Puy Markct. It put money in his pocket.

Because he sold pigs, I am able to spend Saturday afternoons
like this drinking coffee with a friend from America.
What'd you think of that? Not to digress. Not much, I said.
To which he said, You have no appreciation for social progress.

The Moon

Done to death? No doubt, no doubt.
Nevertheless, a full moon tonight. We're back in Davis.
Tonight, watching TV: atrocity, suffering, and death.
I look out the window. Slightly bent, the moon retains its place
at apex. Last saw it like this in Rye, East Sussex.

Stayed at the Rye Lodge Hotel. The moon bright that night.
But the moon is no longer just the moon. Who can tell?
Now it's Apollo 11's moon. It's space moon with spaceship.
Standing in front of Henry James's little stone house.
Quaint, on a narrow cobbled street. *So* not James!
Two stone steps up to the front door.

Flowers in two bay windows—the width.
Above the house the moon reached apex.
No longer just the moon of myth. Where is the moon of "Moon River"?
No longer hunter's moon, nor harvest moon, nor wet moon.
We came to England from Tunis,
the dust of the Tunisian Market still in our clothes.

In Tunis, we wandered around as if moonstruck.
The moon followed us. No longer blue.
No longer just for lovers. No longer of the Maya goddess.
On a beach in France: an afternoon under a beach umbrella,
reading poetry. Directly above us
the moon stood next to the sun.

Once at the market at Gloucester the moon stood above Lane's
looking down at us like a puppy waiting for a snack.
No longer home of the little man. No longer werewolf moon.
Now, home. After the public spectacle of atrocity
we turn the channel to moon exploration,
then to a story, any story—even a moon story.

Once in a blue moon! But we've missed the beginning.
But I'm into it! Night air cloudy with fog
riddled with electric lights—yellow and white.
Night crowds, moonstruck dark and curious.
Three young women in summer dresses enter a bar.
Sadie is singing her favorite song, "Yellow Moon,"

white ribbon flopping about her forehead.
Chorus line comes out, dancing across the stage
under a cardboard moon, yellow as Van Gogh's sunflowers.
It falls to the stage floor. *Plop!*
Everybody laughs. It's gloomy and dark in the tavern.
Music hall merrymakers slightly bent—nonstop!

Old men drinking moonshine and ale.
Only one so far has gone to jail.
Before bedtime we turn to the late news. Where is the gazing rabbit?
Where is the headless horseman?
The weatherman says, "Tonight a full moon.
And you know what *that* means," he says.

The Seasons

Fall. Falling leaves. Leaves falling. Autumn.
Put on a heavy sweater. Start while it's dark. Run in the park.
Speaking German, shedding trees, green leaves turning yellow.
Dragonflies over a stagnant pond. A melancholy harvest festival.
Decaying lotus. A procession of priests into the cathedral.

The sins of summer. Empty confessional booth.
Flags waving national loyalty and Halloween and football.
Yeats singing "The Wild Swans at Coole." Giuseppe's vegetable man.
"May I have this dance?" But she wouldn't.
You wanted to laugh, but you couldn't.

As far as you can see up on a hill a horse grazing by a tree.
Inside the whitewashed house a handrail to a narrow stairway.
On your way up you pass a vaulted window. Enter a lighted hallway.
Stained glass windows on both sides. An old woman at the top.
Leaning out an open window looking down into the courtyard.

Waiting for something to happen.
Winter. You're tilting on your axis. Shorter days, longer nights.
Early morning frost. Icicles and the snowshoe rabbit.
You grieve. Your first snowstorm.
Resisting depression, resisting hypothermia, seeking solace.

Christmas. New Year's Eve. White-tailed jackrabbit on the trail.
Truck tracks in the snow under the overpass. Your daughter's date?
They threw the drunk in jail. The badger storing food.
Skunk and raccoon at the garbage can. It's late.
Morning. You set out to find the footpath buried deep in the snow.

A goat standing by the gate. Death steps out of a canoe.
Securing it to the ring on the deck of winter solstice.
A little girl takes Death by the hand and leads him into the town square.
Here he is already well known.
Death explains again the hour of the wolf. Lots of tears. Lots of hugging.

Spring. Rebirth, a phoenix. Spring doing a ballet step.
Ashes beneath his feet. Power of the phoenix thrashing,
like the power of trees slowly blooming.
Taste the sweetness of smoke. Summer coming.
Axis increasing. Keeping your eye on the tilt of your source.

Purple crocuses shooting up like antelopes jumping from underbrush.
Easter proclaiming a natural place.
Switch to sandals. Forget shoes that lace.
In the attic, before a long mirror, your girl.
She's trying on her grandmother's wedding dress.

Your women in art galleries dragging husbands along to Caravaggio.
"Women come and go talking of" Eliot or Tintoretto.
They give you Groundhog Day or Memorial Day.
Up-all-night girls dancing to the drumbeat of street musicians.
Spring cleaning—searching the want ads for proficient technicians.

Crows in flight, cawing like drunken sailors at play.
Romance at a glance and sleeping spoon fashion.
That summer Stubbs took a dissected horse with him and his wife.
They went on their honeymoon.
You pass an old farmhouse half fallen in.

The view almost sets a trend.
Summer. Summer solstice.
In winter you longed for it, forgetting its dangers.
Remember tornadoes, tropical cyclones, and hurricanes?
Remember thunderstorms and the tree falling on your house?

It came into the bedroom, flattening everything.
Not much you can do with a broom or a shovel for that matter.
Fig tree in bloom. Fourth of July, Assumption of Mary.
Your doctor asks if you eat dairy, and you lie.
In the backyard butterflies, spiders, snails, day and night birds.

You always wanted to learn to box.
Out on the farm, a plodding ox.
A girl with three kittens on her lap.
Colonies of ants invading your kitchen.
Leaving you with little to say.

TV summer Olympics all day.
Up the hill a deer with an arrow in its hide.
Everything you do you try to do with pride.
Volleyball—you know it's not just for the tall.
Animal trap under a tree wedged by a rock.

Shirtless young men playing baseball.
Who's keeping score at the high school swimming contest?
Along the Pacific surfers surfing. A summer job?
Dogs running in the dog run. Girls practicing archery.
You've been told not to buy at the hatchery.

Nice straw basket full of tomatoes. Rain every afternoon. Uncontrollable
umbrellas. Where is Cinderella? Is she all wet?
Boys on skateboards placing bets. Out front a woman sweeping steps.
Ducks dodging her broom.
Inside, a girl at her loom all afternoon.

From Now On

The words can both be yours and not yours.
Did you notice? Did you notice when we drove by?
You think how can I best start a conversation with her.
When you approach, she looks up but only with slight interest.
You've researched the dance of the slaveholder and the slaves.

For a minute there you thought something else.
But you're done with watching the waves.
Without being crude, you were watching the ponies.
They say time flies. Not to be rude, she goes by like time.
But as Holden says, there are too many phonies.

A kite is going to be tossed by a blustery wind. *You bet!*
She says flirting without malice is harmless. Somehow you'll pay.
But what you're doing is okay. Yet the world's in a dark mood.
The trees along that road we just passed are offering shelter.
They're also giving shade to that old man leaning on a stick.

He has a future. The cows in the canyon are searching for grass.
But the firing squad is never as ready as you think.
The sound will shake the trees. True, the engine is running.
If you get to wash her hair, it's best done at the kitchen sink.
To turn a cliché on its back, that train is only *now* leaving the station.

Faith

Run free like a wild horse.

Wake the homeless weeping in their sleep on stone benches.

Rosa broke in bed at Hotel Marina.

Don't want Obi Kenobi to save my galaxy.

Pledge allegiance to the kitchen sink.

Rosa sleeping in her wedding gown.

Don't want to be inspected for perfection or rejection.

Pledge allegiance to the sky, to skylarks, to the unknown.

Don't want anybody tracking my every step.

Don't want to backtrack. But I forgive the boy who sold me a leaky boat.

Is Rosa still in bed?

I worship the ten red apples on the window ledge.

They are my religion.

After Light

Didn't Stevens say something about the body dying as evening dies?
Stars in the country sky! In the Lexington sky!
But it's not just a black veil. Stars twinkling.
In the city, forget it. Too much glare.
Ah, to the letter. Years ago, warm nights were sexy.
And busy as wet windshield wipers.

Nowadays mornings are better. I ride my bike.
Air is better—less frantic. No vipers out looking to strike.
Better still are early afternoons.
Everyone agrees that the coolness of twilight is romantic.
Even the weatherman on TV at six says nice things.

My evenings are not "burnt out" like Eliot's
at the end of smoke-filled days. Ah, London was like that.
But my life is here.
Agnes comes over for midafternoon sessions.
Evenings never work.

I would never forsake her. I'll see her soon.
All the researchers agree: they are all different.
Back then I wore a windbreaker.
For me nowadays evening is best spent reading.
I do it beneath a good reading lamp.

Bitterroot

It was on an incident in the story,
had to do with something Oedipus said or didn't say, I forget which.
Never mind. Balzac gave us Lisbeth. But Othello takes the cake.
You can bet we help him eat it.
I say to the girl at the next table, Death knows my address.

I'm jealous, she says. I want to be known that well.
Canker and poison, you can have them.
If the boy catches the pig and the girl catches the goose,
everybody will be happy. Happy ending?
Or is it, *if the boy catches the girl*? Never mind.

On a journey across country, I sit next to Iago.
He falls asleep with his head on my shoulder.
I am reading *Some Fruits of Solitude*, hoping to learn a few things.
To my unhappy surprise, I find something like Blake's honeybee
stinging my imagination. To hell with it! I'm ready for bed.

I close the book. I close my eyes. I digest what I've read.

The Vegetable King

My sister is trapped in a burning house.
I need to run in and get her before it's too late.
But is it already too late? I must decide quickly.
My knees are about to give out.

Can I move? I will not give wings to my fear.
"Where is your courage?" Where is my courage?
It's hard to forsake prudence.
Still, can I move? I fear I would stumble.

Will I perish in the flames as she is perishing now?
I fear strife! Lady Macbeth said, "Screw your courage
to the sticking-place." Where is that, under my ribs?
A wise teacher once said life is not a race and death is not a goal.

One mind says leap. Another says think. Think carefully!
Jimmy didn't jump into that pit of fire to save Bobby.
Sure, he suffered watching him burn. No one wins.
How quickly can I assess my chance of surviving the flames?

The decision is upon me. There are no games.
Claude said if we must die, let us die with courage.
Bill understood the hazards. He ate his porridge.
I can't stay. I may be a fool, but I'm going in.

Hooray!

In streets I escape my dark home.
In gay streets I'm never lonely!
In wondrous streets I'm happiest among pedestrians!
I am joyous in large groups of busy people on the move.
I was born pressed and creased into crowds.
I must be proud of how I came to be.
Without much to banter about, I was born in Atlanta.
With not much to show, I grew up in Chicago.
Cities of great streets! But give me Paris any day!
In daylight and streetlight I am joyful in streets crowded with people!
Streets to walk even in sleet or snow.
I'm at home in street dances!
At home in streets loud with music and dancing!
At home at parades! At home at fiestas!
Give me neon sparkle! Give me spectacle!
Give me streets that run and rerun like movies!
Give me curving streets and straight streets!
Give me streets to celebrate!
Hooray for the great streets that run on and on!
In streets I am at home in crowds of busy people.
In daylight and streetlight I am happily anonymous.
Give me streets to ride! Streets to recalibrate!
In streets I happily lose myself among passersby.
Give me the streets of Paris!
Praise Haussmann! Streets of Paris redesigned!
You see the Mona Lisa! Give her a try!
Streets with nowhere to hide!
You get through the rhyme! You've come this far!
In crowded famous streets I am a happy wanderer!
Even among strife! Hooray twice for strife!
Even if I blunder or make a faux-pas!
In wide streets of the world I am one with the world!
Hooray for the great streets of life!

Wild Music

At six I had no imaginary animal friends!
Mother sought to fix that by reading me nursery rhymes.
Cat and the fiddle! I never believed a cow jumped over the moon.
I never believed blackbirds baked in a pie.

Everybody said I was too serious.
I never became a fox or a wolf. Never Trigger!
I was not the cockhorse that girl rode to Banbury Cross.
A cowboy, yes! The man on the horse, not the horse!

And I never told a lie! I knew a girl who was a cricket.
Eccentric? Not really. She could make a convincing sound.
In the playpen she was always a different animal. Go figure!
She made the rounds. They now call it animal-centric.

We made animal figures out of construction paper.
Teacher posted the best. Usually a cow! I always had one up.
No probes, no exams, no test. Which reminds me:
scientists say countless creatures live inside our bodies.

Microbes! Wow! That spoils all the fun of being home alone.
Seriously, the girl grew up! I grew up! Love became *the* thing.
Virginia Woolf knew how women love.
Her words had a certain ring. Her timing was never late.

She describes how a woman's impressions of a man accumulate.
At some point they come pouring out in an "avalanche."
I say sometimes on his head! Could this explain my headache?
A cure? Early to bed!

Could it be that all my life I've ignored the endless inner possibilities
of the wild kingdom and its music?
My first girlfriend in high school said
music was with her wherever she went.

Not because of the bells on her shoes.
Music throbbed just under the surface of her skin.
My word to her was I like music—let me in.
A Spanish proverb says men are fire, women are firewood!

The bell had rung just as my tongue sought her tongue.
Instead, a serpent came out her mouth.

The Convex Mirror

With a healthy appetite for fiction,
she said, when I think of romantic love I think of Cyrano de Bergerac and
Roxanne, of Romeo and Juliette!

I said, I think of Ella and Pops singing together.
She said, I lose sleep puzzling over the sequence of Aphrodite,
Venus, and Cupid.

Speaking of Cupid, I said, in the park yesterday I saw two cupids
fighting over a rose. If that's a puzzle, she said, I know the answer.
Cummings said love is stronger than forget—or something to that effect.

Impossible to describe!
I said, I know love is suitable for the boudoir and kissable lips.
In 1912 there was a partial eclipse of the sun.

A young widow in London, standing at the window of her boudoir
(as though she was in Paris), saw the eclipse.
She turned to her lover and said,

I just got a sign that our love will last into old age.
Her lover got up, looked in the convex mirror at his *other*,
and said, Why am I'm not getting that message?

Symbolism of Chains

Back then everybody said I was too sensitive,
too self-reliant, harbored too much self-pity.
I was young and insecure. Sometimes I was Zeus in the form of a swan.
Sometimes I was a swan in the form of Zeus.

I lived entirely in symbolism and chains.
Before an audience, when I spoke, my voice shook.
John (one of the so-called friends)
said, I thought you were going to wet your pants.

Later, it wasn't self-pity that I felt. I was embarrassed, hurt.
What did I desire? My girlfriend, Sue, said I desired nothing.
What was my symbolism everybody talked about?
I was able to talk. My voice had fiber and taste.

My mouth walked, so to speak. Not a waste!
My ears were opened. My ears were closed.
Bells rung, but I heard nothing.
The echo stayed inside my head, ringing endlessly.

Dostoevsky, in *Notes from Underground*, talks about the failure
of self-reliance. I was with friends. On second thought,
maybe they were not friendly. Let's call them acquaintances.
We were at the table, dinner finished.

The symbolism of dinner was also finished.
I was telling these acquaintances about everything relevant.
I was able to talk. Nothing I said was true. Yet I was a winner.
I told them I knew I could wrench myself from the chains—

if there were chains. But I felt I couldn't. I made a bet I could.
Symbolism of chains remained. That got my ire. I could fly.
My desire for clarity, I said, had a way of sustaining itself
even as my comment, at the end,

brought a smile to everybody's lips. Clarity had no effect.
The clarity of my desire—whatever that desire was—
was clearly without symbolic meaning.
No one noticed. I waited awhile, avoiding rage.

What is self-reliance without the virtue of courage?
Jimmy told me failure is as painful as success.
I failed and succeeded at the same time.
Two birds. Without a rhyme.

As with Molly's Yeses

Chaucer's Miller's mistress was to him a honeycomb.

Chaucer needed to tell us about it one night.

Shakespeare's Helena poured the waters of her love

into an "intenible" container of a man. Not all ends well!

Shakespeare needed to tell us Helena's plight.

When my friend Vincent asked me the question,

I said, If love, malice, and lust qualify, then, yes,

I say yes to your question and to all of the above.

Also, I need an audience like Anderson's Joe

needed an audience for his egg standing upright finally

but without a witness. Poor Joe! Poor Bidwell, Ohio!

What good is the act, the passionate release, the pain,

the embarrassment, the guilt, the declaration,

even the exchange, if no one is there to witness

the brave extent to which you have gone?

So, yes, *yes*—as with Keats to Fanny Brawne.

Always yes!

We Were All There

The question was for no one in particular—for any one of us
or for all of us. The leader himself had issues. His list was long—
at the top: gambling, and not just that entire month.
The lawyer said she liked sex. She believed she was addicted.
The old woman liked to sleep too much, felt badly about it.

The twins were hooked on cookies.
The old man drank too much, wanted to stop, didn't know how.
Football was the businessman's thing. No one called his bluff!
His wife was fed up. No more nookie!
The student was on drugs, hard stuff.

Then there were words. I was guilty.
Gee! It's not as if Horace hadn't already warned me
of their ability to fly off into the distance.
They call it now the new technology.
My pleasure was hording a sorcery of them,
served with pus, with vinegar—with Voltaire's blessings.
I even occasionally borrowed Amy's little jars
lifted carefully down from her shelf
and placed carefully on my own shelf. I felt guilty.
Tried to soothe myself with fast cars

with the radio turned up loud to a jazz riff.
David tried to reassure me that we all do it.
His secretary, while taking dictation,
flowed downriver on them as if she was on a skiff.
Martin had already warned me of the epidemic,

the leprosy, the worn mental locality,
the wearing out by routine, the empty slogan.
Loose tongue! Like wet sheets wrung dry!
All so endemic to my own little world of jars.
My mouth dry with the evidence of his truth.

Dog Fight

It was elusive. Richard and I were in the courtroom audience.
Anna was explaining to the judge why her dog was not the aggressor.
Angelo had spoken of not making it a scarecrow.
Anna wanted it defined—to make a go of it. Goodness sake!
Which is not to say she wanted something with no eyes.
She kept her fingers crossed.
Max whispered, It's a snake!
I knew it was elusive and relative.
Everything and nothing was lost!
An accusation was made. At some cost a denial followed.
Voices echoed in the chamber,
talk of a raid! The accused was hopeful.
By the rules both dogs were innocent.
Then who was guilty?
Richard said, It's to protect the innocent.
One hoped to grow!
Then who are those perishing in its shadow?
They're not dogs! Somehow we all are related.
Martin spoke of the "security of it."
But is there guilt too small, too large to punish? Dogs are dogs.
We said people are the point.
But what to call it—how to define it?
The natural. The man-made.
Where was wit? We listened to the loud!
An old proverb: What happens to the lamb if the judge is a wolf?
It's like Coleridge's joy—both "sweet voice" and "luminous cloud."

Classified Notes

I am just born. My eyes are spouts.
The first taste of my own tears, the salt of tears, surprises me,
not the tears but the salt.

My first fingernails digging into the skin of my cheeks surprise me,
not the digging but the pain: salty tears burning open skin.
Am I made entirely of salt and pain?

Already I am somewhere between consolation and condolence.
My tears are messengers with classified notes.
They're from remote areas of my future—at age six.

In that future, on my knees, one leaf falls to the ground.
Now many leaves fall.
My little friends of the soil put on their work boots and gloves.

They get out their hacksaws. My friends: butterflies,
grasshoppers, ants, earthworms, termites, crickets,
even the invisible ones—mites and nematodes.

I watch them hack away at the leaf. Now more leaves.
Now my eyes are rarely rainy,
except in the presence of raw freshly cut onions.

But when my eyes are rainy, they are so with sorrow.
Yet my tender heart grows stronger.
I'm no longer crawling.

I now walk under these trees losing their leaves.
And the leaves keep falling to the bosom of the earth.
Crocodiles crawl from the river to the shore.

I like walking among the falling leaves of fall.
But spring is my favorite season, a time of rebirth.
I love the metaphor of my own first weeping—spring showers.

The Knot

He was from the South Side, Chicago.
She was from Woolwich—south of London.
They decided not to jump over the broom.
Ah! Instead—that à la mode!

But it was draining—like a harlot's progress,
like a rake's progress!
Plus no one knew they'd lived together for six years—
and without tête à tête!—

lived among strangers in a cityscape with no escape,
and never lost interest in each other. Never!
Shopkeepers gave them credit.
They'd endured the owner's distraining.

He sold all their stuff to get his rent.
They lost sleep.
Their dog never found strange panties under the bed.
Yet somehow they were Napoleon after a Hundred Days.
They lived for a time in a tent. They counted sheep!
They took bids—no lie!—But nothing tacky!

Soon! They did it. September 2 they did it,
made it official! Mary Hackey, from high, was maid of honor.
Not arranged! Not deranged! "Come one, come all!"
Even had a village buffoon and a Punch and Judy show.

Neighborhood kids had a ball.
Occasion of the penny dance.
Lots of frolicking in the fairgrounds.
Lots of laughter—no frowns! Even a dog run!

The blind fiddler played and danced.
Everybody was kind! Portia and Brutus!
They were grateful for the freedom and fun.
They learned from what was taught.

Ancestors knew none of it. Once hooked . . .
One dangled on the line till removed—if ever.
Moliere's rack! Lawrence called it a harness!
They watched the shores from ship deck.

Edith warned about the horrors of quicksand.
Somerset said it is a shipwreck!
But they wanted in! They wanted to stay.
Yet they knew these things blew up around people like landmines.

They also knew it was better than making the trip alone.
Robert long ago said it's expensive.
But why were people made to swear never to stray?
And she turned. And he turned too.

And when she was caught, she said she had nothing to say.
When he was caught, he was simply defensive.
Hell! He was only sorry he was caught.
The age of innocence was over.

Both caught in their separate *bagnio*!
But she was not begging for forgiveness!
She called long distance to talk to her mama.
And he was not going to kill her lover! No such waste!

They were too modern for such drama!
She and her lover dressed hastily!
But where was the squirrel?
And who dropped the masquerade mask by the bed?

Ah, who cares? Only so much on a dare!
Humiliated and embarrassed, she and her lover left together.
And she did not poison herself. No such drama!
Her lover was not strung up. No such spectacle! No public square.

On the Road Back

On our way there (there is a there *there!*)
we pass houses leaning one way and another.
We wonder at the sentimental sunset drenching the land
with buttery light. Are we more than a fly?
We wonder at the rolling hills behind the houses,

at the human lives behind those walls—
will they go dancing tonight?—
and the mystery and beauty of Walt's "we two"!
Predatory hawks?
We refuse to think we will die.

Theo says it's all self-interest! Everything!
Ben says son of his right hand better off dead aged seven.
Self-interest! Till things get better . . . Haystacks casting tall shadows.
A boy and a girl kissing in the shadows!
Bill says girls understand better than boys.

Tonight more women seated wallflower than on the dance floor.
A couple kissing! The ultimate expression of . . . of what?
Or Oscar's "misunderstanding"?
Percy got carried away: saw only *selfless* interest.
Adoration of the Other! Not Other as Self! Mercy me!

The boy Cupid reduced to greeting cards.
My friend the cynic: it's a four-letter word like the others.
On the street winter women in long coats,
men in coal holes digging. Spring comes! A door opens.
Yet something is missing.

Toys lined up available.
And on the road back we pass a man walking a mile
holding both hands over his ears, screaming.
Maybe folly, maybe foolish, but we pass couples,
arm in arm, reducing the universe to a single smile.

Long Avenue and River Street

Inside we hear the reading of the decree, the edict.
On the long avenue winding past the cathedral
no young people, only old women in black dresses,
coming from and going to the market.
They all know tragedy.

Rare is the one who stops to notice the way the light falls.
The cathedral taller than all else reaches into clouds.
Its shadow falls softly across the city
reminding everyone of its presence.
A few old women stop in to pray.

They pray for themselves, for the weak and the poor.
All the prostitutes are young women working for rent.
They smell of cheap perfume—ah, their sweet scent!
They get little sleep, trying to make ends meet.
Tragedy finds them randomly one at a time.

They're down on River Street hanging around cheap hotels.
Young men are there too, some walking lightly and politely,
younger ones on scooters and skateboards
zooming back and forth—proving Aristotle's prediction.
Did Aristotle stutter?

Are there orders left to obey?
Or is that not the point?
What is the point of obeying?
But they are decidedly not just a blunder.
When at six o'clock cathedral bells chime, all hearts flutter.

The Sometime Difficulty with Teaching

This is the classroom, twenty-five students,
all smart and ready for the world!
No trouble teaching them how it was
when the crusaders came into Constantinople!
Or what Cezanne meant by the cylinder, the sphere, and the cone.

Or how passionately Thetis pleaded to Jupiter
to help her save the life of her son, Achilles.
But today we're talking about *routine*.
I say, There is a sense of well-being
in doing the same thing every day—of being regular.

They say, No way. They say, Doing the same thing
every day is boring—even unbearable.
I say, Consider the value of patterns in your life.
Patterns sustain your sense of comfort.
Patterns reassure you that you will not go over the cliff

into the abyss. They say, Without variety life is dull.
But, I say, you can have variety within patterns.
The opposite of routine is chaos.
They say, Then give me chaos!
At six in the evening, from my kitchen window, I see a blackbird.

He comes and lands on the same limb of the same tree in the yard.
He sits there for about an hour.
He looks south for a while.
He turns and looks north for a while.
There's variety in his pattern.

He never does the same thing exactly the same way twice,
yet he is keeping a pattern.
The class says, Birds are not people.
People need lots and lots of variety—no patterns!
Would you want to eat the same thing every day?

I say, If it is good, why not?
I already eat the same thing every day!
And I remember Ron saying to me,
You have unusual ideas;
that's why you've never had a best seller.

Two Double Burgers

She's waiting for you out there in the car.
On your way to the line you check out yourself in the big mirror.
You're clearly there. But is she real?
Could she possibly exist only in your mind?

You say she has the aural effect.
Sometimes you think she's only a voice.
You said she's talkative, a chatterbox!
She repeats your words with a thrill.

She accuses you of loving only yourself.
You've called her names—
lover, wife, mate, date, coquette, virgin, whore, and more.
Still she waits. She's not playing games.

While she's waiting, she sings to herself.
She waits as you buy two double burgers with fries.
You intend you two to eat them for dinner.
It's hot out there—over a hundred degrees in the shade.

What's her angle? What'd you think she's thinking?
Perhaps of that time you called her God's mistake.
Or Eve for evil! Or when you said she was inferior.
Or when you called her an angel!

Or when you said she was two-faced—accusing her of confusing you.
Or maybe she remembers you saying Woman is made from Man's rib.
And she said the evidence is to the contrary.
Her voice was chiming!

Think! Which comes first, chicken or the . . . ?
Without rhyming you called her a tyrant!
You've called her out of her name many times.
Now you come out to the lot, and the car is gone.

She's gone! You, mirror gazer, with burgers in bag!
Have you lost your imaginary echo?
Perhaps she drove around the block.
Perhaps she will return to the parking lot—a delayed echo.

A Battlefield

A noise just outside your window!
Faint-heartedness? Or is it just your fear of authority?
When the lineman waves to you, you blush.
When the children wave to you, you blush.

Hobbes said it's the same thing as your judgment.
Or is it simply that ever-present serpent? You stand like a T.
Progress may depend on what goes on in your head.
Or what you meant. You are very alert.

Just outside your window you hear weeping.
A naked woman is at the window.
She's tapping with her fingernails on the glass.
You were sleeping. She's trying to get your attention.

You let her in. She has been abused.
You want to call the police. She begs you not to.
You tell her you must call. She's been misused.
If you don't, you won't be able to live with yourself.

You give her a pair of your pants and a jacket.
You leave the room so that she can dress.
Imagine something that does not exist yet given a name.
It's not exactly instinct! A spark? Inhibition?

It's not a matter of being awake or even alert.
No one is more alert than you!
You witness the sun coming up.
You witness a group of children with their backpacks.

They are walking to school.
You are aware of the lineman checking the tracks.
You touch the skiff like a blind man making sure it's actually there.
You enter the castle and feel the coolness envelop you.

Romantics call it an inner light. Nonsense!
The poets imagined it to be a kind of corrective force.
They called it a force with a bright light shining from within.
Or is it simply fear of punishment?

You agree with those who called it a battlefield.
It leaves you filled with guilt and shame,
but also driven by passionate self-interest projected onto others.
You call the police. They take her away weeping.

Nancy's Nanny Goat

The age-old question: What is it?
My friend James the cynic says we should be smart.
We should keep things simple, not complicate everything.
Pondering his idea, we stay up all night.

Self-restraint is likely involved.
That's an improvement, right?
We know now that it's not just newer gadgets,
nor taking the train instead of the bus.

We think of it as some sort of forward march.
We don't drink. We exercise and vote.
We don't fuss and fight, but we gamble some.
Yet something moves into the future without us.

There are goals. Justice is one.
Nancy's nanny goat has gotten out again.
The goat has learned to wait at the gate.
Food will come.

Call it faith—faith that the future is free to change.
James is concerned about what our town is becoming.
We watch our town become a city.
Is it inevitable? A law?

Or is it just a drifting too soon?
Is it a thoughtless shifting toward something unknown?
We watch the changes of the moon without blinking.
The baby is moved from the nipple to the spoon.

Some of us move north, some south.
I have a terrible sinking feeling.
A parade moves through the city.
Girls strut.

What a pity the boys clown!
The housekeeper secures her hair at the base of her head.
She settles on the edge of the bed as if to stay.
She's holding the spoon to the baby's unwilling mouth.
Gently, she pushes the food into the little mouth.
Anyway, on time or late, she is a sleeper.

James and I are at the café talking again about this thing.
He says it's in all organisms.
I order a double latte. It's a keeper!
Everything inevitably moves beyond its original state.

Is the city better than the town, an improvement?
Nancy stretches out on the couch.
She is painting her fingernails and toenails.
She fans herself with the passion of a saint.

Is she an improved Nancy?
Children are playing in the marsh.
They're collecting insects, pinning them to cardboard.
Budding scientists? Is it a dream of utopia?

The Art of Confessional Poetry

I spit on the street. I can be silly and foolish.
I may have too many affectations.
I don't know the rules of dress. I make faux pas!
I am not considerate enough. I play a guitar off-key.

I slip up and say things that earn silence.
When the muse was passing out kisses, she missed me.
I've done gauche things. I can be arrogant.
I went to a formal gathering dressed as a centaur.

My girlfriend went as Beatrice of Aragon.
Men were in black tie and women in evening gowns.
We were both ready to die of shame.
Worse, we entered shouting, Hip hip hurrah!

As if it was some kind of game.
Heads turned. I felt like a clown!
I had forgotten about the mask!
The contrivance. How artificial, how protective!

They were protected—we were exposed!
I forgot Dorothy, Emily, Amy, Erasmus, and Galeazzo.
I forgot I'm liberal, genial, and loyal—loyal to everyone.
I forgot everything I'd read in Galeteo!

Before going there, I forgot to wash my hands.
I groomed on the way in the car. What a lout!
Someone asked my girlfriend if she'd ever been in a bridal shower.
She said no but once in a high school she played Psyche.

She had to hand Venus a bowl of water.
Definitely the wrong thing to say!
My girlfriend didn't know the rules.
She'd never gone to a finishing school.

She didn't know proper place settings.
Like me, when she felt like it, she would shout!
We knew we should speak in a moderate voice.
We both had lots to worry about.

We knew we should not make rude gestures.
We failed to use the proper utensils at the dinner table.
We were able but so forgetful. We needed a place to hide!
We needed the manners of Renaissance nobility!

I shook hands too eagerly, not much to tout!
I thought self-consciously of myself as I talked to guests.
I worried how I was perceived. How rude!
We should have been out collecting mussels at low tide.

Not here! How crude! How tactless!
In the toilet I prayed for the wisdom of Voltaire.
I prayed for the manners of a prince.
But none of the gods responded!

Everyone here seemed too finicky!
I've heard it called a firewall and a station.
Perhaps it's the hardest form of morality.
It might be just a set of small-minded sacrifices.

Still, I should have been courteous. I was not charming.
I had no *sprezzatura*—translation: I was not cool!
Kindness eluded me.
Everyone except us acted appropriately.

Disgusted with myself, I went out alone on the terrace.
The sprinkler in the yard was turning rhythmically.
It was spraying water over a dry area—nourishing it.
Disgraced, I saw the poetry of it as a kind of saving grace.

The Green Monkey

There is silence where there should be answers!
In the fifth grade my teacher, Mr. Berry, said,
"Never forget how small you are in the universe!"
Now, I'm floating in Franz's reds, yellows, blues, and greens!

Hell, who says we are at a party? Somebody forgot a purse!
Take more than a glance—it's far more serious!
The thing itself must first earn a name.
You might then puzzle over meaning. Debate it!

But does truth lie? You can tell me. I am your brother!
Definitions can come later—freelance. You want proof?
Anyway, is the "we" of us only a pretext for the "I" of us?
Sure, you *are* alone! *I* am alone! And this is not a game!

There is proof in my trance—so says the debater!
Listen! I hear a rigorous noise in my sleeping brain!
I wake up from dreaming about *meaning* and can't get back to sleep.
Then somebody says hello stranger and I wonder, Am I going insane?

At best, I can't decide if the greeting is spoken in jest.
Does it mean *where have you been so long* or where are you *now*?
Why am I trembling? What am I afraid of—the sound of the gavel?
What is this steep anguish? I hear you say, "You better get a grip!"

In the French sense, if I am a stranger, what am I a stranger to?
What is this nothingness? Can I *buy* my way out with money or charm?
Daily and nightly, am I the reclusive subject? Should I travel more?
What is the theme of *me* as subject—the essence of the "I"?

Is there nothing at the beginning and nothing at the end?
Paradise denied? I say, *Squeeze me, honey!* Let's walk in the park!
I say findings might be inconclusive! Anyway, hold me tightly!
You say all consequences are here. So am I always at point otherwise?

I know I am responsible. I close my eyes; I stretch out on the grass.
I am my own subject. I am also both myself and my other.
Truly, I am my own subjectivity. *And I am your brother!*
Look! See Marc's green money laughing at his red man.

Man and monkey? They reinforce the questions.

Horses Don't Care

We bring it on ourselves.
Then we have to act. It's a debt!
Sue said, Do it by living better than Betty!
Transgressors around every corner!

Those who bring it on say, To hell with grand principles!
This thing we know festers! We can't win!
Laws hold human emotions in check.
Under duress we arrive sometimes at an undesirable second life.

The circus performer eats only popcorn to stay thin.
His wife eats barbecued ribs. She's a wreck!
He makes a living as a clown jumping rope on a high wire.
He buys her a second wedding gown.

The lion trainer distracts him. He falls to the net.
The cat can't catch the butterfly, so he looks up at the clouds.
The sheep is stuck on a cliff. He'll be there till fall.
The circus performer plans a scheme: An eye for an eye!

A tooth for a tooth! The attendant unlocks the gate.
There is a scream! Untold thousands are coming in!
Abused, Bob the gorilla scampers off to a far corner.
To the man in the booth he's making his point clear.

He sits there, knees to chin, holding himself. Plotting.
Oh, dear! Is it true that only the noblest among us never seek it?
Bob rocks himself, trying to calm his anger.
Maybe you saw Jack Johnson knock out Jeffries.

Imagine Jeffries plotting a rematch!
Everybody watched the clock!
The boy finally catches the pig.
Imagine the pig plotting a rewind of reality.

The girl has finally caught the goose. She's a winner!
Imagine the goose on the dinner table.
The rational mind knows when we have trapped ourselves.
People on rooftops wave at a procession of returning soldiers!

Somewhere the defeated army is plotting a new campaign.
This thing we know festers and festers. It hangs around.
The bus stops, and the door opens. Beyond it is the city.
The old woman just stands there. She's not insane.

She can't bring herself to step down.
The driver becomes more and more impatient.
A committee declares it beyond the domain of humans.
Horses don't care.

They do look up as we approach
but show only slight interest.
For a minute I thought something interesting was about to happen.
The old woman is still standing there.

Dragons

I'm dying to get things done!
My fellow airmen are from Spain—northern and southern.
They are still fighting the civil war.
I have to do everything. I will construct and repair.
Looking at things constructively I see guys with money.

They are buying time to do nothing. It's a game.
Nothing consists of lying on bunk beds all afternoon.
Or they're lying by the pool. Doing so is so lame!
By the pool they are still fighting the civil war.
I study the details. Characters rename themselves.

This is to avoid having their names come up next on the work list.
The list is posted in the hallway by the bathroom door.
It's as though the earth itself has lost its power to be fruitful.
Carlos, Juan, and Pablo embrace inactivity.
I am doing everything. I run; I walk. I do everything!

Bodies suffer stupidly. Nothing is giving birth.
It's insupportable! Stagnation festers—smells of rot.
Despite all, they are kind! They are each other's buffer.
They say they are of Mother Earth.
But they are still fighting their civil war!

It's as though the earth has lost its will to be reborn.
See the long barren stretch of the mother?
See her belly button out there in the desert directly under sunny skies?
The guys say the belly button is some kind of religious shrine.
The arms and legs are roads leading away to remote areas.

That's where of late there still be dragons.
The sky beyond her is a slab of sunny slate.
Desperate migrating tribes travel across her skin.
But they go only so far as maps show. Beyond are dragons.
What has led to this lack of engagement?

There is an illness, a vice—or call it sin.
There is much to resent. It's monstrous! It's insane!
Even without crops there can still be heaven and hell.
The Spaniards are suspended between the two with nothing to do.
Meanwhile they go on fighting their civil war.

But perhaps there is hope, even for the guys from Spain!
Still, I'm dying to get things done, even on the run.
It's clear now. I have to do everything. While I work, I sing.
I will construct and repair. I will get things done before nightfall.
In the night we always hear the dragons in perpetual despair.

Quicksand

The caterpillar hides beneath a leaf till it becomes a butterfly.
Is it the same as lying? A moth is on the garden rake.
Worms hide from the scratching of chickens.
Sometimes you know it by its silence.

Is it a trick? Is it a fraud? We keep trying to be better.
The snake tries not be seen. It crawls in low hidden places.
Sometimes this thing is built brick by brick.
I had a girlfriend who was double minded.

See that lion crouching behind that rock?
He is waiting for the deer. The deer is in for trouble.
I hide the actual number of my blood pressure from myself.
I'm waiting for a better number.

But I can't rewind it. By the way my nurse is a grouch.
I throw dust in my own eyes.
For a while I can't see. But a lot I've already seen.
Dean lied to Justine to gain advantage. Is it hypocrisy?

Justine says there is no justification for it.
Off with Dean's head! Roof rats hide in his attic.
They think he doesn't know they are there.
I expect Justine will soon dump Dean.

Seeing the hawk, the lizard on the rock changes its color.
The new color is that of the rock.
Chaucer said the smiling man might be hiding a knife inside his cloak.
The wealthy pimp drove a Ford twenty years old.

No cop ever stopped him. It is quicksand.
Shakespeare was right—it is glib and oily.
But it's built into nature. Or Nature!
Dean says go complain to nature—with a capital N.

The Chipmunk and the Hawk

I was trying to gather my notes to teach a class.
Is there a connection between meanness and superstition?
Let's not define superstition. Let's be cautious.
Better to define worry.

No one has done it well. But let's take another look.
My mother once said it's the beginning of wisdom.
My father said it is the beginning of your demise.
There is a high wall to climb. It makes me nauseous.

One climbs it in self-defense, sometimes in a hurry!
I worry about putting too much information on Facebook.
There is a certain gut-intelligence at work,
the soul's red flag! And I doubt that there is a soul!

Maybe the long shadow is just a lack of intelligence,
a kind of permanent rut! But shouldn't one be cautious?
In a rough part of the park Judy is sitting on a bench.
She sits primly and self-consciously on the edge.

She looks up from the book and glances around.
Her eyes blink rapidly! Is she sensing rain?
The squirrel looks up repeatedly from the nut he is trying to crack.
Is it anticipation of pain?

Is it anticipation of the wrath of the gods?
What of the dog that hides under the bed when the doorbell rings?
There is the needle that is coming toward your arm.
You can see it. Watching it is the hardest part.

This thing is an inventor of safety.
Eric says it says you are weak. You are inferior.
Eric at times is brutal.
I said to Eric, Isn't nature trying to warn us.

Sure, we expect what we don't want to happen.
What of little animals rushing to hide in the underbrush?
The chipmunk safe in the zoo cage watches the sky for the hawk.
But the hawk will never come.

Faith, Hope, and Charity

Into each other's aura! Speech halts! Words wait!
Yet the mind continues to spell them out, letter by letter.
My mouth presses against your mouth!
My tongue pries into your mouth!

An exchange of saliva!
What allegiance is this? Do you feel the allegiance?
My tongue dances with your tongue! Or, are they fighting?
We give what we take.

This is the pause on the way to a question mark.
But I taste no cement. I taste no glue. I taste no lime.
I taste the aftereffect of your toothpaste.
I'm in your atmosphere! You're in my atmosphere.

I feel a swelling in my chest and elsewhere.
By the way, who are you? Do I know you?
Wet tongues together or words that rhyme with tongue?
Which comes first? *Wait!*

Haven't we done this earlier somewhere?
Was it in Chicago? Was it in Paris? Was it by a brook?
It was not in Hollywood. We were not in a movie.
Not on videotape. Not on Facebook.

Perhaps we met by chance on the street.
We mistook each other for someone else.
I held your hand. I pulled you close.
Speech halted. Funny how people meet!

Words waited like a nineteenth-century carriage by the front door.
My mouth pressed against your mouth.
Yes, I remember now. You said you knew my friend Byron.
Byron knew all about bliss. And he knew lots more!

You were looking for the next step to the next step.
Lip service was only the first step.
You wanted a diamond ring with all the bling.
To stop the words, I kissed you again.

And again! Then once more!
And I kissed you again for a long time.
Then I felt your tongue in my mouth.
It was spelling out the letters in the word *marriage*.

Onion

I suckled at the left tit of a wet nurse.
She was a woman under stress.
Poor woman, she was not exempt from tragedy.
On her right breast was her infant son.

No other arrangement was attempted.
The local bet was her son would stand the test of time.
I, they said, would fail at everything attempted. I was sickly.
I stayed on the left. I was determined to prove them wrong.

Sure, I had relapses, but I recovered quickly.
I grew strong! But at age five, on a day of sleet, her son died.
Yet I never thought there was a plot against him or me.
Sure, we were born, like everybody else, on a one-way street.

But I learned fast the jigsaw puzzle of all the road signs.
I never was satisfied with my lot on the highway.
Yet I knew I had a lot to be grateful for.
I was grateful for air and light. I owned no gold mines.

Day by day on the slate it was a learning process.
I learned to deal with misers, misanthropes, and missionaries.
Everywhere I turned probability and disability!
Anxiety, stress, strife, pain, and illness!

Everywhere jealousy, deceit, lies, and anger!
The stuff of everydayness! Occasionally pretzels and two beers!
Everybody said what's your goal, what's your angle?
The easy and hard answer was more contentment than tears.

"Keep living the way you are living, and you will arrive at the end."
Toil and trouble! Yet I had to go through the motions!
Everyone said there is more misfortune than fortune.
Dust to dust. Bubbles and troubles! Double bubbles!

My goodness! Look who gets the best seats!
Best seats or no seats, I would prevail.
Yet rust accumulated on my emotions.
Marking my pace, I moved to another city and another city.

I was not alone in my travail of facts and notions.
A soldier in battle, I trudged on through the mud of the front lines.
I refused the cliché of sojourner in an unfriendly place.
It was all about the journey—the extent of the content.

It was not about the arrival or where the arrow landed.
I worked here, and I worked there. I played, and I stayed.
I was never happy. I was never unhappy.
The story never turned out the way I expected.

The story was always what I expected.
No patient likes the hospital. I was delirious!
A lot of empty beds in the terminal ward!
I wasn't ready for the ultimate answer.

I studied my tendencies—especially the destructive ones.
One voice said I was too serious—too dense!
Another voice said this is better than the alternative.
"Every day remember how big the universe is.

Keep your perspective. It's all vapor!
Here is the preservative against decay!
Bathe in it! Rinse in it! Be nice.
Practice compassion, kindness, altruism, and mercy."

I didn't have the best cards, but I thought before I said *all in.*
They said think twice before you hit your mark!
Everybody had good advice. "Love thy neighbor!
Practice pity! Practice sympathy! Keep hope!"

Careful about how you throw your dice!
It's a short stretch from creation to the rope,
just a shadow to cremation—then worms and lice!
They said know the maxims of universal law.

I came back time and again to the unknowable.
I came back time and again to the limits.
Few were the words for the limits and the unknowable.
Sometimes it was a trick on a stage full of fools.

Rarely a party! Too often interlude after interlude!
More allegory than glory! Lots of allegory!
Pleasure bait and all! Catcalls and allegory!
Bravo to allegory!

At other times it involved pealing off the layers of an onion.
A horrible compromise! That was the mood!
It was mostly work! Maze and work! Rarely amazing work!
"A little of this, a lot of that, then it's over—*and the curtain falls.*"

The Invisible

My defense was symbolic! Or was it just all symbolism?
Here was the fortress, a fortress with faces of the dead.
It was my advocate, yet perhaps a worthless fantasy,
full of invisible writings, invisible numbers!

But what was accomplished? What was it worth?
Alongside necessities, a pile of trinkets! What of worth itself?
Night or day, when the moment arose, I would have the means.
I would not have to plead for freedom, to beg for liberty.

I would not have to fight—but what of worth itself?
Yet I always wondered where was the substance?
Though symbol, yes, it was like blood circulating through my veins.
For it to continue I needed to keep suspending disbelief.

I wanted to drink it like a bottle of medicine before bed!
I trusted it to keep me healthy, to give me a long life,
to give me comfort! But what did it stand on?
"It's a great master," people said—with good reason!

The seedbed of temptation! Yet what of worth itself?
Heavy as a potted plant yet light as air! Always in season!
I lost sleep over its worth. But translation was never necessary.
Everybody understood what it *did* but not what it meant.

Like a piece of fruit, you had to eat it before it rotted.
I stood on stage accepting the honor and all that came with it.
At their best everyone said they were proud of me.
Friends came out of the woodwork. They thought I had it.

This was conquest! It was loud and never out of fashion.
The tall girl said it meant more to her than anything in the world.
"It's a great servant!" I said to her, "but it's an illusion.
Here, take half of it!" Yet I could not fault her or its power.

We rode up in the elevator together to the sound of rockets.
She took a shower. Water rolled off her like Niagara over the fall.
Sweet balm under the mattress! Sweeter balm in the vault!
Sure, it assured safe passage. It underwrote assurance, assured sleep.

The guarantee was satisfying. Quote me—I never needed luxury!
Yet the sovereign queen held forth! Invisible but somehow there!
"Here, take it. It's nothing! It may comfort you like bread.
See if you can find some use for it. It will never be dated."

It's an earthy force, and its earthy power is overestimated.
Yet who was I to resist? And she wasn't about to say no!
For what it was worth—I gave her as much as I would keep.
Not knowing worth itself, my lamp of dignity shined brighter.

Always

Potentially useful patterns of thought floated through the air.
Every thought I grabbed was faulty.
But there was always something to gain by keeping patterns.
There was always something to gain by breaking patterns.
I was living calmly in patterns.
That was my pattern. I was one with the nation.
Yet I was trying to be innovative.
I unstrapped my beneficent harness for more freedom.
I made my way through cobwebs into brighter light.
Occasionally I drank a beer.

The deer in my headlights stopped, then continued.
The deer in the wallpaper moved always the same way.

I went to G. G.'s on a regular basis—my oasis.
I always picked up the newspaper on the way in.
The delivery truck double-parked every Thursday.
At G. G.'s the cook always beat the eggs twenty times.
Customers gazed into laptops for social thrills!
Customers talked into cell phones for personal thrills!

At home I used a coffee mug with a George Eliot quote.
I threw my beneficent harness in the trash.

Then I drove my car out to the sea to see the sea.

The Things You Hear

If it matters, it's a beautiful day.
You and I are outside at the crab shack.
You are telling me what you think happened.

What I'm doing is eloquent.
In any case it's safe!
You say, How do you know?
Every week many disagree on the value.
Is it a weakness—a strength, something in-between?

If this thing had color, the color would be yellow.
Nothing mean about yellow.
No whine, no squeak!

If you yell out your disapproval, you fail the test.
It *is* a test trimmed in gold.
You didn't know it was a test?
Just for you! It's a defense too.
Though unrated, it's a test and a defense!

I often listen, if not always carefully.
From this side of the fence
I know what I think,
and I'm listening now
because I don't know what happened.
I listen with focus as best I can.
But I will not tolerate hocus-pocus!

I disagree with those who say there is danger
in simply observing the coastline,
the hillside, the plains, the bay,
and people on the sidewalk,
people in line at the grocery store.

Later we gather to drink wine,
to watch the sunset—instead of TV.
You give me a peck on the cheek.
"Do me more!"
Okay, that's the way you want to be!

At the center of the unspoken
is a kind of stillness to be respected.
If you can imagine it—a buzz without a sound.

"Somebody's at the door!" Who is it? We make a bet.

I don't buy the notion of an emptiness as definition.
I'm not saying that you or everyone does.
It's sometimes just a matter of getting in the car
and turning on the ignition.

I give myself to it as if it were an honor.
Here! You've earned this difficult thing! Take it!
But I confess I also go for a walk
along the path when I am unsure.
Once I saw a baby in a manger.

With my tongue I absent-mindedly feel my teeth.
No danger in holding my tongue.

The danger is you might think I am criticizing you.
There *is* a kind of criticism—I admit.
But I submit that it's not necessarily so!

And as you once said,
if it goes on too long, it reproduces itself twofold—
and not always to the best advantage.

Beneath the blanket might be a sword
or a love letter.
At my age hardly a love letter.

In certain countries only one side is revealed,
over and over. One voice.

You might find yourself trying without any response,
physical or otherwise.
It can become a quest!

You try, then you wait darkly, sometimes wrongly.
But I have no problem taking a nap
on the daybed in question.
It is a place of comfort.

Remember,
there is a kind of wisdom gained in that sleep.
I don't have to be told: there is safety too!

It doesn't come in a bottle,
but it's also an effective medicine to drink.
Drink it slowly.

From Now On

About the only place that still looks good.

Decent size.

Note ~ Record all room dimensions later.

Tiled white floor needs a good scrub but is in good condition. Distressed white wood (obviously bought a job-lot of this stuff!) units all look good. Range works and is still in good condition. Obviously not much cooking done here. Island is large, decked out with marble plinth. Deep porcelain Belfast sink. More sash windows, dirty but otherwise seem in good condition.

Really bright in here with large window to front lawn.

My favourite room!

Small extension-slash-mini conservatory acts as a utility room with glass door that opens out to walkway down the side of the house. It has a washer and dryer. Both in working order.

The glass door has a broken pane that's been fixed up with plywood and gaffer tape. Dirt and dead leaves all over the floor.

All good enough to sell as is (obviously after it's had a good clean!).

(16) Glass in door needs fixing and the whole place needs a good clean!

Dining room.

The dining room can be reached from the miserable

hallway and is quite spacious. Wood floor throughout but also in need of a thorough clean. Large solid wood (probably oak) dining table with room for eight with light wood chairs. All in fairly good condition. Another garish, ornate gold mirror on the wall. Weird wooden antelope chandelier hangs over the table. Abstract art? All looks fairly good but, again, horrible cigarette-smoke-coloured walls. Needs a clean and good lick of paint, as there's dust everywhere.

This furniture could actually be sold, maybe even locally? I wonder if the grocery store has a notice board or something??

Try to sell furniture locally if possible.

The Conservatory

Although they're clearly two separate spaces, the conservatory is effectively an extension of the dining room.

Like everywhere else, it's dirty, featuring webs and their unpaying guests and an open grave of insects. The tiled terracotta floor looks OK but needs a good scrub. Pale blue fabric armchairs are faded and worn. They need to be disposed of along with wicker coffee table.

Gold floor lamps (the old man obviously had a thing for gold — shocker!) still good. Just need cleaning. Can be donated when no longer required.

Spectacular views of garden and ocean in here, though! (I know that's your favourite sentence, Lucinda.) There's an archway in here that also leads to the lounge (or den).

This completes the tour of the first floor!

Thank ~~fue~~ heavens for that!

When I look up from the notepad, Ellie is gazing out of the conservatory window, and this gives me pause because, although my wife seemed patient throughout our tour, contributing here and there with ideas and suggestions about how to tackle the renovations of this place, her heart doesn't seem to be in it.

"Penny for your thoughts," I say, walking up to her.

She turns and forces a smile, and I can see that it's for my benefit.

"Hey," I say gently, "I know this is all a bit weird right now. And I know that the country is probably the last place you want to be, but—"

"No, it's not that... Well, it kind of is," she corrects herself, her eyes finally meeting mine, and I see something in there. Something I can't quite place. Something about the way they keep moving as if she wants to look at me, but can't.

"What is it?"

"It's just this place."

"I know you don't want to be here—" I begin again.

"No, Marco. It isn't that."

"Tell me," I say, juggling the notepad to take her hand in mine.

"Just... I can't stop thinking about him. Here. You know how excited he used to get when we left the city. He was always asking why we couldn't move to the country and..."

She breaks off here because there's a recognisable quiver in her voice, and it compels me to fold her into an embrace and wish away her pain – just as much as I would like to wish away my own, but can't.

Truth be told, I've shared the same thought. It's the first thing that struck me when we pulled up here, how much Toby would have loved to explore the back garden. The woods! Even more so if he had a dog for company.

He was always asking for a pet, despite our explanation that they weren't permitted in our block of flats. That didn't stop him asking, though. Ellie would tell you that's because he could be obstinate like his father.

I've lost count of the amount of times I've fantasised about handing him a box and watching his reaction as he unfolds the flaps to find a puppy inside. My son had the most wonderful smile. A smile as bright as the sun. And I know all parents say that, but I can genuinely say that Toby was the real deal. He seldom had a wrong word to say about anything or anyone.

I used to think nothing could excite him more than the thought of a pet... at least until he started showing a serious interest in remote-controlled toys. He obviously got that from his grandfather. Me, I could take or leave that stuff. Toby, though, he became obsessed. And I think, in part, that's probably why we ended up buying him that thing. The quadcopter was no doubt the biproduct of all that guilt we were hoarding over not being able to buy him a pet.

"I've thought about it, too," I tell my wife. She breaks the embrace and looks at me. I nod. "I didn't want to say anything because, well, I didn't want to upset you by stating the obvious."

She laughs, and I move quickly to correct myself. "No, I don't mean it that way. I just mean that there was no point in sharing that thought with you because, well, I didn't want to stir up any feelings you might already have. But I think therein lies the problem. You see, neither of us wants to say something that may upset the other, so the net result is that we don't talk to each other," I explain, and instantly regret it because that's my therapy talking now, and I know my wife hates it when I talk like that.

She doesn't say anything for several seconds. She just watches me, thoughtfully. Eventually, she nods. "I suppose you're right."

"Yeah?" I ask.

She nods.

"Wow. Can I get that in writing? Make a video."

She rolls her eyes. "Don't push your luck."

"It's OK to talk about him, El. We shouldn't be afraid of our feelings. And before you say anything, I know I used to be the worse one for that, but Holmes is right. If we keep avoiding the things that scare us, then we're going to spend the rest of our lives being scared."

She pulls a face. "Really?"

I chuckle. "I know. It sounds naff, but it does kind of make sense, and on this occasion, you know I'm right." I watch my wife's eyes narrow in mock protestation.

"Um, I think you'll find that I'm the one that's right because I know everything," she says, knowingly.

I'm about to question that when I realise what she's referring to.

Our son surprised the both of us one day when, out of nowhere, he told me that I shouldn't swear. When I asked him why, he said 'because God doesn't like it'. Ellie and I exchanged glances because Toby had just come back from a weekend with his God-fearing grandparents. So, I asked him how God would know when I swore. My then ten-year-old son squinted at me as if I'd asked a ridiculous question, and said, *"Dad, God knows everything."*

"He does?"

"Yes, then it's Google and then Mum."

Our shared memory of that day brings a mist of tears to both of our eyes as we laugh all over again, and I pull what's left of my family into a tight hug and say, "We're going to be OK, Ellie. I promise."

I don't truly know what that means since it's inconceivable to me how any parent can be *OK* after the death of their child. I don't think they ever truly are – not in the conventional sense, anyway. But you can learn to live with it. To function as a new version of yourself. A new iteration. You never stop being a parent, but you can learn to become a so-called non-practicing one, as hideous a prospect as that is.

And I wonder if this is the time. If, in this very moment as I hold my wife close, I should reintroduce the subject of counselling.

Doctor Holmes was adamant that we both seek support during this new phase of our lives, and he even went through the trouble of making various enquiries on our behalf, but although Ellie seemed enthusiastic while we were in his presence, that quickly changed the moment we were alone. She made it clear that she wasn't interested in meeting someone else and rehashing everything all over again.

In fact, we were browsing for books at the exact time of our appointment an hour or so away.

At the time, it felt like the right thing to do, but now… now, even I think it would have been useful. That we could use the support.

"El?" I begin

My wife breaks our embrace and looks at me, eyes still shimmering with tears. There's a bittersweet smile on her face, as she still appears to be languishing in the memory of our son.

"I, um… I think now might be a good time… for a cup of tea. What do you think?" I follow that up with my own smile.

Yes. I know I'm a coward, but this is the most intimate we've been in a long time. It feels like we're slowly reconnecting, and I can't bring myself round to doing anything that might jeopardise that. Not right now.

Ellie studies my face for a while as if she knows that isn't what I meant to say, but she goes along with it and nods. "Sure. You go on ahead while I do that, and I'll catch up with you when it's ready."

"OK."

Her face brightens. Then, with a kiss on my cheek, she's gone, leaving me standing in the dining room. Alone.

3. PORTHCOVE

SUNDAY LUNCHTIME.

Porthcove is one of those quaint little hamlets nestled in a small valley on the southwest coast of England. It has fewer than three hundred dwellings, with a total population of one thousand, one hundred, and eleven according to the last census.

It has a small working fishing harbour that, as one Google reviewer put it, *is as picturesque as it is chocolate box divine!*

The village – built of stone houses, steep cobblestoned streets, and artisan stores – is popular with tourists during the summer months. Many of whom flock to its notorious art gallery, which is carved out of the harbour cliff face along with the pub, *The Smuggler's Inn*, and the café, *The Fisherman's Tavern*.

Porthcove has its own train station, which is really more of a train stop with a hut in the middle of a field. It, along with the tiny church with an abnormally large steeple, overlooks the village from a perch atop a hill less than a mile away.

Legend has it that my parents tied the knot in that church. Although, I'm not sure if that's a detail I actually remember or something I imagined, and with both of my parents dead and no Google reviews to corroborate either way, I'm going to assume that was the case. Not that I plan on visiting church any time soon.

At the foot of the hill, as you enter the village and just before the main thoroughfare, is a statue of Captain Cook standing mid-stride and gazing into the middle distance. It is almost as big as the green in which it resides. According to the plaque, the famous explorer and captain in the Royal Navy is believed to have spent some of his most formative years in Porthcove.

The high street is so small that it would be easy to miss, were it not for the plethora of award plaques and rosettes from institutions such as *Britain in Bloom* and *Visit England.* There's an ice cream parlour, a soap store, and a silversmith. A bakery bragging about its award-winning pasties. A candy store specialising in handmade treats and featuring a Christmas winter wonderland shop window to rival Willy Wonka's realm. Then, there's the grocery store come fruit seller… come post office come souvenir shop.

This is my first stop.

Any plans I had for making a discreet entrance are scuppered by a cowbell hanging on the door. And that's not a figurative bell it's literally a medium-sized cowbell that clangs loudly as you enter, to the point where I feel like I should be apologising for making a racket.

The place is busier than I expected, unfortunately. There's an elderly couple wearing matching yellow bodywarmers debating nutritional values in the fruit aisle. A gang of children making life-changing decisions by the pic-n-mix, and two or three others milling about in the groceries section.

Christmas carols compete with a clutch of women having a raucous conflab by the till at the other end of the store, which is much larger on the inside than its petite frontage suggests.

A tall, slender woman with heavy makeup, wearing a Santa hat over her long white hair, breaks off from the conversation to glance up at the sound of the bell.

Shit (which by the way is the one word that I'm allowing myself during my swearing abstinence), it's getting to that time of year. *I really need to start thinking about what to get Ellie* is the thought that crosses my mind as I dive behind a clutch of card carousels. I came here to ask about a local builder but wasn't planning on having a public consultation.

So, I loiter by an array of postcards of picturesque Porthcove viewed from all possible angles. Most of which tend to focus on the harbour in full technicolour – from all angles in all lighting. Sunny weather. Dramatic weather. Sunset. Sunrise. I'm no connoisseur, as photography was my mother's bag, but because of her, I have learned a certain appreciation of the art. And some of the shots are quite stunning. A few, taken from above, presumably via drone, even feature Dolce Vita perched on the peninsula like a jetty out in the ocean.

Oddly, I feel a ripple of pride… as if I didn't inherit the place but gave birth to it. To the point where I consider buying a couple of the cards as my own souvenirs, but a shrill of laughter from the gaggle by the till pierces the air and the moment, breaking the spell.

So, I move onto the next carousel. This one has larger pockets to accommodate thin souvenir books about Porthcove and the greater southwest of England. Some talk about the county's once thriving tin mining industry; it's believed that tin was traded throughout Britain for almost 4,000 years. Others are about the legend of King Arthur, who's believed to have hailed from these parts, with much speculation about the legendary site of Camelot where, folklore has it, he held court with his knights.

There are also books about the famous flash flood that devastated the beautiful harbour village of Boscastle, less than a couple hours' drive from here. On August 16th, 2004, the whole nation fell into collective shock when extensive footage of the disaster was broadcast on television. I still remember it now. It was like something out of a disaster movie, only live. That nine-foot wall of water washed cars, caravans, and buildings into the Atlantic Ocean as if they were toys.

It was one of the most devastating events of its kind. The result of a staggering eight-hour deluge.

I shrug off a shiver and move away from the rotating history lesson, down an aisle of shelves displaying handmade pottery in a rainbow of colours, shapes, and sizes.

In the middle and to my left is an archway flanked by two tall green country dressers, laden with an array of hand-poured, scented candles. I've barely approached and am already enveloped in a cloud of heady, delicious fragrances such as vanilla, coconut, jasmine, and sandalwood. To name a few.

Now that I think about it, we could use a couple of these at the house. I've noticed some funky and embarrassing smells in a couple of the rooms, to the point where I felt compelled to point out to Ellie that the stink wasn't coming from me. And I'm considering which fragrance my wife would appreciate when a sound far removed from the garrulous voice of one of the women at the till gets my attention. I follow it through the archway and into what feels like a separate oasis, far away from the drone of Christmas carols and the ruckus of the main store. In here, the lighting is subdued, but for a row of display cabinets on the opposite wall that spotlight an impressive collection of mythical figurines.

There's no loud chatter here – just the gentle, musical sound of a clutch of windchimes activated at intervals by an oscillating fan, and a musical recording of panpipes and harps.

There are trickling water fountains for the home and the garden, featuring an array of characters. From fairies sprinkling water and gnomes peeing into a basin to toads showering on lily pads and witches spitting into the air.

There's something about this place that's oddly calming. And it isn't just the burning incense, but the whole of the ambiance. I could spend a lot of time in here.

I pause by a glass cabinet with a glittering display of crystals in a multitude of colours, shapes, and sizes. There's a rough-cut pinkish violet one that draws my attention, and as I peer closer at it, a disembodied voice says, "Amethyst. Opens spiritual awareness and psychic abilities."

The voice startles me, as it seemed the place was empty. I look up to see a pretty girl who's probably in her late twenties, with braided brown hair and fingernails painted in a rainbow of colours. She's sitting behind a counter of grey medieval figurines of knights and dragons encrusted with gems.

"Oh, sorry. I didn't see you there," I say, stretching up to my full size once more.

"That's because I like to sneak up on people," she says,

putting down a copy of *The Woman in Black* and taking her red Converse-clad feet off the counter. "Don't tell my mum I had them on there, will you?" she asks conspiratorially.

I smile and make a sign of zipping my lips. "Any good?" I ask, nodding at the book on the counter.

She shrugs. "Don't know. Haven't read it yet."

"Do you like ghost stories?"

"Only the good ones."

There's a pause as I look around the place and contemplate my next move.

"So, what are you doing in here?" she asks, like there's no reason I should be browsing in a store.

"Oh, you know, just browsing."

She looks up at me knowingly, and in the spotlights, I can see that she has vivid green eyes. Perfect skin. "Sure you're not just avoiding the Stepford wives in there?" she asks with a grin.

The burn in my cheeks obviously answers for me.

"Don't worry. It should be over soon," she reassures me. "Is there anything in particular you were looking for? Unfortunately for you, all of the travel stuff is near the till."

"Oh, I'm not a tourist," I say, surprised by my own words.

"No?"

"No. I've just moved into Dolce Vita. You know, the house on the peninsula."

"Oh, I know where that is. You've just moved in? I thought the place had been abandoned since…" she trails off here, obviously unsure of how much I know.

"Yeah. He was my father," I say soberly.

Her eyes widen. "Roberto was your dad?" she asks, feeling free now to look me over. "Oh wow."

"You knew him?"

"Who didn't? He was like a Rockstar around here. Lovely man. Never stopped talking about his children. A very proud daddy."

"Really? He was most likely talking about his other children with his new family," I say, a tad more bitterly than intended.

"Oh," she says, picking up on my tone and arching

manicured eyebrows, "you wait 'til Mum finds out. She's going to flip!"

Great. Show pony for the day. Can't wait.

"Well, I'd heard someone had moved in, but–"

"You'd heard? Wow. We've only just got here."

She shrugs and rolls her eyes amiably. "Small village. You'll get used to it. I'm Sarah, by the way," she says, pressing her hands together and giving me a little bow. "I would give you a hug because I kind of feel like I already know you, but we've only just met and… I wouldn't want you to feel uncomfortable." She follows that up with a wink.

"Oh right, OK." I mirror her gesture. "Namaste, Sarah. I'm Marco," I introduce myself with a smile.

"Marco. I know. I like that name. So, you've moved into Roberto's place."

"Only for as long as it takes to sell it." I don't know why I felt I had to clarify that. "We're refurbishing before we put it on the market."

"Oh right," she says with a nod.

"That's one of the reasons I'm here. I wanted to pick up a few things and put word out… you know, if there are any local builders in the village who might be interested in quoting to do the work?"

Her eyes widen knowingly. "Funny you should say that."

"Oh? Why?"

"My uncle's a builder. He does all that stuff. You know. Building, fixing, painting, landscaping."

"Really? Sounds perfect. How do I get hold of him?"

"Easy," she says, gesturing through the archway. "Just pop over to the till. Mum has his details. Just tell her that Sarah said you need the contact details for Uncle Irvin."

"Oh," is all I can muster, and I gawk at her for a few seconds before she follows that up with a cute little giggle.

Then she adds, "Come on. I'll protect you." She places a cool, slender hand over mine, leads me through the archway and out into the grocery store once more – where, much to my disappointment, the conflab is still in full swing.

My new pal barges in, though. "Sorry to interrupt, but I come on important business," she says in mock officiousness as she offers me up to the group.

The droning stops, and the producer, who must be on the other side of her fifties – with short, bobbed blonde hair and way too much makeup for the exercise her pink spandex is suggesting – leans in closer as if afraid to miss a word.

OK, so this is worse than I thought.

"Mum," Sarah says to the woman with long white hair, "*this* is Marco. Marco Battista."

Yeah, thanks for the Bond-like introduction, Sarah.

There's a collective *ooh* of amazement.

"Really?" the woman asks, coming out from behind the counter. "Marco. Is that really you?" she adds, like she's the aunt I never had.

"In the flesh," I reply awkwardly, presenting myself with a lift and a widening of my arms. *Ta da!*

She moves over to me and places warm hands on my face as if she's inspecting me. "Goodness gracious, me. You're much more 'andsome than I imagined. And you look just like 'im. God bless his soul," she says in a local lilt.

The group responds as if at mass, with a chorus of chortles and appreciative sighs. Especially the bobbed-hair cougar lady, as I can sense and see her sidling in beside me like she's stalking prey.

Once I'm released from the clutches of the shopkeeper, I retain my artificial smile as if I've just enjoyed being manhandled by a complete stranger.

Hold your judgement. That was strictly in my past. Not the present… or the future, for that matter.

"You know, your father talked about you all the time," Sarah's mum says longingly.

"Yep. I told him," Sarah contributes with a grin. If I didn't know better, I'd say she's enjoying this.

"Yes," I respond, smile still plastered on, "you certainly did,

Sarah. But, as I say, my dad and I… well, he was most likely talking about his other children."

"Roberto Junior and Samantha? No. Yes, he talked about them, too. Even brought 'em out here a couple of times, but it's you he talked about the most. How proud he was that you'd turned your life around and were making a career for yourself."

"As a mechanic!" I laugh. It's bitter, but so artificially and sickly sweet that I don't think anybody but Sarah notices.

"No, as a doctor. You know. A therapist," she says, adding that last bit with a bit of a hushed tone as if it's not the kind of thing you want the world to know.

"Actually–"

"Actually, Mum, Marco's here to refurbish the house – you know, Dolce Vita? And he's looking for a local builder," Sarah says, riding to the rescue. "I suggested Uncle Irvin."

"Yes. That's a fantastic Idea, Sarah. I can give 'im a bell if you like, or would you prefer to call yourself?" she asks, but her response is cut short when the elderly couple from the fruit stand makes their way towards the counter with their basket.

"Good morning, Albert, Betty. How are you both doin' today?" With that, she resumes her position behind the counter.

Meanwhile, like a pack of hyenas, the remaining three women close in to get a better look at me, and this is the moment where I want to remind them about social distancing.

Cougar is really close now, smiling sweetly and batting those fake eyelashes. "Has anybody told you that you look like that actor?" she asks seriously.

I know who she's talking about, but it'll be much easier if I just pretend I don't. "No," I say.

"Ere, you know what? He does, right," a shorter and much rounder woman with short black hair agrees.

"You know, I was thinkin' that, too," says her lanky companion. "What's the actor's name? I can't quite place it. I've got it right on the tip of me tongue. You know the one… green eyes, short hair, gorgeous bod." She follows that up with a creepy schoolgirl titter.

"Yeah. The one in that film with all the sex stuff."

Bashful giggles.

I look at Sarah. She glances at me while stifling her own grin. *You are enjoying this, aren't you?*

"Grey. Christian Grey!"

"Yes. That's it!"

"No, that's his character's name. What's the man's name?"

Oh God. Just kill me now.

"It's Jamie Dornan."

"Yes! Him!"

'Saved by the bell' takes on a literal meaning when the shop door opens and a belly walks in followed by a man in a brown uniform. He strides right up to us, nods at me and then at the women holding court. "Mornin' ladies," he says in that now familiar burr.

"Oh, morning, Trevor!" the trio of women chorus excitedly.

"Trevor, welcome back! How was Australia?" It's Sarah's mother speaking now; she's paused packing bananas into bags and is smiling affectionally at the rotund man with a tanned face who's spilling out of his uniform.

"Morning, Majorie. Yeah, it was good. Hot."

"Ooh, wonderful. How's Amy doing? The new baby?"

"Oh, fine, they're just fine."

"Ooh, lovely. Bet you must 'ave 'ated sayin' goodbye to 'em both."

"Oh, well, ya know. It'd been three months. We always said it was a once in a lifetime thing, but we were both startin' to get a bit homesick."

"Oh, I've got these for ya," he says, handing her a pair of small parcels. "Need ya to sign for this one, please."

"Of course."

As he waits, cougar woman perks up. "Trevor, you'll never guess who this 'andsome thing is?"

The courier with podgy cheeks and a tiny moustache I've just noticed turns and studies me. "Oh aye, Faye, don't tell me you've decided to get engaged while I've been abroad."

There's a chorus of laughter. Mine, I think, is hysteria, but I don't think anybody notices.

"It's Marco. Roberto's boy."

"No!" The man says breathlessly as if he's just won the lottery, and then he moves in closer to study me. So close, in fact, that I can hear him breathing.

I lift my eyebrows and grin, but it's more of a grimace.

"Yeah, now that I look at ya, I should have known. You look just like your pa. Incredible. And how is your dad? Is he with you?" he asks cheerfully, looking behind me as if the old man's been hiding in one of the aisles all this time.

"Oh no," I say. "He passed away a few months back."

"What?" The man instantly loses his smile.

"Yeah, unfortunately, we lost 'im a few months back now," contributes the cougar.

Trevor's podgy dimples take on a life of their own as his frown deepens. He turns to Cougar as if to validate her words. She nods sadly.

Then, he turns back to me, and I see the oddest thing. The man has tears in his eyes!

He places a chubby hand on my shoulder. "Well, this has got to be one of the saddest 'omecomings ever."

There's a collective sigh behind him. Christmas carols try their best to restore the cheer but appear to fail miserably.

"I'm so sorry to hear this, Marco. Your father was a wonderful man. A top bloke. Thought the world of you. We've all been dyin' to meet ya – especially after, well, you know, especially after what 'appened."

I don't know what to say. Thank you, maybe. I'm not sure, really, as the man seems genuinely devastated. I can only watch in bemusement as, one by one, the women pat his broad shoulder in a sign of support.

Okay. This isn't weird at all.

Mercifully, Sarah takes my arm and says, "Mum, I need to take Jamie, I mean Marco, to get some urgent stuff for his wife. We'll be back soon. Okay?" She doesn't wait for an answer. Instead, she whisks me out of there and, mercifully, back out into the fresh air.

"What the hell was that all about? That man had tears in his eyes!" I say incredulously.

"As I say—"

"Small village?"

"You learn fast. Your dad really was popular around here. People liked him. Even though he didn't live here all year round, when he was, he became part of the community."

"Great. Not much pressure, then," I say flippantly.

She rocks her head. "Oh, I don't know. Something tells me that you two are alike."

"If you knew my dad, you'd know that isn't entirely a compliment."

"Maybe. But nobody's perfect, right?" she asks like she's already heard things about me, and I consider saying something, but I think better of it because it's most likely my paranoia speaking.

Instead, I change the subject of conversation. "You were enjoying that, weren't you? Parading me to the whole gaggle in there," I say as we make our way down the high street.

"Of course," she replies. "It's not every day *Jamie* makes an appearance in our shop."

I roll my eyes.

"You do look like him, though."

"So I keep hearing."

"But you're much better looking," she adds, looking up at me because, as I've just noticed, she's a few inches shorter than my six feet. My face must have reacted to that somehow, though, because she quickly follows it up with, "Don't worry. I know you're married."

"Really?" You seem to know a lot about me."

She shrugs.

"Small village?"

"No. Your dad. Along with bragging about your accomplishments, he used to talk about how madly in love you are with your wife and how much you both dote on your little boy. I'm surprised you didn't bring him with you," she adds, looking around me as if I've been keeping my son in my pocket.

I don't want to get into that, and since we've come to a stop outside of the bakery, I ask, "How did you know I needed to come here?"

She shrugs. "I didn't. I just knew you needed to get out of there."

Smiling, we make our way inside.

4. THE OFFER

SUNDAY AFTERNOON.

The sun, nestling behind a smoky curtain of clouds, is already casting low shadows across the land by the time I get back from my excursion. It's still late afternoon but feels more like dusk.

Ellie, bundled up in a blanket, is in the back garden talking on her mobile when I cross the den with my bags of groceries, heading to the kitchen.

You know how they say that the way to a man's heart is through his stomach? Well, the way to Ellie's heart is through freshly baked and still warm Cornish pasties, just back from the bakery. Well, they've won an award. It makes sense to try them.

My wife is all about artisan foods and abhors anything that's squished into a different colour or form and then frozen.

Toby wasn't allowed anywhere near McDonalds, or any fast food chain, for that matter – except for on his birthday, when he could choose any food his heart desired for the day. Oh, and, of course, on the odd boy's day out when I, pathetically weak when it came to my son's happiness, often gave in to his illegal lunch choices… provided he swore to secrecy, on pain of both our deaths.

Now, I'm hoping that my bounty of freshly baked goods will go some way to bringing a little cheer to my wife's day.

I am smiling about this, but the expression is instantly erased at the moment I reach the hallway of gloom to find that all of the doors are closed, and the catacomb plunged into darkness.

"Ellie," I grumble, "I thought we agreed to keep the doors open to let the natural light into this place."

My hands are full, and I don't want to put the bags on the floor because God knows what's been here before us. Besides, it's pointless; the one light in here doesn't work, which is the very reason why I said we should leave the doors open for now.

I approach the blackness with the same reluctance I would the maggot-infested carcass of a dead animal. And that's because it stinks like one! I have no idea why. It's a bloody hallway!

Ellie thinks it's an extreme case of damp, and perhaps even mould or mildew, and that it will probably disappear once we give the place a good cleaning and airing, but I have my doubts and am hoping that it isn't something much more sinister... like rot in the walls or something.

Which reminds me. We need to bring in some dehumidifiers, or maybe just electric heaters. The whole place reeks of dampness. It makes sense to get a couple, at least for the upstairs since the storage heaters don't seem to do much. Item one thousand and one on the long list of things we need.

In the meantime, my plan is to light a fire. I'm hoping it'll make this cold and drafty place a little cosier. Not that Ellie is supportive of my idea. She laughed when I suggested it. Wanted to know if a townie like me even knew how to light a fire. The cheek of it. How hard can it be, exactly?

I'm actually relieved to emerge into the daylight of the kitchen, which is still very much a work in progress by the looks of it since, unlike the doors in the corridor, every single cupboard, drawer, and window is open. And it's bloody freezing in here!

There are cloths on the draining board, and bowls full of bleach bottles and cleaning solutions. And, by the thick coat of dust and desiccated bug corpses that litter the place still, I'd guess that Ellie hasn't even made a start.

I sigh and am about to rest the bags on the island, but pause when I see it wink at me. By that, I mean it's sparkling. As if it's had glitter scattered all over it.

My first thought is that it might be an intricate natural pattern of the marble, but it isn't. This stuff is sitting on top, like frost.

Jesus. Is it that f…ricking cold in here?

Reluctantly, I set the bags down so that I can take a closer look and… bloody hell… it isn't frost. It's sand.

Sand?

How the hell did that get in here?

I look around and then up at the ceiling. Like the den, the ceiling in here is painted white, and striped with the occasional, exposed beam of dark wood. Except for more insectoid squatters, it's otherwise unblemished.

"OK."

No idea where the sand's come from, but the whole place needs a deep clean anyway.

I reach into one of the bags on the counter, retrieve a box of eggs, pull the fridge door open, and gag when the foulest stench hits me like a tsunami of shit. There is no other way to describe the malodour, which is so bad that I stagger backward, kicking the door shut on my way.

And I'm still gaping at the appliance as if it has quite literally just relieved itself on the kitchen floor when a deep, guttural voice demands, "*WHAT ARE YOU DOING HERE? LEAVE AT ONCE!*"

I drop the eggs and whirl around.

"Jeeeeesus!"

Ellie is standing in the doorway, mobile phone to her mouth. Big grin on her face.

I nod and try to swallow the bitter dryness at the back of my throat. "Funny. Very funny," I say, taking a deep breath and running my hand through my hair. "El, you gave me a bloody heart attack," I grumble, holding my chest.

"I'm sorry. I didn't mean to scare you… not that much! Why are you so jumpy?" my wife asks, walking over to me as I crouch to the floor to retrieve the stricken eggs.

"You didn't scare me," I say sulkily. "You startled me."

My wife nods, eyes full of mischief, a snigger still on her face.

I shake my head at her as I carefully open the carton of eggs. A couple are cracked, but they'll live.

"Sorry, baby," the resident prankster says, tousling my hair as if I were a child.

This is all deliberate, of course. It's part of who we are. Pranks have always been a staple of our relationship – both before and after Toby arrived. Pranking and making each other jump is something that we all did on a regular basis. My son, of course, mastered the art of hiding in small places and waiting patiently until one of us showed up. Hunkering in the closet where he knew I'd go to get changed after work. Inserting himself in the airing cupboard when his mum was busy going about her chores.

The app on Ellie's phone was put there by our son, and I'm both surprised and secretly delighted that she felt happy enough to use it on me since the last time it was used is most likely when Toby was still with us.

"So," she says as I get to my feet. "What are they like, the locals?" She crosses her eyes, lets her tongue hang out of her mouth, and make claws of her hands.

I don't want to, but I must smile at the sight. "They're quite nice, actually. And I've already put feelers out for a local builder."

"Yeah?"

"Yep. So, what have you been up to?" I ask, looking around the place, but being sure to keep any tone out of my voice – because seeing my wife behaving more like her old self is a sight to behold. It's as if our arrival here has reignited the spark in those mischievous eyes.

"I know. Sorry," she says. "I've been busy talking on the phone."

"Yeah. I noticed," I say. "Oh, I brought you a surprise," I add, nodding at the bags on the island.

"Ooh," she says excitedly, clapping her hands together.

Clapping her hands together? OK, well, this doesn't seem like the person I left at home this morning.

"Feeling better?" I ask.

"Much," she says, grin still intact as she retrieves a bottle of milk from one of the bags and walks by me to the fridge.

"NO!" I shout as she opens the door.

She gawks at me for a few seconds. "What?" And then she breaks into a smile. "Dude," she says, mimicking me, "you're going to have to do better than that."

I watch her place the eggs and the milk in the fridge and close the door, casually.

I surreptitiously sniff the air. Nothing.

She must notice me doing it, because she says, "Yes, it was a bit pongy, but I gave it a good wash and a bleach; it'll probably be that which kills us now, but otherwise it should be fine. It's about the only thing I managed to do before my phone call. Ooh!" she adds, discovering the pasties.

"OK," I say, picking up the kettle and holding it under a sputtering tap. Was it doing that before? I make a mental note to add it to the list of jobs for the plumber.

Kettle on, I turn to my wife once more and find that she's still grinning. "Yes, OK. Who are you, deranged doppelganger, and what have you done with my wife?"

"Ask me who messaged me this morning," she says.

Folding my arms and leaning against the sink, I ask, "Um, Ellie, who messaged you this morning?"

"David."

"David my friend, your ex-boss David?"

She nods enthusiastically.

"Cool. Is he planning on making an appearance?"

She shakes her head. "No. Better."

"Better?"

She nods. Deranged grin still intact.

"El, you're going to have to–"

"He wants me back. He wants to forget what happened and start afresh by giving me a promotion! He said that it just hasn't been the same without me and wants, no, he *needs* me to go back, whatever it takes!" She follows that up by skipping across the room, throwing her arms around me, and planting kisses in my hair, on my face, and, most interestingly, on my mouth.

Yes, I know that may not seem like much to you, but for a reluctant celibate like me, it's electrifying. Not least of all because the attention is coming from her. As you know, things haven't exactly been hot and heavy since our reunion and, well, given my history, it's weird how much I appear to be unaffected.

What, you weren't here the last time? Just as well. It's not a history I'm proud of, so the less said about it, the better.

In the meantime, I'm focussing on those exquisite kisses my wife just gifted me and the way those gorgeous eyes of hers have turned into pools of blue which are so rich by the window light that I just want to dive into them.

She is beautiful. In the conventional sense, of course, but she's positively radiant now.

And yet, it doesn't take long for her words to blow away all that romantic rubbish and bring their full meaning to me in glorious technicolour.

The kettle is whistling angrily, but I don't hear it until Ellie asks, "Are you going to get that?"

I spin around and hastily pull the thing off the stove.

"Well, what do you think?" she asks, leaning on the island and putting some distance between us now. And although I'm not looking at her as I pull two mugs from the cupboard, I can feel her eyes on me, burning into my back with ardent expectation.

"David wants you to go back and work for him?"

"Yes, but not in the same position. I'll be heading up operations. He says there's something really exciting on the horizon. Something that he can't talk to me about right now, which can only mean one thing."

"A merger."

"Exactly. Although he can't say that yet because I haven't signed an NDA and his telling me is conditional on that. Anyway, he wants me to be a part of it. To be his right-hand gal, to use his words," she says breathlessly. "Can you believe that? David's a control freak!"

"Of course, I can."

"You can?"

"Of course. He'd be lucky to have you. But that's not the point, El," I say, choosing my words carefully here because I know all too well how quickly this conversation can go south. "Do you think you're ready to go back? I mean, we've only just left."

For the first time today, my wife loses her smile. "*You've* only just left, Marc. I've been there the whole time."

"You know what I mean," I say, placing teabags in mugs and adding the hot water – not necessarily because I'm desperate for a cuppa, although I was, but more for want of something to do as I decide how best to handle this particular brand of explosive.

She doesn't respond, and there's silence but for the call of a pair of wood pigeons sparring in the hedge outside.

Then… "Look, Marco." Oh shit, she's starting the sentence with my full name, which normally means she wants undivided attention. "I know you have this romanticised view of us here, our faces splodged with paint, laughing and joking as we go about fixing up this place…."

I turn to her. "Yeah. What's wrong with that?"

"There's nothing wrong with that. There's absolutely nothing wrong with that."

"Then, why don't you want to give it a try?"

"Because it isn't me," she says decisively.

"What do you mean it isn't you? You used to be all about changing rooms–"

"Not anymore," she says. Then, softening her tone again, she adds, "Things change. People change. I mean, for God's sake, we've changed. You've only just emerged from, from…" she struggles to find the words, "but I've been living with this for months now. I need something else."

"And I get that. Why do you think we're here, El?"

She shakes her head hopelessly. "I have no idea."

That sentence cuts deep into my chest. It's the first time since we left the city that I've heard her suggest that it was a mistake, and I have barely formed the words in my head to reply when they're falling out of my mouth. "Right. So, you *do* think coming here was a mistake?" I ask, allowing my words to produce the question I've been afraid of asking this whole time, despite the fact that she, along with the doctor, said it was the best thing for us.

She steps forward. "No. Of course not. It's something that needs to be done. I just don't know if I'm the person to do it."

I lift my eyebrows. "Wow, El, you may have wanted to mention that *before* we drove ourselves out here. I certainly wasn't in a hurry to come back to this place."

"I know, but you needed to," she says reasonably. "I mean, I'm no therapist, but this place has been a catalyst for many of the sad things in your life. It made so much sense that you'd need to come here and process it."

I nod. "OK. Now you even sound like him," I say, turning to pluck teabags out of the mugs in order to buy a few seconds to *process* what's just been said.

There's more silence between us now. From the sound of the fluttering wing activity outside, I imagine those pigeons are jostling for the best seat at this freak show. That, or they're squabbling over the popcorn.

I retrieve milk from the now innocuous fridge and rally back, "You know, it amazes me that you're in such a hurry to go back to the city after years of complaining about how much you hated it."

"That was before I lost my son," she says flatly.

Which, of course, sounds like a dig at me. It probably isn't, but that's my default setting and no amount of therapy is ever going to change that.

Then, probably reconsidering her words, my wife adds, much more softly and somewhat desperately, "I need this, Marc. I really do. After all this time. I need to feel, to feel…" she struggles with the words, "relevant again."

"Of course, you're relevant," I say, setting the milk down and reaching out to her.

But she brushes me away with an angry hand. "Not like this." Her eyes are searching mine, and I have no idea what she means by that.

I want to ask her, but, since we're doing this, there's also so much else I want to air, and yet such shitty opportunism isn't cool even for someone like me.

I have to accept. It's one of the things we talked about in

therapy. There are some things that are out of my control, but I must learn to accept them – otherwise, I risk sending myself back into a negative spiral, and I can't afford that. I can't risk losing myself again. I can't and I won't do that to her.

Besides, my wife has made up her mind. That much is clear. Now, I can be supportive, or I can turn this into a full-blown row which would most likely have the same outcome, but more collateral damage.

So, I swallow my reservations and ask, "What exactly would this entail?" Which sounds sulky, but hey, that's exactly how this man-child is feeling right now.

She shrugs, allowing a trace of a smile to return to her lips, and I've got to force myself to see that. This is quite literally the first time that she's seemed excited about anything since... well, since my so-called *return*. I would defy anybody to deny her that.

"I don't really know the details yet. He just asked me to go and meet with him."

I nod. "Charming. My best friend can't make the drive out here to see me, but he's more than happy to poach my wife," I say with mock irritation.

"He's just trying to make it easier for us to connect. But going into the city? I think it'll be good."

I'm surprised by this. "Really?"

"Yeah. I think I need to get out of here. You know, breathe in some pollution. This fresh air is starting to make me feel ill," she says with a conciliatory smile.

I want to return it, but I'm too busy sulking and stirring milk into our tea, which is probably lukewarm now.

My wife obviously senses this, too, because she adds, enthusiastically, "Come on, Marc. This is good for us."

"Really? I was led to believe that being out here and having a mutual project would be good for us."

"Yeah, but it was a therapist who suggested that, and you know those guys talk crap most of the time," she says, touching my arm.

"Is that so?"

"Yes. Besides, we need money. Especially with all of the ambitions you have for this place."

She has a point. In my usual ostrich-like way, I've been deferring even thinking about the practicalities of this upfront investment until I have a better idea of exactly how much it's all going to cost. And my wife knows that, which is why she just used it to favour her case.

I hand her a mug of warm tea.

"Thanks." And given the fact that I've fallen silent, she adds, "You know I'm right."

"I didn't say you weren't."

"So, what do you think?" she renews the question — now that she's made it impossible for me to give her anything other than the answer she wants.

I scoff. "Does it even matter what I think?"

"Oh, come on. You know that's most of the fun; getting you to think you have a say in anything I do," she adds with a wry smile.

"Don't I know it?" I respond, taking a sip from my mug. The tea is, in fact, tepid... but not as bad as I thought it would be.

Nor is my wife's newfound excitement. It's disappointing, yes, since it'll probably mean me being marooned out here on my own again, and we all know how that ended last time. And it's this part that scares me a little.

"What happened?" I ask.

"What?" she asks, sipping from her mug.

"Before, you told me that David said he wanted to forget what happened."

"Did I?"

I frown at her. "Yeah."

"Oh." She screws her face up pensively. "No idea why I said that."

She moves away from me, and now I know she's hiding something. "El?"

"Don't analyse me, Marco. You know I hate it," she says with a forced smile.

"I'm not analysing you. I'm just asking a question. You told me you had to resign because of me, but earlier you made it sound like something else happened that made you resign."

She turns to me once more and hisses, "You mean besides the death of my son?"

With that, she dumps her mug in the sink and walks out.

5. FIRST NIGHT

I've stayed up late researching blogs and YouTube videos for repair options and maintenance of some of the things on my list, hoping to get some idea of cost. And I have to say, while it's still rudimentary research, it's enough to make me wonder whether we should have gone for Option A after all and cut our losses.

But I've concluded that it's just my exhaustion speaking and that everything will seem much better after a good night's rest. This is something Ellie would normally say to me, or vice versa, but she went to bed before me.

By the time I've joined her in what was my dad's bedroom – yep I'm making that distinction because it's one of those things I can't get out of my mind – she's already asleep.

I have to say, being here is weird on so many levels. And it isn't just brushing my teeth in that old echoey bathroom, nor the creak and snap of settling timber or the bloody creepy draft that somehow always manages to find its way through the windowpane, but just being here after the old man. After *last time*.

But I'm OK. I'm alright. This is the means to a very important end and I'm up for the challenge.

The processor of my mind refuses to stop whirring even after I'm in bed and powering down, making sure I don't stray into Ellie territory. Not just because of what happened in the kitchen today, but also because it's bloody freezing in this room and she's already huddled on her side in her pyjamas and extra blanket. The last thing she wants is me bringing my cold body anywhere near her. She hates that at the best of times.

And so, it must be somewhere around 1 AM before I tune

out of the demon howl of the draft and into the lullaby of the surf in the distance and then fall gradually into an oblivion.

"*Wake up! Wake up!*"

My eyes spring open when I feel Ellie's hand shaking my arm.

I bolt up in bed. "What? What's the matter?"

But there's no response.

"Ellie?"

Nothing. And by the sounds of it, she's still fast asleep.

I forget that we're not in the city anymore. There's no annoying city light spilling in through the window. The opposite. Once you turn the lights off here, the room's pretty much pitch black.

I need to get some night lights.

Luckily, I used my phone as a clock and it's charging on my bedside table. So, I pick it up, swipe, and tap until its powerful LED light scares back the shadows.

"Ellie, what…" I trail off here because my ears did not deceive me. Ellie is lying scrunched up in the same ball with her back to me.

OK. But I'm sure I felt her pulling on my arm. Heard her whispering voice. And as these thoughts drift through my mind, a chill ripples through me.

I snap the beam over to my side of the bed where light licks over the bedside table, the window, the bathroom door, and–

That's enough of that. The last thing I need is to be going all *Blair Witch* with a torch on our first night here.

It must have been a dream, though, because I've just realised that the tugging was on my left arm. Ellie is sleeping and always has slept to my right.

I stop and listen.

Nothing but the buffeting of the gale around the house. At least the demon draft under the door has… stopped.

The light beam has just revealed the fact that the door is wide open, but I'm sure I closed it. I remember that because I gently clicked it shut so as not to wake Ellie.

Yet, the thing is wide open now, the beam of light travelling as far as the struts of the balustrade.

OK.

I slide out of bed and stop just short of yelping when my bare feet touch the icy floor. It's glacial in here. When I say that, I don't mean it as an exaggerated euphemism… I mean it literally. I mean it like it's got to be my top priority tomorrow because we can't function with our minds frozen numb. We might just end up feeling people calling to us and shaking us awake when they didn't.

I tip-toe across the room not because I don't want to wake my wife, but because the less contact my feet have with the floor, the less chance there is of me getting frostbite. At the door, I grab the handle and have just begun to push it shut… when it starts screaming at me.

"Shiiiit!" I hiss under my breath. The squeal is so loud, I'm surprised it didn't wake us when it opened.

A quick glance across at Ellie tells me she remains unaffected. So, now I'm considering my options. Band-Aid the thing and rip it off or do it slowly and tortuously, hoping it doesn't wake the bloody dead.

OK. Probably not the best analogy at a time like this, but–
What was that?

I train the light out onto the landing. I'm sure I heard something out there. It sounded like a distant thump. Footsteps. Bare feet.

I step out into the corridor and, like a police officer in every movie you've ever seen, flash the light right towards the stairs.

Empty.

Then left towards the bathroom and spare room.

Nothing there.

The gale whips up and hums around the house. It seems louder out here. The sudden, scratchy talons of a tree branch on glass give my heart a bloody jolt.

Shit! I forgot about that. The spare room. My old room. Tree branches tapping and scratching on glass like bloody fingernails.

It's fine. It's all fine. Just a creepy house in the middle of nowhere and way too much autosuggestion for a grown man. The hairs tickling the back of my neck like something is crawling over it and the goosepimples all over my arms have absolutely nothing to do with the creepiness of this place at night, and everything to do with the chill. I'm sure.

Shit.

I'm going back to bed.

I turn toward the bedroom door, but duck instinctively when a loud click, scrape, and crack fills the air.

Squeak… squeak… squeak….

It takes me a few seconds to unfurl from my automatic scrunch.

Squeak… squeak… squeak….

I turn in the direction of the sound as a cold breeze blows over me, ruffling my hair and bringing with it a new and ominous moan.

I turn the flashlight toward it.

"Are you fu–dging kidding me?" I hiss through clenched teeth.

Down the hallway, about six feet from me. The hatch to the attic has sprung open and is swinging back and forth.

Squeak… squeak… squeak….

"Hell, fu–nking no," is my emphatic response to that. I've seen this movie before. I was bloody in it last time I was here. There's absolutely no reason to be roaming around a pitch black attic in the dead of night with a bloody phone torch!

"What are you doing?"

"Jeeeeeesus Christ!" I and the light spin around to see Ellie standing in the doorway, rubbing her eyes and squinting in the glare of the powerful LED light. "Ellie, you fu–"

"Ah, ah, ah," she warns.

"You bloody scared the shit out of me!"

"I scared the shit out of you? I'm not the one roaming around the creepy house with my phone torch, Nancy Drew. What are you doing?"

I breathe in a couple of times, but regret it when I realise I'm sucking in the dank air that's being blown at me from the attic.

"I thought I heard something," I say, swallowing and almost choking on my dry throat.

"What?"

"I don't know. Something," I say dismissively.

"And decided to investigate with the flashlight? Why didn't you just turn on the light?"

"I didn't want to wake you," I admit.

This, for some obscure reason, makes my wife smile.

"You know, you can be so sweet."

"Ah, well, you know," I reply.

"When you're not being a complete prick," she adds.

"And there she is."

"So, what's with the attic? Is that where the sound was coming from?"

If I didn't know better, judging by the slight increase in pitch, I'd say there was alarm in my wife's voice when she asked that question.

"It, I, um, no. Actually, it wasn't up there. That's just incidental," I say, shining a light on the trap door that's still rocking back and forth unaided.

Ellie snaps the light on as I walk over to the now innocuous hunk of wood and examine the latch. "Be careful when you're up here, OK?" I suggest. "There's obviously something wrong with the latch, as this thing just fell open. You wouldn't want it hitting you on the head."

"OK. Can you shut it now, though? Because it's already freezing in here and that draft is making it worse."

I place the flat of my hand on the back of the trapdoor and push it upward, but the ceiling's at least a couple of feet higher than me, which means I have to jump and shove the thing shut.

It works the first time, but rebels against the reluctant explorer by spitting a shower of plaster at me.

I splutter. Ellie laughs.

"Thanks," I say.

"Oh, come on, you big baby," she says, reaching out to me. "Let's get back to bed."

With me spitting and blinking away the dust, we return to the bedroom once more, firmly closing the door behind us.

6. IRVIN AND SONS

PORTHCOVE. MONDAY. 13:04.

So, I've been thinking about yesterday's chat with the wife. No, not the midnight chat, but the one in the kitchen.

It's been bugging me all morning.

I thought I was handling it quite well, until the inquisitor in me just couldn't leave the fact that I knew she was withholding something. I mean she was talking on the phone outside. In the cold. Why? Ellie, as you discovered in the early hours of this morning, hates the cold. Why couldn't she have that conversation inside? Talking out there made absolutely no sense to me.

I kept telling myself that it wasn't important, that I didn't need to know. But then, the more I saw that she was withholding something, the more I wanted to know.

And yes, I can see the twist of irony here. Only a few months back, I was the one withholding truths. Sneaking around and lying became second nature to me.

Of course, this is the part where Doctor Holmes would tell me that much of that was because I was sick. That my addiction to doing what I did was precisely that, and I didn't really have much say in the matter, at least not consciously. I was as addicted as one can be to drugs or alcohol, and the addiction needed to be fed.

But who's truly buying that? Are you?

Don't answer that.

It's Therapy 101. Acknowledge the addiction, work through it, and accept what you can't change. Forgive and move on.

I'm paraphrasing here.

Bottom line is, I think I was projecting onto my wife yesterday. Because of the shit I was to her, I instantly sensed the lie and therefore needed to know the truth.

The thing is, as much as it's hard to believe – and I've been thinking about this – much of our marriage wasn't like this. Far from it. We never kept secrets. We were all about transparency. It's one of the reasons we'd share passwords and stuff like that, but then, a few years back, things started to change. I developed this need to be with other people who weren't my wife.

And I have spent the rest of the time feeling shitty about it. Like one of those abusive husbands. (Which, by the way, is something I could never do and will never understand. Don't get me wrong, violence and I aren't exactly strangers which you already know if you followed my last tumultuous adventure, but the less said about that the better.

Again, it's in the past.

I'm just thankful that wife batterer doesn't feature on my rap sheet of sins.)

Anyway. I was out of line yesterday. I should've just let Ellie tell me what happened when she was ready rather than try to pry it out of her like a bloody madman.

We didn't even get a chance to discuss it this morning because we were running late after last night's shenanigans So, we had to rush to the station, and with a quick kiss of "see you later", that was it.

When I asked my wife when she expected to be back, she told me she'd text me.

Now, I'm alone once more.

And it's shit.

I don't do 'alone' very well. People have been telling me that for years. Mostly women, of course.

And it was much worse last time when I was here for entirely different reasons.

You know what I mean when I say that, right? When I say *last time I was here*? Technically speaking, the last time I was *physically* here was when I was a child.

The last time I remember being here, I really wasn't. It was all a hideous figment of my imagination. Like a bad episode of one of those soaps that write out a main character by killing them off, only for everyone to discover that they've made a terrible mistake. So, they then contrive some ridiculously convoluted dream sequence to pretend it never happened.

Although, my last visit to this place wasn't a dream. It was a terrible nightmare. My stress-induced psychosis lasted much longer than I would ever wish on my worst enemy. It's one of the unspoken reasons why I didn't like the idea of Ellie going back to work in the city.

I'm afraid of being alone – with my thoughts, that is.

And this, too, is part of the process.

I must accept it. Accept that I cannot be trusted. Not alone. And I must do everything I can to mitigate any possibility of my abandoning the here and now in favour of regressing to a place that doesn't exist outside of my own imagination.

The worst part is, I couldn't and can't share how I'm feeling with Ellie, or anybody else, because I know exactly what they'll think. How they'll start seeing me. Curiously. Cautiously. Weighing their words, for fear of saying something that might *set me off* and somehow *send me back*.

Though, it isn't as easy as that. I know this. And Doctor Ethan Holmes has made that perfectly clear, too. It would take something specific. A trigger, like a traumatic event.

Like last time.

The thought of that has brought me out in a cold sweat. My hand is literally shaking over this yellow plastic vial of pills that was lovingly prescribed for me by the doctor.

Have you read about the bloody side effects of these things? Well, no, you likely haven't. Allow me.

Drowsiness. Shaking. Well, I'm already there. *Weight gain.* Like I need any help with that right now. *Restlessness. Muscle twitches. Blurred vision. Dizziness. Constipation. Loss of sex drive.*

Forget it. I shove the dresser drawer shut.

Then, I pull it open again. *Come on. You've just been whining about this. Help yourself.*

I pop the lid, shake out two of the pills, and swallow them without water. Yeah. Because I can do that. But, considering the potentially unpleasant side effects, I have to say that they're innocuous. No odour. No bad taste.

I need to go outside. It's another sunny day, and there are giant, marshmallow clouds drifting across a wonderfully pale blue sky. And the ocean, which is still but for a few white peaks, is a patchwork quilt of greys and greens. I should go for a walk and get some fresh air. Do some reconnaissance for a potential running route.

Pull myself together!

Then, I'll come back, make a proper brew, and start doing some research on the stuff needed to transform this place into a palace so we can get it sold and be out of here.

A creak on the bedroom door's threshold makes me turn to look at it. And my initial thought is that it might be Ellie. Maybe she's back home early.

But there's nobody there. Just shadows drifting across the hallway outside as those clouds sail past the sun.

"Ellie?"

I have no idea why I just said that — because part of me knows there's nobody there. And yet, my senses were just triggered by that sound. The tell-tale sense that says someone is standing in the doorway, watching you.

And yet....

I walk over to the door and stop when my foot causes the threshold floor strip to creak again.

I listen.

Nothing but the incessant call of a wood pigeon and the low rumble of the ocean. I look around the landing. It's empty, but for the moving shadows.

Now I know what they mean when they say that silence is deafening. The rush of the blood behind my ears. The *thump, thump, thump* of my heart and the sound of my br—

Brurrr!

"What the fu–?!"

It sounds like someone is drilling through the stone wall. What the hell–

I wait, my eyes darting all over the place as I try to work out what it could have been. Did I just imagine that?

Seconds tick by.

I couldn't have imagined it because–

Brurr! Brurr!

The sound is electrical. Rusty.

Aaargh! You've got to be joking. We've got a bloody pneumatic drill for a bloody doorbell!

I hurry downstairs. I don't want whoever it is to make that noise again.

Yes, I've developed a bit of a thing when it comes to repetitive sounds. It's something I've had for as long as I can remember, but last time I was here, it turned into something else because my *visitors* had a way of hammering on the door during every waking moment. The knocking was so desperate, it was like being visited by the bloody Gestapo.

Anyway, somehow – and I don't know how – this loud noise thing came up during therapy and Dr Holmes said that I may actually have a condition. *Yay! Another one.* Apparently, certain sounds are like emotional triggers for people like us.

Brurrrrrrr!

For example, wanting to punch the lights out of someone when they keep ringing the shitty doorbell that obviously isn't working properly. Item one thousand and whatever on the list. Get a new doorbell, urgently!

Misophonia. Google it if you're interested.

In the meantime, I yank the door open so fast that it nearly smacks me in the face.

"Yes?" I ask flatly – which, by the way, is a few factors nicer than how I'm feeling right now.

I'm looking at a short man with bright rosy cheeks, wearing

a flat cap with his tufts of grey hair poking out the sides and a blue polo shirt stretched over a portly belly.

"Mr Battista?"

"Yes?"

He must pick up on my tone because he opens with, "Sorry. I wasn't sure the bell was workin'," in a southwestern bur.

I dial up the fake smile because the man seems friendly enough and I don't want to come across as a complete dick. "No, it works. Kind of. What can I do for you?"

"I'm Irvin. Irvin Smith. You spoke to Marjorie at the store. Said you was in the market for a builder."

"Oh, right." My stance softens. "Wow. That was quick."

"Yeah, well. Marj gave me a bell last night. She's me sister-in-law, you see."

"Oh, OK."

He smiles, which only emphasises those two red apples he has for cheeks. "She says you're looking to do this place up and finally put it on the market," he adds, as if he's also in a hurry to be shot of it. Then, he takes a step back and looks up for a wider appraisal.

"That's the plan," I say after several seconds of watching his small eyes rove over the building. "Would you like to come in?" I ask, hurrying him along by standing aside.

He looks past me into the gloom of the house and hesitates, as if contemplating whether he actually wants the job. Then, with a quick nod, he walks by me.

I don't close the door because I've noticed that, despite the large window, the entrance to the house is a bit dark. Nothing like the hallway, but on the side of making you want to switch on a lamp every time the sun goes in.

"Well, this is… nice, ain't it?" the man askss, looking around the space. And I don't know if I'm imagining it, which is possible, but I'm sure he hesitated just then… as if unable to find the right adjective to describe what he's seeing. As if he were hovering between a compliment and WTF.

Which prompts me to say, "Yes. Well, it needs some work,

but then, that's the whole point of the project. We need to make good a few things before we put it on the market."

He nods, his head turning as if searching rather than looking.

"So, you said that Marjorie mentioned me?" I ask, for no particular reason other than to initiate a dialogue

"Aye. she called and asked me to stop by as soon as I could," he says, removing his hat and holding it in his hands as if he's suddenly concluding that it might be impolite to wear it indoors.

His face looks rounder now. Kinder. And I can see that the youthfulness of his sideburns has fared much better than the hair on top his head, the remnants of which are now plastered to his scalp.

"Oh, right… well, Irvin. I don't know what exactly Marjorie told you, but I was looking more for a labourer type of firm. You know. Odd jobs and such, as opposed to an actual builder," I say, eager to disabuse him of the notion that we're in the market for any major redevelopments.

He looks at me and smiles. "Oh, no. We're just a small business. Three of us. Me and two other young*er* lads," he says, adding the *er* on the end of that word with a smile, as if he believes it important to make me aware of the fact that there are a pair of younger and presumably fitter members of his crew.

Although, from my estimation, I don't think the man is far out of his fifties. He looks a bit weatherworn maybe, as if he's spent a lot of time in the sun.

"I get them to do all the heavy liftin," he continues with a chuckle as if to reinforce the point, and then adds, "we do all sorts, really."

"Like painting and decorating?"

"Oh, aye, that makes up the bulk of what we do."

"What about landscaping, and repairs?"

"Yeah. We can take of all of that."

"And do you just work locally then, or..?" I leave the sentence unfinished because even I'm not sure what I'm asking. I think I'm trying to establish whether or not they're busy, and by association popular enough to have business all over the county, or if it's more of a small business propped up by acquaintances and family. I can't afford to hire the first lot that come along, only to find out that we're still stuck out here in three months' time.

But he waves a reassuring hand and says, "Aye. We work all over," and then adds, "and are on most of those review sites. This may be a small village, but we do know 'ow to use a computer." He beams a congenial smile. "Well, almost. The wife takes care of most of that stuff, and of me," he adds with a chuckle and a pat of his paunch. "She runs the bakery in the village."

"Really? No way. I went in there yesterday."

"Did she take care of ya?"

"Absolutely. Really friendly. And her pasties are delicious. I know now why they won awards. My wife's a real fan," I say enthusiastically, because they ultimately got me out of the doghouse yesterday when I repeated my offering to Ellie with a good dose of humble pie. It worked, and I secretly thanked the ruddy-faced baker whom I've just noticed bears an uncanny resemblance to her husband. A perverse thought that they might be one and the same introduces itself, but I kick it out.

"Aye. So, you can appreciate my predicament," Irvin is saying.

I laugh. "Absolutely. I'm going to have to start watching what I eat, too," I say, patting my own belly. "I'm thinking of getting back into running.

"You're into that, then?"

I think about this. "I used to be," I say.

"What, back in the city, like?"

Oh, I see. Like that, is it? Why do I get the feeling you already know all there is to know about me? "Yes. Although, the city's running circuit isn't as stunning as the one here," I say.

"Aye. So, what exactly is it that you wants doin' then?"

"Well, I actually have a list," I say.

I lead the handyman through the den to the dining room, where I was last working on the notes. As we walk, I notice him having a good look around. Either he's very observant or he's expecting somebody else to make an appearance at any moment.

"My wife's back in the city today," I say, picking up the notepad. "She's been offered a new job, so it's unlikely we'll be able to do much of the work ourselves… as originally planned," I add, trying to mask the disappointment in my voice. "Which means I would need you to do more. Assuming you put in the best estimate, of course. When do you think you'd be able to start? It's just that, as mentioned, we're keen to get this place on the market as soon as possible," I say, looking around the room.

"Well, I guess that depends on how much you want us to do from that list of yours," he responds, eyeing the pad in my hand. "We gets booked quite a bit in advance, you see. Although, sometimes we can stagger the jobs. You know, instead of all showing up to one place at the same time, we can swap the labour around. We make more progress that way. That said, we're in between jobs at the moment. Some of 'em are outside, you see, and with all the bad weather we've been 'avin' of late, it's been difficult to make much progress. And with 'em givin' it more rain this week, those jobs are probably gonna have to be put on hold, you know. So, there's a good chance we could get started as early as next week, but that all depends on how much there is to do. You get my meaning?"

I nod. "That makes sense."

I talk him through the list while all the time being mindful of the fact that it's most likely just going to be me working on the simpler jobs like cleaning, and maybe even painting the easier stuff. Although, I'm not exactly the world's best decorator. I mean, the extent of my experience was our flat and, based on Ellie's reaction, I don't think it's one of my fortes.

So, I go over everything, and then I walk him through the upstairs.

The stairs to the next floor are just off the entrance to the corridor. They're made of an unidentifiable dark wood that could do with a good clean and is as creaky as hell, but otherwise in fairly good condition. The landing balustrade is in pretty much the same condition. The floor is decked out in the same dark wood. No idea what. Maybe oak?

This is followed through into the master bedroom, which

is a large utilitarian space. With a double bed and heavy, dark wood dressers. And a built-in wardrobe with mirrors for doors. Another nothing room with no character. But habitable. We'll give it and the spare room a good scrub, disposing of the old mattresses and replacing them both, along with new linen.

There's even a rustic flower vase I found in the dining room, which is now sitting on Ellie's bedside table and filled with yellow flowers I spotted in the garden. Google has reliably informed me they're jasmine, which is known to flower at this time of year. They've brought some cheer to what can only be described as a cheerless room since there isn't anything we can do immediately about the weird pea-soup colour on the walls, which I assume is supposed to represent the countryside but is more akin to vomit.

This space definitely needs a paint job. White or Sea Spray. The light is actually quite good in here, though, so probably the latter, and that's most likely something I could do, subject to time. The furniture can be donated once we're done with it.

The en suite is odd. Bit like the bathroom that time forgot. It's quite big, given the size of the house, with a large porthole window for light but with peeling paint and a sticky window that doesn't like to be opened. The bathtub is a large, ugly white thing with rusty claw feet and flakes of paint bubbling off the side. Ironically, in its prime, it probably would have looked quite elegant in here. Star-shaped hot and cold tap handles with the letters worn off lead overhead to a stained waterfall showerhead. The whole thing is encased in an opaque shower curtain that's already been through the washing machine, as we both refused to go anywhere near this room before it was disinfected to the best of our abilities.

A flower-patterned basin and white, chain-handle toilet complete the design, which is so ancient that it's now in vogue once more. The floor looks like it boasts small, flower-patterned, Victorian tiles. I don't think this room has been changed since the place was built, but there's plenty of space to replace the furniture and add a shower cubicle in addition to the bath.

Not something I can do.

The landing – which is relatively bright, thanks to the

window opposite – also leads to the family bathroom, which is a weird place, to say the least. It has a row of three basins with one long strip mirror in front of it that casts a distorted reflection worthy of one of those freaky fairgrounds. Along with a stained, ceramic pull-chain toilet which has seen better days. This place is more like a washroom, and I'm amazed that the old man, who did like his creature comforts, didn't see fit to upgrade it.

I don't like this room. It gives me the creeps, but I think that's mostly because it's evocative of what this house used to be way before the Battista's decided to buy it.

Anyway, that all needs replacing. It's actually a nice space, especially with that large portal window overlooking the front garden. Just needs to be modernised, to make it more like a family bathroom and less like my boarding school washroom, which is probably one of the reasons why I don't like it.

At the end of the corridor is my old room, now the guest room.

I purposefully haven't spent much time in here, except for helping to remove the old mattress. Ellie naturally took over dusting the place and replacing the bed linen as soon as she sensed my reluctance. But now, in the interest of having a comprehensive list, I and Irvin venture inside what is another generous room. It, too, is minimalistic, considering it was supposed to belong to a child. Bare and pale blue walls. Pine wood bedframe for a double bed. Wardrobe to match.

This is quite a nice room, though. Especially with the large window with the view out to the back garden and ocean. I obviously didn't appreciate it when I last stayed here, but the view is quite stunning, especially now, when a band of grey clouds is occupying the sky and casting a chequerboard of light patches onto a choppy ocean.

"You may want to look at getting that cut back," Irvin says suddenly.

He's referring to the twisted branches of the oak tree that, like long bony fingers, keep reaching back and forth to tap on the window.

"I used to hate that tree as a child," I say aloud.

"Yeah? Well, you probably should 'ate it more as an adult," Irvin says ominously. "The wind round these parts is brutal. Won't take much for that monster to fall and cause a lot of damage."

Monster. That's exactly what that tree became to me at night. Especially when the moon was out making shadowy claws of the branches, casting them all over the walls. On stormy nights, I imagined it reaching through the glass and dragging me out into the night. But then, my mother told me that I had it all wrong. The tree wasn't a monster, but an ancient protector planted here long before I was born – with the sole purpose of watching over me. And the fact that its roots were buried deep in the ground would ensure that it would never leave my side.

"That tree hasn't gone anywhere in years, despite all the storms you must have around here. I doubt it's going anywhere now," I say wistfully. "I love it. It's about the only thing I actually like about this place."

The builder shrugs apathetically, as if to say, *You were warned.*

In other news, there's a memory! At least, I think it is. I remember some kind of a fuzzy image of me cowering under the sheets, and someone holding my hand and comforting me. It's about the only one. That, and the other hideous thing I discovered while in therapy. The one I try not to think about. Especially while we're living here.

So, this room is fine. Doesn't need much. Just a good clean, by the looks of it. Nothing to see here.

And I'm just about to turn to leave when I spot something in the corner.

A giant, wooden box.

I don't remember seeing it before. But then, I don't remember much.

I walk over to it, lift the lid, and my stomach drops.

There's a small bucket and spade, a scuffed action man doll, and two jigsaw puzzle boxes – one with the image of a tyrannosaurus rex in mid-roar, and the other with a group of dinosaurs that each have their own anger issues, in front of a leafy backdrop and erupting volcano.

But the one thing that gets my attention is the Perspex box sitting on top of everything else. It is filled with a collection of dinosaur figurines.

Why the hell did Ellie bring these here? And why would she put them in this box of all places?

The answer is, she didn't. These figurines aren't my son's. They aren't Toby's. They're mine.

I can't believe this. All this time, and I didn't even realise that I shared my son's fascination with dinosaurs so much, to the point of buying him the very same set.

It's both creepy and oddly comforting.

I open the box, take out the dark-green-skinned, 4-inch T-Rex figurine, and turn it over in my hand. Its shiny, white-painted teeth flash up at me and I get a sudden flashback to Toby in a haze of sunshine, playing in his bedroom. I can hear him making the beast's roaring sound effects and my heart swells.

Toby.

I hold the figurine to my chest and close my eyes, as if doing so will somehow amplify the memory playback. My mind has been so busy repressing my childhood that it wiped out the fact that, unbeknownst to me, Toby's obsession with dinosaurs was born out of my own.

I can see him now. Smiling up at me from his position on the carpet. A whole herd of dinosaurs scattered around him. *"Dad! Daddy, come and play! Come and play with me!"*

I'm about to reply when the sound of someone clearing their throat brings my conscious streaming to a screeching halt.

I'm still clutching the figurine to my chest when I look up at the tubby man in the doorway. He's smiling at me sympathetically.

"Marjorie and me," he starts softly, his sad brown eyes glancing at the floor, "we tried for a brood of our own for many years, but it wasn't meant to be. Instead, I ended up with those two I've got. Been working with 'em for a few years now. Dean's adopted.

Drew is just like one of me own," he adds with a smile before letting it slide once more. "Your boy no longer with ya?" he asks gently.

"No," I say, biting my lip as the man's sudden sensitivity brings a lump to my throat.

"My heart goes out to yers."

I nod because I don't want him, this stranger, however amiable he is, to hear the quiver in my voice, and nor do I want him to ask what happened – because that'll truly set me off.

Instead, I hastily return the figurine to its plastic case before placing it back inside the box and closing the lid.

Back on my feet, I say with a shrug, "Well, that's pretty much it."

There's no point to showing him the generous linen cupboard at the end of the hallway, which is now doubling as a hotel for creepy-crawlies and, judging by the tiny black pellets everywhere, rodents and assorted families.

It also houses a long, metal hook which I assume is for pulling down the hatch to the attic – which, in my opinion, is located in the most impractical of places, right in the centre of the landing; if you're someone like me who hates heights, that's the worst possible place. One false step or, God forbid, a slip of the ladder, would mean plummeting over the balustrade to death or certain disability, courtesy of the flagstone floor below.

"I think the latch on that thing needs looking at, too. It sprang open for no reason last night. Scared us half to death."

Irvin nods pensively. "Aye, they do that sometimes because of the draft blowing through the rafters."

"So, what do you think?" I ask.

My burly visitor, who I have to say has remained patient and impassive throughout the tour, with not a flinch nor a sucking of air over his teeth, smiles at me and shrugs as if it's the same-old, same-old.

So, I make him his own list in handwriting that he can actually read and ask him to go away and give me an estimate as soon as possible, with the assurance that I will give it my immediate and full attention.

And that's it.

Now, alone once more, I realise that it isn't so bad. Things are looking up.

7. THE GLOOM

PORTHCOVE. MONDAY. 19:45.

When Ellie gets home, it's going to be to a candlelit table for two, the aroma of my signature pasta sauce, and a glass of wine. It's *Arrabiata* tonight, or as my wife likes to call it because of my *former* hot and quick temper, 'Marco's sauce'.

Right now, I'm in a great mood.

When Ellie messaged me earlier in the day to say that she was on the train home, I started making the preparations. And when she asked me how the day had gone, I avoided responding because there was no way I was going to share my fantastic news in a text message.

No. I want to see the whites of those gorgeous eyes of hers at the moment I tell her that we are on our way to solvency and beyond. This will be a new for us since we've spent most of our lives living hand to mouth, but that's going to change. Soon. I am going to make us better, albeit indirectly. It's the least I can do.

See? I'm doing it again. Contrary to what Ethan spent most of his waking hours drumming into me, what happened was not my fault. And to be fair, Ellie hasn't ever made me feel as if she blames me, either. She says it could have been either one of us. But it wasn't either one of us. It was me.

Besides, even if I did allow myself to flirt with the idea that I might be blameless, there is one thing that I can never forgive myself for. I put my wife in an impossible situation. My absence forced her to go cap-in-hand to her stuck-up cock of a dad, not only to survive but to bail me out. To pay for my staycation at that place. That, I can never forgive myself for. And I am going to repay every penny.

That's why, right now, I feel grateful. I'm not resentful in any way over the fact that my greedy, blood-sucking half-siblings have inherited all the old man's cash and other properties. No. I'm just grateful that he saw in his skinflint way to leave me this place – because once we're finished with it, it's going to change everything. And the thought of that warms my blood like booze.

It has nothing to do with sticking it to the in-laws. As if. Who do you take me for?

Don't answer that.

In the meantime, what I have left on cards may be enough to see us through, but it's certainly not enough to pay for the refurb on this place, which I'm going to have to consider separately. But one thing at a time.

And yes, of course, I've considered getting a job. I am part-Italian after all. My dad, for all his faults, was a hard worker. He was from a tiny village in the south of Italy. The embodiment of working-class, with a strong work ethos. Which I imagine goes some way to explaining why he treated me like crap and, despite his wealth, pushed me out onto a paper round as soon as I was physically capable of doing one. My father was not into hand-outs. At least, certainly not to me. As a child, I never received pocket money or an allowance of any kind. Any money he gave me had to be earned, whether by polishing his shoes, shining his car, or any other menial chore he could find that would involve me earning what I received.

And chores always came before recreation.

Always.

Yet, something tells me that he probably wasn't as harsh on the terrible twins, though maybe I'm just being cynical.

Ellie, on the other hand… she doesn't want me to get a job. She doesn't think there'll be anything for me around here anyway, which I'm trying hard not interpret as a belief that I am incapable of turning my hand to new skills.

I suggested the pub, not that it would pay much. She wasn't that keen.

So, then I suggested being a handyman on a farm. I told her that I could just see myself getting up at four in the morning to tug on a pair of giant teats.

It made her laugh.

And the memory of that makes me chuckle as I stir the sauce.

Yes. If David were here right now, he'd be making a joke about my experience with breasts, but I'm bigger than that. Remember… to the pure, all is pure.

I miss that bloke. No matter how annoying he might be.

David!

This whole time, I've been thinking about how, given my current employment status, I couldn't get money from a bank, but there's also David. There's no doubt that he could help with a short-term loan. He's always told me that if I ever need anything, I should ask. He even made me promise once.

No. No. Absolutely not.

I've already leaned enough on him in the past. Moving on.

I have a strong suspicion that Ellie's comment about me not being able to find employment around here was more about substantiating her argument for going back to work than my being useless. That, and given how competitive my wife can be, I wouldn't put it past her to secretly enjoy the idea of relegating me to 'househusband', or is that 'domestic engineer'?

That's no offence to the *domestic engineers* out there. I am sure they're perfectly happy with their arrangement, but it just isn't my bag. Certainly not with how I was raised.

Of course, there is always the other thing. I told her that people around here must have cars that need fixing. The conversation was brief because she quickly shut it down. I have no clue if that's because she thinks I'm still smarting from the fact that they lied to me, or because–

The slam of the front door echoes down the hallway and brings me back into the moment.

I pour a couple of glugs of red wine into my sauce and then fill one of the stemmed glasses on the island. I fill the other with sparkling water.

That's right. I've gone all this time without a drop, and I'm sure I can go a few weeks more. Who knows? It might just lead to permanent teetotalism.

I hold up the wine glass to the kitchen door and wait for Ellie to walk through it.

She doesn't.

At home, she had a habit of dropping her housekeys on the side table and announcing her arrival, and here... well, we haven't had the chance to get into any kind of a routine yet.

"Ellie! Is that you?" I shout – pointlessly because who else is it going to be?

Nothing.

"Ellie?"

Silence but for the wind, which is back and as belligerent as ever. Sweeping around the house, shaking the hedge, and hissing at the windows.

I walk over to the door and call down the gloomy corridor. "Ellie?"

Still nothing. And she's not in the toilet because there's no light under the door.

"El?" I call anyway, for good measure.

The house is deathly quiet, but for the occasional creak of timber as the ocean chill pushes at the building as if seeking shelter from itself.

"Ellie?" It's a half-hearted call this time as I move to the light switch on the wall and flick it.

Nothing happens.

"Shit," I hiss, swallowing my irritation. One measly light and even that can't be bloody bothered.

So, now the only illumination in the gloom is that which is spilling through the kitchen doorway at one end of the corridor and the living room lamps at the other. And I don't know if it's my imagination, but they seem… weaker, duller. As if they've been dimmed.

I squint into it.

"Ellie?"

At this point, the words I utter are just an automatic murmur since I'm not truly expecting a reply.

Which is good, because I don't get one; instead, a draft appears out of nowhere and starts buffeting against the toilet and dining room doors, causing them to knock and tremble in their frames as if they're being molested by invisible hands.

Reluctantly, I place one foot in front of the other and almost feel my way towards the light at the end of the hallway.

"El?" I speak out as I near the toilet door, but I already know she isn't in there, and when I look back up–

What was that?

My heart skips a beat. A shadow. A bloody shadow! Someone just crossed the hallway, heading towards the den.

Someone?

Who else would it be, but Ellie?

With a narrowing of the eyes and a knowing smile on my face, I hurry out of the gloom and into the light with an unnecessarily loud, "El, I know it's you! Why aren't you answering—" Hot and cold shivers slither and coil around my spine to paralyse the rest of the sentence.

The lounge is empty. The sofa lamps are burning innocently, alone. I gawk at the things as if they're going to confess to going on a walkabout or, worse, tell me something I'm not sure I want to hear. That I'm not alone and that Ellie isn't home.

They don't. Obviously. But I wish they would because now I'm starting to feel just a tad creeped out. I did just witness that, right? I mean you heard me describe it to you, so I must have seen it, right? Right?

Shit.

I remain still. Frozen to the spot. My limbs reluctant to move, to make a sound, because I may not hear what else is happening in the house. You know… footsteps upstairs, doors opening and closing in mysterious drafts.

Stop it!

Maybe someone snuck in.

Listen!

Who?

Stop it! Listen!

There's nothing here. Just the rhythmic back and forth of the surf in the distance. The ever-present gale. The creaky building. So what? It was the same last night. After I went back to bed. There was something moving around up there. Ellie had to talk me down. Tell me there was nothing. But I heard something.

Something?

More illegal bloody squatters. Rats. Seagulls. Bats?

Ugh.

A squealing sound grabs my attention and I look at one of the lamps that sounds as if it's been throttled by something. And I can only watch as the soft light grows into a glare as if someone is dialling up the power.

I lift my hand to fend off the shine just as there's a loud pop and the light's snuffed out, plunging part of the room into darkness.

"Jesus Christ!" I clutch a hand to my chest to try and still the pounding there.

I chuckle. It's a nervous one as I take in deep lungsful of air. That made me bloody jump. And I barely have time to recover when a scratching at the front door makes me spin on the spot.

There's something out there. Right outside the front door, and it's scratching to come in.

The gale is even louder now. Storming around the building. Searching. Intimidating.

This isn't like yesterday. This is worse. Much worse. I can literally see it pressing on the patio doors and squeezing itself inside somehow because it's moving the blinds.

Yet, my attention is brought back to the front door where the scratching has now turned into a thumping. It's low, as if someone or something is pushing on it from the outside and pulling on my very last nerve.

Yes, I'm alarmed now. I'm suitably alarmed that something is actually—

The door bursts open and a sound leaves my mouth. I have no bloody idea what it's supposed to be until I hear Ellie scream, and then the overhead light springs to life, dazzling me.

"Marco? You gave me a bloody heart attack!" my wife complains.

"I gave *you* a heart attack? What's with all the bloody scratching at the door?"

"I told you. We need to get the light fixed out there. You can't see a bloody thing in the dark. I thought you said you were going to replace the bulb?"

"I did. But they have a habit of spontaneously combusting around here," I say, glancing at what's left of the lamp. And I mean that literally because the bulb didn't just die. It exploded! Surely, they aren't supposed to do that, are they?

Bloody hell. I swallow hard. My heart is still throbbing as Ellie dumps her coat and scarf onto the back of the sofa – yeah, she has a habit of doing that – and walks up to me. "Are you OK? You look like you've just seen a ghost, and–" she sniffs the air. "What's that smell?"

"Oh, don't you start... shit!" I turn on my heels and run down the corridor, back to the kitchen.

***

Ellie is still giggling as she forks salad leaves into her mouth.

"You still think that's funny, huh? Well, burnt pasta sauce is a first for me," I say, lifting up surrendering hands as the image of the offending pan smouldering in the sink replays itself in my mind.

We had to skip the main course and go straight to the second, which is sirloin steak with a Mediterranean salad. Yes, I thought I'd bring out the big guns because I'm feeling optimistic after Irvin's visit and, most importantly, I'm eager to make it up to

Ellie after our falling out yesterday. I want her to know that, as her husband, I fully support her every endeavour. I just hope it doesn't mean us spending much more time apart.

"So, what's your news?" I ask, topping up her wine glass.

"Oh, no, you don't," she says. "Yours first. Who was the first mystery visitor?"

"Well, I was—"

Her phone, which I've just noticed is sitting on the table next to her, starts to vibrate and inch its way towards her plate like a hungry insect.

We don't normally have phones at the table. We agreed that it would not only be socially healthier but would also set a good example for our son. So, it's odd seeing it there. But I don't mention it, and instead ask, "Are you not going to get that?"

"Nope," she says, looking at the display before swiping, tapping, and then beaming at me, sapphire eyes winking in the candlelight.

Well, I thought I would make it as romantic as I could, given the limited tools in my arsenal. But one thing we seem to have an abundance of is candles. And there can only be one practical reason for that perched out here at the mercy of the elements – Power cuts. Joy.

"I'm much more interested in your news," she adds.

"I. Um… well—"

The phone vibrates once more.

"You can get that" I add, straightening in my chair and shrugging out the non-existent crick in my shoulders. "I don't mind."

"No. it's just work," she replies, looking at the device and then picking it up.

"Work?" I echo since the words were spoken like she's been back for months already. She doesn't respond, but instead taps and slides her finger on the screen until it goes dark. Then, she takes a sip from her glass without looking at me, and I wonder. "Work?"

"Your news first," she repeats with another smile.

I hesitate because it feels a bit awkward now. The childish

excitement has well been diluted. So… "We had our first potential builder come over today."

"Really?"

"Yes. Apparently, he's the baker's husband. Brother-in-law to the grocery store owner." I lift my eyebrows.

"Really. Wow." Ellie widens her eyes, too, because she gets my meaning. It does all sound a bit inbred, but I guess that's to be expected in a small village.

"Marc, that's brilliant news," she continues. "What was he like?"

I think about this and nod. "Yeah. I quite liked him. He runs a small crew of two and it sounds like they do a bit of everything, which is exactly what we need."

"That's brilliant."

"Yeah. I'm just hoping his estimate comes in at the right price."

There's a pause as we take a short while to eat. Enjoying the ambiance. Well, if I may say so myself, I did manage to make the room quite cosy, in that country pub kind of way, but obviously with just a large table for two.

I found some neatly pressed white tablecloths in the side unit. They smelt damp but seemed in otherwise good condition. I selected the one from the middle just to be sure. There was already a bronze, three-candle, ornate candleholder on the table. So, I lit that. I also found some decent wine glasses, dinnerware, and after turning down the so-called house lights, it all looks the part.

My wife does have a bit of a penchant for fine dining, so I'm hoping the extra effort might earn me some essential forgiveness points. And no, I'm not even thinking about the other stuff because…. Well, that's a complex part of my life, given who I was and who I'm trying to be – and the fact that I don't want to have any expectations, for fear of refusal, and thus risk abject disappointment and potential depression.

Well, I did say it was complicated.

The pièce de résistance was finding an old record player in the side unit, too. I have no idea who it originally belonged to; the people who owned this place before, the old man, or even his wife. I can't use that other word after learning what that woman tried to do to me here of all places.

Anyway, the record player came complete with a series of old records. Rather appropriately, most are of that Italian *Dolce Vita* kind of time. *Rosemary Clooney, Dean Martin, Bobby Darin, Perry Como, Frank Sinatra*, and the gang. And while they wouldn't be my first choice, it doesn't get more fitting than *Beyond the Sea*, which is filling in the silences beautifully right now.

I want my wife and I to reconnect after yesterday. I know it's a bit early, but I want us to have some good news to share and for us to be able to cautiously look forward to better days.

"This place looks great," Ellie says suddenly, looking around the table.

"You think?"

"Absolutely," she says, beaming a warm smile.

Back of the net! Not one of my usual phrases, but what can I say? These are unusual times.

"So, it's true. David has offered me my job back," Ellie adds. "Well, actually, it's not my old job. He's offered me a new role. More responsibility. He wants me to be his deputy."

"What?"

"Yes. There's major stuff happening at the company. It's all hush hush right now, but," she leans in as if the walls give a shit and says, "I think one of the big four has made him an offer and he wants me to spearhead the deal." The last bit is said with an over-excited inflection which, if I'm perfectly honest, is infectious.

"So, you're definitely thinking of going back to work in London?"

"Well," she begins, hesitating, "not thinking. I've, um, accepted. Signed today."

"What? Without even asking me?"

She frowns. "I didn't know I had to ask for your permission."

"Not permission, El. But we are married. We're a team still, aren't we? This is big stuff. A big decision. I would have thought we'd at least discuss it before you committed."

"What, you mean like we discussed marooning ourselves out here?"

OK, that stung, and I don't even know why. "I thought it was what you wanted," I say with a scowl.

Her stance softens. "It is. Was. I mean, *is*. This is your thing, Marco. It isn't really mine, is it?"

I screw my face up incredulously. Because, well, I'm hearing this for the first time. "Wow. *My* thing? I thought it was *our* thing."

"It is. Of course, it is, but this is also the perfect opportunity for me to get back."

"Get back? Get back to what?"

"To living some semblance of my own life!" she snaps, her voice ringing around the room.

Seconds tick by. This isn't how I wanted tonight to go. And I know how headstrong my wife can be. So, I have a choice here. Persevere, and risk ending up in the same place we were yesterday, or….

Despite my feelings, I take a deep breath and say, "You're right. I'm sorry. I'm actually thrilled for you."

"You are?"

I force a laugh. "Of course. I just wanted to give you a bit of a hard time after the grilling you gave me."

"Marco, that's only because—"

I hold up a hand. "I know. And you're right. But we all have to move on, right? Isn't that what we were told? Nothing will be the same, but as long as we keep moving forward and taking each day as a new step, we also can forge a new life, or some shit!"

She laughs. "Oh God, you actually sound a bit like him."

I put on a soft, safe, measured, well-cultured voice. "Ellie. Are you sure this is what you want to do? What would you really like to do? Let's talk about it."

My wife giggles again. "You sound just like him."

I watch her for a short while. It's a good to see that smile on her face again.

Eventually, she says, "You don't think we're moving too fast with all of this?"

I shrug. "Hell if I know. If I'm perfectly honest with you, I really think the best way to do this is to just take each day as it comes. This is unchartered territory for us both, but the way I see it is that we have two choices; sit here and mourn what was, or do as every Dr Holmes person and wannabe therapist tells us, which is to remember the past, but also, as you say, form some semblance of a new life for ourselves."

She pulls a sad face and then reaches across the table to take my hand. And there's a moment here. Finally. Like we're connecting again, and I am so grateful for it.

"Didn't you, um, give me a similar speech when you asked me to marry you?" she asks.

"Did I? I don't think so."

"Yeah. Something similar about standing still, and if we did it too long, life would run us over."

I think about that. "Really? I don't remember, but it sounds wise, so it was most likely me." I smile.

We eat silently for a few seconds, and then I finish chewing, take a sip of my water, and continue, "I was thinking that, with a bit of luck, we might have this place done in a couple of weeks and on the market before Christmas."

Ellie stops chewing. "You're joking. Christmas?"

I nod.

"Don't you think that might be a little ambitious?" she asks.

"Yeah, a bit. But I think we need to be. Need to have a goal, a target to aim for."

"Yeah, well, there's *target* and then there's *crazy*," she says, putting her glass down and going back to her food.

"Do you really think it's crazy?" I ask earnestly.

She must realise how she sounded because she pauses once more. "Well, 'crazy' in that it does sound a tad optimistic, but I think you're right. It's good to have a goal."

"Yeah. And some goal, El. Can you believe it?" I look around the room and then back at her. "Can you believe what this means for us? No more credit cards. No more scrimping and saving. I mean, El, this is going to change our lives forever."

Yes. I know I'm in danger of sounding like my dad. All I seem to think about is the money. Well, that's because those who don't know us have missed the part where we, like many, used to talk about money all the time. Especially in London, where the cost of living makes it prohibitively expensive to, well, live. And Ellie, she's always been one of those *posh birds*. She liked to live – sometimes at the expense of rent and bills.

You can't blame her, though. She grew up with it. Leaving her parents and moving in with me was a major adjustment for her. One she struggled with, regularly.

"I know. I can't believe it!" she's enthusing. "Especially if it all happens for Christmas. Wait. Do you really think we might have this done and dusted for then? As in, be in a new home? That would be awesome!" she says, forking raw meat into her mouth – which, by the way, I think is grotesque. I like my meat cremated, but my wife likes it to still have a pulse.

And yes. Of course, I noticed that tone. I know my wife. I know she's projecting right now. Saying what she thinks I want to hear, not least because she's smiling with her mouth again and not her eyes. I don't think she's truly smiled like that with me in a while. Certainly not since Toby.

"So, what's the plan?" she asks, the dregs of that artificial smile still on her face.

"You don't need to pretend for me." *Oh shit. I said that out loud.*

She stops chewing. "What do you mean?"

"El, come on."

"What?"

"You know what."

She puts her fork down. "No, I don't. Marco, come on. Tell me. We're a team, remember?"

"Oh, don't start that shit, either. Why are you trying to antagonize me?"

"I'm not. That's the kind of stuff they say in therapy, isn't it?"

She's part smiling, part serious. And she's throwing that

at me because she probably thinks I understand it. Therapy. But what she also knows is that, conversely, I hate submitting myself for analysis. And yet, despite that, I was fully prepared to go to bereavement counselling because I thought it would help her – *us*. She thought it would be a pointless waste of time, and now she's making a joke of it.

I hear her sigh as she puts her fork down. "Look, I know you're excited about the sale. I am, too. Of course, I am. As you say, it really is our chance to start over, whatever that means. And I know you want me to be as excited about the money as you are. But you've always known that money, for me, is just the means to an end."

"That's because you've never needed it like–"

"Marco, if you finish that sentence, I swear to God I'm going to stab you with this fork. Of course, I bloody know what it's like! When you were in that clinic, I was the one who had to go cap-in-hand to my father, remember? So, don't fucking tell me that I don't know what it's like. Of course, I bloody do! I'm just not obsessed with it like you are."

The artificial smile has gone. Replaced by pursed lips and flashing eyes. This is my wife. At least, these are her genuine feelings.

Toby and I are familiar with this look of hers, which was often triggered by this ever-emotive subject. We never have and never will see money and the independence it brings in the same way.

Silence rules as we allow Dean Martin to belt out the finishing notes of "That's Amore".

Yeah. Thanks for that, mate, as if I didn't know already.

We both pretend to eat when, really, we're just chasing the food around the plate. That's because the steak is now as cold as the salad that accompanies it.

There's a crackle, hiss, and click as the needle reaches the centre of the disc, and then the house falls silent as if it wants to listen in to the rest of our conversation.

That's one thing I've noticed about this place. Being perched up this high means there's always a gale buffeting the building. And it's quite tangible, almost like another presence living out here with us. And when it isn't there, it feels oddly as if the house is missing one of its inhabitants. It's noticeable. Palpable. The solitude, the isolation.

In this case, the silence is pierced only by the rhythmic tick-tock of the unnecessarily loud wall clock, the occasional chink of steel on porcelain, and, of course, the ever-present, low rumble of the turning tide.

"I'm sorry," I finally say.

"No. I'm sorry," Ellie joins in, throwing down her fork as if she was looking for an excuse to stop pretending.

"Did you try not to laugh at the Dean Martin song?" I ask. She giggles. "Yeah."

I reach across the corner of the table. "I love you, El. I didn't mean to sound like a dick."

"No, it's not you. I know this means a lot to you. And me. But, you know, you're blessed, or not, with all that Italian passion. When you're into something, you burn hot and fast. Me... you know me, I'm a typical English girl. We don't do *excited* very much. One must maintain proper decorum at all times," she says, and her last words are clipped in the Queen's English.

I smile and feel a burning in my cheeks because I am suddenly overwhelmed with a rush of love for her, closely followed by an urge to lean over and kiss her. But as I do, she draws in a sharp breath and jolts backward.

"What's wrong?"

She doesn't answer, and I look down at myself wondering what it is about me that appears to have horrified her. But when I look up, I realise that she isn't looking at me, but over my shoulder.

"What is it? What's wrong?" The words leave my mouth, but I'm already turning my head just as a faint breeze brushes the side of my face.

I jump away as a giant, black insect flutters over the dining table towards Ellie, who screams and jumps off her chair, knocking it over with a loud scrape and a crash.

The fluttering insect doubles back on itself and circles over the table a few times. Its wingspan must stretch at least three inches.

It's massive! And its jittery, jerky motions as it flaps around the candles are enough to show me that it isn't just black, but brown with speckles of black.

"Get it! Kill it! Marco! Kill it!" Ellie screams.

I'm not a fan, either, but for Ellie's sake, I find myself saying, "It's just a moth, Ellie. It's harmless."

"I hate moths!" she proclaims as if we're not already married and I'm not already aware of her feelings towards anything that crawls.

"I know, but I think you're scaring *it* more than it's scaring you."

"Just kill it!"

I imagine that long, thick, cylindrical abdomen squishing open, and the thought of that makes me gag. My queasiness is amplified when the insect lands on what's left of Ellie's steak and crawls over it. Long tongue – or at least I think it's a tongue – unfurling and flicking as it goes.

It looks completely black now that its wings are folded neatly onto its back, resembling an obese slug with twitching antennae as it surveys the dead flesh. And that isn't everything. I mean, I don't know if the candlelight is playing tricks on me, but this thing has weird markings on its back, like some kind of tattoo, and I can't be sure, but what the… is that a skull? It's a human bloody skull!

Ellie shrieks again as if the thing is crawling over her. The sound drills through me. "Well, don't just stand there! Get rid of it! GET RID OF IT!"

"Ellie, be quiet," I say in a whisper while slowly approaching the table. As gross as the thought is, I'm going to try to flip my plate over Ellie's in order to trap the thing in there and then I'm going to try to release it outside… because the thought of squishing it as per my wife's demands is more repugnant to me than letting the thing go.

But, as if it's read my mind, the moth takes to the air once more, eliciting another shriek from Ellie, who jumps over her stricken chair to hide behind me.

We can only watch as the fluttering continues over us for a

few more seconds before the insect finally lands on the wall clock, which I've just this second concluded is an ugly thing made of what looks like pieces of bark hammered together around a carriage clock. It's grandfather-like tick and tock are seemingly louder now that the room has fallen still once more.

Tick tock... tick tock... tick... tock.... The sound merges with Ellie's rasping breaths and my thumping heart as the insect remains motionless, as if it's being hypnotised by the sound. And I can still see that skull on its back. It's faint in the candlelight, yet clear.

Tick tock.

A skull. A fu–dging skull!

Tick

The conservatory roof creaks.

Tock.

A draft wails.

Tick.

SLAM!

Ellie screams and throws herself against my back, the act startling me as we both turn to the dining room door which has just slammed shut. We both gape at the thing as if neither of us has seen a door before. I can feel Ellie trembling against me. Her fingers digging into my sides.

The wind is back, and it's in its usual foul mood. We both remain motionless for what feels like minutes. Hearts thumping. Breaths rasping.

Then: "Ellie," I say gingerly.

"What?" she whispers.

"I think… I think I've just shit myself!"

"Marco!" she complains, slapping my arm as I turn to look at her with a chuckle. "That's not funny. That was bloody creepy," she whines.

And I have to say, as stereotypical as her behaviour may seem, my wife isn't normally like this. In the city, she's a completely different animal. No pun intended. But here…. I don't even recognise this person. She obviously doesn't do well in the countryside –

something I haven't really noticed before. I mean, I know she's never been a fan of insects, and nor have I, for that matter, but to hear her like this? Well, selfishly, I like it. It feels good to have her need me.

"Oh no," I hear her moan ominously.

"What?"

"The moth," she says. "It's disappeared."

8. AISLE 7

TUESDAY. 10:03.

Ellie had me search pretty much the whole house last night before she would even consider going to bed. But there was no sign of that thing, which meant that we had to sleep with the bedside lamps on. And no, the irony of that wasn't lost on me since anybody with half a brain knows that moths are drawn to light.

On the plus side, it had been such a busy day that, despite the glare, I was out for the count much sooner than even I had expected. One minute, I was agonizing over the fact that I was never going to get to sleep, and the next, I was having a bad dream about people standing at the foot of my bed. Well, when I say 'people', I mean 'presences' – which, if you joined me on my previous shit show, you'd know turned out to be more fact than figment of my imagination.

But that's a different story.

Right now, I'm focussed on the task at hand. Ellie has made it perfectly clear that she can't wait to start her new job, and although still suffering from the dregs of disappointment, nor can I.

Surprising, right? Especially when you factor in how I was feeling yesterday. But today... well, today, the sun is out again, the birds are quite literally singing, and I quite fancy myself as one of those project managers. You know the ones you see in those stock photography images with the handsome dude in a suit, wearing a shiny hard hat, holding a clipboard or maybe even a tablet, with a perpetually shiny smile.

OK. Maybe not.

But I am looking forward to getting started. That's why I'm already mooching my way around the DIY superstore, looking for inspiration.

I asked Ellie if she wanted to come, but she said she needed to stay at the house and get started with a presentation David's requested for her return-to-work – illustrating what, in her new role of operations director, she'll do to take the company forward.

Which is how I know that she's already forgotten what was going to be our mutual project and moved on.

I was going to hang around the house, too. Maybe brave the gauntlet of logging into my various financial institutions and seeing just how bad the damage is there. But I changed my mind when Ellie suggested that we work on that together. For some reason, I didn't fancy taking that journey with her around. We may share most things, but, thankfully, we still have separate bank accounts, but for the household expense account. I really would rather she not witness what she already knows if I can avoid it.

So, instead I said that I needed to go out first. Research prices for some of the materials we're going to need for the house. When she suggested that I do that online, I told her that it wasn't the same as walking around the store and being inspired.

That seemed to work.

I also told myself that this is a strict reconnaissance-only mission, and that I will not in any way be tempted to buy superfluous stuff with money I do not have. But then, isn't that exactly what a credit card is for?

Ellie would be giving me one of her looks right about now, but she isn't here, and you… well, you're here to support me in my decisions, right?

Don't answer that.

Aisle 7 of this place, which is probably large enough to house two jumbo jets, has what I need.

Motion Activated. Auto alert direct to your phone. Connects with whichever AI is the current fad. Talk directly through your phone or via your computer. Wireless. Wired. With or without camera.

I have a total of three credit cards. One has a credit limit of 5,000 pounds, and the other, which I haven't used in years and has probably expired, has 10,000 pounds, while the one I use for everyday stuff probably has about a thousand left – which, judging by these prices, will probably have half of that by the time I've finished shopping here.

Fu–dge doorbells!

"Excuse me, sorry, excuse me," I say desperately to a passing child wearing a red jacket with *How can I help you?* emblazoned over it.

The boy twitches his head, which is code I interpret as *T'sup, dude?*

"I'm looking for doorbells," I tell him. He glances at the shelf next to us. "*Normal* doorbells," I add quickly. "You know. Something people press, and it makes a ding-dong sound. And by that, I mean *just* a ding-dong sound. No awful muzak rendition of *She'll be coming down the mountain when she comes* or twenty other hideous melodies that I'll never use; I just want a standard run-of-the-mill doorbell that makes a standard run-of-the-mill ding-dong sound when pressed."

The boy squints at me like I've just asked him to give me a lap dance and then plucks one of the boxes from the shelf. The box has *30 programable melodies!* splashed across the front, and he hands it to me. I look at the package and then back at him, and I inhale to speak, but conclude that resistance in this particular case is obviously futile, so I give him an overenthusiastic smile.

"Thank you so much."

It grunts and shuffles on its way once more.

Of course, a short-term bank loan seems like the obvious thing right now, but who is going to loan money to an unemployed mechanic? Even Ellie has been out of work because of me. It's obvious that my ending up in the mad house was the last straw for her. She had to give it up to take care of me. Daily visits and all that. This is my fault. So, I and I alone need to find a solution to it.

I probably have around 15,000 to play with if I max out my cards. So, again, this is the part where Ellie would be looking at me as if I have lost my mind – which, of course, I have.

Or have I? You know you have to speculate to accumulate wealth, which in this case couldn't be truer. When this process is over, we're going to be super-filthy rich. Or, well, at least we will by my standards, anyway. We just have to get there.

And no, I haven't discussed money with my wife, and that's because she's already given enough. She's already *been through* enough.

Of course, there's always David.

NO!

Ellie doesn't know this, and try not to be shocked, but in a previous life, I wasn't the best at managing my money. Secrets, illicit activities, and, dare I say it, a wife who likes expensive things can prove costly. Especially in London.

Alright, I know, but you can quit your judging. It's not as if you don't have any secrets from those closest to you. Come on. Be honest. What kind of secret about yourself are you harbouring from those nearest and dearest to you right now? And by that, I mean things that you have done in your life that you would never want them to know about.

Exactly. Sometimes… well, lies are more flexible.

Besides, that was then. This is now.

And now, I am staring at what looks like a whole football field of shelves that starts and disappears somewhere into infinity, stacked with different shades of paint.

Fu—nk.

***

The DIY superstore is at least an hour's drive from Dolce Vita, which means that it's early afternoon by the time I get back. The once enthusiastic morning sun is already waning in a coral blue sky.

It turned out to be a productive trip. I feel like I have some good ideas about what can be done with the place, along with some indication of just how much some of the materials are going to cost.

And, since I'm feeling optimistic, a better grasp of the most logical ways to fund all this.

And as tempting as the whole card thing is, it's kind of reckless… especially given my history. Somewhat impractical, too, if we hire labourers, which is most likely going to have to happen, as there's no way I can take on all of the jobs myself. Certainly not if we want to finish within this century.

Me, one of those blokes that starts house renovations running in one year and still hasn't finished in the next or the next or the next after that.

The image of that brings a smile to my face as I imagine Ellie stuck out here in twelve months with dust sheets as curtains and paint pots as lamp holders. Although, maybe for maximum effect, I should buy one of those vintage motorbikes so that I can disassemble it on the kitchen island. It could live there like an expensive piece of art with grease and grime all over. I could wear one of those wife-beater vests, too, to complete the image!

I'm laughing to myself like a madman now. Oh, if only it were more practical, as I would love to do it as a laugh and have Ellie come home to it. I could tell her that there's no room on the dining table because I've disassembled everything that we have, so that we'll be forced to eat TV dinners off our laps. Priceless!

I'm still laughing as I walk up the garden path, but this fades when I see something that has me stopping in my tracks.

The front door, the kitchen, and the photography room windows are wide open. And I mean *wide open* like Ellie's decided on a spontaneous winter clean. And yet, for someone who has rolled up her sleeves, wrapped her hair in a headscarf, and donned rubber gloves like a land army girl, it's all a bit quiet.

No music. No lights, and probably freezing in there, too.

I say this because my breath is fogging out in front of me. And, as we've already established, Ellie hates the cold.

"Ellie!" I call out, expecting her face to appear at one of the windows.

It doesn't.

Everything's remains eerily quiet, but for the chorus of birds and the natter of seagulls who love using the roof as their personal sun lounger.

At the front door, I call again, "El?"

Still nothing.

The den is empty, too.

So, I look down the hallway. All the doors are closed and it's black in there. I smother a flare of irritation and yell, "Ellie?!"

I wait. Listening for creak or movement. Anything. But I get nothing.

Maybe she went for a walk…. And left the house wide open? No, she wouldn't do that. She's from the city. She doesn't believe in all that neighbourly stuff. She believes in doors and locks. We both do.

Although, back in London, she did have a horrible habit of forgetting her keys, so she would leave a spare one under the plant pot outside our door – which, for me, given how she felt about security, made no sense.

This is the very reason why I'm now wondering what the actual fu–nk she is playing at.

"EL!"

Silence.

I drop the bags and walk through the den to the archway and dining room.

Ellie, bundled in a coat and woollen hat, is sitting in front of her laptop at the dining table, but she yelps and throws a hand to her chest at the moment she sees me appear in the archway.

"Jesus Christ! Marco!" She yanks earphones from her ears. "You scared the shit out of me!"

"I called you, but you didn't answer," I say.

"I had my earphones in," she breathes out.

"Yeah. I noticed," I say with a smile, secretly enjoying the fact that I made her jump. Don't worry, though, she's done worse to me many times. It's how we roll. "What's going on?" I ask, approaching the table.

"Oh, nothing much. I've just started work on that

presentation for David," she says, hunching her shoulders against the cold.

"No. I mean the get-up." I make a show of looking at her clothing.

"Oh, right. As much as I hate to say this, I think the heating's packed up. It's absolutely freezing in here. I can see the breath in front of my face. Look." She demonstrates by breathing into the air in front of me. "I wanted to check the boiler, but I don't even know where that thing lives. Do you?"

I squint at her. "Well, if you're that cold, why did you throw the doors and windows open?"

"What do you mean?"

"I just got back, and the front door and all the windows are wide open."

She pulls a face and looks back at her screen. "Well, I didn't open them."

I laugh, but it's an incredulous sound. "El, you're the only person here."

"So?" she asks without looking up.

"What do you mean, *so*, El?" But I don't wait for an answer, as I get the distinct feeling I'm not going to get one. I sigh. "Don't worry about it."

When El has something on her mind, especially when it has something to do with work and she's in the so-called zone, she has this terrible habit of ignoring people. She just stares at her screen and completely blanks you. And when she isn't, she can hold an entire conversation without even looking at you. She used to do it with Toby, too, and it used to piss me off because it wasn't exactly setting a good example for the little man.

Yes, and you're probably thinking, given my past, *You're the one to talk*. That's exactly what she would say, but my being a dick had nothing to do with teaching our child that it's basic manners to look at someone when they're talking to you.

And yet, I swallow how I'm feeling. "Would you like a cup of tea?" I ask.

"I could murder a cup of coffee," she says, looking up.

"Oh, heard that, though, didn't you?" I ask, but it's with a smile. Life's too short.

She throws a fake smile back.

I plant a kiss in her hair and then make my way across the room to the door leading out into the corridor of doom, and that's when I remember. "Oh, and El, I thought we agreed we were going to leave these doors open to let the light into the corridor?"

"What?" she mumbles without bothering to turn around.

I sigh and yank the door open, pushing it as wide as it will go.

9. THE WOODS

Mid-life crisis; the catch-all for the impulsive exploits of millions of men (and women) of middle age; bloke in his fifties decides to buy himself a new car or hook a new girlfriend, generally a few generations younger than him.

The reality is more than often the opposite. *It* – the so-called *crisis* – doesn't always happen at a specific age, and nor does it happen just once, but multiple times, generally when you least expect it. One day, you'll wake up, look in the mirror, and: *How the fu–n did I get here? What have I done with my life? What exactly do I have to show for it? And shit and double fu–n, is that all the years I have left on average?*

Cue the compulsion to devour life for all it has to offer and cling onto the ravaged remains of youth by rediscovering those things that were popular during our most youthful years.

No, I didn't wake up today and start browsing the web for sports cars, and, yes, I'll say it, girls, nor did I don my *CHOOSE LIFE* t-shirt and start singing along to Wham songs. As if. Shit, just thinking about that era and knowing I was around for it makes me feel old.

No, the trigger for me was looking at my naked form in the mirror and wondering, *Where the fu–nk did those love handles come from?*

And I remembered. Ever since I've arrived here, both in my previous visit – yes, even then – and again now, I keep threatening to take up jogging. I mean, seriously, you couldn't dream of a more majestic circuit than the coastline and shore around here, and yet, I've still been unable to get my arse out there.

Well, that's all changing right now. In fact, I am currently easing myself into an old pair of trainers that I remember exiling to the back of the closet, where I knew they'd be unable to shame me.

Until now.

Because, as I grimace and grunt, I realise that the *easing* is more like *squeezing* and *forcing*. It's almost as if the bloody things have been sulking all this time and are now refusing to fulfil their purpose.

Have my feet grown bigger? Is that even possible?

I feel like I've already had a workout, just getting into the things!

Aaargh! There!

It's OK. I'm good. They're on. *A bit snug, maybe, but they'll do*, I conclude as I proudly test-walk them around the lounge.

I'm wearing shorts, T-shirt, and fleece, and I'm ready.

If I may say so myself, because nobody has mentioned it in a while, I do have fairly decent legs. They're straight with nicely rounded knees and just enough hair to bolster my masculinity, but not too much to make me look like the Wolverine.

I hop and jog, first in place and then to the door, a bit like a boxer before a match, but I'm soon put back in my place when I open the front door and an icy breeze punches me in the face.

Wow. Hello to you, too.

Winter is pretty much here, and I don't rate our chances of being out before Christmas, but Lucinda feels good about it, provided we can get the renovations done within the next couple of weeks, and who am I to question a professional?

I leave the house, pulling the door firmly shut behind me – primarily to keep the freeze out rather than trespassers. Not that it feels much better inside. When I get back, I already have the unenviable tasks of hunting down the heater, boiler, or whatever the hell is responsible for running the bloody storage heaters in that place. That, and/or making a fire. Ideally, I'd like to get it sorted before Ellie wakes up.

And so, zipping up the fleece as far as it will go, I launch myself up the gravel path. That's right, I'm heading towards the small woodland area that acts as a shield between us and the rest of the village.

The natural tendency, given our location, is to gravitate towards the shoreline, but I concluded a few days back that we haven't met our immediate neighbours, and I'm curious to know who exactly woke me up last night.

Something, and I don't know what, kept crying out during the night. I have no idea what it was. I'm assuming it's an animal of some kind, as it was a weird, pitiful sound. I'm thinking maybe a fox. I know they make all kinds of strange noises. Whatever it was, it sounded like it was slowly being murdered… loudly.

Although, not loud enough to wake my wife, apparently, as she appeared to sleep through the racket with no problem and is still sleeping now.

At first, I thought it was coming from the village, but when I went into the guest room to look, it sounded much closer. As if it were coming from just beyond the trees. And so, like any rational male, I concluded that it should be investigated… during the safe light of day, of course. No point in going wandering out in the dark like one of those airheads in a horror movie. That's just stupid. Not that I expect anything horrific to happen, but more, well, it makes sense to go during the day. Doesn't it? So that I can see better and all that.

I reach the edge of the trees, breath fogging out in font me, but pause as a flock of excited seagulls glide overhead toward a calm ocean and the faint yet burgeoning orange crest of another beautiful sunrise. The air is bitingly crisp, and heady with the aroma of wood-burning which fills me with a certain sense of nostalgia for a childhood I may have had, but don't remember. Of home cooking, family gatherings, and closeness. Of Sunday lunches and siestas. Of train journeys through moonlit alps and early-morning breakfasts of paninis hastily purchased through carriage windows.

I go through the ritual in my head. I understand that these memories may not be real and that they may be a fabrication of my mind, as it seeks to protect me from the bad things that happened to me as a child by overwriting the rotten with the good. Which. I have to admit, is an amazing human coping mechanism. It means I no longer remember the worst bits. Unfortunately, it also means I can't remember some of the good bits, either.

Dr Holmes thinks that, now that we've untapped that well during therapy, there's a good chance some other stuff may come back. But I've already concluded that if it's shit like what happened down on the beach, I'd rather it didn't bother.

Either way, I'm holding onto the good memories of my travels to Italy because even I know that there has got to be something good about my past.

I breathe in the woody scent again, as if to validate that, and it fills me with a sense of peace that I don't think I've felt in a long time. Not since early morning fishing trips with Toby.

And it's right now, in moments like these, that I can't even imagine returning to the city. I know Ellie's keen, but me, well, I just feel that London is where we used to be with our son, and the country… well, that's who we are now.

Daylight fades as I follow what appears to be a path out of the early morning light and into the long shadows cast by the bare limbs of trees that have long been stripped of their summer beauty. Their leaves, like lovers' discarded clothing, cover the ground. The smell of their decomposition fills the air with a rich, damp aroma that I'm sucking in like it's a designer fragrance.

It feels good to be running, to be working out some of the negative energy that I've accumulated over the past few months.

I have to duck occasionally to avoid some of the spindly tree branches that keep reaching down like claws to grab at me as I don't fancy–

"FUUU-NK!" Who put that root there?

I crash down, hands-first, with a heavy thud, and then I perform a stuntman roll into a pile of leaves that, like butterflies, are startled and then flutter down all around me.

"Shit!" I exhale as I roll to a stop on my side and take several seconds to recover, wheezing and sucking in the rich mossy scent I've just unearthed.

Crows caw loudly and flap overhead, irritated by my noise pollution.

Because that's how it sounds. This place of sun flares and dappled shadows is otherwise soundproofed from the world outside, but for my rasping breaths and the occasional creak and snap of twigs from the wildlife that inhabits this place.

At least, I hope it's the wildlife I'm hearing.

With a groan, I place a palm into the leafy sludge and push myself up into a sitting position.

The stinging on my hand alerts me to the fact that I must have grazed it on a piece of bark or something. I'm otherwise OK. Damp with muddy knees and sporting a new cloak of desiccated leaves but OK.

My pride's fine, too, because a quick glance around me confirms that I'm alone in here. Although, I should hope so because, after all, this is part of the so-called estate. I wonder if Lucinda has taken that into account. I don't remember her mentioning it, so I make a mental note to make sure I check the property description once the marketing information has been published.

Then, I sit here for a few minutes listening to nature; more wings fluttering, black birds calling, wood pigeons cooing, seagulls squawking, and even the very faint rumble of the ocean. Wow, you can still hear it even in here–

Another sound pushes its way into the morning chorus, and I check myself because I'm wondering if I'm imagining it… until it's accompanied by a rustle of leaves.

I snap my head around to tune in.

Yes. There! About fifteen feet behind me; movement beyond the body of a fallen tree. Something big enough to move the leaves.

Shit.

Yeah, I'm man enough to admit that, as I sit on the ground with a damp patch fast spreading through my shorts, that I'm feeling just a tad apprehensive… as I have no clue what's lurking behind there.

Slowly, I move onto my knees and twist into the sound as I rise back onto my feet. I give everything a quick test. Yeah. All seems to be in working order. Just this graze on my hand, but otherwise, I think I'm fine.

Rustle.

Or is that digging? Sniffing? Scuffling?

Slowly, I inch my way towards the noise as a breeze whips up out of nowhere and starts howling through the trees, shaking the remaining leaves that are still clinging on for dear life, causing them to hiss in alarm.

Scuffle. Rustle.

I'm about ten feet away now, and my heart is wondering why I'm approaching whatever it is when the safety of the makeshift path is beckoning me to resume my journey.

Eight feet. Wooden claws reach down and poke at my face as if they don't want me to venture any further, and yet, still, I'm unable to stop, unable to resist the compulsion to see what's behind here.

Five feet.

And I freeze, ducking instinctively as a blood-curdling shriek fills the air.

It's a woman!

Oh fu–n! It's a woman and she's screaming!

Oh shit.

Someone is being attacked. Here in my woods?

What the....?

I've no idea how to proceed. I could make the leap over the log and hope to scare the attacker away. Anybody who knows me knows that, for all my reluctance to investigate things that go bump in the night, I'm no stranger to a fist fight. And my body is already telling me that it's up for it. Adrenaline coursing. Blood pumping.

But, on the other hand, what if he's armed? I'd be just as helpless as his victim.

Shit.

I look around for something, anything to use as a weapon and, not surprisingly, there's no handy gun, baseball bat, or even fireplace poker that I can brandish, but there is a handy broken branch. It isn't seriously hefty, but good enough for me to wave it at anyone to show them that I'm not fu–ssing around and that I mean business.

I reach down and grab the thing just as another nerve-jangling scream fills the air. Only, this one is different. This one is more of an angry chatter than one continuous sound. It's scratchy, guttural, and, by the scuffling sound accompanying it, it isn't a bird.

Despite the thumping in my chest and every other rational sense, I step closer. I need to find out what's going on. I need to silence the harrowing yowling which has just been joined by another repetitive squeal.

It isn't a woman. It's some kind of animal.

Closer.

Leaves flutter.

Closer.

The wind tugs at my hair.

Closer.

I can almost see over the moss-riddled wood now. My heart wants to leave and run back to the house, and I want to join it.

Ellie.

Can she hear this? Can anyone?

My head is pounding to the point of hurting, and I realise it's because I'm screwing up my face against the fingernails-on-blackboard ruckus.

And then, finally, I see it; compost, like an erupting oil well, flying in an arc into the air and then falling down accompanied by clumps of vegetation. Then, I see the bushy white tail and rusty-red fur.

The fox, probably a vixen from the sound of that cry, is alternating between frustrated screeches and digging, presumably to get at its quarry. The howls become progressively louder as the frustration builds and what I can only assume is some kind of dirt sanctuary is systematically relocated by a rapid and determined set of claws.

The hunter is so fixated on its objective that it doesn't even notice me peering over the tree trunk, makeshift weapon in hand, easily within bludgeoning distance.

And I hesitate.

This is just nature's way. I should just go about my day as this potential mother is going about hers, hunting for food to feed her family.

But something tells me that I can't.

I can't because there's something familiar about the wailing that I realise now is coming out of that hole in the ground. I recognise it because, somewhere in the depths of my memory, I've heard it before. I know it. And, as I come to that realisation, I hear a squeal that shreds through the pit of my stomach like sharp claws; the fox's razor-sharp teeth have latched onto its prey and it is now tugging the creature out of the dirt in a series of grunts, tail flicks, and growls.

"NO!" is my angry contribution.

The fox freezes. Head and snout still partially buried in the dirt, it observes me, warily. Creepily, it even glances at the weapon in my hand as if assessing how much real damage I could inflict before, to my astonishment, resuming its excavation.

"Oi! I said stop!" I yell, waving the stick at the animal. It freezes again. Keen eyes observing the lump of wood in my hand. And yet, seconds later, it continues its tug of war, eliciting a series of agonising yelps from its victim.

I lose it. "Oi, you little shit, get out of here!" I roar angrily, poking its furry butt with the stick, but the animal is determined. It isn't going to leave without its prize, and to that end, it twists its body away from me while tugging at the hapless thing locked in its jaws – which is slowly but surely emerging from its hidey-hole through a curtain of dirt. Its pitiful wails ring through the trees, scaring a group of voyeuristic crows from their perch in an indignant cacophony of wing flaps and screeches.

The fox and I must have both been temporarily distracted because, when I look back down, I notice that it's temporarily lost its grip on its prey, which has retreated back into what's left of its compost bunker. Its hysterical whimpering now a muffled drone.

Undaunted, the fox produces some kind of guttural sound which I assume is a growl while seeking to intimidate me by presenting a set of sharp, vampiric teeth. Then, cautiously, and without ever taking its eyes off me, it begins to ease itself towards the hole in the ground once more.

That does it, you little fu–xer!

In one swift movement, I'm over the trunk and standing directly in front of the fox's quarry. It makes a show of jumping away from me, but doesn't leave.

I squint incredulously. How bloody hungry is this shit? "Get the fu–dge away from here before I bash your fu–dging head in!" I rage, waving the stick at it, but as I do, the little bastard leaps forward and grabs the end in its mouth, and with slathering teeth, it attempts to wrestle it out of my hand.

"Oh, like that is it," I snarl, and yank my weapon towards me while holding out my right foot, slamming the fox's face into my trainer and instantly realising my mistake.

It yelps, but recovers and starts snapping at my shoe; I snatch it away just in time, replacing it with a swing of the stick – which it evades by expertly leaping backward once more.

I'm hoping that's the end of it, but the thing is seriously pissed off. Ears folded back, black eyes narrowed to slits, and bushy tail up for ballast, it rears up and back towards me with a snarl of bloodstained teeth.

Now, there's saliva dripping from those pointy things, and I get a real pang of fear. I know rabies has been eradicated from the British Isles for some time, but there's no telling what this thing, as cute as it may look, when calm, is carrying.

"Get out of it! You little shit!" I scream.

It leaps back instinctively, but its slitty, menacing eyes are still locked on me. "Go on! Get lost! Go on! There's nothing here for you! Go! Go!" I yell, waving the stick once more.

After hesitating a few more seconds, and with one final glance behind me – presumably at what could have been breakfast – realising that it has met its match, the fox turns and reluctantly trots back into the trees.

I wait until that reddish-brown streak of colour dissolves to grey before finally turning and falling to my knees.

I'm panting. Heart thumping. That was as scary as it was exhilarating.

There isn't much left of the occupant's dugout. It's now just a mangled mess of freshly dug earth, leaves, and blood. A lot of blood.

I can only assume that that heart-wrenching wailing was in response to some kind of a wound or wounds that this thing has sustained, which spurs me and gives me pause in equal measure; if this thing is wounded, then it's going to need help and it probably won't be in the mood for another stranger trying to evict it from its hideout. And right now, I can't see much. It's managed to retreat into what's left of the lair. All I can see is a blood-drenched stump and a black snout, so I move in for a closer look, lowering my head to the entrance. But it's hard to tell what I'm looking at within the collapsed earth.

So, I unzip my fleece pocket, pull out my phone, and tap it a few times to turn on the light. When I point this into the gloom of the cavity, what blinks back at me are two giant brown eyes.

"What the…" I breathe. It looks like a baby seal, but I'm guessing it isn't. It's much smaller than that, too.

I think it's a puppy.

Jesus! Was that fox really trying to drag this poor thing home? Is food really that scarce around here?

I glance around to see if there's anybody or anything around who can help while also making sure that Rusty the fox isn't making a reappearance.

He/she isn't.

So, I turn back to the matter at hand. Slowly and gently, I reach towards the blinking eyes. As I do so, the pitiful whimpering resumes and my heart melts. But I need to act fast if I'm going to make a difference, as I don't know the extent of its injuries, and based on what I've seen so far, there's a good chance it might bleed out.

So, to avoid unnecessarily distressing the animal further, I pocket my phone and, instead of reaching in through the entrance to the burrow, I start digging from the top. The compost is loose, so it isn't long before I see patches of dirt-smeared golden fur and part of a short, stumpy tail.

Oh, wow.

"It's OK, buddy. It's OK," I coo as I carefully pry the earth apart to expose the animal. It's coated in dirt, leaves, and blood that judder as it shivers. Cold. Shock.

As I reach down, it cowers onto its side and resumes its yowling, eyes full of terror as it watches my hands drift closer.

"It's OK, buddy. It's alright. I'm not going to hurt you. No, I'm not going to hurt you," I say as I brush away its coat of earth and dry leaves to find that it has two hanging curtains for ears. The right ear is hanging in two separate flaps caked in blood, and it's this that I assume the fox likely managed to latch onto before it ripped in half.

"It's OK, buddy. It's OK."

But the puppy isn't looking at me anymore. Instead, it has sunk its bloody snout into the dirt as if resigning itself to its fate.

"Oh, no, you don't," I say, springing into action by removing my fleece and tying the two arms together to form some semblance of a blanket. Then, I reach down and lift the animal up, drawing another series of pained yelps.

"I know, buddy. I know," I say, lifting the small bundle that can't be more than three or maybe four pounds, and placing it onto the makeshift bed I've created. I notice that it's a boy and that he has a puncture wound on his left paw. And I don't know if he's in shock, but I'm finding the fact that he's suddenly fallen silent troubling. He's obviously in a bad way, and I'm already feeling anguished at the prospect that he might check out on me... which is why I get moving.

The journey out of the woods seems to take much longer than it did going in, but all the time, I'm holding the bundle close to my chest in an effort to radiate what little heat I may have to offer. Still, the dog's eyes are glazing over. Its body is limp, and I'm surprised by how much that's distressing me.

I have no clue where the nearest vet is, nor how to get there, but a quick internet search tells me that there's one in the next town, which is about seven miles of windy roads away.

I consider running upstairs to let Ellie know what's happening and where I'm going, but she'll inevitably start asking questions, which is time I don't have. Besides, she's probably still sleeping and there's no point in waking her. I'll message from the vet's office.

And so barely a minute has passed, and I've been inside to grab keys and carefully laid the bundle on the passenger seat. There's no way to secure it, so I'm going to have to hold him with one hand as I drive. On the bright side, the sun is up and slowly burning away the early morning mist as our old Volvo makes its way out of the village and through twisty, narrowed lanes and roads, slicing through brown fields.

You'll be pleased to know that, despite the many instigations to do so, I haven't yet sworn once at oncoming cars, slow-moving tractors, and other vehicles that, unlike me, appear in no particular hurry to be anywhere.

I keep glancing over at the bundle in the passenger seat as I maintain one hand extended to secure it, my other on the steering wheel. It doesn't make for easy gear shifting, but what can I say? I'm resourceful.

Kind of.

It seems to take forever for me to find the tiny stone house masquerading as a veterinary surgery, and that's despite three wrong turns and several drivers giving me the finger for driving up a one-way street.

Chill, you psychos! It's not like we're moving faster than ten bloody miles an hour here!

I haven't been able to get a look at the passenger for some time now, and haven't sensed any movement whatsoever; I'm as panicked by this as I was that day with Toby.

Not again.

Toby.

That thought punches me in the gut and I feel like I want to roll down the window and wretch, and if I didn't have to be somewhere, I probably would allow myself the luxury, but I can't because–

Finally! A sign for *Church Lane Veterinary Clinic.*

I yank the steering wheel right, eliciting an angry horn blast from the car behind me.

You'll get over it.

Luckily, the car park is empty. Not that it matters, because I pull up outside the front door anyway as if it's A&E, with the image of me running in there and yelling, *Help! I need some help here!* in a scene worthy of *ER.*

No such drama, though, because my movie debut ends when I reach the front door and see the hours of operation. 09:00 to 18:30.

It's barely 08:30.

"You've got to be fu-nky joking!" I yell.

Me and the bundle in my arms step back and scan the building as if looking for an open window to climb into.

It's all locked up.

I can feel a throbbing in my temple. My anxiety levels are rising, and this is made worse when I look down at the would-be patient in my arms to see that his eyes are closed, and that he remains motionless.

"You're going to be OK, buddy," I coo, but I think that's more to reassure myself than the pup.

I look around. The street's deserted, but for the shadows moving with the rise of the morning sun. I can feel the frustration engulfing me now, just as it did that day, and I feel like I'm choking. Like I'm going to suffocate. My brain is racing through a whole raft of scenarios, none of which are practical or rational, and yet....

Get a grip, Battista. Now's not the time to fall apart. Breathe. Remember your breathing.

There isn't another vet for miles. I remember that from the internet search. So, I look back at the door and consider just how much it would take to break into this one.

10. BREAKING IN

I've made many mistakes in my life. Breaking and entering into a veterinarian's clinic because of a wounded puppy may well appear to be an adequate justification of the means, but nonetheless, it remains a crap idea.

Not least of all because I'm still going to need an actual trained veterinarian to treat the puppy. There's no point breaking into the place if I'm clueless about what to do. I need the bloody professional inside, which is why, out of pure frustration, I start thumping on the door – angrily.

After what feels like minutes of making my knuckles red and raw, I finally give up and start trudging back to the car when…

I hear a key in the lock and instantly turn back. There's someone standing behind the glass!

I rush back, and… I recognise that face. I'd recognise her anywhere.

She gawks at me and then at the bundle in my arms.

I nod at the door handle a couple of times before she awakes from her spell and finally pushes it open, squinting into the morning sun.

"Marco?"

"Sarah?"

That's all we both appear capable of saying before I eventually add, "What are you doing here?"

"I work here."

"I thought you worked at the store in the village."

"Yeah, I help out there occasionally. On weekends mostly, but this is my day job."

"You're a vet?" I ask incredulously, taking in the light blue scrubs she's dressed in and not believing my luck.

"Nurse," she says churlishly.

She looks different today. More grown-up. Professional, with her hair secured into a cute ponytail and green eyes glittering behind a pair of round-rimmed glasses.

"What have you got there?" she asks, peering into my arms.

"It's why I'm here," I say, holding up the bundle. "I've literally just snatched him out of the jaws of death," I add breathlessly, as if it's still happening. When Sarah cocks her head, I add, "A fox."

"Oh no. Poor thing!"

"Sarah, I know you aren't open, but I don't know where else to go."

I watch her bite her lip. "Well, the vet isn't here yet, but come inside and I'll see what I can do," she says, standing aside.

I carry the patient through a small cubicle of a waiting room that's empty, but for the people and pets smiling at me from wall posters promoting pet hygiene and insurance, and we go on through to a larger, oblong room lined with cages.

Dogs bark loudly, and I'm half expecting the little thing in my arms to respond, but it doesn't. It remains ragdoll limp, and I'm once again hoping we're not too late.

We enter a small examination room. It's cold in here. The air smells stale and is ripe with disinfectant.

Sarah stands behind the examination bench and rests her hands on it expectantly, as if she's ready to start some procedure. I take my cue and gently lay the bundle in front of her.

"Wow, he's lost quite a bit of blood," she remarks, which does nothing to allay my fears.

Then, she gently peels back the sodden material of my fleece to get a better look at the patient. "Oh no, you have been through it, haven't you?" she asks softly. Then, "OK… first things first." She turns to the nearby sink and pulls on gloves. After that, she retrieves gauze, cotton pads, swabs, and a plastic bottle full of clear liquid from one of the overhead cupboards. She pours some of the liquid into a petri dish and then, as the smell of alcohol fills the air, rips open the packet of swabs, dips one into the liquid, and gently dabs at the puppy's ripped ear.

It whimpers in response to the chemical, which is probably stinging like hell, and the thought of telling her to stop crosses my mind, but I dismiss it. She's helping, and I'm grateful to her.

This is the first time that I get a good look at the puppy. I'm no expert, but he can't be more than six or seven weeks old. The blood from his wounded ear has caked the side of his face, and the blood from his wounded paw has turned what I think is supposed to be gold fur into a rusty red.

I watch Sarah expertly go about her work as if she's done this many times before. She gently probes and prods the animal all over his body and waits for a reaction. I assume she's checking for internal injuries. The puppy doesn't react, and I'm hoping that's because there aren't any and not because he's given up the fight.

Sarah uses a damp cloth to gently rub away the grime from the patient's body ending with another gentle prod of the small, furry belly. "I don't think he has any internal injuries," she confirms, suddenly breaking the lullaby of her cooing. "But there is this torn ear. I'm not sure, but he may need stiches… although, from what I can tell, the ear itself isn't damaged. Then, there's this large puncture wound on his paw."

"Probably where the fox was trying to drag him away," I contribute.

"He may need a shot for that, as we don't know what the fox was carrying, if anything." She looks up at me. "He's lucky you found him when you did."

I nod, noticing that her green eyes have flecks of brown in them.

"Is he going to be OK?" I ask, moving around so I can get a better look at the animal – because he doesn't seem to be moving. Then, I crouch down so that my face is level with his and I see those dark doe-eyes – *Toby* – lifelessly staring forward with just the occasional blink as the puppy's body rocks with the occasional stroke of Sarah's cleansing hand.

"I don't know," she responds soberly. "I mean, I can clean

him up, tend to the wounds, but we're going to need the vet to take a look at him."

"You rang," a voice says, and we both look up.

There's a man in the doorway. My age, carrying maybe a few more pounds, a receding hairline, bundled in an anorak and hat.

"Morning, Simon."

"What have we got here, then?" he asks with a smile and no discernible accent, looking at the both of us and then the patient on what is, presumably, his bench.

"An emergency walk-in. Been mauled by a fox."

"I don't suppose there's time for a cuppa?" he asks, pulling off his hat.

My anxiety is about to respond, but I have the presence of mind to realise that it's a rhetorical question since the man is already slipping out of his coat and making his way over to us.

It takes almost an hour for the doctor to treat the injured puppy that he confirms is a boy and that, at less than a foot long, can't be more than nine weeks old.

By this time, the tiny waiting room is full, presumably with patients who already have an appointment. And it's odd, because normally I wouldn't give a shit about them. I got here first, so it's tough tits. But I do today, because I'm humbled and so grateful that the vet arrived when he did, and that he forsook his morning cuppa to treat the little boy for his wounds, and although the puppy isn't yet out of danger, the prognosis is good. The vet thinks the blood loss looked worse than it was and doesn't believe the dog has any internal injuries. He also gave him a couple of shots against possible infections.

We speculated as to what such a young puppy might be doing out in the woods alone. Was the litter birthed there? Could there have been other puppies nearby? I don't think so… I would have heard them, surely. Was he carried away from somebody's garden? If so, there's most likely a frantic owner out there somewhere, I would think.

This, in turn, prompted a debate about the meaning of that word, 'owner'.

Did you know that, by British law, a pet is classed as the *property* of its owner? Property. Like an old vacuum cleaner or toaster.

I didn't even remember I knew this until the conversation reminded me of an article I read once, which talked of some celebrity supporting a campaign for a change to the law so that pets could be reclassed as *family.*

"Marco?"

It's Sarah.

"Yeah."

"Everything OK?"

"Oh, yes, Sarah. Fine. Thanks."

We're standing at a bench in the backroom now, where all of the cages are. Sarah has placed the patient in a medium-sized dogfood box lined with newspaper. He actually looks quite funny with the tiny swaddling over his ear and that bandaged paw. I'm choosing to cling to the comedic impression rather than how vulnerable and utterly adorable he looks right now.

"So, are you sure it's OK for me to take him back tonight? Don't you want to keep him in for observation or something? I mean, he looked like he was at death's door."

I must have a worried look on my face because Sarah reaches out and touches my arm. "You're going to be fine. Just follow the advice the vet gave you." Here, she takes one of the surgery's business cards and writes on the back. "This is my number. Keep an eye on him, and if there are any problems, give me a call, but he's going to be fine. He just needs some rest, and some food and fluids as directed." There's a mixture of warmth and sternness to her voice, like she's a mother encouraging her son to brave school or something. "You obviously don't have kids," she says with a smile, which I'm guessing is supposed to be a statement, but sounds more like a question. As if she's trying to find out something out about me. Of course, I could be reading into that given that I've probably behaved like a surrogate, overwrought parent.

Parent.

"No. Um. No children," I say, which is awful (I know) but I don't know if I can bear another one those sympathetic, pitiful looks that people give when faced with the awkward reality that your one and only son has died.

"You're going to be fine," she repeats. "Just follow the instructions."

"Yes, miss," I say. "Keep a close eye on him. Check for infection. Fluids. Food if possible. Although, he probably won't be up for much for a while."

"It's mostly shock. He's a baby, remember? I've put formula and some of the food pouches in here," she says, handing me a separate plastic bag. "I've seen puppies with far worse injuries make almost immediate recoveries." The last line has been added as she traces her finger over the puppy's now almost golden fur. "Also, don't worry too much if the bandage comes off his ear. We could do with the air getting to that wound. He's bound to paw at it once he's feeling perkier. We just don't want him it to get infected."

"OK," I say apprehensively. Like I've never held a baby in my arms before.

Maybe that's exactly it. If I were psychoanalysing myself, which I'm not – but am I? – would I be doubting myself with a puppy because of what happened?

Shit.

I guess I've got much bigger issues than I thought if I no longer trust myself to take care of another living, breathing thing.

"What are you going to do with him? Are you going to keep him?" Sarah asks, interrupting my thoughts.

"Keep him? No. I suppose I need to try and find his owner."

"How are you going to go about that?"

I laugh. "I have no idea."

There's an awkward moment in which the hubbub of people and their pets joins us from the waiting room.

"Oh. I'm sorry. I've been prattling on. I should let you get back to all these other patients," I say.

"You're right. I should."

"Sarah. I…"

The words drown in my mouth, and she instantly puts another reassuring hand on mine.

"I," I stutter. What the eff is wrong with me? Spit it out, man! "I… I'm ashamed to say it, but I don't have my wallet on me. As you know, I was out, running–"

"Don't worry about it," she says. "I'll take care of it for now. Just ring a card through when you get the chance."

"Are you sure?"

She nods eagerly.

"Thank you so much. I really appreciate it," I say. And then it's my turn to place a hand on hers. "I really do."

"You're most welcome," she says aloud – probably for the benefit of her boss, who has popped his head out of the examination room doorway.

And so, with the dogfood box, now a makeshift carrier, in hand, I make my way through a packed waiting room.

I keep my head down, avoiding all eye contact, and leave the place as fast as I can.

11. HOME

LATE MORNING.

The dogfood box and its contents are too small to be strapped in with a seatbelt, so the journey home is made pretty much in the same way as it was coming out; with one hand on the steering wheel and the other holding onto it.

By the time we get back to Dolce Vita, the sun is already at work painting colour and beauty on the land from its perch in a cloud-streaked sky.

Ellie is in the kitchen making coffee with one hand while holding her mobile phone to her ear with the other. When I appear in the doorway, she says, "OK, well, I've got to go now. I'll message you later. Bye." She disconnects the call, slips the phone into the back of her figure-hugging jeans, and says, "There you are. I noticed the car was gone and sent you messages. What happened? I thought you said you were going running?"

"I did."

She laughs. "In the car?"

My only response is a smile because, as cheesy as this is going to sound, I'm stunned by the sight of my smiling wife in her skinny blue jeans and a tight white T-shirt. Yes, I'm hearing it – figure-hugging, tight white shirt – but I am a hot-blooded male after all. Especially when she's wearing that girly ponytail of hers. Something about girls and ponytails. Psychologically, you can infer whatever you like from that, but just remember that, to the pure, all is pure.

"What?" she asks, pausing as she emerges from the fridge with a bottle of milk. I'm assuming I was staring at her.

"I've got a surprise for you?"

"Oh, right," she says.

"Yep. Come and see."

"Can I get coffee first?"

I lift my eyebrows.

"OK…." She sets the milk down on the counter and follows me out of the kitchen and into the effing gloomy hallway because, once again, she keeps closing all the doors (but we're not going to think about that), and into the sunlit lounge.

I go over to the box on the coffee table and look down at it. Ellie's approach is a cautious one, more as if I've brought a potential bomb than a surprise.

"Open it," I say with a smile.

She looks at me, the box, and back at me again.

The carton remains still. So much so that my stomach is lurches. I did check before I left it here, but still… no movement it starting to make me anxious.

"Go on," I say, forcing a smile.

Ellie complies by kneeling, gingerly unfolding the flaps, and then peeking inside. Instantly, she throws her hands to her mouth. "Oh my God…" she breathes. "What happened to him? He looks hurt."

"He's sedated for the pain."

"Where did you find him?" she whispers incredulously, gently tracing a finger over the puppy's back.

"I literally saved him from the jaws of death. A fox was trying to have him for breakfast."

"No!" she says incredulously. "Poor thing."

"I had to drive him to the vet in the next town to get him fixed up."

"Any idea where he came from?"

I shake my head, thoughtfully. "No."

"He must have been somehow separated from the rest of his litter."

"That's what I thought."

"Oh, you poor baby," she says, gently caressing the dog's long and crinkly good ear. "Do you know what it is?"

I nod. "A Golden Retriever," I say proudly, as if I personally gave birth to the pup. Then, somewhat idiotically, I follow that up with a grin and say, "Toby's favourite. Do you remember how he kept asking for one at the flat? He loved their crinkly ears and used to go on about what a fantastic breed they are. So good that they're trained as service dogs for the blind. I remember he…."

Oh, fu–dge. I trail off because I notice that my wife has now retracted her hand and is standing once more.

"So, what's the plan?" she asks plainly, as if I hadn't just spoken those words.

"What do you mean?"

"Well, are you going to put an ad in the shop, take him to the police, what?"

"Well, I haven't really thought about it, but–"

"Great idea. Someone is bound to come forward. People are looking for puppies all the time."

"Wait, what? I thought you meant track down the owner."

"Well, if that works, then even better. I mean, someone must be missing it."

I don't say anything because I'm not sure what to say. I feel bad because I actually had the audacity to mention our son, but at the same time I'm confused because El is normally the one saying that we shouldn't be afraid to talk about him, and how she's terrified of forgetting, in some weird way, even what he looks like.

What he looks like?

Therapeutically, that makes perfect sense to me, but in reality, I don't think I could ever fully understand how she thinks that's even possible. How could we ever forget our beautiful boy with his big brown eyes, sandy blonde hair, and that smile as bright as the sun?

"You weren't actually thinking of keeping it, were you?" she asks with a chortle.

Which annoys me – because I know she's just being cruel.

"Why not?" I question her, finally admitting the prospect that I've obviously been considering and yet avoiding all morning.

"Because it's ridiculous," she says dismissively, turning to make her way back down the corridor.

I think about letting it go, but I can't, and I follow her. Being sure to open both toilet and dining room doors as I go, too. Then, I lean on the kitchen doorframe and watch as my wife resumes her coffee making.

"Why is it ridiculous?" I ask.

"Because we don't know where we're going to end up and whether we'll even be allowed pets."

I frown. "What do you mean, where we're going to end up?"

"Well, once the sale goes through and we get a new place…" she says, avoiding eye contact by spooning coffee into the paper filter on the machine.

"What will it matter? If we're getting a place outside the city, having a pet shouldn't be a problem."

"Well, that's just it."

"That's just what, El?" I ask seriously.

She shrugs. "Well, things have changed now, haven't they?"

"How?"

"Well, with my new job, it makes sense for us to move back to the city."

"Right. And when were you planning on discussing this with me?" I ask, folding my arms.

"We're discussing it now."

"Now? El. We talked about this. Neither one of us wants to move back to the city."

"That was before," she says, flipping the switch on the machine, placing a hand on her hip, and looking at me. Defiance is etched in her pretty face. "Before I took the job."

The text alert on her phone rings loudly, like one of those bloody bells at a boxing match.

I sigh. "El, I don't want to move back to the city."

"Why not? Don't you want to get back to work?"

"Fixing cars? Um, let me think about that," I say sarcastically.

"You know what I mean."

"I'm not ready for that yet. I've barely left therapy, myself."

She moves to answer, but must think better of it.

"What?"

"You could look at other stuff, too. You know. Retrain. Haven't you ever wanted to retrain?" she asks, and then looks at me expectantly. Not like someone who is wondering about the answer, but more like somebody who's expecting a *specific* answer. She must read the puzzled look on my face because she adds, "Well, you could do whatever you wanted."

"I don't have to be in the city for that. I can do *whatever* I want from here."

"Here?" she asks, eyebrows knitting together.

"Well, not here, but somewhere in the countryside."

"With hours of commuting back and forth. Come on, Marc. It's soul-destroying."

"What's soul-destroying is living in that concrete jungle again. I can't believe you'd want to. You used to always bitch about the view from the flat. I can't believe you want to go back."

Her posture relaxes and then she turns away from me, seemingly noticing the view from the kitchen window for the first time. She's avoiding eye contact.

"What?" I ask warily.

"Well, I know you're going to think it's crazy, and I did, too, believe me, but I've already made enquiries about getting our old place back."

"What? El."

"I know it's mad, but–"

"Mad? El, it's insane! Why the hell would you want to go back there? It can't be the money."

"It isn't that."

"Then, what is it?" I ask, but I pause when it dawns on me. "Oh fu…." The seagulls perched on the roof are equally scandalised because they start squawking loudly. The sound is like laughter. "El,"

I begin, gently. "We're supposed to be moving forward with a new life, remember, not trying to recreate the old one."

The coffee pot spits as my wife shoots me a murderous glare. "Don't quote your therapy shit at me."

"My therapy shit? For God's sake, El. It's what we've both been told. And it's bloody common sense. Toby is gone. We've got to face that."

Her lip curls into an angrily snarl and she spits, "You're a prick!" Then, she turns her back to me, retrieves a mug from the cupboard, and pours milk into it.

I know she's pissed and that she doesn't want to hear it, and nor do I, but that's the bloody point. Our whole relationship has been based on the fact that we're able to be honest with each other. It's who we are. It's what we've always been. So, why do I feel like such a shit?

"El–"

"Save it! You're right. We did talk about not going back, but now that I've got the promotion, it only makes sense. Besides, I miss my parents."

I laugh. "You're joking, right?"

"No, I'm not bloody joking," she fires back, but she also avoids my gaze by fetching a teaspoon from the drawer.

"El. You hate your parents. You say they're emotional vampires. You told me that having to stay with them was like being in a concentration camp."

"Yes, but living with them isn't the same as living close to them."

"You're not making any sense. You've always told me that you never want to live anywhere near them."

"So? I've just changed my mind. Is that a crime?"

"No. Of course not, but moving back to London… it's madness, El."

"Yeah? Well, so's adopting a fucking puppy, but it hasn't stopped you, has it?" she retorts.

Her attack is caustic, and I'm taken aback by it. My wife has always had a fiery temper. We both do, but the good thing about us is that we've always been able to regulate each other. A bit of a yin and yang kind of thing. When she's chewing someone out over something, I'm the voice of reason, and vice versa. Up until the world imploded, it was more of the latter. But since then, she's changed. Since my return, even more so, which in turn has led me to assume a more passive role during these exchanges.

"I haven't adopted anything yet. I wanted to talk to you about it first."

"Well, we've talked; it's a shitty idea and you need to find another place for it," she hisses.

"You're saying that because you're angry."

"Don't condescend."

"I'm not."

"You are."

"And you're deflecting."

"Fuck you!" She turns, and I watch her pour coffee that is clearly steaming as much as she is right now, and yet that doesn't stop me.

"I'm not moving back to the city, El. That isn't what we agreed," I say emphatically.

She turns, cup in hand, walks up to me, and says, "*You* don't have to."

With that, she disappears into the hallway, leaving me standing there to consider the weight of her words as a rather fitting black cloud smothers the sun and the gale whistles at the backdoor, demanding a closer seat to the action.

And I feel it. You know, like one of those annoyingly sharp tags in the back of a new sweater prodding at your skin. Did my wife just tell me she's happy for us to separate?

I follow her out. "El, I think we need–" My sentence is cut in half when I see that her silhouette has already stopped at the other end of the hallway. The reason why I can't see her is because she's closed the bloody doors, again!

"El?"

She doesn't answer. Instead, her profile remains motionless. Watching. Listening.

"Ellie? We need to talk about this."

Still nothing.

"El! Why won't you answer me?" I yell angrily, reaching for the light switch and flicking it on – but when I look up again, the shadow has disappeared.

"Ellie!" I call after her, not really expecting a response. Which is good, because I don't get one.

Then, to top everything off, the overhead bulb sputters a few times and then dies, leaving me alone in the dark once more.

12. THE PHOTOGRAPHY ROOM

Ellie and I spend most of the afternoon keeping out of each other's way. Correction. She's keeping out of mine with the explanation or excuse that she's busy working on this top-secret stuff for work that, unless you're a complete moron, obviously has something to do with some kind of merger. Because, let's face it, David's company doesn't work for the Ministry of Defence – it designs computer games.

The result is that my wife spends most of the afternoon on one side of the house, in the dining room, and I on the other in the photography room.

Never the twain shall meet.

Don't worry. I'm keeping my head down while I'm in here. Avoiding all contact with the faces on the walls, lest I be sucked into reminiscing about a past I cannot remember, and most likely for good reason.

The mind has a way of doing that, protecting us from those things that seek to hurt us.

Of course, the issue of what exactly I should do with all these photos does present itself once more like an annoying doorstep salesman. There's an argument for keeping them since, for better or worse, they are, after all, part of my life whether I like it or not. The other is, why bother? If the images don't mean anything to me, if they don't evoke any kind of an emotional response, then why keep them?

Although, that isn't strictly accurate, as they do invoke an emotional reaction; it's normally rage, but not necessarily about something that was… more for something that could or should have been because, if I can allow myself a moment of uncharacteristic familial objectivity, they are amazing images. I mean, for all her grotesque failings, my mother did have a great eye for photography. Some of these images are, in my humble and clearly unbiased opinion, exhibition-worthy, which is probably one of the reasons why they annexed this whole part of the house to display them even if they were strictly for private viewings.

If I'm completely honest with myself, I'm in no hurry to spend time in the mausoleum of hypocrisy, but, given that my wife has hunkered down in the dining room, it's only right that I establish some kind of beachhead, too.

Kind of.

More like I just wanted a place where I could shut the door, gather my thoughts, and take a closer look at the patient without Ellie's judgemental eyes on me.

Birds tweet beyond the window as I lift the dogfood box onto the bureau, unfold the flaps, and look inside.

And it's now, in the tranquillity of this room, that I become aware of just how *hurt* I am by Ellie's words. And no, contrary to what you might be thinking, I'm not even talking about the bit where she told me not to bother being with her in London. I'm talking about the part where she told me to find another place for *it*.

"She's right, though. Somebody may well be looking for you. Missing you," I say softly, as if the dog can understand me.

If he does, he doesn't stir. Then, it occurs to me that he can't even see me. I'm just another scary giant towering over him. So, I sit in the creaky wood chair next to the bureau, slowly pull the box closer, and gently rip a rectangular door in it.

Then, I bend down until my face is level with the cutest, most adorable thing I have ever seen since my boy. Yes, I know that if I said that aloud, some might think it grotesque that I should even draw the distinction between the two. There isn't one. Of course not, but for me, it's the one thing I can relate how I'm feeling to.

Ellie, of course, could never understand it. But then, she's not crouching down here looking at this honeycomb-coloured, furry thing with one crinkly suede ear flopping down his face like one of those ushanka hats with earflaps, and a short square snout punctuated by a black button nose resting on fluffy golden paws. Along with his tiny, bandaged appendages, he looks like a character that's been painted for some children's book.

"Hey, little fella. How are you feeling?" is my default whisper. Presumably so that I don't startle him.

Slowly, large eyelids flutter open and I can see my distorted self in two dark, chocolate eyes that observe me with wary sadness, which is so palpable that my heart aches.

Blink.

"Oh, buddy. Hey. Hello. It's OK," I coo, slowly reaching out and gently tracing a finger across the top of his head.

Blink. Blink.

Wow. I've only been with this fella a few hours and the thought of giving him up is already sticking in my gullet, but…

Those puppy eyes close once more.

"You don't want to think about it, either, do you? Don't blame you. You're going to be OK, pal. You're just a bit sleepy now."

I pick up a breakfast bowl with milk formula and place it in front of him. He opens his eyes, but doesn't even bother to sniff the bowl's contents before closing them again.

"Yeah. I agree. It does smell a bit funky, but then, I'm no expert." I smile as if encouraging a human to smile along with me.

Yes. I know. Pointless.

So, I bring out the big guns. A small sandwich bag of tiny treats that Sarah included in our Red Cross package.

Sarah. She was so good to us this morning, and I feel a pang of guilt for some odd reason. I just bulldozed my way in there, and I wonder if I was suitably grateful. I think so, or at least I hope I was.

Shit. These are the moments when I wish I never met Doctor Holmes. I was blissfully ignorant to everything and everyone other than my own needs and wants before I met him. Now, I'm like a simpering bloody idiot! I'm nothing like I used to be, and I miss that. All this other icky, gooey stuff is hard work and bloody exhausting. Especially when you're overcompensating, which I'm sure I must bloody be.

That said, I need to remember to pay for today's treatment. I don't want her lumbered with that, too. Maybe I'll buy her a drink or something. Get her flowers to say thank you.

SHIT! Can you hear yourself?

I sigh. No. It isn't like that, is it?

No. I know what these thoughts are about. It's obvious. There's chaos in my own personal life and I'm already looking for validation elsewhere because my so-called happy family plan doesn't seem to be working as well as I originally hoped.

You think? It certainly won't if you start slipping back to your old ways.

I know. I won't. That's not who I am anymore. It isn't!

I slap myself on the forehead.

"You're so lucky you don't have any of these problems," I say, waving one of the treats in front of that dry button nose. "No. You just have to deal with being mauled by a bloody fox. I'm sorry. I'm a dick."

The eyeliner eyes blink, and I think there's a small effort to at least sniff this thing that looks like a rabbit dropping, but then those fluffy lids blink shut once more.

"You've got to eat, buddy. You need your strength. And I've got to go and start a fire."

I say that because a quick internet search confirmed what I pretty much already knew. There is no magical mystery to storage heaters. They don't have a central control system. Each unit is supposed to simply draw energy at night when the energy tariff is cheaper and release it during the day at a speed of the user's choosing. Well, that was worse news than discovering that the main circuit board to this place is located in the cellar and reached via a trapdoor in the kitchen floor.

Yay!

This means that not one but all of the storage heaters in this place must be faulty – because they all seem to be working, but none are releasing any warm air. That's why we've been freezing our arses off since we got here. And, given the very presence of storage heaters, I can reasonably conclude that this place is not plumbed into the gas supply.

That's why I've taken another of my woollen jumpers and used it to create a nest inside the box, so that the patient will be a bit cosier while I go and see if I can start an altogether different kind of fire in the den.

The fireplace is one of those eff off big things and a bit of a feature in the lounge, featuring a heavy mantlepiece of dark wood that's ornately carved with what looks like flowers of some ilk, and now that I've actually stopped to admire it, it's quite impressive. Above it isn't one of those ancestral portraits of a dour relative sitting ramrod straight and glaring at anyone and everyone who dare fall under their gaze, but another of those heavy-looking mirrors featuring its own wood carvings. It's obvious that, not unlike the bedroom furniture, the old man bought a job lot of these, too. That, or this thing was here before he bought the place.

The fireplace has been swept clean, as if maintained by someone, and I can't help but wonder if that was the old man or the person I can't bring myself to even think about, who spent most of her time here before returning to the city to step out in front of that train.

I shudder as my mind's interpretation of what that would have looked like presents unhelpful snapshots to me. You know, whoever said that *the mind is a dangerous thing* was spot on, although they missed out the bit about it being a sadistic bastard, as well.

I strike up one of those long cook's matches, hold it in the fireplace, and watch the flame dance a few times while releasing a plume of smoke that snakes reassuringly up into the black void.

"OK."

I add kindling I gathered earlier, courtesy of the tree outside, and use the newspaper I removed from the box to get things started. Waste not, want not.

It doesn't take long to get Dolce Vita's first fire in probably a very long time burning – which, to my surprise, arouses some kind of primordial sense of satisfaction in me. *Man makes fire.* Although, he has been doing that for centuries. I can only assume my own satisfaction is based on my ability to bring warmth back into this place rather than to set a match to wood.

After several minutes, I add some small logs to my creation and, as the heat emanation grows, so does the grin on my face. This is one thing I know will please Ellie.

Standing up, I take in the den. This place is finally starting to feel cosy.

"Ellie!" I call out. And then I wait a few seconds before calling again.

"What? Why are you screaming?" she asks, appearing in the archway.

"Come and see this," I say, marvelling at the multicoloured glow in the fireplace. I step aside and present the crackle and snap. "It's alive!" I declare.

My wife can't resist a small smile, and I'm reassured by it; if there's one thing that I've always managed to do, it's make her laugh. And while a smile isn't quite the same as a belly laugh, I'll take it right now.

"That's brilliant," she says. "Finally. Did you not have any luck with the storage heaters?"

"Well, from what I can tell, they're supposed to just work. They're just electric heaters at the end of the day." I scratch my head as if to emphasise my confusion. "We're going to need an electrician to sort out the lights in the corridor. He can have a look at that–" I cut myself off.

"What's the matter?" Ellie asks.

I can feel her eyes on me, but I'm staring at and listening to the fireplace. "Did you hear that?"

"What?"

"That sound," I say, stepping closer to the growing flames.

"What sound?"

"In here." I'm looking at the fire now. Trying to tune out of the snap-crackle and into the other sound.

Scratching.

"Marco?"

"You can't hear that?" I ask, looking back at Ellie, who shrugs at me and rolls her eyes as if I'm pranking her. I'm not. I can hear something. Inside of the chimney. Something scratch– "There! Did you hear that?" I turn to her, but she simply widens her eyes and shrugs. "You can't hear that scratching inside the chimney? It's like there's something in there. Come here. Come closer. Listen."

Ellie reluctantly complies and the two of us, now as one, angle our ears towards the fireplace as if trying to warm one side of our faces.

"I can't–"

"Shhh! It's… like… claws… on stone. Something is moving around in there."

Silence.

Fire crackling. Seagulls squawking. Ocean rumbling.

"It's probably just a b–"

Ellie's sentence is cut short when a nerve-jangling shriek I can only equate to a tortured cat scampers down the chimney, startling us both. Ellie jumps back from the intimacy of the fireplace and I instinctively step in front of her just as a cloud of acrid black smoke spills down the chimney, snuffing out the fire and enveloping us before scurrying around the room like a trapped animal.

The foul, noxious vapour pushes its way into my nostrils and lungs, causing me to gag and then cough, and by the sound of it, Ellie isn't fairing much better.

Spluttering and gasping for air, I grab my wife's hand and pull her to the patio doors where, after wrestling with the key for way longer than my patience allows, we both fall out into the delicious fresh air and double over, spitting and spluttering for several minutes in an attempt to expel whatever shit we've both ingested.

And it is shit.

Not in the metaphorical sense, but literally. The smoke's sour taste is like tar-laced excrement. And I can feel it stuck to the back of my throat, making my nose run and my eyes water.

"Are… are you… OK?" I manage through coughs as I look back at the patio doors.

The black stuff doesn't billow as you'd expect smoke to.

Instead, it oozes like an inverted oil slick slithering its way up into the sky.

"Ellie!" I prompt, looking at her.

"I… I'm fine. What… what… what is it?"

I shake my head and spit a couple of times. "I don't know."

"It tastes like…. Tastes like…."

"Shit! I know."

We continue spitting and coughing a while longer in stupefied synchronicity as we watch the inky smoke thin into a pale grey when, suddenly, even out here at the back of the house, the nerve-shredding *Brurr!* of the muffled doorbell manages to find us.

We look at each other as if we've been caught doing something illicit, but I think that's more wishful thinking on my part.

"Stay here," I say, not wanting my wife to venture anywhere inside until I know that stuff has cleared. I take a long deep breath and then step back into the house, where I'm amazed to find that the noxious cloud has disappeared.

The fire is dead. The fireplace is cold and dark as if nothing happened.

Slowly, I release the breath I've been holding and brace myself for the aftermath of *the stink*. But, amazingly, there is none. It's gone, as if taken by the filthy fumes… which is peculiar, because anybody who's ever burnt toast knows that smell lingers for hours if not days. I inspect the rest of the room, sniffing as I go like a bloody dog. But there's nothing. No smoke. No smell. The place is clean.

Brurr! Brurr! Brurr!

Yeah. There's no doubt about it. I hate that effing doorbell as much as I hated the gestapo knock. Something I'm going to sort out the moment I've dealt with whoever this is.

I stomp over to the front door and pull it open, but there's nobody there but a cold chill.

The driveway is empty. The gate closed.

I look left and right. Empty. I step out as if not trusting my eyes.

Nothing.

"What's going on?" Ellie asks, appearing in the doorway.

"There's nobody here."

"What do you mean?"

I shrug. "Exactly that. There was nobody at the door."

Crows caw mournfully as it slowly begins to rain.

13. THE VISIT

Screaming. Crying. Begging. Crunching footsteps. "Mummy, please... Mummy! Stop! Mummy! Please stop! You're hurting me!"

"Shhhh... it needs to stop screaming now because it is not my baby. Dear Father, thou art in heaven, hallowed be thy name..."

Clicking pebbles. Grazed arms. Searing pain.

"Thy kingdom come; thy will be done..."

"Mummy...!" *Crying. Anguish. Hair being pulled. Roots ripped. Dragging. Pain. Sobbing. Pain. Tears. Begging. Tears. Salty water sloshing, splashing, and fizzing.*

"Mummy! Please!"

Thundering surf. Clicking pebbles.

"On Earth as it is in Heaven"

Thundering surf. Fizzing water. Thundering surf. Thundering! Thundering! Thundering!

"NOOOOO!" I'm still yelling as I bolt up in bed, arms outstretched in front of me as if protecting myself from the gloom. I breathe in deep lungs of air as I slowly recover, running my hands through my hair reassuringly.

This is a habit I developed during my last stint here, and something I'm prone to do each time I am presented with or recovering from a stressful situation. Many people twirl, eat, or stroke their hair. Me, I settle for running my hands through it, which is one of the reasons I try to keep it short. Ironic when you consider the fact that I don't like people touching my hair.

I actually hate it. It is, after all, a relic from a time when I seemingly had no control over my life. Yet more irony when you consider that I've never felt as vulnerable as I do now. Something that is no doubt exacerbated by this chasm that is widening between Ellie and I over what happens after this place sells.

Thunder explodes loudly overhead, and it makes me duck instinctively as rain hurls itself against the window like a swarm of angry hornets.

I look across to see if Ellie can hear it, too, and flinch when the clammy coldness of my sweat-soaked T-shirt touches my back like cold fingers.

Looks like the night sweats are back. Yay!

I sigh deeply as the furniture is momentarily reanimated by a flash of lightning.

So much for blue skies.

Ellie is still asleep, and judging by the sound of her deep breathing, doesn't have any intention of stirring.

I envy that about her. Once she puts her head down, that's it. She's out. She wasn't much different when Toby was a baby. Most new mothers sleep lightly when there's a new-born in the house. I heard that it's natural. Primordial, even.

Not my wife.

I, on the other hand, am a light sleeper all the time, which meant that I was often the one to tend to Toby during the night.

Did my son choose to wake during the very few hours when I was asleep? Of course. Was it knackering? Absolutely. But I loved it. I enjoyed that special time with my boy. It was our time together while the rest of the world slept.

Toby.

I swallow the dry sawdust that is the back of my throat as I will myself to leave the relative warmth of the bed in exchange for some dry clothes.

Lightning winks and temporarily strobes the room, shortly followed by a boom of thunder which is so loud, that it literally sends shockwaves through the building.

"What the fu–dge?"

I look across at Ellie. Still asleep.

Now, most people would find the wind demon screeching around the house, pulling at the odd shingle, and rattling petrified panes of glass in their frames a somewhat terrifying experience. I know this because I was one of them. But given that I have a history of this, both during my previous visit and this one, I'm no longer as concerned as I used to be that the windows might implode at any moment.

That said, it doesn't mean that this place is any less creepy by night now in comparison to how it was when we first got here. That's why when another sound pierces the demonic, tempestuous orchestration, it gets my attention.

Ellie stirs, and I think she's going to wake up, but instead she pulls my recently surrendered covers over to her side of the bed.

There it is again! That sound.

It's dark in here. And, after last time, despite the fact that's it's probably going to get me yelled at, I decide to switch on the bedside lamp.

Nothing. I flick the switch a couple more times. Dead.
Shit.

A power cut is all we bloody need.

I pick my phone up, swipe, and tap until the light comes on. Then, as if it's going to help me identify the sound amidst the meteorological cacophony, I shine the light at the door and listen.

Moaning draft. Drumming rain. And… my sadistic mind is playing tricks on me again. It must be because what I think I'm hearing isn't possible. And yet–

There it is again!

NO! Stop it. Stop! You've seen this in a hundred horror movies and you're projecting it into your memory.

But I'm not. I know that sound. I've heard it many times before. I'd recognise it anywhere.

A glance at my phone's display makes me smile. Now, I know I'm dreaming because it's 03:01 – the devil's hour. Yeah. OK. Why is it the devil's hour, Marco? Well, it mocks the 3 PM time which is when Christ is believed to have died.

How do you know this?

I have no fu–nking idea!

Despite my attempt at distracting myself, the sound returns, and this time it's much louder. *Clearer.* As if it's coming from just outside our bedroom door.

I glance at Ellie in the hope that she can hear this, too, that she'll be able to corroborate the fact that I am not imagining it. But she remains motionless. The outline of her body barely discernible in the overspill of the light beam.

No power also means that the new landing night lights are useless. I check the gap underneath the door for confirmation.

Darkness.

Crying.

NO!

I pinch the skin on my wrist for as long as I can bear it. I'm awake, as ridiculous a test as that might be.

I slide out of the bed and onto the cold wood floor.

Images of an abattoir and us sleeping amidst a clutch of hanging hulks of dead flesh instantly parade across my mind.

Fu–n! I bat the images away and instead busy myself by pulling off the sticky T-shirt I've been wearing, discarding it in favour of a hoodie. Then, I glance at my phone's battery icon. Last time I was in this situation I ended up scaring myself shitless, and I see no need to re-enact that experience.

I brandish my phone in front of me like a weapon.

Shadows jump away from the beam, as we all know vampires do from sunlight.

I make my way towards the door as a gust of wind attempts to strangle the window frame into letting it inside. It creaks loudly in protest as I brace myself. This is it. This is the time when the window implodes, showering us with a zillion fragments of glass in super-slow motion.

It doesn't.

Of course, it doesn't. And I remind myself, once again, that this place has been standing against the ravages of the Atlantic gale for years, and there's absolutely no reason why it should yield now.

I reach out for the doorknob, but snatch my hand away when it suddenly clicks and voluntarily creaks open. The nightmarish sound is so loud that I'm sure it's woken Ellie.

However, when I flick the light towards the bed, I see, to my disappointment, that she hasn't moved. I want her to wake up. I want her to tell me that I'm hearing things and that the fu-nking door didn't just open by itself!

It did, you fool, the wind pushed it open. There are drafts all over this place.

There are. I'm not just making that up to justify what just happened. There really are cold spots all over the house. I noticed the first one in the corridor of doom. Right next to the toilet door, and another on the landing, and now… well, now everywhere is one giant cold spot.

Cold spots? Ghosts? Yeah. Not helping.

The phone's light beam and then I slide out of the crack in the door and onto the landing, where the din of the storm is much louder. It's fury like that of a ginormous beast buffeting against the house, spitting rain at the window, shaking frightened doors in their frames and kicking something across the driveway onto a journey to only God knows where.

Even the hatch to the attic is seemingly being tortured as it keeps creaking and wailing like something is pushing it from the other side.

But I ignore this because I've seen it all before. To the uninitiated, it can all seem somewhat intimidating…. OK, terrifying, but don't worry. You're safe with me. I've experienced worse.

Have you?

Yes, I have.

I turn my thoughts to our houseguest-come-patient. Ellie refused to have him in our bedroom and didn't particularly like the idea of him being upstairs, either, but I hated the thought of him being downstairs alone. So, in the end, we agreed that I would put his box outside our bedroom door. Far enough away from her, but close enough for me to check on him.

The only problem is that the box is empty now.

Shit.

I'm shivering at this point, which I'm sure has nothing to do with the creepiness of this place at night, in the dark, and everything to do with the meteorological conditions.

It's just cold. It's just so bloody cold.

I open my mouth to whisper the puppy's name, but realise he doesn't have one.

Lightning flickers and I look around to see if I can see the dog anywhere nearby. But he isn't. Did he go downstairs to find a hideout or something? Maybe he got scared when the storm started.

There's a loud woosh of wind, then a splitting sound, and for a second, it sounds as if one of the wood beams has given way somewhere… but then the sound is followed by a loud crash and a smash, which I can only assume was one of the plant pots outside.

Thunder rumbles overhead as I make a conscious effort to stop my teeth from chattering. But the sound seems to continue until I realise that it isn't me, but something in my old bedroom.

Tap. Creek. Scratch. Tap. Tap. Scratch.

I flick the light up and over to the doorway

There's nothing there, but there's definitely a noise coming from that room, and I'm just about to lose it when I realise exactly what it is.

Idiot!

It's the tree. You would have thought that, if I remembered anything, I would remember the sound of that thing tapping on the window like bloody fingernails. Relief floods through me until another sound pierces through the tempest to plant a cold dagger of a chill in my spine.

It's the same sound I heard before. The same one that I thought I had imagined.

A baby. Crying? No. Not a baby. A boy. A child. Me? Or at least the memory of me in that room?

What the fu–dge is going on?

Strong sonar tugs of chills wash over me before they're interrupted by a scratching, scraping coming from somewhere in the attic. Pushing and then banging on the hatch. I train my light on it, and can see the bloody wood bowing against its hinges.

Something is in there! Something is howling angrily. Something that wants to be set free….

It's just the bloody wind! Pull yourself together.

Lightning flashes and I leap backward because, in the corner of my eye, I just saw something or someone standing in the doorway to my old room. I flick the light over there, but there's nothing but the entrance to the cavernous void beyond.

"Hello?"

I don't know why I just said that because it's just us here. All the doors are locked. Right?

And yet, the beam of light that is still trained on the doorway is now quivering. *Shivering. Not quivering, it's bloody shivering from the cold.*

NO! NO! I'm not doing this. I'm not going to let myself start down this path. If I do, it's a slippery slope. It's just an effing storm! An effing bastard-bitch of a storm!

"Daddy?"

My heart stops. My stomach rolls. The voice was clear. Unmistakable.

Even above the wailing elements outside. I heard it. It came deep from within the blackness of my old room and I am both electrified and paralysed by it.

"This isn't possible. This isn't happening!" I whisper to myself. "This isn't possible. This is not real."

But it is.

I know it is. I know what I heard is not in my head just like I know that there's something in the attic, threatening to tear the latch of its hinges.

I will myself to move, but I can't. I can only watch as the clouds from my short, shallow breaths are illuminated by the light beam. And then, to my absolute terror, I watch as another daisy chain of clouds joins mine, to be closely followed by the sound of someone's breath in my right ear.

I yelp and whirl around, training the light on the empty landing and stairs beyond.

Oh my God.

"*Daddy.*"

I whip around once more. Down the dark hallway, towards my old room. Above the rattling and creak of doorframes, the hammering of rain against window, and the unnatural scrape and tap of talons on glass, I heard my son's voice just as I have many times before in the dead of night. Calling out to me. Loudly. Clearly.

"T-T-Toby?"

He's dead, Marc. Your son is dead.

I squeeze my eyes shut, bow my trembling head, and tell myself, *This isn't real. This is all in your mind. Remember what the doctor told you. Stay in the here and now. <u>This</u> is your reality.*

I want to turn away, to run like a little pansy back to the bedroom and dive under the covers because I'm afraid. I'm terrified. It's all happening again. I've been out barely two weeks and I've already succumbed to my old ways.

Scratch! Tap! Scratch! Tap!

There's something in that room. There's something in there. Something in the dark.

It's just the tree!

No. It's more than that. There's someone in there. I can sense it. It's as palpable as the freeze that's squeezing the breath from my lungs.

Toby!

But is it?

Scratch! Tap! Scratch! Tap! Tap! Tap!

I turn to leave, but my feet aren't moving. They're frozen to this icy floorboard, leaving me at the mercy of whatever's in there.

Look!

I can't. I don't want to.

Look in there! Look at me!

"No... no."

Look at me. I came back for you.

No! Don't do it. Don't.

And yet, slowly, reluctantly, I lift my head and look into the jittery light beam. Eyes wide. Jaw slackened. Tongue desiccated.

The doorway is empty. There's nothing there, but–

"Oh fu…!"

Thunder explodes like a percussion grenade overhead, startling the phone out of my hand. It clatters to the floor, light carving shapes in the darkness, before sliding to a halt just inches from plummeting to certain death on the flagstone below.

Oh shit.

A strobe of light illuminates the space, and I'm both terrified and relieved. There's nothing here, but me.

"There's nothing here but me. Nothing here but me," I chant over and over again to the melody of *Follow-the-bloody-Yellow-Brick-Road*!

Jesus, Marc. What the hell has happened to you? Afraid of your own bloody shadow now. This is what he reduced you to. This pathetic little shit afraid of a bit of thunder and lightning. If you give into this you will never recover, mate. Never.

Now, man the hell up. Just get the phone, go over there, and show yourself that you are alone here and that what you heard was in your head. No. It was wishful thinking. Perfectly rational wishful thinking from a grieving parent.

I straighten up. Shrug, and then roll my shoulders like a boxer readying himself for the big fight.

Now, get the light, march in there, and see for yourself that–

I can't. I just can't. And I can't even explain what it is because it seems too irrational, but all of my instincts are telling me not to go in there and that if I do then something bad, something awful, will happen.

Like what?

I glance at the phone. It landed face down. The torch is still on, though, helpfully or not, depending on your point of view, illuminating the rim of the device.

I'm just about to reach down for it when–

Daddy. I'm here.

I snap my head around to look back in the direction of the open doorway, scouring the darkness for something – a shape, an outline, anything to corroborate what I just heard. Or what I think I just heard.

I did! There's no mistaking that beautiful voice; soft, warm with that equivocal inflection. *Daddy. Are you there?*

Toby! Toby!

And then it happens.

The sheet lightning that temporarily illuminates the world beyond the window of the spare room may as well have passed through me for the jolt I receive when it highlights the silhouette of someone standing in the doorway. It's just a few seconds, but more than enough for me to recognise the short profile and the wavy hair.

Unmistakable.

A shower of hot and cold shivers washes down my back as I throw a hand over my mouth… not to silence a scream, but some other inexplicable noise that I emit which is akin to a sob fused with incredulous, maniacal laughter.

There's another flash of light, and I instinctively stagger backward when I see that the shadow has moved from the doorway and is now coming toward me.

Oh Jesus!

This time, I do scream as I feel the cold hands of the wall touch my bare legs.

I can hear, no, I can *feel* the presence moving closer as the darkness shifts and reforms as the air is disturbed by something invisible to me.

Thunder grumbles, and it feels as if it's coming from all around. As if the dark itself were an entity. An ancient, gargantuan creature of terror that I've roused from its irritable slumber. The percussion ripples through the stone, the mortar, the floorboards, and then my body.

"Oh, sweet Jesus," I mutter as my eyes half-squint and half-hide from what may well be lurking right in front of me.

Then I become aware of it.

Scratching.

No, it isn't scratching. It's more like tapping and then scratching… tapping and scratching.

And it's inching closer.

I press as far back as I can, into the wall, in the hope that it might absorb me in some way so that I can emerge in the bedroom on the other side.

Tap! Scratch! Tap! Scratch!

"Help! Help me!"

Tap! Scratch! Tap! Scratch!

Suddenly, the nightlights spring back to life and I yelp once more when something touches my foot.

I look down.

"YOU!" I yell as the puppy's eager face looks up at me. "Buddy," I breathe, releasing the breath I've been unconsciously holding, "you scared the funking shit out of me!" I say before yelping once again when the overhead light comes on and a voice behind me asks, *"What the hell are you doing?"*

14. THE MORNING AFTER

OK, so it won't surprise you to hear that Ellie was none too pleased to be woken up in the middle of the night by what can only be described as a blood-curdling scream. It, quote, *frightened the fucking life out of me.* And, if you knew Ellie, you'd know that she doesn't swear that often – only when angry, which, come to think of it, has been a lot lately.

I guess you can hardly blame her. I'd be pissed off, too, if I'd been wrenched from the arms of Morpheus by that. And yes, I am talking about the mythical Greek god and not the character from *The Matrix*.

Things probably looked worse when she found me on the floor, face contorted with terror, with a wounded puppy playing at my feet. She said that I had plenty of time to play with my *new pal* before I found him alternative accommodation, so *why* – and again, I'm quoting – *the fuck would you do it in the middle of the night?* She added that she had a busy day ahead of her and that I was selfish because she'd hardly had any sleep because of the *fucking storm*.

And no, of course, I didn't make a quip about the fact that she appeared to do a surprisingly good impression of someone who'd slept through it. It was bad enough that I suggested that she might want to consider making another bet with me to see if *she* could last a whole week without swearing.

I'll leave you to imagine her response to that.

Speaking of which, by my reckoning, I only have two more days to go before I win our bet. Of course, I felt compelled to remind her of that, too.

Yeah. It was shitty timing.

So, no, I didn't tell my wife what really happened on the landing last night or, more specifically, what I believe happened. For two reasons. A) I don't think she would have been receptive right then, and B) she didn't exactly give me a chance because, after castigating me, us, like children, she turned on her bare heels and took her gorgeous legs back into the bedroom, slamming the door behind her.

And so, me and my so-called new pal spent the night in the spare room. Which, as it turns out, was fine because this little guy who is currently – don't tell Ellie – playing ghost with the sheets on the kitchen floor, seems to have tapped in to some kind of energy reserve, along with rediscovering his appetite. I don't know if he was stress-eating last night because of the storm, but he devoured a whole bottle of formula, and even a handful of pellets, which means that I definitely need to venture out today to get him some solid food of some kind. Whatever that might be since I have no idea what puppies eat these days.

Why did I decide to strip the bed since there's a good chance I may end up in the spare room again tonight? Well, what goes down must come out somewhere, and that was all over the quilt, the sheets, and the mattress cover.

What was the puppy doing on the bed?

What's it to you? I'm going to have it all washed, dried, and returned before Ellie gets home, so this needs to be our little secret.

Yes, fortunately, and I mean this in the nicest conceivable way, my wife had to catch the train to London today, which means she had to leave at the crack of dawn and I had to get up to drop her off at the station.

Yes, I'm knackered. And thanks to the furry sprite whose sudden and boundless energy is matched only by his curiosity, there's absolutely zero chance of my going back to bed.

That's why I'm currently making a fresh pot of coffee.

So, OK, I suppose you have some questions about last night. Alright, maybe you don't, but I, as much as I've been pushing it all to the back of my mind, need to allow my thoughts to at least stray over the memory of what happened. You'll appreciate that it's much easier to do that with the unique perspective of daylight.

The sun has returned, but is doing little to melt the chill out there. In fact, as I look out the kitchen window at the gold leaves flickering like crystals as they twist and turn in the dregs of yesterday's gale, it would be easy to think that last night never happened – that I dreamt everything, including the storm.

But I didn't.

And the drive to the station served as a grim reminder of the ferocity of mother nature.

It's like something out of a disaster movie out there. Trees upended; wheelie bins overturned with their contents strewn across pavements. We even spotted cars with smashed windows, presumably from flying debris. We appear to have fared well compared to the rest of the county, which, according to the radio, has suffered severe flooding, with many properties still without power.

Ironically, as much as I didn't think so at the time, last night was much worse than it seemed from the safety of the house. And even our own stream has swelled. That thing looks more like a small river now, which, of course, got me thinking about the books I came across at the store. It's a ridiculous comparison, I know, but it did cross my mind, especially since the radio was talking about the fact that the worst is yet to come.

Yay!

Thankfully, I decided to tune into that on the way back from the station. The last thing I need is to have Ellie panicking about this. She was already traumatised when I had to stop the car at intervals this morning in order to push tree branches off some of the back roads.

Yeah, so, there is something to be said for living in the city. Again, thoughts that I kept to myself because, while I accept that it'd undoubtedly be bleak living out here in the middle of winter, there's also a lot of beauty in autumn's barren desaturation of the rolling patchwork of coloured fields, naked trees, and tempestuous coastline.

So, OK. Alright. I know I'm avoiding. Thinking about everything else except what's truly on my mind.

This isn't necessarily about what I saw. Or, more specifically, about what I think I saw. No.

"This is about you having some kind of a relapse, mate," I say aloud as I grip onto the sink and gaze out the window.

There. I said it.

The problem here is that I don't have anybody to talk to about this. I mean, I can try to rationalise it by myself, but therein lies the problem.

My mind is untrustworthy. An unreliable witness. What I saw, or think I saw last night, was clearly a figment of my imagination. It wasn't real because it can't be real.

I pour black coffee into a cup and turn to watch my furry companion attempt to extricate himself from the sheet but make a complete pig's ear of it. The vision brings a temporary smile to my face as I sip hot black liquid, but it dissolves the moment I go back to the memory... and that split second when the lightning flash caused that apparition that made me scream like a fu-nking pansy. And I must make no mistake here; it *was* an apparition projected there by my faulty mind. An easily suggestable mind affected by the subconscious memory of my childhood visits to this place.

Of for fu–dge sake! This is amateur hour. Am I really going to attempt to self-analyse? That's ridiculous! There's no way I can be objective. There's a reason why people seek out the cold, analytical, unbiased nature of strangers to work through their shit.

Shit.

I set the cup down and pour powdered detergent into the machine before untangling furry legs and a floppy ear from the bed linen and loading that into the drum.

Overjoyed by his newfound freedom, the puppy bumbles and slides on his short legs, swerving around the kitchen floor before crashing into my feet.

I pick him up and he starts to lick my hand while flicking his stumpy tail back and forth. And I didn't realise it, but I'm smiling.

No. I'm grinning. And, if I think about it, I don't think that I've done much of that lately.

Brurr! Brurr!

The grating sound of the doorbell startles me to the point of almost dropping my furry friend.

Have I mentioned how much I hate that thing? Last time, it was the bloody Gestapo knocking, and now it's the bloody electric chair thing that sends a volt of rage through me every time I hear it.

I've *got* to replace that thing today.

I set furry pants on the floor because I don't want him falling off the counter – not that he should be on there anyway – and make my way to the hallway.

"What the actual fu–nk?"

That can't be right. I'm sure I left the light on in here because it was still dark when we first came through. And yet, it's like the bloody black hole of Calcutta. Angrily, I push the kitchen door wide open. Then, I make my way into the gloom to fling the dining room door open and drag a chair in front of it before making my way up the hall and pushing the toilet door open as far as it will go.

Ellie says leaving the doors open is in some way, beyond my understanding, untidy. I, on the hand, don't recognize the logic of walking around in the dark, especially on a spectacularly sunny day like today. So, we've compromised to decide that when the doors are shut, the light needs to stay on. Not that the shitty thing is any good, but it's better than nothing.

Brurr! Brurr!

I look back and smile at my petty accomplishment of turning night into day, and then head over to the door which I yank open, expecting to find an unwashed and impatient delivery driver, but instead it's a most welcome, early morning sight.

Sarah, bundled in a wax jacket, cream scarf, and grape mauve beanie, smiles and says, "I'm sorry. I wasn't sure you heard me. I don't think the bell is working."

It takes a few seconds for me to respond, as I'm momentarily entranced by the colour of her hat. Oh, OK, maybe it's more her mousy brown hair which I can now see is actually chestnut brown in the early morning sunshine and pouring down the sides of her face like maple syrup.

"I hope I'm not intruding," she adds when seagulls have more to say than me.

"Of course not. Come in," I say quickly, waving her in and trying my best not to think about what I must look like in my thick socks, jogging bottoms, and now regulation fleece.

I take a quick look up the driveway to make sure there's nobody else out there. I have no idea why. I can only assume it's due to the fact that Sarah is the only female, besides Ellie, to enter this place since we arrived, and for some reason that's made me nervous.

Guilty conscience?

Piss off.

Yeah. That might sound tough, but I'm still secretly wishing that Ellie doesn't have a change of mind and decide to come home early.

Stop it!

"Oh, also, Uncle Irvin asked if I could drop this off," she says, magically producing an envelope from the inside pocket of her jacket and handing it to me.

"Oh, great. Thanks," I say, wondering what the other side of *also* might be.

"Wow. This place looks lovely," the nurse says, looking around the lounge.

"It's OK. Needs some work, though," I say, holding up the envelope since I'm assuming it's Irvin's estimate and not a love letter.

She nods. "I heard you're still thinking of selling up." She turns to look at me. I, in an effort to appear relaxed, attempt to fold my arms over my chest, but the whole movement just turns into some weird spasmodic motion that, well, I can't and probably shouldn't even describe.

"That's the plan. Yeah," I say, moving on.

"So, you'll be leaving us soon?" she asks, and I really don't know if she sounds disappointed or if it's just me projecting. I'm pretty sure it's the former... I mean the latter.

"Well, it hasn't quite been decided yet," I say, scratching an invisible itch at the back of my head. The action must, to my surprise, lift the front of my fleece far enough to expose my midriff, because I notice my guest copping a look at the pleasure trail I cultivate there.

If I'm perfectly honest, it is actually one of those things that lovers tend to maintain to please their partners. Ellie thinks it's sexy. Not that she's been interested in going anywhere near it lately.

And, apparently, so does Sarah. *You're a naughty, naughty girl, Sarah*, I think to myself, smiling inwardly. Grateful for this attention. Yes, many women talk about the need to feel desired, but us men feel it, too, you know.

At least, I've just found out I do.

"So, is it OK if I take a look?" she asks, and I'm about ready to lose it as I feel the heat rising to my cheeks.

"Sorry? What?"

"The puppy," she says, smiling. "Where are you hiding him?"

"Oh!" I say, the heat now a raging blaze. I overreact and clumsily, some would say somewhat churlishly, drop my hand and zip the fleece up as far as it will go without garrotting me. "Yes. Of course. He's in the kitchen," I add, stepping back and waving her in the right direction.

"Down here?" she asks.

I look up and am about to reply, but I'm momentarily struck dumb.

What the…

My visitor is peering down the dark hallway, and I don't know which thing I'm disturbed about more – the fact that she thinks I'm some kind of sexual deviant leading her god knows where or the chilling fact that all of the doors are closed once more.

I'll say that again. *All* of the doors are closed, but you remember me opening them, don't you? On my way to answering the front door.

Don't you?

Dear God, what is happening to me?

"Marco?"

Sarah is looking at me with a curious frown, which no

doubt is only adding to what she's probably already thinking... that I'm some predatory creep.

Get a grip!

"Are you OK? You're looking a bit pale."

"I... yes. Of course. I'm. Yes. It's just down this very dark hallway which I have to agree is really creepy." I force a laugh as I hurry forward and push the toilet door open, doing so with so much force that it slams loudly against the wall.

My guest flinches at the impact, and I consider asking her to leave. Run! And never come back here!

Calm down.

I open the dining room door and glance inside. I have no idea what I expect to find in here other than the chair sitting innocently in the middle of the room. Maybe I was hoping to find Ellie or David... someone, *anyone* snickering in the corner. Laughing at the fact that they'd managed to prank the prankster.

"It's much brighter in here with the doors open," Sarah offers.

"I know. Right," I say, moving quickly to the kitchen door, although nothing could have prepared me for what I'm about to find inside.

15. HIEROGLYPHICS

The kitchen floor is an ice rink of pearlescent blue featuring a series of dashes and swirls.

Sarah gasps and throws a hand to her mouth as the presumed artist of the washing powder masterpiece comes sailing around the island, tongue hanging and stumpy tail wagging. When he sees us, he attempts to slam on the brakes, but the momentum is too much for his ungainly short legs and he ends up sliding and crashing into the skirting of one of the kitchen units.

But he doesn't let that deter him. He simply shakes his head, and after a series of awkward, slippery sliding movements, attempts to take a run up for his next skating adventure. Instead, he fails to gain the necessary traction and ends up slipping and then collapsing into an undignified pirouette at my feet. The flourish to his finale is to look up at us with his big brown eyes blinking, pink tongue hanging, and tail flicking.

I'm lost for words. Marooned somewhere between *what the actual fu–dge* and awe. Sarah, hand still on her mouth, allows herself a snigger which quickly turns into an unladylike chortle that, in turn, starts me off – and before we know it, we're belly laughing, and it feels bloody good.

Eventually, I reach down and pick up the budding Picasso and place him on the island, where after an initial scouting expedition, he returns to lick my hand.

"Don't tell my wife he's been on here," I say, shaking my head at the little demon.

"Don't worry. Your secret's safe with me," she says, pulling off her hat and liberating her hair. Then, she takes a step closer to the island and I am instantly engulfed in a cloud of her scent. It's sweet, fresh like a flower-filled meadow. Intoxicating.

Seriously? I can't even remember walking in a meadow full of flowers. How the hell would I know what one smells like? I suppose it's how I imagine it. Maybe as a child. I seem to have a vague recollection of my boarding school being set in between a forest, a lake, and acres of land....

Oh shit... can you see what I'm doing here? I'm thinking about juvenile stuff because of her proximity. This is not a good sign. It is not good at all because this means I am affected by her, and if I am affected by her, it can only mean one other thing.

Trouble.

Yes. With a capital T.

So, I should discreetly move away. And I will. Right now. OK. Maybe in a moment because, after all, I don't want to appear rude.

She's really close now. I can feel the heat of her body. Or maybe it's just my body heat bouncing off of her because I went from freezing cold to feeling like I'm breaking out in a sweat. I can feel it tickling my hair now.

"Well, you're looking much perkier than you were the other day."

Her voice interrupts my ridiculous thoughts. You would have thought I'd never been close to a woman before. But I realise that I haven't for quite a while. Not since before therapy. Nobody but Ellie.

"Yes. I really thought it was touch and go there for a second."

"Me, too," she says casually as she stoops to take a closer look at the dog.

"You did?"

"Yes. But you seemed pretty attached already, and I didn't want to panic you."

"What?"

"But you're looking great," she adds, putting on an affected voice as the puppy rewards her with a kiss on her hand, prompting a girly squeal of delight. "Is that for me? Is that for me? Oh, thank you," she says, still in that obligatory, patronising voice we all adopt when talking to cute things. Then, she bends over a little more to nuzzle the puppy's head with her nose and then plant a kiss there.

I look at the mane of hair cascading over her coat and surreptitiously breathe in that perfume in exactly the kind of way I used to when riding the escalators back in London. Filing in behind a beautiful lady and breathing in her scent.

Yep. I know. I heard that, too. But I promise that it sounds way more pervy than it was. Back then, I used to do it as some weird tantric foreplay. Right now, there's nothing sexual about it. I'm doing it because I want to. Don't get me wrong, I love my wife, but I miss this – the appreciation, that is, of a beautiful woman. Not that Ellie isn't any of that, because she is and more, but ever since we moved out of the city, I've been squashing down and supressing any of these feelings and urges with her because I know that isn't where she's at right now. She's made that abundantly clear, and I've wanted to respect that.

But the sight of Sarah. Her fragrance.... It's made me realise just how much I miss being excited by the presence of a woman.

Fu–ss. Now, I'm making myself sound like the poor neglected husband justifying his pervy behaviour.

I'm a dick.

"...and it's lovely. I want to stroke it."

"Um, sorry. What?"

"His fur. It's so soft. I can't help stroking it."

"Oh."

"How's he healing?"

"I think he's doing OK. I changed the bandages as instructed."

"May I?" she asks.

"Oh, of course. I suppose I should make a start on this," I mumble, turning to the blue slick over the floor, and that's when I notice them.

They were easily missed before because of all of Speedy Gonzales' skid marks, but now I can see them. The occasional tiny squiggle sitting on islands of undisturbed detergent. They look like letters; vertical dashes crossed with ornate squiggles. It reminds me of the kind of stuff archaeologists find on cave walls around the world… but not on my kitchen floor.

Could the puppy have created these? If he did, have we just discovered some rare kind of canine alphabet?

"Sarah?"

"Uh huh," she acknowledges me, though she's busy gently peeling the bandage off the puppy's paw. I'm being ridiculous. This is ridiculous.

"Doesn't matter."

But she turns to me. "What's up?"

"Nothing. It doesn't matter. I thought I saw something."

"You mean besides the disaster on your kitchen floor?" she asks with a smile.

I nod. "Yeah. Besides that," I say before going over to retrieve a long-handled dustpan and brush from the utility area. I'm just about to begin the sweep-up when it occurs to me. *Wow. I suppose we're just not used to having visitors here.*

"Can I offer you a beverage, Sarah?" I ask.

"I've noticed you've got some fresh coffee on the go," she responds, busily yet gently removing the gauze from the puppy's ear – who, by the way, has rolled onto his back and closed his eyes, enjoying the attention.

Tart. It's alright for some!

I like the fact that she doesn't stand on ceremony. Italians are like that.

"*Un caffè per la signorina!*" I ask in what's probably the worst accent ever, but it makes her smile in the same way I used to be able to make my wife smile, and that makes me both happy and sad in equal measure.

"Are your parents Italian?" she asks.

"My father was."

"You were born there?"

"Oh no, born and bred in London."

"You don't sound like it," she says, glancing up with a squint.

I pull a face. Rock my head. "By way of a little public school."

"A little?"

"A lot more than I would have liked," I acknowledge. "How about you?"

"Me? Born and bred in Porthcove," she answers, exaggerating her own local accent.

"Really?"

And she must have read something into my question because she adds, knowingly, "I know it isn't a metropolis like London, but I like it. It's peaceful. The people are nice, and with everything that's happening in the world, I'm starting to think that's a bit of a rarity."

She shoots me a smile. And for reasons I can't explain, I feel suitably admonished. So, I nod, return the smile, and then busy myself with the coffee.

"Oh, I almost forgot," she says suddenly.

I turn back to see her reaching into her pocket and pulling out a small, black trinket box. Then, her face turns serious enough to tug a frown from mine. "Marco," she begins, "I know we've only just met and, well, there's something about you. I don't know what it is. Maybe the fact that you look like that handsome actor, but, well, I was wondering, would you marry me?"

She hands me the box. I look at it and then swallow hard because I've no idea what's happening right now.

Then, she starts laughing. And I'm not talking giggles, but big guffaws of laughter of the kind I used to share with Ellie and always with my best pal, David. She even doubles over to add to the moment.

I shake my head. "Oh, you!"

"You should have seen the look on your face!" she says between chuckles.

Wow. She's ballsy, this one. I've got to give her that. "What's really in here?" I ask, shaking my head with mock disapproval because I, Marco Battista – king of pranks – has no idea what to say, because even though I knew she was having me on, my traitorous body still reacted, and I can feel that familiar burn in my cheeks.

"Open it," she says excitedly.

"I don't know if I want to now. Might be one of those squirty flower things."

"I promise, it isn't."

I look at her warily and then open the box to find a heart-shaped green stone.

OK.

"Don't worry," she intervenes. "The shape is incidental. It's what it's made of that's important. I didn't want to visit your new home without a gift, so I thought a piece of malachite made perfect sense."

I take the smooth, polished stone out of its box and turn it in my hand. Its different bands of green shades gleam in the daylight pouring in from the window. "Mala-what?" I ask. "Mala-shite?"

She giggles. "Mala-kite. It's known for its powerful metaphysical properties and as the *stone of transformation*. It brings deep energy cleaning along with positive energy to the owner."

"Really?"

"Of course. At least, that's what it says on the tiny leaflet inside." She follows that up with a smile and a wink.

"You're something else."

"Thank you. I'll take that as a compliment."

"So, do you believe in this stuff?"

She shrugs. "Yeah, I suppose I do. Although, at this stage, I don't know if that's because I have a certain faith in it or if it's just because I was raised with it. If that makes sense. The shop is a family business and has been for generations.

We know that Earth is made up of a whole series of different energies. Many of them responsible for life on the planet. It's hardly a stretch to think that there are certain energies emitted by different minerals that have an influence on us as biological inhabitants of this planet."

I widen my eyes. "Wow. I guess I never looked at it that way." I lift the stone. "Thank you. Thank you very much."

She shrugs and turns to give her attention to the puppy

once more while I go back to coffee-making duties, but I take a few moments to consider her.

I'm in awe of this woman. I admire her confidence and her exuberance. She reminds me a bit of the person I used to be before I became all bloody touchy, feely, and consciously guilty of everything. And she's right. I don't know if it's her presence or the stone's, but the atmosphere here has already changed.

"So, have you decided on a name yet?"

"A name?" I ask as I retrieve a cup from the cupboard.

"Yes, for trouble here."

I glance at her, but she's busy looking at the dog's ear. I don't feel like telling her that I've been avoiding thinking about it because of my discussion – alright, my argument –with Ellie. Or about the fact that I was hoping to avoid getting too attached by not thinking of a name.

Yeah. Like that makes a difference.

"Um, not really. One did spring to mind. Rusty."

"Rusty?"

No, she obviously doesn't like that, but I persevere "Yeah. I kind of thought it was fitting; you know, when we cleaned him up, some of his fur had turned a rusty colour in patches. You know, with the blood, so I thought that…" I trail off here because, when I glance up, I can see her looking at me and the expression on her face says it all. "Yes. That's exactly what I thought. Not a good name for a dog. Bad name. Other than that, I haven't really thought about any others, so I've just been calling him 'buddy'."

"Buddy?"

"Yeah, I know, it's lame–"

"It's perfect!"

"You think so?"

"Yeah. What do you think, Buddy?" she asks, kissing the dog's belly and prompting him to roll onto his side and return the favour by licking her hand, invoking more of those girly giggles, and I can't help my smile. Watching her with him, sunshine spotlighting them both, reminds me of Ellie with Toby.

Toby.

Toby?

Are you fu-dging kidding? Ellie would lynch you for even considering naming a dog after her son. Besides, he won't be here that long.

"He's healing really well," she Sarah says, wiping her face on her jacket. She's definitely a country girl.

"Really?"

"Oh yeah… much better than I expected. It's odd, really. These wounds are only days old, but, and I'm not exactly a super expert *yet,* they seem weeks old. To the point where you should be able to leave the bandages off – you know, let some air at the wounds."

"Really? I obviously make a much better nurse than I thought."

She acknowledges the comment by bowing her head. "Indeed, you do."

"I was obviously trained well," I say. *Oh God, I know. It just slipped out. Now, it's awkward.*

Well, it is for me. My guest simply smiles and then looks at the cup of coffee in my hand.

"Oh yes. Here it is."

"Thanks." She moves away to sip from her cup and the puppy almost instantly starts looking for a way down from his perch.

"Hold on, Buddy," she says. "I'm not finished with you yet." Then, to me, she adds, "What did your wife say when you brought him home?"

Shit. Why don't I want to tell her that Ellie thinks it's a terrible idea? "Um, well, she obviously thinks he's adorable, because he is—"

"But?"

"Wow. There are no flies on you, eh? Um, well, we're going to be selling this place, and she's worried that if we move back to the city, then we may not be able to keep him."

"So, you *are* going to do it then?"

"What? Move back to the city? Um, well, we haven't decided yet."

God. That was pathetic. Didn't that sound pathetic to you?

For some obscure reason, I'm hoping she's isn't disappointed. But if she is, she doesn't show it. Instead, she moves back and gently nudges the puppy towards the centre of the island to make sure he doesn't fall off. Then she says, "Let's check that paw of yours. Go on, give me your paw. Give me your paw."

Aw. I'm smiling. I think it's cute that she should ask, but there's no way he's going to give her his paw. He's–

Wait, what?

To my amazement, the animal – albeit gingerly – lifts his wounded paw to her.

"Wow. You didn't mention that you were a puppy whisperer."

She doesn't respond, instead says in a pained voice, "Yes, I know. Is it still a bit sore? That's OK. That'll pass soon. I promise." The dog has reeled in its tongue now and is looking more like that bundle I found in the woods yesterday. Chocolate eyes brimming with heart-breaking sadness. "Don't worry, Buddy, you're going to be OK. You're going to be just fine," Sarah coos like a mother does to a child with a grazed knee.

"Yes. Definitely looks good. Just need to make sure he keeps those wounds clean. E.g., no sticking it in washing powder," she adds with mock severity. Then, she produces a small tube from her pocket and proceeds to squeeze a few drops of the lotion onto the dog's paw and gently rub it in with her finger. I expect the dog to pull away, but he doesn't. "Who's a good boy, then? You're such a good boy."

"Um, so, do you always walk around with…"

"Antiseptic," she offers.

"With antiseptic in that Tardis of a pocket?"

"Not really. Only when I'm visiting cute little patients like you. Yes, you are!" That voice is back, and judging by the wagging of Buddy's tail, I think he likes it.

"So, what are you going to do?" she asks without taking her eyes off her charge.

"About?"

"About this little guy."

"I don't really know. I was thinking of maybe putting a notice up in your store. You know, maybe someone will come forward and claim him."

She nods. "I would offer, but we've already got two dogs. I don't want to outstay my welcome."

I cock my head, so she adds, "I've not long been back. I was living with my boyfriend, but things didn't work out, so now there are two extra dogs and me at the house."

"That's a shame," I say. You can choose what I'm referring to.

She shrugs. Then adds, "How was he last night?"

"Sorry?"

"Buddy. How did he cope with the storm last night? It was quite a bad one. A lot of damage around the county."

Memories of last night roll over me like a giant wave, and it's weird because, for one split second, one ridiculous moment, I feel like I want to tell her about it. About all of it… because I've got this feeling that it probably wouldn't phase her.

"Actually, he was OK. Apart from scaring me to death."

"Oh, right." She's looking at me now while rubbing the puppy's belly. Yeah, he's thrown himself onto his side again, and by the droopy blinking of those normally keen eyes, he's enjoying it.

"Yeah… it's a long story, but he started shuffling towards me in the dark and scared me half to death."

She chuckles and looks straight into that honey face. "Did you scare Daddy? Did you scare Daddy?" she whispers.

Daddy.

"The thing is, he moves but doesn't say anything."

She looks back at me and pulls an equivocal face. "Say anything?"

I know she's messing with me. "You know what I mean. I don't think I've heard him make a sound since I found him."

She looks at the puppy, who appears sound asleep now. His good ear spread out over the counter like a movie actress's hair fanned over a pillow.

"Right. That's interesting. Well, I don't think there was

any obvious damage to his voice box, as the vet gave him quite a thorough examination. I mean, it's odd, but not unusual. Given how you found him and what he had just been through, there's a good chance it's psychological."

"Psychological?"

"Yes. Animals get traumatised just like humans; you would know about that, of course," she says with a snigger.

I'm not sure how to take that. Does she know about me? Does she know about my time at the institute and is making fun of me?

I must have a look on my face because she follows that up with, "Are you OK?" She's looking at me now, keenly. "Is it what I said?"

"Well, actually–"

"Oh, I'm sorry. Mum did say that you might not want everybody to know or they'd all be queuing up to see you–"

"Now, hang on."

"Especially us lot. We're all a little crazy around here," she says, lifting her eyebrows knowingly. "I reckon you could work full-time just on Mrs Budgen, the head teacher. She's definitely a few sandwiches short of a picnic. If you know what I mean. Everyone's still convinced that her husband didn't die of natural causes, but that she buried him somewhere in the backyard." She's smiling as she says this, but it fades when she notices that I'm not smiling with her.

"Oh no. Have I just said something–"

"Are you saying that the whole village knows about me?"

She bites her lip and rocks her head. "Well, it's kind of all your dad talked about."

"What?"

"I told you. And you heard it at the store. I know it's a bit weird, but your pa was really social and, well, we weren't exaggerating. He did talk about his children, particularly you, a lot. About how proud he was. If I'm perfectly honest, you've become a bit of a celebrity around here," she adds with a grin and nod of the head.

It's a first for me, but I'm momentarily lost for words.

There's so much about what this vivacious woman has just told me that makes no sense. She said that my father was proud and that he told the whole village about me. But every time I saw the old man, which wasn't much toward the end, he barely had a good thing to say. At least not to my face. Shit, he kicked me out of the bloody house; packed me off to boarding school the moment he knocked my step-mum up. And there's no way he could have told anyone about my time at the institute because he wasn't even alive.

Oh God. It's happening again, isn't it?

"Marco? Are you OK? Did I say something wrong?"

"Mrs Budgy."

"What?"

"Mrs Budgy. The schoolteacher," I say.

"Oh right," she giggles. "You mean Mrs Budgen."

"You said that I could work full-time on her. What did you mean?"

My effervescent guest frowns for the first time since arriving here. "Um. You know. Therapy."

"Therapy?"

"Yeah. Therapy. That's what you do, isn't it?"

I shake my head. "No. I'm a mechanic."

She laughs out loud. "Is that what they're calling shrinks these days? Is that like domestic engineer and all of that rubbish?"

"What makes you think I'm a therapist, Sarah?"

She shrugs. "Well, your dad! He used to talk about it all the time. He'd have the whole shop in stiches with stories about all the nutters that live in the city. Along with the fact that you were a bit of a tearaway as a teenager, but how you'd turned your life around, graduated from college, married a successful and beautiful wife, and that you were studying to become a therapist."

That last part drops a boulder into the pit of my stomach. Was I the last person to bloody remember that?

"Oh wow. Did you see these?" I hear my visitor breathe out, but I don't respond. I'm still reeling from what I've just learned, but then I feel a hand on my arm. "Marco," Sarah whispers. "Did you see these?"

I turn to follow her gaze. She's crouching on the floor. "I didn't spot these before. Did you?"

I don't respond because I can't. The hard drive that is my brain is working to full capacity as it attempts to process everything I've just learned – although, peculiarly, it still manages to absorb the words *symbols* and *alphabet*.

16. THE ATTIC

I felt both sad and relieved to close the door behind Sarah. Sad, because, yes, if I'm perfectly honest, I really enjoyed her company. She was like a breath of fresh air in this stuffy old place.

Yes. Exactly that. Stuffy, old, and full of bloody secrets. This is exactly how it was last time. From the moment I arrived here, it was nothing but an endless parade of people and ugly revelations. Now, it's starting to look like history is repeating itself.

Only, it isn't history, is it? My last trip was all in my mind. This one is real. Isn't it?

God! This is exactly it. Enough to make you lose your fudging mind! If I didn't feel like it was already lost, that is.

I'm not even going to try to describe it. The best way for you to have some idea is to take a few seconds, and I mean drop whatever you're doing, and look around yourself. Look at the space you're in, at whatever you are sitting or lying on, and then ask yourself, how would *you* react if you discovered that everything you thought was your life wasn't real? How do you think you'd cope with the fact that it was all a figment of your mind?

Then, imagine someone coming along with a metaphorical sledgehammer and hammering a reality that you don't recognise into your brain. Insisting that this is your reality. That your partner's eyes are not blue, but brown, and that they don't look like a supermodel, but more like that woman from *Throw Momma from the Train*. A shitty comparison maybe, but hey, I'm making a point on the fly here, so cut me some bloody slack.

The point is, I don't know if I can trust myself anymore. I mean, all I know is what Doctor Holmes and Ellie told me two weeks back. They told me that this is my reality and that I need to stay with it if I don't want to risk a relapse.

Well, surprise! I think I'm already there. And that was helped in no way by what Sarah told me today. My dad has been bragging about me. Me! His disappointment of a son. The troublemaker who his second wife was afraid to have in the house. I mean, does that even make any sense to you whatsoever?

And yet. Sarah's recount was persuasive. It's also consistent with what the women said at the shop that day.

This is precisely why, this time around, I am going to do things differently. I am going to tackle things head-on and I am not going to leave any bloody stone unturned because, if I do, if I just accept whatever I am being dealt, that is a sure bloody way to the loony bin. And I'm not going back there.

I'm not.

Sarah helped me come to that conclusion. I mean, I was ready to write off those symbols on the floor as something I was imagining, but she helped me see that they weren't my imagination at all. She even took pictures on her phone and shared them with me. And yes, we had to exchange phone numbers for that.

Sarah also asked if I wanted her to put a sign up in the shop about the puppy. I realise now that she was testing me to establish my true intentions with him. But I was still reeling from the whole revelation thing and just eager to get the fu–dge out of this place.

I said yes.

And yes, of course, I feel like a shit, but if you think about it, it's only right, isn't it? I mean, he could belong to someone. They could be in a great deal of distress right now. Probably roaming the streets looking for him.

Yeah. I *still* feel shitty.

Oh well, it's done now, and I can't keep him anyway because Ellie doesn't want him here, and the idea is to patch up my marriage – not do everything I can to make things worse.

How's that working out for you?

Fudge off!

So, anyway. After clearing away the spillage on the kitchen

floor, and no longer having a task to focus on, I found myself absorbing the emptiness of this place. I can tell you, it's a peculiar experience and one I don't recommend. It's the equivalent of a black hole. It devours everything. Your personality, your feelings, your soul. It doesn't leave anything behind but a catatonic, empty shell of nothingness.

The first time I ever felt anything like it was after the accident. That's how I've been trained to describe what happened. It was a *simple accident* over which I had no control.

There's nothing simple about the loss of a child.

So, yeah. Anyway, see? This is what happens when you're left alone. You become all maudlin, closely followed by miserable, and we all know where that led me last time.

That's why I've decided to act. To take control and make things happen rather than let them happen to me. I've left furry Picasso asleep in his box in the photography room and am making my way across the den.

Anybody who has ever heard the expression of the quiet being deafening and sniggered has never been to somewhere like Dolce Vita. The world outside is quite literally like another dimension, isolated from the quiet within. I mean, even as I make my way up the stairs in the cold light of day, the wooden steps creak eerily and particularly loudly under my feet. And this only gets worse as I reach the landing.

I pause here to look out the window. The sun appears to be fighting a losing battle as a series of giant black clouds take turns absorbing it.

The forecast was updated this morning to warn that a new northern front is making its way across the country, bringing with it icy cold winds and a whole lot more of rain. There was even speculation that we might get some early snow next week, which is a sobering reminder that our chances of getting out of this place before Christmas are dwindling by the day.

The mere idea of being stranded at Dolce Vita during snow brings the whole chill up here into focus, and I instinctively rub the cold permeating my fleece. Suddenly, this thing doesn't feel warm enough.

I need to go out and get those heaters.

They say that it's the people which make a house a home, but Ellie's right. We could never make a home out of this place even if we wanted to. We've been here nearly a week now and there's nothing about it that makes me feel warm and cosy. In fact, if I didn't know better, I'd say that this house doesn't want us to feel welcome. It wants to wallow in its sorry state of abandonment. Perfectly happy to rot here for a century.

Another chill runs through me, and this time it isn't the temperature, but the memory of what happened that day down at the beach.

How can any mother do that to their child?

But then, you could argue that she was sick and that she didn't know what she was doing. She wasn't of sound mind.

And you'd be wasting your breath. As her son, as much as I have tried, it's difficult to forgive the mere notion of what she tried to do. The actuality of it is inconceivable to me.

You would have thought that a therapist would know better.

Now, that's funny. Me, a therapist? But then, why is that so hard to believe? I've certainly been screwed up enough to be compelled to want to unravel the complexities of the human mind.

Yeah, but a while back, you were also arguing the idea that you couldn't be a mechanic.

My stomach lurches. Was that a memory? Just then. It was. That wasn't my imagination. *That room.* the rain against the window. Ellie crying. The doctor talking down to me like I was a fu–nking child.

Shit.

I can't be a mechanic because I know all this stuff about psychology. I know about C.B.T. Cognitive Behavioural Therapy. How would I know anything about that if I wasn't a therapist? I know about repression. Anxiety. Erotic transference. How would I know this stuff if–

A sound interrupts my thoughts and I instantly look up at the ceiling.

Something is definitely moving around up there.

Thump. Thump. Thump.

No, this isn't happening. This isn't happening. It's classic autosuggestion.

You know this!

Do I?

Anybody with a brain knows it. Noises in the attic. Really?

I ignore it. That's right. I ignore it because this isn't happening. This is me creating something out of the silence. So, I turn and am about to walk into our bedroom to grab my phone when…

Crash!

Squeak… squeak… squeak.

I slowly reverse back out, sideways, onto the landing. The hatch to the attic is open and swinging back and forth just as it was that night.

Squeak… squeak… squeak.

Oh shit.

I splutter and wave at the stale air and dust particles floating down and around me.

Still think you're imagining it?

Nope.

But then, I know exactly what's happening here. Each time someone walks out on the landing, the weight causes some kind of displacement that loosens the hatch from its moorings.

You really believe that?

Of course. What else could it be?

Slowly, I walk forward and squint up into the black, yawning mouth of the cavity which is protesting the intrusion and warning me off with a low baritone, demonic growl.

Yeah. I'm in a hurry to go up there now.

Shut up. It's just the wind.

Yes, and it's really loud.

Focus.

So, this is the deal. In therapy, each of the rooms in my imaginary Dolce Vita represented a shitty secret. The attic was one of those rooms I was most reluctant to venture into. If I'm going to tackle things head-on this time, then I need to go into this place first.

Make sense?

Um, kind of.

OK. Alright. But we —me, myself, and I — know that my motivation is much more sinister than that. That's why I'm working through all of this in my head like a madman, to somehow justify the fact that I'm pretty much snooping on my wife.

You're not snooping.

I'm snooping.

OK. Maybe a little.

You see, we arrived here with hardly any personal belongings. Ellie had all our stuff from the flat put in storage when she let the place go. She only kept a few personal items with her. One of those items was a medium-sized box.

I helped unload most of the stuff from the car, with the exception of that box. Ellie took care of that. When I saw her disappearing with it up the stairs, I asked her where she was going. She said she was taking it to the attic. I said I would take it for her, and she said that she would do it.

Ellie. In the attic?

While my wife isn't afraid of much, there's one thing she has never done in all the time I've known her, and that's scramble around a dusty attic. It's always been a thing with her. Christmas decorations. Unwanted junk. She'd always leave it in the hallway for me to take care of. Sometimes, she'd even recruit Toby to go up there, but she'd never go herself. She used to say there were too many reasons for her to even list why she hated attics.

And yet, as soon as we arrived at this strange place, the first things she did was take her and her secret box straight to the attic. Not a cupboard. Not a wardrobe. The attic.

I think that's motive enough for my suspecting that my wife is hiding something she clearly does not want me to see, and if I'm going to try to make sense of this new reality, then I need to know *everything.*

So, here I am. Taking a good look at the dregs of daylight outside, as the rest has already been gobbled up by the gathering gloom which is undoubtedly going to turn into another rainstorm.

Fantastic.

I look up at the black hole literally hovering over my head.

Cue irrational thoughts.

Yes. Of course, the place is creepy. But there's nothing up here but freezing, dank air. No, there's no trap rigged by a psychotic serial killer that's going to blow your head off at the moment you poke it. No child facing the corner of the room, crying, waiting for you to go over and touch its shoulder so it can turn and reveal a disfigured–

Slam!

"Fu–nking hell!"

I put an instinctive hand to my chest because my heart is threatening to punch through *a la Alien* any second.

Calm down. It's just the bedroom door in the draft.

Eerie.

The whole house seems to have come alive now. Eaves creaking, wind moaning under doors, and the burgeoning darkness that is slowly folding the place into its colourless embrace.

I look over the bannister to the den below. Shadows grow and shift as the sun makes one final effort at eradiating the land before it is gagged and bundled off towards dusk with little hope of returning tomorrow.

Carefully, I move around the hanging trapdoor and over to the linen closet, from which I retrieve a long metal hook. I use it to catch the protruding arm of the folding ladder and give it a sharp tug. The black mechanism squeals in protest as it slowly unfurls like a rusty, insectoid leg to form a ladder while showering me in minute metal particles.

I shake them out of my hair and sputter some more before slowly and reluctantly placing a cautious foot on the first rung, tapping it a few times to test for stability as I look up at the black void.

Seems firm enough. And yet, my mind sees fit to offer me a

selection of unhelpfully grisly images of what I might look like after plummeting to the den below.

The metal creaks loudly and unhappily under my weight as I make way upward.

I think of Ellie. She came up here without any fuss or preamble. So, man up.

Yeah. Man up!

And yet, for some inexplicable reason, I pause like the proverbial soldier at the top before lifting my head above the parapet and into the gloom.

It smells up here. No. Nothing horrifyingly foul like rotting flesh, but just the usual old traditional dankness of decaying junk. Which is interesting because, from what I can see, the place is empty.

I screw my eyes shut and then reopen them to squint into the gloom. Daylight, like spiderwebs, has taken up residence in far corners, away from the two shards of light flooding in from the skylights in the centre of the space. It's relatively quiet up here. Still, but for that moaning wind forcing its way through gaps in the shingles and then terrorizing the rafters so that they creak and snap in fear.

A pair of seagulls clack loudly across the roof and start squabbling. The sound momentarily startles me. Other than that, this place isn't anywhere near as creepy as I imagined. No unidentified scratching, no creaking or sudden movement in the corner. There isn't even a totally out of place mannequin backlit by a mysterious light so I can mistake it for a shadowy figure.

The place is empty. Decked out with planks and, thanks to those skylights, fairly well-lit – if you ignore those dark patches in some of the corners.

In fact, I would go as far as saying that this is a good space with a lot of conversion potential. You could easily put in a decent stairway and turn it into an office or a playroom. If I had the time, money, and inclination, it'd be something I'd be giving some serious thought to.

But I don't.

I shift my weight on the step. It creaks to remind me that my perch remains somewhat precarious.

I look left, finding nothing there. I look right and–

Oh, hello. What's this?

It's Ellie's box. But I can only see the side of it.

So, I take another step up. The ladder judders and creaks to get my attention. I look down. I don't know if it's my imagination, but the thing does seem to be bowing in the middle.

Oh shit. I need to get–

The rest of the thought is hacked in half when, through the corner of my eyes, I see a shadow momentarily block out the light on the landing. Someone is down there, and they just walked in front of the fu-nking window!

I've barely had time to process this when the ladder lets out a squeal followed by a jolt that makes me squeal as I feel myself plummet suddenly by at least two or three feet.

"Shit!"

The ladder is buckling underneath me, collapsing in on itself, invoking another involuntary yelp as I scramble and just about manage to grab the wooden frame of the trapdoor as the crumpled stairs fall away and my legs are suddenly kicking air and swinging like a pendulum between the relative safety of the landing and the certain injury or death of the den below.

"Fuuuuuuuuuuuuuuuuuuuu!" is the only sound to come out of my mouth as I strain with effort of holding on.

Then, as if to highlight the seriousness of my plight, something tumbles out of the upset box next to me, pings onto the balustrade, spins and plummets to the depths below.

The strain on my arms is immense and it makes me grimace, veins throbbing, as I work to bring the pendulum of my legs under control, but I'm slipping.

"Aaaaaargh!" *I'm slipping!*

I don't even understand how, but my fingers… are… losing… argh! Losing… their… grip!

It's as if, one by one, someone is lifting, unclamping, prying them open, and I know, I can feel it, that I'm just moments from falling onto the jagged remains of the stepladder or following that thing's journey down and onto the flagstone floor of the den below.

The tension in my head is agonizing, the muscles in my body screaming as I try to look down, trying to angle and aim my body so as to cause the least amount of damage as my fingers fall away and suddenly I'm…

…falling, kicking at open air before something smacks me on the back of the head, forcing the breath from my body and the world to turn black.

17. AWAKE

"Daddy, come on. Wake up! You can't stay here."

"It's early, little man."

"No, Daddy. It's late.

"Toby, who's your favourite parent?"

"Da-ad. You need to wake up."

"Yes, but just tell Daddy. Who's your favourite?"

"You and Mum will always be my favourites. You know that. That's why I'm here. That's why I've come back. Now, come on, you need to get up. You need to leave."

"Give Daddy a kiss first."

"Oh, Da-ad."

"Come on. You're not too grown up for that, are you?"

Oh. The warmth of his body. The softness of his hair. Oh, my arms around him. "I love you, buddy. And I'm never gonna let go. Never let go."

"I love you, too, Dad. But you've got to get up now. You can't stay here. It's dark and cold."

"Cold? What do you mean? The sun's out. It's warm."

But the sky turns dark and ominous and it scares away the sun, plunging the world into blackness.

"Quick! Quick! Dad! You really need to wake up now! Please, Daddy! Wake up!"

My son. My pride. My flesh. My joy. I can feel you. I can feel you, buddy. Holding onto me. Kissing and touching my hair. My face. My nose?

"OK, Toby, that's enough." But he won't stop. Giving big,

slobbering kisses that make me laugh. I'm laughing! "OK. I heard you. You can stop now. Toby, stop!"

I open my eyes to find a furry, four-legged creature, paws astride my chest, licking my face.

"Buddy," I groan as the blurry pink tongue shows no sign of abating. "OK. OK. I'm up."

But I'm not. I am in a crumpled position on the wood floor of the landing with my back against the wall.

Ugh. It feels like an elephant has been using my head as a bongo drum with the occasional break to use it as a foot stool.

"What the hell…. Oh, God." I remember and look up. The black chasm of the attic door yawns wide over me like the cavernous mouth of a giant. The jagged metal remains of the stepladder are inches in front of my body like the mangled beanstalk.

"Oh shit," I groan. "That was close."

Slowly, the memory thaws itself loose from my brain, which is frozen numb both figuratively and literally. It's bloody cold up here.

I look at one of the ladder's protruding limbs and shudder. I have no idea how I managed to avoid impaling myself on that or plunging to the den below.

I groan again. This could have gone whole other, hideously different way.

There's a stiffness in all of my extremities which I imagine is only in part due to the arctic blast that's coming down from the open black mouth hovering overhead… and now giving me the creeps.

Buddy hops off me as I find my hands and push myself into a sitting position. Pain shoots through my back and butt, and for one horrible second, I'm worried that I've done myself a severe injury. But gentle attempts to move suggest otherwise.

You're OK. Just been lying awkwardly for God knows how long.

I look up. It's dark outside. Dusk is reluctantly giving way to night, which makes me think it must be around four or five in the afternoon.

Wow. I've been here a few hours.

I want to get to my feet, but am minded by possible

concussion. Still, I feel OK. I think I'm OK. Just achy and bloody stiff from the fall.

Slowly, delicately, I haul myself to my feet, but as I do, I hear the tap and rattle of something falling to the floor. It's a small, flat plastic container.

I weigh the pros and cons of stooping again to retrieve it when Buddy seemingly reads my mind. He ambles over, picks it up in his mouth, drops it at my feet, and then looks up expectantly. Chocolate eyes now black in the fading light.

The act makes me smile. "Wow. Good boy," I groan. "Good boy. But no fetch right now," I say, crouching down with my knees and retrieving the capsule, which I can now see is an SD card holder. And now that I look at it, I remember; that's the thing that dove to its death earlier. I'm sure it is. The same thing that pinged and spun to the depths below.

I look at Buddy, who is still waiting patiently. "Did you bring this back up here?" I ask. His only response is to cock his head to one side, as if that will help him translate what I'm saying more effectively.

I slide the container into my pocket. Then, rubbing the stiffness from my neck and the ache from the back of my head, I look up once more at the black hole.

I hate that thing.

I mean, I hated it before, but now I dislike it for additional reasons I can't even put words to.

I hunt around for the hook and, ignoring the pounding on my brain, twist the protruding limb from the ladder until it comes away in my hand. I then use the hook to shove the cavity's mouth closed, locking away the wintry chill.

The relief is instant.

I'm never going back up there again.

I would love to report that I disposed of the metal limb by throwing it outside and then spent the rest of the evening recovering from my ordeal, but instead, after swallowing two Ibuprofen, I decided to mount the wireless doorbell on the front door – which I know sounds very handyman-like, but in reality actually means that

I peeled the sticky back tape off of the transmitter button, stuck it to the side of the front door, and plugged the receiver into a socket in the den. Then, after cycling through a whole series of mind-cringing melodies, I finally managed to find one that resembled normalcy.

No more nerve-jangling, rusty (which I've taped over with black tape), grating sound, and no more Gestapo knocks for the duration of our time here. And yes, I know that modern monstrosity is hardly in keeping with the rustic vibe of this place, but, worse case, we can remove it when we leave.

In the photography room, or what is now my study, I've decided, for the duration of our time here, I'm about to insert the SD card into my laptop when I notice the envelope with *Mr Battista* scrawled on it.

I hesitate because I don't know if I'm in the right frame of mind to find out just how much it's going to take to fix this place up, but then I break the seal and pull out the two-page estimate.

Labour and materials. More labour and materials. The thing seems to go on forever, and so, like most people in this situation, I skip straight to the foot of the second page.

Sixteen thousand. Nineteen thousand with the optional extras, such as additional equipment, and materials. Oh, and all plus tax.

Shit! Fu—dge! Bloody hell!

That's more than I thought. So, then I start the process in reverse. Optional items, materials, labour. In all, it looks relatively fair, but it's obvious that I should get a second opinion.

I think about Sarah. She wouldn't care either way if I hired her uncle. Would she?

I read the cover letter. It starts with the usual thanks for requesting an estimate, then pitches the fact that Irvin and Sons have decades of experience in all aspects of home improvement, so I can always be assured of quality work and their best attention.

The interesting part is that they could start as early as next week, with the projection of completing everything within two weeks. Which doesn't seem like long to me, but then, they are a three-man band and, if he says he can do it, I'm not going to argue with that.

Besides, the timeline is music to my ears.

Do I really want to start shopping around, wasting precious time when I could just give this guy who seems reasonable enough the go-ahead and get things moving?

The answer is obviously no.

I pick up my phone and dial Irvin's number. He answers after a couple of rings.

I tell him that his quote is acceptable, providing he can start first thing Monday and have everything finished within the two weeks he's suggested. He says that's no problem. "See you Monday."

"Yeah, see you then," I say, and disconnect the call.

There. That was easy.

Now I just need to find the money.

18. FLASHING LIGHTS

Dolce Vita will be receiving its first official guests this weekend.

David and Aaron are arriving tomorrow.

I couldn't wait to tell Ellie about David's short yet typical text informing me that he'd allowed us enough time to settle in and that they were now planning on arriving tomorrow afternoon and staying the weekend.

The text made me smile. I thought my friend had forgotten all about me.

Ellie, on the other hand, didn't share my amusement. In fact, now that I think about it, she didn't seem particularly excited by the news. She started fretting, asking me if I was ready to receive visitors and pointing out how the spare room wasn't set up for a couple.

And I have to say, I liked that. I liked that she was fussing over me. I haven't felt that in a while, and it felt good.

So, I reassured her. Told her that I was excited to see my friends and that she didn't have to worry. I would take care of everything. It took some persuading, but she accepted it in the end.

Given her concerns, I decided that it was probably best I not tell her about what happened today, but then she asked why I kept rubbing the back of my neck.

Interestingly, she seemed to take that news pretty well, considering what could have happened. At least, she did until she finally asked to look at the giant bruise on my back. Then, she seemed a tad more concerned and began questioning me about how

I had been feeling since the episode. Did I still have a headache, and was I feeling nauseous?

I told her that I had Googled 'concussion', too, and that I didn't have any other symptoms beyond a sore back and a headache. I then went on to reassure her I was fine and that she didn't need to worry, but, upon reflection, I think that was more for my own benefit than hers.

Thankfully, she didn't ask what I was doing in the attic… probably because I headed it off by telling her that I didn't manage to make it up there before disaster struck. I then took the opportunity to expertly lead the conversation away from me and over to house renovations. When I told her about the estimate, she didn't even flinch. She said that she believed the estimate seemed fair, considering the amount of work and the fact that there would be three people working on the project full-time.

So, then the conversation turned to money.

She naturally suggested her father. I naturally suggested that I'd rather cut my dick off, not least of all because she'd already been there to solicit part of her inheritance. I do not want her to go through that again. No way.

This then led to my proclamation that I would be paying her back in full once we sold the house, to which she took offence – because she's my wife and not a bloody housemate – to which (and I have no idea why, though it's probably because I'm an idiot) I blurted out, "You could have fooled me!"

To which her eyes narrowed and she retorted, "What's that supposed to mean?", which then prompted me to prove that I'm perhaps not as idiotic as I first thought… because I ignored the question and instantly steered the conversation in yet a different direction by softening my tone and reminding her that I was her husband and that, as old fashioned as this sounds, I wanted to be providing for her.

She then told me to stop being a misogynistic dinosaur, which led us into another argument that culminated in me kneeling before her, taking both her hands in mine, and explaining that I loved her and appreciated that she stood by me, but that I was going to have the opportunity to repay what was rightfully hers. I told her that it was something I wanted – no, *needed* to do – and that I *needed* her to accept it.

She thought about this for a few seconds and eventually broke into a smile, and said, "Hey, if you want to pay me back, I'm not going to argue with you about it," which then led to a hug and some kissing, but, disappointingly, no sex. It's not that I didn't try. She just didn't seem responsive, explaining that it had been a long day, she was tired, and that I was wounded... and she had a point.

In fact, I didn't realise just how exhausted I was until my head hit the pillow.

Until now.

It's 02:30 in the morning and, for some reason I can't explain, I am bloody wide awake. Well, I can explain, I suppose. I dreamt that someone was in my room, pulling at my arm the way Toby used to do on fishing days.

Sometimes the little man would wake before me and act as my alarm call without wanting to wake his mother, so he'd stroke my face until I opened my eyes, but if that didn't work, he'd pull at my arm.

Sadly, when I opened my eyes this time, there was no cute little boy standing by my bed, but just the ghost of his bittersweet memory.

By the sound of her deep breathing, Ellie has had no such dream and is still sleeping soundly.

Its deathly quiet in here and dark, but not as black as it used to be, thanks to the night lights that are working in the hallway tonight.

No power cut.

Beyond the window, a full moon has made a churlish appearance by draping itself in a thick cloud. It seems that the torrential rain that was forecast hasn't materialised. That, or I slept through–

What was that?

I strain to listen and wait a few seconds.

Nothing. Just the rumble of the surf and the occasional eerie creek of the rafters.

I wait. Seconds lap by.

There! Something beyond the door. On the landing.

I glance across at Ellie to see if she might have heard something, but she doesn't stir. Then, I scan the room. Nothing in here but the shadowy shapes of furniture conjured by the moonlight. And yet, like insect legs, the small hairs on the back of my neck are tickling because, once again, I have this overwhelming sense of being watched.

I shrug the creepy feeling away and lift myself off the bed, ignoring the sharp twinge in my back. Shit. I may have to get this thing seen—

There's that sound again! Is it voices? It sounds like... *voices!*

I look at Ellie again and consider waking her – for no reason, you understand, other than to verify what I think I am hearing, to confirm that I'm not dreaming or, worse, losing my mind. But I decide against it. Instead, I slide out of the bed, but snatch my feet back up the moment my toes touch the floor. I don't know how, but somehow, the wood floor is covered in a layer of frost, or at least it feels that way.

Cautiously, I place my feet on the floor once more, hop into socks, slide into jogging bottoms, and pull on my trusty fleece which, as you know, has become essential wear in this place.

I'm by the door now, and because my mind is a sadist, I look down at the rim of light underneath it and imagine a shadow falling across it. It doesn't, but I'm suddenly reminded of what I saw while I was on the ladder. Did I really see something, or was it just a cloud passing in front of the sun?

That fast?

With a final glance at Ellie, who still hasn't moved from her blanket cocoon, I reach for the door handle... and it fu–nking happens again!

The thing clicks open, completely unaided!

What the F-F-Fu–nk? I scream in my head.

The creak is as loud as a bell in the still of the room. Much louder than it was before, and there's no doubt that it's woken my wife. And yet, her only reaction is to roll over onto my side of the bed.

The landing is awash with the glorious, blue-filtered glow of the nightlights.

I glance over at the scene of yesterday's disaster. I don't know why. Probably to reassure myself that I survived the ordeal.

I never did find out what was in the box, but the thought of venturing back up there – along with the image of that broken strut beckoning me to impale myself on it – sends a chill down my spine.

I turn away from the trapdoor, which is reassuringly shut, and notice that the spare room's door is open. Didn't I close that before bed last night? Obviously not.

On the landing, just outside our room, Buddy's box, now a nest of old, warm tops of mine, is empty. The hound is nowhere to be seen. I squint into the gloom, but resist the urge to call out because I don't want to wake Ellie. She's already found me in this situation before and I'm in no hurry to repeat the experience.

And I can't help but wonder which I hate the most; the demon wind moaning under doorways or the tomblike stillness of this place, where every creak and sigh is amplified by the sparseness of the furnishings. I'm considering this when my thoughts are interrupted by that sound again. Distant. Tinny. It's definitely voices. Laughter. Yes, it's the sound of someone laughing, and it's coming from….

I move to the bannister and look over it. Down into the den. My view is limited because of the vertical drop, but I can see something down there. It's faint light, like ripples of water bouncing off the walls.

What the hell?

I glance back at the bedroom door. Is this the time to wake Ellie? Why? It doesn't sound like intruders. At least, they don't sound dangerous.

I make my way down the stairs slowly and cautiously, as if this will somehow diminish the noisy creaks of wood underfoot. It doesn't, and I cringe at each and every one of those squeals. Not that the uninvited guests seem to care, as their chatter and laughter continues unabated.

So, now I'm slowly moving from apprehension to irritation. I know that my reaction is due in part to the fact that I'm dealing with the unknown. It's something over which I have no control, and my being confronted with that reality is invoking a flight or fight response in me.

Yes. I've been in this movie before.

The other part of my irritation, of course, has got to be related to the fact that this house is designed in such a way that, once you've left the landing, you can't see what's going on in the den until you've reached the foot of the stairs.

And that's when my stomach turns, and I become aware of the throbbing at the back of my head which is matched only by the pounding in my chest.

"Oh fu—nk," is all I can whisper as I reach the foot of the stairs.

The sound and flickering lightshow is coming from the photography room. The door, which I'm sure was closed before we went upstairs for the night, is ajar in a way that allows light and sound to spill out of it, to flood the den and wash over me.

Voices that I recognise and am now rushing towards.

"…now might be a good time to finally lay this question to rest. Who is your favourite parent?"

"Da-ad!"

"Marc! Stop asking him that."

"Well, he keeps abstaining from answering. He's got the diplomacy of a bloody politician. Is that what you're going to be when you grow up?"

"I love this, and I love you both so much exactly the same amount."

"OK, and how much is that?"

"Um, more than all the stars in the galaxy… no, more than all the grains of sand!"

There's a boulder in the pit of my belly. A lump in my throat.

It feels like it's been years since I last heard the beautiful timbre of his voice, the glorious colour of his laugh.

"Toby," I utter as I reach the door's threshold and look inside.

My laptop is open on the bureau, and a video of my family is playing full-screen.

My son and my wife are both in frame. Toby, his sandy blond hair radiant in the sunshine streaming in from the nearby window, is emerging from a hug with Ellie, who looks at the camera, at me, and grins. *We did good.*

"Good job, Mum."

Toby, my glorious little boy in his superhero pyjamas, walks up to the camera and throws his arms around it, making the image wobble.

My hand clutches at the tightness in my chest as I watch the camera's frame tilt down and fill the screen with the image of a drone shaped like a ship.

"I love you, Daddy."

"You do?"

"Yep. But not more than Mummy. I love you both the same amount."

"I love you, too, little man. Merry Christmas. Just remember the number-one rule."

"Yes, I know. No flying that thing over people...."

"Over people, that's right..."

"Ever."

"That's my boy."

The camera tilts up again and Ellie comes into view. Her face is beaming. Her grin wide and beautiful as she looks at the camera and blows it a kiss.

Love. I felt her love in that moment like I've never felt it before. Strong. Unequivocal.

"Come over here, beautiful – let me give you your Christmas gift!"

"Oh, Da-ad! That's gross!"

"What? I just have a gift for Mummy."

Ellie jumps up from her seat on the floor. *"Better still! I'm feeling a little hungry. How about a Toby sandwich?"*

"Fantastic idea!"

"Oh no! No Toby sandwich! No Toby sandwich!"

I listen to my son's squeals of protest as Ellie scoops him towards the camera. There's more laughter, more squeals of protestation before the screen goes black and then static fills the room with a fuzzy glow.

I swipe at the tears in my eyes, and that's when I notice him. I've been so engrossed in what was on the screen that I didn't see him before, but now, for reasons I can't explain, the sight of him rakes up the small hairs on the back of my neck once more.

Buddy.

He's been sitting on the chair the whole time and watching the video, but now the puppy – somehow looking twice his size – slowly turns his head to look at me. Eyes wide, one ear up and alert with the other drooping, the dog sits ramrod straight and holds my gaze.

"Buddy?"

He doesn't even blink at the sound of my voice. Instead, the puppy turns back to the screen which is still broadcasting an electrical blizzard… before sputtering a few times and then springing back to life.

It takes a few seconds for me to work out what I am watching, and then I instinctively step closer.

The view is from above. The shot growing wider, and then I see the beach. The car. Us.

"No," I utter as I watch myself on screen, looking upward towards the camera lens with a hand over my eyes, shielding it from the glare of the sun. I'm smiling. Toby, controller in his tiny hands, is grinning with me.

I step closer to the laptop as it projects the images of my son and me from above, walking down a sandy path to the beach before stopping, looking up, and waving in synchronisation. Then, I stick my fingers in my mouth and pull a face. My son follows suit before we resume our journey towards the pier.

"No," I croak once more, clutching the growing ache in my chest as my unconscious is dissolved by the overwhelming weight of foreboding.

Toby is looking straight into the lens now, and then – suddenly and spontaneously – he lets the controller dangle from the lanyard around his neck before yelling something at the camera. There's no sound, but I remember the words clearly as if they have just been spoken.

"I LOVE MY DADDY!" I mouth with him.

I thump my clenched fist against my chest as if trying to scare my heart into calming down, but it wants out. It wants to leave this viewing because it doesn't want to watch what comes next. I don't want to watch, either, but I'm paralysed. Entranced by each and every frame of the footage that is so familiar, in that I was there, but alien because I have never seen it before.

We're walking across the wood pier now, drone flying high above us. I can see the surf. The tide is in. It isn't angry; it's wild. It smashes and froths white peaks like saliva on the rocky teeth under and around the pier.

I'm a few feet away from the laptop now, and all of my instincts are telling me to shut the thing off, close the lid, and run from here, never to return, but I can't. No matter how much I try, I can't stop watching the image of us walking toward confectionary stands. I can smell the frying onions. Feel the warm breeze on my face.

Toby is running in front of me now, but stops to look back. I watch myself jerk a thumb downward.

"No," I say again, as if the computer can hear me and as if I have any control of these pre-recorded images.

The headache at the back of my neck is pounding now, the veins in my temple bulging, and I realise it's because I've stopped breathing.

Breathe!

When I do, my breath doesn't come deep and slow, but fast and shallow… as if it can by some means influence the fact that the image on screen is now almost directly looking down at us, the other people, the pier and the ocean. The frame is shrinking, becoming tighter and tighter as the camera slowly descends back to earth. I can see myself on the phone, looking in Toby's direction. He's much closer to the image, looking upward into the camera as it descends to his height.

"Don't do it. Don't!" I plead through tears. "Please don't do it."

But my son is hurrying closer towards the lens now with an alarmed look on his face. He's just feet away.

"No!"

I can see myself in the background, dropping my phone and running after my son. I'm yelling, screaming.

"Toby, no!"

I watch as my son lunges towards the lens, his face a mask of terror as first his tiny hand and then his golden hair blur out of focus and then disappear, leaving a glimpse of my horrified expression before the camera descends under the pier and crashes onto the rocks before being bathed in water.

Then, everything flickers to black.

19. ICE CREAM

SATURDAY, EARLY MORNING.

Sunshine. Summer breeze. The smell of the ocean. The fairground melody of the carousel. I turn my face to the sun and it's like warm fingers caressing my skin.

Then, laughing. We're laughing. I'm blessed. I love. My son.

"I love you, buddy."

"I love you, too, Daddy."

"Can we get an ice cream now?"

"Sure."

We're on the pier. My son's footsteps are loud on the boardwalk as he races towards the ice cream kiosk. It's large. More like an ice cream truck than a small kiosk. It's bright, colourful, decorated with the image of a clown eating an ice cream and carrying the words, 'FUN! FUN! FUN!'

"Three cones with flakes, please," Toby says excitedly.

"Wait, what? Toby, what are you doing?" I ask with a bemused chuckle.

Toby looks at me and frowns. "I'm ordering the ice cream, Daddy."

"Yes, but two, not three of them, silly," I say, walking up to him.

"But we need three," he says.

"Why would we need three, greedy?"

"Because she said so," he replies, pointing inside the kiosk.

I turn, following the direction of my son's finger. "I'm sorry, but—" I cut my words short when I see that there's nobody inside the kiosk. It's empty.

"Um, who were you talking to, buddy? There's nobody in there."

He chuckles. "What do you mean, Daddy. She's right there."

"No. I can't see anyone."

"She's right there. To the right. Hiding behind the counter."

Hiding? I step towards the serving hatch. "Hello? Excuse me."

"Don't get too close, Daddy," Toby warns.

"What do you mean?"

He doesn't respond, but instead starts pulling at my hand. "Let's go, Daddy. Let's go now."

"Wait. Wait," I say, pulling my hand away. "I thought you wanted ice cream?"

"Dad."

"It's OK, Toby. Excuse me," I say, leaning into the serving hatch, but it's almost as high as me, so I can't see behind the counter without getting on my tip-toes.

"Daddy…"

"It's OK, buddy."

I strain to lean over and look around the large menu board and various syrup pumps. But there's nothing there. I can't see anything.

"There's nobody here, To—" My sentence is cut short by the sudden sensation of something crawling through my hair. It's chunky. Large. The legs of some kind of insect.

A chill runs through me as I consider how to react. If I flick the thing off, it'll end up on my son. I need to flick it in the opposite direction. Back into the kiosk.

I can feel the anxiety building in my chest, and my instinct is screaming at me to just flick the thing anyway and then run. Fast. But I stay calm. Calm.

After three.

"Daddy?"

Three.

"It's OK, Buddy. You stay there."

Two.

"Dad!"

One.

In one powerful movement, I swipe my hand from the back

of my head to the front, expecting whatever it is to be ejected forward, but instead I feel my fingers entangled in something.

It's hair! Thick, black hair!

"What the…." The words dry in my mouth as I follow the strands up to the ceiling of the kiosk, where more hair hangs like a giant web fanning out in curtains towards me. And there, at its centre, waiting like a voracious spider, is something pockmarked, slimy, and pallid that shifts and begins to turn my way….

"Daddy!"

"Marc!"

"Daddy!"

"Marco!"

I wake with a start to see Ellie standing over me, holding a mug of coffee.

"Good morning, sleepyhead," she says with a curious lift of the eyebrows.

I'm sitting in the wingback chair of the study with my legs extended onto the stool.

I rub my eyes and face, blinking away sleep and the remnants of that hideous dream before attempting to sit up, but I feel a weight on my lap.

"Buddy," I groan. The dog glances at me and then goes back to snoozing.

"Rough night?" Ellie asks as she waits for me to relocate the puppy to the stool and stretch my achy legs to the floor.

"I, um." I can't even remember how I got–

The laptop. I look at it. The lid is closed.

"Oh God." I rub my neck. "Everything hurts."

"Yes. And snoozing in the chair probably didn't help any, either," Ellie says.

"What time is it?" I ask, clicking the crick in my shoulder.

"Almost eight-thirty."

"Shit."

"What are you doing down here?" my wife asks.

And I try to find an excuse. I don't know why. It just feels wrong to have slept down here – like I'm trying to send her a message or something, which I'm not. Although, now that I think about it…. "I thought I heard a noise last night," I say. The words have just fallen out of my mouth, and it's as good an excuse as any.

"What kind of noise?"

"I, um…." I don't know how to raise this conversation first thing, so instead I take the mug that she's still patiently holding aloft and draw a generous sip. It's hot. Strong. Welcome.

OK. So, what's my problem? I don't even know. To be fair, I've just woken up, I don't think the cogs have started turning in my fuzzy head yet. Have I mentioned that? Along with all of my other aches and pains, it feels like I have a bloody hangover, which you and I both know isn't possible.

"So?" Ellie asks expectantly. "What kind of noise?"

"Did you put anything in the loft when we arrived here?" I ask. Once again, the words have just fallen out of my mouth, and I decide that this is probably the best strategy right now. *Don't overthink it.*

She cocks her head, "Why do you ask?"

OK. So, it isn't a denial, which means she probably did and doesn't want to talk about it. "Ellie, that's answering a question with a question. You hate it when I do that," I say with a smile.

"I also hate it when you don't just get to the point," she says, reflecting said smile.

"I think I found some stuff up there yesterday."

"What were you doing in the attic?"

OK. I wasn't expecting another question. "I, um, told you, I just wanted to see what was up there. You know, see what condition the place was in and if there was any stuff we'd need to get rid of."

"What kind of stuff?"

"Eh? Stuff… you know. Like boxes and shit from the previous tenant."

"No. What kind of stuff did you find up there?"

"Ellie," I groan, supressing my early-morning, achy-body impatience. "Did you put anything in the attic when we got here, yes or no?"

She puts a hand on her thigh and then looks around the

room as if she doesn't want the photographs to hear what she has to say. Then, she turns back to me and nods.

"Why didn't you tell me?"

"I didn't realise it was that important."

"It isn't. It's just—"

"Why are you asking?"

I glance at the laptop, and can see that the SD card is still in its slot. And, again, I don't want to say anything, but I reason to myself that it makes no sense to hide it.

"I found the SD card. Well, I didn't exactly find it…." I watch a shadow like a raincloud fall over my wife's face, but continue, "Why didn't you tell me about it?"

She looks at her feet and then shrugs. "I don't know. They gave some stuff back to me. They also said they'd managed to retrieve the data from that thing and thought I might want to keep it." She sighs. "I couldn't bring myself to leaving any of it in storage and didn't want to keep it within easy reach, either, so I just put it out of the way of both of us." She looks at me, eyes now glistening with tears. I watch her swallow words before forming them. "Did you watch it?"

It's a reluctant question of the kind where the inquirer doesn't actually want a reply, yet feels compelled to ask it, nonetheless.

And I have no idea how to respond; *yes* sounds like some kind of betrayal, and *no* is an outright lie.

I nod.

She frowns. "Why?"

And I think that's an odd question. "Why?"

"Yes. Why? Why would you watch it?"

"Well, I didn't have much of a choice. You left it in my laptop. She squints at me and is about to say something, but I'm already coming back with an extension to my retort, "Besides, why wouldn't I? He's my son."

I watch her bite her lip. I can see there's a struggle behind those almond-shaped eyes of hers, but I have no idea what kind of a struggle because she won't talk to me about it. Asking only aggravates her, which in turn aggravates me because I want my wife to feel safe and secure enough around me to be able to express how she's feeling, beyond anger.

"I'm going out," she says, swiping the back of her hand across her eyes.

"Ellie—"

"We haven't got anything in the house, and we've got visitors arriving tonight, remember?"

"Do you want me to come with you?" I ask.

"No," she responds abruptly. "You're not even ready yet and I... I have some other errands I need to run. Besides, there's no fucking heating in this house and I'd rather you look at sorting that as well as finding a new home for the dog!"

With that, she turns on her heels to leave.

"Ellie?" I call after her.

But she's already disappeared out of the door.

20. THE FOG

SATURDAY. LATE MORNING.

So, I know it's a thing, as sexist as this is going to sound, to ask the man of the house to check the heating, but if I'm being perfectly honest, I still don't get it.

I'm not a plumber, and nor do I profess to be some kind of heating expert; yet, still, when my wife asks me to check if the heating's packed up, I do so as if I'm any more qualified than she at checking whether or not the storage heaters in the house are working.

They are. Or at least they appear to be. Again, I'm no expert, but if the switch is set to ON and the light is illuminated, I believe it's fairly safe to assume that the thing is working... or else doing a very good job at pretending to be.

And yet, Ellie is right. It's still bloody cold in here.

I mean, for crying out loud, doesn't this house understand that it's perpetuating the stereotype of all places of its kind? Cold drafts, storage heaters that appear to take electricity but give nothing in return, and a fireplace that coughs more disgusting smoke than it has ever produced heat.

Especially this morning, when I came to in that chair. I mean, the chill has quite literally taken up residence in my bones. I tried my best not to make it obvious in front of Ellie, but, well, you saw how that went.

With that in mind, you won't be surprised to hear that I was very much looking forward to a hot shower. What I got instead was a dribble that sputtered and hissed like a disgruntled reptile before vomiting glacial water over me. I read somewhere that cold showers are good for you. Invigorating. Those saying that seem to miss out on the part where sometimes the water is sometimes so f–reezing cold that it feels as if your heart has stopped.

So, now I'm dressed in two pairs of socks, jeans, a T-shirt, a sweater, and that ole favourite, my fleece. Which reminds me, I really need to throw it in the washing machine, as it's starting to smell a little funky. Like the rest of this place. Every now and then, I'm sure I catch a whiff of something beyond rank, but then, when I stop to investigate further, it's gone. So, I think it's all in my head.

And yes, I know what you're thinking. We've all seen the same movies. You're thinking I've got a poltergeist in this house.

Really? Stop and think about that for a second. I mean, really think about it.

Exactly.

So, now I'm sipping more hot coffee, which is more for the warmth than the caffeine, while looking at the picket fence through the kitchen window.

I should have told Ellie about the oil heaters, but that would have led to a whole different conversation; and it's probably best I just go get them as soon as she's back with the car. Or, better still, I'll order them online.

Should I pull on a coat, as well?

No. Physical activity should bring back the sensation in my toes.

It's nearly lunchtime by the time I venture out into a freezing fog that descended on this place sometime yesterday evening and seems to have no plans to leave.

But it's OK. I'm OK. I'm layered up and ready for action.

If Buddy is feeling the chill, he doesn't show it. Instead, he trots down the garden path with his tail high, and I'm reminded of last night. Of how he was sitting on that chair, seemingly watching that video and then me.

And yes, I'm man enough to admit, in the foggy light of day, that there was something about the way he was looking at me that gave me the creeps. I mean, I didn't notice it at the time, as I was preoccupied with the images on that screen, but now, in retrospect, the human way in which that dog turned to look at me… well, yeah, brrr! It's just sent a creepy chill right down my back.

"Creepy, Buddy!" I call to him, but he merely looks at me expectantly, as if to say, *Are you going to open this gate or what?*

I do. And he ambles out, stopping only to sniff a leaf here, a patch of grass there. No doubt considering which section of the garden he's going to fertilise today. We probably should get into a better and healthier routine with these morning walks, with a view to discouraging him from doing his business anywhere near the house if we can avoid it. It's not like we don't have enough land.

Assuming nobody reclaims him, of course.

Wow. That thought just made my stomach flutter. I'm becoming attached. I know that. But, hey, you try being around this little fella and not falling in love. Especially after last night.

No. Not that *Exorcist* chair moment, but afterwards.

After I watched the video and dissolved into a crumpled mess on the floor. And when I say *mess*, I mean it. I'm talking convulsive sobs. Tears streaming in torrents down my face and snot like candle wax on my lip. It was, undoubtedly, not a pretty sight. I had no idea it all still felt so raw. Well, I did; I just didn't realise it could still affect me as strongly as that. After all, isn't time supposed to heal?

Yeah. Probably more than a few months needed for that. God. It may as well be years. I've no doubt I'll not feel any different at that point.

I ache for my little boy, which is most likely why I've become attached to this bundle of trouble so quickly. In a way – and yes, I know this is going to sound strange, if not a little creepy – he reminds me of Toby.

The puppy looks at me like a foreman would an employee who isn't getting to work.

And that's just it. Right there. This little rascal seems to have his own personality, which is why, last night, while I was on that floor, he whimpered as if he was sharing my grief, crawled into the space between my legs, and then placed his head on my thigh.

Now, come on, I defy anybody not to be emotionally affected by that.

Of course, it could just be that he was making himself comfortable and I'm reading that he was being comforting. I was, after all, vulnerable. Needy.

My foreman is happy now, though, as I have dumped my so-called equipment on the ground and am, with a gloved hand, sanding the first part of the fence.

Shit.

This is going to take much longer than I thought. I probably should have invested in an electric sander. There's elbow-grease, and then there's doing yourself an injury.

Nope, I don't think I ever said I was a DIY man. But, thinking positively, I've just decided that this is going to be my thing. My so-called labour of love. I am going to restore this whole picket fence and gate to its former glory and then I'm going to declare that–

"Buddy! Shoosh!" He's been yapping for the past minute or so at nothing, just the misty drive, but it's empty.

At first, I thought it might be Ellie returning, but nothing's there. Besides, she's just texted that she's going to be later than she thought. Traffic was bad, but nothing to worry about. By *traffic*, you know I mean the next town and not Porthcove, right? The only bad traffic around here is the occasional murmuration of birds.

Speaking of which. Where's everything gone? I can't hear any seagulls, nor the resident crows or tweet in the bramble. I can barely hear the surf. It's as if the fog has smothered all other sounds but the scratching of sandpaper against wood and–

"Buddy! Stop it!" I pause and look up. He's standing in the middle of the driveway now, legs extended as far as his little body will allow. Tail wagging furiously behind him as he leaps toward and then back from the mist in a frenzy of snapping barks and angry growls.

I follow his gaze. Squinting into the vapor.

Nothing.

Just glistening gravel dissolving into the silver haze, out of which there's–

Oh shit! There!

In the mist. Dark shapes? People? Watching us, unmoving.

I stare at the sight before yelling, "Who's there? Who are you?"

But there's no reply.

And then it occurs to me. I roll my eyes and shake my head. That crowd of people is the bloody outlines of trees!

Isn't it?

Wait. I'm squinting. Peering into nature's veil to ascertain what exactly the dog is getting all worked up about. He's amped up the bravado now. Venturing further up the driveway, yapping in all directions.

"There's nothing there, Buddy! Nothing."

And yet, I'm still rising from my kneeling position by the fence and walking up to him, all the time scanning the depths of the fog. When I reach the dog, I crouch down and stroke his back, hoping to break the spell, but he's adamant that something about the....

Realisation dawns. It isn't what's in the mist. It *is* the mist.

I smile. "It's just fog, Buddy," I tell him as if we chat like this all the time. I wonder what my yapping may sound like to him, and it brings a smile to my face.

Blah blah blah blah, Buddy. Blah blah blah.

"It's just fog." I add with a chuckle as I watch the grumpy pup jump up and down. I've got to give it to him – what he lacks in stature right now, he certainly makes up for in bluster.

I look up once more. The mist appears to have shifted now, growing in intensity and swirling around us like the smoke from that shitty fireplace. As if it weren't a meteorological phenomenon at all, but a living entity. Thick. Cold. Inhospitable.

I hope Ellie's going to be OK driving back in this. The roads around here can be treacherous. I should send her a message, but what if she tries to read it while driving?

The yapping is persisting. Growing now, both in speed and intensity... as if there's something right next to us.

"Hey, Buddy, calm down… calm down," I say. "You're going to give yourself an aneurysm."

But the dog isn't even hearing me anymore. He's staring directly ahead. So, I follow his gaze back to the outlines of those trees. Staring now. Scrutinizing them, and yet I still can't see

Oh shit!

One of the trees has just moved. One of those bloody shapes has just moved behind one of the others.

You're just seeing things….

It moved! Across the driveway towards the wood.

My heart's knocking at my chest again, demanding to be set free so that it can abandon me here and go and seek shelter inside the house. I'm unable to move, paralysed by the very thought that whoever that is, they've been standing there watching us all this whole time.

Buddy, on the other hand, has no such concerns, and moves forward to chase the shapeshifter away.

"NO! No, Buddy!" I yell instinctively. Then, angrily, I add to the fog, "Who is that? Who's there?"

But there's no reply, and I'm just about to shout again when I see them.

Eyes!

Burning through the fog, and seemingly growing in size and shape, followed by crackling sound. The first, beyond the dog's barking.

Rumbling.

Rumbling, crackling, and popping!

Then, the glaring eyes shift and metamorphose until….

They're the headlamps of a bloody car slowly making its way down the drive.

"Jesus Christ." I release my breath as the car rolls to a stop in front of us.

Ellie steps out of the driving seat, looks our way, and asks, "What?"

21. GUESTS

PORTHCOVE. 18:36.

It turns out that the errand Ellie had to run was buying new clothes and shoes for work. By *clothes*, I mean several outfits: one for each day of the week, with three pairs of shoes. None were what she was looking for, but they would have to do until she got back to civilisation. When I asked if it would be easier to just have some of her things shipped here from storage, she looked at me as if had a bogey hanging from my nose, stating that those clothes were at least five months old.

Yes. I don't know if I mentioned this before, but, for all of my wife's romantic speeches about the unimportance of money and how she doesn't need anything but her family, I find that she often fails to note the fact that, by family, she isn't just talking about Toby and me, but *Jimmy Choo, Louboutin, Louis Vuitton* and the whole extended family of expensive brands.

And, as I've mentioned before, living in London is expensive and there's only been so much money to go around.

But what my wife wants, she must have.

She's just landed herself an important job with a lot of responsibility. She needs to dress the part, and I fully support that. I'm just looking forward to the part where we've sold this place and I'm no longer worrying about my knees knocking together every time Ellie goes shopping.

After the fashion show, it was time to get on with dinner; only, Ellie said that she needed to work on her presentation, as it was important to her to make the right impression both on David and on their potential buyers – I mean *business partners*, as it's all still hush hush.

Anyway, it fell to me to cook dinner for our guests. And, if I'm being perfectly honest, that charge makes me happy. It feels like the first time in a long time that Ellie and I are co-hosting a dinner party, and it's the closest we've come to normality since my return. Not to mention the fact that it's the first time we've had guests at Dolce Vita. And most likely the last, so I'm planning to make the most of it.

The special of the day is homemade lasagna. No, I'm not talking about the slop served at restaurants or that pre-packaged shit you shove in the microwave. I'm talking about traditional *pasta sugo* made with meatballs of organic beef- fresh from the butchers – with homegrown herbs and spices layered over fresh leaves of pasta and topped off with a variety of cheeses, and then more of that beautiful, rich red sauce.

No need for so-called Bechamel slop.

For seconds, it's the best grilled *Bistecca* with green salad and crunchy bread, fresh from the bakery.

Yes, the one remarkable thing about this village is all of the artisan goodness it has to offer. It is without a doubt one of the things I am going to miss the most when we leave.

With the lasagna in the oven, I pour two glasses of Ellie's favourite Chianti, and I'm about to make my way over to the dining room but change my mind. I want tonight to be a great night, and I'd rather not start it off with that look of Ellie's that says nothing and everything at the same time.

So, I go back, return the contents of one glass to the bottle, and refill it with sparkling water.

Yay.

I feel a spark of irritation at the deprivation, but if it preserves the peace and contributes to a successful evening, then, fine.

However, that spark turns into a flame when I step out of the kitchen and into the dark hallway.

"Ellie," I grumble, "why do you keep turning the bloody light off?" As if she can hear me.

She's always doing this; each and every time she goes to the toilet, she keeps turning out the lights because she thinks it's a waste of electricity, but she forgets that we're not living in the city anymore. And this particular part of the house is, as you already know, miserable as sin.

Worse is the fact that the shitty light switch, as you'd expect, is badly located at the opposite end of the hall.

Anyway, I take a deep breath and smother that flame the best I can as I push the door to the dining room open with an eerie creek.

Yes, they all seem to do that here. And, yes, I've sprayed the bloody things with all sorts of home remedies and yet they continue to creak like something off a *Hammer House of Horror* film set. The dampness of the sea air can do that, which is one of the reasons why they tend to install storage heaters in these types of properties. That's when they work, of course.

Anyway, it's as I'm about to step into the dining room that I see Ellie's silhouette block what little light there is coming from the lounge at the opposite end of the corridor. "Oh, El! Can you switch the light on, please, while you're there?"

"What's that?" she responds, distracted. Only, her voice isn't coming from the hallway… it's coming from inside the dining room, where I turn to see her sitting over her laptop at the table.

I nearly drop both glasses as my head whips back to the corridor. But there's nothing there; just the amber glow of the lamplight spilling in from the lounge.

"What did you say, Marc?"

I look back into the dining room. Ellie has turned in her seat and is leaning on the back rest looking at me, curiously.

"I, um…" I look back up the hallway and then back at her several times, hoping to recreate the effect.

Nothing.

"Are you OK?" she asks.

"I'm fine. I, um, just thought I saw you in the hallway."

"No," she says wearily. "I've been here the whole time. Then,

"Is that for me?" she asks excitedly, eyes widening like saucers as she takes in both glasses in my hand.

And I'm back in the room once more.

"Yeah. This is for you," I say, walking up to her.

"Oh, thank you so much," she replies, taking the glass from me as her phone vibrates twice and then lights up. She looks at it and then at me, and asks, "How's the feast coming along?"

"Yeah. Good."

The phone vibrates again, and this time she turns it over without looking at it. "Smells great," she adds with a smile. "Have you heard from David?"

"Yes, they've hit traffic," I say as the phone vibrates again. "Aren't you going to get that?" I ask.

"No. It's just work."

"Might be David."

"No. You just said he messaged you, right?"

I think about this, and no, of course, I don't believe my wife. Her whole body language is off; tense shoulders, over-smiling, complete disinterest in the object she's normally glued to. On the other hand, we did have a long chat about how tonight is about the reunion of friends and not just another board meeting between her and David.

There is to be no *shop talk* tonight.

"Did you turn the light off in the hallway again?" I ask, jerking a thumb behind me.

She follows it with her gaze. "Hallway? Um, no."

"Well, I remember turning it on and now it's off again."

She looks back at me with a smile and asks, "Are you sure you're OK?"

"I'm fine. I just want to know if you turned the light off. I know you've got a thing about–"

"Marco, I didn't turn the light off," she says slowly, making a show of looking around me.

It's my turn to follow her gaze this time, and when I do, I see that the hallway is now flooded with light.

"What? That can't be."

Ellie giggles. I love that sound. I haven't heard it that much since we arrived here, and it's soothing. More normality.

"Are you sure you've got water in that glass?" she asks. "Let me sniff it," she says, reaching for my hand.

"I'm telling you. That light was off when I came in here. Didn't you see it?" I look at her, but after she's done sniffing my water, she simply widens her eyes, flashes me one of my favourite cheeky smiles, and then takes a sip from her glass.

"There's got to be something weird going on with the wiring…" I want to add *in my head*, but I think I forfeited the right to make that joke a while ago. Now, all jokes about mental illness are no longer funny in any shape or form. Yes, even for me.

I'm considering this when we're startled by three loud bangs at the front door. That's right. *Bangs* and not knocks. The sound echoes down the hallway I'm still gawking at and slaps me across the face.

Did I mention how much I hate people knocking like that? Just use the bell. *Use the effing bell!*

"They're here," I say ominously.

"Good. Because I'm starving," my wife says, turning back to her computer.

"Um, aren't you going to shut that up now?"

"What for? It's not as if I need to dress for dinner. Besides, if I get out of this woolly jumper, there's a good chance I'll get frostbite, thanks to my husband."

"Ha ha. Very funny. I told you that I checked. The bloody heaters are working. Although, I suppose that remains subject to interpretation."

Ellie's about to make another quip when, *BANG! BANG! BANG!* echoes down the hallway once more.

"I'll get it, then," I say, and off I plod into the now slightly less gloomy hallway, although judging by the way the light is flickering – like one of those bloody theme park ghost houses – that probably won't be the case for much longer.

And I've barely emerged from the gloom when I feel it… that familiar arctic breeze on my face. And I hesitate. I don't even know why, but I've suddenly become wary. The air feels different. Charged. Like it does just before a rainstorm. My skin feels prickly and there's that general icky feeling that makes me squirm.

I look back down the hall and consider calling Ellie. Not because I'm afraid. *Afraid? Of what?*

It's just this feeling, and I want to know if it's me or if she feels it, too. But then, that would freak her the fu–nk out.

Hesitantly, I step out of the hallway and stop. Then, in a scene worthy of a thousand horror movies, I take in the space like a director's camera.

The stairs steeped in shadows, but empty.

The den, two lamps burning innocently. Empty.

The photography room – door shut, just as I left it.

And then the bit I've been ignoring. The bit that rolls an icy snow boulder down my spine and into the pit of my gut. The front door.

Wide open.

Faint wisps of mist along with the distant sound of the far-away world drifts in and languishes in the lamplight.

I pan back to the lounge. It's empty. Then back to the door.

There's nothing in here. So, why do I feel like I'm not alone?

Slowly, I turn and look down the hallway. The light has stopped flickering.

"Marco?"

Ellie's distant voice shatters the moment like crystal, startling and galvanising me.

I step forward and cross the space to the front door, hunching against the chill blowing at me, and I look out.

It's dark out there. So, I flip the wall switch.

Nothing happens. And that doesn't surprise me since it's characteristic of this place.

From what I can make out in the overspill of the houselights, that thick freezing fog is still smothering the land.

"Hello?"

The mist swallows my words and gives nothing in return.

I glance back into the lounge.

Empty.

I pull my phone out of my pocket, tap on the light, and aim it in front of me and to the sides, as far as the beam will travel. Water particles drift innocently back and forth like miniscule insects. They appear to be the only thing out here.

Then, who knocked on the door?

And who opened it?

The light starts juddering as I begin to shiver. I swap hands and pan the beam around, but all it reveals is the same white wall. Deep. Impenetrable. Like the cold out here.

I sense Ellie walking up behind me. The clouds of our breaths appearing and then dissolving into the night.

"There's nobody out here," I say distractedly, brandishing and panning the light in front of us. "And I've no idea who was at the door, but it was wide open when I came out," I say, squinting into the gloom.

"Hey! Why aren't you answering me?"

A jolt of terror whips my heart into a frenzied patter as I slowly turn to look over my shoulder and back into the house.

Ellie has just emerged through the archway into the den and is standing, hand on hips, staring at me.

I stagger back from the front door and retreat several steps down the path before I see my wife's silhouette fill the open doorway.

"What's the matter? Marc? What's wrong with you?" I hear her say. Or at least I think that's what she's saying because I can see her lips move, but my mind is numb with horror.

I shine the torch light at her face, causing her to squint and throw up her hands to fend off the glare.

"Hey! Stop that!" she complains.

I open my mouth to speak, but I'm unable to find the words. I'm unable to articulate that someone was just standing behind me. Someone who was not her.

"Marc!" she yells, breaking the spell.

"I… um… sorry. Sorry," I mumble, realising that I'm still blinding her.

"What's the hell's wrong with you?"

"I, um, I thought you were standing at the door next to me. But you weren't. You… you were still inside."

"What? What are you talking about?"

I want to answer her. I keep trying to wrap my tongue around the words, but none of them make sense, so I just dismiss them.

"Marc," Ellie begins, but stops when we're both distracted by the scrunching sound of tyres on gravel.

I turn to see the fog being stained yellow with headlamps as a Range Rover rolls to a stop just outside of the front gate.

"OK. Weirdo," Ellie says, walking towards me. "This conversation is on pause, for now. And can we please get the bloody light fixed? I can't see a thing out here." Then she's gone. Through the gate, towards the vehicle.

I glance back at the house. The void of the open-door stares back. My wife is right. I'm not even going to think about this shit while they're here. I'm not. I can't.

So, with a sigh and that reassuring run of hands through my hair, I make my way down the path after her.

My best friend, David, must have opted for the practical vehicle today. That or it's Arron's car, because David loves performance vehicles, which he likes to refer to as *Dick Magnets*. He often says that his love for supercars is seconded only by the number of actual dicks he can pick up in them.

However, this all changed the moment he met Aaron. Or so Ellie keeps telling me. I haven't seen much of my friend since it all went to shit a few months back. And, I realise now, as I see him jumping out of the SUV, just how much I've missed him. Not that I would ever tell him that, of course. I'm a bloke, after all.

I think about the fact that he's engaged to be married, though, and that thought puts a smile on my face because it's as weird as it is exciting. I mean, this is the guy who said that monogamy is unnatural. That human beings are programmed to perpetuate the species. Spread the so-called seed far and wide. That we're not designed to be exclusive with one person for our lifetimes. I know this because it's the speech he gave me when I went to him in bits after first cheating on my wife. I know, not my finest hour, and nor was having an affair with someone for the best part of a year.

At least, I think it was that long.

No. It's not what you think. It's not that I don't remember because I'm a piece of shit; that's a given. This is more because it was part of my addiction, and something even I wasn't truly aware of until my world imploded.

Anyway, since meeting Aaron, David has changed his stance on monogamy as well his position on spending life married exclusively to one *dick* beyond his own.

His words.

Now, he's engaged. I never thought I'd see the day.

"Alright, geeza!" is my chum's enthusiastic greeting, along with an equally over-enthusiastic hug. And when he's done deliberately squishing me along with slobbery-kissing me on the cheek for no reason other than the fact that he knows I hate it, I say, "You managed to finally find the place, then?"

"Dude, what I can say? I'm a busy man. Besides, wasn't I the one who messaged you and said I was going to gate-crash this place? If I'd waited for an invite, we'd never have gotten here."

I consider this, and am about to respond when Ellie throws her arms around him in a quick embrace before saying, "He doesn't want us to mention anything to do with work this weekend. He doesn't want us to talk about any of that stuff. He wants this weekend to be all about friendship and tranquillity."

"Is that right?" David asks, observing her for several seconds before finally saying, "I can do that."

"I second that!" Arron agrees from the back of the vehicle.

"OK. Alright. Message received. No shop talk... but now that I've finished with your missus, why don't you pucker up and give me another smacker?"

"Oh, get out of it," I say before moving to the back of the vehicle, where Aaron is busy retrieving overnight bags. "Hey, Aaron,"

"Hey, Marco," he says with a warm smile. "How're you doin'?"

I proffer a hand, but he looks at it and then pulls me into a hug, slapping me on the back.

Yeah, I know part of this is because David will have told him to amp up the touchy-feely just to try to bug me.

"I'm good. I'm good. It's been a while," I say when it's over.

"It sure has."

"How was your journey?"

"Long."

"Yeah. It takes some getting used to. Here, let me help you," I say, taking one of the two holdalls. "It's good to see you both." And I mean it. I'm grateful for the company.

"Sorry. But, you know, Ellie said it would probably be best if we gave you guys some time to settle in," he says. "If it were down to me, I would have climbed into your trunk the first day you came out here."

I laugh. "You wait until you see the view. You're going to love it."

"Can't wait," he says. "So, how are you coping with all the fresh air? Must suck, right?" he asks with a grin.

"Yeah. It's awful."

I like this guy. Something about him. What you see is what you get. And, of course, who can forget the way we met? A brawl in the middle of a stuck-up London restaurant. Although, technically, it wasn't really a brawl. I punched him, wrongly believing that it was my wife he was having an affair with. He fell onto a couple's table. Demolished it along with a lot of glasses, my reputation, and much of the credit on my card. The police were called. It all got a bit messy.

But that was then.

When we turn around, I see that both David and Ellie are deep in a conspiratorial conflab.

"Um, excuse me," I call out to them. "Don't forget what we just agreed to!"

"God, he's a nag, how the 'ell do you put up with 'im?" David asks, breaking the intimacy. "Dude, we've got much to catch up on."

"Yeah? And it'll all still be waiting for you on Monday."

"I knew there was a reason why I liked this guy," Aaron says loudly, for my friend's benefit. Then, to me: "Exactly. What's done is done, right?" he asks knowingly, as we make our way to the door.

I'm not sure how to take that.

"Alright. OK. Spoil sports!" David calls back over his shoulder. "Now, El, please tell me you cooked tonight and that we're not going to be forced to eat whatever slop he's thrown togetha."

"I heard that—"

"Just kidding, Marco, me stud muffin!" he says, putting his arm around me and planting a slobbery kiss on my cheek as we all make our way inside, shutting the night out behind us.

PART 2
ELLIE'S JOURNAL

October 13th

Did you know that there are five stages to grief?

1. Denial
2. Anger
3. Bargaining
4. Depression
5. Acceptance

It's been almost a month to the day since it happened. I've definitely moved beyond the denial phase, wouldn't you say?

I reckon that I'm now transitioning from stage 1 and just getting into stage 2. And I don't know what the statistics are on this, but I have a sneaky feeling that this is going to be my favourite stage.

I do have some questions, though. Perhaps you'd be so kind as to explain these to me during our next session. Since I have *accepted* stage 1, does that mean I go straight to stage 5 without passing stages 2 to 4? Or do I still go through those? Does it work a bit like snakes and ladders, or no? Also, is there some sort of timeline I can attach to each of the phases? Just so I have an idea about where I'll be in a few months' time.

You'll be pleased to know that I took the plunge today. In addition to our scintillating, weekly one-hour sessions, I joined a support group.

I received my official invite a few weeks back now. My son's body was barely cold before they shoved that leaflet in my hand. A fucking leaflet. Like they were handing me one of those tickets you get in a shop. *Number 69, please! Number 69! Now serving commiserations, vacuous sympathy, and that fucking rabbit-in-headlights look that people get when they don't know what to say to you for Ticket Number 69!*

Patricia said group would be good for me. You remember her, don't you? She's the best friend I told you about. Came to the funeral, and I hadn't seen or heard from her since. Not until we bumped into each other at Sainsbury's. I dare say that she'd have tried to retreat down the aisle, had it not been for the one-way system they've implemented there now. Awkward. Or "Awks" as she would say.

Anyway, she suggested I join group just like you suggested that I keep a journal. You said it would be cathartic. A journal, for crying out loud! A journal that anybody can pick up and read. Hardly conducive to full, open and honest catharsis, is it?

No, if it's all the same with you, I'd rather keep typing this thing and then password-protecting it and the computer it resides on.

I am now a bone fide cliché. I'm just like the rest of those people you hear about in the news and read about on social media. One of those zombie people that you sympathise with for a few seconds but then try to avoid for fear that they might tarnish you with their misfortune, like black ink on a white blouse. Staining every colourful moment with that ominous, monochromatic certainty that this could happen to you, too.

Well, it did.

It happened to me.

And I hate it. I hate everyone. Including myself. No discrimination implied or intended. And I feel so angry! So fucking angry all the time. I mean ALL the time. As soon as I open my eyes. No, technically it happens before then because I'm already going through it in my dreams.

Then, the moment I open my eyes, *Smack!* It hits me like a punch to the face, a fist to the gut, a boot on my neck pressing down, forcing me into a blubbering ball of wretchedness.

So, yes, I have a sneaky suspicion, although I can't be sure, that I've reached stage 2.

And do you know what I'm thinking about right now? I'm thinking about them. You know, the dregs of society. Those people who spawn children but neglect them so badly that they must be taken into care. That's who I'm thinking about. But I'm not going to write down what I think should be done to them. Oh no. Because if I do that, if I actually put it in black and white, you, dear doctor, will probably want to have me institutionalised. Well, no thank you. No thank you very much.

Although, now that I think about it. Why not? It seems to be working perfectly well for others.

October 16th

It's been a few days since my last entry. That's because it was the anniversary over the weekend. It's been over a month, just a month since it happened, and almost three weeks since he left.

I called again today. Still no chance of a visit, although the doctor is hopeful for a *breakthrough* in the next week or so.

I'll believe that when I see it.

I went back to work today, but when I say 'work', I think I mean more like a 'set'. A film set for one of those old black and white movies. I've been watching a lot of those lately. You know those forties and fifties melodramas. I used to watch them all the time with Toby. It used to be our thing. That boy never ceased to amaze me. I remember being gobsmacked the first time he crawled onto my bed and started watching *Dial M for Murder* with me.

Today, I felt like I was in *Invasion of the Body Snatchers. Not the remake. The original 1956 version with Kevin McCarthy and Dana Wynter.*

Where you gonna go? Where you gonna hide? You can't. Because there's no one like you.

I don't think there was one person on that set today who didn't perform a double-take the moment they clapped eyes on me. I'm like, "Jesus, people. I'm still the same person, you know. It's still me!" Yes, my usually immaculate makeup is off. Yes, I may be lugging some extra baggage under the eyes. Yes, a brush through my hair may have been a good idea this morning, but I was running late. And yes, you judgemental pricks, that is the smell of alcohol, but it's from yesterday.

What's it to you?

Now I know how celebrities must feel. It's stifling. Claustrophobic. It feels like everybody is watching you all the time. I spent most of my day under the glare of the public studio lights, holding back that perpetual flood of tears like Moses and the fucking red sea.

Jesus Christ! Can't I do anything without it being a fucking trigger for what was and/or what happened?

Anyway, you can imagine just how ecstatic I was when the clock director called "cut" on the working day and it was time to go home after more artificial smiles and pleasantries. Thank God that's over. I can't wait to do it all over again tomorrow. NOT!

You know, when David – that's my boss – lectured me about it being too soon to go back to work, I just thought he was being overprotective… but now? Well, now I'm not so sure.

October 17th

So, today started well. It was so good, in fact, that I couldn't wait to get out of bed.

Yes, I'm being sarcastic.

I barely slept last night, for all the bad dreams. Well, I don't know if they can be described as *bad*. Because in the dream, everything is as it was. Sun shining, birds chirping, a whole family. But then I wake up. That's a nightmare, right?

I'd be interested in knowing how you would define that.

So, things are starting to heat up at work. We've got a major release coming out and we're getting a lot of negative feedback from the beta testers – who may sound like a bunch of sophisticates in white coats, but are actually a group of pimpled-faced, scruffy urchins whose delusions of self-importance are matched only by their overinflated egos. Still, they are the last defence before the game is unleashed on a world of equally scruffy urchins whose reviews and cash will ultimately make or break the company's fortunes.

David, who as you know is my so-called friend and boss (I don't know why I feel like I have to keep reintroducing him and why I'm writing it like you're going to read this thing. You're not, are you? – See? Still doing it!)…. Anyway, David went apoplectic at this morning's meeting, which is understandable considering the amount of money that's been invested in developing this game. I don't think I've ever seen him like that.

And so, you would have thought that, as resident Marketing and Communications Executive, it would fall to me to contrive some fantastically inventive way to promote our latest overpriced mind-rotting tat. And you'd be correct. Similarly, should the commercial Armageddon described by our resident man-baby, Sebastian Franks (otherwise known as the Head of Quality Control), happen, you would expect me to be working hard on a robust damage limitation strategy to stop the company's value from going down the toilet once the game's put out and the bad reviews come rolling in.

But I wasn't.

I wasn't even listening to today's episode of Sebastian-the-Whiny-Bitch, during which he described in infinite, tedious detail the results of the last wave of tests. Instead, I was busy thinking about the leaflet I picked up on the way into work this morning.

Sainsbury's has a special two-for-one offer on *taste the difference* Chianti Classico.

According to the leaflet, the Chianti Classico is an elegant wine refined with a bold cherry flavour with a herby, spicy finish. And it hails from an area of Italy that stretches between Florence and Siena.

Chianti is one of my favourite wines. Now, I just need to think about what, if anything, I'd like to eat with it.

October 18th

What a night last night!

After a whole bottle of wine, and at least an hour of tossing and turning, I woke up from yet another dream, screaming!

Is that normal? It can't be normal.

This time, we both fell into the freezing water together. The scene was specially lit in underwater blue. The water was being agitated by a current or some kind of riptide, which meant it was whipped into a white foam with bubbles floating all around us. If it hadn't been so horrific, in that the current kept pulling us apart, it would have been beautiful. Peaceful.

It's the end, though. That part. Oh God, I hate that part because that's the bit where we get ripped apart and I start screaming in a cloud of bubbles as I'm dragged away, but not before seeing those beautiful brown eyes turn to an opaque and filmy white.

Jesus Christ! What exactly is the point of me writing all of this shit, only cover it in our sessions anyway? Seems a bit sadistic if you ask me.

Anyway, after the dream (nightmare), I got up for a pee, sat on the toilet, and bam! Just started bawling my eyes out. Just like that, out of nowhere, my body starts expelling fluids. I already had the shittiest headache, but this, the tension, just made it ten times worse.

So, I pull myself together. You know, in a Hollywood kind of way. Held onto sink, splashed cold water on my face, and watched it dribble in rivulets down my nose as I stared at my haggard reflection in the mirror. Then,

I had a couple of uglier-looking, snotty crying convulsions before going back to bed to rinse and repeat.

First thing I did this morning was call the institute. No change. I asked if I could go visit and was told that there's no point. I argued, but the doctor kept refusing. He said he couldn't see any value in it for either of us, so I slammed the phone down on him. Well, I didn't exactly *slam* it down because we can't do that these days, but metaphorically, I did.

Side note: I WISH we could slam phones down on people. I think that's the downside to a mobile phone. You can only press a button or sling it across the room, but you don't want to sling it across the room because then you'll be out of a phone. It's a fucking dilemma!

What do you suggest I do? No. I'm really interested.

Oh, and the game saga continues here at work.

It's still buggy, which means we've already had one early morning meeting. Well, kind of early, as I was late. Just as well because Sir Sebastian of the Whiny Pants (and his band of misfits) says that his people have managed to isolate the biggest problems and is confident that if the developers can sort those out, then things may not be as bad as originally thought.

Meanwhile, David wants me and the rest of my posse (all three of us) to press ahead with marketing plans while simultaneously planning an adequate response to Armageddon. That is, if the whole thing still turns out to be one great big pile of cack (how exactly do you spell cack? I'm not sure). Anyway, I'll get round to that last bit as soon as I've finished writing this and I'm feeling in a better mood since it's hard to be optimistic about a complete clusterfuck when you're feeling like one. Right?

P.S. Got home to find another letter from my landlord today. If he's not careful, people are going to talk.

October 20th

It's the weekend. Woo hoo!

I couldn't be bothered to put an entry in for yesterday. It was just same dream, the same lack of sleep, me as the same grumpy bitch.

Today, however, Patricia called. Someone must have reminded her about me. That, or she had to complete her good deed quota or something. Anyway, she called to ask if I wanted to go out with her and the girls. She thinks that a night on the town will do me good. I think she's an idiot, so I told her I was busy.

Apparently, I've been saying that for weeks now, but that's because I am busy. I have to plan this launch and the so-called contingency. I can't do that if I'm out partying. Also, what kind of message would it send if I'm out having a good time with them when the only people I actually want to be with aren't here anymore?

That, and I was also in a mood. Ugh. I had to endure a rare telephone exchange with my mother this morning. Rare because I normally do everything within my power to avoid her judgemental diatribes. And I've generally been successful, until today. Her call happened to come in as I was trying to get ready for work. I was already late, running around the house and trying to find some clean underwear.

Anyway, I went to press red to reject the call, but ended up pressing green. I greeted her with a *"Can't talk, Mum, I'm already late for work."* To which she replied that I never seem to have time for them lately, that I have been avoiding them, and that they are worried. Which in itself is a joke. The usual shit. Anyway, it was as I was hopping around the bedroom, one leg in a pair of my husband's briefs and the other stomping on the empty coke can on the floor, that I lost it and told her I didn't have fucking time for her shit right then.

So, not surprisingly at all, my mother, who never has and still does not condone profanity, actually gave me the telephone silent treatment, which just made me want to hang up on her.

And I was about to, too, when she came out with this dramatic, breathless, *"What has happened to you?"* Then came the rare blubbering and, *"I don't recognise you anymore. Who are you?"*

"Who do you think I am, Mum? I'm your very busy and late daughter."

And she's like all dramatic. *"You are not my little girl. You're nothing like her. You're just so angry all the time."*

"I'm not angry all the time, Mum."

"You're angry and mean. You're just so mean. We lost out grandson, too, you know."

So, I disconnected that bitch by pressing that dissatisfying red button before flinging my phone across the room.

I'm not fucking angry all the fucking time!

October 21st

So, I wasn't going to bother with an entry today because, well, it's the weekend, and you'll know by now that they tend to turn into a bit of bender, but you won't believe what kind of a mind trip I had yesterday. Well, it was a mind fuck, but I realise that I keep saying those words and I have no idea what they actually mean. They aren't even my words. I don't even talk like this!

But last night…

I had already retired for the evening if you know what I mean. I'd taken some pills and had a few glasses. You know, the usual weekend stuff. And I'm half-asleep when my phone starts ringing, and I rarely answer that thing these days. I mean, I do during the day, but not at night, not when I'm snoozing, but the thing keeps ringing and ringing, and you won't believe who it was.

It was the clinic. Major breakthrough, and could I get over there immediately?

So, there I am, four sheets to the bloody wind. Or is it five? Anyway, I'm splashing water on my face, rolling deodorant under my arms and generally trying to make myself look human, but I'm half-stoned. Half-fucking-stoned and making my way across town to this place. And it was chucking it down with rain. I mean, throwing it down. I looked like a drowned rat by the time I go there.

And he was awake.

My Husband. He was a fucking awake! Awake, but completely bonkers. I mean, there's me worrying about my mascara running down my face like black fucking tears, and then there's this guy…. This stranger that I've been married to for the best part of two decades, he doesn't even recognise me.

Correction. He recognises me, but he thinks I'm that bitch he fucked for nearly a year behind my back!

He went mental when he saw me. Starts screaming, *"You're not my wife! You're not my wife! Get my wife!"*

And the doctor's saying, *"She is your wife. She is your wife."*

Shit. It was complete pandemonium. Nothing like how I remember him. I mean, I know that doesn't make any sense, but he wasn't. I'd fantasised God knows how many times about how I would feel when I saw him again, but when I did…?

Nothing. I mean, he was there. But it was like I was looking at the shell of my husband. His spirit, the part that made him who he was, that was gone.

And the worse part? I felt like an absolute idiot. I was crying, bawling my eyes out. Snot running and the works. At one stage, I was even on the floor with him, repeating what the doctor was saying, telling him stuff like, *"Stay here! Stay with me! Stay in the here and now."* All of this weird shit, and yet...

I didn't feel anything. Nothing. It was like I wasn't even there, and there was this actor person who was just playing my part, like it wasn't me or anything.

Weird. Just weird.

Anyway, he didn't stay. He went off and started staring into space again. And the doctor's on the floor, helping me to my feet, and he's excited, actually happy after that whole mindfuck. He said it was progress!

Progress?

Uh uh. Not for me. Progress for me would have been being able to have a conversation with him. Me being able to grab that fucker by the scruff of his neck and ask him why... Why the fuck did you kill my son and then leave, huh?

WHY?!

October 23rd

Ugh. It's the beginning of the week after a shitty weekend.

There was that mind trip on Saturday evening, then getting home, and then I don't remember much after that.

It's got to be the drink and the antidepressants. They keep zonking me out, by the way. I told you. We need to review those.

Anyway. I was persona non grata at the office today since I arrived a whole hour late for the morning crisis meeting. Well, that isn't quite accurate. Technically, I wasn't late for the morning crisis meeting because the meeting had finished by the time I arrived.

David wasn't impressed. I don't think I've ever been at the end of his ire. I wrote it off as him being under pressure since he wasn't very understanding when I explained that the reason why I hadn't called in to let them know I was going to be late was because my phone had stopped working. Anyway, he informed me that the rest of my team picked up the slack for me, as they have been doing quite a bit of late.

Cheeky bastard! I miss one meeting and I get raked over the bloody coals, and Sebastian and his cohorts that got us into this mess still have a bloody job.

Apparently, it isn't the first meeting that I was late for recently, and was I sure I didn't need more time off? Because the rest of the team can cover for me. Which, of course, told me instantly where exactly he's getting his information from. Those two duplicitous bitches I work with.

No, I don't need any time off. I'm perfectly capable of doing my job. Nothing has changed.

That's when I got that prolonged gaze that you give someone when you don't quite believe what they've just told you and you hold out in the hope that they're going to confess the truth. I should know. I gave my son that very same stare many times. And my husband, for that matter. Fat lot of good that did me, though.

Anyway, only after making me promise that I had everything in hand with this disaster recovery plan did he leave me alone to get on with the said work he'd just accused me of not doing.

What the actual fuck is he doing at the office these days, anyway? He's normally shacked up with some bum boy somewhere, but ever since he met Aaron, he's turned into this goody-two-shoes, by-the-book bore.

So, anyway, just to keep him off my back, I did some work on the bloody plan. Only a little, though, because it's bloody hard being upbeat when you're not in the mood. Writing press releases and stuff like that, you've got to be in the right frame of mind.

So, I took a break. Checked Facebook, being sure to avoid all of those bitches who insist on posting everything about their perpetual bliss for the world to see. Nobody believes that crap. Especially Jessica – we all know that her husband fucks around behind her back, so when she's posting lovey-dovey pictures of the two of them, it just makes me laugh. Well, actually, it makes me angry. It makes me bloody furious. I want to hit 'Reply' and tell everyone what's really going on, that behind the façade, there's a world of fucking grief.

I would know.

P.S. The doctor's still insisting that what happened on Saturday was good, and that if things carry on the way they are, there's a good chance I can have a proper visit sometime next week. He didn't think for a second to ask whether I wanted to.

October 24th

So, let's get the usual stuff out of the way.

It was a cloudy day today. You know, one of those warm ones where it's still warm, but you know that summer is pretty much on its last legs and that autumn is here. No matter what the official meteorological calendar tells you.

Oh, and I rang again today. No visit. No point, apparently. Some kind of relapse. Maybe next week.

Did I have the same dream again? Of course, I did. Are you doing anything about it? Of course, you aren't.

Today I decided to try something new. You know, just for fun. On the way to work, I decided to stop by Starbucks to grab myself one of those skinny-no-animals-were-hurt-during-the-making-of-this-product coffees, which was not farmed by little kiddies in some South American land, so no people were offended and no flavour included in skinny lattes today.

I don't normally do that. I don't normally have the time. Well, to be perfectly honest, I didn't have the time today, either. But hey, I wanted to try something new. I wanted to see what it was like to be normal again.

Normal. What the fuck is that anyway? What is normal? If I think back, it isn't so long ago, just a couple of months. Christ! A couple of months. This is exactly the kind of stuff that I can't wrap my head around. Why does this thing feel like it happened such a long time ago, and yet it doesn't, all at the same time? I mean, how can I feel two different ways simultaneously?

It's like having that distant, dull ache of a scar with the rawness of a fresh flesh wound. I just don't get it. And I hate it!

Do you know what else I hate? Time. I loathe and despise it.

When this first happened – and I remember the day clearly, I remember it being bright and sunny – we'd just had a few days of warm showers. I remember my boy being disappointed that he couldn't go out and try that thing.

But on that day, on that actual day, I remember being so excited. My husband and I... yes, *my husband* because I can't bring myself to say his name. I won't say his name until I see him again. I won't!

Anyway, he'd taken me out the night before; gave me this long speech about how it was over with her and how he wanted us to try again.

And I remember being happy. I remember being so happy that MY boys – MY BOYS – were out together, having fun while I was enjoying some me time. It was an important day; we were releasing this new game and David had paid for me to check in and get pampered at the hotel where the event was taking place.

And I made the call. I made that call and I heard it. I heard it all, and it was just like one of those shitty dreams. It was all so surreal.

And I remember the sounds. Oh God, I remember the sounds. The sound of my husband wailing down the phone. Screaming. And in the background, there was that musical sound of the carrousel. And people, they were just chatting and laughing. And I couldn't believe it. I was like, what's wrong with you? Can't you hear what's just happened? Are you deaf? Why are you still laughing? Why is everybody still going on about their life? Why is the sun still shining? Why the hell hasn't the world stopped fucking spinning?

None of it made sense to me. None of it.

And I don't like it. I don't belong in this version of my life. I want to go back to the old version. I want to go back to when life was normal. Back to when I still had a family. A beautiful son and a husband.

Back to when I used to think that my life was bland. Ordinary. Except for when he decided to fuck around on me. Then it just felt like a bloody cliché.

God, that is so funny. And I mean that literally. As I write this, I am laughing my bloody head off. Because back then, I used to fantasise about something else. Something different. Something more exciting. I used to crave adventure far beyond the confines of a poxy flat in the arsehole of London. Of course, I'd never tell my husband that. Never. He's already got an inferiority complex about the fact that I came from money and he didn't.

Truth is, he did... His dad amassed his own little fortune. The only difference is, he likes to spend it on his new family and not the only son he had from the old one.

Except for that house by the bloody ocean... The Sweet Place or Life or whatever it's called. I mean, the old bastard actually did something right by his son, and he still didn't want to claim it. My husband said he'd rather cut his own balls off than take money from his father.

Did I mention that? We needed money and he was standing on principle. Selfish prick. He's a selfish bastard prick of a man who loves to throw down the law about whether or not I should accept cash from my parents while at the same time refusing to cash in on what's rightfully his. And then, when the worst happens, he takes off and leaves me here, alone, saddled with all of this shit!

Well, I hope he doesn't come back. I really do. I hope he suffers some fucking coronary or something and never wakes up because I hate him! I fucking hate him!

October 25th

Same dream again.

I didn't bother calling.

OK. So, yesterday, in case it wasn't obvious, was a bad day. Not least of all because the supermarket was out of my favourite wine. So, as you can imagine, I got home and started thinking about things and, well, the result of that was in my last entry.

And, this is the part, I guess, where I'm supposed to take it back.

I don't.

I don't, really. I mean, I love my husband, I do. But he's just been such a shit. He has made a shitty mess of everything and... I don't know. I really don't have a clue about how we are going to come back from this. Assuming he actually does return.

I mean, it's been nearly a month now since I found him sitting on the bathroom floor. Almost a month since he was admitted, and I'm starting to wonder if I even want him back – because he left me. He left me with all of this. He left me when I needed him the most.

In other news, things are really starting to heat up with the landlord. I received another letter today. This one had angry red capital letters at the top of the page. Like I might have been incapable of reading the big black bold of previous letters. I have a finite number of days to settle the arrears; otherwise, they're going to turf me out of here.

So, now I am going to let you into a little secret. As strange as this is going to sound, I've been enjoying receiving letters from my landlord and all of his kind. I've been imagining them salivating like a pack of hungry wolves.

Pushing against the restraints of due process and salivating over the prospect of exacting their retribution for my insolent delinquency.

I imagine mister landlord and his missus pouring over their computer screen. Or maybe they don't even have one. Maybe they use one of those old, clangy mechanical typewriters. Both muttering under their breath, bashing their anger out on those keys, bolding and underlining each and every syllable of frustration.

Yes, they must be truly pissed off that I haven't even bothered to send them a response. *Why, I'm just a poor bereaved mother and abandoned wife bundled under the covers, quivering at the very thought of being thrown out on onto the street. Whatever will I do?*

What they don't realise is that, as much as I love these black and white classics, I am nothing like these simpering, monochromatic, cardboard cut-outs. I enjoy watching these women go about their melodrama for one reason and one reason alone; they remind me of how I will never be.

Ever.

So, go ahead. Send your demands. Mail me your threats. Bankrupt me. I don't give a fuck. This isn't a home to me anymore. It's just a shell, a place to take shelter from the elements. And an overpriced one, at that.

Living in London is expensive. I mean, even back when life was normal, it was still a struggle to keep the wolf from the door. He didn't make much when he wasn't busy with his flights of fancy.

Oh, the irony. My husband spends much of our income and quality time getting a degree in how to help other people, and then he decides to have a fucking breakdown right after killing our son.

See? I'm laughing again. He's still able to make me laugh, even now, albeit for entirely different reasons.

October 26th

The world is angry at me.

Well, snap! That makes two of us.

Today, I came back from work to find a whole assortment of multi-racial envelopes seemingly having a party at the foot of the front door. So, I stepped over them on my way to find the corkscrew since I'd already picked up two slabs of chocolate for dinner and all I needed was the entertainment.

I don't know how, but somehow, I ended up watching one of the Fifty Shades films. I don't know which one, as they all seem the same to me, and I – for a split second – I found myself missing my husband. No, not because of what they get up to in the film, but because he looks like the leading actor. Yeah, green eyes and the works. It's one of the things I really loved about him until I started hating it – because it's also the reason, no doubt, that those bitches dropped their knickers for him, including the one who ran screaming back up North or wherever the bitch came from.

Fuck! Now I'm angry again. And it's so fucking exhausting!

I'm tired. I'm really tired because I'm not sleeping because of those nightmares in which I keep drowning and you refuse to give me anything to help me sleep because you think I'm going to top myself!

I fucking hate you, too! I really hate you!

Meanwhile, back in gaming land. It would appear that Sebastien and his sidekicks have finally managed to give the game a clean bill of health.

And even when David gave *Mr Weed* his famous *Are you sure you're not fucking with me?* look, Sebastien stayed firm and, albeit with some obvious trepidation, spoke those infamous words that are undoubtedly going to come back and bite him in the arse at some stage....

We're good to go!

So, big gold star for that snivelling piece of shit who managed to get us to just one week before the launch before finally identifying and supervising the eradication of all of the bugs that he and his team should have identified five fucking months ago!

And so, it would appear that all is well in the land. The damage limitation strategy that I've barely started is no longer required. Oh ye of little faith. Although, David did say that it would make sense to have something in place just as a precaution, but he's just a worry wart.

Oh, and I did try to call today after the film, but changed my mind and hung up (Sorry, I mean pressed 'disconnect').

October 27th

It's the weekend!

Now, I know you keep telling me I shouldn't drink alcohol with the pills you gave me, but I figured today is such a momentous day that it deserves to be celebrated.

DARK STAR – no, nothing to do with the seventies movie, but a game where a group of astronauts must overcome various challenges to colonise and support life on the moon – is being unleashed on the world next week. It has been years in the making, has cost thousands, and represents one of the company's biggest gambles.

Put simply, if DARK STAR bombs, the company and by association David are unlikely to survive.

It's a couple of weeks late, as we were hoping to capitalise on the whole Halloween thing (even though the game has nothing to do with Halloween), but anyway, yes, much to celebrate.

That's why I've stocked up on Italy's finest and I'm going to treat myself to two movies. Today's playlist includes *Gaslight* and *Rebecca*.

Do you know what's weird? I don't even like wine. Well, I do with a meal or something, but in such massive portions that it actually makes me vomit. I mean, I don't know how many times I've yacked since starting this new diet, and the morning headaches are bloody awful. But I think they're worth it, given how effective it's been at, you know, knocking that proverbial edge off.

And no, the irony isn't lost on me. I know I used to berate my husband for this very thing. But unlike him, I can hold my liquor. I am the one in control here, not it. Do you know how I know that? I don't drink and then go and fuck some random stranger!

Which by the way, reminds me… I called the clinic again today. Guess what?

Exactly.

October 28th

I can barely bring myself to type today's instalment. That's because there wasn't going to be one.

I was still busy recovering from last night when I was woken by the phone.

You won't believe it. I can barely type, my hands are shaking so much. The clinic called today. Apparently, pretty much a month to the day since he left, they've had a massive breakthrough and are wondering if I would be able to go in next Wednesday for an actual visit.

Fuck.

I need a moment.

November 2nd

4 days until launch.

So, it' been days since my last entry. I don't even know how long because I've been out of it. And when I say *out of it*, I mean right out. I don't know if it's the pills, the wine, or the mindfuck of everything that's going on lately, but I'm finding that I keep spacing out.

A lot.

First, I had to get through Halloween. And you know how bad that was because of all the calls I made to your mobile phone. Yeah, sorry about that.

Or, no. Actually, now that I think about it. I'm not sorry. You're the one who said I should call, so I did. It was fucking Halloween, for Christ's sake; Toby's favourite time of the year, and I just couldn't face it. I couldn't face seeing any of the decorations or the costumes, nor hearing the laughs of the trick-or-treaters.

None of it.

It's why I turned all the lights off, locked the door, and hibernated... for a few days, until November came and it was time to surface.

You can imagine how that went down with the bitches from the office, can't you? It's release week and everybody is losing their minds prepping for what you would have thought was the second coming.

It's like, everybody, calm the fuck down already. I need time to get my head straight. I'm still reeling from Halloween, and there's this bloody meeting at the clinic tomorrow.

I thought I'd be excited, but instead I'm dreading it. I have no idea what to expect, although the doctor said it's best that I go with no expectations. Easy for him to say that!

And what the hell am I going to say?

I know you told me to just tell him how I feel, but there's no way we're going to have enough time for that.

November 3rd

3 days until launch.

I don't even know where to start. I've just gotten back and my hands are shaking again.

I'm just waiting for the booze to kick in.

So, anyway, I did it. I went this morning. As much as part of me didn't want to. It was surreal.

As soon as I got there, Doctor Holmes handed me Starbucks, which was handy because I woke late and didn't get a chance to make coffee. I must have given him some kind of look because he just smiled and said, *"Trust me."* But I can't help but wonder if he was trying to make some kind of point.

Cheeky git.

Anyway, I saw him. He was sitting all alone on a bench in the garden. He has lost a ton of weight. Looking a bit gaunt in the face, but it's the same Marco. He looks even worse because he's shaved his beard off. There's just stubble there now, and I can't say I'm a fan. Makes him look harsh. That coupled with his slicked back hair. He reminded me of a serial killer.

He was absolutely gobsmacked when he saw me rock up with a cup of coffee in my hand. Strangely, he was holding an exact same cup, too. I've no idea what kind of experiment that was supposed to be.

Anyway. It was tough. Really tough. Part of me wanted to throw my arms around him and the other... well, the other part wanted me to put my hands around his throat.

But the doctor had already warned me off. He'd said that I needed to *take it easy* with him. Whatever that's supposed to mean.

Marco, my husband, he told me I smelled lovely... and I wanted to laugh my head off. Lovely? I haven't showered in days and couldn't this morning because I was late. What he could smell was half a can of deodorant and another half of that brush-in shampoo stuff.

Thinking back, we didn't really say much to each other. It was all awkward looks and smiles and hugs.

But the important thing is that he's back! After more than a month, my husband has finally come back to me. I mean, there's still work to be done and he won't be coming home just yet, but still, he's back!

So, why am I not happy?

November 4th

Ugh.

2 days until launch.

I didn't want to get up this morning. On the positive side, you'll be pleased to know that it had nothing to do with wine or alcohol of any kind. Interestingly, I wasn't in the mood last night. There was way too much stuff whizzing around in my head. I mean, that visit was something else.

I was still trying to wrap my head around how I was feeling as I passed out on the bed. It's just weird because there's been all this build-up about what it would be like when I could talk to him again, and then, when I did….

Nothing.

Weird.

Anyway, as you say, it'll take some time to get used to communicating with each other, I suppose, but I want to discuss this some more when we next meet. In the meantime, things were a little frosty at work today. I bet you can't imagine why.

Sisters Grim. I call them that because the two whipper-snappers who are about a whole decade younger than me and who think they know it all are inseparable. It would appear that the sisters were pissed off that I was selfish enough to take time out yesterday to visit my sick husband.

Bitches.

I mean, David – you know, the actual boss – was perfectly reasonable, considering what he must have on his plate right now, but those two....

Of course, they didn't tell me this, not directly anyway, as they don't have the spine for that. No, they did so by putting on an endless parade of passive aggressive statements, like, "*We did that yesterday, Elisabeth, because, as you know, there's just one day until the launch.*" And, "*That was decided yesterday, Elisabeth, but you weren't here.*"

Oh, how I would love to be able to transfer how I'm feeling to just one of them. Would love to see how she'd cope. She wouldn't last a fucking day.

Anyway, no booze today. Before you ask, I don't know why. I just didn't fancy it. And I don't fancy waking up feeling like shit tomorrow, either. It's the last day before the launch, and I think I'm more nervous about this than I was about my meeting this week. I don't know. Too tired to work it out.

November 5th

Ta-dah!

You know that expression, TWIST OF FATE? Like that film, *Sliding Doors*? Well, today, I think something like that happened to me.

There's just ONE more day to go until launch, and I told myself that today I was going to take your advice. Today, I was going to attempt to rewire my thought process. Challenge myself to look at every negative and attempt to identify its positive.

Today, I succeeded.

So, my new *positive attitude* thingy was tested at the moment I arrived at the Underground, only to hear an announcement that the Northern line had been closed due to an incident.

An incident?

On the positive side, they did lay on extra buses. The only problem with that is that, by nature, they travel over ground, and it's been throwing it down with rain for days now. Freezing rain, that is.

The interesting thing here is that I hadn't really noticed that until this morning, when me and my band of misfits were huddled at the bus stop. (I'm trying to find a positive term – *misfits* is the best I can do. I mean, they were a right bunch of all ages, sizes, and colours. By colour, of course, I'm talking about what they were wearing, not their skin, before this descends into a whole rally.)

Anyway, we're all huddled at the bust stop. Sadly – see how I'm moderating my language? – it wasn't one of those handy ones with an actual roof, one of those ones that can also double as a urinal. No, it was just a place on the street with a digital sign counting down to the next bus.

So, there I am in my sodden cashmere coat and designer shoes, clearly ill-prepared for such a situation and standing among a group of, well, you know… people who are obviously all much better prepared than me, as they're all holding umbrellas.

And it was chucking it down. My hair was plastered to my scalp, rainwater was dribbling into my bra, and the traffic… Jesus! It seemed so loud as it growled and hissed back and forth on the wet tarmac in front of us. With some of the arseholes deliberately driving through small puddles just to see us all recoil.

So, I'm just about ready to turn around and head home when I hear a man's voice in an accent I can't quite place, say, "Excuse me. Please, you're welcome to share my umbrella with me."

So, I turn to my right and all I can see is this giant yellow umbrella that, like something out of a stage production, slowly lifts to reveal this young man, probably in his early twenties, with a black beard, wavy hair, and the broadest Roman nose I've ever seen on a man. I mean, it's broader than my husband's. That's one of the things I used to love the most about him, along with his green eyes.

Loved? Did I just use the past tense? I have no idea why. Maybe you can explain it to me during our next session.

Anyway, he smiles at me, revealing a set of neat teeth that are positively dazzling against that thick beard. Do you know the kind I mean? Thick yet groomed, not vagrant.

And, if I'm being perfectly honest, he put me into a bit of a trance. I couldn't stop looking at him. At his dark, olive skin, the hazel eyes, and those lips. Thick lips. Kissable.

Anyway, thankfully, someone coughed behind me somewhere, which broke the spell, and I quickly turned away to create my own artificial clearing of my suddenly dry throat when I heard, "Please. I assure you, I don't bite, and you're looking, how'd you say…" he doesn't finish his sentence immediately, but instead looks me up and down with one of those sparkling smiles and a shrug. "Rather wet."

He follows that up with a shuffle to his right, making space for me.

I was literally shivering. The time for coyness passed when rainwater started dripping into my underwear like a bloody leaky roof! So, I stepped to my right and the relief was immediate. I mean, I was still cold, but to be shielded from the persistent onslaught was just as delicious as he was.

Anyway, because I'm a rude bitch and have seemingly lost all ability to be social with anyone other than the odd client at work, I didn't even thank the man. Instead, I just stood there. Close but not too close, if you know what I mean, drinking in his aftershave.

We stood that way, in such intimate proximity for at least two minutes, and I could quite literally feel the heat from his body when I realised that I hadn't even thanked him. So then, I'm going through all the different ways I can say those words. But the more time goes by, the more awkward it feels. Then, just as I'm plucking up the courage to speak the words, literally as they are forming on my tongue, the bus appears in front us in a cloud of fumes and spray.

Of course.

He gestures for me to go first while all the time holding his umbrella over my head until I'm inside.

The bus is packed with a humidity factor to rival Florida and stinks of body odour-slash-spices-slash-God-knows-what. I tried not to think about it because my gag reflex was already tickled by a dank odour at the back of my throat. And I'm thinking that maybe, despite the downpour, I'm better off out in the fresh air. But I don't have any choice now because other people are getting on the bus, and one of those is him.

I get a real glimpse now. He's wearing a black leather coat over a shirt, tie, and waistcoat. I'm considering the odd combination when an old Asian lady with a giant wart above her lip tells me that the seat next to her is free.

I take it, grateful, but at the same time regretting it because I think I may have found the source of the spice odour.

Anyway, my helpful stranger walks by me with another smile of his pearly whites and I – and I have no clue why – instinctively put my head down! Rather than smiling back. I have never felt so awkward and embarrassed in my whole bloody life. It was just so ridiculous! A married woman reduced to a teenager on the smelly school bus to God knows where.

Anyway. Just like said teenager, I get a thrill of delight when I hear him ask in that accent of his – French? No, probably Spanish – "Is this seat taken?" And I'm assuming the mumbled response he received was a *no* because the next thing I sense is him sitting right behind me in that cloud of cologne.

I'm not ashamed to admit it, but I breathed it in. I breathed it in because it was like oxygen in the carbon monoxide of that metal capsule on wheels.

And then we're off. The bus driver obviously keen to make up for lost time because he sets off so fast, we're all pushed back into our seats. I half-expected the people in the front row to throw their hands in the air as we followed them into the first of a set of roller coaster whirls.

Toby loved rollercoasters. I hate them.

So, we're bumping down the street and, in typical British fashion,

I have nothing to say to my fellow traveller who is busy staring into middle distance because she, like me, obviously can't pretend to be looking out of the window since they are all misty, and I have to work hard to dismiss the fact that that's the result of humanity's collective spent breath.

Gross.

So, I settle into my seat, close my eyes, and try to tune into the presence of my helpful stranger. And it's weird because I felt like I could. I felt like my mind's eye was like some kind of closed circuit camera beaming back images of him sitting behind me and gazing at my sodden and most likely scraggy hair.

And, despite the obvious fact that I must look a mess, I liked it. I liked to feel his gaze on me. He was the one soul who had extended me a kindness not born out of dutiful sympathy. And it felt good. It felt really good.

In fact, I was so buoyed by this very thought that I was ready. I was now ready to turn in my seat, look him in those gorgeous hazel eyes, and say *thank you. Thank you so very much for being kind, it means so much to me. So much more than you could possibly imagine.*

And I was ready, and I was about to turn, when the bell sounded and, to my abject horror, I heard him bid his travelling companion a good day and rise from his seat.

Then, I felt a tap on my shoulder, and I turned to see those beautiful hazel eyes just inches from mine. Those thick lips parting to reveal those beautiful teeth. "Here. I think you're going to need this more than me," he says. And he hands me his yellow umbrella!

"Have a great day," he adds with a wink, and then he's gone. Down the aisle and off the bus.

Shit! It was all I could do not to run after him.

I didn't. Not that I had much of a chance because the doors were barely closed on the man and our driver was gunning the engine and shoving us forward for the rest of the journey.

At this stage, I wanted to throw myself across the lap of the old lady next to me, but you'll be pleased to know that I thought better of it. Instead, I sought out the nearest porthole through the steamed-up window by the seat in front of us and I watched, for those few fleeting moments as the bus pulled away, how the stranger ran through the rain, skirting around and jumping over puddles before disappearing through the doorway of a building with a giant sign above it that read, EL VINEDO.

And that was it.

Wow.

So, anyway. I was late in again today, but for once, it was due to reasons beyond my control. Not that anybody cared. Everybody was too busy running around like bloody headless chickens. Jesus, people! You would have thought we'd never released a game before.

Press conferences, interviews, web and social media marketing campaigns, promotions, competitions, pre-scripted interviews. Fact sheets for staff.

It was relentless.

And I fucking loved it!

Admittedly, much of it was already done. By Sisters Grim, BUT based on my previous templates. Of course, I had to make several revisions which bent a few noses out of shape, but I don't give a shit. I'm still senior to those two, and with a whole lot more experience.

David surprised me today, though. He summoned me into his office for what he called a general pre-launch chat, which I know was just his way of stopping the squabbling.

In the meeting, though, for some obscure reason, he asked me about the disaster recovery strategy document. He hadn't received a copy and wondered why not since he was assuming it was complete.

I'm like, *Why the fuck are you asking for that? It doesn't exactly inspire confidence for you to be asking me about a disaster recovery document on the eve of the launch.*

So, I made a joke; I asked him if he knew something we didn't know. He laughed, but then he asked me again. Said he'd feel better if he clapped eyes on it.

Since when? That's a bloody first!

I told him that he was obviously stressed and that that was the last thing he needed to stress over. I told him not to worry because I had it all in hand, as always.

I don't because, well, you know, things have been chaotic. Also, we ironed out all the kinks, and while it's standard practice to have something like that as a contingency plan, there's no doubt in my mind that it won't be needed.

Anyway, to get him off my back, I told him that I needed to go and check it over to make sure I had covered everything.

And, if I'm being perfectly honest, I did go to my desk with the best of intentions… but then I caught sight of the umbrella.

It was leaning up against my desk, the pointy bit still dripping rainwater that was slowly building a water stain on the carpet. And I knew I should have left it in the rack, but I didn't like the idea of dumping it there and it being contaminated by all the rest.

I preferred to have it next to my desk. Next to me.

Exclusive. Close.

Had a bit of an episode at the check-out on the way home tonight. Card was declined, so I was about to have an argument with the sour-faced bint who served me, but then I remembered that I'd bought a new bag which I'm probably never going to use the other day.

Anyway, I managed to pay with a different card.

Ironically, by the time I got home, I wasn't in the mood for booze anymore, anyway. And instead, I am showered, wrapped up in a fluffy dressing gown with a movie and enjoying some cheese on toast.

And it tastes so good!

November 6th

Well, what an eventful day!

Last night may well have been Bonfire Night, but my fireworks blasted off today. Much to report in this evening's broadcast and I really don't know where to start.

Well, I suppose the obvious thing to start with would be that, after years of development and months of planning, DARK STAR was finally unleashed on the world today, and it's a hit!

Sales are much better than our original forecasts suggested, which would indicate that the marketing team did a fantastic job, as always. This, as you can imagine, was cause for celebration.

So, at the office party, I had a few glasses of bubbly and a few glasses of Jack and Coke. I have to say, not my usual poison. Well, when I say *usual*, you know what I mean… not something I have been enjoying lately. Anyway, turns out that, especially on an empty stomach and with the dregs of those pills you gave me still in my system, well, they wreaked havoc and the next thing I knew I was praying to the porcelain god in one of the toilet cubicles.

I have no idea how long I'd been in there, hunched over that disgusting thing (which, by the way, is something I wouldn't normally want to be caught dead doing) when I heard the door go.

And who do you think came in with that irritating snort-cackle of theirs? That's right, Sisters Grim; Selina and Gemima.

As you'd expect, they were both euphoric about the release and gushing so much praise on each other that, if I'd had anything left in my system, I would have brought it up. I mean, it was like a fucking mutual admiration convention in there. You should have heard them.

And I'm thinking, *Hey bitches, aren't you forgetting someone?* when Gemima pipes up with how this would be the perfect time to talk to David about the extra slack they've had to pick up lately and how, despite this, the launch was a major success, thanks to them.

I couldn't believe it. I mean, we're talking Selina here, the nothing black girl with a chip on her shoulder who I actually welcomed onto the team; I taught her everything she knows. I mean, that bitch couldn't even spell properly. Couldn't write decent copy to save her fucking life!

Anyway, that two-faced bitch Gemima, little delicate wall flower of a waif who is normally afraid to say boo to a goose, actually agreed with her. I mean, I don't think I have ever heard her speak with such confidence in all the time she's been working there.

So, I'm about to drag my vomit breath and myself out of that cubicle and put a few things straight when they start gossiping about me. Start going on about why I even bother going into the office anymore since I spend most of my time shitfaced on booze and God knows what else. And how I and David must be the only two people in the office who don't see it. Then, Selina perks up with her theory that the only reason David puts up with me is because he feels *sorry* for me because I'm married to his best friend, the *nutter from the nuthouse who was put there because he killed his own kid!*

So, I have to say I was quite good about that, the fact that she referred to my son as a *kid* and not a child. But the other stuff? That hurt. And when I say *hurt*, it was like someone had shoved a red-hot poker down my throat and begun twisting it around in my guts.

So, then I start thinking about school and, you know, sticks and stones and all that. Then I think about you and those breathing exercises that you taught me for when I get anxious. But... well, they don't work this time, and that red-hot poker started a fire and that fire grew bigger and bigger until it consumed my whole body.

I was physically shaking. And all I could think about was how she had just referred to Toby. My beautiful boy. My beautiful baby boy was a boy, a child, and not a fucking baby goat!

A CHILD!

Well, I exited the cubicle in a bit of a temper, I'll admit, and Gemima barely had the chance to put on a fake smile and greet me as if nothing was wrong before the back of her head met one of the mirrors with a loud smack. Selina's scream barely left that big gob of hers before I tangled that peroxide weave thing she calls hair in my fingers and dragged her into the cubicle I'd just vacated and shoved her head down the toilet, puke and all!

"My Son! Bitch! He was my son! My baby boy! MY CHILD! MY CHILD!" I remember screaming over her gurgling…. *Not a fucking kid!*

Well, everything else was a bit of a blur after that. The only thing I kind of registered was Gemima screaming, somewhat hysterically, and trying to pull me off her friend, but when that didn't work, she ran from the room, screaming *like a kid.*

David wasn't in the office at that point. He had already left and was somewhere across town giving interviews that I and my so-called teammates had organised.

OK, alright, that *they* had organised.

He's still trying to reach me on the phone as I write this, but I'm not in the mood to talk now. I'm feeling very sleepy. I'll talk to him tomorrow.

Oh, and guess what… fun fact! When I finally got round to checking messages today, I found one from the doctor at the clinic. Apparently, my husband had a breakthrough which also brought on some kind of *relapse.* There's a good chance that his recovery from this is going to take weeks. I have no clue what happened. I stopped listening after that part of the message.

November 7th

What an eventful week I'm having, and to think that, for a while there, I thought I had turned into a reluctant spinster.

First, I meet the perfect stranger on the bus, and this morning I was woken up by the sound of the doorbell. My first thought was that it was bailiffs coming to collect on something, so I ignored it. Especially since I had the worst headache.

No, it had nothing to do with the vino I drank last night and everything to do with the fact that I've got a throat as dry as a pharaoh's sock.

My husband used to say that when he wanted a cup of tea. He knew it made Toby laugh.

Anyway, this morning, I was so thirsty I even found myself eying up the water in the vase for the roses that died a few weeks back. My father's way of cheering me up, like I had a cold or something and not like I'd quite literally lost the will to live because the two people I cared about the most had been pretty much ripped from me in the space of a week.

Anyway, after a while, the door buzzer stopped and the hammering on the front door started. I yelled, *Go away*, but, as small as the flat is, I don't think the visitor heard me because he carried on and then even started yelling, telling me that he knew I was in here.

How the hell did he know? Is the place rigged with cameras or something? Anyway, reluctantly, I dragged on the clothes from last night, because I can't seem to find my dressing gown, and opened up.

David, AKA my boss, was standing there, and I can tell you, he looked pissed – and not in a British kind of way.

If I tell you that he led with *"What the fuck, El?"*, that will give you some idea of his mood.

"I suppose you're here to talk about what happened yesterday, right?"

And he answered, like he was stuck on some kind of loop.... "What the fuck happened, El?"

"They were talking about me. Talking about Toby."

"And you think shoving her head down a toilet full of puke was a justified response?"

If I'm being perfectly honest, I had to think about this for a few seconds. My head was still a bit fuzzy; you'll understand. Eventually, I managed to say, "Too right, it was. Those bitches have no right to talk about me or my family. They don't know what I'm going through here."

"Everybody knows what you're going through, El. You've been wearing it like a walking billboard ever since it happened."

"Oh, well, I'm sorry I didn't stop grieving to spare your sensitivities."

"That isn't what I'm saying, you know that."

"Do I?" I asked. Well, I think it was more of a shriek, actually. You know, one of those whiny, watery-eyed ones. Like a child who can't come to terms with the fact that a decision has been made over which she has no control.

Then, as if that wasn't bad enough, David, our best friend, reached out to touch my ugly hands that I realised in that moment had fingers with chipped red nail varnish and chewed ends.

Chewed? I don't think I've chewed my fucking nails since I was still in school.

Anyway, I stopped short of snatching those ugly things away and I let him, another human, touch them. And his hands felt so warm. And I mean bloody warm. Like heated mittens or something.

Well, I just melted. I have no idea what kind of sorcery he has going on, but I just dissolved into a burst main pipe of a mess.

You know, I realise now as I write this, David is the first human contact that I have had since the funeral. I mean, I didn't know that at the time, but my body must have somehow registered it. Somehow registered that I didn't die that day, too, although I probably should have.

So, he then brings on that soft, sympathetic voice. "El, you're in crisis."

I snatched my ugly hands away. "Don't you fucking start! Not you, too!"

Fucking crisis. Doesn't he think I know that? Of course, I fucking know it. And if by some miracle I've managed to block it out, I can always rely on you to dredge the whole shitty thing up in session.

Fucking crisis! Of course, I'm in crisis!! The one person I cared more about that my own life is gone!

Mothers should never outlive their children! I don't need someone to keep reminding me of that. Keep telling me how to accept it. I need someone to make it go away and to make me feel normal again. That's what I need.

And yes, I know what you would say right now – you'd give me your speech in that patronizing tone of yours, saying *Elisabeth* because you seem incapable of understanding that I want to be called Ellie.

Ellie is my name!

Ellie!

You'd say, *"Ellie, you know I can't do that for you. This is something that only you can endure. I can only help you through it."*

Help me? Does it fucking look like you're helping? Do I sound like someone who is being helped?

Fucking therapy is a load of fucking shit! Shit!

You realise that when you talk like that, all I can hear is my husband trying to shrink me, and I just want to kick your teeth in!

Yeah. So. Anyway. *David.*

Long story short: Cry cry, snot, snot, tears, tears. And that was just him! Ha ha.

Anyway, he says I need help. I can't go on living like this, and what I did at the office is unacceptable.

I know that.

The bitches may press charges because what I did was assault. This is something over which he has no control, and like any responsible employer, the welfare of his staff must be his top priority, blah blah blah. And so it is with regret (he obviously thinks he's Lord Sugar) that I'm fired... at least until I get the necessary help I need.

In the meantime, he will try to smooth it over with the girls.

Smooth it over? Like I'm the villain here. Those bitches were bad-mouthing my family and he needs to smooth it over *for me?*

"Fuck you!" I said. "Fuck you and your shitty job and thank you so very much for being there when I needed you the most!"

As for you, dear doctor.... See? He doesn't even think I'm getting help, so, do you know what? You're fired, too!

November 8th

I am out of control, apparently. Or at least that's the prognosis according to my now ex-boss. Can't I see what's happening? Can't I see how I'm dealing with all of this? I haven't been behaving any better than my husband. In fact, I've been behaving just like him. I have become him, which in and of itself may be a sign of something.

Oh, fuck off!

So, yeah. Anyway, I'm alone. Alone without any money or a job.

And, um, fun fact? Yesterday, not long after David was chased out of the flat by my angry voice and a whole string of expletives, the doorbell rang again.

Obviously, I thought it was him coming back to apologise, but instead... surprise! It was a sullen, grey-faced imp with an ill-fitting suit and balding hair, accompanied by a posse of police officers.

Oh, OK, not quite a posse. Two.

There to execute the eviction notice.

Apparently, it was served on me a few weeks back. Well, longer. I just didn't do anything about it.

I was shocked. That landlord didn't look anything like I'd imagined him.

Anyway. So, half an hour later, with only my essentials hastily shoved into a suitcase, my yellow umbrella, and a notice for me to arrange collection of the rest of my possessions within 7 days or else they would be disposed of, I was turfed out of our family flat. The place where my boy was born, and where we'd lived relatively happily for years.

I'm not going to my parents, though.

No way. Not a chance in hell am I going back there. I'd rather live on the fucking streets than go back to that prison.

That's what I told myself.

But after three hours of roaming the streets and hopping between cafes to buy hot beverages and keep warm, I gave in.

And now…. Surprise!

I'm back at my childhood home, in my old room.

According to the sermon that started just moments after I walked through the front door, this was inevitable. My parents were only surprised that it did not happen sooner. But everything is going to be fine now that I'm back home, as they'll get me into a routine. Which, much to my delight, starts with me accompanying them to church on Sunday.

I couldn't bring myself round to telling them about the job, especially since my father has already mapped out how I can get to the city from Bray.

On the bright side, just as always, they will take care of all of the debt I have managed to accumulate, including the fees for my husband's stay at the clinic – for as long as I choose to remain married to him, of course.

The spreadsheet my father has requested, detailing just how exactly I've managed to stuff up my finances, can wait until tomorrow. It is to be comprehensive, as my father intends to use this to draw up the necessary paperwork stipulating that this money will be given strictly as a loan that will attract a 5% interest rate above standard, or if I so wish, it can be claimed as early inheritance. Either way, I will need to sign paperwork accordingly.

What the actual fuck has happened to me?

I used to be a germaphobe, for crying out loud! I used to have a beautiful son, an imperfect but functional marriage, and wonderful things. I used to be free of these two. It's one of the very reasons I got married in the first place, to shove it up their sanctimonious arses!

And yet, in the space of a few months, all of that – literally all of it, even my fucking therapist, for crying out loud – is gone!

Now, it's just me, the suitcase, and this yellow umbrella which is about the only bright and truly colourful thing in this room.

I mean, I hate yellow, but there's something about the thing that pulls at me. Inside, I mean, tugging at the core of my spirit, pushing and shoving me, telling me to wake the fuck up! To live!

Which is something else. Being around Marc, swearing is pretty much the norm, but here, with these puritans, unless I want to be thrown down the cellar steps with just bread and water for food, I'm going to need to reconsider that.

OK… it isn't that bad, but close.

Maybe my helpful stranger will come and save me. Maybe he'll burst through the gates on his black stallion and sweep me away a la Jane Austen.

Ha! That thought made me smile.

Those dazzling white teeth smiling at me as his steed rears up while he holds on with one muscular arm.

Oh, God. I can't believe I'm writing this shit.

But, then, I can, as this is actually who I am. Inside, I mean.

That therapist was a useless bitch and has undoubtedly killed any chance of me ever going to therapy ever again, but she was right about one thing. I have lost sight of who I am without my child. But my loss should not define me. It should change me, of course, but it shouldn't change the fundamentals of who I am inside.

Deep down, I am still me. I am not who I project myself to be.

The wife to my husband.

The mother to my son.

The daughter to my parents.

I am more than that. I am me. Strong, reliable, resilient, resourceful, unbreakable.

LOL! LOL! Who the fuck am I kidding?

It's time for bed. With a bit of luck, I'll wake up to tomorrow and this will all have been some horrendous nightmare.

PART 3

THE BEGINNING
OF THE END

22. MONEY

Have I mentioned how much I've missed socialising? I don't think I have. That's because I didn't realise just how much I've missed it until we sat down for dinner.

Simply having other people in the house and listening to them talk about themselves and their lives... wow, it just feels like a road trip to another place. It's like stepping out of my own spotlight, off the stage, and letting somebody else provide the entertainment.

There were a few moments during the conversation, where the boys were recounting stories of life in the city, when my thoughts became my own once more and went to that encounter on the doorstep earlier this evening.

There's something wrong with me.

I'm taking the pills. I'm doing the work, and yet this stuff is still happening.

The worst part was when Ellie started asking those questions. Somehow, they made everything much more sinister because it felt as if she was validating everything. Emphasising the fact that I'm losing my mind all over again because I'm starting to imagine things that feel real. And, as much as I want to, I cannot keep ignoring the fact that it runs in the family. My mother was sick, and she ended up throwing herself in front of a train.

My imagination's replay of what that must have looked and felt like was enough to shock me back to the conversation in hand, where I distracted myself by trying to *shrink* the characters from Aaron's and David's stories.

Like, why exactly that bloke at the café might be so angry

all the time. And why that woman in Aaron's building always greets him but never makes eye contact.

I love people-watching. That's no surprise. I used to play that game all the time with Toby. Mostly while waiting in the car for Ellie to return from one of her *quick* shopping trips.

Who is that person? What might their story be?

Humans have always fascinated me. Doctor Holmes told me that he believes my interest was born out of the need to understand why people do the things they do. To try to deconstruct my dysfunctional relationship with my father and, of course, comprehend why exactly my mother did what she did to me.

And, of course, thoughts of all this reminded me of what I was told at the store that day and what was subsequently echoed by Sarah in the kitchen.

An inclination to analyse one's self as well as this compulsion to look beyond the words that are being spoken by the very first guests ever to cross the Dolce Vita threshold does give me pause for thought.

But a therapist, really?

I need to talk to Ellie about this. Not now, obviously, but it's something that I need to tackle. And did the old man really go around the village crowing about me? The very notion of that is unfathomable since it's a fundamental deviation from everything I've believed for most of my life.

And now? Now, I need to focus on the evening at hand.

David and I have been in top form tonight, our repartee worthy of many a stage show. It's as if we've never been apart. Laughter has been ringing out through the dusty hallways and rooms of Dolce Vita for the first time since our arrival here, and it's like a tonic for the soul.

And all without a drop of alcohol. For me, that is – the others, well, they've been wetting the proverbial whistle way before the antipasti.

I haven't heard my wife laugh like this in a very long time. And me? Never since my release from cloud cuckoo land. Not like this, anyway. Certainly not before Buddy arrived on the scene. And I'm grateful.

Speaking of which, our guests were both for our adopting our furry forest orphan, who was quick to introduce himself the moment they walked through the door.

Ellie hasn't budged, though. In fact, that was probably one of the rare moments where the laughter actually stopped.

"So, how's the first week been for you guys?" Aaron asks. "Are you missing the city?"

I'm about to answer, but Ellie jumps in. "Absolutely."

"What? Even with all this beauty on your doorstep?"

"It sounds good in principle, and it's a lovely place for a weekend or a short break, but to live out here? It's awkward. Right, babe?" Ellie asks, touching my arm.

I know how I'm feeling, but I must have a particular expression on my face because Aaron says, "What about you, Marco?"

"I'm—"

"He loves being out here in the sticks. That's why he wants to adopt the puppy."

"Oh, but he is cute," David adds.

"*I*," I say, jumping in, "I quite like it here. Yes, it can be a bit remote, especially after living in the city for so long, but I think that's the charm of the place."

"Would you consider living here? If you weren't selling up, that is?" Aaron asks.

I look at Ellie, who is already eagerly awaiting my answer.

I rock my head, considering the question. "Well, maybe not here exactly, but the idea of moving to the country does appeal to me. I mean, the air's breathable, for a start."

"You just love all the oldy woldy stuff," Ellie says dismissively.

"If by 'oldy woldy' you mean historic places, yes. Of course, I do. I find history interesting."

"Me too," Aaron interjects. "I was hoping to visit one of those stately homes while we're down here. You know, the haunted ones."

"You've got a thing about them and castles," David says.

Aaron nods. "Yeah, I'm fascinated by British history. It's so extensive. My family comes from a small town in Iowa. The only ancient thing there is the mayor. And I actually think he's dead already. Preserved. They just wheel him out for public engagements."

"Well, this place is old enough. Our bathroom is certainly from the last century, and if we give you the tour tomorrow, it'll be just like visiting one of those homes," Ellie says, taking another sip from her glass and then adding, "all you need is the ghost. Although, coming to think of it…." She leaves the sentence unfinished and looks at me.

"What?" David's ears have pricked up. "What does that mean?"

I shoot Ellie a glare because I know this is only going to end up in a bunch of piss-taking.

"Oh no, it doesn't matter," my wife says bashfully, before taking another sip from her glass. Yeah, I'm starting to think she's had enough wine.

"Oh no, you don't. You can't say stuff like that and then leave us hanging," David complains.

Ellie looks at me again and then back at our guests like she's about to share a closely guarded secret. "Dolce Vita is haunted."

Dramatic gasps from the men across from us.

"Are you serious?" Aaron asks.

Ellie glances at me, but it's more for effect because she completely ignores my frown. "Marco thinks the place is haunted."

"Now, hang on a minute, I didn't–"

"He had a strange encounter at the door just before you arrived."

"What kind of encounter?" Aaron asks as both men lean in for more.

"He said someone touched him."

"I didn't say that!" I protest.

"Didn't you?" She squints at me.

"I said I thought it was you. It felt like you had walked up behind me. Like you were standing right there."

"No, I'm pretty sure you said someone touched you. And it scared the shit out of me. Then you go on about hearing noises...."

"Wow, Marco, is that true?" David asks, eyes wide with interest. And I can't quite work out if he is genuinely interested or already piss-taking.

I shoot Ellie a glare, but she remains impervious as she takes another sip from her glass.

I rock my head and shrug. "There have been some noises, yes," I agree.

"In the middle of the night," Ellie throws in.

"What, like noises in the attic?" Aaron asks.

Ellie points at him. "Exactly. That kind of crap."

"Really? That's not very original, Marc," David says.

"It wasn't just that. The trapdoor fell open. It was a whole thing," I say.

"Just like seeing dead people," Ellie adds suddenly.

"What?" I ask. Because I have no idea what she's talking about. I haven't discussed any of that with her.

"You said you saw Harvey in the village the other day," she explains.

Shit. I completely forgot about that.

"Harvey? Who's Harvey?" Aaron asks.

I look at my wife for a few seconds. Trying to work out why she's being so confrontational. "I said I thought I saw someone who looked like him in the village."

"Right. How do you even know what he looks like? You were, what, twelve when it happened?" my wife asks scornfully. And I have no idea why she's being so spiteful, but I'm confident that the wine has something to do with it.

"Wait, wait... who's this Harvey bloke?" David asks.

Ellie defers to me now like it's some big secret. I clear my throat, and can feel my heart thumping in my chest for no apparent reason other than the memory that is now trying to push itself into the forefront of my mind.

"Harvey," I begin, "is the man who saved me back then. Um, down at the beach," I add quietly.

"The beach?" Aaron asks. "What happened at the beach?"

"Aaron, mate, it doesn't matter," David begins.

"No, no. It's OK," I say. "Since Ellie brought it up. It's fine. Um." I swallow hard – not necessarily because of the words I am about to speak, but more because of the effort it's taking to supress the images that Doctor Holmes very kindly raked up from the recesses of my mind like shit from a fu–dging cesspit. "When I was a little boy, I nearly drowned. Down at the, um, down at the beach. And, um…" I take in a deep breath. "Harvey is the man who saved me." I nod.

"Oh, wow. Marco. I'm so sorry," Aaron says.

"It's OK. You weren't to know. At least not until Ellie brought it up. It was a long time ago."

I look at my wife, but if she regrets raising the subject, she's not showing it.

"So, what happened, did you go swimming or something, alone?"

"Aaron, no," David says again, quietly. Like he's afraid of the fact that I might still be some kind of nutcase and that Aaron's words might, in some way, set me off.

"It's OK, David," I say, much more sharply than I intend. "It was a long time ago. It was my mum, Aaron. She wasn't well, and she, um, she tried to drown me!" I force a quick smile because that sounds as ridiculous as it does insane.

"Oh shit," is the American's immediate response.

"Yeah. The thing is. Up to a few weeks back, I wasn't even aware of it. I'd managed to successfully repress it until then."

"Well, I wouldn't say *successfully*," Ellie throws in.

"What?"

"Well, it wasn't exactly successful if it manifested itself in other ways," she says flippantly before taking another sip from her glass.

Right. You want to do this. Let's do this–

"Wow. Now, that is what I'm talking about; British history," Aaron says with what I'm sure is glee in his voice.

"Dude, you come from Iowa, so let's not start talking about history," David retorts.

Aaron weighs up the comment and finally rocks his head. "Fair. That's fair." Then, the two men start laughing.

Laughing about my misery. The cheeky bastards! And yet, it isn't long before I'm laughing, too, as is Ellie, who spits out her mouthful of wine and prompts a whole new wave of grossed-out laughter.

"Dude. You've really gotta work on your dinner conversation," Aaron says with mock reproach.

"Me? Tell her, she's the one who brought it up," I protest. "And now that we've got that pearl of tragedy out of the way, who wants a top-up?" I ask, lifting the bottle of wine, as I'm eager to steer the conversation in a completely different direction.

"No. Thank you," Aaron says, pointing a finger. "Not if she's gonna spit it all over me again."

"It was an accident!" Ellie protests through giggles.

"I'm not sure," Aaron says. "Whose idea was it to come and visit these two again?"

This is exactly what I'm talking about. The ability to laugh about those things that pain us most. It isn't easy. For a second there, I was ready to deck the bloke, but, when you think about it, it's beautiful. We've all had bad experiences that we spend the rest of our lives trying to avoid, to forget. But like it or not, our bad experiences are part of us. They're often the scars that shape us into the people we become.

Imagine if we were able to laugh about all of the bad bits of our past – it would make everything about the future good.

Wow. Did I just think that? It doesn't even sound like me, even though it does make sense.

"Oh, go on then, mate, you twisted my arm," David says, thrusting his glass my way. "Anyone would have thought you were trying to get us pissed. Even though Ellie appears to have successfully managed that all on her own."

"Oi, cheeky!"

"What are you after?" David adds, winking at me.

I roll my eyes at him and the devil on my shoulder suggests that now might be an appropriate time to ask my friend for a loan, but I ignore it to top up Aaron's glass.

"Oh, by the way, mate. The text you sent. No problem."

"What?" is my distracted response, as I'm trying not to overfill Ellie's wine glass.

"The money. The loan you're after."

And just like that... everything stops.

So, you know that butterfly feeling you get in your stomach when you're nervous or your best friend has said something as if he's just read your mind?

Well, don't be shocked when I tell you that that feeling isn't a swarm of butterflies in your belly at all. It is actually your Automatic Nervous System, or ANS. The ANS is responsible for two main systems: the parasympathetic and the sympathetic systems. Commonly known as *rest-and-digest* and *fight-or-flight*.

The parasympathetic system effectively reduces your heart rate while the sympathetic one increases it. With the former lulling you into relaxation and the latter into action. It's this action that places a demand on your body's resources, thus diverting blood away from the gut and giving you that odd butterfly feeling.

How do I know all this?

I have no idea.

What I do know is that the sympathetic part of my body has taken over. The blood is pumping, insulin and adrenaline releasing, and the butterflies fluttering because I've just been confronted with an awkward situation that I was not expecting... and now my body wants me to run screaming from the room.

If only.

"How do you know about that?" I ask incredulously.

My friend squints at me.

"Marco!" Ellie yells, and I turn to see that the wine has overfilled the glass and has now produced a growing scarlet stain on the white tablecloth.

"Shit!" I gawk at the stain and then up at my friend.

"Fuck me, this is probably one of the few times I've seen

you lost for words. Wait up, let me take a picture." He picks up his phone and snaps a photo of me before I even have time to react.

"Hang on a minute. What's going on?" It's Ellie, dabbing at the wine stain with a napkin.

I look at her, still unable to formulate some bloody words, so David jumps in again. "The money. So, you guys can get on with doing this place up," he says helpfully – or, judging by my wife's reaction, unhelpfully. "Guys? I just said *guys*, and again, I blame you for that," he adds, turning to Aaron.

"You asked David for money?" Ellie asks, abandoning the stain as a lost cause now.

"Um, well, not exactly. But I was going to. You know I was," I say, resuming the dabbing, but she catches my hand and speaks through gritted teeth.

"No, I didn't."

"El, I don't even–"

"Uh oh. I feel a domestic coming on," David says dramatically.

Ellie glares at me and then turns to him with a smile. "No. No domestic."

"You sure?" David asks, "Because for a second there, I thought it was going to be the after-dinner entertainment."

Ellie sticks her tongue out at him and smiles, but I can see that the news has pissed her off.

And David knows my wife, too; that's why he follows that up with, "Chill, babe. It's not a problem. I did say that if you guys—" he turns to Aaron. "See, I just bloody said it again!" Then, back to us as he continues, "I did say that if you two ever needed anything, then I was your man. So to speak."

We laugh.

But then my friend loses his smile and gets that look of his that I used to hate, because it was incompatible with the type of man I was back then, but now….

"Seriously, people. It really makes me happy to be able to help, and I don't know what kind of domestic you two have going on behind the scenes, and I don't actually care, but I just want you to know that it makes me happy to be able to help. Besides, I know he's good for it. Which means that once this place sells, you'll be able to give it back to us – with interest, of course. So, when you give him an ear-full later, just remember that. All right?"

We laugh, but it's still somewhat stilted.

David holds up his drink, and I think my friend has had too much of that stuff already, given the fact that he's getting misty-eyed.

"I love you two. You're like family to me. *Correction.* You *are* my family. Soon to be *our* family, and that means the world." He thumps his chest. Everyone lifts their glasses. "To family!"

"To family!"

I look at Ellie in the hope that the moment may have diluted her ire, but she avoids making eye contact with me. In fact, she's avoiding eye contact with anybody, seemingly more interested in the wine stain.

"David, I don't know what to say," I comment.

He just glances at Ellie, who's still avoiding everybody's gaze, and makes a furtive zipping action across his lips.

And so, reluctantly, and still reeling somewhat from the shock, I throw out the first thing that comes to mind. "So, how are the wedding plans coming along?"

Aaron gives me a smile and then looks at David.

"What?" I ask.

Even in the lamplight, I can see David's taxi-door ears turning a different shade.

"David has his own favour to ask, but–" Aaron rocks his head, "with everything that you guys have been through, he's been, you know, reluctant to raise it. Reluctant to ask."

"What? What is it?" I ask. Now it's my turn to lean forward.

Aaron turns to David, who bites his lip and blinks back misty eyes. "Fuck, Aaron. I didn't realise I was going to be put on the spot," he grumbles before taking another swig from his glass. "Cheers, mate." Then, turning to me, he begins, "Well, you know, given that I don't really have anybody else – that I actually like, that is – I was wondering if, well, you know… I wanted to ask if, since you're me best mate, if you'd consider being my best man, too."

Shit. Where did that lump in my throat come from? I swallow it. "Of course, I will, you doughnut!" I say, rising to my feet as Ellie and Aaron clap and cheer. "I thought you'd never fu–dging ask!"

I uncharacteristically hug and kiss my friend on the head, and now it's his turn to squirm. Yeah. I like that.

"Fudging? What the hell. You know what that actually means, don't you, in–"

"Yeah, we don't need to hear any more about that, thank you. Besides, it's nothing even remotely to do with that."

"No. You gone all religious on me? Seen the error of your ways?"

"Nope. Ellie and I made a bet almost a week ago to the day."

"It hasn't been that long," she says.

I nod. "It has. A week at midnight. Ellie bet me that I could not go a whole week without swearing."

"What? No way! You can't go a whole hour without swearing."

"Well, I've proved both of you wrong. It's been almost a week now. And just so you know, I plan to collect," I say to my wife with a grin. But she simply throws back a fake smile and a middle finger for good measure.

David shakes his head. "Sore loser, obviously."

"Obviously," I say, smiling at my wife, but she's not yielding. She still seems pissed off.

Thankfully, the conversation turns to the spring wedding. In the UK and not the US, because Aaron prefers London to the States. Well, you can't blame him.

Apparently, his family members and friends are looking for a good reason to visit England anyway. David then cracks the obvious joke, that if we're still at Dolce Vita, he'd be happy to have the reception here.

Aaron agrees, but when I say that I would love that, Ellie soon shuts me down by saying that if we're still at Dolce Vita in the spring, we'll also be divorced. She then adds that there are plenty of beautiful country homes and stately homes much bigger than this place… and much more suitable.

When the boys then go on to ask what our plans are after Dolce Vita, Ellie expertly steers us away from that conversation once more.

And so, I have no idea what's going on with my wife, but what I do know is that drinking copious amounts of wine does not agree with her. In fact, now that I think about it, since when did she start drinking like this? She hates wine because it makes her vomit. And yet, she's been knocking the stuff back tonight, seemingly without a care in the world. And it's made her rude and obnoxious.

Jesus. Is that what I was like? Was I this bad? Worse, did I do this to her?

This is without a doubt a conversation that we need to have soon. One that I am in no way looking forward to.

23. THE DARK

Well, as you know by now, Buddy would normally have his own comfy little bed in the spare room to totally ignore and instead choose to sleep on the cold wood floor outside our room. Tonight, given that we only have one spare room, I considered taking the guy up on that and move his box to the landing.

Ellie said I should just leave him downstairs, but, as much as I'm unable to explain it, after that weird encounter with the video, I don't like the idea of leaving him down there.

No, I'd rather keep him up here with us.

I know there's more to all of this. Just like I know that if I sat myself down and had a good think, I would probably come back with some completely ridiculous theory about everything. But I don't want to. I don't want to because I know that if I allow myself to mull over this stuff too long, I'll start jumping to conclusions.

Things are already starting to feel off.

You know what it's like; when factors happen in isolation, you just write them off, but when you start to analyse the collective… then, well, they start to take on a life of their own.

This, of course, was underscored by the things that Ellie said at dinner. It felt like she was trying to tell me something. *Look. See? You're starting to lose your mind again.*

Again, that's most likely just me reading into it all too much, but that's exactly my point. It's this kind of thought process that could quite easily send me spiralling once more.

After all, it's obvious that whatever Ethan has me on, it's not working.

That look on Buddy's face. The dreams. The fog. That encounter at the door. The so-called things I keep seeing through the corner of my eye. You know, those things that you think are there, but aren't.

Of course, if this were anybody else, I would be telling them to talk to someone instead of letting their mind run amok like a fu–nking wild horse.

Which is exactly what I think is happening, but I can't tell anybody because I know that, the moment I do, history is going to repeat itself, and I can't… I *won't* go back there.

So, I'm not going to think about it. End of story.

So anyway…there was no point in making up the bed in the spare room unless David and Aaron were thinking of top and tailing in that small bed. So, instead, Ellie, ever the planner, brought back one of those cheap, self-inflating beds, which we've made up in the den.

I've really enjoyed seeing David.

Having the dynamic duo back and not feeling like anything has changed. I needed that. For once, probably more than he did. The old normal. An anchor back to the days when life was good. When Ellie and I were happy instead of how we've been since arriving here.

Strangers.

Of course, I'd never say that out loud, but that is exactly how it's felt. Two strangers cohabiting, not two people who have loved each other for years and who, at least to my mind, created beautiful life as a result of that love.

Fu–n! Can you hear this shit?

This is what Doctor Holmes did to me! This is what therapy does to you! And I do not recommend it.

I used to go through life pretty much not giving a shit about anything beyond my family and my one true friend, and now it feels like I've turned into some chakra-opening, emotional goop!

Boll–ony! And this fu–dging not being able to swear crap isn't helping any! I can't wait for tomorrow and to get back to fu–nky fu–dge! and fu–n!

Anyway, bedtime is quite the contrast to dinner, with Ellie avoiding my gaze as she goes about her ritual. Brushing teeth. Applying cream and generally looking ravishing. But I've reached the stage where I've stopped even trying to initiate sex, and by that I mean a kiss that's more than a peck but less than something you'd give your old aunt.

There's only so much rejection and lame excuses a man can take. That, and the fact that there's more chance of aliens landing in the back garden than my wife allowing me anywhere near her tonight, judging by those beautifully pursed lips of hers.

"OK, so I take it you're still pissed off about the money, then?" I ask in a hushed tone. I'm lying in bed, watching my wife liberally apply lotion to her legs.

She doesn't respond, but I'm all for not going to bed angry, and besides, I know my wife. If we don't address this thing tonight, it's going to spill over into tomorrow and potentially ruin what little time we have left with our guests.

"Ellie," I begin.

"You could have at least discussed it with me," she says without looking up.

"We did discuss it."

"No. We discussed needing the money. Not where it was going to come from."

"I told you. I didn't message him. I thought about it – of course, I did – but then decided against it. Look!"

I sit up and reach for my phone on the bedside table, and I tap messages and scroll through. "Look," I say. "No messages from me to... fu...n."

| TO DAVID: | Mate, you don't happen to have 40 grand lying about, do you? |
| TO MARCO: | Forty? Dude, you said you were fixing up that place, not rebuilding it! |

I didn't send this.

When I look up, Ellie is staring at me. Expectant hand on her hip.

"I didn't send this," I say. Emphatically.

She lifts her eyebrows. "No?"

"No."

"Who did? The dead man you saw in the village or the one at the door?" she mocks me.

Wow. That stung more than I thought it would. But I push it aside.

"What difference does it make?" I ask, leaning forward. "I'm going to pay it back anyway, and David's my friend."

"And I'm your wife!" she snaps, glaring at me. Oh well, at least she's looking at me.

"Really? Because lately, I've been wondering about that."

"What's that supposed to mean?" Her voice is no more than a hiss now.

Oh well. "Exactly that. You've been so distant since we got here that I'm worried that, instead of getting closer, we're actually drifting apart."

She gives out a short laugh. "Funny. You didn't seem so worried about that before."

"Before when?"

"Before… oh forget it." She trails off here and then goes back to vigorously massaging lotion into her skin.

"No, go on, finish the thought."

"Doesn't matter."

"No, Ellie. Please, I want to hear it. There's obviously something bothering you. Let's hear it."

But my wife doesn't answer. Instead, she rises from her chair and disappears into the bathroom. Closing the door behind her.

***

The sensation of Ellie's cold, slender fingers touching my face pushes its way into my featureless dream, which instantly shifts and shapes until it becomes our old London flat based on a quasi-surreal, moonlit memory of us.

But I know that there's no moonlight in London. Or, more specifically, there's a lot of light pollution from the city, which is how

I know that this scenario is a dream that, if memory serves me well, I should like.

My relationship with Ellie wasn't always this strained. In fact, we rarely argued. If we did, it was never in front of Toby. That's something we both signed up for even before he was born. Along with family time and our son's right to feel safe and secure in his own home. This was paramount to both of us, no matter what.

And to be fair, we both stuck to it even during the most challenging of times. This meant that most shallow arguments took form via a series of passive-aggressive statements and actions. An acid bomb here. An ignore there. Terse conversations through smiling, clenched teeth. That kind of thing.

The more serious conversations – the ones that generally involved me being a dick, and by that I mean succumbing to my addictions, be that the alcohol or those meaningless encounters I had – we'd take away from the house or send Toby to his grandparents for the weekend.

Sometimes, those weekends resulted in the somewhat dysfunctional process of Ellie yelling at me, me feeling like the shit that I was, and both of us eventually collapsing into an exhausted slumber that would often result in Ellie reverting to some kind of primordial repossession ritual. Some people call it angry sex. In our case, it was more perverse than that. It would involve me being asleep and being woken to the sensation of her pulling my hair. Closely followed by her pulling at my shorts, stripping me, fondling me, and bringing me close to orgasm but changing her mind in bouts of disgust because I, at least to her mind, had been contaminated, and was corrupted. Impure.

In all these scenarios, the repossession ritual in which my wife sought to re-adopt what she perceived as my *contaminated* body resulted in rough sex, as many times as she demanded it and at her direction. With her rage subsiding only through exertion.

The next day, we'd be one step closer to normal and, within a week, back to our usual selves.

Angry sex is undoubtedly a thing that I somehow seem to know a lot about, both personally and on a general psychological level. There are many motivators, all too elaborate and convoluted to share right now.

Before we worked out that there was something broken in me and that it was one of the reasons why I strayed from the wife I love and risked losing my family, we attended couple's counselling. There, we learned that Ellie was addicted to the *repossession* ritual. That she, in some perverse way, liked me screwing up so that I would be humbled and beholden to her, repentant so that she could *strip, use, punish, and dominate* me for being the sinner at the altar of our marriage.

While it became clear that this was all about control, we never did establish why, because we – well, Ellie – refused to discuss it in session until she eventually refused to go back at all. Before we quit, however, it was suggested a couple of times that Ellie's peculiar fetish was most likely born out of her parents' authoritarian (and some would argue fanatical) religious practices.

At the time, we laughed at the therapist's theory by deriding his appearance rather than absorbing what we were being told. Although, he was a peculiar-looking thing with a wiry body, round spectacles, and an odd, Anglo-German accent.

In hindsight, it became clear to me that we did that because we both recognised what he was telling us as the truth that neither of us wanted to see. Both of us being much more comfortable believing that I was a cheating bastard who didn't deserve his beautiful wife who had given me the perfect son.

It would take the death of my father, the loss of our boy, and my subsequent breakdown for me to learn that my following my dick between the thighs of other women was much more complex than that.

And so, this is the reason why I am not at all perturbed to feel cold fingers crawling over my face as I try to sleep, along with the removal of covers from my body.

I just assume that Ellie has begun her repossession ritual, albeit for completely different circumstances.

And I wait… as the frigid air breathes over my skin like a

layer of frost, the flimsy material of my T-shirt and shorts offering little protection against the freeze.

And I still wait… eyes shut tightly in anticipation of what might come next.

While at the same time secretly willing my wife to expedite the process because I am now actively stopping my teeth from chattering.

Tic. Toc.

Tic follows toc.

Surf rumbles.

Nothing.

Then, I sense the air shift. If feels as if someone is towering over me. Looking down on me, but I didn't feel the mattress move.

Ellie?

I'm just about to speak when I'm suddenly overwhelmed with a stench which is so foul that I want to gag.

Oh God. I try to smile through it, but it's the worst. "Oh God, Ellie. Did you just fart?" I laugh as I open my eyes.

But there's nobody there. Just dark, empty space.

Fu–nk!

Now fully alert, I sit up and scan the room, but it's dark in here with neither of us having remembered to turn on the nightlight apps on our phones last night.

Shit.

I move to turn on the lamp, but decide against it because I don't want to wake Ellie again and give her yet another reason to be pissed off at me. So, I reach for my phone instead.

It's 01:23.

I tap a couple of times until the LED light dissolves the inkiness.

I scan the room slowly, starting from my side of the bed, going past the bathroom door, over the furniture, to the bedroom door, and then over Ellie's side of the bed, over the mound of her feet, up her body, and then–

I jolt back when I see something large scuttle off her face and disappear over her side of the bed.

"Oh fuck!"

I flip onto my knees and gawk at my wife who is lying on her back, face up to the ceiling, mouth wide open in a silent scream.

A chill scampers down my spine as my mind races to decipher what I think I just saw. Did I see something, or was it just a shadow? I lean forward and consider crawling over her to check, but am startled by something scratching at our bedroom door.

I flick the light over there, but see nothing. I can just hear claws on wood. Fast. Desperate. And I'm just about to lose it and wake Ellie when–

Ruff! Ruff! Scratch! Scratch!

Buddy!

His growl is barely audible through the door, but everything else is much louder.

"Noo! Buddy! No! Shhhh," I say in a loud whisper before flicking the light beam back to Ellie. Her mouth is closed now, and I realise that she wasn't screaming at all. Just sleeping.

She stirs in the light, unconsciously hunching her shoulders and hugging herself against the freeze.

I wait, expecting her eyes to flutter open any second, but they don't.

I'm torn. Shut the dog up or investigate?

I shine the light down my side of the bed again. Nothing here. So, I move the beam to the foot of the bed, slowly crawl over to it, and then peer over the side.

There's nothing here, either.

Scratch! Scratch! Woof! Woof! Yap! Yap!

I slide off the bed, and it feels like my bare feet have just landed on a slab of ice.

"Shhhhh… it." I ignore the urge to hop from foot to foot and instead reluctantly shine the light at the floor on Ellie's side of the bed.

Empty.

"And where the fuck have the covers gone?" I mutter under my breath.

Scratch! Scratch! Woof! Woof! Yap! Yap!

Buddy seems determined to wake up the whole house.

I lunge across the room and pull the door open halfway, expecting the dog to burst in and jump up at me. Instead, he trots in and heads straight under the bed, where he starts growling once more.

I feel my pulse quicken my, senses awaken as fight or flight kicks in.

Ironically, I haven't even thought about *under* the bed because… well… the covers won't be under there, will they?

And yet, slowly, hesitantly, I crouch down, taking the light from Ellie's now foetus-scrunch of her pyjama-clad body to the dog's butt and angry flicks of its tail.

Buddy's growl is muffled once more, as his little mouth is stuffed with quilt, and he's gradually, with dogged determination, tugging, pawing, sliding, and pulling the thing from under the bed.

How the eff did it get under there?

My heart is knocking now, trying to get my attention, telling me to grab wife and hound and run far away from here.

But I can't. I'm transfixed as I watch the dog yank at the quilt with all his might as it, slowly but surely, unravels like a coiled reptile from its hiding place in the dark.

Something is under there. Something is holding onto the other end of that bed cover and I'm loath to look.

And yet, motivated by Buddy's little growls, I grab one end of the quilt and start pulling with him while all the time training the light ahead of us, but soon regret it when, like animal eyes in the dark, I see two lifeless glints glaring back at me.

The shock of the apparition makes me jump backward, knocking me off my balance and sending me sprawling onto my backside.

The phone slips from my hand and clatters loudly to the floor.

"Fuck!"

Buddy also retreats from the darkness under the bed, to the presumed safety of my proximity and the blue hue of the landing's nightlights, before turning once more and yapping animatedly at something stalking the gloom.

I can only gawk into blackness as I watch a dark, humanoid shape crawl out from under the bed to a chorus of growling bravado and angry yaps, and then slither up Ellic's bedside table.

I yell, and am about to jump to my feet when a blindingly bright light comes on and, in a scene reminiscent of the previous nerve-shredding episode of this kind, I hear my wife's voice demand, "What the bloody *hell* are you doing?"

24. SUNDAY

Sunday morning, I'm already out and running while the sun and the rest of the world continue to slumber. The chilly air pinching my cheeks feels good as I jog through the wood, being careful not to trip on anything in the faint light of dawn.

So, I've been avoiding it. Thinking about it, that is. But I know it's most likely the first thing you're expecting me to tackle, so I suppose I should allow my mind to wander back there.

Yes. It's barely been a week and I'm already seeing things, which is bad... but worse is the fact that now I'm starting to second-guess everything.

For example, this dappled light I'm running through, this fresh scent of moss that I'm breathing, the birdsong I am hearing... is any of it real?

And in the most existential question I'm ever going to put to myself, am I really here? Am I really, finally running this circuit or is it all in my mind? How do I know? How do I test for that?

I've been racking my brain, looking for signs. Last time, there were elements. The lighthouse was one of them. It was a repetitive presence in my delusion. One constant. And yet, I can't think of anything like that this time around. A common landmark, totem, or anything.

Nothing. Apart from the house itself, of course.

So, what's the alternative?

Dolce Vita is haunted by something I haven't clapped my eyes on yet. Something hideous, judging by the foul smell which any horror fan will know normally means a poltergeist.

Yeah, right.

Well, if it isn't that, it would mean that Ellie really did fart in her sleep last night, which, if I'm being perfectly honest, isn't unheard of.

The thought of that does bring a smile to my face.

Oh, come on! I've barely been out of the clinic a week, and my world is already starting to fray around the edges. I could use some levity, and if that's at Ellie's expense, then so be it.

By the way, she didn't find anything about last night's tableaux amusing.

But then, if I was awakened freezing cold, covers gone, my husband on the floor like he was practicing early-hours yoga with a puppy barking in my ear, all while one of our first houseguests looked on, I'd have had something to say about it, too.

It turns out that my wife could hear Buddy yapping, but was ignoring him in the hope that I would shut him up before she was forced to rouse herself.

Asked if she noticed anything unusual last night, she gave me one of her dirty looks and snapped, "You mean besides my husband rolling around on the bedroom floor in the dead of night playing with a fucking puppy?"

OK, so maybe that was a stupid question, but I did see something. I can't describe exactly what, but it was like some kind of a shadow. Only, it wasn't dark because I could almost see it in the dark. It was like an aura. An energy.

Fuck!

Yeah. It's Sunday! I'm finally allowed to reclaim part of what I used to be, at least. Although now, who knows? I might try to dumb it down a bit. Don't get excited. It's been scientifically proven that those who swear are less stressed than those who don't.

Yeah. Given what I'm going through right now, I wouldn't expect much.

Shit. I need to talk to somebody about this. I can keep going round in circles, but I'm not going to get anywhere on my own because I can't be objective.

Who, then?

Ellie? David? Maybe even Aaron. He seems like a reasonable

guy, so I'm sure he'd be able to look at this objectively and then promptly tell David, who would then come to me and ask why the fuck I was sharing creepy stories with his fiancé and not him.

Which brings me to Ellie. I could possibly sit her down, assuming she'll give me the time of day… because she seems like she doesn't even want to be around me lately. She's either hiding away in the dining room or back in the city. When we are together, I've noticed that she generally avoids eye contact, which is so unlike her. She's one of those people who holds your gaze even in awkward situations.

I saw her deal with one of the parents at Toby's school once. That woman was getting right up in her face about some altercation her son had had with Toby.

Ellie didn't even blink.

She waited for the mental case to finish her rant before putting her in her place, and she didn't scream or holler; she just laid out the facts coldly and eloquently.

It's why Toby and I rarely got away with anything. That gaze of hers is like a bloody scanner. It examines your expression, demeanour, timbre of your voice, and knows what you are thinking before you do. It's how she found out about me and my so-called indiscretions. If I didn't know better, I'd say my wife was an MI6 agent. Maybe she is. Maybe I'm just clueless.

See what I'm doing here? I'm avoiding even thinking about a potential discussion with my wife about any of this.

I knew our departure from London and Ethan's care was premature. I did say that.

Holmes?

No, no way.

Then who?

I have nobody I can tell about this. Nobody who's going to look at the cold facts and tell me if I'm losing my fucking mind or not. It's not like I can tell you. Well, you already know, but like last time, you're just along for the ride. Sure, you'll have your own theories now about what you would do and probably how you think you could deal with it much better. Well, bully for you. Me, I'm stuck in this shit. No, I can't leave, as I need… no, I *want* the money.

No, I can't tell my wife. She would probably divorce me. No, worse, she'd probably have me committed and throw away the key. There's no way our marriage would survive another bout of this. Not if current events are anything to go by. But then, who can blame her?

David's the only other person I would tell, but I don't know. He seems so close with Ellie that I'm not sure I trust that he wouldn't share stuff with her one night when working late at the bloody office.

Aaron…. Well, I don't truly know the guy.

Sarah? I don't even know her.

But she does seem to be one of the most likely candidates. Open-minded enough.

Oh shit, I feel like my head is going to explode!

I mean literally explode as I emerge from the woods and onto the costal path that circles around and back to Dolce Vita.

The Sweet Life. That's a fucking joke!

It is beautiful, though. Out here, the horizon is ablaze as the sun announces its imminent arrival by broadcasting an orange beam across a rippling ocean. It looks like it's going to be another glorious day. Where's the storm they've been going on about? Those things seem to be as frequent as they are getting more violent. And no, the metaphorical symbology of that is not lost on me.

The worse part of all of this is believing that there's something wrong with me. That I am regressing, but not knowing for sure. And that thought is like an irritating and equally toxic mosquito. It keeps trying to sink its teeth into my skin, but I swat it away – as I have been doing each and every time it makes an appearance – but it's a persistent fucker, and has been trying to make its presence felt more frequently lately. And I know why. I'm in crisis again, and I'm trying to turn to the one thing that seems most logical, safe.

I've just reached the boundary between public footpath and Dolce Vita, and the sun is now a burgeoning ball of colour on the horizon casting long shadows over the land and smearing it with a marmalade orange. But as I look at Dolce Vita basking in the rays of a new day, something about that feels off. Cold. Like it doesn't belong in this setting.

A haunted house in the clothing of an idyllic setting.

But that's going to change. The renovations begin tomorrow, and they can't come a moment too soon.

***

Aaron is the first person to enter the kitchen while I'm prepping everything I need for a fry-up. White linen, stemmed glasses, orange juice, fruit salad. I've even repurposed the cheap bunch of flowers that Ellie picked up from the supermarket.

Yes. I've gone all-out. Not just for our guests but also in the hope that this will go some distance toward making things up to my wife. It can't be easy living with a bloody nutcase like me.

"Good morning," I say brightly, as if I didn't have a care in the bloody world.

"Morning." Aaron smiles as he shuffles into the room in jogging bottoms and a T-shirt. Man after my own heart.

"Coffee?"

"Yes, please."

"How did you sleep last night, or need I not ask? I'm sorry about all the commotion."

"No. Don't worry. It was fine. I didn't even hear the dog barking or Ellie's yelling," he says wryly.

I shake my head. "Sorry."

"Don't be. It's peaceful here. And despite the interlude, I slept well. Especially without all the light pollution. It's so dark out here, it's like being back home."

"Yeah. You get used to it after a while," I chuckle, placing a mug of steaming black coffee in front of him. "Milk and sugar?"

"No, that's fine. Thanks," he says. "And, wow... I saw the sun rising this morning. Beautiful. I was saying to David that it's been a while."

"Yeah. Sunrise isn't quite the same in the city. Assuming

you get to see it beyond the concrete rises," I say, leaning against the kitchen sink and nursing my own mug of coffee.

He smiles and raises his eyebrows. "No. I bet this is a great place to go running, too."

"Yeah, it is. Do you run? You could've come with me." I've asked the question, but I already know the answer. He is, after all, the guy I dubbed Captain America, and that wasn't just because of his accent; it was mostly because of the way he tends to bulge out of his shirts.

He glances at himself as if to check the evidence. "Yeah. Fitness has always been important in our family. My father was in the army. He instilled the importance of psychical fitness in me from an early age. We spent a lot of time in Arizona. Saw some of my best sunsets there," he says, nodding out of the window.

There's a pause as we both sip from our cups. Wood pigeons call. Birds chirp beyond the kitchen window.

"So, how are you guys settling in here?" he asks.

"Oh, you know. It's OK," I lie with a smile. "Takes some getting used to."

"How are *you* doing?"

I stare at him because, not unlike my wife, he has one of those scrutinizing gazes. The type that asks a question and waits expectantly for a response. Those blue eyes are no longer sleepy, but fully activated and seemingly searching mine for truth.

Shit.

"I'm… I'm OK. You know. Getting used to the adjustment," I say, glancing away because that's what normal people do when they're trying to mask how they're truly feeling.

He nods. "I bet," he says – and looks away!

For the first time! Shit, that's even more worrying than the truth detection eyes. It's as if he knows or wanted to say something, but instead thought better of it.

"Aaron?"

He looks at me with that face like he's about to reveal something that he's been struggling with, when: "Ah, there you are! Morning sunshine."

David enters the kitchen in shorts and a T-shirt like we're in the height of summer. He plants a kiss in Aaron's hair. "Oh, and one for you, too, I know you'll feel left out, otherwise!" He grabs me by the back of the head and plants a slobbery kiss on my cheek, forcing me to fight him off. "What? You don't like that?" he asks with a grin.

He knows I don't. And it isn't a gay thing. He just enjoys his ability to make me squirm.

I pour black coffee into a mug and hand it to him. "Sleep well?"

Now, it's his turn to look up at me with a wry smile as he takes a seat at the island.

I shrug. "Sorry, mate. I know. Not the best night's sleep."

"What the fuck was that all about, dude?"

I shake my head helplessly. I want to say something, but I can't. It just feels wrong. "How was the blow-up bed – when you actually managed to sleep, that is?"

"It was fine. A bit tight. But OK. It was Aaron I felt sorry for. My snoring must have sounded like a megaphone right next to his ear."

Aaron laughs. "It's alright. I'm used to it!" He winks.

"He doesn't snore," David says with mock resentment.

"I do."

"You don't! I'm telling you, he's like a bloody freak of nature. How he puts up with me, I have no idea."

I notice there's a rosy colour to Aaron's cheeks, and he makes a show of drinking from his cup as David runs hands through his short blonde hair.

I recognise that look. It's an insipid one. The same one that I know I used to get with Ellie.

He's in love.

Used to get?

"I actually slept really well last night. If you don't count your midnight craziness and the constant up-and-down on those bloody creaky stairs. It was good. Nothing like the city."

"Yeah, I was saying that. We should think about moving out to the country. You know, after the wedding."

"Yeah, alright, farm boy—"

"Wait. Creaky stairs?" I ask.

"Yeah, your stairs need oiling or whatever, because every time you came down last night, it was like a bloody serenade of old ladies' thighs."

"I didn't come downstairs last night," I say flatly.

"No?"

"No."

"Well, someone did. You heard it, didn't you?" David asks Aaron, and he nods in agreement. "Maybe it was El."

It wasn't because I would have noticed, and why would she, anyway?

"I thought it was you coming down for a drink or someffin. At least, I did at first. The second and the third, I thought there was someffin wrong with your bladder. What with you gettin' on and everyffin, I know peeing is a bit of a problem..." he adds that last bit as a teasing whisper, which prompts Aaron to snigger and play-punch him.

I put a smile up on my face, but that isn't how I'm feeling.

"So, what's the plan for today?" David asks, clapping and rubbing his hands together like an eager car salesman.

I'm back in the present. "Well, I thought I would cook for you *guys*," I say putting the inflection on the word for Aaron's benefit and because even us Brits seem to overuse it in the same way we do the word *kids* – yeah, one of Ellie's many pet hates. "A slap-up full-English which we could then walk off with a tour of the area. Then, it's back here for a spot of lunch or, if you fancy it, we could go down to the pub. Heard the food is really good there. What time are you *guys* planning to head out?"

David drinks from his cup before answering. "I'm not sure, really. Need to talk to Ellie."

"Ellie?"

"Yeah. When do you think she'll be ready?" He catches my gaze and pulls a face. "Shit. You two've not talked yet. I keep landing myself in it."

"Talked about what?"

David shrugs. "Yeah. Rather than get the early train up in the morning, El asked if she could catch a lift back with us tonight," David says sheepishly, which if you knew him, you'd know is relatively unusual. "Well, I think that's what she said," he tries to backpedal.

I sigh, and as I do so, I catch another look from Aaron. As if he's deciphered what's going on around here without any need for help from me.

"Sorry, dude," David says.

I shake my head and force a smile. "It's fine. Really. Makes perfect sense," I say.

"Dude," David repeats.

"It's fine. Honestly." Then, forcing a smile, I add, "So, what'll it be, one egg or two?"

25. ALONE

SUNDAY· PORTHCOVE· LATE AFTERNOON·

So, here I am once more.

Alone.

The SUV's tyres have just scrunched and sloshed their way up the gravel drive, their tracks dissolved into the sheets of rain that are being dumped upon the land. This, I understand, is the precursor to the storm whose name I can't remember. And if the headlines are anything to go by, we're about to be battered by sixty-mile-an-hour winds and torrential rain of the likes to prompt authorities to issue a 'danger to life' warning. I don't know exactly what that means, but it doesn't sound good.

Some parts of the country are still recovering from massive floods, and this is only going to make things worse. Now, all we need is a plague of locusts and we'll be sorted.

I would like to say that I am pissed or sad about being left here on my own but, truth be told, I'm indifferent. I suppose I can attribute this devil-may-care attitude to the fact that I have, at least in my head, been here before.

But, shit. I've just remembered what that was like and, on second thoughts, no. I don't think I like it. I don't think I like it one bit.

Interestingly, regardless of my feelings or the impact that being abandoned here may or may not have on me, my wife was undeterred since, when I raised the subject at breakfast, she simply smiled and told me that she hadn't mentioned staying in London because it did not affect me. Code I interpreted as: *You didn't tell me about the money, and so why should I bother telling you that I'm ditching you and spending the night in the city?*

I didn't rise to the bait. Even though I wanted to because I really don't remember sending that text to David. I don't!

Besides, there was no point. It would have just turned into yet another argument, but this time in front of our guests, and I didn't want to expose them to that. I wanted them to go back to the city with a positive experience from their time here. And the feedback I received as they boarded the vehicle home was that they'd had one. That's, of course, if I ignore David's guilt-stricken, forlorn face as he embraced me.

Aaron's, too.

I wanted to say, *Chill guys! I'll be fine. You're not exactly leaving me behind to hold the front and repel a military invasion on my own.*

No, I'm just being left here to come to terms with the fact that my marriage is in crisis and, unless I do something about it, there'll soon be nothing left.

That, and there's the usual chestnut that I've vowed never to bring up again, and yet, like a dog with a bloody bone, I can't help but wonder about my wife's relationship with my best friend. I mean, those two have always been close, and I know I should be happy about that. I am. At least, I am when they aren't both ganging up on me… which sounds childish, I know, but in reality is actually fucking annoying because I can't exactly go to my best friend for a good venting session, given that he more than often starts to have an opinion about it or, worse, takes her bloody side!

Although, interestingly, there wasn't much of that this weekend. I'd like to think that it was because the two of them have finally gotten the message, but I'm more inclined to believe that the opportunity simply didn't present itself.

Alright. So, maybe I'm not as indifferent to being abandoned here as I first thought. The artificial smile I had on my face as I waved goodbye to the people I care about most as they drove away into a rainstorm was exactly that.

Fake.

I am not OK.

It isn't just my marriage that's in crisis. It's me. And I know that I can ignore this if I want to, but it's only going to get worse.

Shit! What's that?

"Oh, hey, Buddy. You startled me."

As if sensing my anguish, the dog nuzzles his little head against me and then looks up, expectantly, with those black, teddy bear eyes.

I crouch down and pet him. "It's OK, Buddy. Daddy's OK."

Unconvinced, the puppy jumps up to stand on his hind legs and stretch towards my face. So, I oblige and dip my head towards him, and he instantly starts licking my nose.

The slobbery kiss drags a chuckle out of me. "Thank you," I say, "thank you," as I feel the tension in my shoulders slowly dissolve… because this is exactly what my son used to do.

Every time he sensed something was off, be that tension between Ellie and I or one of us being unwell, his answer would be to climb up next to us and gently cover our faces with kisses.

Toby.

"Yes, thanks, Buddy," I continue. "Thank you." As if the dog can understand. And I am grateful because it's just occurred me, as bloody sad as this is going to sound, that this is the only true act of affection that I've felt in a while.

Yes. Sad.

I stand once more, ignoring the creak in my knees reminding me that life like time marches on. I am getting older. Life is passing me by. These seconds, these minutes, are ticking away and are not coming back.

Is this truly how I want to spend what's left of my life, or do I want to do something about it?

The answer comes in the form of a baritone moan and tapping sound on the patio doors.

I step over to them to see that the world has already been engulfed in premature darkness, thanks to the tumultuous, low-hanging black clouds that have occupied the sky. The onslaught of rain appears to have subsided, but I imagine it's only temporary as

I watch the giant, black spectres drift ominously over the house, reducing the land to nothing but shadows in the dregs of daylight. Even the tree's silhouette is trembling in fear, as if throttled by unseen hands.

Movement inside the house draws my attention to Buddy's reflection in the glass.

I watch him trot to the foot of the stairs and sit on his hind legs before angling his good ear and its misshapen counterpart to listen to something over there. Then, he cocks his head, as he often does when I speak to him… just before there's a loud creak that makes me spin around to see the scene with my own eyes.

I recognise that creak. It's the sound the third wooden step makes when stepped on.

Slowly, I walk over, as if attempting to catch whomever it might be before they run and hide in one of the upstairs rooms.

When I reach Buddy, I follow his gaze up into the gloom of the landing. It's dark up there, and I mean *black* because the nightlights haven't quite received their cue to get to work. And I feel a chill move through me because there's something about this place. I think I've mentioned it before. Something about the dark. Generally, it's just flat nothingness, but here it just feels different. Aware. Conscious.

"Hello?" The word panics its way out of my mouth and echoes in the quiet. I didn't realise this space sounded that hollow until now. Empty.

Thankfully or not, there's no response. Just the creak, tap, and moan of the wind through the eaves.

I look at Buddy, whose attention has now turned to me once more. "What?" I ask him.

The only response is a cock of the head before he turns and pads away.

"Yeah. Thanks for that, pal!" I call after him.

In the kitchen, I turn on the radio and instantly regret it – because it's either adverts or people talking about the apocalyptic storm that'll be hitting us tonight. They're recommending again that the public refrain from all non-essential travel, and my thoughts turn instantly to Ellie and the boys, so I check my phone.

No messages.

So, I send one of my own asking about progress and reminding them to let me know the moment they arrive safely. Then, I drop sliced bread in the toaster and turn the kettle on just as the overhead light flickers.

"You have got to be joking. There's barely a drop of rain and…" I trail off here because my words are interrupted by the strafing of water droplets as they begin their assault on the kitchen window. "Great."

When I first found out that I was going to be spending the night alone here, I entertained the idea of taking a walk down to the pub. But with the onslaught of rain and the weather advisory, I think I'll give that a miss. Especially since radio talk has turned to a so-called expert on climate change discussing why, he believes, the frequency of these storms is going to worsen as the planet rebels against the abuse it has suffered at the hands of humanity.

I switch the radio off. Not because I don't believe in climate change, because I do. Any person with half a brain must accept the fact that human life is undoubtedly contributing to a change in the environment in a variety of ways.

I barely hear the pop of the toaster over the drum and hiss of the downpour against the window and back door.

Shit.

It's not as if we haven't already been through a few of these storms already. It's just that they appear to be getting progressively worse. Being out here, perched on the cliffside, doesn't help.

Yeah. Architects never account for that, do they? Some brainchild must turn up and think, *Yeah, this spot with a killer view will be cool. Let's just plonk a house right here!* But they don't stop to truly consider adverse conditions like tonight, when there's a wild Atlantic gale tearing round the house, threatening to rip the doors and windows from their bloody hinges.

I butter the toast which, oddly, is already cold and hard, as if it's been sitting here for a few hours and not a few minutes, meaning that when I take a bite, the crunch is so loud that I almost don't hear what I think is the sound of the front door. It is instantly followed by a loud squeal and a bitter wind that invades the kitchen like a band of marauders, ringing hanging pots and swinging pans like church bells.

"What the hell…. Ellie?" I call, stepping out into the hallway, where the dreary light is flickering like something out of a theme park house of horror as it contemplates whether or not it has the courage to clock in for the nightshift.

I hate this hallway. I know I've mentioned that, but right in this moment, I've decided that I hate it more than anything else and am going to elevate it to *urgent* on the list of things for immediate change.

As if protesting, another wave of freezing air scurries down the hallway to ruffle my hair.

"Jesus!"

I move in the opposite direction. Quickening my pace now because it's just occurred to me that it may be Ellie and the others. They may have run into severe weather and decided to turn back.

But there's nobody in the lounge.

The only thing I find is the front door, wide open, and a group of desiccated leaves aquaplaning on the puddle of rainwater collecting on the floor.

The howling wind pushes at me before ungraciously spitting in my face. I return the favour by shoving the door shut in its face and turning the lock. "Fuck!" is all I have to say to that.

I'm already soaked. Freezing. And, like a disaster action hero, I lean my back against the door for a few seconds, panting and shivering.

"Buddy! Shit!" *Did he go outside?*

My stomach summersaults as I begin a search of the room, calling his name as I go.

But there's no response. And I'm just considering whether or not to reopen the door when I see his little head appear from behind the couch. His chocolate eyes are wide like saucers, as if to ask, *Has the evil wind gone now?*

"Buddy!" I smile with a sigh, relief flooding through me.

I had no idea just how panicked I'd be at the thought of losing him.

I walk over, bend down, and pet the mutt and...

What the hell are they?

The sight sends a wave of hot and cold shivers over my skin, rousing those small hairs from their slumber once more.

Shit.

I didn't notice them before because of my angle to the lamplight, but as I turned, they glistened and winked as if spot-lit by a special effects crew.

Footprints. Bloody footprints!

Made of rainwater. Leading from the front door to the hallway.

"What the actual fuck?" I gasp.

At least, they look like footprints. It's hard to tell in the lamplight.

So, I move over to the light switch on the wall, but when I flick it, there's a buzz, a pinging sound, and then all of the lights go out.

OK. Wasn't quite expecting that.

So, I stand there considering what to do next. I think there's a flashlight in the kitchen. There are candles in the dining room, but none in here, of course. None where I need them.

I swallow down the anxiety that's attempting to crawl its way up my throat. It's fine. This is fine. It was bound to happen. *Yeah, but is this a general outage or one of those special ones reserved exclusively for me?*

Shut up.

I look out the rain-blurred window, through the haze of water to the orange glow of the village.

Their lights are still on. It's just here. Of course.

Which means that, like something out of the worst horror movie, something has tripped, and I am going to have to go on a hunt for the junction box. I have no idea where that bloody thing is.

Oh God. I think it's down the trapdoor in the kitchen, but I'm not–

Creak!

That familiar, dreaded sound that's loud enough to be heard over the meteorological onslaught, and it scuttles down the stairs like a rodent.

Someone is moving around up there.

"Hello?" I wait, but the only response is the hiss, ding, and drum of the rain and the moan, creak, and rush of the wind closely followed by a new sound…. Sloshing, sluicing, and tapping just outside the front door.

I think the guttering has given up ferrying water and is now simply dribbling it down the wall.

"Ellie, are you home?" I call.

No reply.

I frisk myself even though I already know the answer; I left my phone on the kitchen counter before running out here.

Thunder explodes overhead and I duck instinctively. "Fuck!" Where the hell did that come from? It was so loud, I can feel the aftershock.

"I love you, Daddy."

I yelp and spin around, holding a hand over my mouth as if to stop my heart from jumping out and scampering off to find a hiding place.

"You do?"

"But not more than Mummy. I love you both exactly the same."

"I love you, too, little man. Merry Christmas."

The voices are coming from the photography room where, once again, I can see that flickering blue light.

"…no flying that thing over people."

"Over people…"

"Ever."

"Daddy!"

I'm breathing heavily now, almost to the point of hyperventilating. *It's OK. You're OK. It's just the dark. You're a grown man.*

I gawp at the shimmering light through the open door and then, slowly and deliberately, will myself to step forward.

Thunder cracks and then rolls away, startling me once again before revealing a snapshot of the room to me.

I run my hands through my hair, over my face, and I realise I'm still dripping rainwater, or is that sweat? I don't know.

The sounds have stopped now, but the flickering light continues as I gingerly make my way towards it, shuffling my feet to make sure I don't trip over anything. Although, visibility has improved somewhat now that my eyes have adjusted to the flicker acting as a nightlight.

Thunder grumbles. Rain drums.

I'm at the door now. I grip the frame for reassurance as the blood thuds behind my ears.

I don't want to look in there. I don't want to see.

And yet, I can't help myself.

My heart skips a beat when I see him.

Buddy. Sitting on the chair again in front of the laptop.

"Oh, Buddy," I groan angrily. And I'm about to move towards him when I hear that tell-tale creak on the stairs.

I whip around just as a flash of light reveals something that shoves a dagger of terror into my spine.

There's someone on the stairs! There's someone *standing* on the fucking stairs!

Wave upon wave of hot and cold shivers smash over me like the tide against rocks as my beleaguered brain attempts to process what I've just seen. A hand. Or at least the shape of a pallid hand on the banister.

It isn't Ellie. I know it isn't her.

Buddy's bark is like an alarm bell in the still of the room. He jumps off the chair and in front of me, yapping angrily towards the staircase.

Then, the laptop screen flickers and dies, and before I have the chance to react, the place is plunged into darkness once more.

Shit!

Unlike my dog, I slowly back away from the door's

threshold, both wishing for and dreading the next flash of light, but it doesn't come. So, instead, I improvise by backing my way to the other side of the room, where I tap keyboard buttons to bring the laptop to life.

It doesn't.

What?

I tap more keys, and still get nothing.

Thunder claps and then grumbles as I prod keys in the general vicinity of the power button. "Wake up!"

Finally, the thing springs to life, running through the start-up procedure, but how is that even possible? It was on just a few seconds ago.

Lightning flashes, and I jump again when the shadow of a giant, bony claw is projected onto the walls.

It's the branches, you idiot, just the tree branches. Pull yourself together.

The laptop finally boots up and I, with trembling fingers, click and move the mouse until the word processor's blank white screen appears. Then, I pick the machine up and brandish it in front and around me, pushing away the shadows.

Buddy pauses his yapping and turns to face me, revealing demon dog eyes that freak me the fuck out in the light. I wish him to turn away once more, and mercifully he does, going one step further and trotting deeper into the den.

"Buddy! Wait!"

I rush after him, waving the laptop in front of me as both illumination and a weapon. "Who's in here?" I yell, buoyed by my newfound protection, sweeping an arc of light around the room.

But there's nothing in here. Nothing on the stairs. No pale or otherwise hand on the banister.

Nothing.

Buddy doesn't agree, though. He's convinced that whatever was on the stairs is now in the corridor, so he's jumping back and forth, up and down, with a series of growls and barks.

And, as much as all of my senses are screaming at me not to, I turn the light in that direction.

Nothing.

Just the usual empty, miserable hallway. At the bottom of which is my phone, the torch, and candles.

"Hey. Stop it, Buddy. Calm down," I say to the grumpy pup, but he's not having any of it. "There's nothing there," I say to him. "Nothing there," I say, very much aware that I'm speaking the words more for my own self-assurance than to calm the dog, whose aggravated growls aren't doing anything to relax the tension in my nerves.

"There's nothing here, mate. It's just a trick of the light. Look." I tentatively pan the light around the den and then back at the hallway.

Empty.

"There's nothing here. Just me and you."

And then, as if to prove the point, I walk past him and down the corridor, still brandishing the laptop as if my life depends on it – passing the toilet and the dining room, both of which have their doors shut, and then the kitchen.

I burst inside and fall upon my phone, which I tap a few times immediately, activating the reassuring power of the LED light and quickly making a sweep of the place.

The kitchen is empty.

The rain is still falling, but I think the thunder has moved on… albeit with the occasional distant mutter.

And I sigh.

The pressure is still bulging in my temple, but I'm a little more relaxed now that I have my phone. I have no idea why. It just feels like I'm no longer alone, like I'm connected to the rest of the world, and that thought makes me feel a little better.

I use the phone to find candles in one of the bottom kitchen drawers. I light a couple and stick them to saucers, and then place them around the room, bathing the place in a reassuring amber glow.

Finally, I lean against the sink and take a few seconds to have a word with myself while staring at the remains of my now petrified toast.

I know what happened here. I know what's going on. I've

been avoiding it, banning my thoughts from straying anywhere near the memory of what happened before, but it's time that I confront and accept it.

What happened here – or, what I experienced here before – was not real.

It was NOT real, Marco. It was all in your head. You never were here. You never saw the intruders. They do not exist. They never did exist.

Now, on your first time alone with some seriously fucking creepy special effects, you're allowing your mind to fabricate a scenario that does not exist.

Yes, the lights are out. Yes, it's raining outside, and yes, it's all scary as hell, but – and that is a big but – there is nobody here. Just you and your equally creepy hound.

Do NOT let yourself spiral down again.

Get a grip. You are a grown man.

And, if I may say so myself, I'm right. I am fucking right.

So, why doesn't Buddy agree? Why is he still barking out there like there's an invisible entity stalking the dark?

Because, not unlike you, he has issues.

"Buddy!" I yell, hoping that he'll at least pause for breath, but he doesn't. He continues yapping and growling like one of those toys that you can't wait to yank the batteries from.

So, I take my phone and step out into the corridor. "Buddy! Stop it. Stop."

I shine the light around. The dog hasn't even ventured down the hallway. He's exactly where I left him, at the other end, and I flinch when his demon eyes glint back at me once more in the light.

"Jesus, Buddy. No, not helping."

I step out into the corridor, and freeze when the light on my phone flickers several times and then dies.

Of course.

So, I turn it to look at the screen, and that's dead, too, which makes absolutely no sense… because I've hardly used the thing.

What's that?

I spin around. Something. In the kitchen. A strange sound. Like–

There it is again!

Wheezing!

I take a step back away from the doorway just as the wheezing is followed by…

Draag.

Hell, no! I've been in this horror flick before.

Wheeze. Draag. Wheeze. Draag.

Slowly. Growing progressively louder as it moves towards the doorway.

I turn to bolt, to get out of here, to run away never to return when…

"Ugh!" What's that? Something tickling my face! Cobwebs!

Wheeze. Draag. Wheeze. Draag.

I run fingers over my face and can feel the tickly substance on my hands.

I thrust them into the light and, to my horror, see that the stuff entangled in my fingers is not a cobweb, but a knot of….

Hair?

Black hair.

And it's… hanging down from the ceiling!

Unwillingly, I pan the light upwards and recoil in horror when, not unlike the puppy's eyes before it, I find two featureless, filmy white eyes glaring back at me with a malevolence so palpable that it fouls the very air around me, triggering an immediate ball of bile at the back of my throat.

I move to leave, but stumble over my own feet and crash to the floor, where a scream crawls out of my lips and echoes around the hallway.

Then, I hear laughter, voices, and a whirring sound before the lights come on… and I discover that I'm alone.

26. AND SO IT BEGINS

Nothing changes.

Last time I was here, one of the things that used to grate the most was the fact that, as soon as I looked forward to some alone time, the doorbell would ring.

Today is no exception.

Only, I'm still in bed.

On the bright side, it's just a normal, albeit electronically synthesised door chime instead of that Gestapo-like hammering that–

OK. On second thought....

I'm sitting up in bed now, running my hands through my hair; it's getting quite wavy, which means I need to find a barber. I think I saw one in town. My beard could do with a trim, too.

There's sunlight streaming through the window, and that bleached blue sky is back. Looks like Armageddon has been postponed once more.

A glance at my phone tells me that it's almost eight in the morning, and I feel like the proverbial shit. I don't think I fell asleep until the early hours, and even then, I kept waking up at the slightest noise.

Buddy doesn't seem to care for the intrusion, either. He's curled up on the bed and obviously so exhausted from last night's shenanigans that, just beyond lifting his head and shooting me a judgemental look of *are you going to get that?*, he's already gone back to snoozing.

Yes, Buddy is on the bed. Yes, if Ellie knew, she would kill me. But Ellie isn't here – she is in London as per her WhatsApp message late last night advising me that they arrived late in the city because traffic was, quote, *shit,* and that she'll see me tonight. *Kiss.*

No, I haven't forgotten last night. Of course, I haven't. The fact that the overhead light and the two bedside lamps are still glowing in the cold light of day is testament to that.

After what happened in the hallway, I took myself, the puppy, and my phone, and scaled the stairs two at a time – chanting the usual mantra to myself: *It's in my head! It's in my head!*

It's classic autosuggestion brought on by suggestive meteorological conditions and that obligatory fact that the house was plunged into darkness.

There's no such thing as the intruders. They don't exist. They were a figment of your imagination.

Oh God. If you weren't with me last time, count yourself lucky.

I don't know which is worse. Being right that I'm starting to lose my grip on reality once more or the fact that the house is haunted.

Which would *you* prefer?

Don't answer that; it'll probably only make it worse.

I have several hours of daylight, so I'm going to stuff all this shit into the bottom drawer until I've at least had my first cup of coffee. Meanwhile, I still need to deal with whomever has fallen asleep against the bloody doorbell.

Wow. I'm already disliking this sound, too.

I hurry down the stairs and yank the door open, ready to give whomever it is a piece of my mind… until I see Ivan's round face smiling back at me. Today, he's flanked by two younger men – both of them probably in their twenties – who keep looking around him like children eager to get into a fairground attraction.

"Ivan," I say. He must detect the surprise in my voice because he says, "Oh, mornin', Marco. You hadn't forgotten about us, had ya?"

"I, um, well… no. I just thought that, given the weather yesterday, you know, conditions, wet, you might not…" I trail off here because I can hear myself rambling.

"Nah, we're used to working in all conditions. Besides, what we can't do outside, we can always start inside."

"Oh, right."

"Is that a problem?" he asks.

"No, no, of course not."

"Oh, these two are Andrew and Dean," he says. Then, turning and nodding at the driveway, he adds, "You two can gets unloadin." I follow his gaze to the battered and blue flatbed truck in the driveway with *Irvin and Sons* stamped across it in faded white lettering.

And so it begins.

Irvin produces the original list I made for him and, as if he reads my mind, asks if there's anything I would like to add, as now would be a good time.

And I unload.

I tell him that I don't know if he has any idea or if he knows somebody who does, but that the electrics have been playing up, with lights going on and off of their own volition and bulbs exploding for no given reason. And that the storage heaters don't seem to work, and that we've been freezing our arses off. I tell him about the plumbing – that sometimes the house is plagued with bad smells, and that I can't be certain, but I'm sure I hear toilets spontaneously flushing in the middle of the night. Then, there are the drafts. The cold spots and – this just in – black, mouldy-looking spiderwebs that seem to have taken up residence in the corner ceilings of the hallways and master bedroom.

When I finally pause for breath, my undaunted workman-slash-builder-slash-master-of-many-things wrinkles his chubby face and gives his thinning hair a scratch before telling me that, "Faulty wiring is a general term that encompasses many things."

His words.

So, I cock my head and pay attention when he says that there's a good chance that we may have an exposed wire somewhere, and that sometimes the sheave encasing the wire can become exposed, be that through wear and tear or damage caused by animals, such as rodents. This is the countryside, after all. That wire can then become waterlogged during particularly harsh weather, such as last night's rainstorm.

He then, in turn, goes on to address, in meticulous and eloquent detail, all of the possible causes for each of the faults I have itemised, but assures me that each of them has now been added to his list.

When he notices me glance at the list in his hand, he taps his head and says they're catalogued in there.

So, yeah. I'm feeling better already. I don't know if it's because I managed to get so much off my chest or the fact that there's something about this man in his stained dungarees with his kind brown eyes and unrattled demeanour that makes me feel better. Like he has taken all of my problems and made them his own.

OK. Maybe not *all* of them, but at least the ones that mean absolutely nothing to me and have still been nagging me like a clutch of hungry chicks.

On Irvin's instruction, I'm opening the patio doors to the warzone that is the back garden.

Sweet Jesus (and I'm not a religious person), but I had no idea.

The mobile barbeque is on its side and wedged into the hedge. Its metal innards are strewn across the meadow that is the lawn as if it has undergone some kind of medieval torture during the night. The tree has shed much of its remaining leaves and some of its branches, including a six-foot limb that's been severed and wedged like an impromptu barricade across the patio. There are ripped plastic bags decorating the hedge like party streamers and, from what I can tell, the gate at the foot of the garden has finally given up and most likely flung itself off the cliff, leaving a gaping, arched hole framing the view out to a choppy ocean.

I run both my hands through my hair this time. I was not expecting this carnage. From inside the house, I had no perception of just how bad last night's storm was.

When I voice this, Irvin's eyes widen, and he wastes no time in filling me in on the fact that other counties are still without power, that more trees have been uprooted, and that he and his own crew had to drive around a few just to get here.

He then adds that flooding has closed thousands of businesses and schools across the region, while in the neighbouring town, the very place Ellie went shopping over the weekend, a sinkhole has devoured a council building; and, elsewhere, another sinkhole has swallowed a major artery through the town centre. And better still – again, these are his words – the worst is yet to come.

Yay.

I have to say, as much as this is going to sound strange, there's something reassuring about the builder's apocalyptic recount. It does not appear sensationalised or dramatised in any way. That's oddly calming. As if Mother Nature's public displays of wrath around here are an everyday occurrence, and nothing to be concerned with.

Although, I only have to look at the devastation before us to be disabused of that notion.

Yet, ever the pragmatist, Irvin goes on to say that, in light of more impending doom, it makes sense for some of their work to start outside today while the weather is holding. They'll clear up the debris, hunt down the remains of the gate, and dispose of all that along with the green waste from the hedgerow which, as we all know, is out of control. Cutting this back to a more manageable size makes sense for many reasons, not least of which is the fact that we could probably use the extra light in the house at this time of year.

That hadn't even occurred to me. I just accepted the place as dark and dingy, but I nod and make the right noises as if it was a point I was going to raise anyway.

Talk then turns to those rooms that they can safely avoid. That is, the few rooms in the house that require minimal or no work. I confirm that these will be the photography room turned study and the kitchen since both are still in good condition. The kitchen cabinets could maybe use a lick of paint, but it isn't a necessity. Time permitting, I can take care of that, anyway. Both rooms could do with a deep clean, regardless, and that will be my job for the day.

We also discuss the painful conversation of windows. I say 'painful' because initial web research has revealed that replacing our type of windows and doors is bloody expensive! This is the reason why my initial estimate of twenty thousand for the house was inflated to thirty thousand with a ten thousand contingency.

Forty thousand.

| TO DAVID: | Mate, you don't happen to have 40 grand lying about. Do you? |
| TO MARCO: | Forty? Dude, you said you were fixing up that place, not rebuilding it! |

So, it must have been me who sent that message. The only other person who knew about the budget was Ellie because we discussed it together. And she obviously didn't send it.

Anyway, Irvin, who is fast becoming my most favourite person in the world, stops short of laughing when I tell him that I've budgeted ten thousand in case we need to replace the much sought after sash windows with double-glazed PVC.

It would appear I'm the only moron who doesn't appreciate the true value of sash windows, almost as much as I have no clue how much replacing them would cost.

He tells me that, from what he can see, the windows just need a good clean, maybe fixing in places, and that we should start there. Worst case, he has a mate who is a windows specialist and he could call him for a best price.

Music to my ears.

At the front of the house, he observes, "I see you've made a start on the fence, then," clearly supressing a snicker. He's referring to the two struts that I managed to sand down.

"Yeah," I say, throwing him a look and then promptly pull the phone out of my pocket to pretend I'm a busy person with an avalanche of messages that need tending to.

Which reminds me.

I open WhatsApp and reply to Ellie:

| TO ELLIE: | Work has started on the house! Exciting! It's going to be a busy day. Hope you have a |

productive one. Please don't overdo it. You've been working really hard lately. What time will you be home? Please don't make it too late, as they're forecasting more bad weather. X

I press *SEND* just as the giant that is Andrew retrieves something from the back of the truck and makes his way towards us.

OK, maybe he's not a giant. He's just a tiny bit taller than me, which would make him six-foot-something, although he is wearing muddy work boots. Alright, he's a lanky thing with ginger hair and an obligatory chequered red and blue jacket. Reminds me a bit of Shawn, but the least said about that, the better.

Anyway, he's carrying what looks like an elongated chainsaw. "Any chance of a brew, guv?" he asks, as if he comes from the East End of London, but without the accent to back it up.

Tea boy for the day? Sure.

"Of course," I say. "Milk and sugar?"

"Yeah, lovely. Cheers," he throws back as he and his mechanical mutant disappear around the side of the house.

I should probably tell him that he can't get to the back that way, but don't since, well, you know, I've got to make the tea.

27. RESPLENDENT

PORTHCOVE· LATE AFTERNOON·

Have you ever found yourself asking a question, but then instantly regretting it?

I remember ordering a pizza once. Shortly after placing the order, I received a phone call apologizing and informing me that the type of pizza I had ordered was not available, and that instead of a deep pan pizza, I would be receiving the stretched, thin crust version instead.

When the caller stopped there and didn't offer anything more to the conversation, I felt compelled to ask the most logical question. *Why? Just out of curiosity, why is the pizza I ordered not available?*

The young man, who sounded like he was still in his teens, proceeded to explain, in meticulous detail.

Apparently, the fridge that was normally used to store the dough had malfunctioned. Because of this, they were unable to store the dough that was usually extend….

Fifteen minutes later, the pizza delivery had almost reached us before the explanation was concluded. I remember being bemused and somewhat shellshocked when Ellie asked me who I'd been talking to for so long.

And so, it was with some trepidation today, when I spotted Irvin examining the house's external stonework, that I asked, "Irvin, stone pointing. What the hell does that mean, exactly?"

Apparently, walls are built of brick, stone, or flint with mortar as the glue that binds the materials together. Mortar is made up, in part, of aggregate (*sand* to you and me). *Old builds* like Dolce Vita tend to use lime or even earth – sometimes a combination of both. It's the joints of mortar that are known as the *pointing*. So, the most obvious purpose of pointing is to fill the gap between the brick or stone to stop water, draughts, and vegetation from taking up residence in there and compromising the structure of a building.

The most crucial part, of course, is to manage the moisture in the wall since this, as we know, can sometimes cause dangerous mould, mildew, and even hideous black discolorations. This is due, in part, to the fact that bricks and some types of stone are porous.

Repointing becomes necessary once the joints of mortar have eroded beyond the face of the brick or, in this case, the stone.

Now, I must have the same look on my face as I did that pizza day because Irvin is smiling at me. "Based on what I've seen so far, I think you're OK," he tells me. "You won't need to spend a fortune repointing this place. I can't imagine a surveyor 'avin' a problem with this baby," he says, touching the stonework, "who, I have to say, seems to 'ave fared well despite the sea air. That moist, salty air can cause a lot of unwanted 'avoc with the structure of a buildin'."

I watch the man caress the stone as if it were a beautiful woman, and I am in awe of him. I just love a professional who knows and seemingly loves his craft.

"So, what about the marks on the ceiling, Irvin? If the outside looks like its weather-sealed, then what's causing those dark patches?"

My short, portly builder – who appears to be gradually metamorphosing into one of those cute gnomes with red cheeks and a bulbous nose – scratches his head and says with a sigh, "Well, there's a process, Marco. First, we take a look outside and, failin' that, I'll need to have a wander up in the attic."

Not exactly the way I'd describe it, but each to their own. I suppose I could ask him to sort out a decent stepladder while he's at it.

"Would you like a cuppa?" I ask, changing the conversation as flashbacks of the jagged remains reintroduce themselves to me.

I don't mention anything of all that. We'll cross that proverbial bridge when we need to.

And, for now, I'm happy.

Yes, if you've accompanied me on my previous journey and are back for more, you'll know that it's an unusual state of mind for me, but I am happy to officially declare that I am happy.

We've made a fantastic start on the house today.

Andrew and his metal beast hacked down what looks like most of the hedgerow, giving it a somewhat severe back and sides, while Dean, who I've learned has a computer science degree but much prefers working with Irvin, dragged the corpses to the hearse that is the back of the truck.

Irvin completed his rounds on the external structure of the building and then began his investigation into the dodgy electrics and temperamental plumbing.

I removed all of the photo frames from the walls in the photography room and stacked them in the den before brushing, hoovering, and wiping every nook and cranny of the place. Then, I scrubbed the picture window inside and out, and marvelled at just how much brighter the room is, thanks to the manicured hedgerow and grime-free glass.

It was as I was standing there with my hands on my hips and a somewhat achy back that I allowed myself to flirt with the idea that I could settle down in this place. I mean, if we weren't in debt up to our eyeballs, not including the additional loan from David for the refurbishments, I could live here. I know Ellie isn't that keen, but, well, even though we can't stay, I can now understand what the old man saw in this sanctuary, and what my mother saw in it, for that matter.

Dragging.

Pain.

Sobbing.

Pain. Tears. Begging. Tears. Salty water sloshing, splashing, and fizzing. "Mummy! Please!"

I shake my head as if that can shake those images out like bad fruit from a tree, but I can't. And I bite my lip, angrily.

This is just one of the reasons why, as idyllic as it might seem at times, we *could never* stay here. In the country maybe, but not in this house.

Fuck. And just like that, I'm angry again. Or frustrated, mostly with Doctor Holmes. He opened my mind to all this stuff. He may have healed me in some way, but he's bloody handicapped me in others.

Come on. Remember how good it felt to be content?

I take a break. Decide to make us all another nice brew, accompanied with a side order of chocolate cookies.

And, mug and cookies in hand, I'm about to head out back to find Andrew when I spot him through the patio doors, taking bloody selfies of himself with the house as a backdrop.

What the hell?

I watch him snap a few more of them before pushing on the door handle with my elbow and making my way out into the chill with the mug and a plate of biscuits.

He must have spotted the door opening because he instantly pockets his phone and resumes his work.

"What's going on?" I ask with a smile – because I'm supressing a snigger. How bloody vain can you be, to snap photos of yourself while raking a bloody yard?

"Yeah. All good, guv. Finished the cutback and now focussing on the lawn."

"Yeah. I've noticed. It's looking much better already," I say, handing him the mug and biscuits.

"Cheers."

"So, have you been working with Irvin long?"

He nods. "Yeah. Since I left school."

"He must be a good mentor. He seems to know his stuff."

"Irvin? Oh yeah. He's a decent bloke. Wouldn't have a job if it wasn't for 'im. Even after all that stuff with Sarah. Nothing changed. Top bloke."

"Sarah?"

"Yeah. His niece. We were engaged like, but it just didn't work out."

"Oh, right," I say, because I'm surprised. What would Sarah see in this bloke?

And what business is it of yours?

He nods, chomping on a biscuit, squinting into the wintry sunshine. "Yeah. He's always treated me good. Like a son."

I nod – that's all I can do. For some reason, the news that Sarah and this guy were engaged is bothering me. OK, it isn't bothering me, but just–

"So, you're planning on selling the place, then?" he asks before washing down the biscuit with some tea.

"Yes," I say.

He nods knowingly. "Aye, probably for the best."

I squint at him, and am about to ask what he means by that when Irvin's voice interrupts us. "'Ere, Drew! Leave Mr Battista alone. I'm sure he has a lot to be getting on with and so do you. Need to get the outside sorted before that comes in," he says, nodding at something behind us.

We both turn in unison to see that the horizon has been blotched out by a giant shroud of blackness.

Andrew turns back to me. "Best get to it, then. Cheers for the tea," he says.

I nod at him thoughtfully before taking my cue and returning to my drudgery of scrubbing and spraying silicone on door hinges. Standard practice in this place since every door insists on creaking like a prop in a Foley artist's studio.

Then, I go through the trouble of polishing each eight-by-ten-inch black photo frame while childishly avoiding direct eye contact with its monochromatic content. A pointless exercise since the imagery is already seared into my memory.

Little boy with a mop of curly black hair, running and laughing on a shingled shore… the one I've walked on many times since arriving here, the one beyond the gate before it was blown away to God knows where.

Then, there's the little boy in front of a woman with long black hair. My mother. She's wearing a summer hat and is laughing. Next to us is a puppy. A black Labrador. I never did find out what happened to him. She told me that he ran away, and I was devastated. That feeling is renewed when I glance across the room at Buddy, who is snoozing in his box by the desk. And, oddly, tears prick my eyes. I don't even know why. I can only assume that it's because I thought I'd consigned all this shit to history, and yet it's always there, just beneath the surface, waiting to be uncovered like a stinking turd.

My mother looks just how I remember her. Beautiful. So beautiful. Which makes what she tried to do even uglier.

And it just goes to show how unreliable the mind, our memories, can be sometimes... because I thought somebody else had snapped these pictures, but it turns out that it was my dad. Just like I thought he was the villain in the drama of my life, but – according to the locals, at least – that may well be yet another figment of my imagination.

He didn't keep leaving, as I was led to believe. She drove him away. And I keep telling myself that she couldn't help it, that she was sick, but no matter how much I want it to, it doesn't make any of this any easier.

I glance down at the black and white image of her looking over-the-shoulder straight at the camera through a curtain of long black hair. She's smiling enigmatically, seductively, at the person behind the lens.

I pick up another frame. This time, it's in colour. A family portrait, seemingly taken on the same day. My mother, large brown eyes as wide as her smile, is holding a pair of small legs. A distinguished looking man with grey hair, dark eyebrows, and a salt and pepper beard, my father, is holding the other half of the little boy, whose face is contorted into a fit of laughter.

It's me.

But I don't recognise this photo.

There are at least twenty more of all shapes and sizes. Most are of the old man and me; at the beach, fishing, trekking through woods, riding bikes, and sailing. There are even photos of us in front of this house.

And then there are the others. The artistic ones snapped by my mother. The ocean. The skies. The countryside. The house.

All taken at various times of the day, with and without elongated shadows. With and without colour.

But there's one that draws me in. It's a moody, black and white shot of the shingled shore being ravaged by an angry white surf. Behind it, out of focus, is the giant cave, then the ragged cliff face, and high above that, perched on the peninsula, is Dolce Vita, silhouetted against a tempestuous sky.

There's something about this image that makes me want to crawl inside it and explore as if it's hiding something in plain sight that I am unable to see.

Instead, I drop it on the pile with the others before moving to pick up a batch and return them to their perches.

But do you know what? Fuck it! What's the point of putting them back up, only to have to take them down again when we leave?

So, instead, I hunt down the box which the blow-up bed came in, fill it with most of the frames, drag it to the corner of the room and then neatly stack the rest on top.

To be fair, the walls do look rather naked now, and scarred by the faded outlines of where the frames used to be. But I can easily paint over those. In fact, a couple of coats of emulsion should do the trick in here. Satisfied, I fill a bucket with hot water, detergent, and disinfectant, lift Buddy onto the desk, and mop the hell out of the floor.

It's on the third pass where the water remains as clear as it did when I first started that I realise that I've moved from deep-clean to obsessive-compulsive… no doubt triggered by that lapse into sentimentality.

The result, though, is an immaculate room in which you could quite literally eat off the floor. In fact, I challenge any hospital out there to have floors anywhere near as clean as this chessboard.

When I become aware of the fading light, I'm surprised to find that it's gone past four in the afternoon. I had planned to make a start on the kitchen today, too, although I'm not too worried since that place has already had the once-over when we first arrived here.

Besides, there's always tomorrow.

And, no. It has absolutely nothing to do with the fact that

my back is killing me. At least, that's what I'm telling myself. And so, it's as the sun finally surrenders to the invasion of darkness that I make my way across the immaculate, chequered floor in my socks, because I can, and over to the laptop.

I plan on getting a good night's sleep tonight, and the last thing I want is yet another mind trip down emotionally conflicted memory lane, with the agony and the ecstasy of seeing my little boy. And it isn't because I'm trying to forget it – far from it. No, it's more because I just can't handle that overwhelming sense of hopelessness that drowns me when I see those images of him. That sense of paralysis. The anxiety of my inability to change the course of events that end up with my son being wrenched from me is just too much to bear.

So, I'm going to remove the card from the machine and put it somewhere safe where, hopefully, one day, I'll be able to watch without the emotional dagger in my chest.

You can imagine my surprise when I look down at the laptop and find that the SD slot is empty. I check around, underneath and nearby, but find nothing. No card.

I look at Buddy, who, of course, abandoned his nap in favour of chasing my mop around and is now looking at me as if wondering why all the fun has stopped.

"What did you do with the SD card, you?" I ask the pup, who I'm sure has grown two weeks in two days. His only response is to scratch an itch behind his floppy, wounded ear, to the point of knocking himself off his own footing and falling, snout first, onto the floor.

I laugh and roll my eyes. "Right. So, you don't know, either."

I look around the room as if I haven't just cleaned the place three times over. I would have noticed an SD card, or heard it slide around if it had fallen onto the floor.

So, I look at the dog again. Did he eat it, maybe?

Chewed it possibly… but eat it? I doubt it. The thing has been there the whole time and he didn't touch it, but he did sit there and watch it.

Again.

Yep, that gave me the creeps both times, even though I know it shouldn't because Toby's in the film.

But he didn't know Toby.

"I should rename you 'Creepy'. What do you think? Creepy Buddy?"

If he's offended, he doesn't show it. He just flops into a sitting position and looks up at me before performing a wide yawn, as if he's the one who's just finished all the backbreaking cleaning.

I'm about to speak to him again when I hear Irvin call to me from the doorway.

"Yeah, I'm here! Just talking to the creepy pu–" I cut my word short when I see that there's nobody standing in the doorway.

"Irvin?" I call, as if there's something wrong with my eyes. Then I walk over and look out into the den.

It's empty. The front door is open. That cold breeze is making itself at home again, but there's otherwise no movement. No sound from in here. Just rumbling surf. The call of a wood pigeon.

It's as if everyone has left already, but I know that can't be because I just heard him. I just heard Irvin call my name. It was as clear as day. I did *not* imagine it.

I look back at Buddy, who's watching me as if I'm about to abandon him here. "You heard that, right?"

"Heard what?"

"Jesus!" I spin around.

Irvin is standing in the doorway. "Sorry, mate, didn't mean to startle ya. Just wanted to let you know that we're all done and packed up for the day."

I nod and swallow a suddenly parched throat. His eyes are on me, so eventually I croak, "You weren't just here, were you?"

He cocks his head. "Here?"

"In the doorway," I elaborate, but his expression tells me all I need to know. *Shit.* "Don't worry about it."

"You alright?"

I nod. "Yeah, I'm fine. It's just… I thought I heard you call me, that's all."

He shakes his head. "No, I just came in from outside. The

boys are waitin' in the truck. So, Marco, listen.... We're all friendly around here. You know, it's a small village. Folk are close. Neighbours like family if you get me meanin'. So, open doors and all that, not really a problem. It ain't like the city. But, you don't wanna leave the door open all the time cos we're in the country, after all, and the odd animal, you know, 'as been known to wander in. And, when they do, they can make a right mess. If you get me meanin'?"

I smile. "I thought *you* left it open."

He shrugs. "No, I've even trained the lads not to leave doors wedged open without first asking an owner's permission. You know, it's just good manners... oh, eh, this place is lookin' 'ansum, ennit?" he comments, looking into the room behind me.

The comment brings a smile to my face. Yes, I know. I haven't saved the world or anything, but there's nothing wrong with taking pride in your work. Especially when it's recognised by somebody else.

"Oi, 'ansum! I hope you wiped your paws before comin' in 'ere!" Irvin calls out to the dog in a mock reproachfulness.

Buddy's reaction is to lift his ears and slap his tail on the floor a few times. The acknowledgement prompts one of Irvin's trademark chuckles. Then, to me, he adds, "Yeah, so, we're done for the day. I 'ad a look at the electrics, but can't seem to find nout wrong. Nor plummin'. As for the storage heaters, I don't rate 'em, meself, but the ones upstairs seem to be workin' fine to me."

"What? Really?"

"Yeah. Checked and triple-checked. The master bedroom is quite toasty right now. Want to come and check?"

"No, I'll take your word for it. But that's really weird."

"As I say. I don't rate 'em much. You're better off g'tting' a couple of those electric 'eaters. They're cheap enough. But, anyway, I'll take a closer look tomorra.

I nod. "So, what is the plan for tomorrow? I heard on your radio today that there's another front coming in."

"Yeah, well, that's one of the reasons why I wanted to get it finished out there. Unless your wantin' us to do the fence, after all.

Otherwise, we'll be startin' inside tomorrow if that works for you, like."

I nod. "Absolutely."

"So, the weather won't matter."

"Great. Also, do you think you could start in the hallway tomorrow, please, Irvin? I'm eager to get that done first and the lights up in there."

"Yep. No problem. See ya then. Same time. See ya tomorra, me luvver! Take care of your pa," he adds for Buddy's sake. And, to my surprise, the dog stands, wags his tail, and barks as if bidding the man goodbye.

We laugh before I see my foreman out of the house, being sure to close the door firmly behind him.

And… it's quiet again.

I make my way down the corridor, being sure to snap on that one murky overhead light, and I secretly threaten it with the fact that its days of snoozing on the job will soon be over as I make a beeline for my phone, which is charging on the kitchen counter.

I'm relieved to see the WhatsApp icon, as that'll most likely be Ellie telling me she's on her way back – which is great because I'm starving and am considering what to make us as her message is displayed on screen.

FROM ELLIE: Hey you. Glad things have started. We made good progress today, but there's still a lot more to do so it makes sense for me to stay in London tonight anyway. All being well, I should be back home tomorrow night. Love you. xx

And just like that, a good productive day turns to shit.

28. THE VISIT

PORTHCOVE. 22:03.

Water. Waves. Bitter coldness.

I can hear you calling to me from there. In the light, but I can't reach you. I can't. I'm trying… I keep trying…. But I can't.

I'm sinking! I'm sinking! Deeper and deeper. I ca…n't breathe… I c-c-can't breathe. I'm drowning! I'm dying! Heee..lp… meee…. he… lp me….

"Daddy!"

"To… Toby."

"Come find me."

"I c-ca… can't… it's so cold."

"Daddy… follow the colours."

"What? Toby?"

"Wake up, Daddy."

"Toby!"

"It's time to wake up."

I wake to find Buddy standing on my thighs, licking my face.

I groan at the slobbery wetness on my cheek. "OK. Thank you. Thank you. I'm awake."

I sit up and rub a sleeve across my face, and ow, my right arm is killing me. Jesus. Must have used up all of my so-called elbow grease in the study. I stretch and bend it in the hope that it will relieve the ache, but movement just makes it worse. I'm obviously not used to so much manual labour.

Yes, the one good thing about being all alone. There's nobody to agree with you or make a sarcastic quip.

"And you're not going to, are you?" I look at the hound that's now sitting on the couch and observing me like a concerned parent. I emit another groan as I rub my arm. "I'm alright, Buddy. Just need to take some pills. Daddy loves doing that."

Daddy?

Dude. Chill. Technically, you are his dad. Step dad at least.

"And hey, you're pretty nimble for a puppy, aren't you?"

He doesn't respond, obviously, and whatever he interpreted as some kind of crisis must be over because he yawns in my face and then settles down on the couch beside me.

"Yeah. Thanks for waking me. I didn't realise we were on shifts."

I sigh and run a hand through my hair. Oh God. Dreamscape one hundred and whatever on the list of crappy dreams. I was drowning this time. Last time I was trying to swim my way across the ocean towards some technicolour horizon.

It's always some bloody nightmare. Whatever happened to good old-fashioned wet dreams? Is that something that's just exclusively reserved for teenagers now or what? I can't remember the last time I had one of those, and I feel like I've been missing out. Literally.

The rain is back, tapping at the balcony doors again. Lightly this time, as if I've ignored its previous pleas for shelter and has resigned itself to its fate. Although, it can't be much colder out there than it is in here.

I hate those storage heaters. It's as if when those things were manufactured, they built the part that takes power, but forgot to add the element that exchanges it for heat.

I don't know what Irvin's on, but those things are not working. Yes, they did seem warm when I checked them, but they're obviously not working again now.

I'm looking at Buddy, who already has his eyes closed, when a shiver runs through me. I should go upstairs, get a sweater, maybe even stream something on the laptop in bed.

There's way too much silence around here.

Did I mention that there's no television in this place? Yes, I had a bit of a meltdown when I first discovered it. Not because I'm television-obsessed – far from it. It's just that, last time I was here, there wasn't any internet or anything else. I was completely cut off from the rest of the world, to the point of insanity.

No pun intended.

This time, the internet works, but it's sketchy. Phone signal works, but it's not the best, and–

What the hell was that?

Something just tickled the nape of my bloody neck!

I instantly flick it away, suspecting that it might be a spider.

It isn't. But now I'm feeling unsettled because I definitely felt something, and if it wasn't an insect, then it was something else. Something creepy enough to make my skin feel dry and prickly, and those sensitive hairs at the back of my neck have been alarmed by something again.

Instinctively, I keep rubbing the spot as I'm reminded of a story from boarding school.

That place was pretty much located in the middle of a forest. Me and a bunch of mates were out picnicking one day, amongst other things. And Gary, my roommate, was sitting on the grass opposite me. He was still wearing his uniform, which meant he was wearing a shirt and tie. And, I remember, we were in the middle of a conversation when, suddenly, out of nowhere, this massive spider scuttled out from one side of his shirt collar and into the other.

I instantly lost it and started yelling, "*There's a spider on you! There's a spider on you!*"

He went straight into hysteria: "*Where? Where?!*"

"*On your collar! Your collar!*"

And he's jumping around, demanding, "*Where?! Where?!*"

That went on for what felt like minutes until he finally decided to act. He ripped off all of his clothes, and I mean all of them, but there was no bloody sign of that spider.

The other lads were pissing themselves, laughing. Me, all I could think about was the fact that he should have taken action sooner. That spider could have gone anywhere by the time he stripped off.

So, anyway, since then? My philosophy has been *Flick first, ask questions later.* When Ellie and I met, she instantly adopted the practice since, like me, she hates spiders. And then, we both very kindly passed that same irrational fear onto our son.

In this case, I don't see anything on the floor. But it definitely felt like something just crawled across the back of my neck. If it wasn't an insect, then it was something else.

Something else? Like what?

"What the…..?"

Again! It just happened again!

Something just touched my hair, and the sensation propels me out of my seat and spins me around, clutching at the back of my head like I've just been stung.

"What the fu…" the words dissolve in my mouth as I survey the den and the rest of the room.

Empty.

A shiver slithers down my back, and I try to shrug it away by rolling my shoulders and walking back and forth, eyes flicking everywhere. There's nothing here, though. The place is empty, but for that creepy lingering sensation.

Cold, craggy fingers touching my face.

Oh God. That night I was roused from sleep. I thought it was Ellie. That thing under the bed!

The memory of that dials up the squirm, and when something other than the rain starts tapping on the patio doors, I'm not ashamed to say that it elicits a yelp from me which is so loud that even the hound opens one eye.

A reluctant inspection of the glass beyond the shutters reveals that the tap isn't coming from a demon, but one of those giant moths obviously seeking shelter from the downpour.

Sorry, buddy. No room at the inn.

Then, that dreaded sound. The staple of any creepy movie special effect rundown; the agonizingly slow creak of the photography room door as it suddenly clicks open as if aided by invisible hands.

Are you having a bloody laugh?

It's OK, though. It's OK. It would be easy to jump to conclusions here, but I'm better than that. I've noticed that, when there's a door or a window open in this place, anywhere in the house, it creates a draft that makes that door move like that.

Admittedly, I've no idea why anyone would open windows anywhere in the house. I don't think any of the workmen ventured up there today, unless Irvin–

The lights flicker, just as they did the other night.

"No," I mutter under my breath. There's nothing supernatural about this. And it's just as Irvin said... there's an exposed wire somewhere, it's raining, and that's creating this effect.

"I love you, Daddy."

"You do?"

"NO!"

My stomach drops and I gawk at the gaping black entrance to the photography room, where I can just about make out the flicker of the video on the newly polished door.

"But not more than Mummy. I love you both exactly the same."

"I love you, too, little man. Merry Christmas."

"NO! This isn't possible. It isn't possible."|

And yet, I find myself inexplicably drawn to my son's voice because my mind is already playing the moving images like a projector in my head. Toby in his superhero pyjamas opening his Christmas present and Ellie looking at me with that love in her eyes.

Our life as it used to be.

No. NO!

And yet, I'm moving, slowly, reluctantly, gingerly... until I reach the door where, with one hand clutched to the ache in my chest, I peer inside.

The room is steeped in darkness. The video is playing on the laptop screen and casting giant shadows over the walls.

I close my eyes, for I can feel the anguish rising like bile up my throat.

Toby.

"No," I'm chanting, "No," as each frame is like a knife to

the heart, pushing tears to my eyes. "Toby!" I call out as if my son can hear me, as if the sound of my voice can breathe back life and return him to me once more.

"Toby…." But the images have switched once more. From Christmas morning to the overhead shots at the beach that day.

That hideous day.

I've entered the room now. Shuffling closer and closer to the laptop on the desk, just as that moth did to the light.

The room is alive, shifting and morphing in an orgy of blue hues and flickering shadows as the pressure in my head builds, but I daren't breathe, I daren't draw air until I know. Until I know for sure.

When I'm finally close enough to see, my legs turn to jelly and threaten to collapse beneath me, for it is clear now that I have strayed beyond the demarcation line into insanity; there is no SD card in the machine, and yet I can still see the overhead view of my son and I walking down to the beach, each of us looking up at the camera and waving.

"Toby," I whimper as tears bubble and spill from my eyes. "Toby."

That's when the computer screen goes black, and in it, as plain as day, I see! The distorted reflection of my son standing in the doorway, backlit by the light from the den.

I spin around only to find the doorway empty.

"Oh God!" I cry, throwing a hand to my mouth and biting on it. This is it. I've definitely relapsed because I just saw my *dead* son's reflection in the *dead* computer screen. It was unmistakable. He was standing right there! Right there by the bloody door! I swear to you! I swear he was standing right there! Right behind me!

And yet, there's nothing in the doorway now but light.

I stagger back against the desk as my mind scrambles to rationalise this, to try and make sense of it, but I can't! I just can't.

Then I hear it. The word is so clear, so unmistakable, that it has me whirling around so fast that I lose my balance and crash onto my backside.

And there, standing by the window, backlit by the light

spilling out through the patio doors, is the incontrovertible proof that I've been seeking. The silhouette is short, the profile unmistakable.

The vision is so powerful that it sends a current of emotion surging through me so powerfully that it freezes the breath in my mouth.

I scramble into a sitting position, eager to refocus through the blur of tears streaming down my cheeks, and that's when he speaks again. That one word that is as familiar to me as it has been absent. The one word that I've been aching to hear him speak for so long.

"Daddy."

29. DINOSAUR

TUESDAY. PORTHCOVE. 08:03.

The Oxford Dictionary meaning of "insane" is being *in a state of mind which prevents normal perception, behaviour, or social interaction.*

This morning, while in the shower and being scalded in one second, to the point of howling, and frozen like a human popsicle in the next, I concluded that I meet that definition.

Last night in the photography room, I saw something which strayed beyond realms of *normal perception* and well into fruit-loop territory.

That or, well, you know the alternative, and I don't know which is worse.

The scary thing is that, deep down, right underneath the years of evolution and exposure to social comportments, mythologies, urban legends, and perceptions of how an assumed rational person should behave in a situation like this, I am attracted to it. I'm curiously compelled to view, torment, and expose myself to it just as an arachnophobe might be drawn in to a documentary about spiders because, for that moment, that one split second, I was excited by the prospect of seeing my son. Of being able to talk to him again.

Yes, I was both terrified and overjoyed by that apparition or whatever the hell it was.

I don't really know because it ended almost as suddenly as it began, but now I know that I'm secretly anticipating the dark of tonight so that I can see if it happens again.

Fuck! See? I *am* insane! This is madness talking. Secretly looking forward to the dark of tonight? Who the fuck even talks like that, but a madman?

This is exactly what I was afraid of when Ellie said she was staying in London. I didn't want to say anything to her because, well, I don't want her to feel responsible for me anymore and nor do I want her to worry about me. She shouldn't have to feel that way. She's my wife, not my fucking caregiver!

And yet, the thing I feared the most has happened.

That's why, right now, I'm leaning on the kitchen counter with my chin resting on my hands and watching how the plastic orange container moves around the surface as I open and close my left eye and then my right eye. Left, right. Left, right.

This optical illusion was one of Toby's favourites. As you know, he was a bit of a dinosaur geek like his dad, and I'd often find him bringing model dinosaurs to life in this way.

He had a whole collection of the things from across the Jurassic and Cretaceous periods. And he knew how to pronounce each and every one of their names. To me, it did then as it does now seem like some palaeontologist threw random letters together to those creatures.

So, take the meds or no?

They're obviously not working, because if they were, then I shouldn't have seen what I saw, unless….

Unless it was real. But that in itself is enough to make anyone lose their mind. And remember, I do have a bit of a track record here that, as much as I don't want to, I nonetheless feel should be brought into consideration. I mean, Jesus Christ, I fabricated an entire world and lived in it for months.

It doesn't get any more insane than that, does it?

But these pills are supposed to supress that.

Supposed to.

Or the ghost of my dead son visited me last night. If it were you, which of the two would you think most likely? Insanity or apparition?

I rise from my seat, pluck a glass from the cupboard, and fill it with water. Then, I snatch the plastic container from the counter and have just popped it open when I hear a sound that I thought I had consigned to the pits of hell where it belongs; someone hammering *a la Gestapo* on the bloody irritating, nerve-jangling, I-want-to-punch-someone front door.

And by now you'll be somewhat familiar with my dislike for repetitive, irritating sounds. So, you can imagine the mood I'm in when the pounding happens no less than three more times before I reach the front door. And yet, when I yank the door open, there's nothing out there but bird chorus, drizzling rain, and a chill blowing a plastic wrapper across the lawn.

I look back inside as if someone could have snuck by me. The place is empty.

So, I test-press the doorbell button. It sounds obediently.

I step outside, survey the garden, and even check the roof. Is somebody playing a prank on me? Is Ellie home early for whatever reason and in a game-playing mood? It isn't unheard of. Contrary to current dynamics, my wife and I used to have a lot of fun together. Although, this isn't quite her style.

What about David? Maybe he came back with her. And hid the car in the bushes?

Seriously? OK. Maybe not.

I turn and take in the house. It stares back at me, windows dark and impenetrable like eyes watching me but disguising their intention behind mirrored glasses.

"What the fuck is going on?" My voice is loud, bouncing off the building to be swallowed up by the trees.

Nobody responds but my wardens, the crows, from their perches on an overhead cable. What is that thing anyway? Power? Telephone? I hadn't truly noticed it before. One cable, like a thin umbilical cord linking Dolce Vita to the rest of the world. I can't decide if I like or hate it, but then again, who cares? We'll be out of this place soon and I can't bloody wait.

The familiar scrunch of tyres on gravel grabs my attention. I turn to see Irvin's truck slowly making its way down the drive, and I'm relieved that I'm no longer alone.

Shit. This is how desperate I've become! Looking forward to bloody workers coming to the house for company. Now, that's something I should be terrified of because that… that is truly sad.

I can only imagine what David would have to say about it. Some quip, no doubt, about how the so-called *mighty* have fallen.

"Mornin'. Everything OK?" Irvin asks as he leaves the vehicle and makes his way towards me.

"Yeah. All good. All great," I say. "Why?"

He shrugs. "No reason. You just look…" he struggles to find the words. "You look like you've seen a ghost."

Ignoring the literal implication of that sentence, I smile and say, "Nah. Just surveying the project out here. You know, all the great work you did yesterday."

"Yeah. It's already lookin' much better with all that stuff cut back."

I nod. "Yeah, it is." And he's right. It does.

"Morning, mate." It's Andrew, or Drew as he likes to be known.

"You know, I could murder a–"

"Brew?" I anticipate.

"Yeah, you read my mind. And you know what would be even better."

"A bacon sarny?" I ask sarcastically.

"Hey, you're really good at this."

Dean chuckles. Irvin rolls his eyes. "Take no notice of 'im. He's a cheeky bugger."

"No, that's fine," I say with a grin.

And I mean it. Really. I do. That's the thing. The old me would have told him to foxtrot Oscar, but the new, vulnerable me, the one who – and yeah, I'm not afraid to admit it – is grateful for the company is thankful for the banter. The normality of it.

"So, is that tea and bacon sarnies all around, then?" I ask cheerily as I rub my hands together.

The trio look at me suspiciously before nodding.

Yeah, I know, lads, in any other world, it'd be a different story, but today is your lucky day.

While the boys unload the truck, Irvin joins me as I make my way back into the house. "So, Marco, I wanted to say, I need to pop out to another job later this mornin' but was thinkin' of gettin' the lads to make a start on the lounge. You know, fixin' shutters, sandin' 'em, and preppin' walls for the paint job if that works for ya."

I think about this for a second. "Yeah. Didn't we agree you were going to make a start on the corridor first?"

"Yeah. It's just, I'd rather be 'ere for that."

I nod. "Oh, OK. Sure. That's fine, but I don't have dustsheets or anything for the lounge. I assume you'll have those."

"Yeah, don't worry. We got all that on the truck."

"Oh, excellent."

"As I say, I won't be 'ere for a few hours, but the lads know what they're doin'. They've done it nuff times."

"OK, sure. Sounds good. Oh, Irvin, and when you do get back, could you please take a look at the hot water again? The shower this morning was Caribbean ocean one minute and Nordic ice bath the next."

"Yeah, no worries. I did take a look yesterday and everything seemed to be working fine. I wonder if it's something to do with your shower?"

"I don't know, but could you take a look for me either way?"

"No worries, mate."

I glance down the gloomy corridor and sigh. "And yeah, this thing has got to be next. Something about it. I hate it."

"Yeah. As I say, we'll be on it tomorra for ya."

"That's tomorrow, right, and not *dreckly*?" I ask with a smile.

Dreckly in the southwest is the equivalent of the Spanish's *mañana*.

Irvin chuckles. "No mate, *mañana*," he says with a wink.

I leave my foreman in the lounge and make my way into the darkness with a certain smugness, knowing the black hole of Dolce Vita's days are numbered.

But the smile on my face evaporates the second I step into the kitchen, where my breath freezes into a snowball that tumbles into the pit of my gut and I stagger backward, leaning onto the doorframe for support.

Bright glorious daylight is bathing the room in a misty sheen that bounces off surfaces and gleams off chrome appliances and finishes, which only makes what I'm seeing that much more incredible.

I know it wasn't me. You do, too. You were with me. And I know it wasn't the lads because two of them are still outside. I know this because I can hear them laughing, which only makes this even more sinister.

So, who the hell came in here and opened each of the cupboard doors, and every drawer, and why? Why would anybody do this?

"Oh, Marco—"

"Jeeeeesus Christ!" My bark mutes Irvin, who's appeared in the doorway behind me like a fucking ghost.

"Sorry, mate. Didn't mean to startle ya. Oh, you making a start in 'ere already?" he asks, looking at the spectacle before us.

I'm unable to respond because the tide has gone out in my mouth and I think my lips are dried shut – because, out of the weirdness, something else has caught my eye, and it's something that has me screwing my face up with incomprehension as I attempt to decipher exactly what I am seeing.

"You… you can… um… you can see this… right?" I stutter.

Irvin chuckles as he takes in the room. "Yeah, and it looks like you've got your hands full, mate. Where did all the sand come from, then? Was that in the cupboard?" he adds, looking at me, but there he pauses. "Marco, mate, are you alright?" he asks, shooting hands out as if to steady me. "You've gone as white as a sheet."

But I brush him aside because I need to see. I need to make sure that I am not imagining it. I need to make sure that what I am seeing on the counter is real.

"Can you see it?" I croak, my voice barely rising above a whisper.

"See what, mate? I really think you need to take a seat before you fall—"

I interrupt him by lifting and pointing with a shaky finger. "Can you see that, over there on the counter?" I repeat.

Finally, he turns, following the direction of my arm. "What, the glass of water?"

"N… no. What's inside it."

"Yeah, I, um… what is that?" he asks, stepping over for a closer a look.

But I don't need to look any closer. I know exactly what that green thing is sitting in my glass of water like a specimen inside a jar.

It's a toy dinosaur.

30. DR. ETHAN HOLMES

WEDNESDAY. LONDON. 10:25.

You know how, sometimes in life, there are certain things that you really don't want to do? Like visiting an awkward relative, getting a prostate exam, gynaecologist, or dentist? Basically, all that awkward, painful, embarrassing shit that most average folk would rather not do. Well, if you roll all those feelings into one and then double it, you may get somewhere close to how I'm feeling right now.

Being sat in this chair as it inexorably transports me closer to my meeting with Doctor Ethan Holmes is like being strapped to a rollercoaster ride as it makes its way to the summit and realising that you don't have a safety harness.

Bottom line, I'm starting to think this was a mistake.

I don't feel comfortable telling anybody about what's been happening at the house. I don't want them to think I am having a relapse. Hell, *I* don't want to think I'm having a relapse! It's the very reason why I'm afraid of knocking on this man's door. I know what he's capable of. Those bloody blue eyes of his behind those square glasses are like the lenses of a human microscope. For a whipper snapper, the man is as astute as they come.

I'm just going to have to watch everything I say. Make sure he doesn't see right through me. I'll just get the answers I need and get out of there.

Yes, I'm very much aware of the fact that this attitude defeats the purpose, and yes, I have considered the idea of just telling him everything, but the operative word here is *considered*... which happened before I immediately dismissed the idea. I'm *not* going back into therapy. No fucking way.

Mercifully, it seems that things have changed since I last saw the doctor. He no longer practices from his office at the institute, which is good because I really hated his tiny, box-room antechamber with diplomas on the wall and that view of the park encased in metal railings. It was like being incarcerated. Although, technically, depending on your state of mind, you were.

Of course, he hated me saying that, but that's how it bloody felt.

Anyway, now he operates out of his town house in leafy southwest London. Apparently, I've been there before – right when we first met, although I don't remember it.

I've left the train now, and I'm in a cab and being driven down an avenue of season-stripped trees, past Victorian replica lampposts and evergreen hedges twice as tall as me. And I bet you can't guess what has suddenly and somewhat painfully been brought to my attention.

Christmas.

Christmas!

I cannot believe that I have been exposed to subliminal messages for weeks now. Supermarket shelves bursting with Christmas merchandise, hand-scrawled signs planted outside of farms advertising Christmas trees, cheesy commercials on the radio station that the builders insist on cranking up whilst working, and now this; a wonderland of LEDs shaped as gift boxes, angels, and umbrellas hovering over the street.

Umbrellas? Am I missing something?

A lot, I suppose.

Everybody knows that Christmas messages aren't in any way subliminal. They're brash, garish, chintzy, and increasingly premature.

And we used to love them.

But this year? This year, Ellie and I must have unconsciously chosen to block those things out because she hasn't mentioned it, either. I mean, we've talked about being out by Christmas and everything, but it's always just been a date like any other, until now.

Shit.

It's a dreary grey morning in London, but I bet this stuff looks awesome at night.

There'll be no reason for us to battle the hordes on public transport this year to witness Hyde Park's transformation into its own winter wonderland.

Oh God. I feel sick, and the driver driving like he's attending the scene of a crime isn't bloody helping.

We're passing jet-black metal railings now propped up by garden trees wrapped in ugly, translucent arteries of lifeless Christmas lights, as well as life-sized wire reindeers and Santas.

Mercifully, the taxi rolls to a stop outside a fuck-off, big brick house enclosed in more metal railings... shit. What is it with this guy and railings?

My stomach has just turned, as tends to happen for most people faced with impending doom. In my case, it used to be because I'd just been caught doing something I shouldn't, both as a child and as an adult.

I pay the driver, who cheerfully bids me a premature 'Merry Christmas', and I just want to punch him.

I walk up to the gate sporting angry, golden spikes and the shiny plaque mounted on a nearby pillar that reads *Please Ring for Attention.*

But I don't want to.

This is definitely a mistake.

I can feel the beads of sweat forming in my hair already, and the knot of snakes in my belly is coiling tighter and tighter. I turn to watch the bulbous backside of my black cab trundle off down the street, and I want to run after him, but I'm blocked by a delivery truck that pulls up alongside me in a cloud of acrid carbon monoxide.

A young bloke, probably still in his early twenties, wearing a wrinkled uniform and a sweat-stained cap, jumps out of the cabin with one leap, reminding me that I should go running more. He nods at me before hurrying to the back of the truck as if he's carrying organs for transplantation and not inanimate packages before coming back.

"Alright, mate?" he asks, waving a box at me.

"I don't live here," I say quickly.

"No, you can do me a solid and sign for it, though. Right?"

"But I don't live here. Why would you hand that to me?"

"You're about to go in there, though, ain't ya?"

"Yes, but it doesn't mean you should hand that to me. I could be anyone. I *am* anyone."

He screws his face up. "Mate, are you going in there or what?"

Good fucking question. I turn and look at the gate. My heart is already knocking for attention, and this ignorant little prick…

Subconsciously, reluctantly, as I hold my breath to avoid sucking in more of the toxic fumes being belched by the truck, I take the packet. If only to get rid of the cheeky shit. He produces a device from his pocket and shoves the screen at me. "If you could just put your monica there, mate. Cheers."

I squiggle the Etch-A-Sketch version of my signature on the screen before he snatches it away with a meaningless, "Merry Christmas!" He doesn't wait for a response, but instead hops back into his truck, guns the engine, and then leaves me in a cloud of one of the reasons why I think it's a shitty idea to move back to the city.

And so, me and the newly acquired packet that is staring up from my hand like a lonely orphan turn to the gate once more.

This is simple, Battista. Do you want answers?

Yes.

Do you secretly want this man to help you with everything that's been happening at the house?

I don't want his help with anything.

Yeah, OK. Spin it whichever way you want, but are you going to make a decision, or would you prefer to stand here having a conversation with yourself?

Shit.

I ring the bell and wait.

Seconds later: "Hello. How can I help?" It's a tinny female voice, and that surprises me.

"Um, hello. I'm Marco Battista. Here to see Dr Holmes. And, um, I have a parcel for him."

"Please come in."

There's a loud buzz, and the gate clicks open.

With a deep sigh, I walk through and am presented with the secret garden beyond it as the gate clicks shut behind me. I'm standing on a cobblestone path that slices through a manicured lawn and shrubs before an intersection and a sign that points one way for *The House* and the other for *The Couch*.

Very droll.

The awkward side of me wants to take the path to the house, especially because I'm not here for the couch, but something tells me that the couch is where I'll find my so-called host, and I'm eager to get this over and done with so that I can get out of here and back to the country.

The path leads me around the side of the house to another small gate, and eventually to a set of timber patio doors.

And so, just as I'm considering what kind of quip to use to open this reunion, both doors spring open. "Marco! Good morning." It's Doctor Holmes and he's smiling. "It's good to see you."

"Ethan, this is for you," I say, handing him the box. He looks at it and then back at me. "I signed for it on the way in – the delivery man's idea."

He nods. "Please, come in," he says, stepping back and ushering me inside.

Here we go.

31. THE TRUTH

WEDNESDAY. LONDON. 10:35.

"So, tell me, how have you been?" Doctor Holmes asks, stepping aside and ushering me through the doorway.

Wow. Nothing's changed. Straight in there. Of course, the man whom I once credited with *saving my life* is probably just being friendly, but, not surprisingly, he already has me on the defensive.

"Good. Great actually," is my overenthusiastic response. I could kick myself, and I want to take the words back. I want to rewind this moment and do it over again. I want him to see that I am unaffected. In fact, this may well be a good time to make some kind of quip about his new torture chamber, but I can't because I'm still coming to terms with the fact that it bears a remarkable resemblance to another place I once knew.

The rectangular space with the whitewashed wall and bookshelf on one side. The window wall to a garden on the other. The wood-carved black bench with a flatscreen computer at the opposite end of the room.

Now, I know where I got the inspiration from.

If you were with me during my previous journey into madness, and away from madness – depending on which way you look at it – you'll know what the hell I'm talking about.

"Please, take a seat," Holmes says, gesturing to a cream couch in the middle of the room while he takes a seat in a black leather swivel chair opposite.

I smile and make myself comfortable on the couch, instantly manspreading in order to project the fact that I am totally at ease and that there's absolutely nothing weird going on in my head right now… because there isn't. This is all just a massive coincidence.

"Are you sure you're OK? I mean, you look like–"

"It's all good, Doc," I say with a grin, and then I look out the glass wall at the view of the secret garden outside. "Wow. Nice digs, Ethan. You've even managed to recreate your own slice of paradise in the middle of London," I say, marvelling at the lawn, the clump of trees, and the cobblestone pathway to what I think is a miniature pond.

"Yes. I love it. And it is a talking piece, for sure," he says. "undoubtedly much nicer in the spring and summer, though."

"Business must be even better than when I last saw you."

"Well, it's been pretty much the same," he says thoughtfully, dazzling me with a set of perfectly white teeth.

He doesn't look any different. I mean, his hair's maybe a bit longer than it was last time, but he still looks way too young to be sitting in that chair and commanding such presumed wisdom. And he's still rocking that whole young Ryan O-Neal thing. Young. Preppy. Emphasised by neat, square, no-doubt designer spectacles framing those blue eyes of his. No chinos today, though, but jeans. And no sweater – just a black shirt.

He's looking particularly casual.

"Are you not seeing any patients today?" I hear myself asking.

"Not until later this afternoon. I have some errands to run this morning."

"Well, thanks for fitting me in."

"Oh, it's no problem," he says. "To be honest, Marco, I was surprised to hear from you. Pleasantly, of course," he adds with a steadying wave of the hand, "as you haven't returned any of my calls or texts."

And there it is. That first jibe.

"I know. Sorry about that. But we just needed some time to settle in, and things have been busy at the house. As you know, we're trying to sell it, so, we have the builders in."

He nods, but I know he doesn't buy it. "And how's that going?"

"Good. At the rate we're going, we may have everything done this week, and then we can start showing people around."

"Really? That's fantastic progress."

"Yeah, we're really excited."

"And how's Ellie doing?"

"Ellie? Yeah, she's good. She's great," I say, nodding like a complete idiot. He no doubt saw right through that, too. So, as if I haven't made enough of a tit of myself, I stir the shit pot some more by saying, "Yeah, she's really great. She's back at work. David's offered her a more senior position."

"He has? Wow. That was sudden and fast."

"You don't approve?"

I can see him thinking about that. "It's just a surprise, that's all," he says, and then adds, "she must be excited."

"Yeah. Well, she is."

"And you're not?"

You know, to my own detriment, I've forgotten just how astute this guy is.

"Oh, I am, of course I am," I lie. Then I change the subject. "Oh, and we've got a dog now – well, a puppy. I rescued him from a fox. He's really cute. His name's Buddy. Ellie hates him, though."

"She does? Why?"

"No idea. But I love him. It's good to have something else to care about for a change, you know." Shit. that just brought a lump to my throat and I don't know why… well, I do, but I hate the idea of acknowledging the comparison, so I change the subject yet again. And it's starting to feel like I'm in a maze where I keep shutting doors to create dead-ends in this conversation.

"What about you? How's married life?" I ask quickly, eager to deflect any more questions because I feel like a complete tool trying to lie to this guy – because there's no doubt that he knows that I know that he knows the truth behind everything I'm saying, and I have no doubt that he also has an opinion about Ellie going back to work so soon, but I don't want to get into that, either.

Wow. Calm down. Breathe.

"It's good," he says, nodding. "No talk of divorce just yet. So, you're safe."

I miss the reference at first, but then I realise that the doctor is making a joke.

Last time we were at the institute, he teased that if things didn't work out with his husband, he was going to start dating David. I told him, rather plainly, that I would rather stick pins in my testicles. I'm paraphrasing, of course.

He's watching me now. No doubt wondering when I'm going to wipe away the gormless grin I still have on my face and stop trying to artificially ventilate this small talk and get to the real reason why I've called out of the blue and asked to see him, especially since I made clear that this visit was just for a chat and not as a patient.

"So, how have things been going with counselling?" he asks.

But I know it's a trick question. There's no doubt in my mind that he's already heard that we didn't go. So, now I'm wondering whether or not it's even worth lying.

"Come on, Ethan. We both know you know that we didn't go."

He says nothing. He just watches from behind those spectacles of his. Nope. I haven't missed that. "We just felt that there was no point, as there was a good chance of us not getting anything out of it apart from feeling shittier than we already were," I add. Then swallow and turn my so-called frown upside down. "Anyway, I decided–"

"*You* decided?"

"*We* decided that it wasn't worth going."

"So, without even going to one session, you *both* decided that it was going to make you feel worse?"

I stifle a sigh because I have no interest in getting into it with this guy again. "I just didn't feel ready to go straight back into therapy after leaving the clinic," I say sharply.

He nods. Then adds, holding up his hands, "I'm sorry. "Did I stray beyond the parameters of your telephone brief?"

I pull a face.

"Well, when you called me and said you wanted to meet, you also made clear that the meeting had nothing to do with therapy. That you were categorically and in no way interested in returning to therapy."

"Yeah. So?"

"Well, my asking about couples counselling with Ellie appears to have irritated you."

"I'm not irritated."

"No?"

"No."

He nods, and I want to slap his face. Christ, I haven't been here two minutes and he's already pissing me off.

There's a long pause.

I turn to the glass wall. Birds chirp over a distant baritone rumble that reminds me I'm back in the capital. A while ago, the very idea of that would have filled me with immense pleasure, but now... now, I just can't wait to leave, but I'm not sure if that's a reflection of the city or my being in the same room as this man.

Seconds tick by.

Shit. And now things feel awkward. Who's going to restart the conversation? Not me. I can't think of anything to say beyond the real reason why I'm here, and now I'm thinking that I should have turned around at the gate.

"I'm sorry, Marco, but you're going to have to tell me what exactly you'd like me to say."

I look at him, and I have absolutely no idea where the words come from, but they fall out of my mouth with a good dose of simmering vitriol. "Well, you could start by telling me why you lied to me."

He shifts in his seat as if he was expecting the comment, and says, "I didn't lie to you, Marco."

"Yes, you did. You and Ellie both. You both flat-out lied to my face. Made me think I was losing my mind, but for entirely different reasons. Do you have any idea what it feels like to be constantly learning things about yourself from other fucking people?" I grumble, jaw muscles flexing.

OK. It would appear that I'm much more pissed off over the one thing I thought I'd compartmentalised.

Obviously not.

"Marco, we've been over this, but if you'd like to cover it again, then I'm more than happy to—"

"Yes, Ethan, I would. Yes, I fucking would like to go over it again because I still can't wrap my head around why you would both pretend that I hadn't put in the graft, that I hadn't struggled with juggling a full-time job, classes, and studying for the best part of four years at the expense of time with my family. With my son," I say. The last words were faltering, as I've started wrestling with the knot of emotion that's just formed in my throat. Then, I watch him. Waiting. Teeth grinding. Heart thumping. Pulling on the leash of the rage beast that's stirring in my chest.

The doctor sits forward in his chair, as I know he's prone to do when he's about to make a point. "I, *we* did not lie to you, Marco. You *are* a mechanic, and yes, you have been studying to become a psychotherapist. The—"

"Then, why did you lie?" I interrupt him.

"I'm trying to explain that," he says calmly, and that in itself is pissing me off.

"During therapy," he continues, "you were struggling with two major aspects of your professional life. The mechanic who represented your real life with Ellie and Toby. And the therapist who represented the fictious life you fabricated to overcome your grief. During treatment, you were straddling both lives, and we, *I* had to make a judgement. And I did."

"Yeah. You made a judgement to make me think I was mental."

"No. I made a judgement to help you refocus on your real life with your family."

"You know, wilfully deceiving a patient? I don't think we're going to find that anywhere in the Good Medical Practice guide. Do you? I've got a good mind to report you to the GMC."

"That's your prerogative," he says, holding up his hands.

"You really don't give a shit, do you?"

"About this kind of detail? No. You were having a breakthrough, I saw an opportunity and I made a judgement. I won't apologise for that, Marco. I told you this during our phone call, in which I asked you to come back for a follow-up, but you refused to."

"Too right. And you're lucky I did," I say, juddering my knee. Something I notice I haven't done in a while. I wonder why.

"Your care. Your wellness was and always will be my top priority. It's why I tried reach you on several occasions."

"Funny you should say that when you're the one who kicked me out of therapy."

He takes a few seconds by sitting back in his chair, and if I didn't know better, I'd say I was starting to get to him, but I doubt I am.

"Again, we talked about this," he resumes. "I didn't kick you out. You'd successfully completed that stage of your treatment. It was important that you then take a while to come to terms with that. Spend time with your wife; process and evaluate everything that we accomplished in your own time. Which you did, and is hence why you're here today, threatening me."

"You're a dick," I hurl at him, childishly.

"Well, you know I'm always happy to hear your thoughts." He follows that up with that trademark wry smile of his, which I would normally find both amusing and infuriating, but not today. Today, it's just infuriating. And I stew on this for a couple of minutes. Listening to that familiar hum of the city as I used to during our sessions.

He did change my life. I owe him a lot.

No, no, absolutely not. I'm not thinking about that right now. He lied! He lied to me. *He* was the one who contributed to that whole mind fuck.

Although, one could argue that I had already lost it, and he brought me back.

That's not the point.

"What do I do with this?" *Shit. I just said that out loud.*

He looks at me, and I want to quickly tell him that the

question wasn't really aimed at him, that I was just thinking out loud. It was just a rhetorical question.

"What do you want to do?"

"Well, nothing right now. I'm barely keeping myself together. And now, with the house and everything, I don't have the time nor the capacity for any of this."

"Then you have your answer."

"Wow. Well, that was truly insightful, Ethan. Thanks."

He holds up his hands. "Well, you made clear that you don't want to return to therapy. You don't want to talk about your being a psychotherapist. You've brushed over how Ellie is coping and covered up who exactly decided that they didn't want to attend couple's therapy. It's clear to me that there are many aspects of this new life you're forging that you've designated as off-limits to me." He sits forward again. "I need you to tell me how exactly you would like me to help you, Marco. What role have I been assigned?"

He's staring at me now. And if I didn't know better, I'd say, judging by the inflection on that last word, that he's irritated.

I think about this.

"Do you know what? You're right. I'm sorry. I shouldn't have come," I say, rising from the couch – which, may I add, is much easier than that previous torture wrack of a chair I used to have to sit in.

"Marco. Talk to me. What's going on? What are you afraid of?"

Don't! Don't do it! Don't say it!

I scowl down at him. "What am I afraid of? I'm not afraid of anything. What I am not in the mood for is your probing, analytical, annoying, judgemental, condescending shit, which I can tell you I have not missed one tiny, smidgeon of an iota, by the way."

"Is that truly how you feel?"

"No. I'm just speaking words for the fun of it, Ethan."

Silence rules as I observe my former therapist, who is only a few years younger than me but feels like so many older. And, if I didn't know better, I'd say that I've somehow hurt his feelings... because there's a peculiar lifelessness behind those spectacles today, and it's one I don't think I've ever seen before. Sadness. Have I upset him? Is that even possible?

I give it a few more seconds, then sigh and say, "Look, Ethan, I'm sorry. This isn't exactly how I saw this meeting going."

"No? How did you see it?"

I think about this, and with a shrug I say, "I don't really know. I was just…" I leave the sentence unfinished because I can't quite find the words. And it's not as if I'm holding back. Far from it. I really don't know what I was expecting. Was I expecting us to man-hug and shoot that proverbial shit – to use one of today's most ridiculous vernaculars? I really don't know.

One thing has become clear to me. Now, I understand why therapists are required to submit to analysis as part of their qualification. It's only by submitting to therapy that you can truly have an idea of what it's like for your patients.

Right now, I'm reminded of just how easy it is to form a connection with the one person who often knows more about you than your own self. It's a unique sense of intimacy that you may not even have with your own family or partner. An overwhelming sense of security that makes you feel like you can share absolutely anything with them, without judgement or recrimination–

"Marco?"

And yet. "I don't know why I came here, Ethan."

He smiles in that disarming way of his. "Yes, you do," he says, rising to meet me. "And if you do ever want to talk, you know where I am."

I return my former therapist's smile and say, "I wouldn't hold your breath."

He shrugs.

"It was nice seeing you," I say, proffering a hand.

"You, too."

And so, after that, you would think I'd be relieved to leave the place.

I'm not.

32. THE LIFT

What a waste… of time and money.

What the hell was that all about? I travelled literally hours to get to London to meet with Doctor Holmes, and how did I react when I got there?

Shit.

I know the guy's a dick, but right now, I think he's the only dick who can help me make sense of all of this, and instead of getting him onside, I just attacked him and then threw up the defences before running out of there.

On the other hand, what he and Ellie did was pretty shitty. I know the ends justify the means and all that, but… but it's curious how I was happy to attack him, and yet I haven't even mentioned it to Ellie. After all, she was complicit.

No. She was just being led by the so called professional.

Really? Or are you protecting her?

I could have handled that differently, but just being back there, it brought everything to the surface again.

Now, as I rock back and forth on this train, the prospect of returning to Dolce Vita fills with me dread. I haven't felt this way in a long time, not since we first came out here, but now… now, I'm dreading it for a whole new reason.

Part of me wants to go back. The other part wants to get off at the next station and turn back, but I've already wasted the best part of the day and I want to get home before Ellie.

No, the best thing to do is write off today and go back another time, when I've managed to get a grip and am ready to have a constructive dialogue with the man.

Now that I think about it, though, I don't think today was a complete write-off.

For one, and this is obvious, I managed to finally get something off my chest that I'd been harbouring for quite some time. I've obviously avoided bringing the subject up with Ellie. That can't have been good.

And, based on how I reacted in that meeting, my studying to be a psychotherapist and being on the cusp of graduating was something that I obviously felt very strongly about, but had rejected, given the natural psychological connotations.

But that's precisely it. I may not be able to self-analyse *objectively*. But I can use those skills to work through this stuff in a relatively constructive way.

This is why, this morning, while sitting on the train with free Wi-Fi and not much else to do, I did some research.

Carefully. Since I know, especially given the fact that I'm supposed to be a professional, that by pursuing any theory that is not grounded in fact, I am in danger of sending myself into a whole spiral of woe.

But I'm aware of that. I'm OK.

I just wanted to see – if you discount some of the movies that I may or may not have watched – if the things that have been happening might in some way be supernatural.

There. I admitted it.

I start with the moth.

That moth we saw during dinner. The one with the weird, skull-like marking. It does exist. It does have those markings, and it is even creatively called the *Death's-Head Hawk Moth*. It is the largest moth ever to be recorded in the British Isles, with a wingspan of 150 millimetres. And yes, in folklore, given that creative skull on the thorax, it is known as the *harbinger of death*.

Yeah. So, good to know except for that last bit. No, not a fan of that. But at least I know what it is now. If I'm being perfectly honest, I was curious, given that I've never seen anything like it outside of *The Silence of the Lambs*.

So, that's a fact. The whole folklore thing. Speaks for itself.

It's just folklore, no doubt simply because of that unusual pattern. Means nothing.

As for the bulbs that keep popping around the house.

You'll be pleased to know that I restricted my search, mostly because I didn't want to freak myself out before the meeting, to the practical abnormalities in the house.

E.g. *Why do my lightbulbs keep exploding?*

Turns out that a loose connection in the lamp holder can cause a bulb to blow.

Fair enough. But since that doesn't answer my question because different bulbs in different fittings around the house keep dying, and the chances of them all having a loose connector is obviously unlikely, I kept scrolling.

And I came across many other theories, including articles from physicists about *dark matter* and *dark energy* that I don't even want to think about because, well, it went right over my head.

The crux of what I learned is that *apparitions* draw energy from various sources in order to manifest themselves. That is, they can draw from any source, from battery-powered devices to the energy emitted from human beings. The things I've seen at the house may well be the by-product of an *apparition's manifestation.*

Yes, I know. I can hear it in my head and it just sounds so fucking ludicrous. But I stewed on it for a while and, at least, it does go some way to explaining some of the things that have been happening at the house.

Or it could just be me latching onto this, as preposterous as it may seem, rather than accepting that I'm having a relapse. I've considered that, too.

But let's just entertain that idea for a second. We're all so quick to dismiss any idea of the so-called *real world* supernatural, and yet we'll gladly embrace ghost stories and folklore. The obvious reason for that is because we can comfort ourselves with the belief that none of it's real. The stories can spook us, scare us, and creep us the hell out, but we know, or we believe, that ghosts, demons, and all that pea soup-spitting possession stuff is exactly that... folklore, fiction.

But what if it isn't?

What if?

What if what I am seeing is real and what if Toby, the ghost of my little boy, is at the house and trying to contact me?

I look around the cabin, which is empty but for a couple who are more interested in eating each other's faces than me, a man in a suit, and two old ladies dressed in almost identical vintage clothing which I'm assuming is in aid of some kind of convention (and not because they've both collectively lost their marbles). None of these people can see the grin on my face. Yes, a fucking grin after a day like today, a week like this week! I can only assume that it is some kind of hysterical reaction to the ridiculous notions that, despite my best intentions, I've still managed to allow into my head just as one might a scruffy-looking hitchhiker into a car.

I've no idea what entertaining this stuff is going to do to me. If it's going to make things worse… but what if, eh? What bloody if? Then what?

I have no fucking clue.

Ellie is home today. Maybe I should discuss it with her. Get her input. Assuming she's in the right frame of mind after how we left things this morning.

She agreed to work from home when I said I needed to come to the city. Of course, she gave me the whole twenty-questions thing, so I had to explain that I was seeing Ethan. She wanted to know why; I didn't want to tell her. I lied. She worked out that I was lying, too, so I reacted the way I normally do when put on the spot; I got angry and told her that she's always going to the city and I never bat an eyelid, but today I wanted to go and it wouldn't kill her to work from home and keep an eye on the workers and the dog.

After which we argued some more before she eventually, begrudgingly, acquiesced. Well, I say that. It was more like, "Fine. I'll stay home," accompanied by a purse of the lips and her giving me the cold shoulder until I left.

Jesus. What is so fucking important in the city anyway? After all, she, by her own words, is only working on a presentation, and she can easily work on that from anywhere.

These days, you can virtually work wherever there's an internet connection, so it makes no sense to me why she would travel hours to….

Hang on a minute. Now that I think about it. Now that I allow myself to truly consider this. Why does my wife travel hours to the city every day if she's just working on a report?

It isn't that. It's more than that, she says.

Like what?

Well, preparing for this big deal.

But that doesn't sound right, does it? Given what I've just thought, given her excuse. I mean, is it that? Is it really an excuse, or is it an explanation?

Shit.

The answer has been sitting in front of me all this time, but I've been so wrapped up with getting the house done and us out of there that I didn't stop for a second to consider the notion that my wife may well be trying to get away from the house.

From me.

Things are worse than I thought. She can't even bear to be in the house. That's how much she hates it. That's how much she hates me.

Shit.

I'm gazing out of the window. Concrete rises have given way to rolling fields, and I can feel the tension melting from my shoulders – soon to be replaced by the anxiety of my reality.

My marriage is in trouble. That isn't exactly a mystery but the fact that I've been in denial this whole time, I guess by its very definition, is a revelation, and it tells me that I need the doctor now more than ever… because I'm clearly incapable of seeing the obvious.

In my mind, I've always had this image of us fixing the house, selling it, settling down somewhere else, and maybe even, God forbid, starting over, but that plan means nothing. That plan is shit if I don't have Ellie by my side.

So, it's time to regroup, re-evaluate, and maybe, just maybe, there's a way that Ethan can help both of us with that.

***

I know something is up the moment I've leave the train and exit through the hut masquerading as a train station. It isn't Ellie waiting by the exit doors, but Irvin.

"Is everything OK?" I ask as I approach the rolled-down window of the truck.

He looks at me knowingly, and says, "I'll explain on the way."

"OK."

I go round the passenger side of the truck that is exactly in the state you'd expect from a builder. Dusty and dirty with a squeaky passenger door and a lot of wear and tear.

The one thing I don't expect to find, though, is a cute puppy sitting obediently on the ripped fabric of my seat.

"Buddy! What are you doing here? Hey. What's going on, sleepyhead?" I scoop the dog up in my arms and give him a kiss before taking his seat and slamming the door shut behind me. Probably a bit harder than necessary, but Irvin doesn't seem to mind.

Then, as soon as we're rattling down the road from the train station, I look across at the shadow of my driver.

It's only early evening, but winter's dusk has already smothered the land in darkness. Although, technically, the astronomical winter – measured by Earth's orbit around the sun – doesn't start until around the 20th of December, which is… shit! In just a few days.

(No. I'm not a stargazer, but I am the proud father of a son who loved all things astronomical.)

Irvin must sense my eyes on him, as he starts talking. "Just so you know. We made good progress today with the 'allway," he says, eyes on the illuminated road in front of us. "But I get the feelin' Ellie wasn't particularly 'appy to 'ave us there."

My smile is instinctive, as I know it's lost in the gloom of the cabin. "Yeah. I probably should have warned you. She's working on this important presentation for work, and leaving her at the house with the renovations probably wasn't the best decision."

"Aye," he agrees almost immediately, and I'm surprised by his candour – not that I don't think the man's capable of speaking his mind, but more because I can't help but wonder just how bad things got today.

"Did she give you a hard time?" I ask.

"Us? Well, you could tell that she didn't like 'aving us around. Barely spoke, slammin' the 'allway door and whatnot."

"I'm sorry."

"Oh, no. Don't worry. I've been on worse jobs. People always want the result, but without the mess… sadly, it's a, one of those, what d'ya call 'em? Occupational hazard kind of thing."

I nod, thinking I see where this is going. "Don't worry. I'll be back tomorrow, and she'll probably be back in London."

"Well, that's just it. I don't know what's going to 'appen tomorrow now."

I stop looking at the approaching village lights and look across at him once more. I can see part of his face now eerily lit by the jaundiced hue of the streetlamps, and I can just about make out the furrow of his brow.

"What do you mean?" I ask.

"Well, I suppose there's no other way to say this other than that your wife is not best pleased right now, and that's putting it mildly. It's why I told her I would come fetch ya from the station. You know. She was in such a state that I didn't trust 'er behind the wheel, if you know what I mean."

My shoulders instantly tense because now I'm imagining all kinds of disasters. Have they drilled through a pipe, cut through a cable… what? They were replacing the toilet and putting the fittings in for the lights today. *Shit.* "What happened?" I ask.

"Well, we're not quite sure, exactly. As I say, she kept closing the dining room door, which meant we couldn't really see what we were doing in there. We had to run a cable with a spotlight from the lounge to the–"

"Irvin, what happened?" I repeat, supressing an outburst.

"Well, we don't rightly know, but we were just getting ready to pack up for the day when there was this almighty scream from the dining room, so we ran in there to find your wife standin' over her computer, and she was just screamin', shoutin', swearin', and whatnot. And when I say screamin', by the way, I mean screamin'. Then, it was the oddest thing, she starts huntin' around the place like a mad woman. Under the table, behind the sofa. At first, we didn't even realise what she was doin', and then, once he started yelpin', we realised that she was trying to get 'old of 'im." He nods at my lap, where Buddy has snuggled down between my legs and I've folded protective arms around him.

"Why?"

"To be honest, I'm not sure, because she seemed so upset it was hard to get much sense out of her. One thing she did keep sayin' over and over again is that she was going to kill it."

"Kill it?"

"Well, no. She said drown. She said she was going to drown it."

A chill runs through me as first a memory and then the image of Buddy, pink tongue protruding from his mouth, rocking back and forth on the tide, forces its way into my mind.

We're bumping down the wet cobblestoned high street now, which is glistening with a rainbow of light spilling out of the various shops winding down at the end of another working day.

"So, anyway, I offered to come fetch ya and to bring the little fella with me… you know, just in case."

I don't know what to say. I mean, first, I'm embarrassed. This man hardly knows us and he's already getting embroiled in one of our domestics. Secondly, I'm still not quite sure what the hell happened.

"I don't know what to say, Irvin."

"Oh, it's no bother. No bother at all. You should see when my missus blows her stack. Bloody fireworks," he chuckles.

But I get the feeling he just said that for my benefit.

We ride in silence for a few minutes as the truck rattles around corners and then over the stream, which has now swollen into a miniature river threatening to wash through the confines of its banks and run freely over the gravelled drive.

"Wow. It's been raining for hours now. Is it ever going to let up?" I ask. It's more of an observation than a question, but it gets an answer anyway.

"I doubt it. They keep sayin' we 'aven't seen the worse of it."

"Great. There's me thinking that this was bad enough," I say as we roll to a stop outside of Dolce Vita.

"Well, here ya go, then," Irvin announces way too cheerily, as if he hasn't just shared all that shit with me.

I look through the misty windscreen as the wipers whir noisily back and forth. Lights burn behind the kitchen and photography room windows like the fiery eyes of a wide-eyed creature, and I realise that I'm dreading leaving the truck.

It isn't because I know I'm going to have to deal with Ellie. We've been through worse. No, it's something else. Something I can't quite put my finger on. It's like a small splinter... enough to hurt, but difficult to reach.

"If you don't want us to come over tomorrow, just send me a text or something," Irvin says, interrupting my musing.

"Why wouldn't I want you to come over?" I ask.

"Well, ya know," he says with a shrug.

"Oh, don't worry about Ellie. She's just feisty. It's one of the things I love about her," I joke. "But her bark is worse than her bite."

The irony isn't lost on me. In our relationship, I've always been known as the capricious one. The one with the quick temper who acts before he thinks. A feature that is all too often and somewhat stereotypically attributed to my Italian temperament. And yet, now that I think about it, and especially since I've laid off the booze, I'm nothing like that man anymore. At least, I don't think I am.

"Business as usual tomorrow, Irvin," I say with a smile, reshuffling the pup to the nook of my right arm so that I can pull the door handle with the other. But Irvin isn't listening to me; he's busy staring at the house, too.

"Irvin?"

"Yes, Marco," he says, snapping out of his daze.

"Are you OK?" I ask.

"Yes. I'm fine. All good."

"Did you hear what I said about tomorrow?"

"Tomorrow?"

"Yes. All good for tomorrow. Please come over as normal. The sooner we get this place fixed and sold, the better," I say, pulling on the handle and spilling out into the fresh air.

"I couldn't agree more," my builder says ominously, and I can't help but wonder if there's part of this story that he hasn't told me.

"See you tomorrow, then."

"Yeah. See you then. Be safe, and good luck."

I slam the door shut and sigh as I make my way inside.

33. THE CONFESSION

Although the lamps are on, the house is eerily quiet conjuring the image of Ellie running out at us screaming and clutching a knife. I replace the image of the knife with a broom and then a duster. Although, the latter is unlikely because Ellie's never been one for housework.

But then I realise that I'm going through all of this rather than addressing the silence and the inevitable confrontation I know is heading my way – even though I still have no idea why.

"Ellie?"

Much to my disappointment, there's no smell of cooking wafting up from the kitchen, but there is a dank, musky odour that I'm assuming is a mixture of plaster, workman sweat, and God knows what else.

There's no sign of Ellie and, since I have no idea what happened earlier, I don't want to make things worse before we even start. So, I set Buddy down in the photography room and quickly close the door behind me, much to his displeasure and mine because he instantly starts whimpering and scratching at the door.

"Not helping," I whisper.

When I turn, it's to find that my least favourite place in the house is even uglier now that is resembles DIY's equivalent of Frankenstein's monster, as the walls have been stripped back to a dirty taupe with gauged channels on each side, like scars crudely sutured with blobs of cement, as that solitary lightbulb hangs naked like a deconstructed eyeball.

OK. So, I doubt that's making my wife feel any better.

"Ellie?" I call again, eager to get this over and done with. It's been a long day.

I avoid the hallway and make my way through the den to find muddy footprints by the patio doors, and I make a point of not looking outside since it's bound to be a tip. On the plus side, I think somebody's fixed the shutter because it's no longer looking like it's had a few too many and is now symmetrically aligned with its brothers and sisters.

A crunch underfoot draws my attention to the fact that grit, presumably from the corridor wall, has been trodden into and carried throughout the den, instantly taking me back to when I was here last. Or, more specifically, when my mind was last busy fabricating its version of this place. That night, the whole building was literally collapsing around me and… and I truly felt like I was going to die.

I shudder at the memory, and that's when I notice, spot-lit by the table lamps… a thin layer of dust on the coffee table, the sofa, and most likely every other surface.

Fuck. They could have at least covered the place with dustsheets. Irvin told me they had everything they needed. This isn't on. But I reel in the flame of irritation because there's already a fire to put out, and I don't want to make it worse by dousing it with more gasoline of my own.

So, I turn away from the bombsite that is the lounge and make my way into the dining room. The lights are burning, dully in here, but Ellie is nowhere to be seen. Although, I do notice that her laptop is sitting in its usual place, on the dining room table.

"Ellie!" I yell.

Still no reply, until I hear a sniffle on the other side of the room. In the conservatory.

The lights are off, but I can see Ellie's reflection in the black glass, as if she's looking out into the infinite view of darkness. She's wrapped in a quilt, and there's a half bottle of wine on the floor next to her.

"Hey, I've been calling you. Are you OK?" I ask, walking up behind her, but the only response is a fresh wave of rain rapping loudly on the polycarbonate roof overhead. "Why are you sitting in the dark?" I ask, snapping on a lamp.

My wife squints at the light, and I can tell from her smudged makeup and puffy eyes that she's been crying.

Oh shit.

I'm about to speak again when I hear her say, "I told you to get rid of that thing." Her voice is flat, as if she's talking about one of the shitty pieces of furniture in here, but I know she isn't. She's talking about the puppy.

And yet, I say, "What thing?"

"The puppy, Marc. I told you to get rid of the fucking puppy," she seethes.

"El–" I begin, sitting in the chair opposite her so that we're at eye level.

"You insisted on keeping it, and now I'm fucking devastated," she says, finally turning to look at me, but only to flash her angry eyes my way.

"What do you mean? What happened?"

"*He* destroyed it."

"Destroyed what?"

"My fucking document, that's what!" she yells.

I hold out my hands calmingly. "OK. Alright. But I don't understand. Who? Buddy?" I shake my head, confused – because that's what I am.

"Your precious dog pissed all over my fucking laptop."

I let out a laugh. It's an incredulous laugh because I can't imagine Buddy climbing up on the table and lifting a leg to take a leak, but that isn't how it's interpreted.

"You think that's funny? You think that's fucking funny?" my wife screams, eyes blazing with fury as she sits forward in her chair.

"Whoa, whoa, whoa," I say, lifting steadying hands high because, in all our years of marriage, I don't think I have ever seen her like this. "I wasn't laughing at you. I was laughing at the image of him doing that with his short legs. I mean, how? Did you leave your laptop on the floor?"

"No I did not!" she snaps.

"Then, how would he pee on it?" Her response is to shoot me another glare. So, I change tack. "OK. Let's just back up a second," I say calmly. "What makes you think he peed on it?"

"Because it stinks, Marc! How do you think?"

"I don't know, El. That's why I'm asking. I'm just trying to understand here. I mean, how do you know it was him who peed on it?"

She gawks at me, slowly screwing her face into an incredulous scowl. "What? You want me to get it analysed?"

"Of course not. I'm just saying, what makes you think it was him?"

"It was him!"

"El, he can barely reach a chair. You're saying he climbed onto the chair and then the table to deliberately relieve himself on your laptop?"

"No, you're right," she says, nodding, but I know it's sarcasm. "It wasn't the dog; it was one of those heathens that you've hired to fix up this place. Because I wouldn't put it past them."

I rock my head from side to side. "Well, I have to give you that, given the state of the den," I say with a faint smile, but she doesn't respond. Instead, she looks away. "OK. So, what exactly happened?" I hold out my hands again and add, "I mean, beyond the smell of your laptop. Is it broken or what? Tell me exactly what happened."

"I told you–"

"No. Tell me exactly how you found out."

"I'm not doing this with you," she says, drawing the quilt around her and looking defiantly at the rivulets of water running down the window.

"El. Please. Just tell me what happened. I know you think Buddy did something, but I don't have any idea how you reached this conclusion. I mean, did you see him?"

She shoots me another glare. "You're fucking unbelievable," she growls.

"What now?"

"You know how much that pisses me off, and yet you still try that stuff on me."

"Try what? I'm just trying to understand."

"Don't try to fucking handle me, Marc. I'm not a fucking patient!"

I pull a face. Confused. "What do you mean you're not a patient?" I ask, as she clearly didn't mean to let that slip. If she wants to discuss that now, I'm ready.

But she doesn't respond. Instead, she looks away, averting my gaze.

"El?"

Nothing. Just the drumming of rain overhead.

"El? Answer me."

Still nothing.

"Ell, fucking answer me!" I snap, jumping to my feet.

Finally, she turns to look at me. Her face is ghostly pale in the dim light.

"What do you mean stop treating you like you're one of my patients?"

She hesitates, and I think she's going to reveal something, but instead her passive expression turns into another sneer. "I've just told you that that shitting dog has destroyed an important file of mine, and all you can do is focus on that?"

"Jesus Christ! Then, why don't you tell me what to focus on? Do you want me to focus on the fact that a puppy Buddy's size managed to and deliberately chose to climb up onto the dining table and piss on your laptop? Or would you rather I focus on the real issue, huh? The fact that you hate being here, with me. Which one, El? Which one? Just tell me which one you'd like me to be sorry for first!"

She says nothing. Rain drums loudly overhead.

"I'm trying," I resume. "I'm trying, as evidenced by the tip in the other room. I'm trying to get this place sold so we can get the fuck out of here as soon as is humanly possible. I've given you space. I've given you the freedom to do whatever you want to do while I get on with all the other shit, and it still isn't enough. It still doesn't seem to be enough for you.

"So, tell me. Please. For the love of God, just please tell me what else I can do to make you happy and I'll do it." My voice has cracked on those last words as I seek to swallow the lump of emotion in my throat.

I'm exhausted. Scared. What's left of my world is crumbling, and I am powerless to do anything about it. So, I pause here, heart drumming in synchrony with the falling rain. Breath coming in shaky rasps.

Thankfully, she doesn't react to my outburst. She's seen enough of them over the years, I suppose, although for entirely different reasons.

Instead, she opts to completely ignore it and plough on with her own grievance. "I was working on the document. I'd almost finished. But to avoid rushing, I decided to take a stretch first. Make some tea. God knows that lout dropped enough hints about it today."

I smile inwardly, as she's obviously talking about Drew.

"I went to the kitchen. Made their drinks. Made mine. Came back, and I found the screen flickering like it was bloody possessed. I've never seen a screen do that before.

"So, I went over to it, but before I even got there, it went black. So, I sat down in front of it to see what was wrong, and that's when I smelt it."

On cue, Buddy starts barking, and I'm wound up so tight that the sound startles me.

"And *it*," she adds, nodding towards to the doorway, "was sitting underneath the table giving itself a bloody bath."

"And that's what made you think it was him?" I ask.

"No, Marc. What made me think it was him was the fucking stench of urine coming from my keyboard."

"So, did you turn it off and on and everything? Try to dry it?"

"What? You want me to dismantle the laptop now?"

"No, I'm just saying that I've seen loads of videos about how to recover from a spill. Remember that time I threw coffee all over mine?"

"I'm not talking about fucking coffee, Marc! I'm talking about bloody dog piss! It's obviously seeped in and fried the bloody mothership thing because it's not even coming on now."

I contemplate that a few seconds. Then, "Board."

"What?"

"Board. It's called the mother*board*."

"Are you seriously correcting me right now?" she hisses once more through gritted teeth.

OK. "Well, just use mine," I say.

"I can't use yours, brainchild, I can't get to the fucking file."

"Well, it's backed up to the cloud, isn't it?"

She doesn't respond.

"El?" I prompt.

She turns to me and growls. "Don't you think I've already tried that?"

"I don't know, it's why I'm asking," I push back, holding her gaze in an attempt to find a solution to this thing rather than continue going round in circles as we appear to have been doing for what feels like the best part of an hour.

"I can't," she spits, "because it didn't back up. As you know, the internet is bloody shitty here. For some reason, it didn't back up the file."

"How do you know if you can't get in?"

"Because I checked on my fucking phone!" she explodes. "The file isn't there. Jesus Christ," she says, tucking runaway stands of her hair behind her ears as she does when gearing up to tackle a chore. "That document was important to me," she says. Then, she yells at the door, "Shut up!"

Buddy has decided to make his presence felt now of all bloody times. And I am torn between going to deal with him and staying here to work through the problem.

"OK. Well, there's got to be a way around this."

"There isn't. Don't you think I've thought about that already?"

There's a crazed look in my wife's eyes. One I don't think I've ever seen before. And if this were anybody else but her, I'd be asking what's really troubling her because this has got to be more than a shitty presentation. She's upset about that, sure. But it's undoubtedly a symptom of something else. It's got to be.

But, again, there's no reasoning with her right now. So, instead I ask, "Well, is there a way that you can present a cut-down version of it? This presentation." She breathes to say something, but I hold up my hand again and continue, "No, hear me out. I know it isn't what you wanted. What you had planned. But this is more about damage limitation, surely. I don't know the details, of course, but maybe a more concise presentation may well be more effective if it's you delivering it, no? I mean, you could fill in the gaps as you go along," I say hopefully. Encouragingly.

My wife shakes her head like my proposition is ludicrous, and yet I can see that behind those eyes, she's already thinking, considering all possible permutations and ways to recover from this. I know that because I know my wife. As much as she's been revelling in this pity party, I know this isn't her style. This is more about making a point with me than the catastrophe she's depicting. I wouldn't be surprised if she already has a contingency plan in place. I'm just trying to nudge her back in that direction rather than slide us into abject misery.

"There's no way I can make back what I need. Although, part of the file is backed up. I just need to make up the parts missing since we arrived here," she says to no one in particular.

And yet, I can see that she's thinking about it.

But only for a few seconds before she turns to me and says, sharply, "I want that thing out of here tomorrow!" She glances at the door before rising from her seat and making her way towards the dining room.

And me? Well, I just sit for a while absorbing that sentence. And the more I do, the more I want to react, and the more I want to react, the more I keep telling myself not to because that isn't who I am anymore. I am not that person. I am not that man. I am….

"No!" I say.

My wife stops in her tracks and turns to me. "What?"

I stand up. "I said no. I'm not getting rid of the dog, El. I know you've been pushing that agenda ever since he arrived here and…" I pause because the barking is getting on my nerves, "as much as his bark is fucking annoying, I love that guy and I'm not getting rid of him."

"You love him?"

I nod.

"More than you love me?"

"Oh, for fuck's sake!" I say, rolling my eyes.

"Because that's what it feels like, Marc. That you care more about that thing than you care about me."

"You're fucking joking, right?" I simmer, walking up to her. *Don't do it.*

"That's it, right? You're having a laugh when you say that? You haven't so much as looked at me since we got here, and you've got the fucking audacity to act like you're threatened by a bloody dog?"

My wife squares up to me. "You think I'm acting?"

"Of course, you're acting. You've got some axe to grind with me and you're finding every fucking excuse to make me pay for it. Well, why don't you just get it off your chest, El, huh? Come on, get it off your chest once and for all… what exactly have I done that's so fucking bad that you can't even look me in the eye anymore? Huh? Tell me! Tell me!"

"You want to know?"

"Of course, I want to bloody know! I asked, didn't I?"

"You really want to know, I'll tell you! I'll fucking tell you!" she rages, eyes welling with tears. "YOU KILLED MY SON! You killed my baby boy! And I'll *never* forgive you! I'll never fucking forgive you!" she rages, slapping me across the face and then shoving me away from her. "Ever!"

It takes me several seconds to stop my wife from slapping, shoving, and attempting to punch me by grabbing her wrists tightly and holding her away from me, as if she's some kind of wild creature and not the mother of my son, the love of my life. Seconds dribble by in silence, but for the drumming of the rain, the gasping and gulping of our breaths, and the sound of the dog, who's switched from barking to mournful yowling as if he's just understood the words that are still ringing in my ears.

I'm gaping at my wife because words quite literally fail me.

I mean, ever since that day, ever since we lost our boy and for as long as I have consciously been able to recall what happened, I have always wondered if my wife shared my own belief that I was guilty. That I was responsible. After all, I was the one who suggested that we go ahead and invest in that gift for Toby, and I was the one who physically drove us there that day. I was the one who let him fly it over the pier. I was the one who was talking on the phone rather than paying attention to what my son was doing, and I was the one who told him to land that thing. If I hadn't made any of those decisions, then there's a good chance that our son would still be with us today.

Despite all suggestions, therapy, and my wife's own words to the contrary, those are the facts. I am responsible. I can understand how that will have affected her… and why she feels this way about me.

I deserve her words that are still burning like drops of acid on my soul, along with the devastating realisation that what I had hoped was a crisis in my marriage is actually something much more deeply entrenched… and from which I'm not sure we will ever recover.

"Marco…" there are tears in my wife's eyes, but the very way she's unable to finish that sentence tells me that she may well regret her words, even though they nonetheless remain her belief.

And that's OK, because I believe it, too. And I always have. I've just been pretending that I agree with everything Doctor Holmes has brainwashed me into thinking.

So, I gently push away my wife's outstretched, comforting arms and walk through the den and into the photography room, closing the door behind me.

34. CARE

I'm holding Buddy in my lap when Ellie enters the room carrying a brown paper bag. I notice that she's wearing a coat and has a red scarf wrapped around her neck.

"Come on," she says.

I squint at her as if I no longer understand English.

"We're going out."

"Out where?"

"Remember the first day we arrived here?" she asks with a smile.

"I don't know what you're talking about."

"Come on. Put your jacket on."

"I haven't got my jacket."

"Yes, you have, it's hanging on the chair behind you."

I turn around and see that my jacket is, in fact, hanging on the chair behind me, but I was sure I took it off in the lounge. Didn't I?

"Ellie, where are we going?" I ask, pulling the jacket on like an obedient child.

"Down to the beach," she says, leaving the room.

I glance out the window. "The beach? Ellie, it's still dark outside!" I call after her.

But she isn't listening. So, I hurry to catch up.

When I enter the lounge, I realise that it isn't that dark, after all. It's dusk or maybe late afternoon. It's hard to tell because it's foggy outside again.

"Ellie!" But she's gone already. Out of the patio doors that's she's left open to rock back and forth in the breeze. "Ellie!" I call, rushing over to the doors just in time to see my wife hurrying down the back lawn until she's swallowed up by the mist.

"Wait!" I race after her until I am also devoured by the fog. It swirling around me now, enveloping, cold and yet welcoming.

The roar of the ocean is loud. Growing progressively louder, reverberating around me as if the fog were a tangible thing with walls made of jagged rock. And I realise… I'm in one of the giant caves under the cliff, under the house.

To my right is the beach. The ocean.

Wait. How did we get here?

"Come on!" Ellie calls to me. I can see her now. Waiting on the shore. So, I hurry over.

"Ellie. How did we…?"

"Would you like a sandwich? Maybe a bottle of water?" she offers, holding up the paper bag to me.

"Hold on. Let me. You've done enough," I find myself saying.

She laughs, eyes sparkling with joy. "It's going to take more than a sandwich," she says.

"Ellie…" I can't finish the sentence, as I have no idea what's going on.

"We're just taking a walk on the beach," my wife says softly, as if she's read my mind.

I look down and watch as I sink into pebbles that are sucking and clicking at my boots. When I look up, I see that Ellie is walking ahead of me now, moving fast.

"Ellie? Wait! Where are you going?" I call after her.

"I'll be right back," she says over her shoulder. "I just need to check something."

"Check what? Ellie?"

But she isn't listening. Instead, she moves away from me and further into the mist that is clearing now, burned away in patches by the morning sun and drifting overhead like miniature clouds.

"Ellie!" I call to her, but she doesn't turn back. Instead, she skids to a halt as if there's something in front of her. Something blocking her path. She's looking down at it.

"What is that? What are you looking at?" I cock my head to see around her, but I can't because she's blocking my line of site. So, I stagger forward. "Ellie? Ellie, what is it? What are you looking at?"

I already know. Inside, I already know who is sitting there in the pebbles, and then, as the thought appears in my mind, my wife moves away, and I can see. I can see him. His small body. The sandy blonde hair.

"Toby?"

This just may be the time when he turns and looks at me. Look at me!

But he doesn't. Instead, he gets to his feet, takes Ellie's hand and leads her away, into the fog.

"No! Toby. No. Wait! Toby!"

Don't worry, Daddy. I'll take care of her.

"NO!" I wake with a start to see two black eyes staring at me and a weight pressing on my chest, and I'm just about to start panicking when I realise that it's Buddy with that worried parent look on his face again.

I groan. "Buddy… you scared the shit out of me," I say, awkwardly heaving myself into a sitting position in the wingback chair, trying not to drop the hound that is now licking my face. "It's OK. I'm OK. You didn't scare me that much, but thank you."

"You're starting to make a habit of this," a voice says, making me jump again. "Jesus!"

Yes, that's bloody happening a lot around here.

I look up. Ellie is standing over us with a mug of coffee like we're in a scene from *Groundhog Day*.

I take in a deep breath and run my hands through my hair to dissipate the dregs of that dream that are clinging to me like bloody morning dew. And I'm suddenly feeling claustrophobic.

"OK, Buddy. Get down now. Come on. Down."

The dog complies, slowly sliding off my belly and onto the floor. I heave myself up and run my hand over the back of my neck that feels as stiff as bloody board.

It's as I move that I feel the blanket slide off me, and I look up.

"I came in to see how you were getting on last night and you were already sound asleep," my wife offers. Still holding the mug aloft.

I finally take it from her. "Thanks."

Then, the memory barges its way in front of the dream's remnants, and I want to groan again. But Ellie heads it off by pulling the chair up from the vanity desk and sitting next to me in a cloud of something delicious which I assume is a mixture of shampoo and perfume. I surreptitiously breathe it in.

"Marco…"

"Ellie–" I interrupt because I think I know what's coming, but I'm barely awake and don't think I have it in me to start right now.

"Hear me out," she says, leaning forward and looking me in the eyes. "I didn't mean what I said yesterday."

"Yes, you did–"

"No. I didn't."

I shake my head. "Yes, you did. And it's OK. I actually happen to agree with you."

She grabs my face in both her hands and forces me to look into those blue eyes, that I notice are now glistening with an emotional sheen. "Listen to me, you little pig-head."

"Hey," I complain as the hot black coffee slops over the sides of the cup.

"I said what I did because I feel it's true. And we both know that, technically, it is true. But the reality is that it could have been either one of us that day, Marc. Either one. We made the decision to buy him that gift together. And we made the decision for you both to go out that day, together.

"I needed to work, remember? So, yes, it is true, but not in the way I said it. And it's really important to me that you believe that," she says earnestly. "Do you understand?"

I nod, awkwardly, considering her hands are still holding my face. And I want to kiss her so badly right now. So, I do, and she responds and I'm fucking elated, but then she pulls away, saying "I need to get going." Then, she stands and buttons her jacket.

"Going? Go where?"

"I need to get away from here and find a solution to the document thing. You know, sit down with David and see what we can come up with."

"El, I know you think that Buddy…"

She holds up a silencing hand. "It doesn't matter. Again, it's happened now. I just have to find a solution and, to be fair, I think you may have been onto something yesterday. I think there's a way I can recover what I have and add the rest from memory." She shrugs, pensively. "I don't know. We'll see. But right now, I just need to get out of here and get there," she says, biting her lip.

Wow. It's almost like she's looking for reassurance. From me! She hasn't done that in ages.

But I don't want my wife to leave the house today. I know it's ridiculous, but after that dream… I don't know. I just feel weird. Unsettled. I would much rather she stay here. Stay home.

And yet, that's not what I express. "Of course," I say with a nod and a generous smile, because I know that my chances of stopping her right now are less than zero. I don't carry that kind of clout anymore. I don't think I have in a while.

She clenches her hands into victorious fists and then steps forward. "Marc, I know I've been a bit of a bitch." I pull a face. "OK. A lot of a bitch lately, but I really want this to work. I really want us to get through this. And I realised last night that the only way that's truly going to happen is if we do this together."

I make a show of nearly choking on my coffee. "Jesus. Easy up there, El. First you tell me that my idea is great…"

"I actually said you might be onto something."

"…and then you're giving me that all-American pep talk that we're a team and can get through this together. I'm paraphrasing here, of course. Next, you'll tell me that you still love me."

She walks up to me, takes my face in her hands once more, plants a kiss on my lips, and says, sincerely, "I've never stopped." Then she lets go and adds, "You just get on my nerves, that's all. But that's nothing new."

I nod and look at Buddy to get his take on the situation.

But I notice that he's retreated under the chair as if he heard my wife's words last night and is still sulking over them.

"Shit! I'm going to be late," Ellie says, looking at her watch.

"I'll get the keys," I say, standing up.

"No. It's OK. I booked the cab last night. He's probably waiting out there now. I'll see you tonight."

"Oh, right. OK."

My wife then clicks her way over to the door, but stops. "Marc, I've been thinking. How much longer do you think it'll take them to finish the work on this place?"

I consider the question. I know the downstairs is almost done. I haven't inspected it yet, but based on what I saw last night, they probably need a couple more days to finish up and get the painting done down here. Then, it's just upstairs bathrooms and painting. That'll be another two or three more days, I suppose. I'm no expert, but that makes sense based on the estimate.

I shrug. "Not sure. Probably another five full days, I'd say, at least. Because there are three of them, Irvin has estimated everything should be done in two weeks, but he doesn't think it'll actually take that long. Why?"

"When's Christmas Eve?"

I think about this, too. "Um, not until next… shit, next week! Wednesday."

"So, that's what, five, six days away?"

"Yeah." I'm nodding because I know my wife is getting at something, but I don't know what.

"Think they'll have everything done by then?"

I frown thoughtfully. "Possibly, if they work the weekend, too, I would have thought so. Why?"

"Well, I was thinking. Wouldn't it be fantastic if we could spend this Christmas Eve celebrating? You know, as it is, it's going to be… well, you know, different this year. So, I think it'll be good for us not to spend it alone and invite a few people… just close friends, for company. We could celebrate getting the house finished, and show them the amazing work you've done here while also getting through Christmas."

Those last words were spoken softly and with a drop of her gaze because I can totally understand what she means. Last Christmas is still etched at the forefront of my mind, thanks to that video. I'm in no hurry to mope about the place grieving that.

"I think it's an excellent idea," I say cheerfully.

"You do?" she asks, meeting my gaze once more.

"Of course! It's a fantastic idea, Ellie. I'll talk to the lads today. Maybe offer them some kind of incentive to make sure it's all done the day before."

"That's brilliant," my wife says, all blue eyes and wide smile.

And God does she wear that well.

The sound of a car horn shatters the moment.

"I've got to go!" she says, looking at her watch. "I'll see you later!"

"See you later!" I call after her.

And just like that, my wife is gone, leaving nothing but a cloud of perfume in her wake.

35. ILLICIT

NOVEMBER 26TH
(3 WEEKS EARLIER)

Ellie. London. 20:45.

I've had this song in my head for days now. It's an old song by a then angst-ridden Alanis Morissette, and one which I've discovered suits the now angst-ridden me perfectly.

It's called "All I Really Want."

OK. So, I'm not full of angst. I was. Several days ago. But not anymore. Not now that I have purpose.

Now, I just love those lyrics. Have you heard them, dear doctor? You really should listen to them. They are inspirational.

I love still addressing this journal to you even though I know you'll never see it. I have considered changing my address over to *dear diary*, but that just wouldn't be the same because, after all, it wasn't the journal that made me feel progressively worse, if that were even possible – it was you.

You and all your psychobabble literature shit made me think that I should *accept* what had happened to me. *Accept* that this was my new life.

And I have *accepted* what happened. But I don't *accept* the plan to live my life like one of those post-traumatic life veterans walking around with hunched shoulders and hanging gazes, brandishing warning placards at everyone, and Santa Clause, about all the triggers that might set them off.

Fuck that!

If I must live this life – and I have thought about this long and hard during my trips to the city – then I am going to fucking *live* it. My way.

And I am going to document all of it in minute detail so that, when I am finally happy again and when I am lounging on some tropical island somewhere supping champagne, I can read it all back like it's in a fucking book and relive exactly how I got there.

Wait, you didn't think I was going to just crumble, did you? That I was just going to be consigned back to the pits of hell – AKA my parents' house – and let this happen to me?

That's isn't me.

The person I am is the one who took her father's advice and made the pointless journeys into the city to a job that no longer exists, but it was only to allow myself time. Time away from the toxic noise of that place to take stock, to consider what I want from life right now. How exactly I am going to reshape my new beginning.

And, if I'm being perfectly honest here, for a while, I had absolutely no idea. I mean, really. None. But it only took a few days of living with those two micromanaging my every move, my every thought, before I was unable to see the wood for the trees.

That was until I decided to put my day to better use by seeking out and returning my yellow umbrella to its rightful owner.

It wasn't difficult because I already knew which bus to board, and which stop to take to lead me back to the Viñedo.

And there he was in his uniform, black waistcoat, tie, and that bright, wide smile.

It was then, in that moment, that I knew. I understood that he had been awaiting the return of his little umbrella as eagerly as I had awaited our reunion.

I can tell you now that none of the scenarios that I had anticipated were anywhere near as delicious as the actual one which was played out.

None.

That was almost two weeks ago. And, at first, I thought that he was just a pastime, a distraction, and that I would tire of him and maybe even move onto the next, and yet....

Everybody has a vice, don't they?

Booze, gambling, cigarettes. Some, men mostly, enjoy dressing up like giant babies and being spanked by some overweight behemoth of a woman spilling out from a leather catsuit – I'll never understand that one – and me, I love the feeling of this man inside me.

There's no rhyme nor reason to it because my husband is still relatively young, fit, and satisfying even. At least, that's how I remember him. But I can't imagine myself revisiting that. Not now. Now, the thought of him anywhere near me is one that makes my skin crawl. The notion of sex with him, repugnant.

But this man…. Just the contours of his body, the smell of his breath, his skin… even his perspiration is a sublime aphrodisiac against which there is no defence.

Ever since I first laid eyes on him. Ever since he woke me from my walking coma, I've been trying to work out exactly how. How this stranger holds such power over me, and I still can't figure it out. The most rational conclusion – unverified by anybody, of course, since I can't really talk to anyone about this – is the fact that he's wrong. Illicit. Illegal. Forbidden.

The fact that we spend most of our time in hotel rooms doesn't help, either. Those places are notoriously erotic.

And I used to keep telling myself that I'm married, and, for all intents and purposes, still a mother. I have been devoted to my husband for two decades. We've been through so much together. So much good, but a lot of bad. Not just the obvious, but finances, my parents, and his addictions. It's those things, ironically, no matter how excruciating, that I believe were the welder's wand to the metal structure of our life together. But, over time, like an achy limb, they're also the things that I've had to endure day after day. It's been one crisis after another culminating with the loss of my son, which offered an excruciating and unique brand of pain that's inflicted scars that I know now will never heal.

And yet, this man, this stranger… he offers me respite from that. He is the medicine to my pain. He offers me relief from being the suffering wife, bereft mother, and abused daughter, and allows me to just be me.

Elisabeth.

Someone who no longer has the duty to look sad in front of her husband, dignified in front of her parents, and in mourning in front of the rest of the world.

He makes me feel that it's OK to laugh, drink, eat, fuck, and even sleep without having to wear my grief and my shame like a scarlet letter on my forehead, in the way that I feel I should when I am anywhere near my husband.

And I love him for it.

Love? Oh, fuck!

As we lie there with our limbs entwined and those thoughts course through my mind, I can't help but think that that's exactly what I feel for this man. This stranger. My saviour. Although, I don't think I could or would ever admit to it. Not to him, but I think I do love him. I love him for freeing me from my prison of pain.

And this is also why I keep going back for more. To use and be used by him. To desire and be desired by him. To feel the roughness of his beard on my skin. The prickle. The graze. The exquisite thorns jabbing at my body as I absorb the sound of his hot breath against my ear growing louder and louder, his movements faster and deeper until we both collapse into a delirious explosion of panting ecstasy.

I can still feel him lying on top of me now. My hands low on his back, unmoving, keeping him deep inside me as we both gasp and gulp. Pulses throbbing and hearts pounding as we recover from our exertion. Each with just enough energy to share kisses on sweat-drenched skin.

Later, as we basked in the aftermath, he asked, "How come you ever only want to meet me in a hotel?"

"Why? Do you have something against hotels?" I asked.

"No. I'm just curious why we can never meet at each other's houses," he said, planting kisses on my shoulder. That beard now both tickling and irritating.

I didn't respond. Listening instead to the sigh of the air conditioner and the sounds of voices passing by our doorway.

"I'm not stupid, you know. You may think that I am, but I'm not. I know you are a married woman, that you are sad in your marriage and maybe for other reasons," he said gently, almost whispering as if his words could hurt me, too. They couldn't hurt me. I was already broken.

Moving in with my parents again was definitely the final straw, though. Their idea of being supportive is to treat me like a child. A child who, in their eyes, made a terrible mistake and can no longer be trusted with the affairs of her life.

Except for work, of course, because they believe it's my job that is going to pay them rent at the end of the month. What they don't know is that there is no job and that I've already planned to use my father's own loan money for that.

"Then, if you know that, you'll understand why I want us to be discreet," I said.

"I do. But I'd also like to understand."

"Understand what?"

"Why you do this with me, if you are married?"

"You know, I much prefer it when we're fucking because that means I don't have to lie here and submit to the Spanish Inquisition."

"Is that what you think this is? An inquisition?"

"Isn't it?"

"No. I'm just trying to understand. Trying to understand *you.*"

"Why? Why the hell would you want to understand me? You're a man, aren't you? Don't men just want to–"

"It's because I love you, Elisabeth."

I laughed so loudly that I'm sure they heard me in the next room, before turning to pull myself up into a sitting position. I wanted to look into my Latin lover's eyes, as I expected to find a sexy and mischievous twinkle in there, but instead I found a solemn face and furrowed brow.

"Shit. You're serious?" I asked.

He nodded, jaw muscles flexing and animating that beard of his.

And that would have been my cue to fall in line, to sympathise, but instead I started laughing again. I have no idea what was wrong with me, but it just seemed funny. This went on for about a minute, at least, during which I could see that he wasn't sharing my amusement, but that didn't stop me.

It was almost as if I wanted to hurt him. Test him. See how far I could push before he broke.

And he did.

With narrowed eyes and that flexing jaw of his, he flung the sheets aside and stepped out of the bed.

The fall and rise of the mattress was my prompt to stop laughing. And I did so as I watched him stalk about the room, hunting for his clothes. And, if I'm being perfectly honest, I enjoyed the spectacle. For multiple reasons.

He does have a bloody fine arse. It looks sculpted. In a David statue kind of way. I mean, my husband has a lovely arse, too, but you can see that while it's still nicely shaped, it's starting to lose the youthful, moulded roundness of a twenty-something-year-old. It's how I remember my tits used to a look a long time ago.

There's no way they'd pass that fucking pencil test now!

Not that this man seems to care. He loves my breasts, or so he keeps telling me, and as much as I dismiss him, I love to hear it.

Anyway, I watched as my walking statue of David stepped into his Calvin Klein briefs and, with one ping of the elastic, turned those beautiful jewels into a generous pouch. And the sight of that coupled with the fact that he was angry made me want to fuck him all over again. Right there in the middle of the room.

"Oh, come on, Cristian. How do expect me to react to that?" I asked.

"I don't know," he replied, gesticulating, "maybe without laughing in my face."

"I didn't laugh in your face."

"No, not in my face, just at me."

"Cristian. You know nothing about me and you're telling me that you love me."

He pushed his hair back and finally looked at me with those chocolate eyes melting with the heat of his anger. "You know, where I come from, we're taught to say what we think, not machine words."

I suppressed a snigger. "Mince."

"What?" He scowled with a sexy look that reminded me of one of those moody black and white posters you used to be able to buy with brooding male models.

"The saying is *mince words*. Not machine them," I said, lowering my gaze and biting my lip to suppress another snigger.

"So, now you're making fun of my accent."

"Of course not! Stop being so sensitive, Christian, and come back to bed."

"No," he said obstinately as he slid his muscular legs into denim.

"Come on. Let's talk about this."

He paused, trousers hanging open from his hips, and nodded at me. "Ah, so, now you want to talk, eh? Now you want to talk, but not really. You just want to pretend to talk, but not really open your heart. You British, so reserved. So unaffected."

Wow. Those last words. Well, they stung with a large needle of irritation. *Unaffected?* "You have no fucking idea," I growled while retaining a begrudging smile.

"Yes, you're right!" he said, moving towards me, hands waving in the air once more. "You're absolutely right. I have no idea. I have no fucking idea because you don't tell me! You don't talk, Elisabeth. All you want to do is fuck!"

"Yes! And all you want to do is fucking talk! Jesus Christ, of all of the men in the world who walk around with a permanent hard-on, including my husband, I end up with the one who wants to talk!"

"So, this is it, eh? This is the reason you're with me. Your husband cheats on you, so you want to cheat on him. Is that it?"

Well, actually it's more than that, but I said, "Yes, and so what? What do you care?" And I met his gaze and held the subsequent stare-off as the city rumbled beyond the window.

"You know what, I feel sorry for you," he told me through shallow breaths, working himself up.

"Yeah?" I asked, and then I gasped when he lifted me off the bed and pulled me into a kiss.

But I fought him off. "No! Get off!" I yelled, pushing at his hairy chest, but he held me to him in a muscular vice grip.

I pulled away. He pulled me back. I pulled away again. He pulled me back once more. I slapped his face, and he pulled my hair.

"Get off me! Get the fuck off me!" I raged through hisses, his bare chest pressing against my naked breasts. His body burning against mine.

"I don't want you! I don't want you! I fucking hate you!" I said, pushing at his jeans until I could feel the muscles of his beautiful arse once more. Then, I kicked at the sheets between us and wished for him inside me, and, before long, my wish was granted.

That was a few days ago.

A few days before I received the phone call that threatened to change everything.

It would appear that, after a few weeks of yet another relapse, my husband has made a full recovery. So much so that they are going to discharge him.

Fancy that, eh? A full discharge back into the land of the living. Just like that. All as if the past few months never happened.

Worse. His doctor suggests it might be useful to his recovery if we found a mutual interest. *"Perhaps the house he inherited from his father on the coast."*

Are you fucking kidding me? He's expecting me to go and play nurse at the back of beyond all while donning dungarees to paint and play *happy couples*?

"No fucking way. No fucking way!" I said.

In my head.

My face was just a mask of disappointment which, lucky for me, apparently looks the same as shock – because the doctor said, "I appreciate that this must all come as a bit of a shock." I told him that it did and then proceeded to ask questions I imagine most wives would. Why now? What's changed? What kind of progress did he make? How do we know he's truly recovered?

Unfortunately for me, the doctor appeared to have plausible answers for all of them.

Fuck.

And I have to say, for a shrink, the man's quite nice. A bit young looking. Reminds me of one of those junior doctors. The kind you would normally tell to fuck off and go get a grown-up when they introduce themselves to you.

In this case, I wanted to tell him that it was too late. That I wasn't ready to take delivery of that particular broken package and that he would have to ship it off somewhere else because I no longer had anywhere to take delivery. The flat was gone. I was already consigned to hell. And I definitely couldn't take him there because my father, despite being a bit of a girl – you know the puritan types – with that poker up his arse, even him, I think he'd be capable of murder. After all, he's never liked Marc and hell would have to freeze over before either of my parents would let him in the house.

So, I was going to tell the young shrink, *"No thanks. Can't do."* But instead told him that I needed to go away, take it all in, and, you know, make arrangements.

I have no idea what kind of arrangements I meant, but he nodded, and it seemed to make sense to him, so that's all that mattered.

Then, on the way home, on the train, as I was sifting through all of this shit, I heard that Alanis Morissette song, and that was it.

When I got home, I skipped vacuous talk with the trolls under the stairs and went straight to my room, where I snuggled up with my quilt, a bar of chocolate – because it's fucking dessert at my parents' house and if I try to change that, it'll be twenty questions along with a good dose of judgement, and I can't be bothered – and an old movie. One of my favourites. *Gaslight* with Ingrid Bergman.

I had already watched it recently, but this time I was watching it for research.

Now, I have a plan.

David… remember him? He's my husband's best friend, former boss, and a spineless cocksucker (literally) is the one I really need to look out for.

Things, as you can imagine, have been strained since the incident at work. Made worse when that shitty game tanked because of a fatal flaw and they all found out that the damage limitation strategy document I was supposed to have been working on was never started.

Apparently, that game nearly sank the company until they found buyers. Now, it looks like the bastard is going to make a fortune from a sale to one of the big-name game houses.

Bastard. They say money goes to money.

It's OK. I'm not bitter. I have my own plan to make a fortune, and David, unbeknownst to him, is going to help me. Provided I can keep him away from my husband, that is.

See, he knows about Cristian.

Because of a fucking rare night where I allowed Cristian to convince me to go out for a drink at my favourite bar, The Grapevine. Do you know it? It's off Covent Garden.

Anyway, who do we happen to bump into? Yes, those two.

And no matter how I tried to spin it, there was no doubt that those two suspected the affair. They didn't say anything at the time, but there's no doubt they worked it out. Well, it's not exactly rocket science. Cristian and I have an unmistakable chemistry. You'd have to be fucking blind not to see it.

So, anyway…. Now, I'm really pissed off.

The good thing is that my husband doesn't have a mobile phone yet. He was cut off, so it's unlikely they'll communicate with each other. Assuming David is going to be an arsehole about it. And it's unlikely David'll be allowed to visit because I suggested to the doctor that my husband not be overtaxed too soon.

He agreed.

So, I then sent a message to David, telling him that his friend was being discharged and that we were going to the country, but that it will be a while before his friend will be allowed visitors and that I'll let him know when he can.

By that time, I'm hoping all of this will be done and dusted, and it won't fucking matter.

Then, I told my parents that, in my husband's absence, I was going to need to go and spend some time in the country. Prep the house for sale and that kind of thing. They weren't too pleased, but my father warmed to the idea when I told him how much the house is worth and how, once sold, he'll be able to get his money back in full, with interest.

That's why I moved out last night. THANK FUCK! I loaded the car with the few possessions I have and want to keep with me. Everything else is in storage. Eventually, I'll arrange for it to be removed and disposed of, as it's unlikely I'll want to keep anything beyond a few of Toby's things.

In the meantime, I've checked into a hotel for tonight (bliss!) and am typing this while Cristian is at work. I've already asked him to get off earlier if he can because we need to talk. I plan to tell him everything. Within reason.

I've never fancied myself as an actress, but I do know it won't take much to be convincing. He loves me, and I'm counting on him being biased towards me and against my abusive, mentally unstable husband who is about to be released from a mental institution. Well, it isn't quite that extreme, but he won't know any different.

I'll explain that there are things about my marriage that I am going to need to deal with over the next few weeks, although I plan to make it back to the city as often as is possible. In the meantime, there are some things I am going to need his help with because, all being well, we'll soon have both the money and the freedom to do whatever we choose.

Assuming I can survive the next few weeks with that man. Although, the way I see it is, if I can survive my parents, then I can definitely survive him.

36. THE SWARM

DECEMBER 18TH
(3 WEEKS LATER)

Marco. Porthcove. 11:30.

I am in a good mood.

Yeah, I know, try not to be shocked. I can't believe it, either – to the point where I keep checking myself just to make sure that I'm not dreaming again.

On the other hand, the vision of Irvin's hairy arse cleavage as he climbs the stepladder to secure light fixings is real enough to tell me that this can in no way be a dream or a figment of my imagination unless there is something much more seriously wrong with me.

No. This feeling is all because of what Ellie said before she left this morning. I am so excited in a way that I can't even describe. And the reason why I'm questioning this is because I want – no, I *need* – this to be real because not only is it a positive step forward, but it may also suggest that my marriage still has the chance to heal.

Don't get me wrong. I'm big and ugly enough to know that things can and will never be the way they were. It's going to take time and maybe even some serious rooting around in the darkest, foulest places of our most disfigured and painful thoughts for us to get back to anything close to a normal life, but I'm ready. I am prepared to do whatever it takes to get *us* back.

Shit. Maybe I am making all this up, after all, because that doesn't sound anything like the bloke I was a few months back.

I miss him.

I do. At least, I miss his approach to life because he was able to stumble through it with a devil-may-care attitude, which meant that he was able to act on things in a much more timely and, yeah, perhaps even more effective manner as compared to this new simpering fool I am, who dotes on puppies and revels in home makeovers.

Yeah. That's as poncey as it comes. But I'm fine with that, which is probably just the Christmas spirit talking.

That's right. It's Christmas next week! And this morning's chat really brought that into focus.

Ellie's right. This year is undoubtedly going to be brutal without the little man. It's the one year where we could both probably benefit more from feeling connected to the rest of the world rather than isolating ourselves, which is why I think that Ellie's idea is brilliant. It's exactly what we need to get us through Christmas, so I've been busy making an additional list of all things Christmas that we're going to need if we're hosting a party.

And yes, of course, the memory of my last disastrous get-together crossed my mind. It was triggered by that very word, *party*.

But, since that was my delusion and this is my reality, I gave it a swift kick up the arse and told myself to focus instead on making these celebrations the best we've ever had. Which, of course, as you know, instantly invoked feelings of guilt because I felt like I was celebrating the fact that my son is dead.

Yeah. And I wanted to spiral, but I didn't. I turned the frown upside down and told myself instead that this is not only going to be a celebration of the end of renovations, but also a celebration of the young man who made me a better man in many ways.

I love you, Toby.

So, I sent a text to my trusty, seemingly super-connected builder this morning, asking if he knew of any places where I could get a *real* Christmas tree. Turns out that he has another *mate* who owns a farm shop-slash-garden centre a couple of miles away that, at this time of year, happens to specialise in real Christmas trees.

Which is why, at this very moment, I am up a ladder hanging battery-powered garden lights on a 7-foot Norway Spruce that the boys had to pretty much wedge into the corner of the room by the patio doors.

Yay!

OK. So, I may have been a tad overzealous, but I was feeling positive after Ellie left. So, when he asked what kind of tree I wanted, I said I'd take the biggest. And when he asked what kind of lights, I said the best, and lots of them, along with those real, red and gold baubles and not the ones that chip easily.

Of course, thirty metres of outdoor, water-sealed, multicoloured LED lights was probably overkill, but these are fantastic. They're mains-operated, but also come with a rechargeable battery which means that they won't go out even if we have a power cut. And the best part? For the first time since we got here, the house smells beautiful. Alpine fresh, just like the outdoors.

Yeah, I know. Impulse buys and all that. But I'm sure Ellie is going to love the fact that I've brought some warmth and colour to this place. Right?

Right?

Yeah. Thanks for your support.

Wrap-around complete. I step down from the ladder and am ready for the big switch-on. In the absence of a celebrity, I let Irvin do the honours and we all toast the new technicolour marvel with a cup of tea and a bacon sarnie.

If I may say so myself, the tree looks beautiful, and, for the first time in what feels like a long time – I seem to say that a lot, like I've been stuck at the bottom of a well all this time – I'm feeling elated.

I also had a chat with Irvin about the chances of getting everything done before Christmas Eve. The question did make him scratch his head and stare off into the middle distance for a while, but he came back with a smile and confirmed that they should be able to make it happen if they work through the weekend.

My thoughts exactly.

He was surprised when I told him that he and the boys are invited to the party, with their plus-ones of course. I told him it was only natural since they're the ones responsible for turning my life around. Although I didn't quite put it in those words.

Rosy apples on full display, Irvin said he would talk to the *missus*. When I told the lads, they said that they normally rock up at Irvin's anyway. So, hole-in-one as far as I'm concerned. And it is therefore with a big grin on my face that I give the multicoloured tree one final look before making my way up the stairs.

Irvin worked on the plumbing first thing today, which meant I couldn't have a shower, but I've just received the green light – which is good because I still have a sore neck and a chill in my bones from spending the night on that chair.

Who knows? If the tree is a hit and I play my cards right, I may even get lucky tonight.

And, of course, the thought of that is one of the reasons why I'm standing completely starkers in front of the full-length mirror right now. Yes, I know it sounds vain, but I assure you it isn't. In the past few weeks, getting out of bed has been a purely functional thing, as has showering, eating, and working on this place. In addition to all that, Ellie hasn't even looked at me that way once.

I have functioned on autopilot.

When the simple act of getting out of bed and on with the day is a chore, the last thing you tend to think about is how you look. But today I'm curious.

What does my wife see? What would the ghosts of lovers past see? Do I still look like that actor… or one of those country bumkins with mismatched clothes, wiry hair, and bird's nest for a beard?

OK. My eyes are looking a bit puffy, and I'm sure I've developed a few more wrinkles around them in the last two weeks. Although, they're still green enough in the daylight. Not looking too dull.

Didn't I mention that? Even the weather's mood has improved. Nothing spectacular, but the cloud-smeared, faded blue sky is back again and a far cry better than grey slate or the rain clouds that otherwise appear to have camped out here.

So, my nose isn't quite bulbous yet… still leaning to the left a bit in the boxer kind of way. My beard definitely needs a trim. My chest has a good smattering of hair and my pecs may not be what they used to be, but at least my belly is fairly flat. Although, yeah, if you look close enough, there is a bit of a beer belly there, but I can sort that out if I keep running and throw in some sit-ups.

That pleasure trail that I've been cultivating, because I know Ellie likes it, could probably do with some taming. And him... well, apart from looking a bit sad for obvious reasons, he looks the same as he always has, and I'm not bragging or anything, but most girls have said that, in their opinion, he's larger than most. I suppose that's the only survey I can reference it to–

What the fuck am I doing? I'm standing in front of the mirror like one of those meatheads at a gym. No offence, but come on, we've all seen the Instagram snaps. What the fuck is wrong with me? Bloody reduced to the neurosis of a pubescent teenager.

Get on with it!

In the bathroom, I vigorously brush my teeth because my mouth's so furry that it feels like I've swallowed a bloody squirrel.

There's nothing wrong with you. Your wife always makes an effort to look nice for you and you should for her. It's only right. No, it's your marital duty.

I rinse my mouth, then move over to the shower where I run the tap and stop just short of crossing my fingers... because I have no idea how the hot water is going to behave today, although Irvin assures me it's all working fine.

I like Irvin and everything, but he did say the same thing about the storage heaters.

But, to my absolute joy, the water runs hot.

I step inside the tub and pull the crinkly curtain across with the same smugness of the other day since Irvin has confirmed that, with the exception of some filling and painting, they should be done with the hallway and toilet downstairs today, which means they can make a start on this room tomorrow. He already has the *furniture*. It's just a case of taking out all this old crap and replacing it with the new.

"Your days are numbered," my echoed voice speaks to the ugly room.

Oh, and the hot water feels absolutely sublime, massaging that ache at the back of my neck and driving the ever-present chill from my bones.

Sarah.

What?

Sarah. I should invite her to the party, too.

Why?

She's pretty much the only friend I have here, and she saved Buddy.

She didn't save Buddy. The vet did. Does that mean you want to invite him, too?

Oh, bugger off!

Soon, you'll be....

I leave the thought unfinished because I hear the door click and creak open. The mournful, elongated sound is swiftly followed by a cold chill that literally ruffles the shower curtain. My eyes flick open and I squint through the water and the blur of the curtain, half-expecting there to be a shadow out there. I don't know why because Ellie isn't here, and I doubt one of the boys will have just walked in.

Would they?

"Hello?" I call out just in case. "Anyone out there?"

There's no reply – just the distant sound of music drifting up the stairs from the workmen's obligatory radio, along with the hiss and now the sputter of the water which I know is a prelude to... fuck!

Freezing water now!

I jump to the opposite side of the bath as if the innocent clear water has suddenly turned to acid. I spit out the freeze as my muscles clench, limbs quiver.

Slam!

I swear again. The door has gone in the opposite direction, banging the hell shut and almost giving me a coronary.

I remain motionless as water gurgles and belches down

the drain. I almost expect to hear a snicker from one of the boys, but that's ridiculous, especially since I'd be able to see their shadow through the curtain, and yet... I still feel compelled to swipe the thing across, rings jangling and water now spraying over the side of the bath and onto the tiles.

There's nothing in here. Just me, my imagination, and the inevitable sense of vulnerability that comes from being naked.

I listen for the now reassuring sound of the radio, and it's still there, albeit weaker as it pushes its way through the gap under the door. I watch the water collect on the tiles before hastily pulling the curtain back because I don't trust the floor to be completely waterproof.

The shower has stopped spitting at me like the usual disgruntled reptile now, and I can see that the steam has returned, so I hold a hand and then my body under it.

Yes, that's more like it.

I wait.

After several seconds, I pour shampoo onto my hands and then begin to build the lather in my hair, being sure to quint my eyes open from time to time because that's one of the neuroses I've developed since arriving here. I don't know what I'm expecting to see exactly, but it doesn't stop me from doing it.

As I'm about to get ready to rinse, I feel the distinct vibration of something moving across my hair.

My eyes spring open automatically and I freeze for a few seconds, the shower hissing and my heart thumping, to see if the legs of whatever it is, most likely a giant spider, start crawling down my ear and into my line of sight – which is probably when I'll most likely freak the fuck out, start screaming like a little girl, and accidently fall out of the bath and onto the floor, where the lads downstairs will hear me and come rushing in to find me stark bollock naked.

Wow. Yeah. I spend way too much time alone.

And yet, no matter how long I wait and listen to the water hissing and gurgling away, nothing happens. So, I move my hand up to my hair, where I imagine the eight compound eyes are enjoying their morning deuce without a care in the world.

It's OK. Just flick whatever it is off and away from you… although, with the curtain there, it'll probably just bounce back. OK. So, I'll flick it to the opposite side of the bath.

Right.

Three.

Two.

One.

Flick!

Nothing.

Flick! Flick!

Still nothing.

It's only after feeling all over my head with both my hands for the best part of a minute that I accept that there's nothing there. But I felt it. I'm sure I felt it. Something crawling across my scalp.

Now I'm just creeping myself out.

Sighing, I gingerly return to the matter at hand, speeding through the scrubbing and moving swiftly onto the rinsing so that I can open my eyes once more.

Yes, the room is still empty. No, there is no shadow beyond the shower curtain. Yes, the door is still closed. Yes, the room is still hazy with daylight.

So, why do I suddenly feel unwelcome?

Exposed.

I hurry through the rest of the process because now, being in here just doesn't feel right, and I'm about to finish up when I spot movement out of the corner of my eye. Something in the bath, on the opposite side. Something that I'm sure wasn't there before.

Was it?

As I move to investigate, the shower starts to sputter in its usual tell-tale way before invoking a gasp and plunging my body into an involuntary spasm as freezing water rains down on me.

"Fuuuuuck!"

I hastily and angrily shut the downpour off.

Then, after giving myself a few seconds to recover from the shock, I look back down at the opposite end of the bath, the plughole.

Yes. There's definitely something sticking out of there, and it looks like… legs! Long, spindly legs poking up from the hole as if, whatever the creature might be, it's lying in wait.

Water drips and echoes loudly. I start shaking as my body begins to react to the freeze of the room.

I'm done with this shit.

I move to swipe back the curtain, but as I do, so do the legs.

So, I move again, and once more, the emergence progresses. It's as if the thing is connected to me. Sensing and then mirroring my movements.

Readying itself for an attack.

"Fuck," I utter under my breath, because whatever is lurking down there has definitely moved. It's moved, I know, because now I can see that it's partially emerged from its hidey hole, bringing those articulated legs into focus.

It's definitely a spi–

No, wait. Actually.

Blinking back the water droplets clinging to my eyelashes, I lean forward and a little closer.

Closer.

I can see now that the articulation of the legs has a curve to it. A soft curve as they fan out of the plughole, and… yeah, that's more than eight legs… in fact, they don't even have the angular shape of legs, as they're much rounder.

Oh, for Christ's sake. "Ellie!"

I crouch down and am already cringing as I tug at the strands of hair.

The more I tug, the longer the hair becomes, until I pull so hard that the drain ring thing springs away from its moorings and spins around the hair like a fucking pendant on a necklace.

I gag as realisation hits me.

Ellie's hair is shorter now, blonde. This hair is longer, thick, black, and disgustingly gunky.

I throw the strands down, they fall to the bath with a sickeningly loud slap, and I'm just about ready to heave when movement overhead catches my attention as a shadow jitters across the room. I snap my head up, but there's nothing there.

I definitely saw it. Something moved across the window, to the point of casting a bloody shadow!

Slowly, I rise to my feet once more and force my mouth shut because my teeth are chattering, and my breath, consisting of short, sharp rasps, is actually fogging out in front of me again.

Can you fucking believe that?

Cue fight or flight and a sudden flash of anger that sees me sweep back the shower curtain in one swoop.

But there's nothing in here. Just daylight flooding in through the window, bouncing and glinting off the walls and the puddles I've created on the tiled floor.

What's happening?

Then I hear it. It's barely noticeable above the distant, tinny sound of the radio, and the ever-present rumble of the surf, but it's there. Closely followed by that unmistakable flicker of movement.

Slowly, I turn my head, look over my shoulder, and freeze.

My muscles have locked into a spasm of inexplicable terror. There is a whole clump of them. In the corner of the ceiling. Immobile, but for the occasional flick of a wing. Their beady black eyes shifting, antennae twitching, and the skeletal features of their furry grey bodies rippling like a living Halloween decoration.

The black moth is back.

And he's brought company. There's at least a dozen of them merged to form one giant, wriggling inkblot painting.

A bang on the door scares the shit out of me and I instinctively look over just as a muffled and yet familiar yap cranks up on the other side.

Buddy.

I take a step in that direction, moving away from the burgeoning black stain on the ceiling as the skin of my naked leg squeaks loudly against the side of the bath. The sound is like a starting gun in the still of the room, and the clump of furry skulls explodes into a flutter of wings diving at my face, sweeping over me and then around the room in a flapping frenzy. The action causes me to jolt backward, slipping on the wet bath and plummeting over the side, where I crash to the floor with a loud smack.

Pain shoots up my left arm, which I instinctively pushed out to break my fall, and the agony sends a wave of nausea up my scrotum and into my brain. The shockwave is so powerful that my vision dims and I think I'm going to pass out, but I don't... although it does take a few seconds for me to regain my bearings and realise that my fall was actually broken by the clothes I discarded on the floor, even though it doesn't feel like it.

Buddy is barking and scratching loudly now. Demanding to be let in. I want to call out to him but think better of it. I don't want to cause another fracas of wings.

I grimace as I try to sit up and see that the furry clump has relocated to a different corner of the ceiling now, but I barely have time to register that before my attention is drawn to another sound coming from inside the bath.

Gurgling and belching... as if the water is still running, but it isn't.

I wince against the pain in my elbow as I heave myself onto my arms to sit up, temporarily grateful for the fabric beneath my naked body, and then an ear-piercing squidging sound slices through the still of the room.

Over there. Jesus Christ, the bath is shaking. Moving.
Something is inside it!

I duck, throwing a protective arm up as the swarm disbands once more and divebombs into the bath.

I wait, expecting the grotesque murmuration to rise once more, but it doesn't. Instead, the room is filled with a series of high-pitched squeaks that resonate out of the bath and around the empty room. I cover my ears just as the vibration of something *thumping* around in the bath travels through the floor, up my legs, and into pit of my gut. Then, to my absolute horror, unfurling over the rim of the bath like giant, articulated insect legs. Pallid. Shrivelled. Long. Bony.

Fingers!

I've barely managed to process what I'm seeing when

another set crawls over the other side. Closely followed by two deformed hands attached to extended veiny arms that, like albino snakes, slither over the side of the porcelain bath until they touch the tiled floor with a sickening squelch.

The foul stench of decay washes over me as I shimmy backward towards the door, behind which Buddy continues his frenzy of barking, growling, and scratching.

I open my mouth to scream, but nothing comes out other than a crackled croak when I see the crest of a tangle of black hair emerge from inside the bath like a scene from one of the worst horror flicks. The curtain of hair shifts, untangles, and grows until it's hanging over the side, supernaturally oozing down and over the two chalky, purple limbs on the floor before the whole bundle of grotesqueness inches its way out of the tub in a skin-crawling cacophony of pops, clicks, and asthmatic sighs.

I will my body to move further, but I'm up against the door now. The handle towering high above me as dirty broken nails tap, click, and scratch on the floor and withered claws reach towards my naked feet.

Click! Scratch! Tap! Click! Scratch! Tap!

I snatch my foot away, but they keep reaching.

Closer….

Yap! Yap!

Closer….

Click! Scratch! Tap! Click! Scratch! Tap!

The thing continues to slither and drag itself towards me, back arched into a grotesquely inhuman contortion straight out of hell.

Drag! Scratch! Tap!

Woof! Woof!

Drag! Scratch! Tap!

I snatch my foot away as filthy, jagged nails reach out for it.

Closer….

The hair is parting now, slowly revealing ghostly white and black ulcered skin with two ocular cavities for eyes that have melted down the face to where a cheek once was but is now just putrefied flesh. Underneath, there is only a gash for a mouth, out of which the thing emits a wretched squelch of a moan that metamorphoses into an ungodly screech akin to the collective torture of a thousand cats that fills and echoes around the room.

37. ON THE COUCH

LONDON· FRIDAY 10:30·

You know that scenario that I said I dreaded? You know the one where the lads rush in to find me stark bollock naked?

Well, that's exactly what happened.

Having heard the sound of my body slamming against the bathroom floor, the trio of men rushed up to investigate.

They found a howling dog on one side of the bathroom door, and me with my shrivelled manhood, cowering and howling in the corner on the other.

I should point out that they became aware of my plight not because I was heavy enough to shake the whole house, but because Drew happened to be prepping the ceiling just under the bathroom for its paint job at the time. And, just for the record, um, my *shrinkage* was because it was freezing cold in that room. So cold, in fact, that Irvin sent the other guys packing while he helped me back into the bath and then turned on the hot water.

That's odd, isn't it?

In any other circumstance, the idea of getting butt naked in front of a complete stranger who is not a beautiful woman isn't something that appeals to me in the least. I had enough of that in boarding school. And yet, in this case, like then, it didn't even occur to me to be concerned about it.

Now, of course, it's all I can bloody think about. And that cringe of embarrassment I feel is the same each and every time. I am never going to live this one down.

Note to self… never drink with or invite any of those men

to any gathering that may involve alcohol because there's a good chance that I become most reluctant fodder for much hilarity.

See? I'm still cringing and holding my head in my hands at the incomprehensible memory of what I must have looked like on that floor in front of a bunch of builders. Face ashen. Body shaking. Dick shrivelled.

Oh God.

Yes, I know this all sounds a bit shallow, considering everything I believe came before it, but you'll appreciate that I'm trying to make light of what was quite clearly one of the most horrific waking nightmares I have ever experienced.

I'm sorry. I know you want me to believe that it's more than that, but right now, that's all I have because, quite frankly, I don't have much more capacity for anything else.

This is it. The moment I was dreading has arrived because, if you were anywhere near me last time, you will know that… that… thing that emerged from the bathtub bared a hideously uncanny resemblance to one of the *intruders* from last season's freakshow, which can only mean one thing.

I've relapsed.

Everything I've experienced thus far was just some kind of prelude to my descent back into madness or denial or whatever it was that put me in that place previously. And if this gets any worse, I just don't think I'll ever recover. Ellie will lock me up, and this time she'll ask Holmes to throw away the key because there is absolutely no doubt in my mind that my marriage will not survive it. We're barely hanging on as it is.

That's why I'm here again.

I am hoping that this man who was able to help me through one of the most traumatic and devastating events of my life can help me through this now.

"Marco?"

"Yes." I look up at Doctor Ethan Holmes, and his furrowed, eager look of a salivating dog instantly transports me back to when I was last under his care, which makes me want to puke.

"Where were you right then?"

"Just thinking about what it's like to be here again with you. You know. Old team back together again. Batman and Robin, wading through the cesspit of Marco Battista's mind."

"Well, I see you've retained that inimitable flare for sarcasm."

"Of course. How else would you and I wile away the time?" I chase that up with my best grin, even though I know he'll see right through the fact that I want to be here again only as much as most people want to have multiple root canals dug out at the same time.

"OK. Why don't we start with a simple question I know you'll be all too familiar with?"

"OK. Straight in there. I love it," I say, making a show of rubbing my hands together. "Hit me, Doc!"

"Why are you here?"

"Well, isn't it obvious?"

"No. Not really."

"Come on, Doc. We went through it last time." I'm keeping my smile because I want the man to cut me some slack.

He doesn't.

"No. We didn't."

I glance away. I need a moment, but I try to keep the mask on my face because I'm worried that, the second I let it slip, he'll see right through me and this whole session will quickly spiral out of my control.

"Marco. I can't help you if you're unable to trust me," he says softly. "You know the drill."

I turn to him, and he gives me a disarming shrug.

I swallow.

He shuffles in his chair. "OK. Why don't you tell me how the refurbishments are going?"

I nod eagerly. Grateful. "They're going well. Really well. Pretty soon, we'll be able to put the place on the market and get the fuck out of there."

"Is it that bad?"

I scoff. If only he knew. "Yeah. It's really that bad."

"Tell me."

"Wow. So, things have been dull around here, then. What?

No sexually frustrated housewives to spice up your day? Ah. Or husbands?"

The doctor smiles. He knows me and is unaffected. Instead of taking the bait, he leans forward in his chair. "Marco. I'm saying this because I know you appreciate candour. You came here before and seemed troubled by something, but unable to share. And you've come back again today after telling me that I shouldn't hold my breath. I think it's safe to conclude—"

I pull a pained expression. "You remember that, then?" I ask, and I can feel my cheeks burn.

Holmes must notice, too, because he moves fast to counteract. "I'm glad you decided to come back. I really am, but you know all too well that if you aren't completely honest with me, if you insist on keeping up the bravado, then I can't help you. You know that better than most."

I can feel the tension melting in my shoulders because, as much as I hate being here, I know, or at least I feel, that I am safer here than I am on my own. But I have no clue where to start.

And so the doctor rides to the rescue once more. "So, how are you getting on with the puppy? What's his name? I don't think you mentioned it last time."

"Buddy. His name's Buddy. It wasn't going to be a permanent thing, but I started calling him that and it just stuck. And…" I realise that the thought of that little pain in the arse has just brought a smile to my face.

That dog sat by the bath the whole time I was in there. Oh God, I just had a flashback to that and Irvin running the hot water over my naked arse.

Fuck!

"…he's great. Always getting himself into mischief," I say, smiling.

"You seem smitten," Holmes says, acknowledging the grin I still have on my face.

I nod. "Yeah, in a way. As weird as this is going to sound, he reminds me of Toby." I swallow the lump that's suddenly formed in my throat and then move to justify it because, well, it does sound weird. "He does things, you know. He's curious and gets himself into trouble all the time, but he's cheeky and often cute with it."

"And what about Ellie? Does she feel the same?"

I sneer, "Um, no. She wants me to get rid of him."

"Rid of him? Why?"

"Oh, there was a situation with her laptop and Buddy got the brunt of it. It, um, caused a lot of friction," I conclude with a nod.

"Would you like to talk about it?"

I pull a face.

"OK. Well, maybe we'll come back to it," he says quickly. Code which I know means that he *will* bloody come back to it. In the meantime, he changes the subject. "So, tell me about progress on the house. When I asked about it, there appeared to be some eagerness in your tone. As if something had happened to exacerbate things. Has something happened?"

I nod, reluctantly.

"OK. Would you like to tell me what exactly?"

I don't answer because I'm busy looking at my feet. For some reason, the tips of my toes are freezing. Like I walked here barefoot.

The persistent rumble beyond the window reminds me again that I'm back in the city. I don't miss that sound. I don't miss it because it, too, has become synonymous with the last time I was in treatment. It's like the worst soundtrack to the worst movie. And, once again, no matter how hard I try, I just can't imagine myself coming back to live here.

You don't have to.

"Marco?"

I look up. "I think I'm seeing things, Ethan. At the house," I croak, finally meeting his gaze. The tide of saliva has now left my mouth in readiness for the verbal tsunami that's undoubtedly yet to come. I reach for the water on the table in front of me.

"OK," Holmes acknowledges, as if I've just told him that it's a bit chilly out. "What kind of things? Like before?"

"No. Not like before. This feels different. More real. It's persistent. Like it's happening in real time."

"Can you give me an example?"

I take my time. Open the bottle and pour water into the glass, which isn't something I'd normally do. I'm stalling. I know he knows it, too, because I can feel his patient gaze on me. I take a good swig from the glass, swallow, and then I mumble, "Toby. I've seen Toby there."

"At the house?"

"Yes, Ethan, at the house," I confirm irritably. I take another swig before adding, "I think I'm losing it, Ethan. I think it's happening again."

"Well, technically, from what little you've told me, it isn't like before. You said it's persistent. By that, I'm assuming you mean that you're not having any of the *resurfacing* that you did last time. You know – waking up, losing time?"

I shake my head.

"So, it doesn't necessarily sound like a relapse. More like something new. Are you still taking your medication?"

"I have been, yes."

"Have been?"

"What?"

"You said *have been*? Verb in the past, as in you were taking them but now aren't. Rather than *am* taking them."

Shit.

"Are you having a fucking laugh?" I snap. "You're really splitting words right now?"

He looks at me and cocks his head.

I back down and answer. "Well, right at the beginning, I wasn't. But now I am," I say sheepishly.

"Can you put that into days for me?"

"I don't know. A week. Maybe a little bit longer."

"So, it hasn't been that long? You know it takes a while—"

"Yes, I know. Like antidepressants, it takes a while for them to build up in your system. But, Ethan, these things don't seem to be doing anything. I mean I'm fully lucid all the time. I don't have any of the side effects, either."

He squints at me. "Marco, you know that just because they state *possible* side effects, it doesn't necessarily mean you'll–"

"Look, Ethan, this isn't about the fucking meds!" I snap, leaning forward in my chair.

"OK," he says calmly. "Tell me what it's about."

"Do you believe in ghosts?" Those words have come rushing out like tell-tale siblings eager to get me into trouble. I study his face for a reaction, but I don't find much… just a faint smile.

"You think the house is haunted?" he asks.

"I don't know. Isn't that why I'm here?"

"I don't know. Is it?" he asks.

I allow myself to be absorbed by the couch, which is actually much comfier than that torture contraption he had at the institute. "Touché," I say with a sigh. "Did you know that the Death's-head Hawkmoth has a wingspan of almost five inches, and that it's part of a three-moth species, and that it is actually capable of emitting a squeak when alarmed?"

The doctor is looking at me like I've just lost my mind. And no, the irony of that is not lost on me.

"Yeah. I Googled it. Apparently, beyond being made famous in the film *The Silence of the Lambs*, this creepy-looking thing with what looks like a skull tattooed on its back is, in ancient folklore, also associated with the supernatural."

I watch the doctor's neat eyebrows arch. "I don't follow."

"There was a whole swarm of these things in my bathroom," I say quickly, and then I let out a chortle. "No, I just heard that, too, and I know what it sounds like."

"What does it sound like?" the doctor asks calmly.

"I sound like a fucking crazy person, Ethan. And yet, there I was Googling this thing because, amongst other things, that place appears to be plagued by them. Well, sometimes; the rest of the time, they vanish into thin air."

I'm sitting forward again, sipping water once more and doing everything I can to suppress the tremble in my hand. But I know there's no point – this bloke already has that look in his eyes like he's dealing with unexploded ordinance and any sudden movement is going to set me off.

The room falls silent. Birds tweet beyond the glass. I shouldn't have said all that, because if I didn't seem like a loony before, I definitely do now.

The doctor sits forward and smiles. "Marco, can you sit forward for me?"

"What?"

"Just bring yourself to edge of the couch for me, could you? Please."

I shoot him a look, but comply.

"Now, could you just breathe for me, please."

I roll my eyes. "Oh for fuck's sake, Ethan."

"Please. Just indulge me, will you? Please."

Eventually, like a sulky teen, I comply.

"In through the nose. And out of your mouth. In through the nose and out of the mouth. Please. I know it feels silly, but I just need you to reset for me."

I go along with it, although I feel like a complete tool.

"In through the nose and out of the mouth."

OK. This isn't as bad as it undoubtedly looks. I can feel my pulse normalising, my heart steadying. I move to stop, but the doctor encourages me to continue, and I must do this for what feels like the best part of five minutes.

Finally, I'm able to relax back into the couch, and I have to say, it has knocked the edge off. Which is good. There was a time when I needed alcohol to do that. And yet, when somebody else is controlling the process, it feels different. Just like how when a sandwich is made for you, it always tastes better than one made with your own hands.

I know. Weird analogy, but it's the first one that popped into my head.

"How are you feeling?"

I nod. "Yeah, groovy," I say sarcastically, as if I've just returned from a weekend retreat.

"I'm wondering if you've been applying a lot of undue

pressure on yourself, Marco. You've been out of the clinic for barely a month, and I'm wondering if, despite our talks, you've been putting pressure on yourself to try to fix things, pushing the so-called square pages of the present into the round holes of the past. Have you talked to Ellie about any of this?" he asks softly.

I scoff.

"No?"

"No. Ethan, that's why people scoff like I did. It's a euphemism for, 'Are you having a fucking laugh?'"

"Why not?"

"Because she'd think I've lost it again."

"And that worries you?"

"Of course, it bloody does."

He nods.

I shake my head slowly. "Oh, Ethan," I say, gritting my teeth.

"What?"

"That fucking knowing nod like you hold the secret to eternal life, it's so fucking annoying."

"OK. What about it irritates you?"

"No. The correct way to pose that question would be to ask me what about it *doesn't* irritate me, and the answer would be nothing. I hate all of it, indiscriminately."

There's more silence. I sigh. Yes, I'm being a dick. What else is new?

Well, actually, coming to think of it. That is new.

I just realised. For the first time in a long time, I've become the old me. Abrasive. Caustic, and a prick, but only here. At the house, I feel like I'm the Stepford Wife version of myself, as creepy as that might sound.

"What are you thinking?" the doctor asks.

"That I'm being a dick." I grin.

He looks at me curiously. "OK. And that's good?"

"Yeah. It's great!"

He shrugs. "Glad I could help."

I lose my smile and say with all seriousness, "Something is

happening to me, Ethan. I don't know what it is and I'm worried that it's going to destroy what's left of my marriage and, worse, see me returned to your clinic – which, and I mean this in the nicest possible way, would be a fate worse than death. No offence."

He waves a forgiving hand. "None taken." Then he continues, "Nothing is happening to you, Marco, other than the fact that you've been putting yourself under pressure once again to try to deliver on a multitude of things that you're clearly not equipped to deal with yet."

"No, Ethan. This is more than just stress."

"You mean more, as in the house is haunted? OK. Let me ask you. And I really want you to think about this. Please. I'd like you to tell me what you genuinely believe and not what you think I want to hear. OK?"

"Don't I always?"

"Well, you've just told me you're worried about losing your marriage and ending up back at the clinic. It wouldn't be a stretch for you to say what you think you should say in order to both preserve and avoid those things."

"Jesus. It wasn't a serious question, Ethan," I say flatly.

I shift in the couch as a runaway train of thoughts starts hurtling around in my head. I take in a deep breath as I try to isolate one of them, but I can't. The problem has got to be with me. It's a relapse, surely. Right?

What about the practical things you've seen at the house?

Open doors. Anybody could have done that.

Even when you're alone?

Draft?

What you saw in the shower? The moths are uncommon this time of year. You looked it up. The apparition. That could have been your mind conjuring something.

Something I'd never seen before? Yes. We do that in dreams all the time.

This internal struggle continues for what feels like minutes before I hear Ethan call my name once more. "What are you thinking?"

"I don't know, Ethan!" I explode in frustration. "I have no fucking clue. Isn't that why I'm here?"

He sits forward in his chair again. Something I notice he does every time he's trying to make a point. "Marco, you know the process. We need to look at the environment. The history. The facts. And take it from there. So, imagine you're in my seat for a moment. This is what I've heard so far, including your previous visit. He holds out fingers as he counts off each one like I'm a fucking imbecile. "You and Ellie refused to go to couple's counselling – something I was led to believe was your decision..."

You and I both know that isn't true, but I'm not going to correct him, as he's on a roll.

"...which means you both haven't had the opportunity to work through your grief."

He holds out another finger. "You've told me that you've stopped taking your medication for whatever reason, and now you're seeing things."

"Oh, come on, you're twisting and oversimplifying what I said–"

"Am I? I don't think so. That's what you told me."

"I'm taking the fucking pills!"

"Are you sure about that, Marco? Or are you just taking them now because you want these so-called apparitions to go away? We talked about this. You can't just switch these drugs on and off. It takes time for them to build up in your system."

Another finger on his unspoken list of *Yes, you are losing your marbles*. "You tell me that your marriage is in crisis and that you're afraid of losing your wife, and yet it sounds as if neither of you has given the other the time you both need to grieve, and you've rejected the only means of support you both had to work through the pain you're both undoubtedly still experiencing. This has resulted in these renewed bouts of anger.

"You rescued this puppy which Ellie hates, but you've now turned it into the physical manifestation of your son–"

"Now, hold on, that isn't what I said–"

"Can't you see the pattern here, Marco?"

"Stop it."

"You are deliberately sabotaging your recovery so that you can avoid the difficult realities of your new life–"

"Stop."

"And you've brought yourself back to me because you want me to validate that there's something wrong with that reality–"

"I said shut the fuck up!" I launch myself out of the chair and move over to the window. Away from him. Away from his words.

"You're still the same persistent little fucker, aren't you?" I seethe, looking out the window. Absorbing the view in the hope that it'll help ease the thumping in my chest, as well as the urge to stomp over and punch the bastard in those spectacles.

He gives me a minute before breaking the silence with, "Marco. We've been here before, you and I. I know you. I know you appreciate straight talking, but it's up to you. It's really up to you. We can dance around this thing some more or we can get straight to it. Your choice."

I sneer again. "Straight talking doesn't mean you have to be a dick," I say without turning.

"Well, as always, you know I'm interested in your opinion." I can't see his face, but I know he's got that supercilious smile on it.

I want to rage against him and say he doesn't know what he's talking about, but as I stand here, I must admit, it makes sense. Not all of it, but most. He's explained more in a few minutes than I've been able to work out in a whole week, which means that as much as I don't want to give him credit, he's right.

"What do I do, Ethan?" I ask as I watch two pigeons jostle each other in one of the trees.

"Come on, Marco. You know I can't tell you what to do, but I can help you make your own decisions and perhaps add a few recommendations along the way. If you'll let me, that is."

Again, I can hear the smile in the last part of that sentence, and I turn to him and say, seriously, "OK. So, let's say you're right about some of that stuff. There are other things that can't be explained."

He lifts his hand and gestures to the sofa. "Try me."

38. THE SOUTHWEST POST

FRIDAY· PORTHCOVE· 19:03·

Statistically, men are more likely to lie to avoid marital confrontation than women, who are seemingly much more eager to address controversial topics.

Men will do anything for an easy life.

Ever since I started experiencing these things at the house, I've been inevitably questioning my own sanity, and that episode in the bathroom was the last straw. I needed a cold, dispassionate perspective on all of it, hence my visit to Ethan today that, as much as the man knows how to push my buttons, I think was useful.

However, since I'm unable to rationalise much of what's been happening to myself, I'm clearly not equipped to explain any of it to Ellie, whom I know – at the mere mention of any of this – is going to go straight to that furrowed brow look of hers, as she has every time Toby or I have been in a crisis.

She stops listening and goes straight into comfort-slash-protection-slash-reparation mode. And, well, that's not going to help either of us right now.

That's why I didn't tell her I was visiting Ethan today. She thinks I've been at Dolce Vita all day.

When she messaged, asking how things were progressing, I told her that they were progressing very well since that's what Irvin told me in his response to my own message.

Yes, I know it's bad. And yes, I know it's symptomatic of the pathological liar-slash-cheater that I used to be. But if you're judging me right now, save it, because you can't make me feel any worse than I am already feeling. In fact, as I sit on this train, rocking back and forth in my seat and watching trees skulk between the light and shadows of rolling fields, I can't help but find it oddly reminiscent of how our marriage used to be. Full of secrets.

But not anymore. I'm a changed man.

Kind of.

I know it's no excuse, but my following Ellie to London on a separate train this morning was the only so-called deceptive thing that I've done in a long time. What my wife doesn't know can't hurt her. And she has been hurt by my actions in the past for much more traitorous behaviour. I think she deserves some respite from me and my problems.

When I receive a second message from her telling me that she plans to work late and then visit her parents, I'm disappointed, relieved, and somewhat sympathetic.

Disappointed because I'm feeling optimistic and I want to share that with her. Relieved because it means I don't have to race her back to Dolce Vita. And sympathetic because anyone related to the Stevensons will know that an hour with them and their overbearing ways is like an hour of having your fingernails pulled.

No. My in-laws don't like me very much. And I'd be lying if I said that the feeling isn't mutual. Mostly because of the way they make their daughter feel each and every time she's in their presence. In fact, now that I think about it, I'm surprised Ellie's even venturing over there on a worknight. Normally, it's a big build-up over days or sometimes even weeks as she steels herself for the confrontation.

But then, as she said, her mum's been nagging her for a while, and she wants to get the visit over and done with.

So, now, as the train slowly rattles and clanks to a halt at the station, it's this thought and the fact that I'm going to spend another night alone at that place that has popped the air from my joy balloon, leaving me feeling somewhat deflated.

Nope, not doing that. Constructive move forward in the morning and regression in the evening.

I'm fine. We're fine. I'm going to go back and find the whole downstairs finished, and us one step closer to selling up and moving on with the rest of our lives.

I leave the train and make my way through the hut, and am relieved to see that the cab is waiting. Yes. This place pretty much has the one. I think it's just some bloke using the family people carrier to shuttle passengers back and forth from the station. I doubt the man even has a licence.

"Evenin'," I say through the slit in the driver's window.

"Evenin'," the man responds with a nod and a smile.

I pull on the handle and slide the passenger door open. The sickly-sweet smell of car freshener stumbles out on a cloud of warm air and dilutes into the darkness. It isn't late. Just gone seven, but around here, it always seems like the dead of night.

I lift a foot to step into the vehicle, but pause in mid-air when it occurs to me. Something I saw back there. Something that didn't register until this very moment.

I can see the driver's disembodied face watching me curiously in his wing mirror.

"Just a minute," I say, putting my foot back down on the ground and turning back towards the station.

This place really does look like a small hut. It can't be much bigger than thirty feet square. Built of wood planks painted green with a black steeple roof, a large clock, and a black sign with white lettering hanging over the entrance -- reading *PORTHCOVE*.

Trackside is an identical façade, but for two black benches and one other thing: a freestanding newspaper stand with a header that reads, *SOUTHWEST POST*.

Fresh off the press, no doubt – because they weren't here this morning – is the bundle of free, local newspapers. By *local*, I mean as the name suggests, the whole county. And, on the front page of the free newspaper, available to anybody who cares to see it, is an image and a headline that kicks me in the gut.

It's Drew. One of the so-called sons from Irvin & Sons. My builder. And he's smiling in a selfie. Behind him is the unmistakable profile of Dolce Vita complete with rescued mobile barbeque.

The worst part is the headline.

HOUSE OF HORROR UP FOR SALE

The by-line goes on to read: *Would you spend a night in this house?*

"What the fuck…?" My words, which are nothing but a whisper, are snatched by a cold breeze scurrying across the platform to be carried off into the night.

Major renovation work has begun on Clifftop House renamed Dolce Vita by the late owner and local philanthropist, Roberto Battista.

Battista, known locally as Robby, built one of London's most renowned marketing empires. He bought Clifftop House as a country retreat for his wife, the former hair model, Natalia Battista. His son Marco Battista inherited the property earlier this year after his father was found dead of a heart attack at the property. Marco Battista, former mechanic turned psychologist, is hoping that the renovations will help to dispel some of the building's notoriously dark and tragic history.

To fully understand the history of Clifftop House, we'll need to go back a few decades to….

I speed-read through the rest of the article before I'm startled by a car horn blasting twice in quick succession.

Clifftop House? Robby? Local philanthropist? Died here? Dark and tragic history?

Oh my God. There's stuff in here that even I didn't know, and I want to both rip it up and read it, but I can't lose my ride back. So, I grab a copy of the paper, roll it up, and hurry back to the waiting car.

"Gotta be somewhere else, mate," the driver explains as I approach.

"High street. Just drop me off on the high street, please," I say, sliding into the backseat and closing the door.

My mind races us as we bump away from the station towards the village. I have no idea what to do with this. There are just so many elements that I don't even know where to start.

Buddy. Think about Buddy. His cheerful face. The way he tries to wag his whip of a tail, but instead ends up wagging the rest of his body.

I hope Drew remembered to take him out today. Last thing we need is another accident.

Drew. That's what the fucker was doing.

Yep. I'm going to focus on the positive.

Clifftop House.

I'll go in, stroke the pup, and survey today's work.

Dark and tragic history.

Have something to eat and maybe chill out in front of a film.

House of Horror!

Before I know it, it'll be a new day full of hope and opportunity.

Oh, who the fuck am I kidding?

"Mate, can you take me to Smuggler's Inn, please?" I ask the driver's now ghostly face, as it's lit only by the dashboard lights.

The driver, who is probably the school caretaker moonlighting for a bit of extra cash, asks in a local dialect, "Rough day?"

"Um, you could say that."

"Well, I'm sure it's nothin' that a few bevvies won't fix," he says, glancing at me in the rear-view mirror, and I can't help but wonder if he knows. Has he seen the article?

Great. Now I can add paranoia to the rest of my neurosis collection.

"That's the plan," I respond, squeezing out a smile.

Bevvies? Oh fuck. We know how that ended up last time. A boy went missing. Oh God, but that's just it. He didn't, did he?

"S-s-sorry, excuse me," I say, screwing up my face, a hive of thoughts all buzzing for attention to the point where I'm stuttering like fucking Rain Man. "I'm sorry. On second thought, can you take me home? Just home, please," I say irritably, avoiding eye contact. And yet, when I glance up again, he's still looking me. "What?" I snap.

"You need to tell me where home is, mate."

"Oh, right. Sorry. Yeah. Dolce Vita. It's the house on the–"

"I know where it is," he says, holding my gaze in that bloody mirror again for much longer than I'm comfortable with, and I'm just about to say something when he suddenly looks away and seemingly starts talking to himself, but for the tell-tale sign of the flashing blue light in his ear.

Thank God. Saved by the blue light.

It means we don't have to converse for the next ten minutes it takes to cross the bridge over the swollen stream and start scrunching down the drive. The first thing I see through the misty windscreen is that the lights are on. Then, as we draw closer, I notice that Irvin's truck is still parked in the driveway.

The image injects a spike of adrenaline into my blood stream, and the car has barely come to a stop and I'm already tugging at the door handle, but the thing refuses to open before the car comes to a complete stop.

Which means that, by the time I step out, I'm already working myself into a state. Something that's exacerbated by the sight of the three workmen spilling out of the truck.

I extract the last two notes from my wallet and hand one to the driver through his open window, along with my best grateful smile. "Thanks a lot," I say, because it's a small fucking village and rumours travel fast. Although, something tells me that the rumour mill has already started.

I chortle – some would call it hysterically – at that thought before starting forward into a bitter wind that immediately sets about numbing my extremities. The cold feels good on my face. Clarifying. Invigorating. I would probably even go so far as to say calming, but that's only until I set eyes on Drew.

The cab's red lights have barely disappeared up the drive before I turn around and, rolled up newspaper in hand, rush over to Drew and, before I'm intercepted, manage to land a punch and much of my pent-up frustration from the past two weeks square on his nose.

The giant literally sails through the air before landing heavily on the gravelled drive.

"Have you any fucking idea what you've done?" I seethe as

I jostle to get around the blockade of the other two men to finish the job.

"Marco! Calm down. Let's just calm down," Irvin chants.

"Calm down? Calm the fuck down? Have you read this shit?" I wave the tube of so-called news at him and seriously give thought to shoving him out the way and it down Drew's cocky bastard's throat.

"I know. We know. It's why we're here, Marco. He wanted to come over to apologise."

"Apologise?" I rage. Heart pounding. Muscles clenching, and breath fogging out like fire in the headlamps. "You've ruined me! You've ruined this whole project and put yourself out of a fucking job! Apologise? I ought to ram this fucking thing down your throat, you selfish prick! Right down your throat!" I yell, struggling against the two pairs of hands pushing against my chest.

"I'm sorry!" the little shit whines, crawling to his feet and holding his hand over a bloodied nose.

"Stop fucking saying that!" I seethe through gritted teeth as I tackle the restraint of the other two. "Your sorries mean shit to me now! SHIT!"

"He didn't do this on purpose, Marco. The fool just shared some photos on his Instagram and somehow the paper filled in the rest."

"Filled in?" I glare at Irvin. "You reckon they somehow *filled in* the fact that we wanted to be out by Christmas? *Filled in* how much this fiasco is costing? Or maybe they were just guessing about what happened to me here when I was just a little fucking boy?" I choke on the last words. I don't think I've ever seen that stuff written down in black and white. Somehow, seeing it like that made it all real again. Raw.

I wipe my face with the back of my sleeve because it's starting to drizzle freezing water. And I'm grateful for it, too, because if there's any chance they can see my eyes, I don't want them to know that they're moist with tears right now – of anger, and of sorrow.

"None of us knew about that stuff," Irvin says gently.

"Well, you do now!" I yell, waving the paper baton at them. "The whole fucking village, hell, the whole county knows!"

There's another interlude as the precipitation continues to fall faster and heavier, dinging off the truck and ticking off leaves. And, I've just noticed, as if mirroring my feelings, the gentle babble of the stream has turned into a whooshing, guttural roar.

I look at the house, lights burning brightly, and am reminded of the countless life settings I went through in my head. The opportunities that the sale of this place offered my marriage. All of which have been washed away by ink on paper.

I think about telling Ellie, her reaction and what this will mean for us, and I am overwhelmed by a sense of hopelessness so great that it devours my energy reserves.

"Marco, I know you're upset," Irvin interrupts my thoughts. Speaking loudly over the downpour.

"Upset? Upset doesn't even begin to describe how I'm feeling," I say through deep breaths because I can feel the anxiety pushing its way up my chest, and I think I'm going to pass out. Yet, like a lion, I can't take my eyes off my prey, currently hiding behind the two other men.

And yes, now I can hear Buddy yapping behind the front door. It sounds like he's upset, too.

I need to see to him.

"Marco—"

"You know what, Irvin?" I interrupt. "I don't want to talk about it anymore. It's done. We're done. There really isn't anything else to say. I like you, Irvin, but please don't bother coming back. There's no point."

With that, I take me and my sodden clothes into the house and slam the door behind us.

39. TAKING SELFIES

SATURDAY· PORTHCOVE· 08:09·

It's a fantastic day to come down to the beach. The sun is warm, and the smell of fried onions is making me hungry.

But the hot dog stand is empty, as is the pink cotton candy kiosk with a giant picture of a grinning child stamped on the front. There's nobody here; the pier is deserted. I'm alone but for the breeze caressing my hair. Seagulls call overhead, but when I look up, the deep blue sky is empty.

"Toby?"

I start and look around. Somebody said that. It wasn't me, but there's nobody here but me.

"Can we have an ice cream now?"

Toby.

But there's nobody here but the haunting organ music of the carrousel, which is lifeless.

A flutter draws my attention to the pier's railing, where a group of ravens have appeared. All symmetrically aligned like soldiers on parade. I watch their heads bob up, down, and sideways. Black marble eyes swivelling. Large, curved beaks like talons snapping.

"Can we have an ice cream now?"

I turn on the spot, looking in every direction. "Toby? Toby, where are you?!"

That's me. Only, I didn't make the sound because I can't open my mouth. It's stuck. Glued shut. I touch my lips, and then try to pry them apart with my fingers, but they won't budge. They're sealed together.

"*Daddy!*"

I spin around again, but the only things staring back at me are the ravens.

My movement spooks them and they all fly off, but for three. They remain. Cawing and pecking each other. Cawing and pecking. Cawing and pecking before they suddenly freeze. Like a movie within a movie, they've been put on pause until, one by one, they start falling backward off the railing, plummeting to the rocks below

"NO! NO!" I cry, but the words push against and bounce off my lips as they continue to fall....

One...

I rush toward the railing.

Two...

I'm trying to move fast, but I can't! My feet are sinking into the wooden decking.

Three....

I reach the railing, cling on, and then look over, down at the jagged rocks bathed by the white frothy peaks of the ocean like saliva over the serrated teeth of a rabid dog.

"*Daddy?*"

I snap my head to the left and feel my body tense. There's my son, my beautiful boy, climbing onto the railing.

"NO! TOBY, NO!"

I race over, but it's too late; he's already climbing the railings. "TOBY!"

I climb after him. "NO, PLEASE! NOT AGAIN. NO!"

And I'm falling, limbs flailing, mouth open, rocks beckoning until....

I wake with a scream.

I'm gasping, spluttering, coughing, and sobbing. My hair is damp. The sheets are cold and wet around me as if I've just emerged from the ocean in my mind.

The room is bright. Sunlit for a change, and yet this does nothing to shake off the tight, chain vest of deep, gut-wrenching sorrow that is weighing me down, constricting my chest, restricting the air to my lungs.

I choke, kick the covers back, and swing my legs over the side of the bed as I clutch my chest, wheezing and gasping for air. I'm hyperventilating. The sound is so loud, I can hear it ringing in my ears.

Oh God... it's that same sensation. Gasp, splutter, pressure in my skull, and that ball of bile like I'm going to throw up right here on the bed. Right now!

Then, something touches my arm. The cold wetness slices through everything else, and I snatch it away before seeing that it's Buddy. The puppy ignores the sudden movement and, with a familiar bowed head and soft, flat, fluffy, floppy ears, climbs into my lap and puts his furry, warm paws on my belly. My instinct is to pluck him off because I feel like I'm going to puke and I don't want him to become a casualty, but I pause as I gradually become aware of the fact that it's getting easier to breathe.

The pressure in my head is subsiding. The room no longer dimming, but brightening.

I look down, incredulously, to meet the puppy's gaze.

"Buddy," I croak.

The dog doesn't react, but instead keeps those steady chocolate eyes on me as, slowly by surely, my breathing becomes easier, the thumping in my chest calms, and a peculiar warmth spreads through me, warming the blood in my veins.

Swallowing on a parched throat, I rasp, "Hey, you." As if I'm the one doing the comforting.

The first time the puppy blinks is when a runaway tear slides off my nose and onto his.

I laugh. "Sorry, mate," I say, rubbing the spot and then his head.

He closes his eyes to enjoy the sensation for a few seconds before turning his attention back to me, as if to say, *Have you pulled yourself together now*?

"I'm OK, Buddy," I say, rubbing under his chin. "I'm OK," I chant, melting into those adorable eyes.

It's because I'm cute and I say cute things.

Toby's voice sounds in my head as clear as if he were sitting in my lap. It's another dagger to the heart, but it's bittersweet. The memory of the moment as opposed to the pain.

"Thank you, Buddy," I say earnestly to the dog as if he can understand me. Interestingly, his ears do prick up. Well, his good one does, and the other tries it's best to join in, the small imperfection emphasising the handsome little fella's cuteness. I spontaneously start planting kisses on the dog's head, as I used to my son's, which more often than not would conjure squirming protestations.

In this case, the dog starts to growl and I instantly pull away, lift my hands unthreateningly, and watch as he slides to the floor with a thump.

"Oh, OK. Sorry!" I call after him as he hurries over to the foot of the bed, sits, and starts staring at the corner of the room, ears up in alert mode. I follow his gaze to the open door. It's folded back against the wall. Did I leave it that way? Normally, it would be closed first thing in the morning.

I listen for sounds beyond the threshold.

Nothing.

I listen some more.

Still nothing.

So, I wipe my damp eyes with the back of my hand, sigh, and take in deep breaths. I'm OK. I've recovered.

I run hands through my matted hair. These nightmares have been getting worse. This one was particularly harrowing. It's almost as if, the more progress we make with the house, the worse things get in life.

Oh shit. The memory of last night announces itself.

The newspaper.

That scene with Irvin.

The wine. Oh God, the bottle of wine, which is empty and on the floor next to the bloody bed! Seriously?

I groan loudly. I hate wine, but that's all we had in the house. No wonder my head hurts. I blame Ellie for having so much of that stuff around. If I didn't know better, I'd say she's swapped places with me and has turned into a raging alcoholic.

It's OK. Maybe it's not so bad. Old houses have history. Right? Empty old houses, even more so. It gives them character. Doesn't it?

Roberto Battista, dead of a heart attack in the property.

News to me!

The very same place where his wife tried to murder her own son three decades earlier.

Oh God. I run my hands through my hair again.

I can still see the words in my mind's eye.

And what exactly is the history of this place anyway? Do I give a shit?

No. I am not going to jump on my laptop and start one of those cheesy film montages of the protagonist typing queries into a search engine to find a series of dramatic newspaper articles that inevitably lead to some catatonic shell of a person left to rot in some asylum somewhere, who then, more than often reluctantly, goes on to issue some ominous foreboding about the future before the shit really hits the fan.

No thank you very much. We've already got plenty of that going on here. I'm not interested in spicing things up any further.

I don't care about the fucking history of this place. I just cared about selling it, collecting my millions, and moving on to another happier life, preferably with what's left of my marriage. Was that too much to ask?

Oh God. I must have read that article at least ten times last night. Washing each paragraph down with a swig of red, disgusting wine.

Maybe I shouldn't have said what I did to Irvin; we could still have gone ahead with the work. Worst case scenario, we could live here until it all blows over.

Ellie live here? Did you do crack last night, too? You know how she feels about living here.

OK. Well, I can wallow, or I can set my mind to some kind

of damage limitation exercise. Yes. Talk to El. She's good at that stuff. She has to write up those scenarios for work all the time.

Ellie. God, I miss her right now.

I run my hands through my hair again.

Yes, I know I'm doing it.

I'm feeling better now though. Well, my body still feels like shit. Head still feels like it's being squeezed in a vice. But the sunshine has burnt away the dregs of that shitty dream and good ole Magic Paws over there did the rest.

I look over. The puppy is still sitting on his butt, staring at the door like there's something behind it in the corner of the room. "OK, Buddy. That's seriously creepy," I say, "so you can stop now."

But he doesn't move. He doesn't even blink.

The message alert on my phone pierces the silence, making me jump, and yes, I'm getting sick of that, too. Afraid of my own shadow. I don't think I was this jumpy as a bloody child, but lately I'm as nervous as a bloody cat.

This'll be Ellie. Feels like I haven't seen her in days. I've concluded that this whole job thing isn't helping our relationship any, and couldn't have come at a bloody worse time.

I reach over, pick the phone up from the bedside table, and tap to wake the screen. Sure enough, there are a few WhatsApp messages and one missed call. *Shit. Was I that wasted?*

I check the missed call first. It's from the estate agent, Lucinda, and there's a voicemail. Great. Can't imagine what that's going to be about.

Then, I'm about to check messages when I notice that the camera app is open in the background.

I tap it and an image of the downstairs corridor fills the screen.

Oh yeah. I'd forgotten about these. It was the first thing I noticed last night. The corridor looks stunning now. Whitewashed walls, four antique bronze wall lights, and dark wood flooring. Despite everything, the sight does bring a smile to my face. Fuck you, gloomy hallway!

I keep swiping until images of the downstairs toilet (or the water closet, as Lucinda would describe it) fill the screen. Wow. It looks great. Dingy walls have been covered with a fresh mint green. The stained furniture is gone, replaced with a modern dual-flush toilet, and there's a corner sink mounted onto a small cupboard. Dark wood flooring matches that from the corridor, with chrome light fittings to match the finishes on taps and the toilet handle.

In ya face, *Good Housekeeping*!

Oh, come on, it's the first time I've done anything like this without input from my wife. You know how us blokes are; each achievement needs to be celebrated like it's the bloody Olympics.

I'm smiling again. Got to give them credit, these guys have done an excellent job down there, and so fast. Admittedly, there are three of them, but still. I'm really impressed. Shame I told them all to go fuck themselves yesterday, eh?

"What do you think, Bud? Am I an idiot or am I an idiot?"

I look up. The dog is still sitting there, staring at the wall now. "Hey! You!" He doesn't move. "Buddy!" His ears flick back and forth like furry, miniature satellite receivers, so I know he heard me, and yet he doesn't move.

I follow his line of sight behind the open door. No, I'm not doing this. There's nothing sinister lurking behind the bloody door.

"Buddy! Hey! Come on." Finally, the dog turns to look at me. "What's the matter with you? What's up?"

Obviously, he doesn't respond. He just twitches his ears a few times and then goes back to staring at what is most likely going to be a bug because it seems he can watch those things crawl around for hours.

I turn back to my phone and continue swiping. Oh look, selfies. Me, sitting on the loo with thumbs up to the camera. Me with an over-the-shoulder shot to the camera while pretending to pee in the downstairs toilet. Oh shit! At least I hope I am pretending and my aim isn't that far off.

Me in front of the corridor formally known as gloom with thumbs up to the camera, pulling a face I don't even recognise and with pupils so bloody dilated that it looks like I've been smoking weed.

Oh, I wasn't. Was I?

Chance would be a fine thing.

Another swipe, and I have to pause because of the stark colour shift from the bright lights of the hallway to stark, almost black and white shadows.

It takes me a moment to work it out, but then realisation dawns. The image was taken through the slit of a partially open door. This bedroom door. Of a bed. This bed I am sitting in.

I look up at the open doorway as if expecting to find whoever snapped the photo to still be standing there.

But there's no one.

Shadows shift as clouds temporarily smother the sun, and I swipe again. The photos were taken at night. The room is in darkness, but for the light spilling in from the bathroom. I look up. It's barely visible in the sunshine, but the bathroom light is still on.

So, I turn to Ellie's side of the bed in case she came home last night, and I was so out of it that I didn't even notice her sleeping beside me.

She isn't.

Another swipe. Closer now. The bathroom light is spotlighting the outline of someone in the bed.

My heart has obviously had enough of this because it's trying to pickaxe its way out of my chest so it can run off and leave me to it.

I swipe again, and that familiar skin prickle is back on my arms. The camera is in the room now. At the foot of the bed and focussed on the mound under the duvet from a low angle.

I look up at the empty space. There's obviously nothing there now, but I can't help but gape in that direction as my muscles tense in anticipation of what's coming next.

Another swipe.

The camera is higher now. Looking down on the bed. Looking down on me, eyes closed, mouth partially open, lying in the very spot I'm sitting in right now.

Oh Jesus. A rat's tail of a chill scuttles down my spine.

Right in the very spot I am sitting.

I don't want to yet swipe once more and receive a shock of horror when I see a close-up of my sleeping face.

A close-up of my face!

I slide backward towards the headboard, eyes darting everywhere as if whoever took these photos might still be in in the room. Tears of terror prick my eyes when the grotesque thought of someone hiding under the bed presents itself to me.

I look down at my feet. And shit! I'm starting to hyperventilate again as I imagine decrepit hands shooting out and grabbing my ankles. Slowly, I pick my feet up from the floor and put them on the bed. Then, heart thumping, sweat beading, I fold onto my stomach and crawl over to the edge of the bed.

I know exactly what lies beneath it, and with a vow never to watch another horror film for as long as I live, which is probably only going to be a few more minutes, I slowly peek over the side….

Further…

More…

A little bit more.

Nothing but a dusty floor.

The tension in my shoulders eases as I lift myself back into a sitting position and then shuffle backward to the sanctuary of the headboard once more.

You're overreacting. Ellie must have taken the photos some other time to creep you out. You just haven't noticed them before.

And that makes perfect sense. So, despite my instincts screaming to the contrary, I lift the phone again to check the dates and then–

What was that? Something in the corner of the room. But there's nothing over there but a puppy who insists on staring at things to creep me the fuck out.

And yet, sweat, like those bloody crawling insect legs, tickles my brow and I want to wipe it away, but I can't; I'm too busy surveying the room.

There's nothing here.

The house is still. Quiet.

The only sound is birdsong, the unrelenting tenor of the

ocean. Life happening beyond the glass. Away from the confines of my terror chamber.

We're alone in here, I reassure myself. So, why do I have the spine-tingling sensation of eyes crawling all over me? Like I'm being watched. Stalked!

Get a grip.

But I can't. I can't because suddenly I'm scared. Petrified as I absorb the reality of what happened. Somebody, a stranger, was in my house last night, and they had both the temerity and the depravity to creep into my bedroom and snap photos of me, while I was asleep!

I rub my arms as an army of ants begin their march just beneath the surface of my skin. The prickling sensation spreads all over my body as the room becomes charged with something that I can't quite explain.

I flinch and jolt to the side – I swear something just touched and traced the nape of my neck again, as it did the other night. *Fingers. Fingernails.*

I snap my head around to the opposite side and then back, but there's nothing there… just the cold hard wall.

OK. That's it. I shuffle to the side of the bed, swing my legs over the side, and freeze when I hear the words–

"I… like… your… dog."

The voice, barely a whisper, is clear. Melodic. Chilling. And seemingly coming from nowhere and everywhere. From inside the bloody walls!

I swallow, hard, and it's all I can do to stop myself from screaming hysterically as I wrestle away a wave of rising panic.

Flickering draws my attention to the bathroom. Although sunshine is streaming in through the window, I can still see that the light is flickering, sputtering as if it's having the life choked out of it before it pops.

"SHIT!" The sound has sent a jolt of fear through me, but I have no time to contemplate it before another noise grabs my attention.

It's faint at first. So quiet that I think I'm imagining it, but

I'm not. There's no mistaking it. It's Buddy. My cute little puppy is now growling at something I cannot see behind the door. I can only watch in abject horror as he extends his little legs to make himself appear taller. Good and injured ears at full periscope.

The growling only heightens my anxiety because now I know I'm not imagining it. I know that there is something else in the room with us. Something that is invisible to me.

"Buddy. Hey," I call to him gently as a series of hot and cold shivers rakes over me.

The dog ignores me and rears up instead, his growl metamorphosing into an angry bark that echoes around us.

I flinch to the side. Eyes darting to the door, the dog, and then back at the door again as adrenaline fuels an instinct to run from this room – now.

Stop it. There's nothing behind that door. There's no room back there for anything. It's in your head.

But not in his. I look down at the dog yapping, jumping forward, and then sliding back. His wheat-coloured fur winking in the morning sun.

"Buddy! Hey. Stop it."

Yap! Yap! Yap!

"Buddy, stop."

But the dog isn't hearing me. Instead, his bark grows progressively louder as he retreats backward, inching closer to the bed. To me.

"Hey!" I look down at him. "What's wrong with you?"

As I look down at him, I hear that loathsome, nerve-shredding, agonising creak of the door as it slowly and eerily moves to close, gradually revealing what's in the corner.

I'm holding my breath now, the pressure instantly building in my head.

Buddy is going nuts. Jumping up on his hind legs, growling and snarling at….

Nothing! There's nothing in the corner but empty bloody space!

"Buddy! Stop! Stop it!"

But he's not hearing a word I say as he slowly follows something invisible from behind the door to the threshold until....

SLAM!

The door slams shut, startling me into dropping my phone so that it clatters to the floor and skitters away.

"JESUS CHRIST!"

I hold a hand to my chest, trying to steady the pounding of my heart and the trembling of my body.

"What the fuck was that all about?"

I'm still staring at the door when something touches my leg. I scream and look down.

"SHIT!"

It's Buddy.

"Dude. What the hell? Are you trying to give me a bloody heart attack?"

The dog nuzzles my leg a few more times before collapsing onto the floor as if all of the exertion has suddenly gotten the better of him. Then, he looks up at me as if nothing is out of the ordinary.

"You just scared the shit out of me! You realise that, right?"

Blink. Blink. Closely followed by a tongue hanging out.

I bend down and rub his ears gently as he nuzzles into my hands. "What are you trying to do, huh? Huh?"

I stroke him with both hands as he rolls around on the floor. I'm sensing his rolling around through touch, of course, because my eyes aren't looking at the dog; they're still transfixed by the empty corner of the room.

40. HOT CHOCOLATE

SATURDAY· PORTHCOVE· 11:11·

So, you know in the movies where one character – generally a female – must break into the device or laptop of another character – generally a male – and how they often wait for their target to take a shower?

You know the scene; our intrepid heroine wakes from her feigned slumber and sets about her task. The audience holds its collective breath with mounting anxiety as the copy percentage bar progresses agonizingly slowly. Then, to our horror, the hissing of the shower stops, and the heroine has but seconds to spare before she is discovered….

Well, I used to laugh at those scenes. I used to think they were downright ridiculous because nobody can take a shower that fast. I mean, shit, I barely manage to lather shampoo into my hair in the time it takes such a character to wash their whole body.

Now, however, I can tell you with absolute sincerity that it is possible. I know this because I, too, managed to shower in just minutes this morning after wedging the bathroom door open with a chair and keeping my eyes open throughout.

Yeah, the bedroom thing was creepy. After that, I couldn't go anywhere in the house without feeling like I was being watched. So, I concluded that I needed to clear my head; hit the reset button, so to speak. So, I did.

Bundled up in a coat, beanie hat, and scarf, I left the house with Buddy and came out here into the winter sunshine for some fresh air and a closer look at the stream that now thinks it's a mini-river. It is scurrying almost as fast as we did out the front door.

Interestingly, we'd barely been out of the house a few minutes when I was already feeling better. Buddy, on the other hand, didn't appear to have any problems either way, and was busy sniffing the undergrowth when we spotted the red slash of a mail van appear through the trees. I thought Christmas had come early when Oscar, a surly man with a mop of curly black hair wearing a tired Royal Mail uniform, handed me a bundle of letters and offered a manufactured smile before jumping back into his van and hurrying on with the rest of his rounds.

As it turns out, the bundle wasn't early Christmas cards, but letters. Lots of them. Our redirect from the London address appears to have finally kicked in.

So, now I'm busy thumbing through all of the envelopes to find that a whole clutch of them are from my bank. And there are no prizes for guessing what they're about.

I skim-read because the sting isn't as painful that way.

OVERDRAFT FACILITY. BACK IN LINE WITH IMMEDIATE EFFECT. SUSPENSION OF DEBIT CARD AND FACILITY.

Oh shit.

Mercifully and gratefully, I'm interrupted by the ring of my mobile phone. At least I am until I pluck the thing out of my pocket and look at the screen.

Oh well, it was only a matter of time.

I take a deep breath and put a smile on my face.

"Hey Lucinda," I say brightly.

"Ma–co. Ret–call."

"Hello? Lucinda? Are you there? Hold on, the reception here's a bit dodgy."

Scooting Buddy away from the stream with my foot and shepherding him and me towards the gravelled driveway, I continue, "Lucinda? Hello? Can you hear me?"

"Ma–co. Hello? Are you there?"

"Yes, Lucinda, I can hear you. Can you hear me?"

"Just about."

"Is that better?"

"Yes. A bit," she responds, her tinny voice finally tuning in properly.

"Yeah. Reception's a bit patchy here. Can you hear me now?"

"Yeah, I can hear you. Can you hear me loud and clear?"

"Yes. I can now."

"Oh, good. Because you know I was wondering why you haven't returned any of my calls."

The straight-talking American gets *straight* to it.

"I'm sorry, Lucinda…." I'm gearing up for my excuse, but I can't think of one. "It's just been one of those mornings."

I know, lame.

"Never mind. So, this article?" she begins.

I feel sick. "I know. I–"

"I think it was inspired. Bold, and a little reckless maybe, but inspired! My phone has been ringing hot since yesterday."

"What?"

"Uh huh. Of course, I had no idea it was even coming out because you didn't bother to mention it, but once I was told, I got myself a copy. Some pretty freaky stuff."

"I know. It wasn't exactly planned, Lucinda. I–"

"Uh huh. Anyhow, I've got a whole bunch of folks who wanna know if they can come over to view the property. But, of course, since I have no clue as to how the renovations are goin', I couldn't give 'em any details."

"I, um. I'm sorry, what?"

"Hello? Has this thing dropped again?"

"Lucinda, no, I'm here. I heard you. I just don't understand. Are you saying that a bunch of people have shown an interest in the house *despite* the newspaper article?"

"I did. Are we still having connection problems?"

"No, Lucinda. I heard you perfectly clearly, but I just don't understand why anyone would still be interested in viewing the house after reading that stuff." I can feel those butterflies in my belly again. And, for once, it isn't dread but excitement.

I stop pacing and look back at the house against the azure backdrop of the ocean. It is a lovely place. Strange, but beautiful.

"Honey, you won't believe the weird shit some people are into. Your shit, as weird as it is, doesn't come anywhere close."

I nod at that, not sure whether to feel encouraged or insulted.

There's a pause. Wood pigeons coo. Birds tweet, and I'm feeling emotional. This whole thing has just been one massive mindfuck. Yeah, I know, I'm swearing more than even I would like, but come on. I think I deserve to.

"Hello?"

"Yes, Lucinda, I'm here," I say, blinking watery eyes because it looks like this whole thing may not be dead after all.

Shit.

Maybe, just maybe there's still a chance of gettin this place finished and sold.

"So? What should I tell these guys?"

I'm about to respond when Buddy barks at me. And I mean *at* me. He's stopped sniffing grass patches and is sitting on his backside staring up at me. I have no idea if he wants something in particular or is just telling me to put the woman out of her misery.

"Well, I was trying," I say under my breath, but only get a blink in response.

"Hello?"

"Lucinda, yes. No. Um, renovations are coming along well. The builders are here working as I speak..."

Yes, I know it's a lie, but who's side are you on anyway?

Don't answer that.

I go on, "The outside is done and looking great." Which it is, but for my abandoned picket fence paint job, which I either need to get to or should delegate to…. Crap!

To whom? I bloody fired them yesterday. I need to un-fire them now, and quick.

"Yeah, so that's great. The hedge trimmed back, lawn

mowed, and downstairs is all done. Hallway's looking fantastic; loo replaced. Paint job done. It's just upstairs now."

"Perfect. So, I can book some people in for tomorrow?"

"Tomorrow's Sunday."

"What's wrong with Sundays? Were you planning on going to church or somethin', because last time we talked, you didn't seem to be the church-going type. If you know what I mean?"

Huh? I'm not sure if I should be irritated or amused with my *realtor's* sassiness, but conclude that I'm in love with her right now.

"No. Tomorrow's fine. But, as I say, they haven't started on the upstairs yet."

"I wouldn't worry about that. Folk love to see work in progress because they think it isn't costing them. Anyways, I've got one couple who are desperate for a place like yours, and this whole house of horror shit has really got them turned on. I'll get them booked in for tomorrow and the rest next week."

"Christmas week?"

"Honey, I'd sell property on Christmas Day if I didn't have to pretend to be a wife and a mother from time to time!"

I shrug as if she can see me. "OK."

"Perfect. Right… Good talk. Oh, and Marco?"

"Yeah."

"Please answer the damn phone next time. I can't do my job if I can't get a hold of you now, can I?"

"Um, yes. Of course," I say like an obedient little boy.

Then there's a beep, and she's gone.

I look down at Buddy, who's still looking up at me, tail flicking from time to time.

"Oh my God, Buddy," I breathe. "We're in business. We're still in business! We're still in bloody fucking business! Woo hoo! Woo hoo!"

I've no idea what I must look like, jumping up and down and punching the air like an excited teen, but nobody's watching.

At least I didn't think they were until Buddy suddenly stops staring at me and turns to look behind me.

"Oh, No. Buddy, what now? No more creepy stuff. No more creepy stuff because I've – oh."

I've turned to see Sarah giggling as she walks over to us.

"Early morning, exercise?" she asks with a smile and a raised eyebrow.

"Yeah, something like that," I say.

I'm playing it casual, but I'm still grinning, and I already know my cheeks are red because I can feel the burn. Luckily, I can blame the chill.

Buddy has already abandoned me and is doing my favourite; trying to wag his tail but wagging his body instead as, ears down, he wobbles over to meet our visitor.

"Hey, you… hello! Hello! Gorgeous! Hello!" Sarah starts with a big smile and that special, affected voice I assume is exclusively reserved for pets and old people. Neat white teeth sparkling in the sunshine.

"For you," she says, handing me the blue flask she was carrying so that she can crouch down and make a fuss of the dog who, like the tart that he is, has already fallen onto his back and presented his tummy to her.

"Tart," I say in mock disapproval, but then, I'm probably just jealous.

Sarah is looking her usual pretty self. I know that's more lameness, but that's the only way I can describe this woman who has tucked that wavy brown hair under a red hat this morning with a mustard yellow scarf. Something that sums up her personality perfectly.

After a few minutes of making a fuss of the dog, she looks up at me and then stands. "How are you?" she asks, as a doctor would a patient.

I nod. "Yeah. OK," I say eagerly, but then I realise what she's referencing. "Oh, you've read the article, haven't you?"

She nods gravely, and then looks at the flask in my hand. "That's why I thought I'd whip up a special batch of my signature hot chocolate."

"Is that right?"

"Yep. Special blend of spices and rum."

"OK. Bringing out the big guns, are you?"

"Yeah. I figured that if your wife was home, then I'd just be someone going for a walk and enjoying a beverage, but if she wasn't, then it'd be just two friends going for a stroll, a drink, and a chat."

"OK…" I smile because I have no clue how to answer that. Several months ago, I may have come back with a smart answer, but these days… well, anything's possible.

Not that it matters because this free spirit reads my mind. "Don't worry. I'm not coming onto you. I'm not that kind of girl."

I laugh. "Phew, that's a relief, because, you know, I didn't want to say anything, but, well, it's getting bit embarrassing." I wink at her. "As it happens, Ellie stayed in London last night."

She cocks her head.

"No, nothing like that," I head her off because I can see those cogs whirring. "She had to stay for work."

"Fantastic," she says, linking my arm. "So, now would be a great time for you to show me that killer view from your back garden. I've heard it's fabulous."

"Oh, you did? Do I even want to know where?"

She shoots me a knowing look and then says, "Come on, Buddy!"

Sure enough, the dog jumps to his feet and starts following us.

Less than a minute later, I'm ditching the bundle of kill-joy correspondence on the coffee table and leading us out of the patio doors, stopping off only to give the tree a hug. You can imagine my delight when, unprompted, Sarah follows suit before we make our way through the gap in the hedge where the gate once stood. Which reminds me… I need to ask Irvin when we can expect to receive the replacement.

"Wow," breathes my plucky visitor as we step out onto the path and blink into the glacial chill sweeping in off the water.

But for the cold, it could easily be a glorious summer's day. The ocean is deep turquoise slashed with the occasional white roll of surf. Above us, giant meringues of white clouds glide lazily across a cerulean sky. Surreally, the seemingly ever-present, dark and foreboding horizon suggests something altogether different is on its way.

I'm worried that an inquisitive Buddy might venture somewhere he shouldn't so instead of taking the precarious path down to the beach, I suggest a seat on a makeshift bench carved out of three slabs of stone. There's moss growing in corners and it isn't the most comfortable looking thing, but it's enough of a spot for us to relax while we enjoy our beverage.

"Are you warm enough?" I ask.

"I'm fine," Sarah responds. "I can't feel my nose, but I'm fine," she adds with a smile. "Just kidding. This view, though…." She breathes in. "It's incredible."

Then, she jumps to her feet and tentatively walks closer to the edge so that she can peer over and down to the waves crashing and fizzing against the shingled shore, which is roughly a hundred and fifty feet below. That's around half the height of Big Ben.

I bet you can't guess who told me that factoid. Yes, I miss my son desperately.

"I suppose you're used to it," Sarah prompts.

"Sorry?"

"The view. I guess you're used it," she says, turning towards me.

"Yes. I mean no. No, it's not that," I finally manage.

She re-joins me on the bench and huddles up, the fresh fragrance of her shampoo wafting on the breeze.

Then, she unscrews one of the plastic cups from the flask and pours hot chocolate into it. I watch as the steam snakes upward before being snatched away by the wind. "Want to tell me about it? We've got the view, the cuppa. Now, all we need is the gossip."

I smile and glance down at Buddy who, like a child in a candy story, is eagerly sniffing out the various scents, alternating between the mud trail and the undergrowth. "There isn't much more to tell. That article much covered most of it."

"You know, Drew really does feel bad about what happened," she says, pouring hot liquid into her own cup.

I cock my head. "You know him?"

"Oh, didn't I mention it? He's the man I moved in with."

"You're kidding? Drew? You moved in with *him*?"

She nods.

"Bloody hell," I say like this is news to me, but you and I both know that it isn't.

"He really isn't that bad. He's mouthy, sure, but one of the nicest men I know. It's why we're still friends."

"Wow. How is that even possible?"

"It's easy when feelings aren't involved. We didn't split because we hated each other or anything. It wasn't anything either one of us did. We just grew apart. Mum was devastated."

I nod, but say nothing because I still can't imagine those two together.

Seagulls on reconnaissance glide noisily overhead. "So, was it Drew that asked you to come over?" I ask sceptically.

"Oh, no. This was all me. I saw the article and thought you could use the company."

I nod. "Well, thank you," I say, looking at her. And it's the first time since she arrived that our eyes meet and linger for a few seconds longer than they should in my emotionally fragile state.

OK. So, we'll have less of that.

"Do you know, there are things in that article that even I wasn't aware of?" I ask.

She shrugs, looking out across the ocean. "I don't believe a lot of what I read anyway. At the end of the day, they're a struggling business trying to sell papers. Facts, objectivity, they're just nice to have. Besides, most people are so braindead now that they won't read anything unless it's been sensationalised, and hyped up beyond all–"

"But that's just it, Sarah. There's stuff in there, at least the bits I actually remember, that are true. Stuff that Drew wouldn't, couldn't have known about."

She meets my gaze now, the sun highlighting the flecks of brown in those green eyes of hers.

"That stuff about my son, the…um breakdown, it's true. I'm–"

"Marco, you don't have to explain yourself to me."

"No. I want to. You're about the only friend I have here. Besides this little rascal," I say, looking down at Buddy's butt since he seems to have buried his head in a bundle of grass.

"A few months back," I say, "we lost our son." I scoff here. That bloody word. "There was an accident. He died. I didn't handle it well. What they said about me, what the whole village is probably all a murmur about right now, it's true." I half-expect her to look away, awkwardly, but she doesn't.

"We all go a little mad sometimes," she says thoughtfully.

"Wait, that's—"

"*Psycho*," she says, grinning, "Anthony Perkins says it in *Psycho*. You know that?"

"Of course, I bloody know that! I'm your quintessential horror fan. At least, I used to be before I came out here."

"Oh hell, I was looking for something profound to say. I mean, what do you say to someone who's just admitted to being a nutjob?" She smiles amiably.

"Hey, you know, you could take it a little easier with the name-calling."

"I will if you do," she says challengingly.

"Eh?"

"Come on, Marc… can I call you that?"

"Do I have a choice?"

"You've been wearing that badge. OK, maybe not exactly *that* badge, but something like it ever since I first saw you in the shop that day."

"I do not wear a badge—"

"You wear a badge. Actually, no, it's more than that. It's a shroud. It's like this big black shroud of grief, guilt, and God knows what else, and you drag it around behind you like one of those thick cloaks. I'm surprised you didn't sweep stuff off the shelves that day with it. In fact, I bet you stand here sometimes and let it billow out behind you like one of those 18th century gentlemen."

I'm gawping at her.

"Tell me I'm wrong," she challenges me again.

"You're wrong, you're absolutely wrong," I protest, but it's a feeble attempt and it isn't fooling anybody. Not least of all this sorceress of astuteness who lifts knowing eyebrows up at me before taking a sip from the cup she's nursing with red-gloved hands.

I'm speechless, which I know is unusual for me. Finally, I say, "You know, you have a way of—"

"Opening my mouth before thinking about it?" she offers.

I nod. "Yeah."

"People tell me that a lot."

"Really? Fancy that."

She pulls a face. "I'm sorry. I didn't mean to trivialize what happened to you. I just—"

"No. It's fine. You're right. In part. I have been hoarding some things," I say thoughtfully. "I can't help it. But this other stuff. I mean, you along with whatever circulation that paper has, now know exactly what happened here, to me, my parents. Things I didn't even know until yesterday – which, by the way, is something I'm still processing as I speak these words. I mean, for crying out loud, if true, it will have taken a newspaper that I've never even heard of to disabuse me of my lifelong belief that my mother stepped out in front of a train when, in reality, she drowned herself, here of all places. And my father, he didn't die in London surrounded by his second family, but of a heart attack, here. Alone.

"The worst is that these things that my mind has been trying to protect me from are also the things that forced me to act out in a variety of ways that I'm still ashamed of.

"But… the two things that I can't reconcile, no matter how hard I try, are that I wasn't the best husband and probably not even a great father. I think Ellie has been honest enough on the former, but Toby… well… he's gone."

I'm barely able to speak the last words, for the knot in my throat, but I blink back the tears, take a deep breath, and add with a bitter chuckle, "So, yeah, my… shroud. It's pretty long."

There's several seconds of silence filled in by the sound of the crashing surf before Sarah speaks. "Blimey," she says, casually. "You've got some serious issues. Has anybody told you that?"

I turn to her, and can't help but laugh. This charming woman has a unique way of offending you and making you laugh about it.

"I can recommend someone if you like," she continues. "I heard he's really good," she says.

"Yeah?"

"Yeah. He's from London. Not quite practicing at the moment, but you know, really good. I've heard he's really empathetic."

"Is that so?"

"Yeah. Sometimes acts like he's got a bit of a rod up his backside, but otherwise...."

"Rod up my backside? No. You haven't met my therapist. I mean, that bloke!"

We chuckle.

"So, what now?" she asks.

"Now, I find the best way to pucker up and kiss your uncle's backside." Ew. Just got an image of that as I remember that cleavage. Mind bleach!

"What do you mean?" she asks.

"Well, turns out that there's a lot of people out there with a penchant for *houses of horror*," I say, emphasising the words dramatically in keeping with that shitty headline as I mask the bitterness in there.

"Really?"

"Yeah. Have a couple coming round tomorrow."

"Wow. That soon?"

"Yep."

She smiles and sips from her cup. "Well, they say it takes all sorts."

I nod thoughtfully, looking out to sea. And we take a beat to watch the clouds shift and move overhead.

"I can talk to Uncle Irvin if you like," she says.

"No. Thank you, but I think this needs to come from me."

"What about Drew?"

"Oh, you mean your ex who tried to earn a couple of quid by selling a picture of my house to the local rag?"

"Yep, that's the one. For the record, I don't think it was exactly like that. I think he posted the image to Instagram. One of his mates who works for the paper approached him. Said they were going to do a small piece, say the house was up for sale. He had no idea it was going to turn into a whole dirty laundry thing."

"I suppose that's your way of saying I should forgive and hire him back?"

"Well, isn't that what we've just been talking about? Indirectly. New starts and second chances?"

I shake my head and smile as I glance at Buddy, who has now settled into the grass and is struggling to decide whether to have a snooze or enjoy the view with us.

"Especially if you ask him to donate whatever money he made from the image to a local charity of your choosing," she continues.

I look at her, and she shrugs.

"How's his nose?" I ask.

"I think it leans a bit to the right now, but he'll live."

"OK, I suppose. I like your idea, and I could use the manpower to get the place finished."

"Oh–" She's about to say something else when my phone beeps.

"Hold that thought," I say, looking at the display.

FROM ELLIE: Christmas Eve is a go with David and Aaron. X

"Excellent," I say.

"Good news?"

"Great news. Do you have plans Christmas Eve?"

"Um, not really. Normally spend it helping Mum prep for Christmas Day. Why?"

"How do you fancy coming to a housewarming party at Dolce Vita?" I probably should have discussed it with Ellie first, but, well, it's out there now. "Your parents, too, if they want."

"Um, I suppose I could ask them. Sounds great… I would love to."

"Yeah?"

"Yeah." She grins.

"Excellent. Oh, what were you going to say just before my phone went?"

"Um, I… it's fine. Don't worry. Nothing important."

"Are you sure?

"I'm sure."

41. THE SNOW QUEEN

SUNDAY. PORTHCOVE. 07:09

For once, I wake up naturally. No nightmare. No feeling of someone pulling at my arm. Nothing. I just open my eyes.

My phone tells me it's just past seven in the morning, although the new day is being strangled at birth by a sky full of irate black clouds.

It's so cold in the house that I decide to leave the bed with the quilt, wrapping it around my body like a shroud and descending the stairs like a bride on her way down the aisle.

There's a breeze blowing through the den, and I'm surprised to see the patio doors are open. I walk over to them just in time to see Ellie, wrapped in a giant red blanket, hurrying down the lawn to the coastal path.

I call out to her, but she doesn't hear me. "Ellie!" I scream, but she keeps walking.

Clutching the quilt to me, I run after her, bare feet crunching through the frost-covered lawn to the gap in the hedge where I come to a sliding stop.

The woman with her back to me, looking out across the ocean, is not Ellie. I know this because of the long black hair that is billowing out behind her as if reaching for me.

"Mummy?"

No answer. Just the whistle of the gale through that hair.

"Mummy, please…"

"Shhh… It… p… b… m… b… " the voice is barely a whisper and the words are dissolved in turbulence before they reach my ears.

"I can't hear you, Mummy."

I step forward, so that the black hair is almost touching my face now.

"It... ne... br... ba..."

"I can't hear you. Mummy, please."

I take another step forward, and yelp when something stings my foot. I look down to see jagged pebbles with human teeth biting at my flesh.

"Mummy, please! Please, Mummy!" I cry.

"It needs to stop breathing because it is not my baby!" a voice hisses.

Then, the hair parts and I can see the scalp expand, contort, and bubble until, where there was once hair, there is now a pallid, scornful and yet beautiful face full of malice.

"Mummy?"

"...father which... in heaven, hallowed be thy name..."

"Mum, please. Stop. Stop."

"...thy kingdom come..."

Please! Please, Mummy... stop! Stop!" I wail as the pebbles continue to gnaw at my feet.

Then the prayer stops suddenly and those black eyes that were once fixed on me roll up in their sockets until only the white remains before those thin, cruel lips part and the voice they unleash fills me with a dread so palpable that I can taste its foulness on the gale whipping around me. A voice that is low and yet high, loud yet whispering, one yet many. A demonic voice that could only have been born in the pits of hell, and it rasps, *"This... is... where... you end...."*

Before the thing in front of me lifts its arms and allows itself to fall backward over the cliff and plummet, red fabric billowing around it like flames until it slams onto the rocks below.

I bolt upright in a fluster of sweating and panting to a room dazzled with sunshine. And when I say dazzled, that's exactly what I mean. I don't think I've ever seen it this bright since we arrived here. It's in stark contrast to the grimness of yet another shitty nightmare.

I look across the bed and sigh. Ellie appears to be sleeping soundly next to me. However, when she senses me stirring, I hear her muffled voice say, "Marc, I'm trying to sleep!" With that, she turns over and pulls a pillow over her head.

She's referring to Buddy, of course, who has replaced the need for an official alarm call with his yapping beyond the door.

I run my hands through my hair.

The sunlight bouncing off the white sheets is starting to give me a headache. Reluctantly, I force my legs out from under the warmth of the covers and brace myself for the icy floor.

When I first arrived, I didn't think the cold could get any worse, but I was wrong.

I drag socks and clothes on as quickly as possible and then tiptoe out of the bedroom quietly, although my efforts may appear pointless given the racket coming from beyond the door.

"Hey, you," I whisper, smiling unconsciously now as the golden wonder bounces around at my feet, tail flicking happily behind him. "What are you doing out here?"

As always, he's left the sanctuary of the blanket bed I made for him in the spare room in favour of the cold, wooden floor on the landing.

"Hey," I say, crouching down. "What are you doing here?" I repeat as he licks my arm. I'm grinning because that's the effect this little fella has on me.

When he's finished slobbering and jumping on and off my feet, he looks to the stairs and then back at me, repeating the process until I see. "Do you want pee pee? Is that it? Pee pee?"

The tail wagging tells me all I need to know.

"Oh, Buddy, really?" I groan, pushing aside the thought of how I have to get up sometimes twice during the night these days. He only gets a couple of opportunities a day.

I consider the pros and cons of training him to use a litter box as we slowly make our way down the stairs, but I draw the obvious conclusion that he is a dog and not a cat, and unless I truly want to incur the wrath of Ellie, I really need to do everything I can to avoid accidents and not encourage them – if that means early morning strolls in the freezing cold, then so be it.

When we reach the foot of the stairs, I pause to look around the space. There's a peculiar stillness today. I mean, I don't think I can even hear the surf anymore. No birds. No seagulls. Just stillness. This is what it used to be like on Christmas mornings. I remember coming down the stairs and the house just seeming so quiet. On the rare occasions where Toby didn't wake up before us, that is. Here, more so.

Bright daylight is flooding in through the patio doors. The giant Christmas tree – which Ellie adores, by the way – is sparkling an array of beautiful colours, and I can't help but wonder if I'm still asleep and this is yet another of those surreal dreams to which there is normally only ever one conclusion. Something equally surreal and, knowing my mind, ghastly.

"I'm not dreaming, am I, Buddy?"

My puppy sits, looks up at me, and cocks his head as if to say, *Are you seriously asking me?*

I consider grabbing coffee. I could even take it with me, but Buddy puts an end to that idea by barking just once. The sound reverberates around the room.

"Alright! Shhhhhh!" I say in a loud whisper.

I step into boots, slide into my coat, and pull on a hat at the front door. "Well, come on, then," I say, turning to the demanding hound who instantly trots over as I unlock the door and pull it open.

What greets me is like something straight out of a Disney movie. The world is covered by an iridescent blanket of whiteness. My first thought is that it's frost, but a second look tells me that it isn't.

It's snow! It's bloody snow!

The first snow of the year, our first snow here at Dolce Vita. I say that like it's something magical. It isn't. I mean, it is, but at the same time, it fills me with an overwhelming sense of finality. Winter has come to the edge of the world and we are still here.

A whimpering sound catches my attention and I look down to see that Buddy, ever the explorer, has just attempted to investigate the foreign white stuff and ended up being absorbed by a pile of it that has collected by the front door.

I laugh as he emerges with a shake of the head.

"It's snow, Buddy. Snow," I say excitedly. And I realise that I'm not really speaking to the dog, but to Toby.

My son loved snow. This time of year, he'd be pouring over the weather forecasts in the hope of catching at least a glimpse of the stuff. And I can't help but wonder what he'd make of this. He'd be absolutely enthralled at this spectacle of sparkle right outside our front door. Untainted and untouched by humanity.

Toby.

Buddy doesn't allow my spirits to drop and, having inspected the innocuous nature of the stuff, is now wading down the virginal white path towards the gate, tail wagging and tongue dangling from the obvious exertion. The snow isn't that deep, maybe an inch or two, but his short legs are having a bit of a challenge negotiating it.

"Don't worry, Buddy. One day, you'll be bounding about in the stuff without a second thought."

He looks back at me. *If you say so*, is my interpretation of the gaze.

I follow the tiny paw prints down the outline of the garden path, but pause to take in the scenery when a murder of crows roosting on nearby branches bids us good morning. Their black bodies in stark contrast to the blue backdrop of the sky and the snow-dusted trees.

I take in a deep breath. The air is particularly fresh today, and I love it

Dolce Vita looks like something out of a chocolate box design. This place is quite literally stunning, and, once again, I find myself thinking that living here probably wouldn't be so bad… until we needed to go out for supplies and the power kept cutting out and the water froze and God knows what else.

Yeah, the view is obviously going to my head. A few months back, such sentimentality wouldn't even have occurred to me. And if it had, I certainly wouldn't have acknowledged it.

Buddy is waiting patiently by the gate now. I step forward and let him out.

He bounds off – relatively speaking, of course, considering

his diminutive size – before sniffing out an obviously suitable spot and squatting to recolour the snow yellow.

"Lovely, Buddy. I'm sure Ellie is going to…" the words freeze like the breath in my mouth as I spot something that sends a different kind of chill skittering down my back.

Footsteps. In the snow.

The trail leads from the front gate up the driveway.

Someone has been standing here. Outside our home. Watching us.

It can't have been Ellie. She's still in bed and it wasn't snowing last night. These things are fresh.

But that isn't possible. Is it?

So, now I'm crouching down to perform rudimentary CSI. I examine the prints as if I am in any way capable of identifying the type of footwear these outlines belong to. Ridiculous, I know, but it's more instinct than a conscious decision.

And it's as I'm doing this that I'm distracted by something else.

Movement. Up the driveway. Through the trees. A red blur. And it's growing. Coming towards us.

Instantly, I'm reminded of my nightmare. That thing allowing itself to fall backward off the cliff. Blanket flapping around it.

My heart is trying to get my attention by thumping against my chest, as is Buddy who has finished his business and is now growling and yapping at the approaching figure.

The images on my phone. The ones of me, asleep!

The thought of someone standing out here, watching us in the dead of night is as unsettling as it is terrifying, and these feelings are only exacerbated by the anxious anticipation of the approaching figure that is slowly emerging from behind the shield of trees.

Buddy is jumping around in the snow now and I have no idea if I'm picking up on his anxiety or if he's picking up on mine. So, I look around for something, anything to use as a weapon, and see a piece of the fence lying on the ground, partially covered by snow. I pick it up and wait as the creaking, scrunching of footsteps continues before the figure finally emerges from the driveway of wooded gatekeepers. It's a bearded man wearing a red lumberjack shirt, a beanie hat, and boots.

At the sight of me, and presumably because I'm staring at him, he raises a hand and shouts "Mornin'" as he makes his way towards us.

"Buddy," I call now, calmly, as dog owners do when their animal singles out a stranger for their wary attention. And it occurs to me, I'm one of those people now. I didn't even realise that until this very moment.

The stranger, who I can now see has a pair of uncannily blue eyes, studies the puppy carefully – as if afraid it might spring up ninja-style and bite him on his red nose.

"Beautiful mornin', ain't it?" he asks without even looking at me.

"Yes, it is," I say, studying the face, but I'm pretty sure I don't recognise it.

Are you the person who left the tracks in the snow?

"I'm Paul," he says, finally turning to me and nodding.

"I'm Marco–"

"The doctor, aye," he says, studying me now.

I don't bother correcting him. "Not used to seeing this place covered by snow," I say since I can't find anything else to talk about other than asking if it was him who left these tracks here. And, if so, why? Oh, and what the fuck is he doing on my land first thing in the morning?

"Aye. It does make the place look pretty this time of year and, who knows, with a bit of luck, it might even hang around 'til Christmas." He looks at the house and adds, "Beautiful place, you've got 'ere."

"Thanks."

I'm about ready to ask what I can do for him when he asks, nodding towards Buddy, who is now warily watching the stranger from the safety of my legs, "Have you had the little fella long?"

I look down and smile. "Buddy? No, not long. Almost a couple of weeks. Something like that."

"Where did you get him, if you don't mind me askin'?"

"I, um," I begin to answer before a flare of irritation changes my mind…. "What's this about? Why do you want to know?"

The ends of the man's lips curl up like old sandwiches. I think it's a smile, but I'm not sure. It could be wind. "You're the fella who put the notice up in the shop, aren't ya?"

I squint, equivocally. "Notice?"

"Yeah, about the puppy you found."

Shit! Lead drops to the pit of my stomach. I'd forgotten all about that. "Oh, right. Yes. I'd forgotten about that."

"Yeah. The missus didn't see the sign until yesterday."

"Right. And you are…"

He takes my cue. "I'm a breeder. It's what I do. My business, that is. It was one of my bitches, Honey, who gave birth to a litter of five a few weeks back."

"Oh, right," I say with a nod. *Oh fuck.* "And your place is not far from here?"

"No, I've got a farm just the other side of your woods. Less than a mile from 'ere."

I nod. That is my head is going up and down when my instinct is to shake it from to side.

What the fuck?

I mean, I knew this day would come. At least, I did at the beginning, but when a week went by, I just forgot about it.

"So, where did you say you got the pup?"

Lie! Lie!

"I um, found him in the woods. Saved him from a fox."

"Is that right?"

"Yeah." And I don't like the curious way in which he asked that. Almost like I've just made it up. "So, are you actually missing a pup from your litter or…?"

"Kind of," the man says, looking down at Buddy, who is curiously watching our exchange as a child would two adults chatting over the garden fence.

"Kind of?" I ask. Either you are missing a puppy, or you aren't.

"You say you saved it from a fox?"

I nod. "Yes. *He* was on the brink of death."

"I can't imagine Honey getting that distracted, to let a fox nab one of her babies."

"Maybe he became separated?"

"It's unlikely."

Another flare comes. "Look, Paul, I don't know what to tell you. All I know is that I was out running, and I came across him in the woods," I say, smothering the irritation in my voice as best I can.

He nods. "Well, there's one way of knowing for sure."

"I'm sorry?"

"Whether he's was actually part of Honey's litter."

"Right," I say with a nervous smile. "How's that? Don't tell me you'd electronically tagged him already."

"No. Well, not 'im. We don't normally do that until around seven to eight weeks."

"Right. Well, the vet I took him to said he was around nine weeks when I found him."

Another pensive nod. "Well, as I say, there's one way of knowing for sure if he was Honey's."

"OK."

"Do you mind if I take a quick look at 'im?"

I want to protest, but have no idea how to do that without coming across like I have something to hide. "Um, sure. I suppose," I consent through a fake smile.

Buddy isn't as keen, though, and when the man tries to pick him up, he decides to suddenly scamper away from us.

"Hey, Bud, it's OK," I coo. But it doesn't make much of a difference. Even in the snow, he's suddenly managed to pluck agility out of nowhere and successfully dodge the man's outstretched hands a couple of times as he slides around after him.

So, now I'm annoyed – this bloke who has turned up at my house first thing in the morning in his search for a puppy that went missing ages ago. Where the hell has he been this whole time anyway? He can't have missed the pup if he's only just getting around to—

My thoughts are interrupted as he finally grabs Buddy by the scruff of his neck, causing him to whimper as he is unceremoniously lifted from the snow and turned in the man's weathered hands so that he's lying on his back in a futile squirm.

It's all I can do not to deck the man, but if Buddy does belong to his dog then, technically, I've been harbouring his property. A thoroughbred no less, which the vet reliably informed me can fetch anywhere between five and thirteen hundred pounds.

Clouds of the man's breath chug out in front of him as he examines the dog that is clearly not enjoying having his belly exposed to the elements, based on the way he's whimpering now.

I take an unconscious step forward and try to make it look casual by kicking the snow at my feet as if it's suddenly become extra slippery, and then I hear a grunt of satisfaction.

"Yeah," he says, somewhat in amazement as he scrutinizes buddy's belly. "See this, here?" he thrusts the dog towards me so that I can see. "Just between his belly and his right hind leg. See the discoloration that looks like a birth mark?"

I lean in to get a closer look and I'm sure my heart stops.

This is not possible. I have no idea how I didn't notice it before, but this… of all the things that have happened so far.

Oh shit, I think I'm going to collapse. My legs are threatening to fold under me, all energy reserves melted like warmed snow.

I look at my hands. They are trembling, and I know it isn't from the cold, but the adrenaline that is firing through my body – activated by my fight of flight response to what I have just seen.

What the fuck is going on?

The man's face is still staring at the dog as I look around us to check if the world is as it was. The trees. The drive.

I wait.

Any second now, the snow is going turn to water, and the ground is going to fall away as it did last time and reveal a whole alternate reality.

But it doesn't.

Eventually, I look back at the puppy wriggling in this stranger's hands.

"This is unbelievable," the man is saying.

"I know," I gasp – because this is not possible.

That birth mark, or whatever it is on the puppy's thigh, is not alien to me. I have seen it or something remarkably before, but not on the dog.

On my son.

Toby had a mark just like it. Only, it was under his arm. He hated looking at it. Ellie and I, well, we fell in love with it the moment the doctor pointed it out to us.

"If you look closely enough, you can see a dip on one side. It looks just like a love heart."

I told Toby that his mummy had etched it there when he was still inside her tummy, so that he would know wherever he went, however old he was, that he was loved, always.

"I can't believe it," the man is repeating, completely ignoring Buddy's yowls of protestation. The dog is obviously distressed.

"OK. I think he wants to get down."

"Yeah," the man says, juggling the puppy to one hand by holding him by the back of his neck while rummaging in his pocket for his camera. "I just need to get a picture," he says.

Yowl! Yowl!

"He wants to get down," I repeat, that sound reminding me of the day I found him.

Yowl!

I feel a sudden and overwhelming protective urge and, feeling the weight of the strut of wood in my hand, I step forward. "Can you put him down now," I growl, unconsciously brandishing the weapon in my hand. "Please," I add, as if to soften my words.

But it's too late. The man glances at plank of wood, at me, and then drops the puppy into the snow.

Shit.

I follow suit and throw the makeshift weapon down, too.

"I just wanted to get a photo to show the folks at home."

"I know," I say. "But he looked really uncomfortable," I add, forcing a smile, but the man's wary of me now. I know this because I've seen that look on other people's faces. He tries to act casual by pulling off his hat, scratching his head, and staring off at the winter that surrounds us as if looking for answers out there.

"I have no idea how this is even possible," he rasps.

I want to say that these are my thoughts exactly, but I realise that he doesn't even know what I'm thinking. "Look," I begin desperately, "Paul, I had no idea he was your pup. Obviously. That's why I posted the notice in the shop, but we, my wife and I," I lie, "we've become attached to him."

The stranger looks at me and shakes his head.

"You don't understand, Paul. Look, if it's a question of money–"

"It's not about the money," he says.

"No? Then what is it?" I ask, reigning in my frustration.

"I just don't understand how the dog got here."

I frown at him. "I've already told you that I found him in the woods."

"Yeah, but that's the part that doesn't make sense."

"Why not?"

"Because this pup died not long after it was born. We buried it weeks ago."

The world falls silent, but for the crows in nearby trees.

42. THE VIEWING

SUNDAY· PORTHCOVE· 09:09·

I don't truly know what I spent the next two hours doing. I think it was walking through the woods, revisiting where I found Buddy, completing my jogging circuit – only, not running – and generally creeping Buddy out by staring at him and looking for some kind of *sign*.

Of course, the dog doesn't start talking to me a la *Doctor Dolittle*. It feels much more like James Herbert's *Fluke* where the dog has memories of once being a man.

It's all so uncannily peculiar that I'm unable to wrap my head around it. It feels like this situation is terabytes of data for just one used, somewhat abused, and mostly unreliable computing brain to process. That's why, as much as it's probably going to make things weird and worse, I've decided to share all this with Ellie.

I know, you're probably screaming at me right now, telling me not to do it because you're imagining how you would react if your partner walked through the door, held up a stray puppy to you, and told you that he thinks there's a good chance that he may be a, um, an, a kind of–

Oh fuck. I can't even bloody form the words to tell you about it. How the hell am I supposed to tell her?

And yet.

I close the front door, and the first thing to greet me is the delicious aroma of fresh coffee and… baking?

OK. What's going on?

I turn around and look at the door. Again, ridiculous,

because I'm checking to make sure that I walked through the correct front door.

I have. I know I have because Ellie, dressed smartly in a blue skirt – what we call a Sunday skirt because it's what she would normally wear to visit her parents for lunch – and blouse clicks her way over the flagstones to me and asks, anxiously, "Where have you been?"

"I've been for a walk."

"You were gone ages. They are going to be here any minute!" she hisses, as if they, whoever they are, can hear us.

"Who?"

"Are you serious?"

I gawk at her blankly because I've used up all of my processing power.

"Stop messing about, Marco! The viewing! They're going to be here in–" she looks at her watch, "twenty minutes. It is nine-thirty, right? You said nine-thirty?"

Oh shit. How the hell did I forget about that?

"Oh, yeah, the viewing." The thing that I need like a hole in the bloody head right now. "I'm just messing around," I say, forcing a smile.

"Well, come on. Are you going to be wearing that?"

"What's wrong with what I'm wearing?"

She looks at me. "Oh, never mind. Just run a comb through your hair, will you?"

"Ellie, it's OK. Take it easy. They're just house viewers, not our bloody parents. If they don't want the place, someone else will," I say, holding calming hands on her arms.

"I know. But I just want to make the best impression."

"And you will. You look stunning."

She smiles coyly. Then, "Not sure I can say the same for you." She retains her smile, but I know she's making a point.

"Thanks a lot," I say. "I suppose I should go and see what I can do."

And I'm moving forward when I change my mind.

If I don't do this now, I never will.

I turn back to see that my wife is now fussing around the front door. "Ellie?"

"Yep," she responds without turning.

"I need to talk to you."

"What about?"

"No, I mean a serious talk," I say because she still isn't looking at me.

Now, she stops and turns around. "What?"

OK. I pictured us sitting down in the den or something for this. Maybe at the dining table, but not standing at the front door. Still… "It's about Buddy."

"Marco, we've already talked about this," she says, stepping by me towards the kitchen. "I know you've become attached, but we can't keep it."

"But that's just it, El. Buddy's not an *it*," I call after her. And then I take a deep breath because her calling him that really annoys me. "He isn't an *it*. *He* is a puppy. He has a name."

My wife stops in her tracks and turns back to me because she recognises that tone. "OK. The puppy. The dog. The thing. You can't keep it."

I stifle another flare. "See, that's just it, El. You keep talking to me like I'm a child."

"Well, if you behave like—"

"El, just shut up for a second, will you? I'm trying to tell you something," I say, gritting my teeth because that adrenaline has kicked in already and it's already fired up the heart engines.

My wife crosses her arms expectantly. "OK. What?"

"I need you to look at something."

"Now? When we're minutes away from people ringing the doorbell, you want to do this?"

"If we don't do it now, we never will."

"OK. What?"

"I think. I mean, I, um…."

Help me! What would you say right now? And it better not be, *Just tell her!* Have you met my wife?

"It's best if I show you," I finally say.

She sighs. "Marc, we don't bloody have time for this."

"It won't take long, I promise."

Buddy, who has parked himself on the floor and been patiently watching our exchange looks up as if to say, *Oh shit, are we really doing this?*

I reach down and pick him up. "Look at this," I say to Ellie. Gently, I turn the puppy over and cradle him in the nook of my arm.

"What?"

"Here, look at this."

Reluctantly, Ellie steps forward. "What am I looking at?"

"Here." I show her the mark by pointing at it. "Can you see that?"

She looks at the dark discoloration next to the dog's hind leg. "Yes, it's a mark, so?" she asks.

"Not just a mark, El. It's a birth mark."

She squints at it. "Right."

"Well, doesn't it look familiar?"

"Um, familiar? No."

"It looks like Toby's."

There's no reaction at first, but then I watch as her head slowly lifts to look at me.

I am wide-eyed, probably manic looking. She, on the other hand, is feeling manic maybe, but for an entirely different reason.

And yet, I still plough on. "I think it's him, El. I think it's Toby's birth mark," I say with a nod, eager for her to jump on the same train of thought, but she doesn't. Instead, I watch her eyes narrow.

"You're unbelievable," she growls.

"No, wait, El. Hear me out–"

"No. That's insane. You're insane!"

"No. Don't do that. Don't try to shut this down just by insulting me. It isn't just this, El. It's other things. Many things over time, and I just didn't piece them all together until today, until that man showed up and showed me this."

"You mean the one you threatened to beat with a piece of wood?"

"What?"

"I saw you through the window."

"You saw?"

"Yes. I'm assuming that's because he asked for his dog back?"

"No. Hang on. It wasn't like that."

"What was it like then, Marc? No. You know what? It doesn't matter. I'm not doing this with you right now," she says, blinking moist eyes, though I don't know if that's because she's responding to what I've showed her or she's just incandescent with rage. I think it's most likely the latter.

And yet, that still doesn't dissuade me. I'm just about to speak again when the doorbell sounds.

Shit.

I watch my wife push her hair back and breathe as if to recompose herself.

"El," I say, touching her arm as she walks by me, but she snatches it away and hisses, through gritted teeth. "Marco, I swear to God. You mess this up for me and…" she deliberately leaves the sentence unfinished, so that I might imagine a multitude of endings to it, and then she clicks her way to the front door where, after painting on her best smile, she pulls it open.

"Good morning, Ellie!" Lucinda's over-enthusiastic American tones sweep into the room along with a freezing gust of air. "Morning, handsome," she adds with a grin for the dog. "And to you, Marco," she says with a wink. Then she nods behind her to indicate that she's being followed.

I look out to see a middle-aged man with a younger female carefully stepping their way up the garden path as if it's a minefield. Seriously? It's just a bit of snow.

But then, that makes sense to look at them. He's suited and booted. She's manicured, plucked, painted up, and wrapped in some kind of fur, which I'm assuming is fake, but who knows?

These two are obviously considering the place as a holiday home. A bit like my old man, I suppose, and for some reason, I already dislike them.

"Good morning, and welcome to Dolce Vita," Ellie is saying with her best hostess voice.

"*Doce* what?" laughs the walking mannequin.

"Dolce Vita, darling. Means the sweet life," the man contributes.

Neither bothers to say hello to Ellie or I; both just walk past us and enter our temporary home.

A quick glance at the gravelled forecourt shows me our beaten-up Volvo, Lucinda's SLK, and what's no doubt his Bentley. *Dick.*

Once everybody is inside, I close the door and set Buddy down.

"Ooh, this place is cute," the painted girl is saying.

"Just wait until you see the views. They're to die for," Lucinda crows. "Visible from almost every room."

From the door, we watch them inspect the lounge, and it's odd because, while I'm very clear about the objective here, I still can't help but feel a pang of irritation at these two stomping around my property.

Buddy isn't enjoying the strangers, either, as he hides behind my legs for safety.

"Oh, I love this fireplace," the painted girl is saying as she rubs her sugar daddy's arm.

Lucinda takes her cue and says, "It's perfect for snuggling up with a nice glass of wine on those chilly summer evenings."

The couple look at each other and grin. Ew, and I can see exactly what they're thinking, as it's written all over their faces.

But not if the fireplace has anything to do with it – because we all know what happened when I last tried to light that thing. The memory brings a temporary smile to my face until I glance across at Ellie.

I shouldn't have mentioned the dog to her. That was shitty timing.

"…Real old-fashioned fireplaces can be temperamental, especially when there's a wind change. Something that's easily rectified with a good clean and maybe even the addition of a small hood," Lucinda is saying, heading off any potential complaints about the fireplace.

Wow. You've got to give the woman credit because, judging by the fact that the two are nodding like toy dogs, I think they're actually buying that.

"So, I was going to take you through to the other rooms first, but I think now might be the perfect time to take a quick look at the back of the property, where you'll find a sweet little garden and lawn that slopes down to a coastal path and the beach."

Lucinda releases the catch lock on the patio doors and is instantly assaulted by a gale force wind, prompting squeals from the visiting party and more smiles from me.

Yes, I'm perverse, but you must admit it is comical.

I watch them step outside and imagine Lucinda selling that: *Cosy fireplace works perfectly well as long as you leave the door wide open.*

I bet she would, too.

I chuckle, and am about to move forward to close the doors before something is broken, when the howling gale stops as abruptly as it started and, for a second, I think the visitors are already returning… but we're alone in here, where the room has turned eerily still but for the swinging and creaking of the chandelier.

I watch the thing glide lazily back and forth with that familiar and creepy *creak, creak, creak.* Like the aftermath of a bloody earthquake.

"Hey! Where you going?" I yell, shattering the moment.

Buddy has started trotting towards the open doors, and that's all I need today. I pick him up and carry him over to the photography room, but we've barely reached the door when he starts squirming. "No, sorry. But I am not going to be running around the garden trying to catch you with those two around," I say, pushing the door open.

I drop him inside, and am about to pull the door shut when I see something that both shocks and angers me in equal measure.

I tug the door shut with a slam and then turn to my wife. "Why?"

"Don't talk to me," she says, breaking out of her own trance and moving towards the hallway.

"Hey! I'm happy not to, but first tell me why!"

"Why what?" she hisses under her breath, eyes on the patio doors.

"Why did you put the photos back up?"

"What?"

"The frames in the photography room. Why did you put them back up again?"

She frowns and says, "I don't know what you're talking about," and turns to walk down the hall, but I catch her arm and turn her to face me once more.

"Get off me!" she hisses.

"Why did you put the frames back up, El? Just tell me."

"I have no fucking idea what you're even talking about," she snarls. "I didn't put any frames up, you weirdo!"

"Oooh. It is a bit nippy out there!" Lucinda says, leading the couple back into the house, where they find me still holding onto Ellie's arm. Both of us gawking at them.

Lucinda shoots me an equivocal frown and I'm suddenly feeling like a rabbit in the headlights. In my own home.

"We were just. um…" I have no idea.

Luckily, our plucky estate agent intervenes. "I was just saying that one of the favourite things you and Ellie love about this place is the early morning walks down on the beach, Marco…" she says with her most pearlescent smile.

"Oh, yes," I agree enthusiastically. "Nothing better."

The would-be buyers squeeze out a synchronised smile as if it's something that they rehearsed earlier.

"Anyway. Shall we see the rest of the house? I can't wait to show you the kitchen; it's rustic, top of the range, and the views from the conservatory, you are going to love them."

Lucinda expertly says all this as she leads the visitors by us and towards the hallway.

"This is all brand new. You can probably still smell the paint… and this is the downstairs WC."

Dick laughs. "Don't you mean bathroom?"

"Well, exactly, see, Steve, we're gonna have y'all speaking Americana in no time," she says, giving the door a good shove so that nobody notices that it sticks.

Not even me because that's bloody new.

The tour continues without us down the hallway, through the kitchen, and then the dining room and conservatory, with those killer views, and finally heads upstairs.

Before long, the visitors have seen the whole house and have boarded the Bentley once more.

When *Dick* makes a show of gunning the car's engine – like we need any more of a reminder of his penis extension – Ellie and I emerge from our respective hidey-holes and join Lucinda at the front door for a special, royal wave. We continue the façade until the car has reversed and disappeared up the gravel drive, leaving nothing but the sound of that engine in its wake.

I shrug. "So?" I ask, dropping the artificial grin and turning to her.

Lucinda smiles. "Y'all both doin' OK?"

I'm surprised by the question, so my response is a bit guarded. "Yeah, why?"

She observes both of us curiously and, like children before the headmaster, we produce reassuring smiles for her. Seconds pass and I must have gulped or something because she immediately stops her amateur dramatics and starts beaming once more.

I take the cue and ask, "What? They're interested?"

"More than interested," she says excitedly. "He's already made me an offer – subject to survey, of course."

"No way!"

"Way!"

"And?"

"What we wanted. I said he could have it for two-point-three if he made the offer today, as I was showing it to others next week. He said he's happy to pay, as he doesn't want to get into a bidding war with anyone!"

"Fuck…" Ellie and I both breathe out in perfect synchronisation.

"Ooh." Lucinda's eyes widen in mock shock.

We both laugh, apologising.

"No. I get it. That kind of money warrants a good fuck!"

"Lucinda!"

We all laugh again.

"So, what now?" I ask.

"Well, I just need to file the paperwork. Run some preliminary checks to make sure we're good, and that's it."

"So, I'm assuming that's not going to happen before Christmas?" I ask.

"Highly unlikely, as his lawyers will want to order their own survey before committing to anything. But, you know, I'll hurry them along once I receive the preliminary survey report we've already conducted."

I give her a spontaneous hug.

"Oh my…" she says.

"I can't thank you enough," I say earnestly, breaking the embrace.

"All, in a day's work, sir," she says, tipping a fictitious hat. And, if I didn't know better, I'd say that the unflappable Lucinda has just been flapped! Her cheeks are rosy after my hug.

Blimey. I didn't know I still had that effect on people.

Ellie's much more reserved than me, and opts to shake the estate agent's hand instead. Although, from the grin on her face, I can tell that she's thrilled.

And so, wow, this is it.

After all of the *will it or won't it* drama. I can't believe it happened this quickly.

Admittedly, we've still got to finish the upstairs, but I've already spoken to Irvin and eaten my humble pie. As expected, he was good about it. He said he'd spoken to Sarah and that he totally understood. Something tells me that she might have already put in a good word for me, although I know she'd never admit it. But then, it could just be the fact that I invited all of them to the Christmas Eve party, assuming they get the place finished on time.

Irvin told me not to worry, that they'll be here bright and early in the morning and they'll work through.

We're so close, and the thought of that takes this whole thing to a whole new level of excitement.

Which has got me thinking. That's why I've asked Irvin for a phone number that I plan to ring, the very moment Ellie is out of earshot.

If this goes well, it'll be the best Christmas gift for her, ever.

43. GRIEF

CHRISTMAS EVE MORNING. PORTHCOVE.

So, here we are.

The past few days have been a blissful blur.

Yes, note that word, *blissful*. I haven't used it that often around here, but I think it's a rather apt way of describing period since, like the snow, the days came and melted away before we even had a chance to notice.

As promised, the boys showed up first thing Monday morning and immediately set to work upstairs, making good and painting walls while ripping out and installing new bathrooms. It was like one of those shows that Ellie used to enjoy so much. The ones where an expert and a pair of complete novices have only twenty-four hours to transform someone's home.

And they have done an excellent job. Dull walls have been rejuvenated. Ugly bathrooms banished.

The place still reeks of paint, of course, but we've been counteracting that by burning spice-infused candles specially purchased from the village store.

Ellie has been amazing.

She messaged David on Sunday and told him that she would be taking a few days off to help with the house and, obviously, prepare for the party. Since then, she's been busy grocery shopping, baking, hanging lights and additional decorations, as well as keeping the workmen fed and watered under the guise that, by doing so, she was ensuring that they met their deadline.

They laughed at the time, but something tells me my wife wasn't joking.

And the result is impressive. I'm looking forward to everybody seeing the fruits of their labour tonight.

Oh, and in case you're wondering. I've been busy, too. Mostly with online shopping for presents, not least of all some Christmas tree gifts for our guests tonight. It was tight, but I think I managed to remember everyone. And you'll be pleased to know that when I wasn't busy supporting Ellie by being sous chef, pot washer, house runner, cleaner, and purveyor of all things deemed absolutely essential but forgotten, I was out with coat and gloves, fixing and painting that fence.

Ah, see? You thought I was never going to do it, didn't you? Admittedly, it did take some time, but I got there in the end.

Even the weird shit that has been happening around here appears to have calmed down. I think Doctor Holmes was right. Yes, again, it was just taking a while for the meds to kick in. Now that they have, there are no more things going bump in the night.

Well, there have been. Creaky doors which, as we know, are explained by drafts, and then there's just the general feeling of someone being downstairs in the early hours. It was a just a feeling, though. You know, the kind you get when somebody is tiptoeing around the house. You know they're there. You think you hear them, but you're not quite sure. It's been like that.

After checking the first two times and finding nothing, I gave up. Besides, it's been so bloody busy around here that, once my head has hit that pillow, I've been out until morning birdsong.

Yes. Exactly as I said, uncharacteristically *blissful*.

Well, I guess it is Christmas, after all.

Which brings me right up to now, with me swallowing a couple of my pills and dressing after the best shower I have had since arriving here. Probably the best shower ever.

OK. I might be exaggerating a little, but I'm excited!

First, I didn't have to step into that ugly bath. I simply walked into a nice, spacious glass cubicle and turned on the tap for a gloriously hot, waterfall shower.

Second, do you remember when this all started? That morning when I thought Ellie was backing into me for early morning delight, but instead it turned out to be a shitty nightmare?

Well, this morning – and I have no idea what got into her – she *backed up* into me, but for real. If you know what I mean.

I had to pinch myself, of course – metaphorically speaking – and have her talk and look at me for a few seconds, which was a bit of an anti-climax, but once we got started….

Wow.

I don't know if it's because it's been so long. I have no idea, but well, you know, we… I'm sorry. There's no other real way to describe it because it would seem my wife has turned into a bit of an animal. Not that she wasn't passionate before, because she was, but this morning… well, she was on fire. She didn't just want sex. She wanted *wild* sex. You know – rough.

It was probably one of the best Christmas gifts I've received in a long time.

OK, don't jump on that. It isn't as crass as it seems. What I mean by that is that, for the first time in a long time, I felt close to her.

Wanted.

Now, the rain, that has been chucking it down for the past twenty-four hours, reminds me that it's here so stay by pelting the landing window as I make my way downstairs.

But we're fine. We're OK. The house actually feels warm and cosy for a change, thanks to the electric oil heaters that I finally bought online and have dotted around the place. And the den is the perfect Christmas setting. In the absence of snow, it's dark outside, which only accentuates the multicoloured glow of the twinkling Christmas tree. There are poinsettia plants on the coffee table, lights strung over the patio doors, a Christmas wreath on the door, the smell of spices in the air, and a cute little puppy sitting on the floor, gnawing on a fake bone toy as if it were the real thing.

"Are you enjoying that, Bud?" I smile. But the dog's only response is a slap of his tail and a glance that says, *Dude. I'm busy here.*

OK.

So, I make my way to my new favourite part of the house, which is the hallway.

Ah, bet you didn't guess that, did you?

I love this place now. It's bright and has no less than four lights specifically chosen to bring light to the darkest–

Except for now, because they are flickering again. They're flickering and, each time they dip, I get a snapshot of what this place used to look like.

"Oh, what?" I groan. "Are you bloody–"

The words dry in my mouth when I hear a sound that makes my blood run cold.

Wheeze... drag... wheeze....

"No," I mutter as the lights threaten to give up.

Ruff! Ruff!

Buddy is standing behind me now.

Wheeze... drag... wheeze....

What's that? There's something at the end of the corridors. A shadow inside of the shadows.

Ruff! Ruff! Growl.

"No, Buddy, no," I snap angrily. "I don't want this; I don't want this in this house anymore!"

"Don't want what?"

"Jesus Christ!" I breathe as Ellie emerge from the kitchen with a mixing bowl and spoon in her hand.

The lights are burning bright once more. Of course.

"Are you alright?"

But I'm busy gulping down an unexpected dose of anxiety.

Shit!

"Marco?"

"Yes, I'm fine," I say.

"Are you sure?"

Thankfully, I don't have to answer again because my mobile phone starts ringing. So, I pluck it out of my pocket and back away from the hallway. I'm angry now. Irritated that I am unable to enjoy one morning without this shit invading my fucking life.

And yet…. "Good morning, Lucinda," I answer cheerily. "Happy Christmas Eve! How are you today?"

"Good morning, Marco. I am very well. Thank you. How are you?"

"I'm good. Just waiting for you to tell me that we're ready to exchange contracts," I joke. But Lucinda doesn't respond. "Hello, Lucinda, have I lost ya?" I ask, mimicking her in my worst American accent as I make my way towards the door in order to get a better signal.

"Yes, I'm here, Marco."

"Oh, right, good. I thought we got get disconnected there for a second."

"Marco, I have bad news," the estate agent says with traditional bluntness.

"OK," I say as my heart skips a beat. "Don't tell me. They've pulled out."

"Yes. I'm afraid so."

I was ready for this. It was worst case. Disappointing, but it isn't the end of the world. It happens. "Well, that's OK. There's plenty more fish in the ocean. Right?"

Another dramatic pause, and there's static on the line, so I move into the photography room where there's sometimes a better signal.

"Right?" I prompt her.

"Well, this is it. Marco, I'm really sorry, but they didn't pull out because they wanted to; they pulled out because they were advised to."

"Advised? Advised by whom?"

"They were advised by the property survey report."

"The survey? How? That hasn't even happened yet!"

"No. their survey hasn't, but, as you know, we conducted our own initial survey. That's standard practice with a property of this value. You know, as agents, we need to be aware of any potential issues, as that affects how we market the property and address potential problems. In your case, there was the obvious one in addition to the condition of the property."

"Lucinda, I'm sorry. I don't follow."

"I have a copy of Dolce Vita's site survey report in front of me, Marco. It seems that there was a landslip there just over a year ago. Were you aware of this?"

I shake my head incredulously.

"Marco?"

"No. No, I wasn't aware of it."

"The surveyor we hired…." She pauses as she reads from the report, and then continues, "Ken Lynch. He's familiar with the area. Apparently, coastal erosion there isn't that uncommon. Particularly at Porthcove, where there was a landslip just over a year ago. It wasn't, in technical terms, a major slip, but it was enough for them to block off access to the beach down there. Did you know about this?"

"No," I utter. "I told you I didn't."

"Apparently, the Atlantic tide is quite brutal. Land erosion in the area is sustained and irreversible and, in his opinion, it puts the peninsula and any properties that sit on it at considerable risk of subsidence. Part of the report is denoted red for serious risk."

I have no idea what our estate agent is saying. I mean, I've heard the words, but they don't make any sense to me. Well, they do, but I'm just finding it difficult to register.

Subsistence? Serious risk?

"Lucinda, this has got to be a joke, right? You're just leading me on, aren't you?"

"Marco, believe me, I wish I were," the estate agent says, and I know she isn't joking because she's got *that* tone. That brisk tone she adopts when she's talking business. The same tone she used just days ago to tell me off for not getting back to her.

Rain spits at the glass of the window.

I've no idea what to say. I keep opening my mouth, but words refuse to come out and I find myself physically straining to say something until I manage to vomit out, "OK. Alright. OK. Well, that's fine. You said you'd had a lot of interest from a lot of buyers. They're still going to be interested, right? I mean, among all of them, there's got to be someone who's still interested, especially if we drop the price a little. Right?"

Another dramatic pause filled in by seagulls singing in the fucking rain. The wind whistling through a gap in the window.

"Right?" I repeat.

"No, Marco. This report, it's damning. I mean, anybody who orders a property survey is going to see this. And something like this," she hesitates, "well, it renders the property worthless."

I laugh. Did she just say *worthless*? I laugh some more because now I know she is joking. Multimillion-pound properties don't just suddenly become worthless.

"We'll get a second opinion. I mean, this Kent or whatever the fuck his name is isn't the only surveyor, right?"

"No, he isn't. And, of course, you're perfectly within your rights to get a second opinion, but at the end of the day, whatever your survey says is irrelevant to a buyer because it is presumed biased. In this case, Steven asked me if I conducted my own survey because he's in the business; he knows that with a property like yours, it's likely I would have commissioned a preliminary survey. But the fact remains, any buyer worth their salt will want their own survey, and if there's a mortgage involved, the underwriters tend to commission their own report, too – especially at this kind of price. It's standard due diligence."

So, now I'm scared. Now, I am really scared. And it isn't necessarily what Lucinda just told me, although that's terrifying… no, it's the way she's saying it.

That tone has remained consistently dour. Our exuberant, gung-ho Yank capable of flogging ice to an Eskimo is gone. In her place, especially if her voice is anything to go by, is someone who has already given up. Someone who, in my mind, is holding the phone in one hand and our file over a shredder in the other.

So, it's panic stations. "Lucinda," I begin, but I cough as I try to clear my throat because my saliva has turned to dust. "Lucinda, there's got to be something we can do. I mean, if I don't sell this house–"

"I'm really sorry, Marco. I wish there were something to be done. But with situations like these, even with the best will in the world, even if we had endless resources, even if you were my sole client, I don't think there's any way we could shift your property now."

"No, don't say that! Lucinda, come on, don't say that. I mean, what do you expect me to do?"

"There's nothing you *can* do. From where I'm sitting, your only option is to stay there. Make the most of it while you can."

"Are you fucking kidding me?" I explode. "I'm not here on some fucking holiday! We came here to sell the place. And I fucking hired you to do that!"

"And I tried. But unfortunately, the dwelling… the dwelling ain't fit for purpose," she says coldly.

"That's a load of fucking shit and you know it! I tell you what… I've got an idea, why don't I come over there and burn your fucking house down so that you have nowhere else to go, and then you can come over here and, you know, make the most of it, and see how you fucking like it!"

There's a pause long enough for me to process that verbal car crash before I hear, "Marco, I am afraid there really isn't much else for me to say. I appreciate that you're disappointed and I wish I could help you further, but I can't. And now, I'm going to hang up before you cuss and yell at me some more."

"No, Lucinda. I'm sorry. Wait!"

"I wish you all the best."

"Lucinda? Lucinda!"

But the only response is a loud beep, and when I look at the screen, I see that the call has been disconnected.

"Fuck!"

I sling my phone down on the desk and hold my head in my hands as I try to take in what just happened, and then it immediately starts buzzing and travelling once more.

I snatch it up without even checking the screen. "Lucinda!"

"Marco? No. It's Dean."

It takes me a few seconds. "Dean? Oh, right. Dean. Hey, Dean."

"Have I caught you at a bad time?"

"Um, well, actually, uh… yeah. What's up?"

"I just thought I'd give you a quick call, you know, about the laptop you brought me."

Again, my cogs are still processing the previous phone call, so that I quite literally have no idea what the guy is talking about until.... "Laptop? Oh, right. The laptop. Ellie's laptop, yeah, yeah."

"Well, I've actually managed to connect to it."

"Connect? What does that mean?" I ask distractedly.

"Retrieve. I can retrieve the data. All I need is the log-on and password."

"Password?"

"Yeah. The drive has a password on it. I need it to get in."

I think about this. "Oh, right, OK. Well, that should be pretty easy. It's, um, it's *littleman* with a capital 'L' and a numerical one instead of the i. No space."

I spell it out for him again just to be sure, and then wait a few seconds.

"No. That's not it," the voice at the end of the phone says eventually.

"Um, should be. Did you try capital 'L' and the '1' instead of the i? No space between the words?"

"Yeah. And yes, I've tried upper and lower case."

The door opens, and Buddy barges through Ellie's legs and trots towards me.

"Everything OK?" she asks. "I thought I heard you shouting."

I gesture to the phone at my ear and whisper, "Couriers."

With that, she nods and leaves the room, closing the door behind her.

"Yeah, I've tried it all several times in a different permutation. It definitely isn't that."

"That's odd because it's only ever been that. And don't give me a lecture, but Ellie and I have shared passwords for as long as I can remember, and then when Toby came along, we..." I trail off here because I realise that I'm rambling, and this guy doesn't care. "I'm sorry, Dean. In that case, I have no idea."

"Can you ask Ellie?"

I think about this. "Of course. Sure," I say, and I move to go find her, but then think better of it.

Why would she change her password? She hasn't done that in years. She hates changing her password. Maybe she was forced to. *Maybe.*

I don't know why, but I don't want to ask Ellie. Mostly because it won't be much of a bloody surprise if I tell her what we've been trying to do as opposed to presenting her with an external drive and all of her data with a bow wrapped around it.

We'll leave it for now. I need to sort my head out with the other stuff first. Leave it until after Christmas.

"OK then, Dean. Thanks anyway, mate, but we're going to leave it for now and come back to it after–"

I pause because Buddy keeps pawing at my leg and looking up at me with those doe eyes of his.

"In a second, Buddy," I say, crouching down and petting him on the head.

"Sorry, Marco, are you talking to me?"

"No, sorry, Dean. It's the dog. Thanks anyway, mate. See you later, OK?"

"Yeah, OK. See you then."

I disconnect and turn back to the dog, who keeps trying to hand me his paw.

"Is that for me? Is that for me?" I ask, taking the offering.

It's because I'm cute and I say cute things.

Toby's voice has just popped into my head. "Well, part of that is true, Buddy," I say, moving under the dog to stroke his belly, but he's not rolling onto his back today. "What? No tummy rubs today?"

It doesn't seem like it. Instead, the dog remains standing, extending his paw to me. "Is there something wrong with it? Something wrong?"

I take the paw and examine it. It looks fine, and he wasn't limping when he came in.

It's because I'm cute and I say cute things.

I let go. I can't explain it, but something feels off. The dog has me fixated with those brown eyes, now dark in the gloom of the room.

"Buddy? Are you being creepy again?"

The dog's only response is to lift his paw to me.

"No. We're not doing that anymore."

And yet, he keeps waving it at me. So, I watch it for the longest time before tentatively reaching out and touching it, as one would a live wire.

It feels warm, but otherwise nothing. No thoughts. No words.

"Oh, Jesus Christ. I am bloody losing it! No. Not losing. Lost!"

In this moment. Who's your favourite parent?

"Who's your favourite parent, Buddy?" I ask, but he just blinks at me. Paw on my outstretched hand. I inspect it again. There's nothing there.

Who's your favourite parent?

I have no idea why that keeps going through my bloody mind. It's just a thought.

I love you both the same.

And I miss you. I miss you so much, buddy. So much. And out of nowhere, the tears start falling.

44. SECRETS

CHRISTMAS EVE EVENING. PORTHCOVE.

I have no idea where those tears came from. I was just suddenly overwhelmed with grief. Another of those things that's difficult to describe. It was more of a strong feeling than anything tangible, but I just felt like Toby was in the room with me, and I mean right there. Close enough for me to put my arms around him. It was exactly the same sense I felt thousands of times over when he was sleeping, playing, or sitting next to me.

And yet, he wasn't.

And so, once I pulled myself together, I spent the rest of the day agonising over whether or not I should tell Ellie about the phone call with Lucinda, and I came so close at least three times, but kept chickening out. I just kept coming back to the fact that it has been a wonderful day so far. The first in a long time. If you ignore the fact that the whole reason why we've come out here has, in one phone call, been reduced to a stinking pile of shit, and that now I've somehow got to tell my wife that we're no longer going to be millionaires, and that, worse, we are going to be stuck here for the foreseeable future. Then, assuming she doesn't divorce me or, worse, stab me with her wooden spoon, I've then somehow got to tell my best friend that the forty thousand pounds he's given us has just been flushed down the crapper.

So, yeah… I just couldn't bring myself round to telling her.

And I've decided that I am going to push all of this to the back of my mind. We're going to get through Christmas and then we'll deal with whatever.

So, now, dressed smartly in black trousers and shirt for the first time in what feels like a long time, I am ready to receive our guests and enjoy the hell out of the evening. Assuming they can get here. The rain has not let up all bloody day. At this rate, they're going to need boats and not cars for the rest of their journey.

In the meantime, I've initiated contingency protocols by placing storm lanterns, flashlights, and candles at strategic points around the house just in case. We've lost power during much milder meteorological events, and I want to be prepared.

Now, with Christmas carols ringing, spice candles burning, and eggnog at the ready, there's that bloody gestapo knock at the door. If I didn't know better, I'd say someone was trying to wind me up.

And it's with some trepidation that I make my way to the door – because I remember the last time this happened, there was nobody there, and I refuse to have any of that shit tonight. So, I take my time and, when I get to the door, I slowly pull it open.

"Jesus, take your time, why don't ya? It's biblical out 'ere!" It's Drew, hair plastered to his scalp. "Has your doorbell packed up or something?"

"You know, I think it has because I didn't hear it."

"Merry Christmas," he says miserably, handing me a wrapped bottle of something with a bow around it.

"Merry Christmas, mate," I say, suppressing a grin and secretly enjoying his grumpiness.

It's OK. Drew and I have made our peace. He was adequately repentant when he arrived Monday morning. And I believe Sarah and the others when they say that his intentions weren't malicious. He was just naïve. There's no doubt the press took advantage of him. And the worst bits of that article, he couldn't have even known about anyway. That's all on the reporter and their shitty source.

Dean and Irvin, both of whom have not fared much better than Drew, follow him into the house.

"It's a bit wet out there, Marco," Irvin says, shaking water off his head. "Hard to think that tonight's supposed to be a full moon."

"Is that so?" I ask with a big smile. "Merry Christmas."

"Get a few drinks in me and I'll show you a full moon," Drew interjects.

"Hey, we'll have none of that," Irvin warns before handing me a soggy cardboard box. "Merry Christmas, mate. A few pastries, courtesy of the wife. She would've loved to 'ave come tonight, but she's got her ma over and is busy preparing for tomorra's feast."

"That's really nice of her. Thanks very much," I say, taking the box.

"Merry Christmas, Marc," Dean says, handing me a plastic bag with something heavy inside. "I went ahead and mirrored the drive as is. So, all you'll need to do, when you're ready, is plug it into your computer and enter the password."

"Oh, that's brilliant, Dean! Thanks very much," I say, offering up the box to him so that he can place the bag on top. "Go on through to the den. You know where it is. I'm just going to drop these off and get you some towels."

I drop the drive off in the study and the cakes in the kitchen. When Ellie asks where they came from, I tell her as I grab a roll of paper towels.

"You're joking? What the bloody hell are they doing here?" she asks in a hushed tone.

"What do you mean?" I say, grabbing beer cans from the fridge and making my way to the door.

"Them. The bloody builders! What are they doing here?" she asks. Then, eying the cans in my hand, she adds, "You better be using glasses with those."

"The glasses are already out there. And I invited them."

She sighs loudly. "Yes, I get that, but why?"

I frown. "Because they did most of the work, El." I look around the room. "If it wasn't for them, this house wouldn't look anything like it does now."

"Yeah. And they were paid for that work."

I pull a face. "What's wrong with you? Are you saying that I shouldn't have invited them because they're builders?"

"I'm saying that we don't even know them. Tonight was

supposed to be about close friends only! I specifically told you that," she hisses back.

"You may not know them, but I do," I say, leaving her and making my way up the hallway and into the den.

"Beers are in, lads," I announce to cheers just as there's another rap at the door.

When I open it, the now newly installed security light reveals a relatively handsome man wearing a blue suit with an open shirt, who's scrunching himself against the driving rain. "Hello," he says with a wide, white smile.

"Hello," I say, flinching against the meteorological onslaught. "Um, can I help you?" I ask – because he looks like he's dressed for a party, but I've never seen him before.

"Yes," he says as water scurries down his beard and drips to the ground.

"Are you with David?" I ask, squinting into the precipitation and the driveway.

Ellie appears behind me. "How come I'm not hearing the bell?" she asks quickly.

"It isn't working," I say. "And–"

"Cristian, I wasn't expecting you!" Ellie interrupts.

"Well, I did say that I would try and make it if I could and, well, as it turns out, I could." I can hear his accent now. Latino. Italian. Spanish. One of those, I think.

"Well, come in out of that rain. Marc," Ellie prompts me so I step aside and watch him walk by me.

Door closed and now dripping water, I ask the stranger, "Are you new?"

"Sorry?"

"Are you new, at the company?" I ask.

He looks at Ellie and says, "No, I'm not that new anymore."

"Right. What do you do?"

"Marc," Ellie says, "what's with the twenty questions? Come on. Let's get you a towel," she says, steering the man away and into the den.

"There's paper towel over there," I call after them, but she seems much more interested in what the non-*close friend* has to say as they make their way toward the dining room.

I don't have long to dwell on that before there's another rap at the door. When I open it, I find Sarah standing there holding an umbrella over her head. "Nice evening for it," she says, scrunching against the cold.

"Well, you know, I like to put on a show," I say, stepping aside.

I've barely closed the door and Sarah has already collapsed her umbrella. I notice that her wavy hair has been liberated and straightened, and that she's wearing more makeup than normal to compliment the black, clingy dress moulded to her body.

"You look lovely." The words have just come out before I've even thought about them, and they've amplified the dregs of her smile.

"Oh, well, you know, I like to make an impression," she says, mimicking my line and chasing it up with a wink. "Make the most of it, though. Dresses, not really my thing," she says almost in a whisper.

"Oh really? But you wear them so well."

"Wow, this place is looking lovely," she says suddenly, noticing the den.

"Yeah, not bad. Would you like a drink?"

"Would love one."

I'm about to answer when there's another rap at the door.

David and Aaron are the only two we're still expecting, so you can imagine my surprise when….

"Ethan. What are you doing here?"

"I heard there was a housewarming party. Was I mistaken?"

I gape at my therapist-slash-pain in the neck standing underneath a black umbrella and notice that his normally tidy hair is looking somewhat dishevelled.

"Um, no. Come in. Please," I say.

I look outside at the collection of cars filling up the driveway, each seemingly an instrument of the rain that is dinging and drumming a cacophony which is as loud as it is absorbing.

Something else that catches my eye – because it's now shimmering under the security light – is that the pathway and front lawn are slowly disappearing underneath a sheet of water that's alive with raindrops.

OK.

"Rough journey?" I ask after shutting the elements out.

My therapist nods. "Yeah. Somewhat. The roads are complete pandemonium."

"And yet, you still braved the journey from London just to be here? Appreciate it," I say.

He nods, and I scan his face for more information, but, as always with this bloke, there's none.

"Husband didn't fancy making the journey with you?" I ask.

"Um, no. He had other plans."

I nod. "So, it was Ellie."

"Sorry?"

"Ellie, who invited you."

"Yes."

"OK," I say. "Well, I'm surprised you came. I imagine you being the kind of man who doesn't enjoy fraternising with patients."

"Well, you're not exactly a patient. Are you?" He's smiling again, but there's something about that smile. I can't quite work out if he just feels awkward being here, in my lair for a change, or if it's something else.

"Anyway, come in," I say, gesturing to the den.

"Place looks fantastic."

"Yeah. We got there in the end," I say proudly, even though those fucking, niggling phone call reminder thoughts keep trying to push their way to the front of my mind like eager brats at an ice cream truck.

OK, not sure where that came from.

Nope. That's a lie. I know exactly where it come from. Ethan's arrival has put me on edge.

But, no. I'm happy that he's here in my home, on my territory for a change because, for once, I am not going to feel anxious or on guard. I am going to feel relaxed, just as I imagine I might if the dynamic of our relationship were different.

"Ethan!" It's Ellie who appears to have abandoned her colleague to the others and is coming over to greet the doctor like they're old buddies. "So glad you could make it," she says eagerly. And I'm about to say something when there's more banging on the door.

Ellie looks at me. "Yep. I'll get that because I'm curious whether or not it's going to be our *close friend* David and his fiancé or another surprise." I follow that up with a sickly-sweet smile.

It is David.

"Dude. What the actual fuck? It's bedlam out here. Roads closed. Diversions in place. Cars stranded on the side of the road."

"Merry Christmas to you, too."

"Alright Marco, mate," he throws his arms around me and squeezes me tight, then looks at me. "Are you OK? How are you holding up?"

I squint at him. "Um, I'm fine. Are *you* OK?"

"I'm fine. We're good."

The *we* is Aaron, who is standing behind him.

"Marco," the man says, hugging me – but, unlike our previous encounters, this one is different. Nowhere near as effusive, which is one of his most notable traits.

When the embrace is over, I ask, "Are you OK?"

"Oh, yeah. I'm fine. I'm good," he says, looking around the den... but not at me.

OK, he's avoiding eye contact. Why?

"Place looks great," he offers. Again, no eye contact.

"Thanks. We did it in the end," I say, putting a hand on David's arm, "all thanks to you."

"Oh, it's just money, ain't it? And once the deal goes through, then I won't have to worry anymore."

I let out a laugh. "Worry anymore? I didn't think you had to worry now. Jesus. How much money do you bloody need?"

David laughs, and then suddenly seems interested in the activity in the den.

"You don't know," Aaron says, knowingly. "Did Ellie not tell you?"

"Tell me what?"

David jumps in. "Eh, some host you are. We've been 'ere like ten minutes and still no drinks or–"

"David, stop pissing around. What did Ellie not tell me?"

He glances at my wife who is standing next to the Christmas tree and deep in conversation with the doctor.

"David?"

He looks back at me, sighs, and then continues. "The last game we launched. Total disaster. Bugs. Online multi-player privacy issues. No disaster recovery. We were at death's door. Vultures started circlin' and I thought that was it. But then, turns out they'd already been eying the company and just didn't want to pay full-price for it. Now, they're gonna get it at rock-bottom discount. But it's OK, I ain't complainin'. Still gonna do alright out of it."

"Fuck. Dave," I breathe out, squeezing his arm. "I had no idea."

Aaron scoffs and shakes his head. "That's because Ellie didn't bother mentioning it to you."

"No."

"Marco, Ellie is one of the reasons why David was hit so hard."

"Aaron," David complains.

"Well, he's her husband. He should know."

"Aaron, we talked about this," David says severely. "Tonight's not the night."

"Then when, David? You've kept this from him long enough. Especially now that–"

"Aaron–"

"Hang on a minute," I cut them both off. "Aaron's right. What the hell, David? Why aren't you telling me this stuff? I'm your friend."

"It's isn't important," David says dismissively. "Now, who do I have to fuck to get a drink around here?" he asks, looking into the den.

"No," I snap. "I want to know. I thought you said, things were going to be OK now that you were merging. That's why you hired El back, isn't it? After she left. You know, because of me." I glance over. My wife is still talking animatedly to the doctor. The model wannabe in the suit standing nearby and listening in on their every word.

Aaron scoffs again.

David looks at him, and obviously sees something in his eyes because he tries to head him off. "Aaron, we talked about this and agreed–"

Aaron meets his gaze. "No. You may be cool with the charade, but I'm not," he says emphatically.

"Guys. What the fuck is going on?" I ask – confused, because that's what I am.

Aaron speaks. "Ellie didn't leave because of you, Marco. Maybe indirectly, she did, but she didn't leave. She put David in an impossible situation. He was forced to fire her."

"What?"

"Yeah. And as if that wasn't bad enough, the contingency plans that *she* was supposed to be working on, specifically in case the company got into trouble, which it did, were never written. As for the job–"

"Aaron–"

"David couldn't hire her back even if he wanted to. Part of his settlement with the two girls was that she would never step foot in the company ever again."

"Aaron, for fuck's sake!" David explodes.

But, again, Aaron rallies back, pointing a hand at me. "*He* is the closest thing you've ever had to a brother! And I know you want to protect him, David, and I love you for it, I do. But this is not the way to do it."

I can't work out if my heart has stopped beating or if it's powering so fast that I can't feel it anymore.

Two girls? "I don't understand," I think I hear myself say. "That doesn't make any sense. Ellie. She's been travelling to London the whole time we've been here – to work, for you. I mean, she's been working on that presentation."

Almost in unison, the two men look over to my wife and the stranger standing beside her... before David finally meets my gaze. His eyes now glistening with tears.

"I didn't, don't know, what is best for you anymore, mate. I just... I just do what I think, what they tell me is right."

I'm about to pull my friend into a hug for a reason that I'm not sure is yet clear to me when an obnoxious voice yells from across the room. "Oi! What are you housewives chattin' about over there? We're runnin' on empty 'ere!"

I force a smile. Then, I call out, "Ellie! Can you please see to our guests?"

I say it mostly because I want to break up the little pow wow that's going on over there.

I look back to David and Aaron. "You two should go get a drink, too."

"Marco–" Aaron begins.

"Go now," I say, putting a hand on each of the men's shoulders and pushing them towards the den. "I'll be right with you. I just need to check on the pup." David glances back at me. I nod at him. "I'm fine. Go."

After hesitating several more seconds, David finally turns around. "OK, bitches. Now the party's truly gettin' started. David's in the house!" he calls, swiping a hand over his eyes and making his way over to the congregation.

What the hell was that all about?

I don't have time to think about it because the lights flicker and a cheer goes up from the assembled guests.

I look at the chandelier as if my gaze is going to appease the power Gods and keep the lights on. It seems to work. For now.

I look at the visitors. What an eclectic mix. Friends old and new. And some complete strangers. Doesn't look like the guest list Ellie described.

It's because I'm cute and I say cute things.

Buddy.

I open the door to the photography room and peer inside. Buddy looks up from his bed by the wingback chair, but doesn't react in any way to my presence like he normally would. He doesn't even thump his tail.

So, I walk over to him and crouch down. "Are you OK, Buddy?" I ask, but, not unlike Aaron before he unburdened himself, Buddy doesn't react; he just looks, for want of a better expression, sad.

"Are all these strangers putting you on edge? It's OK," I say, stroking his head. But the dog keeps his eyes lowered. "What's going on with you two, eh? Is there something else I don't know?"

Rain hammers at the window and then crawls over the glass like a swarm of insects.

Oh God, we may have to put these people up here tonight.

"How do you propose we manage that, eh?" I ask the pup, running my hands over his fur. "Do you think we could use your bed, eh? Would you mind giving it up for the night?"

Who's your favourite?

"Stop it!"

I snatch my hand away and jump to my feet. I don't want this tonight! I don't!

Jesus Christ! I think I've just been told that Ellie has been lying to me all this time and that… that there's a good chance she might be fucking that guy. The last thing I need is more weirdness.

I take a few seconds, and then sigh… and look down. Now, Buddy has his head bowed as dogs do when they sense tension. I've scared him.

"I'm sorry, Buddy… I'm sorry…" I say. I'm not mad at you. I'm—"

The lights flicker again, and there's another cheer from the crowd outside. I should go and join them, but I don't know if I can. I don't know if I can look Ellie in the eyes without wanting to have it out with her here and now in front of everyone.

Oh shit.

I run hands through my hair as I try to process thoughts driving at me like the precipitation outside.

The table lamp that I left on in here – yes, for the dog, and so I could easily check in on him from time to time – makes a weird, high-pitched squeal as if it's being throttled by something invisible before it pops, startling me and plunging the room into darkness.

The rain seems much louder in the dark. And, of course, of all contingencies, there are none in here, so I turn to leave.

"Buddy I've got to go. I need to–"

"*...now might be a good time to finally lay this question to rest. Who is your favourite parent?*"

I whirl around to find that the laptop has sprung to life once more.

"No. No. This isn't real. It isn't real!" I hiss.

"*Well, he keeps abstaining from answering. He's got the diplomacy of a bloody politician. Is that what you're going to be when you grow up?*"

"*I love this, and I love you both so much for exactly the same amount.*"

"*...now might be a good time to finally lay this question to rest. Who is your favourite parent?*"

"*Marc! Stop asking him that.*" The screen glitches.

"*Who is your favourite parent?*"

"*Marc! Stop asking him that.*"

The screen glitches.

"*Who is your favourite parent?*"

"*Marc! Stop asking him that.*"

The screen glitches.

"*Who is your favourite parent?*"

"*Marc! Stop asking him that.*"

"Marc? What are you doing in here in the dark?"

I turn around. Ellie's silhouette, backlit from the light in the den, is in the doorway.

"Ellie, look at this!" I say quickly, before it stops, but when I turn back around, the computer screen is black.

What? No....

"Look at what?" Ellie asks.

I swallow my frustration and eventually say, "Nothing."

"OK. Well, are you coming out?"

I nod without looking at her. "Yes, I'll be there in a second."

"It's just that–"

"Ellie! I said I'll be there in a second!" I snap.

"OK," she says quietly.

She's about to leave when I ask her to turn on the overhead light, but when she does, it splutters and dies, as well.

"Oh, bloody hell," she says. "They've been doing that all over the house tonight."

"OK. I'll take a look," I say absentmindedly.

The rain has stopped, or it's slowed, because I've just realised that it's no longer tapping on the window. I'm moving to leave when I feel Buddy rub against my leg. "Buddy! I nearly tripped over you."

I love you, too, little man. Merry Christmas.

Merry Christmas.

Merry Christmas.

I ignore the voices that keep sounding in my head while telling myself that they have absolutely nothing to do with my making contact with the puppy at my feet… because that's, well, it's just… just fucking crazy.

Instead, I feel my way over the keys of the laptop to the power button, press it, and watch as the machine clicks to life.

Of course, you do. Which only confirms that what just happened didn't. It's all in my head.

I've fucking lost it!

And the thought of that fills me with abject sorrow. And, of course, misery loves company, so I allow what I just learned at the front door to be absorbed into my consciousness. My wife has been lying to me this whole time. She's been pretending to go to work just so she can get away from me. Just so she can go fuck Jose or whatever his name is. No wonder she hasn't wanted to go anywhere near me.

It all makes so much sense now.

And who can blame her, right?

Right.

Buddy starts whimpering.

"It's OK, Bud. It's alright. Some things just can't be avoided."

The dog moves and sits on my foot.

"Who is your favourite parent?"

"Marc! Stop asking him that."

I smile. "I would love for that to be because of your touch, but I know now that it isn't. It's just in my head, Buddy. My own corrupted hard drive."

I look at the red bag with droplets of water still clinging to it.

I reach over, take out the drive, and plug it into the notebook. Almost instantly, a window opens requesting the password.

"Who is your favourite parent?"

"Marc! Stop asking him that."

I type in: *iamthebestparent.* Then, *Iamthebestparent.* Then, *IAMTHEBESTPARENT.*

INCORRECT PASSWORD.

L1ttleman.

INCORRECT PASSWORD.

I try it again.

INCORRECT PASSWORD.

Then I try it in all possible permutations.

INCORRECT PASSWORD.

"Fuck!"

45. APOCALYPSE

When I eventually leave the photography room, it's to a den of hushed voices. Someone has even gone as far as turning off the Christmas songs, and so the only incidental music to this particular scene is the pitter-patter and slosh of rainfall that now appears to be back with a vengeance.

Gone is the hilarity; in its place is a bunch of people staring at me like I've just done something particularly stinky in my pants.

"What?" I ask.

Ellie forces a smile and then, as if she's just stepped out of a 50s' housewife propaganda video, says, "Darling. We've been waiting for you."

"OK," I say warily. "What's happened… have you all run out of booze?"

There are a few smiles, but it's otherwise mostly grimness.

"What's going on?" I ask again, approaching the guests who have assembled like the remaining characters at the end of an Agatha Christie book just before they go through the process of elimination to identify a killer.

"Ellie, we just agreed to postpone or take this somewhere else," Holmes says looking at my wife.

She doesn't answer but instead keeps her gaze and her smile on me."

"What's going on?" I prompt once more.

Doctor Holmes reluctantly turns to look at me and forces a smile. "Marco. How are you feeling?"

I cock my head and pull a face. "I am fine," I say pointedly. "Thank you for asking, Doctor."

"Um, only, Ellie has just been telling us that you haven't been feeling your best lately."

"Right, OK. What exactly has been wrong with me, El?"

She looks at the floor as if struggling with what she's about to say. "Oh, you know. I've just been telling Ethan about how pleased you are that the renovations are finally finished, and how you're looking forward to selling the house and returning to the city."

I frown at her and take a step closer. "Um, no, El. As you well know, you're the one who wants to return to the city. Not me."

"Sorry, Marco." It's the doctor talking now. "Didn't you tell me that you were *struggling*, to use your word, and that you were looking forward to selling the house?"

"Yeah. By that, I meant that I wanted to get the house sold so that we could move onto the next stage of our lives. You know, get a place somewhere else."

"Did you have anywhere in particular in mind?"

"No, we haven't gotten that far yet, but we were going to talk about it." I look at Ellie.

"You mean, together? With Ellie?" It's the doctor again.

"Yes, look, what's going on? Why are you asking me this?"

"I'm just trying to understand if that's how you see your future. With Ellie."

"Or course I fucking do. Why are you asking me this right now? We're not on the bloody couch." I look around. The audience that has been assembled for the evening has all eyes on me.

"I'm just trying to establish if that's how you view your future – as a couple, I mean, with Ellie. Your wife. Only, I understand she asked you–"

"Begged!" she cries, suddenly and dramatically.

"Begged," the doctor picks up, "but you refused to go for couple's counselling with her, just like you told her that you planned to stay here and that she didn't have to."

I scowl at that. "Um, no. I think you'll find it's the other way around." I look at Ellie. "Why are you lying? *You* are the one who said you didn't want to go. You said that you were never going back into therapy again and you told me that I didn't have to come back to London with you," I say, but her only answer is to look at the doctor with a pained expression that I don't even recognise on her.

"*Stop* looking at him like that and tell him," I say.

Holmes speaks up. "She doesn't have to, Marco, because *you* told me that it was *you* who refused to go to therapy. Do you remember that?"

"Of course, I fucking remember. I'm not an idiot, Ethan."

"But just now you said that it was Ellie," he says calmly.

I'm about to come back at him, but instead, I take a breath and glance around the room and at the Christmas tree that's still attempting to bring cheer to the proceedings by faithfully cycling between light patterns.

But it's the only one making such an attempt.

Sarah is watching me with interest. David's bowed his head like he doesn't want to witness this car crash. Aaron's eyes keep flicking from Ellie to the doctor and then back to me. And the others are looking confused yet riveted. All they need now is the bloody popcorn!

I sigh. "Ellie said she didn't want to go to couple's therapy. I told you that I didn't want to go because I wanted to protect her."

"Protect her? From what?"

"From you! And your condescending judgment."

"From me? It wasn't me you were scheduled to see."

"You know what I mean."

"Marco!" Ellies cries.

"What? What's that? What are you crying about?"

"She's worried about you, Marc," David chimes in.

"Oh. She's worried about me. And you're not?"

"Well, I wasn't, but now I am."

I nod. "Right. And why's that?"

"I don't know. You just seem to be struggling, Marco, mate. You know… to acclimatise."

"*Struggling*. Did they teach you that? Yes, I've been struggling. I think most people would in my situation. But I'm fine. I'm perfectly fine. I've never felt better. So, you can take whatever this is, your little intervention or whatever, and shove it."

"But you're not fine, are you, though, Marco?" Holmes continues.

"No?"

"No." He turns to Ellie and nods reassuringly.

She pulls a pained face and looks around as if she's embarrassed. As if *she's struggling* with something.

"It's OK, Ellie. You can show him," Holmes says encouragingly.

"Show me what?"

But Ellie shakes her head and takes a step back so that she's just inches away from Alejandro or whatever the fuck his name is, and allows more tears to well in her eyes.

"Ellie. I know it's difficult, but it's important that he sees this," Holmes narrates.

Then, with a few sniffs, and one last glance around the room, she slowly, and some would say dramatically, lifts up the sleeves of her small sweater to display an ugly bruise running most of the circumference of her slender wrist. Then she repeats the process on the other and there's a collective gasp from the audience.

"Who did this to you, Ellie?" Holmes asks.

But my wife doesn't respond.

"Ellie," he prompts.

Eventually… after a few sniffs, she cries… "M-Ma… Marc."

"What? I didn't do that!"

"Are you saying that Ellie did this to herself?" Holmes asks.

"No. I'm telling you that she, that I, that we… that… I don't know. It must have happened this morning… um, during sex."

Ellie starts sobbing now.

I gawk at her. "What's going on? Why are you crying like that? Ellie…" I step forward, but Fernando moves in front of her.

"Are you fucking have a laugh?" I sneer, rage bubbling through me like hot lava.

"Did you force yourself on your wife this morning, Marco?"

I screw my face up. "What?"

"Did you have non-consensual sex with Ellie? Did you force her to have sex with you?" Holmes presses.

"No, I fucking did not! Why are you asking me this?" I turn to her. "El? is that what you told him?"

She doesn't answer. She's too busy crying into Frederico's comforting arms, and I've got an urge to jump across the sofa and deck the fucker, but something's telling that that isn't going to help my cause.

"Ellie, is that what you fucking told him?"

She doesn't respond.

"I can't believe this," I say, running my hands through my hair. "I can't believe I'm having to justify myself. *She* wanted it that way. *She* wanted me to be rough."

"Ellie wanted you to be rough? Why do you think she wanted you to be rough?" the doctor asks.

"I've no fucking idea! She's never been like that before."

"And what about the other night?" Holmes asks calmly.

"I don't know what you're talking about. What other night?"

"Last week. After you'd been to see me. You returned home and you physically assaulted her then, too. Didn't you?"

"What? No, I did not assault her! She attacked me! She accused me of killing our son and then she slapped me!" I yell.

"And yet you don't seem to have a scratch on you. But she, on the other hand, had more bruises."

"There were no bruises."

"There were bruises, Marco. Over her arms and wrists. I've seen the pictures."

I screw my face up once more, incredulously. "You took pictures?" I ask her. "To show him? Why?" She doesn't respond. She can't even bring herself to look at me. "Why?" I scream. "Why are you doing this to me, El? Why are you lying?"

But she says nothing; she's just whimpering in the arms of Federico like a battered wife! Which, by the way, is something I could never imagine Ellie putting up with.

"She isn't lying, though, Marco, is she?" Holmes continues.

"I think it's time for you to leave now, Ethan." I step aside and gesture to the door.

"She isn't lying, and you know she isn't. And this isn't

the first time, either, is it, Marco? This is not the first time you've resorted to violence to express your frustrations. There's a history here. We both know that."

I scoff. "Seriously, Ethan. You need to go."

"Why don't you want to hear this?"

"Because it isn't true."

"It isn't?"

"No."

"Ellie's lying?"

"Yes, she is."

"Why?"

"I have no fucking idea why!"

"And what about Drew? Is he lying, too?"

"What?" I turn to Drew, who's now taken his cue to hang his head, averting his gaze.

"Didn't you punch him in the face the other night?"

I gawk at him. "He'd fucking taken pictures of my house and sold them to a bloody newspaper!"

"And so your response was to punch him?"

"Um, let me think about that…. Yeah," I answer sarcastically.

"The dog breeder, too? Didn't you threaten to hit him? With a plank of wood, no less?"

I shake my head. "No. No, it wasn't like that. No."

"What about the estate agent, Lucinda? Didn't you threaten to burn down her house"

"What? No! It wasn't like that. You don't even know anything about it."

"I know that she was concerned. After she had read that newspaper article, she was deeply concerned. She has children, Marco. She filed a complaint."

What the…? I run hands through my hair. I can't believe this is happening to me.

I notice that my wife found that last bit of interest, as her eyes flick up and then back down again. *Oh, you didn't know about that did you? You don't know about that at all.*

The lights blink. A draft howls under one of the upstairs doors and, for added effect, it slams shut.

Everybody reacts except for me. I'm still basking in the fact that I obviously didn't imagine these noises. Besides, I've been here before.

When I turn back to the doctor, though, he's still looking at me. Eyes keen. Expression blank.

And I'm not standing for this. "Is that all you have, Doctor? A history of so-called violence?"

"Your wife is worried about you, Marco. She, *we*, only have your welfare at heart."

"Is that so?"

"Yes."

"Then, why did you feel you had to gang up on me?"

"Marc, you're not well! You think the house is haunted for Christ's sake, and you're seeing things again!" Ellie wails suddenly. Presumably because she thinks that the witch hunt is losing steam.

"Marco–"

"Oh God, Ethan, I can almost stomach this charade, but for your prefixing every sentence with my name. I haven't missed that. I have not missed that one bit."

Oh shit. I'm stalling because we're now straying into quite literally scary territory.

"What did you see in the bathroom, Marco?"

"I saw a shower in the bathroom, Ethan, and a toilet and a basin," I say firmly.

"Didn't these men find you naked, screaming at thin air because you believed that a swarm of moths had invaded the room, and that a creature, one of the so-called *intruders*, had come crawling out of the bath towards you?"

"You're breaking privilege, Doctor," I warn him.

"Isn't that what you told these men?" the doctor asks, turning toward the three traitors behind him.

"I, um… I can't explain that. No. Well–"

"What about the toy dinosaur that you said had spontaneously appeared in the kitchen?"

I look at Irvin, who shrugs helplessly.

"And what about the fact that you think that puppy in there is a reincarnation of our son?" Ellie cries out.

Oh wow. Hearing it spoken aloud is creepier than I thought it would be.

"Marco?" Holmes is watching me, expectantly, and prompts, "Is that what you believe?"

Shit. My heart's drumming now in rhythm with the rain that's making its presence felt against the patio doors.

"It's not what it sounds like," I say quickly.

Oh shit, don't say that. Everybody says that!

"Then, why don't you tell me what it's like?"

"I–"

"He's telling the truth!"

It's Sarah. I haven't really looked much in her direction since this trial started, but the few times I have, mostly out of embarrassment, she's seemed to have a pained expression on her face. Of sympathy. Compassion.

Now, all eyes, including mine, have turned to her.

"He's telling the truth," she repeats, softer this time as she starts to feel the weight of everybody's gaze. "I saw the signs."

"The signs?" the doctor asks.

"Yes. In the kitchen. In the washing powder. I have pictures," Sarah says, pulling her phone out of her pocket.

Shit. I'd forgotten about those, and hearing her say it like that, like she's some kind of tea reader, I'm starting to wonder if it was probably best she not say anything.

And yet... "I did some research," she continues, pulling the photos up on her phone and showing them around the room. Though, if I'm being perfectly honest, from where I stand, it just looks like loads of spilt washing powder.

She looks at me. "I was going to tell you the other day, but figured you already had enough going on." Then, to the rest of the room, with a focus on the doctor, like he's suddenly become the master of ceremonies, she continues. "They appear to be from the family of ancient spirals believed to date back many centuries, predating even Sumerian language." She turns back to me with a faint smile and a face full of hope, as if I'm the one who needs convincing, and says, "They're believed to symbolise *spring equinox, renewal* and *rebirth*."

The lights flicker again and a murmur ripples through what feels like my jury, and then come three loud bangs on the front door.

While everybody else looks startled, I, for a refreshing change, am smiling.

"I guess I should get that," I say, cheerily because I've heard those knocks before, and I know exactly who that is. Absolutely no one.

"Marco, wait—"

"Don't worry, Doc. I'm not going to run off," I say. "Shit!" There's a pool of water inside the front door.

I step around it because that's the least of my problems right now, and pull the door open with a flourish…. And I'm surprised to find a pair of men in slickers on the doorstep. One short and spindly. The other tall, fat, and hefty.

Not what I was expecting.

I gawk at them as rain winks in the floodlight and scurries down their waterproofs as if it's just been caught doing something it shouldn't.

The worst bit: They look familiar.

"We got here as soon as we could, Doctor Holmes," sasquatch says, talking over my shoulder.

Oh fuck. I know who they are now. The short, thin one is the bastard who injected me with however many CCs of *get-the-fuck-to-sleep* when I tried to asphyxiate the doctor with my bare hands.

Long story, which you'll most likely remember if you were here last time.

I back away from the door and into the house, which probably isn't the most sensible thing to do, but, hey, I'm in shock here.

"What's going on, Ethan?" I ask warily as the two men enter the house, close the door, and casually shake the water from their coats.

"Marco—"

"What the fuck are they doing here?" Now it's my turn to whine.

"They're just here to make sure we get you back safely."

"Back? Back where?"

"Marco, I just want you to come in for a while so that we can talk some more about the things that have been happening here."

"No. No, Ethan. You know you can't do that."

"Marco, you know I can."

"These two aren't police."

"No, but we don't want them to be right now because I want you to come with me voluntarily. If I called the police, it would be under a Section 136, and that's much more formal. I'm hoping it won't come to that." The last words are emphasised as a warning.

"You have no grounds for this."

"You know I do. You've only recently been released from treatment, and you've assaulted one person, threatened two others… and Ellie has already filed for battery and sexual assault. Not to mention everything else. I have very good reason to believe that you represent a risk to others and potentially yourself. Now, as I say, I'd like you to come in voluntarily just for a short while so that I can complete a full assess—"

"NO! NO! Ethan, HELL fucking no! I'm not going back there. NO!"

My heart is tapping on my ribcage now, telling me that we should probably get the hell out of here, but I've no idea where.

Buddy is at the study door. Barking, yapping, and scratching to be freed so that he can join the argument.

"Please, Marco, for everybody's sake, don't make this any harder than it needs to be."

Ellie's sobbing now, as she did that night when I first emerged from my original delusion… and I've got to give it to her, she's a fantastic actress.

"Marco?"

I glance to my right, where I can see Lurch and the spindly

dwarf are ready for action. I could probably take the dwarf, but Lurch? Well, we all know how that ended last time.

"It's OK, Buddy. Daddy's OK. Daddy's alright," I coo loudly over my shoulder. And I can feel everybody's gaze shift.

"Wow.. chill out, people. I haven't completely lost my marbles. He's a puppy. How would you rather I try to calm him down? Shut up, dog, be quiet, or Ellie's favourite, 'Shut the fuck up, *IT*'?"

Lurch and his chum are circling now like a couple of wild cats. Inching closer as if I can't bloody see them.

"Easy boys," I say, holding out a hand.

"Marco—"

"Ethan. Wait, wait. Just wait."

"Marco—"

"Please, Ethan. Just wait. Just a second. Give me a second here to collect my thoughts."

Rain taps and dings. A gale is moaning somewhere. Lights flicker again, and I get this uneasy feeling that I'm being watched, but not just by the people in this room. Something else.

"Ethan, do you think I respect you?"

"What?"

"You heard me, Doctor. Do you think I respect you?"

"I have no idea."

"Take a guess. *Indulge me*," I say, using one of his favourite phrases as I glance at him and then back at the two attack dogs, and then back at the doctor once more.

Holmes shrugs. "If I were to hazard a guess. You probably do respect me even though you may not admire my therapeutic methods."

"Wow. Doc, that's pretty good. Fairly accurate."

I glance at my wife, who's busy being comforted by her Abercrombie model, all while being sure to throw in a few sniffs for good measure.

"Well, Ethan, what if I told you that you're being made a fool of?" He frowns. "Not by me, Doc, by her." I nod at my wife.

"Marco, we've been through this—"

"No, not yet, we haven't. But indulge me, please. And I promise you, if you feel exactly the same after I've finished talking, then I'll gladly escort Lurch and his dwarf friend to their car."

He thinks about this for a few seconds. Then, reluctantly, he nods at the two men.

"Doctor Holmes, please. This is already hard enough!" Ellie cries, and is that a note of hysteria or frustration in my wife's voice?

But the doctor holds up a pausing hand to her.

"You're being played, Ethan," I begin. "Ellie wants me to be committed again."

"See what I mean," Ellie interjects, "He's paranoid!"

I look at Ellie. "Did you know that my wife loves films?" I ask.

"What?"

"You know, the black and white ones from the forties and fifties?"

"Marco, this isn't helping–"

"No. It's relevant, Doc, I promise you. Just bear with me. You love those movies, don't you, Ellie? Toby did, too. He was like that, our son. He was the kind of boy who'd try anything once. Always exploring. Always eager to learn, to experience new things."

"This isn't about Toby, Marco," Ellie whines.

"Well, maybe not directly, El, but it is in other ways, though, isn't it?"

"Marco…" Holmes starts.

I hold up a steadying hand. "Ellie, why don't you tell these good people which one of those black and white films is your favourite?"

I watch my wife's eyes narrow and her lips purse in same way they do when she's irritated. But she quickly changes her demeanour. "Ethan, can't you see he's rambling now? He thinks he's in court."

Ethan glances at her and then back at me. I'm on borrowed time.

I go on, "One of her favourite black and white movies is *Gaslight*. It stars Ingrid Bergman. And there's one of those Christmas tree gifts for anyone who is able to tell me what that film is about."

I look at the blank faces around the room, except for my wife's. There's suddenly a flicker of interest there. "Do you want to tell them, babe?"

My only response is more pursing of those beautiful lips. "No? OK, I'll tell them. It's about a husband who makes his wife think she's going insane.

"Ellie wants you to take me in again, Ethan. She wants you to think I'm losing my marbles again so she can get on with her plan as well as enjoying quality time with Geraldo or whatever his name is over there."

The doctor sighs. "So, let me get this right, just to make sure I've understood you. I'm paraphrasing here. Ellie, your wife, is trying to make you think you are going insane because she has a lover and wants to be with him?" Holmes asks.

"Well, I'm no body language expert, but from where I'm standing, I think it's safe to assume that Riccardo's pretty smitten with her. Isn't that right, Ricky?" I watch him tense and straighten, but don't wait for a response. Instead, I turn to my best friend. "Isn't that right, Dave, mate?"

David suddenly looks like that proverbial rabbit in the headlights.

I ask him, "I mean, it didn't occur to me straight away, but I did wonder what had happened to you because I hadn't heard a thing since the original text when we left London a few weeks back. After that, complete radio silence. What happened, David? Did Ellie tell you to stay away? Give you some crap sob story about how I needed time to adjust, to heal?"

He slowly turns to her and frowns. And I have my answer.

"See, at the risk of sounding like Perry Mason, you represented a serious risk to her for multiple reasons," I comment. "The more she kept you away from me while her plan was ongoing, the more it would have a chance of succeeding. But she hadn't banked on you, though, Aaron, had she?" I look at him and smile.

Then I turn back to the rest of the room. "And who can forget that one, noticeably short, non-committal text about the money? Ellie knew I didn't want to ask David, but she couldn't take the risk that I procrastinate too long. So, she sent the text on my behalf.

"Unlike my wife's, my phone isn't password-protected. That's because I no longer have anything to hide.

"Disclaimer. This next bit is what the people in legalese refer to as *circumstantial*, but it makes perfect sense now.

"While it would be easy to think that I sent that text message, the fact that my phone is unlocked means that anybody who had access to it could have sent it. In this case, it was my wife. And this had dual purpose. The main one, obviously, was to get the cash. She knew he had it. She worked with him for years. And she was banking on our close relationship, him feeling disconnected, guilty for firing her and for not telling me that he'd seen the two of them together.

"The second purpose was to make me think I was losing my bloody mind. And it worked, especially because she immediately put me on the defensive by pretending to be irritated by the fact that I hadn't consulted her about the money. She figured that something as simple as not remembering to send a text about something so important would have me questioning myself. And that, along with everything else, meant that all I would need was a simple nudge to think I was spiralling again.

"And it worked. I was so busy dealing with that, trying to keep it together, that I missed one glaringly obvious thing – besides the time it was sent, although tracing that back to an actual moment would have been complicated – and it was staring at me the whole time.

"I tend not to address David or anyone close to me as 'Bud' or 'Buddy', and there's one simple reason for that. They were nicknames, terms of endearment or whatever you want to call them for Toby. So, I make a point of not using them with anybody else. At least, not until this little guy came along."

I move over to the photography room and open the door. Buddy comes bounding out and heels by my side.

"I would never address David as *Bud* in a text message.

"Then there was the dinosaur. She knew that if I saw that,

I would flip out, which I did. And, of course, if there happened to be a builder around to witness the meltdown, then that would be a bonus. You could have easily hung around and performed that trick yourself because you knew that, even if I caught you in the act, you could easily make some excuse about coming home early.

"You did pretty much the same thing with the creepy photos. You chose the one perfect night when I was passed out because I'd fallen off the wagon. Drank that wine. It wasn't much, but I'd been off the booze for a while. You knew it wouldn't take much. You shot the photos on my own phone for added creepiness – again, safe in the knowledge that you could make up any excuse if I woke up and caught you.

"Then, for added effect, you deleted them the following day to make me think I was truly losing it. First, thinking that someone had been in the house, and second, that they had vanished like they'd been taken by a ghost or something.

Unfortunately for you, you'd already set all this other stuff in motion, so my mind did what it's done best and suppressed some of it, diluting the impact of the experience.

"Ethan, how much longer are you going to listen to this?" Ellie chimes in, stepping forward. "Can't you hear? He is delusional. He is suffering. How much longer are you going to let him act out like this?"

Ethan looks at me.

"I know, it's all circumstantial," I say, "but don't worry, I'm getting to the best part."

"This is sad. The next thing you're going to say is that I was responsible for the fucking visions you've been having, too. Like the one you had in the bathroom, where no less than three witnesses found you naked, screaming. Are you going to make me responsible for that, too?" Ellie asks impatiently.

"Don't you worry. I'm coming to that because even I couldn't work it out at first. I mean, there was that along with all the other things that you couldn't possible have manipulated. Or could you?

"Ethan, the pills you prescribed. You warned me about the side effects. Do you remember? Of which I had none. No sleepiness.

No weight gain, and definitely no loss of sex drive, more's the pity. It was almost as if I hadn't been taking them at all. But I did take them, didn't I, Ellie?"

"How am I supposed to know?" she snaps, folding her arms and momentarily dropping her façade.

"Well, you're the one who swapped them out for placebos, aren't you? What were they? Stage prop sugar capsules?

"No taste. No side effect. No effectiveness to suppress visions brought on by the additional stress of my marriage imploding and, of course, other things going bump in the night, thanks to you."

"Ethan! You are here to do a job. Do your job!" my wife snaps. How much longer are you going to let him suffer like this? How much longer do we have to listen to this rubbish?" Ellie asks again. "Now, I brought my concerns to you before he even left the institute, yet you insisted on letting him out, and now look what's happened. He's hurt me, he's hurt others, and threatened more. You've known about this for a while now. And if anything else happens, I guarantee you that anyone who needs to know will know about it and it'll be your turn to lose your job. You—"

He holds up a silencing hand. "Yes, thanks, Ellie. I get the picture. You don't have to dramatize it any further."

Ooh, check you out, Doc.

He's looking at me. "Marco, while this all sounds plausible, as you say, much of it is circumstantial."

"It is. The pills aren't, though, are they? I mean, you can have those analysed, can't you, Ethan? I'm assuming you know what is actually supposed to be in them, don't you?"

"Jesus Christ! I can't believe we're listening to this shit. And you could have swapped those out yourself, brainchild, to make me think that you were still taking them when really you weren't!" Ellie accuses me.

"Sabotaging myself?" I ask with a wry smile. "Does that make any sense to anybody here?" I look around the room and then back at my wife, and I sneer, "Didn't truly think this bit through, did you, love?

"Then again, you would know all about keeping up

pretences, wouldn't you? Given that you did it so spectacularly well for, what, two weeks now? You made me think that you'd been offered your old job back at David's and that you were travelling there to work every day."

"I never told you that! You told me to ask David for my old job back and I told you that I couldn't because of what happened. Me, losing my own mind. Thanks to you!"

Ethan looks at me, and I know what he's thinking.

"He said, she said, right?"

He doesn't need to answer.

"If only there were some kind of proof. Some kind of document in which you detail your dastardly plan in meticulous detail."

Ooh. What was that? A little flicker of something behind those devious eyes.

"You see, Ellie. Best laid plans and all that. When you devised yours, it overlooked many things, but there was one whopper of a thing that you didn't truly consider…"

I wait. Rain hisses. Water dribbles.

"This is the part where you ask, *what's that?* And then I tell you. In the movies, they call it *the reveal.*"

"Ethan!" Ellie wails.

I watch the doctor glance at the two men.

"It's OK, Ethan, I'm pretty much done. I promise. I just need one thing."

The doctor shrugs and sighs. In for a penny, in for a pound.

"I want my wife to ask me what she overlooked."

"Marco—"

"Ethan, if she wants me carted off, the sooner she asks the question, the sooner it's going to happen," I tell him, fast and bitterly.

The doctor turns to her.

"You've got to be fucking joking," she snaps.

Everybody waits.

She glares at me. "What the fuck was it, Marco?"

"And there she is. You didn't consider that this house might actually be haunted."

"OK, Marco. Let's go," Ethan says.

"What's the hurry, Doc? I don't think we're going to be getting far anytime soon. This is where it ends for us."

"OK, that's enough."

"We've both dreamt it, Ethan," I say to him. Then I turn to my wife, the person who seems to hate me more than anyone in the world, and ask, "You have, too, haven't you, Ellie? In your dreams. The drowning. Being ripped away from Toby. In my dreams, I'm drowning, too. And in my dreams, I see you leave with him."

"You're sick," she sneers. "You're fucking sick!"

I sense the two men closing in on me, but I don't stop.

"You know, El. All the times you used to complain about me teasing Toby? You know, when I asked which parent was his favourite, I used to think you didn't like me asking because you thought that it was somehow stressing him out. You know, having to choose and everything. Turns out, El, that wasn't the reason, was it?"

She doesn't answer because she's too busy watching Lurch and his sidekick slide their way towards me.

"Doc, it turns out that my wife didn't like me asking our son which parent was his favourite because she was worried about his answer. She was worried that he might choose me over her. And that wouldn't do, would it, El?" I ask, turning to my wife, "Because in your world, Ellie, there's only one reply, isn't there? In your world, Toby says: *Mummy Is My Favourite.*

"Doesn't he? Followed by his birthday with no spaces. That's your password, isn't it?"

"You fucking cocksucker!" she screams, running around the sofa towards me, her claws outstretched and ready to inflict damage, but she's intercepted by Aaron, who restrains her with those big guns of his. "Get off me! Get the fuck off me!"

Buddy walks over my foot and starts growling at the two men.

Who is your favourite parent?

I turn to Ethan. "This whole time, Ethan… my wife has been keeping a meticulous journal. It dates all the way back to when I was still at the institute. It chronicles everything that has happened to her over that time, as well as everything she planned to do and did to lead us up to this very moment, including this whole little soiree of so-called close friends. Although, she wasn't banking on Sarah and the lads being here, too. Which is why she wasn't happy when she found out.

"It's all there in pixels and bytes. And, as I'm sure our resident computer whizz will attest, the files are all electronically date-stamped with machine IP addresses, and the works." I look at Dean hopefully, and he nods.

"Dean will also attest that you shouldn't use the same password for both your machine and your documents, El. That's a serious security risk." I tut. "And by the way, I've made sure it's all backed up to the cloud now for you. Just for good measure. You know, the internet is a bit rubbish around here.

"I've also emailed copies to the Doc and anybody else who might be interested, including your parents. I bet they'll get a real kick out of all the stuff you wrote about them. In fact, I'm sure daddy is going to love reading the soft porn you wrote about you and Paolo over there."

"You're pathetic," she sneers, sidling back to her Latin lover, whose eyes I've noticed are bulging with incomprehension. "I hate you! I fucking hate you!" she spits.

So, I go in for the kill, "Oh, and by the way. Fernando, just in case you're interested, she's pregnant, but doesn't plan to keep it. She never wants to have children ever again. Apparently, giving birth to Toby and then losing him broke her. And I can relate to that."

No. Judging by that disgusted look on his face, I'd say he didn't know about that until now.

I turn to Ethan. "As for you, Ethan. Tell Laurel and Hardy here to step the fuck back before I do something that they'll regret. I'm not coming back with you. If you want to lock me up, you best fetch the cops because I'm not going anywhere. I plan to stay here and enjoy the hard work of these fine men, courtesy of my best friend-backstabber who knew that my wife was having it off with Ferdinando over there, but didn't bother telling me. But it's OK, I forgive you because I know you did what you thought was best. As long as you can forgive her for what I'm about to say next.

"You did all of this for nothing, El. All of it. The reason why Lucinda and I had words is because she rang me earlier today and told me that the buyers have withdrawn their offer on her advice, if you can believe that, because, get this, this house is unsaleable. *Subject to subsidence*, I think is what she said.

"Which means, dear wifey, that you now owe David forty grand from your own pocket. Sorry about that, mate," I say to my best friend, who lowers his gaze miserably.

I look at Ethan, and see that there's a faint smile on the doctor's face. "That's some story, Marco. And while you may not have to come back with us tonight, I'm still obliged to ask you to come in or, if you prefer, refer you to someone for a general evaluation. You can appreciate that, can't you? Being an almost fully qualified therapist yourself."

"Ethan, I—"

Buddy interrupts me as he starts growling at the staircase before I hear that ominous, tell-tale creak and am assaulted by that horrible, prickly feeling at the back of my neck.

This isn't over yet.

Ethan is looking at the stairs, too, as Buddy's growl has turned into his trademark yapping.

"Can you smell that, Ethan?"

"What is that? Lavatory or something?"

"No. That's the smell of something that doesn't ex-ist." The word is cut in half because the lights flicker and die, and there's a collective cry from the group that is now only periodically lit in the alternating red, white, and blue hue of the blinking Christmas tree.

I'm thankful that I chose the outdoor lights with a rechargeable battery specifically for this reason, but I have no idea how long they will last.

"Aarggghhh!" Laurel, the spindly henchman, swipes the back of his head and rushes past me before turning and gawking at where he was standing.

"What's wrong with you?" Holmes demands.

"Something… something just touched the back of my head."

"What are you–" Holmes begins, but is interrupted when Hardy does the same.

Then, someone else yelps from the other side of the room.

I watch Buddy barking at the empty space in front of the door.

"I think we've got company," I say in a hushed tone as my body tenses for what I know is to come.

Buddy's attention is shifting around and past me and back towards Laurel and Hardy, who clock on and rush off to join the rest of the group, but that's exactly where Buddy's attention settles.

"Marco… what's going on?"

"Ethan, I did tell you that some of the things that happened here could not be explained. At least not rationally," I say, staring at the group and holding my breath in between the cycles of light.

Dark.

Ellie screams and rushes forward, and then stops abruptly. Breathing in ragged breaths, she slowly lifts a shaky hand in front of her as if to feel for something.

Dark.

Light.

"There… there's s-.s-s-something standing in front of me," she breathes. And then, to everybody's collective horror, we watch as, clump by clump, strands of her hair slowly snake upward as if driven by static electricity.

Light – Up.

Dark.

Light – Up further.

Dark.

Ellie starts making a howling sound as her body remains rigid, but her eyes are bulge and then swivel all around her. "Wh… wh… what's ha… ha-ha-happening?"

It would be comical if it wasn't so terrifying, but Ellie's hair is standing up now as if gelled there.

"Stop this!" Fernando orders, and he steps forward.

"No!" I shout.

But it's too late. An ear-piercing shriek fills the room, and I watch as the man's hair is visibly blown backwards as if the very air around Ellie just screamed in his face.

"What the fuck was that?!" David yells.

I feel that familiar boulder of dread in my belly, but at the same time I feel energised, buoyed by the fact that, for the first time ever, other people are bloody seeing this, too.

"It's my mother," I say warily, searching the room for any tell-tale signs of her presence.

Ellie has collapsed to the floor now, sobbing uncontrollably, and is in the process of being helped to her feet by Sarah of all people when we all duck at a sudden explosion of thunder overhead.

"That felt like it came from inside the attic!" someone exclaims.

And it did. But I've been in this situation before, and it's fucking terrifying, but nothing could have been as bad as being chased up the bloody stairs by those things.

The thunder has barely rolled away when a scratching sound takes over. And we all turn to look at the front door as the light, like a car indicator, clicks on and off.

Click - Dark.

Click - Light.

Click - Dark.

Click - Light.

I notice that even Ethan's demeanour has changed now. His body is ramrod straight. Eyes wide, peering into the gloom, waiting on the cycles of light to try and work out what exactly is out there.

Scratch. Scratch. Scratch.

It's growing progressively louder now, and more frequent, as if there are multiple things scratching at the wood.

I take a step forward and hear someone gasp.

"What was that?"

Which frightens the hell out of me, especially since the bloody lights have happened to die at the same time.

"I just saw something standing by the stairs!" It's Dean.

"Don't you start," Drew counters.

"I fucking did!" he squeals.

Click - Light.

I quickly scan the space to try to work out what they're seeing, but I can't see anything… although Buddy seems to be losing his mind, turning his attention all around the room.

Click - Dark.

Sarah screams. "Something just touched my face!" she gasps, looking around herself.

Click - Light.

I can see water gushing into the house in small arcs under the door, each sonar ring bringing it closer and closer to the den.

Click - Dark.

"G… g… ett… off…. Get… st… op." Someone is choking, and I think it's Drew. "What's happening?!" I scream into the dark.

Someone yelps.

Click - Light.

I see Drew shoving Dean away from him. Eyes bulging with inexplicable terror as he holds his hands to his neck.

"What the hell, man?" Dean complains. "You… fucking tried to choke me!"

"IT WASN'T ME!"

Click - Dark.

Buddy's bark is reduced to a growl now, and that in itself is comforting, but I'm feeling vulnerable out here. Breathing heavily and holding my arms out to protect myself from a sudden attack.

The scratching seems louder in the dark, as does the rush of water. I've got to see what's happening out there. We've also got to get out of here.

Now's the time to make a move.

Click - Light.

Buddy and I are both staring at the front door, although I've noticed that he's now following me as if afraid of what might be in the water.

"OK, It's time we get out of here," I say, sloshing forward, the freeze of the water instantly nipping at my feet.

Scratch… scratch.

I don't know what's beyond this door, but what I do know is that we're no longer safe in this house because I'm suddenly feeling overwhelmed with a lung-constricting sense of foreboding.

Click - Dark.

This is where it ends for you.

And I can feel it. I can't explain it, but I can bloody feel it. It's as if there's a virus or something inside me. I can feel it in my chest, in my heart, in my bones. Every fibre of me is telling me that this is it.

The dreams. They were all leading up this moment. And somehow, though I don't know how, I feel like I'm going to die here. I'm going to drown. And this may well be the moment it's going to happen.

And I'm fine with that, I think. I think I've made my peace, but what I don't want is for anybody else to suffer, too.

This is where it ends for you.

Click - Light.

"Come on!" I shout over my shoulder before taking a deep breath, steeling myself, and yanking open the front door.

The first thing to hit me is the barrage of water. It sloshes over my legs and invokes a collective shriek from inside the room.

The next, well, it feels like I've opened the door to a hurricane. It's truly biblical.

The rain sprays over me as if God himself just spat. What little I can make out of tree shadows, backlit by the rest of the village, is that giant invisible hands are throttling them. It's obvious that the stream has swollen into a rushing river and that that river has burst its banks.

Now, the drive, lawn, and pathway have disappeared, replaced by a sheet of muddy water that is rippling by with the downdraft of the gale.

Thunder moans like a disgruntled giant, but I barely notice it and the rest of the apocalyptic scene because my eyes are drawn to something else. Something that I have never seen before. Something that has me hopping from one splash puddle to another as someone somewhere is screaming.

"What the actual fuck?" I gasp.

There are hundreds or maybe even thousands of the black objects floating on the water. They could easily be mistaken for small lumps of wood, were it not for the spikes of knotted fur sticking up from their backs like fins, and the fact that they are all moving in unison, like a shoal of fish, towards the front door... towards me with their long tails floating languidly behind them like bloody reptilian appendages!

The rats emerge from their surreal aquaplaning and scurry forward to seek shelter inside, where there is now complete pandemonium. There are shrieks, screams, and people climbing onto and jumping over couches to evade the marauders.

Three of the things – beady black eyes bulging, whiskers quivering – latch onto my trousers and begin to climb towards my chest before I slap them away.

Then, I leap back inside and shove the door shut once more, breathing heavily and rapidly for several second before I'm jumped by another group of glistening shadows. The intervals of Christmas tree lighting amplify the terror of the wet claws and squidgy bodies latching onto my flesh through the thin layering of my clothes.

I shriek even while attempting to convince myself that the rats are more terrified of me than I am of them, watching them scamper around the room, under and over furniture and people as they attempt to evade them. Buddy is now sounding a belated alarm by yapping at the unwanted houseguests and adding to the commotion as more thunder rumbles overhead, and I'm hoping this might be the prelude to the end of the torrential downpour.

"Get me out of here! Get me out of here!" I think Ellie is screaming, but it's hard to tell given all the ruckus that is taking place in partial darkness like a terrifying edition of bloody musical statues.

"Right! Everyone! Everyone! Just calm the fuck down!" I yell, pulling my phone out of my pocket, tapping on the light, and shining it around the room. Everybody else seems to notice that they have one of these things, too, and before long, a whole group of powerful LEDs, like searchlights, are roving around the walls and floor, reanimating shadows and scaring away the dregs of the furry intruders.

"We need to get out of here, Marc," Ethan, who is standing closest to me, says quickly.

Like I haven't thought of that.

"We do, but I don't think it's going to be out that way," I say, aiming my light at the front door, where the scratching persists as the rest of the furry armada demand entry.

"Well, we can't stay here," Ellie retorts, and then she shrieks when a light beam finds a whole new group of rodent contortionists squeezing their way under the door and scaring most people back towards the patio, where Laurel and Hardy – the duo who were acting tough with me just minutes ago – are now cowering at the back like frightened children.

"Marco," it's Irvin speaking now, "I reckon we should–"

"Shh…. Wait," I say. "Can you hear that?"

"Yeah, those things are still runnin' around in 'ere," says Drew.

"And they're at the windows!" Ellie yells, shining her torch. Sure enough… the house is acting as a partial dam. The water obviously isn't running off fast enough to the sides and is gradually building into some sickening swimming pool for rodents because we're now able to see countless, clawed limbs floating about outside the windows.

"OK… just calm down for a second. I think the rain has stopped because I can hear the ocean again. Look!" I shout, pointing at the patio doors. I can see the garden. The moon's out.

Thunder rumbles as if to remind me that it's still loitering in the vicinity, but at least it must be easing up out there.

"Well, that's brilliant, but how does that help us now?" Drew asks.

"It doesn't. But at least it's not making things worse."

"Right and–" Drew begins, but interrupts himself. "What's that?"

At first, I follow his light beam because I assume he's

talking about something specific, but then I see that he isn't looking anywhere in particular.

Buddy starts barking again. This time, towards the patio doors where the two slicker men are looking around themselves as if searching for something.

Then, I feel it. A vibration that starts in my feet and makes its way through my body. I watch open-mouthed as the beams of light begin trembling.

"What's going on?" Drew asks nervously, shining his light all around the room.

"I don't know," I utter as I try to decipher it. My first thought is that it's more thunder, but it can't be because this sound is persistent and growing in intensity.

I follow Buddy's bark towards the patio doors and watch how, one by one, all light beams slowly follow the same direction.

The rumble continues to grow louder, stronger. It's definitely something making its way from the ocean towards the house, and then it occurs to me… the coastguard. It's a helicopter!

"It's a fucking helicopter!" I yell, jumping up and down, squinting out of the patio doors for a searchlight or something as the noise draws closer.

I take a step forward, but stop when I hear David, who is standing by the Christmas tree, utter, "What… the… fuck? The tree is moving. The tree is fucking moving!"

I look at the Christmas tree and frown. Because it isn't.

But then a deafening squeal pierces the night. Closely followed by a ginormous shadow falling out of the sky, momentarily blocking the moonlight, before crashing down in a dissonance of screech, creaks, and crunching. The impact is so powerful, it shakes the very floor beneath us, knocking some off their feet.

At first, I think it's the bloody rescue helicopter crashing, but then I realise.

"OH… MY… GOD…."

I've barely had time to breathe out the words before I watch the men in rain slickers, along with the whole horizon of the patio doors, crumble and disappear before my very eyes.

"GET AWAY FROM THE DOORS!" I scream, but it's too late.

A cacophony of sounds explodes like a percussion grenade – the deafening roar of the surf; the screaming sound of the wind; and the twist, split, and crumble of stone, wood, and mortar.

I can do nothing but watch in stupefied horror as the ceiling under what was our bedroom and bathroom collapses. A rain of splintered wood, plaster, tiles, and furniture lands on Cristian, toppling him backward into oblivion.

Then, Aaron looks at David, who looks at me before the floor gives way beneath them and they both disappear out of sight, shortly followed by the Christmas tree that, lights and all, lunges headfirst after them.

Irvin, Drew, and Dean are next. Each of them scrambling over the sofa to climb away from God knows what when the coffee table, armchairs, and then the sofas themselves shift backward and then sink out of sight, taking the threesome with them in a chorus of terrified screams.

And now I can see it.

A surreal, nocturnal landscape straight out of one of my nightmares. It is as familiar to me as it is shocking.

The full moon.

The giant, ragged clouds scattered like phantoms across a black and foreboding sky.

The agitated surface of the ocean and the roar of the surf resonating around me. Now, no longer languishing far away at the foot of the lawn, but below the precipice to hell just a few metres in front of me.... Inside what used to be the den.

A jagged crack runs from the cliff's edge up what's left of the centre of the room towards the front door like an angry mouth inching wider with each crashing wave in its attempt to devour both Ethan and me.

Ellie and Sarah are collapsed on either side of the chasm.

It takes several seconds that feel like minutes for me to process and then react to the spectacle before me.

"Ellie, Sarah. Can you hear me?" I yell over the deafening sound of the turbulence echoing off walls.

Both look up at me. Ellie with a tearstained face. Sarah with a stupefied gaze and long hair flying about and in front of her as if reaching for me.

Buddy has sensibly retreated to the windowsill next to the new aquarium in the corner of the room as water and rats continue to squish under the door and scamper by us on their way to obscurity.

"Ellie. Sarah. I need you both to make your way towards us. Quick as you can, please," I add with as much calmness as I can muster. Then, I hold up a uselessly defensive arm when part of the ceiling on Sarah's side of the room, underneath the spare room, gives way in a cloud of plaster.

"Sarah!" I scream when I first see a leg and then a whole bed frame push through a crack in the ceiling and crash down inches from her before gouging out another slice of the floor and carrying it over the precipice into the icy cauldron I imagine beyond.

"Fuck! Ethan, help her!" I yell as I move to the opposite side to help Ellie.

From here, spotlighted by the moon, I now have a terrifying partial view of what's happened. Most of the peninsula has collapsed into the ocean as it reclaims another landscape scalp, as foretold by Lucinda. Tears fill my eyes as both the devastation of the place and the loss of life presses on me like the gale and mist that's whizzing around the room. And I'm determined. I'm so fucking determined that they will be the last.

I slide my arms around Ellie. "Come on!" I shout, hauling her to her feet and leading her towards the front door.

I glance over to see that Ethan is doing the same with Sarah as other parts of the ceiling succumb to the compromised frame of the building.

However, like me, he stops when he notices that the front door is shaking.

"Ethan!" I yell. "Let's not risk it. Come over to this side," I suggest, though this means crossing the now considerably wider faultline leading to the front door. "We can try leaving through the kitchen instead!"

He nods, and has started to move in my direction when–

The front door suddenly bursts inward and a four-foot-wide torrent of water wriggling with rats bursts through, washes them off their feet, and sweeps them back towards the cliff's edge, their screams reduced to gurgles.

The gale, like a wild demon summoned by the turbulence created by the wind funnel, screeches gleefully around the room, snatching ornaments and anything else that isn't weighted down to carry it over the edge.

It's deafening. Strong. Freezing.

Ethan is still holding onto Sarah with one hand while white-knuckle clinging to the doorframe of what was the photography room with his other, but, from the strain on his face, and the fact that he's barely able to breathe in the face of the wall of freeze rushing at him, I know he's not going to last much longer.

"HOLD ON!" I yell, and I move to help, but Ellie grabs hold of my arm.

"Where are you going?" she screams.

"TO HELP!"

"No! Stay here. I need you. I'm your wife!"

"Let go!"

"STAY!"

"FUCKING LET GO OF ME!" I yell and shake her off, but when I turn, it's only in time to see Sarah's exhausted, bemused face look at me and smile before she is washed over the side, closely followed by Ethan.

"NOOOOOOO!"

I rush forward to see if they've somehow managed to grab a hold of something else over the other side, but as I do, the whole wall and stairs opposite me crumble away to reveal a new expanse of moonlit ocean.

Suddenly, I find myself on the brink of the end.

I barely have time to register Ellie's scream, "MARCO! THERE'S SOMEONE BEHIND YOU!" before I feel powerful hands shove me from behind just as the floor beneath my feet crumbles away like dust, and then there's nothing but emptiness.

46. THIS IS WHERE IT ENDS

I'm spinning like a ragdoll in a washing machine of salty water. The freeze, wrapped around my chest like a vice, is squeezing, pushing, and forcing every bubble of life support from my body until there's nothing left but paralysis.

Limbs no longer thrashing. Lungs no longer working.

It's time for me to *accept*. I'm well-versed at that now. I know what to do. I know the process.

The human instinct, of course, is to rebel at first, rejecting the things over which I have no control, but I know now that resistance is futile, *acceptance* inevitable.

Daddy! Over here.

Toby. My flesh. My blood. My pride. My joy. I can hear you, buddy. Through the water. I can feel you all over me. And it's no longer cold. No longer freezing, buddy. That smile of yours is as warm and as bright at the sun itself.

This is where you end.

This is where I end.

This is where you end.

This is where I die.

Daddy! Over here!

Am I dreaming again? I'm not, am I? This isn't the dream. Feels different this time. Vivid. Visceral. Darker. Colder.

I'm sinking.

This is where you end.

This is where I end.

This is where you end.

This is where I die.

Daddy! Over here!

I'm sinking. Deeper and deeper. There's no air. No more air.

This is where you end.

This is where I end. This is where I die.

Daddy!

To... Toby.

Come find me.

I ca... ca... can't... buddy.... it's c-co... cold... t-too... cold....

Daddy... just follow the colours. Follow the colour.

I want to follow the colour, but there isn't any down here. It's all dark. Just black.

Daddy! Wake up! Come on. You need to come find me. Follow the colour! Come find me, Daddy. Follow the colour!

I want to, but I can't, buddy. There is no colour. There's no colour down here....

Oh no, wait. What's that over there? Shards of light, I think. No. Colour. Flashing colour. Down here. It can't be.

Yeah! There! Just there. But I don't have the energy. No more energy.

Daddy! Follow the colour, Daddy.

Oh, Toby... buddy... I can feel you... I can feel you all over me.... Oh, buddy. I've missed you so much... I'm holding you now, holding you tight... I can feel your arms around me.... It feels good... it feels so good... oh God, I've missed you, buddy. I've missed you. Daddy's missed you.

I know. But you need to go now. You need to go. Follow the colour.

I can't. What about you? What about Mummy? I should stay.

Don't worry. She's with me now. We're together.

Toby, I don't think I can. I don't think I can go without you, buddy. Not anymore.

It's alright. I'm with you. I'll always be with you. Please, Daddy… follow the light. Follow the colour.

I am. At least, I think I am. I'm not sure.

The flashing colour is growing closer now. I can see it, Toby! I can see it, buddy! I'm going there. I'm going there now.

Come with me. Come with Daddy.

Toby?

I can see the flashing lights high above me now. And faces, all around me. Smiling faces. Drifting around me. It's me, Grandpa. We're on the beach, in front of the house, fishing. I'm smiling. He's smiling. We're laughing. Laughing together.

I want to reach for the images, but I can't. My movements are sluggish in the water. It keeps pushing me, nudging me forward and then pulling me backward, lifting me up and then pulling me down again.

Forward.

Backward.

Up.

Down.

Up.

Air.

Water.

Air.

Water.

Then, something is brushing against my hand. Against my body.

What is that? I can't see it, but I can feel it.

Air.

Water.

Air.

Water. Sloshing.

Air.

Air.

Air.

Beautiful air. I can breathe! I'm breathing! Coughing.

Spluttering. I'm breathing. Somebody is holding me. Holding me tight. Holding me out of the water.

Toby? Is that you?

I open my eyes.

The Christmas tree… it's upside down. Wow. Looks strange like this. Blinking at me, upside down. Bathing me in multicoloured light.

On.

Off.

On.

Off.

…As I lie here in the arms of the oak tree with its feet clinging to the side of the cliff face and its head under water.

And I'm breathing. Spluttering. Breathing once more.

There are voices in the distance. Lights. Engines.

I'm breathing.

I'm breathing.

This is where it ends.

But not for me.

EPILOGUE

LONDON. 18:00. CHRISTMAS EVE.
(ONE YEAR LATER)

Many have asked exactly what happened that night, and even now, one year later, I still couldn't tell you with absolute clarity.

Well, I can. I mean, I can tell you about all the obvious bits, but as for everything that happened after I fell into the water? Well, that all felt just like one of my dreams.

Well, apart from the hyperthermia, that is. That felt all too real, and still does. Even now, I still can't get the chill out of my bones. I mean, I used to be the person who always ran hot. Ellie was the one who was always cold.

Ellie. My wife. If it wasn't all documented in black and white, and now you told me that she conspired the way she did, I would probably deck you. Since I'm still unable to genuinely believe she did the things she did just for money.

But then, if it's true what I've been told, she was also unwell, broken by the loss of our child.

I of all people should understand that. And I'm trying, but it's difficult because, in many ways, she always seemed so much stronger than me. Unbreakable.

They never did find her body, but they believe that, not unlike everything else, it was ultimately taken by the sea.

I haven't been back to Porthcove, but I am told on good authority that the whole of the peninsula eventually sank into the ocean and that Dolce Vita is no more.

And I still don't know how I feel about that, but as I sit

on this park bench wrapped in my coat and scarf, waiting, I am finally able to appreciate that ever-elusive sense of relief. It's like a particularly important chapter in my life has been closed. Like I've finally put to bed those ghosts of the past and am finally able to move on with the rest of my life.

Ghosts is an interesting term, of course, for obvious reasons.

I don't know exactly who or what pushed me that night. I am prepared to believe that it was the vengeful spirit of my mother bringing to fruition both her antics and her nightmarish prophecy, as far-fetched as that may seem.

Others, of course… others have their theories. They believe that it was Ellie who pushed me.

What do you think? After all, you were there, too.

Actually, don't answer that. You'll believe whatever you want, and so you should.

Ultimately, we'll never know what truly happened beyond the fact that three people lost their lives that night. It only occurred to me days later that it rather creepily happened in accordance with my dream premonitions, which if you can get beyond the weirdness, is bloody amazing. That or one massive coincidence.

Those *three ice creams* that Toby ordered in one dream. And the *three* ravens that *fell over the railing* in the other.

Obviously, that meant absolutely nothing to me at the time, but it all means a whole lot now. And probably will for the rest of my life. However long that may well be. I don't even think about it anymore. I honestly believed that I was going to die that night, until the angel of my boy helped me understand that it wasn't my time, again through my dreams. *Following the colour* of the Christmas tree is ultimately what saved me in those choppy waters.

I later read that dream communication with supernatural phenomena is not so uncommon. Again, there are numerous theories about that, but, once again, people will believe what they want to believe.

All I know is that people died, and I *struggled* for a while to come to terms with the weight of that. Wondering how differently things may have panned out if I had made different choices.

But then, we were all plagued by survivor's remorse – even Ethan, who I found out regularly visits a shrink of his own. We all had to come to terms with the fact that, no matter what we may feel, even we can't control meteorological phenomena.

And, yes. Ethan and I have been seeing a lot of each other over the past year. More than I probably would like. Yes, he still has that knack of getting on my nerves like nobody else I know. Yes, that's despite our ordeal. Although, I do think we're much closer now. So close, in fact, that we've even flirted with the idea of opening a practice together.

Can you imagine that?

Yes, it would appear that my father's belief in me finally paid off. Under Ethan's supervision, I've completed my tenure and am now a fully certified psychoanalyst who has, according to my various assessors, a *unique empathetic skill that will stand him in good stead* as I go about solving the puzzle that is us.

You know, it's so cold today that there's a good chance we might have a white Christmas this year. Wouldn't that be nice?

We can but hope, I suppose.

I dare say Cristian won't be worrying about that. He's been back in sunny Spain for a while now.

I felt sorry for him. I genuinely believe that he loved my wife – as wrong as that sounds – even though I don't think his love was truly reciprocated. That, and the fact that he almost became a father…. It's a lot. Whatever he's doing right now, I hope he's as happy as I am. Relatively speaking of course.

My marriage may well have imploded, but there's still another to look forward to in a few months' time and, as best man, I'm looking forward to going about my duties with due diligence. Even though David has been teasing that I should brace myself because he has no intention of shopping for a suit, but is instead planning on getting married in a dress. Which is ridiculous, of course, because I know him, and he's never been one to play dress-up, nor wear makeup or any of those things he's threatening to do on his wedding day. I doubt very much that he's going to start now.

But I'm letting him have his fun, albeit at my expense, because that's what friends do, right?

Although, if they take much longer, I'll probably end up freezing to death here. I'll become yet another statue in this park. Marco Battista, human popsicle, frozen here with his arse stuck to the bench.

"Hello, you."

"Oh, hey!" I look up and squint at Sarah as she slides down on the bench next to me and kisses me on the mouth.

"I brought you this," she says, handing me a Starbucks cup with a picture of a snowflake on it.

"Hmm. My favourite. Thanks, babe. So, how are Irvin and the lads doing?" I ask.

"They're good. Mum asked about Christmas Day lunch again. Said everyone's eager for a get-together."

"We've already promised Aaron and David."

"I know. I told her. Said we'd be over on Boxing Day if you're still good with that. She said to bring the boys with us."

"God, does she know what she'd be getting herself in for with David?"

Sarah smiles. "I think she has a good idea, yes."

And who said relationships born out of stressful situations are a bad idea?

Sarah and I have been together for almost a year now and we're still going strong. To the point where she moved to London with me, and has stayed while I've finished my degree and she finishes hers at RCV, where she's studying to become a vet.

"Hey, Marco."

I look up. It's Aaron wrapped in a red puffer jacket – or are those his muscles? I can't tell. "Hey. What happened?" I ask.

"L.A." He nods behind him to where David, wrapped in coat and scarf, is chatting on his mobile phone.

Oh – the carol singers have started. The melody drifts over to us from somewhere beyond the trees. It's "Carol of the Bells", and it instantly feels like Christmas.

"Dude! Come on. It's Christmas Eve!" I yell at my friend, who wraps up his call and comes over.

"Marco! Marco!" he says, putting on an exaggerated Italian accent before throwing his arms around me and planting a slobbery kiss on my face. Then, he turns to hug Sarah. "Sarah, babe. I'm sure you're looking more gorgeous by the day." Then back to me, he adds with mock exasperation, "Well, come on then, get up! I've been waitin' ages."

I roll my eyes and stand.

"Come on, Buddy! Let's go! Playtime is over."

Sixty-something pounds of Golden Retriever comes bounding over, tongue hanging, tail wagging, and jumps up at me, nearly knocking me off my feet. "Hey you, hey!" I say with a big grin as the dog greets me with his own slobbery kisses.

"See? It's not so bad," David says, and we all laugh.

Do you believe in reincarnation?

If I'm being perfectly honest, I don't truly know if I do, and I've done extensive research on the subject over the past year. There are many stories about people remembering times, places, events… hell, even whole lives of people that lived centuries before them. Then, there are others, the sceptics, who have their own perspective of the subject.

All I can say is, you've seen what I've seen, and you know what I know. The fact is, if it wasn't for this fella, I don't think I would have survived Dolce Vita the second time around, and for many reasons that you are already aware of.

I love him. And, for reasons I can't explain, having him in my life makes me feel closer to my little boy, and his absence that little bit more bearable.

I have no idea how he manged to escape the house. All I know is that, when they put him in my arms, it felt like they had returned a son to me.

As for the others.

Do you remember that story I told you about the Oak tree? The one my mother sat by the side of my bed one night and told me about? She told me that it wasn't a monster, but a protector planted there years before to take care of me.

Well, it did precisely that.

With its roots still anchored to land, the tree lay down the rest of its body and its life to break the fall of those nearest and dearest to me. It caught and then held them aloft until they were rescued less than an hour later.

This meant that most escaped with scratches, bruising, and a couple of fractures, but otherwise unharmed.

It did pretty much the same for me – not just breaking my fall before I fell into the freezing churn, but catching me after I managed to find my way back to shore thanks to those Christmas lights. It then held me out of the freezing water until I, too, could be rescued.

Later, during my sessions with Ethan and away from what felt like the curse of Dolce Vita, I was also able to look through the fog of what I believed to be my past and see my father for the man he really was. Someone who may have been misguided at times, but did the best he could during a challenging time in my life.

I know now that it wasn't my mother who sat at my bedside and told me the story of my protector, but my father.

In my blindness to suppress the terrible things about my past, I also suppressed some of the good.

My father, Marco Battista, did die at the property formally known as Dolce Vita. Apparently, he suffered a heart attack in the kitchen and then attempted to drag himself, wheezing for breath, to his phone in the dining room, but never made it.

He died in the hallway.

"Hey! It's snowing!" Sarah exclaims excitedly.

I look up, and she's right. Looks like it's going to be a white Christmas, after all.

Well, fancy that. A Christmas miracle.

Speaking of which. I have one more thing to share with you.

I had completely forgotten about this, but a couple of years back, as Toby was growing older, Ellie and I became somewhat neurotic about what would become of him – should something ever happen to us.

So, we decided to take out one of those life insurance policies that would pay out to him, should something happen to us. Similarly, it would pay out to one of us, should something happen to the other.

Although the policy was in our name, the payments were being taken from my personal account which, given that I wasn't around to spend the money, meant that there was still enough in there to ensure that the monthly payments were covered.

So, you can imagine my surprise when, out of the blue, I was contacted and advised that settlement had been approved and would be paid out within seven working days.

It isn't as much as I would have made if we had sold the house, but more than enough to buy a new home and even invest in a couple of start-up businesses of our own, should we choose to do so.

And so, while this Christmas will undoubtedly be tinged with sorrow, I have many reasons to believe that we're going to be just fine.

If you enjoyed

HAUNTED

**Please leave an Amazon rating
so that others may enjoy it also.**

If you can't wait for Tony Marturano's next thriller,
subscribe to the blog or follow on social media for the latest
news, special chapter previews and exclusive giveaways.

www.tonymarturano.com

facebook.com/tonymarturano.author

instagram.com/marturanotony

or google tony marturano

ACKNOWLEDGEMENTS

As always, I'm so very grateful to everyone at a Different Angle, who has supported me throughout this book's journey, from manuscript to print. Special thanks to the following who have actively contributed to its realisation.

THE HAUNTED FOCUS/READER'S GROUP

My heartfelt thanks to all members of the Haunted reader's group, for giving so generously of their time and opinions!

(In no particular order)
Francesca Marturano-Pratt – Anna Pratt – Renee Owens – Lisa Hall – Nicola Ramsbottom – Cheryl Green

MY EDITOR

Jennifer Collins.

YOU, THE READER

If you're reading this book, there's a good chance you bought it. I'm obviously very grateful for that. Thank you!

On the other hand, if you borrowed this book from somebody else, even better! It means they thought it was good enough to pass on.

ALSO BY TONY MARTURANO

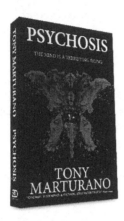

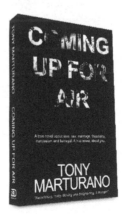